MID-CENTURY

An Anthology of Jewish Life
and Culture in Our Times

Edited by HAROLD U. RIBALOW

NEW YORK : THE BEECHHURST PRESS

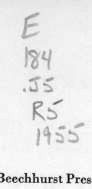
Copyright, 1955, by Beechhurst Press, Inc.

Library of Congress Catalogue Card Number 54–10691

Printed in the United States of America

ACKNOWLEDGMENTS

"Goyim" by J. L. Teller. Copyright, 1949, by *The Antioch Review*. Reprinted by permission of *The Antioch Review* and J. L. Teller.

"My Father Was a Hero" by Shlomo Katz. Reprinted by permission of *Commentary* and Shlomo Katz.

"Do I Have a Jewish Complex?" by Edith Handleman. Reprinted from *Common Ground*.

"The Education of a Jew" by Michael Blankfort. Reprinted from *The American Mercury* by permission of Michael Blankfort.

"A Jew in a Christian Community" by Robert H. Glauber. Reprinted by permission of *Congress Weekly*.

"I Changed My Name." Reprinted by permission of *The Atlantic Monthly*.

"I've Kept My Name" by David L. Cohn. Reprinted by permission of *The Atlantic Monthly* and David L. Cohn.

"Some Melamdim I Have Known" by Harold U. Ribalow. Reprinted by permission of *The Reconstructionist*.

"The Meaning of Jewish Existence" by Abraham Joshua Heschel. Reprinted from *The Zionist Quarterly* by permission of Abraham Joshua Heschel.

"Notes on Jewish Survival" by Menahem Boraisha. Reprinted by permission of *Congress Weekly*.

"When I Think of Seraye" by Milton Steinberg. Reprinted by permission of *The Reconstructionist*.

"Are the Jews a 'Race'?" by Ashley Montagu. Reprinted by permission of *The Chicago Jewish Forum*.

"A Parable of Alienation" by Daniel Bell. Reprinted by permission of *The Jewish Frontier* and Daniel Bell.

"The Lost Young Intellectual" by Irving Howe. Reprinted by permission of *Commentary* and Irving Howe.

"Plight of the Jewish Intellectual" by Leslie A. Fiedler. Reprinted by permission of *Congress Weekly*.

"To the Young Jewish Intellectuals" by Ludwig Lewisohn. Reprinted by permission of *The Jewish Frontier* and Ludwig Lewisohn.

"Troubled Intellectuals" by Charles Angoff. Reprinted by permission of *The American Zionist* and Charles Angoff.

"Repeat Performance" by Milton Hindus. Reprinted by permission of *The Chicago Jewish Forum*.

"The Concentration Camps" by Hannah Arendt. From *The Origins of Totalitarianism*, copyright, 1951, by Hannah Arendt. Reprinted by permission of Harcourt, Brace and Company, Inc. First published in *Partisan Review*.

"The Jews of the South" by Harry L. Golden. Reprinted by permission of *Congress Weekly*.

"The Story That Must Build Itself" by Maurice Samuel. Reprinted by permission of *The Jewish Frontier* and Maurice Samuel.

"Religious Trends in American Jewry" by Will Herberg. Reprinted by permission of *Judaism* and Will Herberg.

"Building Our Future in America" by Jacob B. Agus. Reprinted from *The Menorah Journal* by permission of Jacob B. Agus.

"Hebrew: Revival and Redemption" by Menachem Ribalow. Reprinted by permission of *The American Zionist* and Mrs. Rose Ribalow.

"Literature of a Vanished World" by Naomi Ben-Asher. Reprinted by permission of *Congress Weekly*.

"The Jewish Book" by Jacob S. Minkin. Reprinted by permission of *The Chicago Jewish Forum*.

"Why I Wrote a Jewish Novel" by Zelda Popkin, Ethel Rosenberg, Yuri Suhl, David Miller, Charles Angoff, Herman Wouk, Stephen Longstreet, James Yaffe, and Miriam Bruce. Reprinted by permission of *Congress Weekly*.

"The Dilemma of the Jewish Writer" by Abraham Rothberg. Reprinted by permission of *Congress Weekly*.

"Anti-Semitism and the Jewish Novelist" by Charles I. Glicksberg. Reprinted from *Judaism* by permission of Charles I. Glicksberg.

"The East Side Gangsters of the Paper-Backs" by Meyer Levin. Reprinted by permission of *Commentary* and Meyer Levin.

"Don't You Believe It!" by Marvin Lowenthal. Reprinted from *The Zionist Quarterly* by permission of Marvin Lowenthal.

"Reflections on the Jewish Question" by Sidney Hook. Reprinted by permission of *Partisan Review*.

"The Problem of Ernest Bloch" by Leon Stein. Reprinted by permission of *The Chicago Jewish Forum*.

"Why Jews Stay Sober" by Nathan Glazer. Reprinted by permission of *Commentary* and Nathan Glazer.

"Is Jewish Humor Dead?" by Irving Kristol. Reprinted by permission of *Commentary* and Irving Kristol.

"The Need for Diaspora Zionism" by Mordecai M. Kaplan. Reprinted by permission of *The Reconstructionist*.

"Jewish Culture and Education in the Diaspora" and "On Dual Loyalties" by Hayim Greenberg. Reprinted by permission of *The Jewish Frontier* and The Jewish Frontier Publishing Association.

"America Is Not Babylonia" by Trude Weiss-Rosmarin. Reprinted from *The Jewish Spectator* by permission of Trude Weiss-Rosmarin.

"Whither Israel?" by Horace M. Kallen. Reprinted from *The Menorah Journal* by permission of Horace M. Kallen and Judah Pilch.

"Have Jews a Divided Loyalty?" by Johan J. Smertenko. Reprinted from *Harper's* by permission of Johan J. Smertenko.

"Ben Gurion's Dispute with American Zionists" by Benno Weiser. Reprinted by permission of *Commentary* and Benno Weiser.

"You Can't Go Home Again" by Eliezer Whartman. Reprinted by permission of *The Reconstructionist* and Eliezer Whartman.

"Painting in Israel" by Alfred Werner. Reprinted from *The Zionist Quarterly* by permission of Alfred Werner.

"Zion in Contemporary Fiction" by Harold U. Ribalow. Reprinted by permission of *The Reconstructionist*.

This book is dedicated to the memory of my devoted and gifted father, MENACHEM RIBALOW, one of the great Jews of our time, who was taken from us in this decade. He guided my every thought that went into the making of this book, as his personality, character and integrity will influence everything I ever do for the rest of my days.

CONTENTS

9

CULTURE

ZION

INTRODUCTION

IN THE TERCENTENARY year of Jewish settlement in America, this volume is offered as evidence that the past decade—a mid-century point—has seen the publication of some of the most interesting, authoritative, and provocative American-Jewish writing of the century.

Certainly, the fifty contributors to this book include, in surprisingly large measure, a Who's Who of American Jewry. There are representative writings—all non-fiction—by the most notable names in American-Jewish scholarship, theology, philosophy, culture, and journalism. The essays offered in these pages transcend the dates on which they were originally published because of the timelessness of the material and the manner in which it is approached. Like so many Jews before them and, it is to be hoped, those who come after them, these writers have addressed themselves to the whole Jewish people, and not to a particular Jewish element at a particular time.

The late Hayim Greenberg, lecturing at a Zionist Congress in Jerusalem, speaks to a past, a present, and a future generation of Zionists, impressing upon them the security of the American Jew and the Diaspora problem which Israel's statesmen must face. Rabbi Milton Steinberg, whose untimely death at the age of forty-seven was a loss to Jews everywhere, delivered an address for funds for Jewish causes and called it "When I Think of Seraye." On the surface, nothing seems so dated as an appeal for philanthropy. The passion, the Jewish learning, and the skill which Rabbi Steinberg brought to his address, later published in magazine and book form, made his sermon into a small classic, one which can profit the Jewish reader of any generation. Menachem Ribalow, stressing the immortality of the Hebrew language, drew on spiritual sources which have enriched the Jewish people in every era. Menahem Boraisha's strictures are the strictures of a prophet admonishing his people. The analyses of Mordecai M. Kaplan, Horace M. Kallen, Trude Weiss-Rosmarin remain thought-provoking long after they were committed to paper.

The authors of the articles in *Mid-Century* are the men and women who have been addressing the Jewish people in America for the past few decades. They colored and influenced Jewish life in the past and they and their contemporaries will continue to lead the Jewish community through the decades to come.

Curiously, these essays appeared, in the main, in the much-maligned American-Jewish periodical press. Every contribution is the work of a Jew living and working in the United States, writing in English. All but eight of the fifty-three contributions were first published in an English-language magazine edited for American Jews. The other eight were accepted by the editors of such high-quality journals as *The Atlantic Monthly, Harper's, Partisan Review,* and the now defunct *Common Ground.* The great majority of these articles, then, was brought to the attention of the public in the pages of the Jewish magazines sponsored by Jewish organizations and those few published independently by a handful of dedicated souls.

This anthologist is convinced that the collection of writings found between the covers of this book speaks well for American Jewry and offers an accurate portrait of the American Jew at mid-century. This volume is divided into four separate and distinct sections: a series of personal-experience accounts under the title of "First Person Singular"; a group of essays on Jewish belonging, survival, and alienation in "Belonging and Survival"; a variety of essays on literary and other cultural themes in "Culture"; and a final section on Israel, Zionism, and related themes in "Zion." Each section is prefaced by an introduction which briefly describes the pieces included and the reasons for their inclusion, as well as the magazines from which they were taken. The book ends with biographical notes on the contributors, nearly all of whom have devoted their entire lives to Jewish cultural, political, or communal affairs.

As the editor of two anthologies of Jewish fiction, this writer is delighted to be able to point out that the quality of the prose in this book is first-rate, which should surprise no one, for it contains specimens of the work of such writers as Ludwig Lewisohn, Maurice Samuel, Meyer Levin, Marvin Lowenthal, Milton Steinberg, Abraham Joshua Heschel, Sidney Hook, and many others who are as famous for their style as for their ideas.

It is remarkable that the Jewish periodicals, which have small circulations, are sponsored by Jewish organizations, and can scarcely support the Jewish writer dependent solely on his type-writer, have been able to offer so much fine writing by so many of American Jewry's outstanding thinkers, leaders, and journalists.

While Jewish fiction often appears in general magazines, Jewish material of the kind found in this volume almost always finds its way into Jewish journals. Now and again, of course, a study such as Jean Paul Sartre's *Anti-Semite and Jew* or a discussion of the alleged dual loyalty of the Jew will appear in an issue of *Partisan Review* or of *Harper's*. But such profoundly Jewish essays of the type written by Dr. Heschel or Hayim Greenberg or Horace Kallen are accepted for publication by the editors of the Jewish magazines. That the past decade alone has seen the emergence of *Commentary, Congress Weekly, The Reconstructionist, The Chicago Jewish Forum, Judaism, The Jewish Frontier,* and the continuation of *The Menorah Journal,* is convincing evidence of the cultural outlets for the Jewish thinker and writer. For too long a period has the English-Jewish press been belittled. This book is made possible because it exists, and the material presented in this collection more than justifies the existence of that press.

It is a pity that there are no mass-circulation magazines of Jewish interest which are independently published, but it is, in a sense, rather miraculous that the good Jewish magazines sponsored by conflicting and overlapping Jewish organizations open their pages to so wide a variety of material both in subject matter and in style. The next half-century may see the emergence of a more popular Jewish press in America, but on the basis of what already has been published in the Jewish magazines, the past has been more than a bucket of ashes; it has accurately reflected, at its best and most eloquent, Jewish life in this country. If this book explains or clarifies or illuminates Judaism and Jewish living to a greater audience, it will have fulfilled its function.

Cambria Heights, N.Y.   HAROLD U. RIBALOW

FIRST PERSON SINGULAR

The personal essay written by the Jew about his adventures as a Jew often reflects aspects of Jewish life too inadequately dealt with in more formal writings. The eight "First Person Singular" accounts reprinted in this section describe a wide variety of Jewish experiences. J. L. Teller relives a pogrom in Poland and evokes the horror, cruelty, and fear of an event with which European Jews were frighteningly familiar. Shlomo Katz paints an unforgettable word-portrait of his father, a European Jew who came to America and who—together with thousands of Jews like himself—contributed richly to American-Jewish life. Edith Handleman, a college student, wonders, under the impact of Hitlerism, just how important her Jewish heritage is to her and what she will accomplish as a Jewess. Michael Blankfort, a talented and popular novelist, candidly examines his journey from Marxism to Judaism and concludes that his final turn toward Judaism is a fortunate event in his confused life. Robert H. Glauber, an editor and writer, visits a small town and is shocked to discover that, in spite of his own indifference to Judaism, he cannot—and, in the end, does not want to—escape his destiny. David L. Cohn and an anonymous contributor to *The Atlantic Monthly* argue in the staid pages of this venerable magazine the pros and cons of a Jew changing his name and, thereby, rejecting—or accepting—his Judaism. And a young Jew reminds himself of his Hebrew teachers and speculates on their lasting influence.

These essays appeared in such different periodicals as *Commentary, The American Mercury, Antioch Review, Common Ground, The Reconstructionist, Congress Weekly,* and *The Atlantic Monthly.* However, they have in common their candidness and their valuable insights into the pattern of American-Jewish living.

GOYIM

By J. L. TELLER

M Y FIRST APPREHENSION of *goyim* probably dates back beyond the range of retrievable memory, to a time when an infant's ears absorb sounds in the same fashion as his lips absorb lactation—greedily, lustily, without comprehension. It may have first come to me at an ominous twilight hour in my parents' rambling, single-story house in Tarnopol, situated at the intersection of two streets, one terminating in the railroad yards, and the other leading down a precipitous slope to the fashionable mansions, set in large private parks behind iron picket fences, and to the suburbs and villages that were the city's granaries.

When first touched by memory, I found myself already in the midst of these ominous twilights which came intermittently, in series, and have stayed with me as the keenest memory of childhood.

Our house with its grocery store was usually as open as a circus tent, as if its doors were mere flaps. Customers used to come in by the front door at all hours, from dawn till late in the evening. Neighbors used the rear door, through the kitchen, pounding on it past midnight to purchase mustard for an aching back, rock candy for whooping cough, and in cases of sudden seizures enlist my grandmother's "concentrations" to stave off the evil spirits. My grandmother undoubtedly possessed telepathic powers and even when not in the same room with the ailing person, could relieve, by sheer concentration, some of his physical discomfort.

These awesome twilights, however, would find our house, its doors and shutters bolted, sealed like a clam shell. Inside the shell our family—grandmother, mother (father was in America), my brother and I— huddled around the kitchen stove, backs arched catlike in agonizing anticipation. The kerosene lamp was doused because its reflection might seep into the street. The women moved about in the scant eerie illumination which came from the stove whose door was deliberately kept ajar for that purpose. There was about it all the quality of living on the floor of the seas. Sleep was made fitful by a gnawing semi-conscious trepidation, with morbid dream elements trailing, like saliva, into the state of wakefulness. Tossing in semi-wakefulness I would occasionally whimper and grope for either female. But no sooner did I stir, than I would feel a martinet pressure of fingers on my lips and be hissed into silence: "*Schweig,* or you'll bring on the *goyim* and they'll slaughter us all, *chas ve-sho-lem.*"

It was fear of the *goyim* prowling the streets that kept grandmother and mother from shedding their clothes during these periods of seclusion which dragged on for days, and in consequence the air in our kitchen was close with the stale odor of uncleansed females.

The *goyim* were on the prowl whenever Tarnapol changed hands in the war waged for its possession. Each time an army retreated, it vented its resentment on the civilian population, particularly the Jews, by plundering, butchering and raping. The incoming army would celebrate its victory in similar fashion. And to fill the vacuum between retreat and entry, the peasants would swirl in from the suburbs. Armed with hatchets and knives, and stimulated by their own hot whiskey breath and collective clamor, they would cause greater damage and more casualties among the Jews than the many months of incessant bombardment that preceded each retreat.

On entering and retreating, the armies always poured past our rambling, bolted house along the precipitous slope. On the mornings of such days one could sense a foreboding restiveness in the air. Panicky rumors would start among the Jewish stores and stalls in the marketplace and be quickly carried forward, like *shalach monot* or the communal *lulav,* to all Jewish homes in Tarnopol. On hearing the news, women wrung their hands in anguish, young girls assiduously rubbed chimney soot into their faces, and Jewish males went determinedly about the job of slamming down the shutters.

News from the marketplace always reached us last because we lived up the hill, outside the Jewish quarter. But we were always kept apprised of the imminence of danger by the strange, almost ritualistic behavior of our Christian neighbors. On such days they would appear at dawn in front of their houses, with pails and big brushes and begin painting white crosses on their doors for identification. The hunchback shoemaker would stand on the pavement across the street, grinning and rubbing his hands, and shout to mother the news that "it won't be long now and they'll start killing the Jews." The postmaster's wife, a tall, buxom, childless woman would lift me up and press me to her bosom, sobbing with hysterical abandon as if she had just snatched me out of one of the white infant coffins in which Tarnopol gentiles interred their youngest dead. "Flee, darlings, flee, or put an ikon in your windows," she would cry. Grandmother and mother did neither, and went about grimly bolting the doors.

By midmorning an awesome twilight had descended on our house, as frightful to a child as Yom Kippur eve in synagogue when the adult males assembled in their shrouds. In our Noah's Ark of a kitchen, the horrible vigil had already begun.

We could hear our Christian neighbors talking in the yard, a dog barking and the dull thump of a hatchet biting into a stump. From the distance would come the blast of a military band, rising in crescendo as it approached, climaxing in thunder as it passed our house, and trailing out in the suburbs. Then came the whining sirens of speed-crazed motorcycles, the restive thud and neighing of the cavalry's horses, the relentless surf of hundreds of boots marching in formation, and the low, painful creaking of overladen wagons, harnessed to oxen straining down the slope. Then, as another battalion passed, the brassband again and a confirmation of all the earlier sounds in approximately the same chronology. This generally lasted for many hours, followed by an interminable chrysalis; as the last sentries withdrew, we could hear desultory shooting from the direction of the railroad yards, an occasional excoriating outcry from midtown where the Jews lived, and sometimes a light quick chase just outside our windows, a voice shouting "halt," an instant more of light, quick footfalls, a single shot, an outcry and silence. This was the period of greatest danger, when the local *goyim* moved in to fill the vacuum just before the new army took possession.

There would be loud pounding on our door with fists or iron bars. "Hey, open up or we'll tear the shutters down. Just give up the Jewesses you're hiding. Just the Jewesses." This was sometimes followed by an unintelligible querulous exchange in several voices, culminating in a final, disgusted kick at the door. Our backs arched more rigidly, a challenge to the spine's resilience, and fingers would press on my lips in anticipation of a whimper, as the steps receded from our front door, came loudly past our windows and trailed out somewhere along the slope. Sometimes the retreating steps could be heard approaching again along the gravel path. There would then be even more obstinate pounding on our rear door, accompanied by obscenities in mock Yiddish. This pounding on the doors and probing of knobs and bolts and the gush of obscenities would last sometimes for a half hour or more, the air inside close with sibilant breathing and uncleansed female flesh, but there was always some miraculous intervention, sometimes in the person of the postmaster's wife ("Stop your pounding," she would shout, "they're Christians and have probably gone to bed"), and sometimes in the form of breathless rioters who would run past yelling: "Eh, peasants, on to the marketplace! The Jewish stores are on fire!"

Then there would be the brassbands again, whining motorcycles, the surf-beat of hundreds of boots, and the snap of whips on the backs of oxen straining uphill. Again there would be pounding on the doors, by soldiers who had broken out of line. "Hey, open up, we want women!" But as the brassbands struck up again, they would disappear in the tide of long-coated ranks. Many more hours would pass, and then the postmaster's wife could be heard tapping on the shutters: "Come out my darlings, it's safe now." Slowly, the heavy bolts would be removed. When the door finally creaked open, there was always the hunchback shoemaker on the pavement across the street, grinning and rubbing his hands as he shouted the information that "plenty of Jews have had their throats cut in the past few days, they went after you, too, but I told them you were Christians."

Tall, clean-shaven, immaculate in his vestments, the parish priest would appear in our door, like a visitation, in a cloud of barking, baying and yelping dogs. With a snap of his fingers he would call them off, as frightened I would back into the floursack corner. He looked bemused, standing there, like a disdainful prophet, among his dogs and the Jews; his features small and delicate, and his complexion as white as writing paper which was scarce and expensive in wartime Tarnopol. During the siege, he complained, he had run out of the bread which my mother baked specially for him. He had sent his servant to order more loaves, but when she knocked at the door, there was no answer. So he had to try just any bread. Oh, Jesus-Maria, what a horrible mixture! This was two days ago and he has been sick since. "What would I have done, poor me, if they had killed you along with the other Jews?" He moved toward me, with appraising mockery in his eyes, and felt my cheeks in the same connoisseur manner in which he felt the loaves before putting them in the basket hanging on his arm. He moved out again in a cloud of yelping dogs, and turned back at the door for a final mocking query. "You will give him to me someday, won't you, before he grows up just another Jew, fattened for the peasants' knives? I could use him, you know, as an incense boy," he would say to my mother. In consequence I would sometimes have dreams in which I sat at his tables, wedged in by my foster brothers, the baying dogs, and suffocating on the *tarfuth* odors from the steaming bowls before him.

One morning we woke up to a topsy-turvy world. Soldiers ran around slapping their officers, instead of saluting. Youngsters in mufti scurried about with rifles dropped by fleeing soldiers. Mother had begun bolting the shutters, when the priest came by. "Stay open," he advised in his habitual mocking tone. "This is the beginning of Polish independence. They'll suspect you're in mourning for the alien ruler, if you shut down now." So we stayed open, but out of sight in the kitchen. A little later, the Christian population appeared in its Sunday's best and a procession with crosses, ikons and flags wound its way down the slope, past our house. The priest was at the head of it, followed by the gentry, their mustaches waxed to a fine point, and by their women wearing long, laced gloves and carrying dainty parasols. Then came the students, rifles dangling from their shoulders, and then the mob roaring the national anthem. All wore red and white little bows in their lapels, the Polish national colors.

21

That afternoon, when the procession disbanded, the mob fanned out across the city. A Polish student with a pistol in his hand ran into our store at the head of a half-score panting, perspiring men and women shouting excitedly. Grandmother dropped at his feet, grabbed his hands and pleaded: "Remember when I fondled you in my lap when you were *that* small, and have you come now to kill us?" He flung her aside, and as she scrambled to her feet grandmother waved us all back into the kitchen. The student, his cheeks aglow, his hair disheveled, ordered the mobsters surging behind him: "Take all you want, but don't molest these Jews, so that they won't have cause to say that we Poles are savages." We looked on in fright, as they cleared the shelves, lugged out the sacks of flour, beans and peas, ripping open and trampling whatever they could not carry away. Occasionally a ruffian would rest from his work of devastation and cast a glance in mother's direction, but this did not escape the student who, standing amidst the mob, acted as supervisor of the destruction. "Don't bother them, they're friends of the priest."

This was the beginning of a new relationship with *goyim* and of new fears. The ominous twilight sieges had ended but were replaced with something worse. Mother sighed almost with longing for the old days. "So you would stay locked in for several days, then a new army took possession of the city, and you could file complaints with the commandant. But now the danger is everywhere, and at all times, without respite," she would say.

The danger of the twilight sieges was anonymous and shapeless, a mass of noises pouring like a deluge past our bolted doors and windows. But the new danger was identifiable and bore the faces of many of our neighbors. Mother made her purchases at dawn or during the several hours of daylight when the students were at school; Jews kept off the streets in the evening for fear of the prowling students; synagogues were empty for *mincha-maariv* and private *minyanim* of frightened men mushroomed all over the city. The student across the street, who led the pillagers into our store on that first day, chose me as his special target. I tried hard to elude him.

One day as I came face to face with him, and before I could run off, he grabbed me by the lapels, shook me hard, and commanded: "Jew, lace my shoes!" He slapped me twice across the face as I hesitated, an undersized kid of six looking up at an oversized *sheigetz* of eighteen. Just as I was about to kneel down, his face went pale, his hands and feet twitched as if caught in a trap, his head bobbed like a cork on a tide. He seemed to be working hard to amuse me in some frightful manner, and I stood there paralyzed with fright. His body shook suddenly with a violent explosion, and he dropped to the pavement, foam curling at the corners of his lips like smoke at the mouth of a gun. He had no peace even there, his limbs convulsing and twitching like the priest's hounds before they would subside at the snap of his fingers. He was like Korach about to be devoured by the earth. I yelled with fright and began to back out into a corner; there were no flour sacks in the street among which to hide, but I dropped into the arms of the post-master's childless wife. Tenderly she bent my head down as I began to retch. There were many women pothering around me, all of them *goyim*, but to this day the word *goyim*—not Christians, nor Gentiles, but *goyim*—brings up in my memory none of them, but only the vivid image of the twitching form on the pavement and the sudden tightness in my throat, and there is a bond between us as eternal as that between the Almighty and His People.

MY FATHER WAS A HERO

By SHLOMO KATZ

M Y FATHER WAS always an old man. My earliest recollections of him go back almost forty years, and even then his long beard was streaked with gray. Now his beard is entirely white. He is impersonal and remote, and as I sit before him, his mild gaze seems to imply forgiveness. Though my conscience is fairly clear, I submit to his forgiveness. Who isn't guilty before his father?

He is an old man and his mind often wanders. He begins with the time-honored prologue: "Well, it's this way. . . ." But he gets no farther. I try to draw him on, to reestablish the thread of his thought. The gentleness in his eyes changes into a faraway look that reaches across distances over which I cannot follow. Then he seems to return for a moment, he recognizes me, and asks: "When are you leaving town?"

"In a few days," I say.

"And where are you going?" He is a very old man and his memory sometimes fails him. He no longer remembers that I live in New York.

If it wasn't for his age, and that he is so forgiving of me, I might suspect him of irony. There was a time when the question "Where are you going?" was in place. Each time I left I went off in another direction. But he would only shake his head and say, "Well, go in good health and succeed." Now that I have ceased running off at a different tangent each journey, he no longer remembers where I came to rest.

So every day I tell him anew that I am going back to New York.

He nods assent, but doesn't seem to care. New York is only a name to him. At this point the conversation ends, to be repeated in

24

almost identical words the following day, and the one after that, until I depart a week or so later.

I sit across the table from him trying to sum him up, and I am suddenly struck with the thought that he has been a hero all his life. How is it that I had never seen him in this light? And yet it is quite obvious.

There was that incident only a few years ago, for instance, when he was already in his late seventies. Who would have expected him to act as he did? Yet when it happened it only seemed to be a nice, slightly amusing occurrence.

The neighborhood in which my parents live was once almost exclusively Jewish but was long since abandoned by nearly all except a handful of the aged Jews who no longer move with the stream. In their place, there moved in some Negroes, some poor white people, and many Mexicans. The character of the neighborhood changed. Where formerly there was one bar, there are now half a dozen The streets that had resounded to the sound of Yiddish now ring with Spanish. Outside the bars Mexican boys and young men pass the time and argue volubly. The remaining Jews in the neighborhood utter the name "Mexican" with overtones of suspicion and apprehension. What the Mexican residents say I do not know, but the expressions one can frequently see on the faces of the young men in front of the bars at the sight of some bearded old Jew reveal an uncomprehendingness that seems ready to leap to hostility. One of the half-unused synagogues is now wedged between a bar and a wooden frame house that has been transformed into a Catholic church.

"Well, it happened this way," Father told me when I came on my annual visit that year. "It was afternoon and I was going to the synagogue for *mincha* and *maariv*."

"I was going," he said, but now I recalled that his walk was then already an aged shuffle.

"And on the corner there was a bunch of Mexican fellows, outside the saloon. One of them knocked my hat off. Well, you know, I am a *kohen* and *kohanim* are short-tempered. Without thinking I grabbed this guy by the shirt and pushed him. He didn't expect it and fell. All the other Mexican fellows laughed at him and clapped their hands. 'That's good, old man,' they said, 'good work.' And ever since they haven't bothered me again. I go by there twice every day. Sometimes, when they see me, they laugh and say, 'Good, old man, good work.' But I never again had any trouble with them."

When he first told me about this incident I also laughed; but later, mulling over this matter, there came to my mind two other incidents involving Father that took place long ago in faraway Ukraine during the turbulent times after the First World War.

There was the first pogrom in town—in itself not an unusual event at that time and in that place. As I think back to it I try to reconstruct the mood and the "flavor" of the two days during which the pogrom lasted. It was a warm and cloudy-gray early summer morning when Mother woke me up and without any prologue announced: "Get up, there is a pogrom in town." I leaped out of bed and dressed quickly, suddenly aware of a strange and sharp new sense of being that was not altogether without a pleasant tang. There was an atmosphere of haste in the house, though nothing was being done. Everyone walked about tense, ready to leap, but the time to run had not come yet.

Thus no doubt a flock of chickens in their coop might feel when the housewife announces in the evening that she is going to have one of them killed for dinner the following day. The chase hasn't begun yet. There is no telling which one will be caught. There may still be a last-minute reprieve if the menu is changed. Meantime each chicken feels trapped and nervous and tense—and also chosen.

All of us behaved this way, fearful yet somehow elected, all except Father. He remained calm.

The doors were still open to the summer morning. Outside, Jews nervously congregated in bunches, rehashing the various rumors. Individuals drifted from one group to another in search of the ultimate rumor that would satisfy them. Without any apparent reason, sudden panic would seize the people in the street and they would flee into the houses and quickly lock the doors, only to emerge again a few minutes later. Outside, it is true, one was not in hiding, but neither was one trapped there. And somehow, intuitively, all knew that "it" had not yet begun, that minutes, perhaps hours, would pass before "it" started.

The terror hung heavy in the sultry air. Peasants drove into town in their horse- and ox-drawn carts, though it was not a market day. They scowled and occasionally some muttered something indistinct but hostile. Then other wagons, drawn by horses, began arriving. These carried Jewish fugitives from other towns. They chattered hysterically to the clusters of people that instantaneously formed about them. Then there arose the problem of their housing. By noon we had more than a dozen refugees in our house.

By noon "it" began. Somebody came running down the street; and somebody else screamed that "it" had begun, and in a split second the street was deserted and all doors were locked and all window shades drawn. A last frightened man dashed by shouting something incoherent about what went on downtown, and then the street was silent.

There were about twenty people in the three-room house and in the attic, and all were silent. Occasionally someone would whisper a terrified "Did you hear?" as a muffled cry was heard from afar. Someone would move a window shade a fraction of an inch to peek outside. The street was empty as during a curfew.

Hours passed before the street began coming to life again, in a different way. Peasants who had come early in the morning were now returning to their villages, their wagons loaded with loot. Many of them were drunk and sang at the top of their voices plaintive, drawn-out Ukrainian tunes. Inside the house as many as could crowded near the windows to catch a glimpse of the loot and to learn from it what had happened. A bolt of cloth on a wagon, a few yards of it trailing in the dust, told about the looted dry-goods store and aroused concern for its owner. Pots and pans strung on a rope told the story of the hardware store. Men's and women's clothes had their own stories, though it was impossible to tell to whom they had belonged. A light-colored dress dangling from the side of a wagon was stained with what might have been blood, but it was impossible to know definitely. Small Ukrainian boys appeared in the street shrieking gaily and playing with all kinds of trophies of the looting. Then darkness descended.

Among the twenty in the house there were enough for a *minyan* and the evening prayers were whispered in unison. Then bread was doled out—cooking was avoided lest the smoke from the chimney attract attention to the house—and the terror of the night descended. From the distance came the sound of screams and the glow of fires.

Early the next day a new problem arose. There was no running water in the house. Water was brought daily in buckets from a well some blocks away and stored in a barrel. The twenty had consumed whatever water there was in the house. By noon thirst began to assert itself.

It was then that Father acted. Without saying a word he took the two buckets and went out by the rear door. We watched his progress. Groups of peasants were once again roaming the street, some sober, others drunk. We saw Father nodding a greeting to them and going on his way. Then he was stopped. He was still in sight but too far away for us to hear what was being said. He put the buckets on the ground. The peasants were saying something, then one of them pulled a long knife from the legging of his boot. The knife was passed around and examined. The group seemed to be going through some terrifying mummery.

Mother stood near the window wringing her hands. All others who could had their eyes glued to the narrow strip of window glass between the shade and the frame. Animation was suspended.

Then we saw some of the peasants roar with laughter. One of them slapped Father on the back, and they left him. Steadily he went to the well and returned some minutes later. Three times he repeated the trip, till the barrel was full, then he put down the buckets without saying a word.

The second incident which I remembered took place at about the same time in the same place as the first. This one, too, involved a pogrom, but this time we were in hiding with a family of Gentile friends. In the course of the hasty exodus from home the family treasures, which had been packed in a sack in anticipation of the event, had been left behind. Some hours after we reached our refuge, when things seemed to have quieted down somewhat, Father went to retrieve the "valuables" accumulated in the course of a lifetime. He did not fare so well this time. He returned a while later carrying the sack, but his mouth was bleeding and he had lost two teeth on this mission. He joined us in our allotted alien corner in a stranger's house and sat down quietly.

Since there is so little we can say to each other, especially now that his memory is faulty and his articulation difficult, I become restive after a while, despite my filial intentions. Yet I am determined not to go away before the two hours I assign daily to my parents have elapsed. Rescue appears from an unexpected quarter.

Some friends whom I had promised to meet later at my hotel room
come to pick me up. They exchange a few words of greeting with
my parents and before we notice it, we are in the midst of an
argument on a painful current issue. Who was right during the
Congressional investigations of un-American activities? Those who
named their former colleagues, or the ones who refused to answer
questions about the activities of former friends? The discussion becomes heated. Someone tosses out the word "informers." This puts
things in a different emotional light. Nobody wants to condone
"informing," yet how define it under present conditions?

Even as the argument rages I remember what my father did
about it. This incident also dates far back, to the time before I
was born. I was a child of eight when he told me about it. I then
attended *cheder* and already knew that while it was no crime to
complain to Mother if a sister had taken something I considered
my own, it was an unforgivable crime to report to the *rebbe* anything done by another pupil. That was informing and there was no
more base and villainous creature on earth than a *mooser*—an informer. The only type of informer among adults I then knew of—
the only kind then possible—was a person who reported someone
to the authorities, or, more correctly, a Jew who reported another
Jew to the Gentile authorities.

"Well," my father began, "there was this Yossel and he was an
informer. Regularly he carried tales to the *Ispravnik*. Jews trem-
bled before him. If anyone did a bit of business without a license
or tried to dodge the draft, Yossel always knew about it and informed. People begged him and argued with him, bribes were
offered to him, but it didn't help. A committee once went to him.
'Why do you want to harm your fellow Jews?' they asked him.
'Have you no decency? Have you no regard for anyone? Does it
hurt you if poor people try to earn bread for their children?' But
Yossel only laughed. That was the sort of man he was. He knew he
had the authorities on his side. Just a mean and vicious man. Then
he pulled a particularly bad one. The man he informed on had a
big family and simply couldn't make ends meet. So he began selling
whiskey without a license to the peasants on market days. He
didn't have a regular place, just went around with the bottle from
one to the other, selling it by the drink. And Yossel informed on

him. He was caught and fined, but he couldn't pay it so he had to go to jail for three months and his family almost starved.

"I couldn't stand it any linger. There was another man in town who felt the way I did. He moved away some years ago. So the two of us decided something had to be done. We tried to get others to help us, but everybody was afraid of Yossel on account of his pull with the authorities. They even begged us to leave him alone so as not to cause more trouble than there was already.

"The following Saturday, just as they took the Torah out of the Ark, the other man and I went up to the platform and banged on the table three times. *Ikuv hakriah* it is called, and when anyone in the congregation has very important public business, he does this and they have to wait with the reading of the Torah till the matter is settled. 'We want to make an example of an informer,' we announced and the two of us went up to Yossel. Let me tell you, he was scared. He turned white. He didn't know what we were going to do to him. Maybe he thought we would kill him. As we came up he begged us, 'Don't do anything. I promise. I will never inform again. Don't do anything here, before the entire congregation. I will give you anything you like. I will do anything you say.'

"But we were mad. That last bit of informing could not be forgiven So we took his arms and marched him around the platform three times, shouting 'Thus shall be done to an informer!' I said we marched him around. I should say we dragged him. He was so pale and weak he couldn't stand on his feet. And, you know," Father concluded his story, "it worked. He never informed again and a short time later he left town and we got rid of the informer."

That was long, long ago. Now Father looks at us as we argue back and forth. He does not follow the argument, partly because he doesn't know enough English and partly because the thread of his thought snaps frequently.

In the midst of the argument I wonder: If he were younger, would he know the answer? Of course, it was so much simpler in those days. The authorities were black; the victims white and pure. In our case the issue is more involved. But the fact remains: he knew what was right and what was wrong. He not only knew, he also acted on his convictions.

Father had little formal education. Yet he had the answers to many perplexing questions that befuddled much younger people.

1 often wondered about some of his particularly apt replies, whether he had heard them from others or had made them up himself. Eventually I concluded that they were his own, otherwise he would have given appropriate credit. In his studies of the Talmud he had learned many times how Rabbi X, quoting Rabbi Y in the name of Rabbi Z, said. . . . It became an ingrained habit to shun claiming others' wisdom as one's own.

We, the "younger generaton," were in rebellion against nearly everything that he and his generation of Jews had stood for. His generation engaged in petty business, the enlightened part of the younger generation were all Zionists, singing the glories of work on the land in Palestine, or Socialists, dedicated to the eradication of all business. His generation implicitly believed in the efficacy— or at least the urgent desirability—of prayer. The younger generation sneered at the mechanical recitation of prayers, frequently performed without comprehending the meaning of the words recited.

Father was not much impressed by this criticism. Most of the time he simply ignored it and would not be provoked into argument. But there was one instance when he took up the cudgels on behalf of the practices of his generation.

The particular discussion concerned the recitation of prayers. The "younger generation" felt on solid ground and indulged in some particularly biting sarcasm. How much true religious feeling could one pour into the repetition of sounds without knowing their meaning?

But Father was not impressed. He listened patiently, and when all the fire and thunder had been exhausted, he began his answer in his usually mild manner.

"Why don't you understand?" he said. "Consider it this way. A father has a child of a year, let us say. The child still can't talk. It only babbles meaningless sounds. Yet when the father returns home at the end of the day's work and the child hurries toward him on all fours, babbling its incomprehensible sounds, and it raises its little arms to be picked up, the father beams with pleasure and is convinced that his is a wonderfully bright child and that its babbling is the greatest wisdom ever uttered.

"It is the same when Jews go to the synagogue," he continued. "It is true that many of them don't understand the meaning of what they recite and they mumble their prayers mechanically. But

31

God looks down and sees His children hurrying to His house of prayer. He listens to the sounds they make there and He beams at them with delight. 'What wonderful children I have!' he exclaims. And the prayers are thus perhaps more effective than they would be if everyone understood each word he recited.''

There was no answering this line of argument. There were a few weak attempts at rejoinder; there were some defensive remarks about obscurantism, mysticism. But they lacked conviction.

In late middle age, and later in mounting old age, far from the time and place in which he was brought up and where he belonged, he began to retreat inward. He drifted into the private chamber of his mind where all was clear and where he could commune with his Father, the One who would always understand and appreciate and forgive. He walked about, a strange figure resurrected from a past that extended much further back than his actual age. With a slight change of garb he would have been in place on the ancient plains of the Negev where Jacob's sons pastured their sheep. Yet he passed along the icy streets of St. Paul, by now a walking principle more than a contemporary man.

Because of sickness in the family I was visiting St. Paul. It was midwinter and the temperature hovered around zero. It was Saturday. I came to take him to the hospital where Mother lay sick. Visiting hours were from two to three in the afternoon and from six to seven in the evening. Though the hospital was miles away and the streets were slick with ice, he would not even consider my suggestion to take a streetcar. He did not say "no"; he merely looked at me as if I had said something entirely incomprehensible. We started out at half past twelve. We reached the hospital a quarter after two and stayed with Mother for the remaining three-quarters of an hour. Then he took a seat in the waiting room to spend the next three hours there. I was impatient and went to a cafeteria nearby. When I returned it was after four and dusk was rapidly setting in. The waiting room was quickly filling with visitors to other wards where visiting began after five.

The waiting room had the depressed hush of such places. People whispered to each other, though there was no need for it. Occasionally the silence was rent by the harsh voice over the intercom calling some doctor and everyone involuntarily winced as though it necessarily meant an emergency. Through the thickening gloom outside the windows the bare branches of the trees swayed disconsolately. We in the waiting room felt at the edge of crying, as an abandoned child might cry to be taken home.

The waiting visitors were Swedes, Norwegians, Irish, Germans. Now and then a furtive glance would be directed toward the patriarchal, white-bearded old man, questioning, uncomprehending glances.

Then Father got up and slowly went to the corner facing east. Completely oblivious of the presence of any other people he began reciting his afternoon prayers in an inaudible voice. Only his body gently swayed back and forth. A hush fell on the waiting room. Everyone looked at him. What was the old man doing in the corner? They were mystified, slightly fearful of the thing they did not understand, and also vaguely reverent. There was something about the rocking figure in the rapidly darkening corner that transcended the waiting room, the rasping voice on the intercom, the pain in the wards above. Had they heard his voice they would not have understood the Hebrew words. And if they had understood the words they would have been still more mystified. There seemed to be no obvious point in intoning: "And to Jerusalem the city return in compassion . . ." on a cold winter afternoon in the waiting room of a hospital. But he was probably not considering the meaning of the words either. The old man was again a child speaking to his Father without caring what he said.

Some of the visitors looked at me, as if expecting an explanation. I did not volunteer any.

Later, when we were about to leave the hospital to return home, I saw Father fumbling under the corner of the mattress on which Mother lay. It was a frightening gesture as his fingers searched the end of the bedstead. Then I saw him remove a dime from somewhere beneath the frame that held the spring. He explained the matter to me. "When I go to visit Mother on Friday it is still light and I can carry money, so I take along an extra dime and hide it under the spring. Then I walk home. On Saturday, as you saw, I walk to the hospital in the afternoon but when it is time to return it is already dark and after the Sabbath, so I have my carfare here and can take a streetcar back."

I sit across the table from him. The glasses of tea before us are getting cold. I want to establish some sort of communication with him and find it difficult. He is so far away. I am reconciled. Perhaps true communication between human beings is impossible at any time.

This not very profound reflection brings to my mind a little story Father told me when I was a child. He liked to tell me stories, some of them above my head and others of a kind that modern educators would disapprove of for a child under ten.

He told me about the *lamed vov,* the thirty-six secret saints who live in each generation, and for the sake of whose merits the world remains in existence. They never reveal their true identity to anyone. They are only known to each other. In order not to attract attention, the thirty-six generally engage in some such lowly trade as tailors, shoemakers, or itinerant peddlers; they perform their saintly and sometimes incomprehensible deeds in secret, and then they vanish from the scene.

It happened in the time of Nicholas I, Father told me. At that time small Jewish boys were kidnapped in the streets and farmed out to Russian peasants far away from their homes. When they reached their teens they were taken into the Russian army where they had to serve for twenty-five years. If after all this time they survived and remained Jews—for they were cruelly beaten all the time and in other ways driven to become converted to Christianity —they were free to return home. Those who did return seldom found their parents still living. Grief generally had carried them off.

When a Jewish boy was thus kidnapped he was often held in town for a few days until the authorities could get together a party of boys to be sent away. During this time it was sometimes possible to ransom the child by substituting another recruit.

My story, Father went on, concerns such a kidnapped boy, nine years old, who was snatched in the streets and confined to jail. His parents came to the prison and wept bitterly outside the walls every day. They tried to bribe the guards to let the boy escape but did not succeed. But there lived in that town a *lamed vovnik,* one of the secret thirty-six saints. He could not bear to see the mother's tears, so he volunteered as a recruit to go in the place of the young boy.

He was sent far away to a remote Russian city where there was a fortress. Because he was a grown man they put him in the army right away. He lived on bread and water alone so as not to eat anything that was not kosher.

Often they assigned him to sentry duty. It was then a custom in the Russian army that on dark nights the sentries called to each other every few minutes to make sure that all were awake, because they could not see each other. One sentry would cry out *"Sloo-oo-oo-shay"* ("Hear"), and the one next to him would answer the same call, and so it would go around the wall of the fortress till it completed the circle and they knew that all was well and none of the guards was asleep. But whenever the guard next to the *lamed vovnik* cried out *"Sloo-oo-oo-shay,"* he would mournfully respond, *"Shechinta begaluta vai"* ("The *Shechinah* is in exile, woe").

From a distance it sounded like the regular sentry call.

DO I HAVE A JEWISH COMPLEX?

By EDITH HANDLEMAN

LIFE MAGAZINE AND *Thieves in the Night* join in telling me that there has grown up in Palestine a new generation of Jews. Their striking difference from the traditional Jew is exemplified by the fact that their resistance methods resemble those of the Irish Republican Army, hardly the historic Jewish attitude.

All this, says the modern writer, is due to the fact that they have gained the psychological security of their own land and are free from the tension which besets Jews in other countries. It is enough to convince me that I should be a Zionist, something my Sunday-school teachers failed to do. And it has also crystallized my wondering about whether or not I myself have some complex because I'm Jewish.

I am always robbed in antique shops because I refuse to bargain. The phrase "Jewing down" haunts me.

When we sing the Doxology in our college dining hall, I cannot sing the line "Father, Son, and Holy Ghost." Some superstitious fear makes me slur the words in spite of myself.

Someone once told me that being neurotic was having exaggerated reactions. Slights hurt more than they should; friendship draws us running; sad books make us cry.

All my life I have had all the social, educational, and financial opportunities I could possibly utilize. No one has ever shown prejudice deliberately to hurt me. Yet I feel that I accepted a burden the first day I realized I was a Jew. Being Jewish in today's world always involves some little twisting of thought. I do not know enough about psychological terms to name it. Using the language of the layman, I call it a "complex."

Part of the complex today is a hatred for the word tolerance. How smug the word is—implying, as it does, the enduring of something which cannot be helped. It is the girl who lives upstairs saying, "I could like your Catholic roommate if only she weren't so narrow. If only the Catholics were more broad-minded, like the Protestants, it would be so much easier to like them." Somewhere I have developed a prejudice against the people who assure me that they will tolerate me. Is that my complex—the feeling that I am tolerated as first clarinetist, president of my house, or junior editor of the paper simply because I have earned the position and there is no help for it? The one thing my heart cries for is acceptance.

Probably I am accepted. Undoubtedly, the barrier is in my mind. But I wonder why it is there.

I find that I am continually justifying the two groups in which I live, each to the other. All my family's relatives are close-knit city Jews. Don't we find prejudice in the small town we live in, they ask. Do we really enjoy going to church? And did the rabbi say it was all right? Does my little sister have any girl friends? Would we let her go out with Gentile boys? They find it hard to comprehend the happiness we found when circumstances forced us to live away from the Jewish group; they cannot believe that the community accepts us.

At school the Christian girls, though less frank, ask for explanations, air their uncomprehending views about Jews. "I could never understand why the Jewish girls get so many more parcels of food from home," says the girl across the hall. A discussion follows, an explanation of the reasons why Jewish homes have had to be more close and self-sufficient than others. The fact that dormitory food is strange to Jewish students brought up in Orthodox homes follows, and the mystic word *kosher* is cleared up. The girl across the hall had had queer notions about what the word meant.

I do all this explaining because somehow I feel responsible. I am anxious to give Marie the right impression of Jews—but not for my own sake. I already know that she likes me, understands me. I am trying to help all the Jews she will meet years from now.

Why should I feel this responsibility for people I will never meet? Where did this burden come from?

Incredible as it seems, I did not know I was Jewish, or what a

Jew was, until I was six. With a child's love of colors and textures, I owned the Christmas tree at the home of our friends, the Mullers. We visited there on Christmas Eve, and I remember saying to Mary, "Let's not tell Shirley there isn't any Santa Claus. After all, she's only four." I would go to sleep with the Muller girls and wake with them at midnight to get our gifts. I never understood why, no matter how much I teased, my parents would not let me have a tree in my living room so that I could look at it for twelve days the way the Muller girls did. Although they took me to the Mullers' in the interests of friendship and a broad, pleasant background, they were still too bound by superstitious fear to have a tinseled tree in their home.

My first faint awareness of some difference, then, was that somehow I was being denied this pleasant vision of the tree in my house.

Although I did not connect it with this disappointment, my other early awareness of "difference" was also connected with an unpleasant feeling. Visiting my Orthodox aunts when I was little I had to be told in whispers that one must not ask for butter when there is meat on the table. I was nervous in their kitchen; I wanted to help, but somehow I knew that certain dish towels were for different dishes, and I did not dare ask.

Before I knew what Judaism was, then, I had experienced the feeling of being different both from the Gentile and from the Orthodox Jew.

My first grade in Buffalo was "progressive," so much so that a teachers' college sent delegates to watch the class. They came on Saturday, and we prepared for them enthusiastically.

"If any Jewish children are called on," said the teacher, "you won't want to write on Saturday, so just ask someone else to take your place at the blackboard."

I was not sure if that meant me. I had always written on Saturday. I did not know what a Jew was. My family must have mentioned the word often, though, because I had a hunch that maybe she meant me. I asked my friend Nancy, and she said, yes, I was Jewish, and so was she. It was hard to give up my chance to recite for the visitors, but if Miss Harrison thought I should act like a Jew, I was too proud to admit that in my home I had never been taught anything about the Sabbath. The first time I consciously lined myself with the Jews, then, was both embarrassing and some-what in the nature of a sacrifice.

Other times, since, I have observed my religion more for ap-pearances than for inward comfort. It is no longer as it was in first grade, however, from personal pride, but rather because, as my Sunday-school teachers and my parents said, "People will have more respect for all Jews if they see that you observe your religion."

For my parents realized that I could not cope with Gentiles and Jews without some background. One day when I was ten I came home to find a strange man in the living room discussing "Juda-ism" with my father. It was a new word to me, and I liked its sound, but my mother told me to go outdoors and play. It was not until this moment of writing that I realized the part that stranger must have played in the bringing of my parents "back into the fold." The next Sunday I was sent, with my girl friend Louise, to Sunday-school, and the strange man was my teacher.

To be a Jewish girl there at Sunday-school, following Louise's proprietary advice, was to be a princess. It was better than being a gypsy. I was taught about my heritage. I owned the silver candle-sticks and the velvet-covered parchment scrolls that tinkled their silver bells gayly when they were carried around the synagogue. Everybody else would have to go to school some special holiday, while I could dress up in my best and go to temple.

Later on, I relished the day of fasting and repentance that comes in the fall, starting the new year. Someone had told me that I must not wash my teeth in the morning for fear of swallowing water and thus breaking my fast. I asked my father, who, I proudly discov-ered, knew all about these things. "Yes," he said. "Don't brush your teeth, if you want to be strict and old-fashioned about it." I did want to be old-fashioned. I thrilled to the strains of the traditional *Kol Nidre*. I gloried in the day of fasting, when, dressed in our best ("If God is good it'll be cold enough for them to wear fur coats," said my mother dryly), we wandered from temple to syna-gogue, gazing wide-eyed from the women's balcony in the Ortho-dox synagogue. Below, the rabbi became a high priest and cov-ered his face with the white prayer shawl lest the people be blinded by his glory.

"If you peek now, you go blind," Daddy had said. "I peeked

when I was eight and, as you know, I went blind two years ago. Now, what does that prove?" I didn't know.

I didn't peek. I compared notes with my friends, enjoying the little family traditions they revealed: Muriel's folks broke the fast at sundown with fresh grapes; Eddie's family started their "break fast" meal with grapefruit juice; my own mother, remembering her childhood in an Orthodox family, insisted that we must have orange juice and then wait a while before tearing into the feast.

While my father pointedly looked the other way and the family smiled nostalgic smiles, I stole the special piece of unleavened bread on the eve of the Passover, and then demanded ransom for it when my father came to the end of the service and declared loudly, "We cannot finish this ceremony without the *afikomen*. Where can it be? I will give whoever has it anything she wants." Then one year *I* smiled understandingly, for my little sister was old enough to steal it and claim the traditional booty. She was always afraid of matches, though, so I continued to have the honor of lighting the eight candles in honor of the brave Maccabee brothers during the feast of lights.

I learned in the Reform temple to be proud of the accomplishments of my forbears. I did not learn the theology of my faith, as I wish I had. Instead of learning the guide to living which other religions taught, I was taught justification for my existence as a Jew. I was so busy learning to protect and polish my treasure that I never got a chance to stand and look at it. I could not live normally. I must be ready to answer accusations (they have never come) and to realize the worth of my people.

I am glad I learned about the great philosophers, about the contributions of the Jews to America. But why has no one told me what the prophets left of their wisdom to guide me? My little sister is learning, upon her own request, in the less modern Conservative temple. She learns what the prayers mean, where the eighteen blessings come from, why they carry the scroll of the ark through the synagogue. I envy her. I would rather know that than eighteen rhetorical facts about why the Jews could not have killed Christ.

My first encounter with prejudice—the almost-instinctive, superstitious kind—came when we sang Christmas carols in the fourth grade. Louise, who sat next to me, scowled as I caroled a bit off key that "Christ the Saviour is born." "You mustn't say those words," she whispered, and there was nothing intellectual behind her reproof. She had a blind fear of the cross and the Christ, instilled unconsciously by her parents, to whom the sight of the cross had meant a crowd of crazed peasants bent on religious massacre, a dread pogrom. Louise's warning is still with me; I cannot repeat the responses in Chapel services at school without a fear, which I lay to the more rational feeling that I am playing the hypocrite. There is still a shivering as if the roof might fall in when I say the words "for His name's sake."

By this time we had moved to Boston, and the public school was no longer progressive. New England children that we were, we read *Little Women* in fourth grade, and I asked Miss Roger what it meant when it said that Marmee had given the girls the story of the greatest life every lived. Miss Rogers said, "Oh, you wouldn't know." She seemed embarrassed. "It's—well—I don't know if you —uh, it's the story of Jesus."

I blushed for her thinking me ignorant; I could not stand that in fourth grade. For some obscure reason I read the whole of *Pilgrim's Progress* before that year was out, and years later, living in a small town, I went to the Presbyterian Sunday school so that Miss Rogers would never have to explain things to me again. But the part that impressed me most was her uncomfortable, "Oh, you wouldn't know." I had never told the teacher I was Jewish, yet somehow she thought I might excusably be different. Did my differentness show? Could any person, meeting me, say, "That little girl is different from my little girl—she must be Jewish—there are some things she does not know?" And why the restraint, the murmur? It must be like that question of why babies look like their fathers—evidently better left unasked. This was another of those things people only whispered about. To this day I find it so. The college bull-session takes on a thrilling, daring tension when sex or religion comes up for discussion.

The Sunday school was Zionist; it taught me to accept the burden of the woes of the Jewish world in pre-Hitlerian days. I was my brother's keeper, in more ways than one. My father explained to me how what I did reflected on all the Jews. "Caesar's wife must be above reproach," he cautioned. I felt that I was the focal point for many hypercritical eyes. It is not a healthy feeling for a child: that every action is watched by a world of people capable of hurting others in return for every bad impression he makes.

All this was being built in my mind; the scant anti-Semitism I saw did not hurt me. To a dramatic child, the yell of the boy across the street, "Little Jew," was only another thrilling event in a life full of thrills. It was something to gloat about, especially since the boy across the street was dirty and dumb, and I already played second clarinet in the school orchestra while he played only third.

When my persistent questions brought from my mother the news that we did not go to the Mullers' any more because Mr. Muller had joined some German-American organization, I felt none of the hurt which must have been in her heart. I had heard the name Hitler a few times. This was exciting, as, years later, was the first service enlistment in our family; the world and its affairs were coming into my life.

Anti-Semitism, whatever else it may be, is also an attitude in the Jew's mind. He will either exaggerate or ignore it. Whether he reads discrimination into every slight, or else refuses to accept the fact that prejudice has been shown, his mental attitude hurts him.

I have met some who "blame everything on the weather—or anti-Semitism." Recently I heard a city woman say, "I must move. My children are part of such a small minority in this part of the city and there's so much persecution in the high school." I know her children; I was their counselor at camp. I am prejudiced against them myself. As long as their mother excuses every failure, soothes them and cries "anti-Semitism," they will probably retain their thoughtless, rude ways.

"Oh, no," protests this woman. "I wouldn't have let Beverly join that sorority—and be the only Jewish girl in it. But it's just the idea—why wasn't she asked? Isn't this a democracy?"

Yet if Beverly had said instead, "There is no prejudice in the school. This must be my fault if the girls don't want me," she faces another danger. I have seen it this year, when a friend of my little sister was not chosen to the high-school sorority. Having been taught at home not to look for excuses, she does not believe it was anti-Semitism. Perhaps it is some lack in herself. With teen-age hopelessness she examines herself for the "queer" streak. The doubt is enough to start some little twist in her mind, and the next time there may be a real lack within her.

Here prejudice was shown, but neither accepted the fact. Beverly gets angry; my sister's friend refuses to face it. Both have the beginnings of a nice "complex." They will take the same way out; they are intelligent girls, and they will aim for high marks, school offices, nice clothes. Isn't it the traditional compensation of the Jew? I do not know whose fault the high-school situation is. I do know I cannot change the fact that sororities are organized on religious divisions.

What I can change is my reaction to the world. Three things I can do: I will cease being "proud of my race"—or ashamed of it; I will show Christians and Jews that these differences in our customs and beliefs are not "touchy" subjects but interesting questions, and I will realize that I am prejudiced as any Christian is.

One thing I resent in the "tolerant" Christian is his praising me because Albert Einstein is brilliant, or because Moses was wise. I cannot accept these as my own achievements, or as accomplishments which by some metaphysical means have been communicated to me. If I did, I should also have to make apologies to the world because Lepke Buchalter becomes a public enemy. I had nothing to do with either. If I expect the world to recognize this fact in some instances, consistency makes me shy away from ignoring it in others.

The Christians I meet are eager to learn about Jews. When I mention Judaism casually in conversation and seem ready to talk about Jewish beliefs and customs, they recover from the shock of hearing the taboo word and start asking questions.

With Jews I am more frank—about the question of prejudice as about so many other things—and I present my view without looking for a subtle opening. "Christians do not sit up nights thinking of ways to hurt you," I protest. "They don't even know what you're like, but they're open-minded and willing to learn." And I go off into tales of my town.

Once, years ago, a Jewish girl friend called me an anti-Semite. She said I had no right to talk to Christians about Judaism, that I did not know what it was. She resented my looking for local color in the home life and synagogue. She was amazed, as many Jews are, at my statement that Jews are prejudiced.

I have seen, through living in a small town, attending church, and becoming an intimate friend to many Christians, that it is almost impossible to be an unprejudiced Christian. But I feel that an unprejudiced Jew is even rarer. So much prejudice is excusable that the Jew is likely to rationalize his inexplicable, human dislikes and make no effort to overcome them. "It's self-defense," he argues, as Jewish father forbids his daughter to go out with Gentiles, and Jewish fraternity completes segregation on the campus.

The thinking Jew usually protests earnestly at the assertion that Jews are prejudiced. Or, if he admits the prejudice, he maintains that the main job is to combat anti-Semitism. Eliminate prejudice from the Gentile, and the Jew's defense against it will disappear, he maintains.

I agree with him. But I do not look for the end of anti-Semitism in a hurry. Let the rest of the thinking Jews fight someone else's prejudice. My one voice will be raised against my own flaw. Because I have an excuse, I am inclined to condone my own narrow-mindedness. Newspapers, magazines, preachers support my satisfying theory that it is the Gentile who is prejudiced.

I am not only one of a martyr race. I am one of a group suffering from a martyr complex which blinds it to itself. Playing Caesar's wife is not a healthy pastime.

THE EDUCATION OF A JEW

By MICHAEL BLANKFORT

RECENTLY, IN AN informal reunion of some old friends whom I had not seen for years, the question of the education of our children as Jews came up. In order to make clear a point in my own attitude, I mentioned that I had been attending synagogue services rather frequently in the last few years. I was called on to explain. I replied that I had found in the synagogue, even for the few hours a week, a quiet refuge from worldly stress and with it a spiritual peace.

"But you can get the same thing walking alone in the hills," one of my friends said. I told him that I had tried that but it hadn't worked. And what was more important, the peace and refreshment of spirit which I had experienced in the synagogue became meaningful because it was shared with others, with Jews, and in a place of worship.

"But is it possible that you believe in God?" another skeptical friend inquired.

The question was overlaid with many tones. I could almost hear the echoes of the past two decades, the voices of a generation rising in rebellion against the restrictions and hypocrisies of organized religion, against the values of a society in which we had observed and experienced corruption, decay and impotence; and, finally, our voices rising in defense of another system of values which would, we thought, renew life and bring justice to the oppressed. This system was Marxism, the new materialism, which denounced God in its struggle to supplant the old materialism which had made a mockery of Him.

"Yes, I believe in God," I said slowly, for as I spoke the words I realized that there were even more complex echoes and overtones in the reply than in the question. So simple the answer; so complicated the reasoning.

Some of my old friends understood and revealed their own renewed interest in these matters; but some were frankly critical of what they considered "a withdrawal into mysticism." Now it is not my intention to do a poll on the attitudes toward God of middle-aged Jewish intellectuals, since at best one's views on these matters are one's own business. But I could not help inquiring of myself: Wherefrom and whereto this Hegira? What peace did you seek that you think you have now found? What values in life did you search for which now seem revealed to you in positive and affirmative Judaism?

To start somewhere near the beginning: I was brought up in the Orthodox Jewish home of American-born parents. I was given the conventional Jewish education—that is, I was sent to *cheder* (private Hebrew school) three hours in the afternoon, five days a week for six years, up to the time I was about fourteen. During that time I learned how to read prayer-book and Torah Hebrew, chanted without the vowel signs, and with a speed and accuracy which were miracles of learning by rote. I understood, however, no more than one one-thousandth of what I read. Of course I attended *shul* regularly on the Sabbath and holidays, prayed three times a day, said all the blessings, wore the fringed undergarment, put on the *tfillin* (phylacteries) after my Bar Mitzvah; and outside the home as well as within, I kept the dietary laws.

During my formative years, I felt that I was beset, or more accurately, harassed, by "God's ordinances." I was the object of His scrutiny, the victim of His power. I was in dread of His punishment for my sins. I feared Him mightily. Like hundreds of thousands of others before, and *at* that time, I was the living confirmation of Maimonides' observation that by the constant repetition of the "acts of service to God, such as the reading of the Law, prayer and the performance of other commandments . . . men fear God and are in terror and awe of Him . . ." But I did not know, for reasons too complex to describe now, enough Jewish philosophy, if any, or even enough biblical history to understand or sustain this step in the religious education of a Jew. To be blunt, I was an

Orthodox illiterate. Even those sermons of my rabbi which, as I look back, were often filled with exhortations to an ethical life and God's love, could not compare in impact with those in which he scolded me vigorously for lapses in the observance of the ordinances.

A victim of terror not only fears his oppressor, but also hates him. I could not ever, of course, bring myself to admit into consciousness a feeling of hatred for God, for that would have been tantamount to self-destruction. But He was clearly not a God of love.

Derech eretz (that wonderful Hebrew phrase which in a fairly literal translation means "respect for the land" but which has come to mean respect for the opinions and feelings of others), constrained me to continue with the observances of the Jewish laws long after they had lost meaning for me, long after I had even lost the consciousness of the fear of God and had even lost belief in His existence. But the configuration of values which had been formed within me remained. I had begun a search, though I wasn't aware of it then, for a philosophic understanding of man and his world.

In my twenties, I became a student and teacher of psychology. I was a "scientist," so to speak. My views and values were a compound of behaviorism, pragmatism, Freudianism. Man, I thought, was finite. Given time to experiment, the farthest horizon of human behavior could be reached. Man's soul was merely a higher and more complex system of responses. Change the environment and you change all. Study white mice, conditioned reflex, the learning curve, the establishment of a Gestalt—and all is understood. Man had become a machine.

One could even account for God under the aegis of this new discipline. He was the remaining appendage of early folk-mysteries; He had been the creation of a need to understand the universe before Science had come into its own. But whatever the theory, and there were many, it was obvious that the conception of God was one of man's inferior thoughts.

In each generation of intellectuals, there is a small leading group, the sensitive front-runners, the aristocracy of creative depth and communicability, the pioneers. They set the values; they establish fashions in ideas which are usually vulgarizations of the values. Sometimes these front-runners also make a lasting contribution to our total experience by instinctively giving a renewed emphasis to some eternal verity which may, at the time, have been forgotten or ignored. This residue of intellectual foment is for the succeeding generation to build upon.

In those days of "science," the fashion was to denigrate man's need for God. For me, in those days of the late twenties and early thirties, God was superstition and Judaism was a backward religion. It did not take long, as the Depression deepened, to add that all religion was "the opiate of the people." Marxism had taken the central place in the arena of values in which many of my generation were to become either the victors or the victims. We were living through the break-up of a world, even of the old "science" to which (as we would do with the Marxism which took its place) we had given lip-service and followed its "ordinances" without really understanding them. Breadlines replaced behaviorism in our concerns.

The disruption of the world of capitalism meant poverty to millions, but to many intellectuals it meant a kind of riches. I do not mean this in derogation. On the contrary, the break-up of the world released an enormous creative energy that had lain dormant through the cynical years of the "lost generation" and the "scientific" years of those who were too young for World War I and therefore had not been entirely "lost." A new spirit entered minds which had been deprived of their older spirit or spirituality. The materialism of Marxism seemed not only the necessary reflection of changing times, but also the inevitable outgrowth of the masters who had so valiantly taught us how to criticize Babbitt, Main Street and the Booboisie.

Further, Marxism preached universalism to those who were looking for a way out of the evils of nationalism; it claimed for itself humanitarianism in action; and to those like myself who had devoured the histories of World War I and had learned to hate imperialism, it proclaimed the final answer to war. To the idealist, to the pseudo-realist, to the ever-rebellious young among us, Marxism as a *Weltanschauung* seemed the way to win social justice and the end of the exploitation of man by man.

All these biblical aspirations for which we had prayed in our youth and dreamed about in the vast hours of young manhood could be achieved in our lifetime, we thought, if only the *status quo,* the Authority (the feared God-figure, if you wish), were overthrown. Naturally, we did not like the idea that human blood might have to be shed in the course of this action. We regretted it after we accepted the major premises as much as we regretted the pain and blood entailed in childbirth. But hadn't human blood always been spilled in a long history of bad wars?

Again, the fashion of the intellectual front-runners took hold and colored our thinking. It held sway for almost two decades. The fashion and the values were these: If the ends are good, it doesn't matter that the means toward them could entail hurt to others, even the innocent; in the scale of values only those which further the security of a single political State are worthy, and all others are ignoble, inhuman and depraved; man's character and dignity are totally dependent on the economic environment in which he lives; finally (and most debased), truth is absolute and derives its authority from whoever is the current spokesman of a political party and its special readings and interpretation of Marx.

The literature of disillusion with Communist Marxism is too well known to embroider. But what has perhaps not been stated as often is that such disillusion is not a new experience for the pioneering intellectuals, the people of deep feeling and good will, and the creative workers. Out of such experiences arose many movements which in their time were advances toward a freer life, such as the Reformation, capitalism, even the early socialism. Reaction against absolutism almost invariably leads to an enrichment of the mind. One then doesn't have to fear that, in the long view of history, the bitter turning away from such a dream of social justice as was cast in Marxist terms over the minds of a generation must inevitably lead to black, inactive despair and anti-intellectualism. Nor, it seems to me, must it lead to a reaction-absolutism, political or theological, despite current but transitory symptoms of that trend.

Disillusion had, I think, a progressive impact on me. During the period in which I had accepted the value of Marxism, I remained nevertheless as skeptical of accepting the total faith of a political philosophy which spoke in its name as I had been of religious philosophies. It seems to me now that even during those years I had never entirely lost what was pervasive and lasting in my Jewish experience. There were strains of remembrance even with this Ortho-

49

dox illiterate whose childhood was immersed in prayers ("How can God's judgment on our sins be averted? By Penitence, Prayer and Charity," and a charity which meant Justice). The borders of my consciousness were marked by the weekly repetition of the *Pirke Aboth* ("The Ethics of the Fathers"), the gentle homilies of my grandfather at the Sabbath table, each an anecdote of Talmud, of charity and genuine saintliness. There was more to it than sentiment; there had been deep and unconscious learning which had ingrained a yearning for a charity which was justice, and a justice which did not demand blood sacrifices and the acceptance of an absolutism in order to pursue it.

A dear friend of those years of the melting away of an illusion was a noble Jew, the late Rabbi Milton Steinberg. He made the point clearly when he said that Judaism must reject communism because communism is ready to sacrifice mercy to attain its ends. "For this is an integral part of the Communist program, that compassion must be suspended for a time . . ." And to those who claimed that compassion would be reinstated when the classless society was achieved, he replied: "Judaism says of all such counsels that they overlook the crucial fact about man; that man is always pitiable, even man the capitalist, the Trotskyite, the kulak. Therefore there is not a time or occasion on which we are free not to pity him."

This element and the re-examination and rejection of the Marxist values mentioned earlier led me to withdraw my sympathies from communism, political and philosophic. Of course, one does not sit down coldly and make an analysis and come to conclusions. The dynamic events of the world intensify and clarify such decisions. For me, too, the break was broadened by an approach to Judaism and the Jewish people to which nowadays even Sunday-school seniors are exposed. I began to read the secular histories of my people. From the histories, I moved to the philosophers, the poets, the statesmen, the prophets, the commentators on the Bible, the Talmudists—all in a language I could understand. Slowly, terribly late, I began to shed the old illiteracy. And in becoming an informed Jew, I found that so interwoven are the semi-secular writings with our religious writings that any conscientious study of the meaning of the former must lead to some kind of attraction, if not affection, for the latter.

The way back to the synagogue can be taken by many roads, and there are many kinds of synagogues and many things to find in each. It is no great wisdom to perceive that God is not the property of the Orthodox, nor the property of the Jews. (And I love the Jewish thinkers and scholars for saying this so clearly.) Once I was certain as to who God was and what He did. Now, I am not certain that I even understand what I mean when I say that I believe in Him. But one thing I know: He is no longer a God of fear.

It was with quite understandable joy that after having found this out for myself, I discovered in Maimonides that the purpose of the biblical laws is to lead to the fear of God, and of the biblical truths to arouse love of Him. This love, as Maimonides suggests, depends on a knowledge of God and later becomes the decisive factor in man's relation to Him. (And, I would add, to man himself.)

We who followed other gods, even with all our good intentions, lost the simple knowledge of Micah: "To do justly, and to love mercy, and to walk humbly with thy God." It is particularly apt for our times to note that the commentary on this specific passage in the Chumesh as edited by Rabbi Hertz points out that the Hebrew for the phrase, "to do justly," literally translated means "to execute justice," implying reverence for the personality of every human being as the possessor, by virtue of his humanity, of inalienable rights to life, honor, and the fruit of his toil.

In the communion of Judaism, the identification with my people, my active affection for the Land of Israel, my faltering efforts to live by the precepts of the prophets, I have found a peace of the spirit. They have combined in a set of values which do not have all the answers and perhaps are yet only barely perceptible to me. It is a way of life and understanding by which, as a human being, an American, a Jew and a writer, I can view with more meaning the world around me and the world within.

A JEW IN A CHRISTIAN COMMUNITY

By ROBERT H. GLAUBER

To a man brought up in the overwhelming anonymity of a great metropolitan center, religion, more often than not, is something he either accepts or rejects solely as his inner needs dictate. He is a member of a congregation or not—just as he chooses. It is of as little concern to his neighbors as any other detail of his personal life. In business and in social relationships he goes his own way with an almost infinite number of paths to select from. He shares the general fate of his co-religionists only in an indirect way. He is one of the mass; seldom singled out for specific attention— religious or otherwise. And when such an occasion *does* arise, he usually greets it with profound indignation. He joins Jonathan Swift in asking of his next-door neighbor: "What religion is he of? Why he is an Anythingarian."

I was born and brought up a Jew in New York City. Its vastness is part of me. I was mass-production educated and entertained. I was one Jew (Reform) among two million others. I had a reasonable if not thorough Jewish education. On the High Holidays I went to temple when I was younger because my parents (second generation Americans though they were) expected it. As I grew older, being a scientific rationalist, the God of Abraham, Isaac, and Jacob came to mean little or nothing to me. There was an early reconciliation within me of the dichotomy of Judaism and things Jewish.

My work constantly carried me all over the country. Everywhere I was recognized at once as a New Yorker. I was proud of this. Only in one instance was I challenged as a Jew. At the time, I was as surprised as I was annoyed. I was what I was: one out of many, not to be singled out for special attention.

If I had any specific Jewish consciousness at all, it manifested itself in an interest in American-Jewish history. But I felt no more direct relationship with my subject than a mathematician feels toward a complicated equation over which he works for several months. In short, I was a typical member of the generally disappointing picture of contemporary American Jewry.

Early in September of last year my work suddenly required that I move from New York City to a tiny community on the prairie of central Illinois. The village seemed like little more than a clearing constantly in danger of being swallowed by the vast cornbelt which surrounded it. There was a general store, a post office, a farm-implement agency, a garage and service station, an ice-cream parlor doubling as the bus station, and a short-order lunchroom. That was about the whole of it. The sidewalks along the main street were still sheltered from the sun and rain in the best Western tradition by ancient wood and corrugated sheet-iron marquees. The town pump was the hub from which everything radiated. The current population was listed at six hundred on the road sign just outside of town. But I seriously doubted (and still doubt) this figure. Many old and dilapidated buildings were rapidly crumbling evidence that this village on the plains had seen a better day.

And what of these six hundred people? They were all strangers to me; and I to them. They were Middle Westerners, conservative Republicans, farmers, isolationists even at this late date, willing to interpret the world only in terms of their own immediate interests. In advance, I thought them dull.

They quickly proved themselves to be friendly and cordial. But, by my big-city standards, they were shockingly curious. They asked direct and personal questions about anything and everything that caught their curiosity. And in my first weeks there I seemed to do just that.

In less than four or five days, I was asked by people whose names I did not even know why I was there; where I came from; how long I thought I might stay; how large my family was and when they were to join me; where I planned to live; what I thought of the unseasonably hot weather; and whether or not it was true that the publishing business in the East was overrun with Communists. The constant barrage left me somewhat numb.

After casting about somewhat desperately for a suitable place in which to live, I was finally taken in by one of the town's leading families. The man of the house, who numbered among his fore-bears original settlers of the village, owned and operated a large farm on the outskirts of town. My landlady taught school in a nearby community. As several people hastily informed me: I was lucky to be taken in by—shall we call them—the Smiths.

One evening, over a game of canasta, Mrs. Smith said quite casually: "Robert, you've been here several weeks now. How about coming to church with us this Sunday?"

I was surprised, perhaps even a bit amused. I didn't wish to cause her any embarrassment and, in my own, could only mutter some-thing about being sorry. Church-going was not in my line.

"Well, you might at least try the Sunday school."

No, that too would be difficult.

"Oh, come now, it won't do you any harm!"

Quietly, I explained that I was a Jew and the discussion seemed to end there. We finished the game quite pleasantly without fur-ther reference to the invitation.

Several days later I was button-holed in the lunchroom by the leading town gossip. She was a spinster, thin and cold. Her own life was completely dull and so she garnished it with a vicarious en-joyment of other people's business. In all truth, however, there was nothing vicious about her. She had been pointed out to me and so I felt myself forewarned. Her approach was direct. Without any preliminary remarks she said: "Mr. Glauber, there's a rumor going about town that you're Jewish."

I had expected some innocuous question: how did I like the town? In my amazement, I scalded my tongue with hot coffee. This was an outrage. To me, it seemed that she employed a tone she might have used had she said: "Mr. Glauber, there's a rumor going about town that you're an escaped murderer."

"There is?' I finally answered. "Well, that shows you how wrong rumors can be. Actually, I'm a Druid!"

The lady retired at once. I was not even certain she knew what a Druid was. When I returned to my work, I told my companions about the encounter. They laughed. But inwardly, I burned.

The next day I was stopped on the street by one of the ladies I had previously met at the Smiths. "What do you mean by telling that poor soul that you're a Druid?"

Apparently, no time had been lost in spreading the story.

She continued. "Look, it doesn't matter if you're a Jew or a Presbyterian or whatever. If you'd care to come to church, we'd be glad to have you."

The matter was not to be dropped lightly. Again, however, I thought it best to say nothing.

Perhaps a week passed before I was tackled afresh. I was in my room one night reading when Mrs. Smith knocked on the door discreetly and, in response to my answer, entered carrying three or four books. She put them on the desk and explained that she had been in the middle of preparing her Sunday-school lesson (she taught an adult class and took the job very seriously) and found herself confused on several points. "You see, the lesson is on Isaiah." Then she paused expectantly.

"So?" I said.

"Well you certainly know more about him than I do."

"I? How come?"

"You said you were Jewish. After all, he was one of your greatest prophets. We Presbyterians don't devote enough time to the Old Testament to really get to know it—at least, not well enough to teach it."

Her candor was direct and open. My sophistication might have made me resent her supposition but her naivete would have made anger into brutality. "Just what makes you think that because I'm a Jew I know anything about Isaiah?"

Now she was surprised. "Well, golly, if you don't know, who should?"

For the life of me, I couldn't answer. My apologies and explanations, on reflection, must have seemed lame indeed. There was not a concrete thing I could say.

The next day, unable to put her question aside, I drove to a nearby town where there was a small college. I spent several hours in the library reading biblical commentaries and returned home laden with notes. That night, after supper, I told Mrs. Smith to gather her questions together and I would see if I could answer any of them. We spent several hours talking about the great prophet.

That Saturday morning Mrs. Smith again asked me to come to Sunday school. Her reasons were sound. Being accustomed to study and research, I had obviously gotten more from my work at the library than she had been able to absorb from our talk. Why not give the class the benefit of what I had done? Sheepishly, I consented, but only on the condition that she tell the class I was a Jew.

She shrugged her shoulders. "If that's the way you want it, I'll tell them. But it seems mighty silly to me."

Despite a considerable backlog of work, I went again to the college library during the afternoon. I worked with a research care and exactitude I had not employed since my own college days. I had consented to help Mrs. Smith teach her class and insofar as I was able, I would be prepared.

The class itself was less than I had anticipated. Easily, informally, we discussed Isaiah, his message to the people, his humility and his defiance. They were little interested in theory. The question of the probable authorship of the various sections of the book was mentioned only in passing. Their concern was with the practical. How could they apply the lessons of Isaiah to their own lives? What was his meaning for them?

As I left the building—I was not staying for the service—the minister stopped me. He was a pleasant old man, in the pulpit for over fifty years, almost twenty-five of them at his present post. We had met many times on the street. His greeting was always cheerful and spontaneous. "I heard what you did. It was very kind and we all thank you for it." I was embarrassed and went out quickly.

The following week was Rosh Hashonah. Chance brought a New York paper to me (I seldom read one . . . it was better not to know what I was missing!) and I saw it mentioned. Had I not, the holiday would have passed utterly without my knowledge. As it happened, there was nothing I could do about it. Mr. Smith told me that, insofar as he knew, the nearest community with a Jewish congregation was in P——, and he mentioned a town almost seventy-five miles away. It would have been impossible to get there. So the day passed without the sound of the *shofar* for me. For the first time in my life I could honestly say that I missed it.

I mentioned the holiday at home that night. The Smiths were interested. Just what did the holiday mean? How much was it like the "ordinary" New Year? Why was the date different every year? So many questions revealed their absolute lack of knowledge about even the rudiments of Judaism, and so many others pointed out to me my own scant information. Each time I was forced to say *I don't know* they seemed surprised. I was the first Jew they had ever known at close quarters; surely the first they had ever questioned about his religion. Written behind their eyes was the unvoiced query: are all Jews as uninformed about their religion as this one seems to be?

As the weeks passed I was invited to Sunday school regularly. There was a quiet routine. On Friday night Mrs. Smith would gather what books she had and I, having written to New York for several texts, would bring mine. We studied together. Her questions about Isaiah or Elijah or Hosea (her class was working through the Old Testament prophets) were always keen and direct. It was a process of mutual exploration: what does a Jew think of the miracle-studded career of Ezekiel? And what can a Christian know of the deeper meanings of Jeremiah's lamentation?

The class itself soon took my presence for granted. Strangely, I never could. They were friendly, cordial in every way, tacitly respectful of the irreconcilable differences between us. But there was always a barrier beyond which I could not move. Too often I felt as if I were asked to strip myself mentally naked—to lie unprotected under the Christian gaze. After all, I was a single Jew; a curiosity to be questioned; a representative of the strange people.

Not that there was ever any manifestation of anti-Semitism. To these people, anti-Semitism (since they had never known a Jew and were concerned only with things of immediate interest to them) was as unthinkable as atheism.

But the barrier *was* there.

I had come to the village, a stranger and alone. They had welcomed me in their own curious way. If I missed a Sunday at school for one reason or another, they stopped me on the street to inquire the reasons. Still, I was not part of the community in any but a superficial way. A sense of isolation, of being part yet apart, of—difference obsessed me. I recalled often the lines from Sartre's *Anti-Semite and Jew:* "The Jew is one whom other men consider a Jew." Had this backfired?

What demon is there in me as a Jew that drives me within myself—that separates me from my neighbor *in my own mind?* To all intents and purposes I had turned my back on my religion; completely divorced the cultural manifestations of Judaism from the religious duties and implications; favored one and not the other. And yet, isolated in a Christian community, there was a reversion to type which would have delighted an anthropologist and astounded a psychologist.

Contemporary Jews make so many claims and counter-claims about their religion, lodge so many complaints against it, fracture it into so many mutually exclusive factions that the late-starting novice hardly knows where to begin. It may be lacking (as many during the war claimed it to be—especially converts) in deep emotional outlets in times of stress. It may not abound in the father and mother images necessary for "successful" identification in a Freudian sense. It may be over-intellectualized or under-mysticized. Indeed, it may even be as anachronistic as many people claim all religious concepts to be. I cannot say.

But my experience, from what I can see, has not been in any way unique. Whatever Judaism in the abstract may be in the modern world, whatever lack of enthusiasm it may provoke from the members of an active Jewish community, to me, an isolated Jew in a Christian community, feeling myself challenged on religious grounds (justifiably or not), it proved to be as compelling and irresistible a force as ever.

One is called *Jew*—no matter how—and a wave of racial and historical memory overwhelms one. And, like the more physical waves of the ocean, cannot be stopped by the application of logic— no matter how enlightened.

I CHANGED MY NAME

ANONYMOUS

TOWARD JULY OF 1945 my kid brother's V-mail began coming home scrawled all over with odd pseudonyms. If I knew David, he was after something—just what, it wasn't impossible to guess, even before the final letter that rounded out his campaign. He wanted to change his name.

We are Jews, and our name was forthrightly Jewish. As his letter gingerly put it, the decision to take a new name was related to a taste for travel he had picked up in the Air Force. He had seen New Orleans, the Rockies, the Pacific, Manila; he wanted to see more after the war, and now he sought this means of assuring pleasant globe-trotting.

I think I knocked him out of his cockpit when I wrote that the step he contemplated had been on my mind a good while, and that it appeared advantageous from most angles. Somehow, halfway around the world, and busy with a B-29, he had arrived at my own well-matured conclusion as to one *sine qua non* of the good life in the twentieth century.

When David came home we got out our Manhattan phone directory, pored through the section of names with our initial, and compiled a list of three hundred choice surnames. When it came to making a decision, when we uttered those unfamiliar syllables aloud after our own given names, the project faltered; mutual embarrassment turned us cold. Without our old name we felt as anonymous as a couple of blades of grass.

But at last, having winnowed our sizable list, testing and rejecting, we settled on a name both neutral and euphonious. It might be Protestant or Catholic, it might be French, English, American. It might be anything. Crusaders had borne our name; street sweepers no doubt still do.

Good enough. The less your name says, the louder your actions speak. We hoped ours would do us credit.

Our idea was to find a name soothing to the greatest possible number of preconceptions and prejudices we were likely to meet. Our choice, we had agreed, was not to be pure Anglo-Saxon (although that's such a marketable strain) because we are both dark, resembling our father rather than our mother, a blue-eyed blonde. No telling what shade our children might decide to assume. So, clasping hands in enthusiasm over our own shrewdness, we steered clear of a number of British pitfalls.

Then we paid a lawyer (funny how you always pay for what the court of justice decides is yours by right) and became legal owners of the name of our choice. Incidentally—a tip for careful shoppers —the fee was about the same for both as it would have been for one. Entire families may enjoy this wholesale arrangement.

The required thirty days passed. We put a fine bright new name plate under our letter box and went out curiously into a world that had now and then turned a suspiciously stony face to our efforts. Immediate results were gratifying. For those who hesitate, the answer to "Can I get away with it?" is "You'd be surprised." In my case, though I'm dark, I got the benefit of the doubt. Events showed that most Christians accepted me as just another guy—extended their cordiality without misgivings or reservations.

The right name, I congratulated myself, is a great buy at only sixty dollars.

Later I found that not everybody was fooled, that a small, militant minority penetrated my human disguise and were not averse to showing it; but on various counts these were mostly obnoxious birds anyway, with whom it would have been small thrill to deal— not the impressive people in my field, which happens to be journalism. Make things smooth and comfortable for the latter, and they don't give your origins a second thought.

It was the more bigoted who were apt to spot me. Seemingly they nourish a psychological "set" to which large portions of their waking time are dedicated: eternal, nervous separation of sheep from goats. Such specialists appear condemned to an unsleeping *qui vive,* like Argus. Even among the specialists, however, there were many who took me and my sixty-dollar name into blood brotherhood, confiding how the continued existence of Jews (and/or Negroes, Italians, etc., etc.) added considerably to their burdens. Well, I didn't have to live with them. I just wanted to fool them into the impression that I was human, and I was succeeding.

But while I went around aglow at having joined the human race, fire and brimstone were storing up for me in an unexpected quarter. It was my friends' calling me a coward and deserter—literally, with just not quite enough humor to make it casual—that wiped the grin off my face. Surely there was nothing cowardly about invading what might reasonably be set down as hostile territory? But my accusers were drawing on centuries of stored-up polemic; I was groping an uncharted way to new ground.

Weeks went by before the vague complex of annoyance, logic, and intuition that had been my motivation settled into words. Then my muttering friends found themselves pinned by the lapels and flailed with my rationale of name-changing.

Those very friends who decried my change of name are in the main agnostics; the supernatural has long since departed from their world. Yes, they do sometimes attend services. To worship? The idea would embarrass them. And they were honestly angry with me. Why? What made their eyeteeth show?

I think I know. They have reacted passionately to injustice. They feel passionately that as an Irishman may have his reel, his green, his St. Patrick's Day parade, as each national group in America is entitled to its history, costumes, dishes, songs, colors, so Jews as a matter of simple justice have the right to their traditions. And they will in self-respect defend that right, to the last drop of blood. I am determined to keep my blood, every drop, for more personal ends.

In giving up my old name I had nothing but a headache to lose. My education was entirely secular. I went to school with a generation largely of the opinion that any man who transmits God's desires to you is probably only guessing. My heritage comes to about the same thing as that of any of my college friends whose tastes were academic. The classical tradition satisfied our cultural needs. To the extent that we were not occupied with co-eds, Greece and Rome and Florence were the playground of our young imaginations. There was a period that I shall never forget when, the impetus of my studies upon me, I burrowed through our library and communed, positively communed, with the Middle Ages. Maybe the past, to the scholarly tribe, holds an attraction not fully justified by all of its products. At any rate we got a fund of old art and literature; and the best of *that* was part of, or intimately bound up with, the Christian tradition. Such was the shape Creation took. The culture in which I live springs from twenty centuries of Christianity.

In every field it was the same. Weekly organ recitals in chapel culminated in the liturgical and semi-liturgical works of Bach. Take anything: take architecture. Before my mind's eye the gradual soaring of Early Christian, Romanesque, and Gothic comes unmatched for fascination by the most be-Oscared of Hollywood's 180-minute masterpieces. Now recently I found, scattered throughout New York City, little replicas, little echoes, of ancient basilica and cloister—poor, aspiring imitations at best, yet in continuity with the dreams of those strange, cruel, unsanitary, devout, and lovely days. A faded church in Greenwich Village can harbor a stone column that remembers Constantinople and Ravenna.

If someone says, Jewish tradition is equally exciting, I shall have to confess, Not to me; it wasn't in the curriculum.—Then what do you know about it?—Almost as little as I do of Sanskrit. Like my classmates, I feel well-rounded despite ignorance of both Sanskrit and Hebrew. Given my choice, I'd take Sanskrit to study, for reasons obvious to philologists. However, neither is important to the enjoyment of the great heritage running through Homer, Dante, Rabelais, Shakespeare, Goethe, and Proust. Of course if I had nine or ten lives to live I'd definitely, in the ninth, find time for Hebrew, which is, in America, at least as valuable as Chinese ceramics or Polynesian ethnology.

But don't you bleed, I've been asked, for the Jews trying to get to Palestine?

Yes, but that's another matter. I am appalled by all of man's inhumanity to man, everywhere. The tide of injustice rises, and no one does anything about it, and sometimes one would like to resign not alone from the Jews, but from the universe as well.

The Jews of the Old World all have my sympathy. For one thing, I distrust frontiers; instinct assures me that everyone has the right to go where he wants to go. But I am equally concerned with the plight of the Chinese, and the violence between Hindu and Moslem; and the bell that tolls for Republicans murdered in Java, and Negroes murdered in Georgia, tolls for me.

Today Charity, lovely lady, is denominational. Charity is Methodist and Roman Catholic, she is Scandinavian, Negroid, and Gallic. Greeks contribute scrupulously to Greek relief, Poles carefully earmark shipments to Poland, Jews scientifically raise funds for Jews. Call me naïve or perverse, but I generally feel as bad about a dying Hindu as about a dying Jew. What does that make me—a kind of Christian?

At this or some other point, when a relative begins to look reflectively at me in a withdrawn sort of way, I emphasize the esthetic and humanitarian nature of my sentiments. I will not join a church. People with sincere beliefs have my respect. They are fortunate. But I like best to describe myself simply as a human being. I am a man, and not easy to classify.

The form of family discussion has become as standard as that of a Quonset hut. Names are paraded of brilliant, eminent, important, rich, respected Jews. "Look at Baruch, Frankfurter, Spinoza, the Twelve Apostles, the Rothschilds, Irving Berlin, Matisse, Freud, Einstein, Louis B. Mayer. *They* weren't handicapped."

Mournfully I point out that I am, alas, no Einstein, no Irving Berlin, no Bernard Baruch. I'm an ordinary guy, young, with a taste for security and the amenities of life. Perhaps I could serve as the composite portrait of all undistinguished college grads. And you may want to believe, I add, that the wrong name is no handicap, and you may actually kid yourself into believing it, but you're not kidding me, since I've already found things easier, my entrée smoothed, the new way.

I have a special fondness for the Bright Horizons gambit. "Kindly hold out a while longer. Education will spread the notion that each strain may have something peculiar and original and irreplaceable to contribute. Progress will teach Americans to judge each man fairly on his merits."

There is something to that. Indeed, some day folks may love others for being *different*. Nevertheless, while Education and Progress receive my hearty endorsement, we have only one life to live, and that's pretty brief. Pending the civilization of America, I propose to make mine easier.

So, while the millennium makes its slow way hither, I let my new name open doors. Today I am at the point where background doesn't count, which gives me a pleasant feeling of universality. I once had occasion to visit West Virginia. What sort of people would chance and altered environment send my way? Hillbillies, miners, farmers, moonshiners? I was frankly ignorant, and just as frankly eager. What my considerate hosts arranged was a series of introductions within the Jewish community. Swell folk—but for me it was like accepting an invitation to a restaurant in Chinatown and finding an American dinner ordered. That determined my attitude: Never again; I'm off the merry-go-round. A pox on parochialism.

"How do you like being a liar?" a tough friend will insinuatingly demand, eying me as though he had just connected with a haymaker and was now waiting for me to drop. Well, I think we should be only too pleased to misinform those gentlemen who like to know how to put their finger on Jews. Lies are too good for them, these lovers of an orderly world where each sect and breed comes plainly labeled and Jews good-naturedly make their living at pawnbroking, clothes manufacturing, or junk dealing. Such gentlemen may not always be deceived, but if enough names are changed, they will certainly be confused. Therefore to hypocritical universities, polluted employment agencies, churchgoers ignorant of Christianity, canting business leaders, haters of people they haven't met, it seems a good idea to say: I won't make your dirty work easier, like a sheep considerately running up the plank into the slaughterhouse. Try and find me.

As for the vast majority of folks, decent and kind, this little deception robs them of nothing and makes everybody more comfortable. Actually, there's no need to deceive my Christian friends. I can rely on the sympathy and good sense of those I normally choose as associates. But in a pinch I am exempted from a senseless struggle for my rights.

So far I have glossed over the experience of my younger brother, who was the one to set our experiment in motion. David's story is the story of a bit of cartilage. Now and then my brother comes up against someone so keen and infallible that by looking at the tip of David's nose he recognizes the disguised pawnbroker. My brother may invest still further in his own humanity. He may decide to pay a surgeon to remove enough of that tiny but fatal cartilage to haul him up out of the pawnbroker race—washed sinless in the modern equivalent of baptism of the heathen—up to the shining precincts of individuality, honor, good breeding, ability, personality, talent, and ethics. We don't know—it's a question of percentages; and each month the offending cartilage loses some of its treacherous power. It may stay.

Meanwhile my brother rejoices in the new name on our letter box. He says it brings a sense of freedom as bracing as a good salt wind from the ocean. We can at our ease go anywhere, travel, work, play. Set us down at any crossroads in America, in the world, and we are integrated units, going concerns, operating on about the same basis as anyone else, given, as a matter of course, the same three strikes as other Americans. It isn't anything of heroic proportions to have done, but we have adjusted to environment. And that, if I recall my elementary psychology, conforms to one common, workable definition of intelligence.

I'VE KEPT MY NAME

By DAVID L. COHN

NAME-CHANGING, AS H. L. Mencken has exhaustively shown, is a widespread phenomenon among members of all the racial stocks who compose our population, including the Anglo-Saxon. The most frequent reason for name-changing among Jews is to get jobs in areas where there is marked economic discrimination against them. Others change their names as a prop to their teetering little souls; because they are socially insecure or are ashamed of their birthright. It is not for me to pass judgment upon them. One remembers, in this context, that during the nineteenth century several European travelers succeeded in penetrating to the sacred Moslem city of Mecca disguised as Moslems. Yet Doughty traveled for two years as a Christian in the Arabian peninsula, every moment in peril of his life, as he records; for to slit the throat of an infidel is to store up merit for oneself in the Moslem heaven. But Doughty's *Arabia Deserta* is the greatest of all travel books in the English language for the reason, perhaps, that Doughty was personally the greatest of all among travelers.

I find that keeping my name, far from complicating my life, simplifies it. I was born an American and a Jew, as you were born an American and a Gentile. I am what I am, as you are what you are. "Jews," wrote Mark Twain, "are members of the human race. Worse than that I cannot say of them." But it would not be wholly admirable if I should, by changing my name, reject the fifty centuries' history and tradition of my people in order to gain a hotel room at Newport.

Nor is this all. Bearing an unmistakably Jewish name, I am

spared the crude comments of virulent anti-Semites, for even they retain a modicum of manners in my presence; and, there being no possibility of mistake, I am not asked to join groups that do not "take" Jews. I am accepted by my fellows as a human being, or I am rejected as a Jew, and while I have no apparatus for measuring hatred and love as they move the hearts of millions of non-Jews, I do know this: that Gentiles, knowing me to be a Jew, have all my life taken me into their hearts and homes, with no self-consciousness on their part or mine, with no abrogation of dignity on either side, without condescension by them and without obsequiousness by me.

The fact that I have been free of most of the blatant prejudices that often run against so many of my co-religionists does not make me insensitive to their plight, nor do I detach from them as though I lived upon a private planet of my own. The war between good and evil never ceases. It was once suggested to Luigi Luzzatti, a Prime Minister of Italy and a Jew, that he change his faith. "I do not think of myself as a Jew or a Gentile," he replied, "but only as an Italian. But when Jews are attacked, then the voice of Isaiah rises in my soul." Here it would seem meet to do battle under true colors rather than false.

If I should resort to the plastic surgery of the courts, it would be only because I should like to pass myself off on the community as a synthetic Plantagenet. This, conceivably, could bring me certain dubious "advantages," such as eligibility for clubs that reject me because I am a Jew, or admission to hotels in "restricted" resorts that refuse me for the same reason. With a new name—preferably one suggesting kinship with a high-church bishop—I might even be asked to dine with some newly minted family that, having gouged the government during the First World War, is now almost as pedigreed as a grand champion bull. These considerations leave me cold.

We already have an overproduction of social climbers in this country; folks who, in the telling and contemptuous rural Negro phrase, have "got above their raisin'." There is no reason why I should add to their number; I can derive a sufficient knowledge of their obscene antics, without closer relationship, by reading the considerable American literature that deals with them.

Yet it is not surprising that there should be so many of them among us—Gentile and Jew—seeing that, paradoxically, snobbery reaches its ultimate in a shirt-sleeve democracy such as ours. For snobbery, generally speaking, flows from social insecurity and only two groups are free of it. The one is the tiny group of aristocrats at the top who feel that no matter what they do, they cannot lose their social position. The other is the group of men at the bottom who have no social position to lose. One finds, therefore, few snobs among true aristocrats and truck drivers. The place to look for them is among large numbers of the American middle class—especially its women. Corroded by a sense of social insecurity, they are almost pathologically concerned with the "right thing"—the right friends, schools, resorts, clothes, clubs, addresses. Nothing stops them in their search for social position.

Socially insecure Gentiles do not automatically rule out all Jews. Among them, the social penalty of being a Jew is not Jewishness. What is unforgivable is to be a poor and obscure Jew—or, even, a rich and obscure Jew. Consequently, a Lehman, a Schiff, a Warburg, a Baruch, who are neither poor nor obscure, are forgiven their lack of prenatal wisdom. The welcome extended to men of this kind is of fascinating interest to the cultural anthropologist—revealing, as it does, some of the magnificently absurd taboos of our society. While they may be "good" enough to marry a man's daughter, they are often not good enough for membership in his clubs, nor can they be permitted to swim in the miraculous waters of exclusive beaches.

So, too, socially insecure Gentiles may welcome Jews who are Famous Names—distinguished artists, musicians, playwrights, actors, movie producers. But the Names, by a tacit conspiracy of manners, are expected to sing for their supper while their hosts, whether or not they are bemused by the singing, enjoy the pleasures of vicarious association with the famous.

One also finds in this country "pet Jews" and their Gentile keepers. The latter derive from the association an exotic touch of the fashionable, as certain English families of the eighteenth century found it exotically fashionable to adorn their households with a liveried blackamoor or two. The former derive from the association, one assumes, a certain masochistic pleasure, knowing that the attitude of their keepers toward Jews in general is that of the Duke of Dorset (in Beerbohm's *Zuleika Dobson*) toward Americans. The Duke granted that Americans had a right to live, but he wished that it had not been so easy for them to live at Oxford.

These are worlds to which I might presumably gain access by changing my name. Do you blame me if I reject them?

There are, happily, other worlds in this kindliest of countries. I was born and raised in a good world. It was far more Gentile than Jewish, but I never felt alien there, nor was any attempt made to make me feel alien. I have found that being a Jew has been no deterrent either to my happiness or to my career whether, as formerly, in business or, as latterly, in writing. My rewards, or lack of them, have been, I feel, in proportion to my merits except, embarrassingly, that I have been dowered with kindness quite beyond my deserts.

Shortly after the Civil War my relatives, European immigrants, became cotton planters in the Mississippi Delta, and my parents soon followed them to the then tiny pioneer town of Greenville. There they met with unaffected kindness in an atmosphere hostile to bigotry. There I was born and raised. For as long as I can remember, the Roman Catholic church, the First Baptist church, and the synagogue have stood within a stone's throw of one another. Over them all was the benison of God and the grateful shade, in summer, of leafy oaks and magnolias. Living, their communicants got on well together. Dead, they were buried in adjoining grounds where weeping willows flow and mockingbirds make mimic song.

In that town there walked saints. Whiskey-drinking, poker-playing, quail-hunting, pleasure-loving saints. Sinners hate. Saints hate, too. But they hate injustice. Greenville has always had men who were saints in this respect. Let me tell you about one of them.

In the early 1920's, the Ku Klux Klan came to the town as it came to so many communities of the South and Middle West. But it did not go far. There were two reasons, among others, for this. First, Leroy Percy, a virile aristocrat and the county's most eminent citizen, together with his son Will, called upon the district attorney, who was a lifelong friend and an eminent Klansman. The Percys quietly told him that if the Klan touched the hair of a single person in the community—whether Catholic, Protestant, Jew, or Negro—they would kill him since the burden of responsibility rested with the district attorney. He knew they were as good as their word, and under the circumstances it may be believed that his influence was not incendiary.

Second, Leroy Percy singlehandedly chased an imported Klan organizer out of town. A "Colonel" Camp was speaking in the Washington County courthouse for the purpose of forming a local branch of the Klan. At this meeting, writes William Alexander Percy in *Lanterns on the Levee,* "the Klan organizer made an artful speech to a tense crowd that packed every cranny of the room; and every man was armed. . . . Who had recently bought a huge tract of land opposite West Point and another overlooking Washington? The Pope. Convents were brothels, the confessional a place of seduction, the basement of every Catholic church an arsenal. The Pope was about to seize the government. To the rescue, Klansmen! . . . It was an example of Nazi propaganda before the Nazis. The very enormity and insolence of the lie carried conviction to the simple and the credulous. . . ."

(Similar lies about Jews have been told, and believed, for centuries. They range from the canard that Jews drink the blood of Christian children in religious rituals to stories now current here that Jews—and this is a most extraordinary feat—"own" the country and are also Communist.)

When the speaker sat down, Leroy Percy, hated, uninvited, and hating, arose. Shaking his finger at Camp, his first words were: "Who is this itinerant scoundrel that comes here to set brother against brother?" He told how Catholic, Protestant, Jew, and Negro had struggled together against floods of the great river; against yellow fever, malaria, and all the ills of a struggling pioneer area. He said that together they had conquered wilderness and swamps; had built homes, schools, roads, railroads, levees, courthouses, and cotton gins. They had helped one another in hard times and had managed to live on amicable terms. And now this "itinerant scoundrel" had come to set them apart. He asked upon what field of honor "Colonel" Camp had won his spurs. Whence did he come? Who had besought his presence?

As his anger mounted, ridicule and invective poured from his mouth, searing and burning all that they touched. He spoke to a hostile, sullen crowd, but when Leroy Percy sat down, a wildly cheering throng passed a resolution *condemning* the Klan, while a badly frightened "Colonel" Camp scuttled out of a side door.

In Greenville neither I nor any of my co-religionists, to my knowledge, suffered any indignity or lack of opportunity because of being Jewish. Gentiles and Jews rejoiced together in happiness and mourned together in sorrow. There were bigots in the town, it is true—Jews as well as Gentiles—but they were a tiny minority looked upon commiseratingly by the majority as unhappy aberrants.

There were affectionate relations between many Gentile and Jewish families in Greenville. I shall content myself with one example. My brother Joel, never wealthy, was in the latter part of his life poor. He and his wife lived in a little house in a street of little houses. Once they went out of town, and upon their return were amazed to find that the frayed curtains of their living room had been replaced by new ones. It was not until much later, and by chance, that they learned how this had happened. Their next-door Gentile neighbors, themselves of small means, had taken down their own curtains and hung them in my brother's house.

The good-neighbor tradition of the town lives on. In 1946 Hodding Carter, publisher and editor of the Greenville *Democrat-Times,* won the Pulitzer Prize for editorials on racial and religious tolerance. Last year he published an editorial saying that he had had five crises in his life, and on each occasion he had been rescued by a Jew. A few days later, Gentile leaders of the community quietly collected a considerable sum of money for the relief of distressed Jews overseas.

There are many American Jews who could bear testimony to Gentile kindness, as Carter has borne it with respect to Jewish kindness. My own gratitude to the Gentile friends, neighbors, and teachers of the formative years of my youth is immense. I am deeply and especially indebted to William Alexander Percy. Cultivated and compassionate; a cosmopolitan and an enlightened provincial; writer, soldier, lawyer, and planter, this fellow townsman, older than I, befriended me in my youth. It was a relationship, richly fruitful for me, that endured until his death.

I remember with photographic vividness a present he made me when I was about fourteen years old, a raw country youth filled with furious, inchoate longings. The gift was a number of volumes of translations by Gilbert Murray of Greek plays. They made a profound and lasting impression upon me, for from them I got my first glimpses of truth and beauty; so profound an impression indeed that, years later, I found myself making a sudden decision to retire from business as I stood one day upon the hill of the Parthenon looking down upon the golden structure of the Temple of Theseus.

Long afterward, when I returned to Greenville to write my first book, my parents were dead and my brother had no room for me in his house. William Alexander Percy took me into his own home, where I remained for over two years, as much at ease in his hospitable house teeming with friends and relatives as I could ever have been underneath my own roof, while he gave me, a frightened beginner at writing, his counsel and encouragement. Nor was this the end of my good fortune. For when Percy, shortly before his death, sat down to write his superb autobiographical *Lanterns on the Levee,* he who had hitherto written only verse had small faith in his ability to write prose. Then it was my privilege to do a little for him in the field where he had done so much for me.

I have, for all these reasons, kept my name. The United States is, I repeat, the kindliest of countries; how kindly only those can know whose history is nearly all somber tragedy. But if, unhappily, the United States should ever change, my course would remain unchanged. It is not only that I can do no other. It is also that the upright posture of man, though it is a biological disadvantage, is a great psychological triumph. Speaking for myself alone, it would be too high a price for survival to abdicate that posture which raises man toward the rising sun.

SOME MELAMDIM I HAVE KNOWN

By HAROLD U. RIBALOW

SENSITIVE JEWISH WRITERS, from Hayim Nahman Bialik to Alfred Kazin, have written of the thoughtful Jewish adolescent and the gnarled, impatient, bitter Hebrew teacher, or *melamed*. The *melamed*, as a matter of fact, has become something of a stereotype in Jewish literature, especially in memoirs. He appears, more often than not, as the villain rather than the hero in short stories, novels, autobiographies. In the literature of the ghetto, where the *goy* is not the *bête noire*, the *melamed* is. In retrospect, it is no real wonder. The Hebrew teacher of the immediate past was frequently a man without true status in the tightly-knit Jewish community. He was badly paid, and he was in continual conflict with indifferent or rebellious students. They disliked his classroom manner, which always included sharp clouts with any stick at hand. It was expected that the teacher inculcate Jewish "learning" with the *baitch,* or any equivalent of the cat-o'-nine tails.

It was not "progressive" education, although, in a curious way, it was deeply enough imparted to color and influence the lives of all those subjected to the old-time *melamed*. The smell of garlic, apparently so well remembered by those who disliked their *melamdim,* was less significant than what they absorbed together with the garlic odor.

The *melamed* may have been native to European Jewry; he flourished in America as well, although now he has given way, by and large, to the congregational school and the *yeshiva*. He is still met, I imagine, in the Orthodox synagogues in the Bar Mitzvah classes. The boy approaching the age of thirteen cannot, it appears,

73

learn to compose a Bar Mitzvah speech and read his portion of the Torah simply by attending his Sunday-school class. He needs special instruction—and this is where the *melamed* is resurrected.

I recall my own first experience with a *melamed*. I was raised in a home where Hebrew was spoken as frequently as Yiddish or English. Because it was expected of me that I, as the son of a Hebrew-language magazine editor, should know Hebrew fluently, I was not subjected to the casual Sunday-school atmosphere. Instead, I had a private tutor. He was a youngish man, recently arrived from Poland, whose command of English was remarkably good, considering that, until six months earlier, he had never heard a word of English. He taught me and another young Jew in the neighborhood, a fellow who later became a brilliant student at the Jewish Theological Seminary and a rather prominent rabbi. But when we studied together, he was a frightened youngster of ten, also a recent arrival from Europe. I was the only Yankee in the crowd.

Our teacher was as interested in observing a normal American boy, which I imagine I was, as he was in teaching me Hebrew grammar. He, I am afraid, learned more than I did. The complexities of Hebrew *dikduk* always baffled me; he, on the other hand, rapidly assimilated himself to American customs. He could draw well, and within a few weeks his doodling included some excellent sketches of American automobiles. Perhaps my memory is playing tricks on me, but I now believe that in those days he drew streamlined versions of cars which were far ahead of their time. It is not entirely impossible that his sketches were a bit like the 1953 Continental Studebaker, which, they tell me, is the latest in American automotive design.

I do not imagine it is accurate to call my first teacher a *melamed*. He was a philosopher, who taught only because my father asked him to. He did not use a ruler to slap at our hands. One reason was that he never thought of it; another was that his other student, the little foreign boy who later became a rabbi, was really an excellent student, even then. Years later, when I heard that Avraham was an honor graduate of the Seminary, I said of him what I was not able to say of many other rabbinical graduates I knew, "He always was a good student. I knew he'd make a good rabbi some day."

Within a year, my teacher dropped his students. He became a Hebrew journalist, a very good one and has been one ever since. I am sure that he learned a good deal from teaching us, for I discovered later that, before he could speak English well, he knew the language well enough to translate from it into facile, flowing Hebrew. He also was a baseball fan. For this I still take the credit. I meet him every once in a while at conventions of Jewish organizations or occasional press conferences, and I experience some pride in his calm, easy American ways.

He is, however, as much of a character as any *melamed* in literature or memoir. He devoted himself to philosophy and wrote two fat books, in Hebrew, on general philosophy and on Jewish philosophy and philosophers in particular. The volumes were printed in what was then Palestine, slowly, or just about as he was able to pay the cost of the composition. The printer in Palestine set type on his books only when he sent American money to him. It took a number of years before the books were completed.

Finally, my teacher was a full-fledged philosopher. His tomes were widely reviewed in the Palestine and the world Hebrew press. He was ranked as an important Jewish thinker. But few people bought his books and consequently, he lost money on them. By the time he realized he was in the midst of a losing proposition, he was enough of an American to believe that any work which is performed at a loss is not very intelligent. Now, when I meet him and ask him about his books and whether he is planning any further volumes, he waves his thin hands at me and says, in a rather good American accent, "I am finished writing books. I have nothing more to say." I happen to know many Hebrew writers, however, who often talk about him and his books and point to him at meetings and whisper that he is one of the significant Jews of our time. I suppose I want to believe them. Sometimes I feel that I can. Most of the time, I think of my teacher as a doodler of cars, and I shrug my shoulders with some puzzlement and wonder if perhaps I am not the type to appreciate a real honest-to-goodness philosopher.

My second *melamed* was far from a philosopher. He was hired by my father to prepare me for my Bar Mitzvah, and, while I spoke Hebrew less haltingly than most potential Bar Mitzvah heroes, I was completely ignorant of the melodies for chanting any Torah portion. I was bright enough, I am told today, to have composed two Bar Mitzvah speeches of my own: one in English for my rather large family, the other in Hebrew for the synagogue audience, many of whom knew who my father was and expected me to do something special. I did; I delivered the two speeches, one in English, the other in Hebrew. It was quite a trick, some of my now-elderly uncles and aunts remind me, when we get together at a family function—a wedding, a Bar Mitzvah or a funeral.

But the blessings and the singing of the portion had to be pounded into me. So I met with my second *melamed*. He was the head of the local Hebrew school, a rabbi with a short beard. In later years, I heard tell that he never really had earned a rabbinical *semikah* (ordination); that he was, in other words, something of a fraud. At that time, I did not think so. He was the first ultra-Orthodox teacher I had. And I regret to say that my memories of him are similar to the memories of men like Alfred Kazin when they recall their own *melamdim*. Not that he hit me. I think he was afraid to because of my father. But he did rant, and sometimes he swung at the desk top, just missing my fingers. I was not aware of the reasons at the time, nor do I know them today, but I am certain that he was a highly frustrated man.

He talked to me—and I was not yet thirteen—of the troubles he was having with his family, of how unhappy he was teaching and how he was worried about a daughter of his who, apparently, was rather wild. I did not understand why he talked to me about these things and I did not relish the turn of conversation, for the longer he discussed his family, the longer I had to sit with him. I did not like his apartment—we met there twice a week; on Sundays, we met in the Hebrew school—nor did I care for his method of teaching me how to chant my *haftarah*. He made me repeat it after him phrase after phrase, without ever explaining to me what it was I was singing. I felt unlucky, in that mine was a long *haftarah*. I had noticed how many shorter ones there were and I was angry that I had such a long chore before me.

One day, perhaps a week before I was done with him, the *melamed* stopped the lesson, which consisted of interminable chanting—and I never did have a decent singing voice; in my public-school classes I was a "listener," which meant that the singing teacher had placed me, together with a few others, in the rear of the classroom and admonished us to be still while the rest of the class sang songs— and turned to me with a question.

"You are an American boy," he started, "and you might know. Do you think I should make a rabbi out of my son?"

I was astonished. I knew his son slightly, a gangling tall boy, with sharp features, who was noted throughout the neighborhood as having poor physical coordination. He was a bad ball player and that in itself was enough to make him an outcast. But I was by this time accustomed to the *melamed's* monologues about his family.

"Yes," I offered, giving advice to the bearded man, who at one time had awed me, "I think he'll make a good rabbi." I was thinking, I am afraid, that if he could not play ball, he might just as well become a rabbi. He was lost to us, as it was.

I do not know to what extent he took my advice. After my Bar Mitzvah I saw him infrequently. He did send his son to the *yeshiva*, which later became Yeshiva University, but, as I remember it, the boy became a chemical engineer, a very successful one. I never talked either with the boy or the father again.

Throughout these years, I felt a trifle different from the other boys in the neighborhood. None of them had private Hebrew tutors and those few who were taught their Bar Mitzvah chores, did not have to deliver speeches in two languages. While I was attending public school and taking on private teachers, my friends were playing ball, mostly hockey on roller skates, and I began to feel that either I was missing something or that I was cut out to be something special. What bothered me was that, on the few occasions when I joined the boys in a hockey game, I was quite good. I was fast on my feet and handled the stick and the puck cleverly. Whenever a big game was to come up, however, I could not make it. If it was not one teacher, it was another. I sometimes am amazed that I was not more deeply embittered. Surely, I was less shocked than I should have been when my father told me, after I had graduated from public school and was already registered in the local high school, that he had decided to send me to a *yeshiva*.

"You mean where they wear hats when they play ball?" I remember asking.

He did not know that. He knew only that, if I attended a *yeshiva*, I would become a Hebraist. I was too young, or too unimaginative, to run off to sea. So I allowed myself to be taken to the *yeshiva*.

It is now Yeshiva University. Then, it had many departments: Yeshiva College, the Teacher's Institute of the Yeshiva of Rabbi

Isaac Elchanan, the Rabbi Isaac Elchanan Theological Seminary and the Talmudical Academy, which was the high school. I was a student, simultaneously, of the Teacher's Institute and the Talmudical Academy.

That I lasted five years amazes me to this day. I had been accustomed to the casual school hours of the public-school system: from nine to twelve and from one to three. (I understand that to the contemporary public-school student, these are rather long hours.) At the *yeshiva,* I attended classes from nine to two-thirty, with an hour break for lunch. And then, from two-thirty to six, I was a high-school student. I lived more than an hour away from the *yeshiva,* so that I got home after seven. I was then expected to do homework and study for thirteen different subjects, Hebrew and English. It was sufficiently difficult for the turnover at the school to be greater than that of a major-league baseball club. There was an astonishingly low percentage of graduates, and it was no wonder. I have been told that, since my time, matters have taken a turn for the better. I suppose they had to.

Yet those five years left an impact on me that is still recognizable. For one thing, I meet ex-*yeshiva* students everywhere I go, and nearly every rabbi of thirty-five spent some time within the Rabbi Isaac Elchanan Teacher's Institute or Theological Seminary. Many of them left after a year, frightened or upset by the schedule, and registered elsewhere. In time, they became Conservative or even Reform rabbis. It is a matter of extreme anxiety to the leaders of the Orthodox rabbinate that so many of the young men who come to them first leave them for the other religious Jewish denominations. They cannot seem to understand that the average fourteen-year-old who comes to them is soon made aware that it is an enormous task to stay afloat as a student at their *yeshiva.* Sooner or later, the huge majority of them will leave for schools which do not present such great obstacles to imbibing Judaism.

Nevertheless, once we are safely out of the *yeshiva* and are ten years older, we remember, as people are prone to—even ex-soldiers seldom talk bitterly of the Army; they recall the humorous incidents and the exciting ones of their uniformed careers—those aspects of *yeshiva* life which did us some good.

Nearly all of us fell in love with one of the teachers there, now dead for a decade, and no ex-*yeshiva* student ever talks of the *yeshiva* without mentioning, with deep affection, the name of Abraham Soyer. He was an old man, perhaps seventy, when I met him and he had behind him at least four decades of teaching Hebrew. As he was a professional Hebrew teacher and a European, he was, I suppose, a *melamed*. Nevertheless, he was the best possible teacher any youngster could have. The only other man who could inspire a class or leave a permanent mark on an impressionable young student was, in my experience, a Welshman, who taught ethics at New York University. The two men were completely unlike. The Welshman, whose name was Shepard, was irreverent, bawdy, eloquent and sophisticated. Soyer was gentle, naïve, eloquent in a shy manner, and never irreverent. They were men from two different worlds. They had one gift in common: they entranced their students and taught them far more than the subject at hand. They expanded horizons, deepened visions, brought poetry into lives.

Soyer was a sparrow of a man, slight, thin, neat. His eyes were wide and blurry. He wore a long mustache which muffled some of his words. Unlike many other Hebrew teachers, who were unable to discipline a class, he always had a quiet classroom. It was as though his own gentleness rubbed off, even on the wild boys. He sat, not on his seat behind his desk, but on the edge of the desk, one leg neatly folded over the other. His subject was Hebrew literature, and it helped that we knew that he was a writer of some stature himself. He had written many stories for children, but his work was published in the better Hebrew journals all over the world and we knew it. The other teachers were, in the main, scholars and rabbis. Soyer was not a rabbi, nor was he a scholar. He was a warm human being, and he wrote short stories. We liked him not only for himself, but for the manner in which he differed from the other teachers. He—and this was so rare!—loved to teach. He enjoyed the proximity of young people. The truth is, he was as young in heart as any of us. One day, he came to school on a Sunday, when he had no classes. He had forgotten about it. But he refused to return to his lonely room on Washington Heights. He sat, like a student himself, in the back of the classroom where we were being taught English literature.

Later, I asked him why he sat with us and he told me, in slow, simple Hebrew, "My life is here, and even if I have no classes to teach, I'd rather be with you"—he meant all of us—"than alone. If they did not pay me to teach," he said somberly, "I would teach for nothing."

He was not a "progressive" teacher, perhaps, but there was nothing he would not do to make matters clear to us. He would hop from his perch on his desk to the blackboard and manipulate the chalk cleverly, and birds, buildings, people would come to life. He never talked about his drawing ability; it was part of him. He took it for granted, and so did we. It was not until years later that I learned he was a father of four sons, three of them noted artists, two of them Raphael and Moses Soyer. The sons often used the father as model, and he was an unforgettable one.

Mr. Soyer liked me and I loved him for it, because I was ill at ease in nearly every class but his. I had never been subjected to the Talmud before I came to the *yeshiva*; neither did I know anything about the more traditional studies, like Mishnah or Rashi. I could never learn to read the Rashi script. Most of the other students were graduates of lesser *yeshivas* and what was natural to them was completely new and foreign to me. It made my adjustment that much more difficult. The only class in which I was an alert student was Hebrew literature. I could write lucidly and I could read and understand the modern writers. Unfortunately, I read very haltingly when asked to recite aloud. I do not know why, for I never have had any trouble in reading languages I studied, except Hebrew. I spoke and wrote and read well enough to myself. I was terrible when called upon to read.

The old man was the only teacher in the school who sensed this, and he did so immediately. After the second time, he never again asked me to read aloud, although he took special pains with my writing style and, when grading my papers, he wrote me long, affectionate notes in Hebrew, telling me that I had a future as a Hebrew writer. He hinted that, if I continued to write as I did, I might even learn to read more fluently, although he never quite came out with the thought.

After my first year in his class, I spent part of my summer vacation practicing typing on a Hebrew typewriter which was given to my father. He was incapable of writing on any kind of a machine. He always wrote with a skilled hand, using a steel pen. The typewriter was left with me and so I spent much of my spare time that summer, the summer Will Rogers crashed in Alaska, writing Hebrew compositions for Mr. Soyer. When, that Fall, I returned to school and handed him a sheaf of typewritten Hebrew compositions, he nearly cried with pride. He accepted my book and his eyes grew blurred. He said to me in a quavering voice that I was a nice lad and then he turned away. A week later, he returned my book, with comments on every composition, some favorable, some not so good. At the end of the book, he wrote me a letter, informing me that never before had anyone written so many compositions for him to judge. The very idea, he wrote, that an American boy could spend a summer writing Hebrew was wonderful. He did not seem to realize that he was more than partially responsible for it. I felt, as so few students there did—or anywhere for that matter— that I had an understanding friend, not merely a teacher.

What happend with Mr. Soyer and me must have happened with dozens of others, for whenever I mentioned his name to other fellows, they glowed as they talked. No other teacher elicited more than a mutter. He brought forth warmth.

A few years later, when I was no longer a student at the *yeshiva,* he died. I remembered that I cried when I heard the news. I do not recall why I did not go to the funeral. I think, at that time, I had never been to a funeral and I was, frankly, afraid to go. But I never forgave myself for it, and when I was asked by the school journal editor to write a memoir of Mr. Soyer I did so happily yet sadly. I re-read it recently and I was surprised that I was able, so long ago, to be so emotional about the old man. But I am not surprised when I am aware of how frequently he comes to my mind, or how often my friends, who attended the *yeshiva* with me, so many of whom are rabbis, talk about him. It would seem that in the 1930's and early 1940's, Abraham Soyer was the only worthwhile thing in that *yeshiva.* No doubt there were others. I happen to be unable to think of them.

And when I read about the wicked *melamed,* the one who alienated the sensitive Jewish boy from his people, the *melamed* who whipped and beat boys, the one who was frustrated and bitter, who was underpaid and undervalued, I do not think of my philosopher-tutor, who escaped into Hebrew journalism; nor do I think of the rabbi who may or may not have held a *semikah* and who wanted to know from a child of less than thirteen whether he should make a rabbi of his son. I do think of a blurry-eyed, neat little man, who could draw and tell stories and look into the hearts of boys. He, too, was a *melamed*. And it was he who influenced lives and changed them and shaped them.

BELONGING AND SURVIVAL

The theme of Jewish alienation, together with the problem of belonging to the Jewish community and surviving as Jews, has captured the American-Jewish writer, rabbi, communal worker, and, one is certain, large segments of American Jewry. When, in 1944, the *Contemporary Jewish Record* published a symposium on the influence of Jewishness on a group of prominent American-Jewish writers, critics, and poets, the English-language Jewish press devoted reams of paper to thoughtful studies of the alienation to Judaism exhibited by the creative persons who contributed to the "Under Forty" symposium. When Leslie A. Fiedler wrote "Plight of the Jewish Intellectual" for *Congress Weekly* in 1951, his acute confession became the subject of a symposium in *The Jewish Frontier* and was featured as a news story in dozens of English-language Jewish newspapers all over the United States. When Daniel Bell published his "A Parable of Alienation" in *The Jewish Frontier,* prominent Jewish theologians and literary critics filled the pages of *The Jewish Frontier* with their rejoinders. And when Irving Howe published "The Lost Young Intellectual" in a 1946 issue of *Commentary* he became a prominent personality on the American-Jewish scene.

The lost Jewish intellectuals, as represented by some of the contributors to this section and by Alfred Kazin in *A Walker in the City,* have become an important element of American-Jewish life, although Ludwig Lewisohn, in his "To the Young Jewish Intellectuals," and Charles Angoff, in "Troubled Intellectuals," reply to them persuasively and with passion. Yet, perhaps, these same intellectuals might have become different persons had they been acquainted with the writings of men like Abraham Joshua Heschel, Menahem Boraisha, Milton Steinberg, Maurice Samuel, and Jacob B. Agus, all of whom are represented in this section by some of their most pungent and influential work. Mr. Samuel's essay, in particular, which is ostensibly a review of John Hersey's *The Wall,* is a brilliant example of what a profound Jewish thinker can do with an assignment to review a book. The alienation and the belonging are both part of American-Jewish life today. But there might be a great deal more belonging, and far less alienation, and happier Jewish survival, if the alienated were acquainted with those who belong and never were cut away from the basic Jewish patterns of living.

Ashley Montagu and Hannah Arendt and Milton Hindus, in their own way, clarify Jewish belonging and survival—Montagu as an anthropologist; Arendt as a sociologist and historian; Hindus as a writer, in a personal confession.

Harry L. Golden's analysis of "The Jews of the South" combines a description of Jewish survival and Jewish belonging—and Jewish alienation—as convincingly as any of the other contributors to this volume. In his essay on religion, Will Herberg, one of the most acute observers of American-Jewish life, reveals a trend toward faith, and because his account is both penetrating and authoritative, it is bound to outlast its own time.

The essays in this section first appeared in *Commentary, The Jewish Frontier, The American Zionist, Congress Weekly, The Zionist Quarterly, the Menorah Journal, The Reconstructionist, Partisan Review,* and *The Chicago Jewish Forum.*

THE MEANING OF JEWISH EXISTENCE

By ABRAHAM JOSHUA HESCHEL

THERE IS A high cost of living to be paid by a Jew. He has to be exalted in order to be normal in a world that is neither propitious for nor sympathetic to his survival. Some of us, tired of sacrifice and exertion, often wonder: Is Jewish existence worth the price? Others are overcome with panic; they are perplexed, and despair of recovery.

The meaning of Jewish existence, the foremost theme of any Jewish philosophy, is baffling. To fit it into the framework of personal intellectual predilections or current fashions of our time would be a distortion. The claim of Israel must be recognized *before* attempting an interpretation. As the ocean is more than what we know about it, so Judaism surpasses the content of all philosophies of it. We have not invented it. We may accept or reject, but should not distort it.

It is as an individual that I am moved by an anxiety for the meaning of my existence as a Jew. Yet when I begin to ponder about it, my theme is not the problem of one Jew but of all Jews. And the more deeply I probe, the more strongly I realize the scope of the problem; it embraces not only the Jews of the present but also those of the past and those of the future, the meaning of Jewish existence in all ages.

What is at stake in our lives is more than the fate of one generation. In this moment *we,* the living, are Israel. The tasks begun by the patriarchs and prophets, and carried out by countless Jews of the past, are now entrusted to us. No other group has superseded them. We are the only channel of Jewish tradition, those who must save Judaism from oblivion, those who must hand over the entire past to the generations to come. We are either the last, the dying, Jews or else we are those who will give new life to our tradition. Rarely in our history has so much been dependent upon one generation. We will either forfeit or enrich the legacy of the ages.

Judaism is not a chapter in the history of philosophy. It does not lend itself to be a subject of reflection for armchair-philosophers. Its understanding cannot be attained in the comfort of playing a chess-game of theories. Only ideas that are meaningful to those who are steeped in misery may be accepted as principles by those who dwell in safety. In trying to understand Jewish existence a Jewish philosopher must look for agreement with the men of Sinai as well as with the people of Auschwitz.

We are the most challenged people under the sun. Our existence is either superfluous or indispensable to the world; it is either tragic or holy to be a Jew.

It is a matter of immense responsibility that we here and Jewish teachers everywhere have undertaken to instill in our youth the will to be Jews today, tomorrow and forever and ever. Unless being a Jew is of absolute significance how can we justify the ultimate price which our people was often forced to pay throughout its history? To assess Judaism soberly and farsightedly is to establish it as a good to be preferred, if necessary, to any alternative which we may ever face.

The task of Jewish philosophy today, is not only to describe the essence but also to set forth the universal relevance of Judaism, the bearings of its demands upon the chance of man to remain human. Bringing to light the lonely splendor of Jewish thinking, conveying the taste of eternity in our daily living is the greatest aid we can render to the man of our time who has fallen so low that he is not even capable of being ashamed of what happened in his days.

This surely I know—the source of creative Jewish thinking cannot be found in the desire to compare and to reconcile Judaism with a current doctrine. A noble person does not compare himself with anybody else. The intellectual passion of medieval Jewish philosophers was not bent on making Judaism compatible to Aristotelianism but rather, having absorbed the philosophic ideas of their time, they were anxious to apply and adjust those ideas to the teachings of our fathers. Man is only creative when he is neither apologetic nor propagandistic. It is true, Judaism has no strategic boundaries, being exposed not only to cynicism and the denial of the divine but also to the powerful impact and even deliberate missionary efforts of other creeds. Yet, the strength of truth lies not in refuting others but in understanding itself, in being consistent with itself.

Judaism is a source, not only an object of philosophy. Jewish philosophy is basically the self-understanding of Judaism, the self-understanding of the Jew, just as the paramount topic of philosophic reflection is man himself.

Jewish philosophy is an obligation to the Jewish people. What is going on in the study-rooms of Jewish thinkers has a fateful effect upon what will happen in the lives of the Jews. We have to comprehend in order to prepare for the future of a shattered people. We do not write for a future *Genizah*. We explore Jewish literature because we love and affirm Jewish living.

We were not born by mere chance as a by-product of a migration of nations or in the obscurity of a primitive past. The idea of Israel came first and only then did we come into the world. We were formed according to an intention and for the sake of an idea. Our souls tremble with the echo of unforgettable experiences and with the sublime expectation of our own response. To be a Jew is to be committed to the experience of great ideas, "to act and to hear." The task of Jewish philosophy is to formulate not only these ideas but also the depth of that commitment in vivid, consistent thinking. The task of Jewish philosophy is to make our thinking compatible with our destiny.

In trying to set forth that commitment and that destiny we feel a discrepancy between the depth of our experience and the short reach of our power of expression. What we have seen in the lives of our people is so much greater than what we will ever be able to say. We are all involved in the playing of a drama staged by Israel with God as the attentive audience. Philosophy of Judaism is the attempt to write a review of that performance, to formulate its principles and to say why we take part in that drama.

Philosophy of Judaism has often been formulated as a set of dogmas, shed from nature like catkins from a tree. Yet, the essence is not in the mature fruit; the essence is in the sap that stirs through the tissue. To understand Judaism we must penetrate to its core. The surface may seem to be gnarled and hard like the branches of an ancient tree, but our faith, suffering, striving cut the crust of dogma off the soft, growing cells. Our dogmas are allusions, intimations, our wisdom is an allegory, but our actions are definitions.

Trust in these beliefs is not found in self-detachment, in brooding, gazing, musing—but by striking at the amazing sources that are within ourselves and letting our hidden forces emanate in our thoughts, deeds, words. In exposing ourselves to God we discover the divine in ourselves and its correspondence to the divine beyond ourselves. That perception of correspondence, our discovering how acts of human goodness are allied with transcendent holiness, the sense of the sacred context of our candid compassion—is our most precious insight.

Just as humanity is more than a set of principles, so is Judaism more than a set of dogmas. Judaism is our genesis, not our wisdom; it is not grist for the mill of a mind. It is as real as a law that operates in history, preceding the vicissitudes of contemplation. Not an ideal, a desirable aim of the mind, an eye for the future, but a condition of existence, not choice but destiny. It is impossible for us to survive without the sense of life's earnestness, as if we had given a pledge in advance of our entrance into the concert of history.

Our failure in faith gives us no authority to reject or reduce the inner wealth that has come down to us from our ancestors. Only by applying a clear-sightedness, an urge and a craving comparable to those stored up in the forms of Israel's faith, only by a spiritual intensity equal to that of our teachers who expressed them, and in whose lives the experience of the spiritual has often been like breathing of the common wind, can we reach the depth of meaning hidden beneath the crust of beliefs. On the other hand it is absurd to assume that we can heal our shattered souls by outlawing aggressive thinking, that we can revive our suppressed faith by substituting frantic nostalgia for sober conviction or worship of rituals for walking with God.

One of the maladies of our time is the shattered confidence in human nature. We are inclined to believe that the world is a pandemonium, that there is no sense in virtue, no import to integrity; that we only graft goodness upon selfishness, and relish self-indulgence in all values; that we cannot but violate truth with evasion. Honesty is held to be wishful thinking, purity the squaring of the circle of human nature. The hysteria of suspicion has made us unreliable to ourselves, trusting neither our aspirations nor our convictions. Suspiciousness, not skepticism, is the beginning of our thinking.

This sneering doctrine holds many of us in its spell. It has profoundly affected the character and life of modern man. The man of today shrinks from the light. He is afraid to think as he feels, afraid to admit what he believes, afraid to love what he admires. Going astray, he blames others for his failure and decides to be more evasive, smooth-tongued and deceitful. Living in fear he thinks that the ambush is the normal dwelling-place of all men. He has failed to pick up in his youth the clue of the unbroken thread of truthfulness that would guide him through the labyrinth.

Indeed, life appears dismal if not mirrored in what is more than life. Nothing can be regarded as valuable unless assessed by something higher in value than itself. Our survival depends upon the conviction that there is something that is worth the price of life. Our survival depends upon a sense of the supremacy of what is lasting. That sense or conviction may be asleep, but it awakens when challenged. In some people it lives as a sporadic wish; in others it is a permanent concern.

What I have learned from Jewish life is that if a man is not more than human then he is less than human. Judaism is an attempt to prove that, in order to be a man, you have to be more than a man, that, in order to be a people, we have to be more than a people. Israel was made to be a "holy people." This is the essence of its dignity and the essence of its merit. Judaism is a link to eternity, kinship with ultimate reality.

What are the roots out of which we draw that consciousness, that contact with the sublime? A sense of contact with the ultimate dawns upon most people when their self-reliance is swept away by violent misery. Judaism is the attempt to instill in us that sense as an everyday awareness. It leads us to regard injustice as a metaphysical calamity, to sense the divine significance of human happiness, to keep slightly above the twilight of the self, ready to perceive the constant dawn in our souls.

We are endowed with the consciousness of being involved in a history that transcends time and its specious glories. We are taught to feel the knots of life in which the trivial is intertwined with the sublime. There is no end to our experience of the dangerous grandeur, of the divine earnestness of human life. Our blossoms may be crushed, but we are upheld by the faith that comes from the core of our roots. We are not deceived by the obvious, knowing that all delight is but a pretext for adding strength to that which is beyond joy and grief. We know that no hour is the last hour, that the world is more than the world.

Why is my belonging to the Jewish people the most sacred relation to me, second only to my relation to God? Israel is a spiritual order in which the human and the ultimate, the natural and the holy enter a lasting covenant, in which kinship with God is not an aspiration but a reality of destiny. For us Jews there can be no fellowship with God without the fellowship with Israel. Abandoning Israel, we desert God.

Judaism is not only the adherence to particular doctrines and observances, but primarily the living *in* the spiritual order of the Jewish people, the living *in* the Jews of the past and *with* the Jews of the present. Judaism is not only a certain quality in the souls of the individuals, but primarily the existence of the community of Israel. Judaism is neither an experience nor a creed, neither the possession of psychic traits nor the acceptance of a theological doctrine, but the living in a holy dimension, in a spiritual sphere. Our share in holiness we acquire by living in the Jewish community. What we do as individuals is a trivial episode, what we attain as Israel causes us to grow into the infinite.

Israel is the tree, we are the leaves. It is the clinging to the stem that keeps us alive. Israel has not erred, even though some of its branches have fallen off. Its substance can only be sustained within its roots, within the depth and unutterableness of its being.

There is more madness than sanity in this world. Israel is one of the few healing herbs that have not withered away in the dust-laden winds of history. It is a unique source in the spiritual life of mankind, offering so much of what is valid and fit to guide the soul.

There has perhaps never been more need of Judaism than in our time, a time in which many cherished hopes of humanity lie crushed. We should be pioneers as were our fathers three thousand years ago. The future of all men depends upon their realizing that the sense of holiness is as vital as health. By following the Jewish way of life we maintain that sense and preserve the light for mankind's future visions.

This is a time of simple alternatives. Mankind has arrived at the narrowest isthmus in its history with no possibility of avoiding the dilemma of total peace or total calamity. As Jews, too, we have to face our existence in terms of sharp alternatives: we either surrender to the might and threat of evil or persist in the earnestness of our existence.

To be loyal to Judaism means to affirm it even at the price of suffering. We are attached to life, and still Judaism is dear to us. Our fate is often hard to bear. Yet we bear it for all men. There will be no humanity without Israel.

It is our destiny to live for what is more than ourselves. Our very existence is an unparalleled symbol of such aspiration. By being what we are, namely Jews, we mean more to mankind than by any particular service we may render.

I have faith in God and faith in Israel. Though some of its children have gone astray, Israel remains the mate of God. I cannot hate what God loves. Rabbi Aaron the Great used to say: "I wish I could love the greatest saint as the Lord loves the greatest rascal."

In the face of confusing enigmas we submit our incomprehension to the source of grace and meaning that undeniably fill the world. In communing with stillness we exchange thoughts for light and see the brotherhood of joy and pain, of grief and hope, of mountain and grave.

There is a holy order in the wilderness of history; there is consoling beauty in the fading of cherished hopes. For human hopes are merely the reflected rays of an incandescent promise that never expires. We may falter and fade away but our sacred tears are like dew that falls on a soil that no treason can desecrate.

We who ceaselessly toil and strive to rule the atoms and the stars fail to grasp what it means to be a man. Or have we ever understood what it means to be a Jew? Listening into the past, attuned to the striving of ancestors, we perceive that to be a Jew is to hold one's soul clean and open to the flow of that stream of striving, so that God may not be ashamed of His creation.

Judaism is a gift of God. It is not something that we inaugurate, not our attainment, but our inheritance, the accumulated experience of ages. It is to be acquired, not produced. We live not only on what we have created, but also on what our ancestors have received.

The essence of conscious living is to act according to aspirations, to strive for ends which we set for ourselves. The human will is blind and can never by its own power envision the ends of our actions. Ideals grasped by the mind in history's rare hours of spiritual insight are like sparks of orientation, glittering before our will during the long seasons of obscurity. To Israel the ideals are more than means of orientation. The great events of the past were not visions of the mind but impregnations of the will. Our souls became fertile, waiting to give birth. We have no choice. To us, therefore, the conception of the past is the source of what is vital in the future.

Being a Jew is a part of a continued existence. Suddeness of conversion is alien to our mentality. We carry the past in our will.

Duration does not mean mere survival, mere enduring on this planet. It means that the great events of our history endure in us. We are a channel for the flow of Israel's memory. Words piercing our ears, we may ignore and even try to drive away; yet they do not cease to ring in our dreams. Our duration is our memory.

Without solidarity with our fathers, the solidarity with our brothers will remain feeble. The vertical unity of Israel is essential to the horizontal unity of *klal Israel*. Affiliation with what is undying in Israel, the acceptance of what was unanimous throughout the ages, the endeavor to integrate the teachings and aspirations of the past into our own thinking will enable us to be creative, to expand, not to imitate or to repeat. Survival of Israel means that we carry on our independent dialogue with the past. Our way of life must remain to some degree intelligible to Isaiah and Rabbi Yochanan ben Zakkai, to Maimonides and the Baal Shem.

We do not consider the past to be a model of perfection. We do not indulge in conserving antiquities. Yet whenever we are faced with the alternative of betraying the past and accepting the dogmas of intellectual fashion, we should recall that neither an individual man nor a single generation by its own power can erect the bridge that leads to Truth. By treating lightly that which has been created throughout the ages, we can easily forfeit what is spiritually reliable. "And ye shall not profane the holy things of the children of Israel, that ye die not" (Numbers 18, 32).

Harassed, pursued with enmity and wrong, our fathers continued to feel joy in being Jews. "Happy are we. How good is our destiny, how pleasant our lot, how beautiful our heritage." What is the source of that feeling?

The quest for immortality is common to all men. To most of them the vexing question points to the future. We Jews think not only of the end but also of the beginning. We have our immortality in the past.

As parts of Israel we are endowed with a very rare, a very precious consciousness, the consciousness that we do not live in a void. We never suffer as so many others do from a fear of roaming about in the emptiness of time. We own the past and are, hence, not afraid of what is to be. We remember where we came from. We were summoned and cannot forget it, as we wind the clock of eternal history. We remember the beginning and believe in an end. We live between two historic poles: Sinai and the Kingdom of God.

Israel exists not in order to be, but in order to dream the dream of God. Our faith may be strained but our destiny is anchored to the ultimate. Who can establish the outcome of our history? Out of the wonder we came and into the wonder we shall return.

Belonging to Israel in the Diaspora is in itself a spiritual act. It is utterly inconvenient to be a Jew. The very survival of our people is a *kiddush Hashem*. We live in spite of peril. Our very existence is a refusal to surrender to normalcy, to security and comfort. Experts in assimilation, the Jews could have disappeared even before the names of modern nations were known. Still we are patient and cherish the will to perpetuate our essence.

We are Jews as we are men. The alternative to our existence as Jews is spiritual suicide, disappearance. It is *not* a change into something else. Judaism has allies but no substitute. It is not an analogy of other peoples, creeds or religions. "It is a people that shall dwell alone, and shall not be reckoned among the nations" (Numbers 23:9). We are the only example of a people who has become identified with a religion. The entire people, not just a select group has grown to be a symbol.

The people of Israel groaned in distress. Out of Egypt, the land of plentiful food, they were driven into the wilderness. Their souls were dried away; there was nothing at all: no flesh to eat, no water to drink. All they had was a promise: to be led to the land of milk and honey. They were almost ready to stone Moses. "Wherefore hast thou brought us up out of Egypt, to kill us and our children and our cattle with thirst?" they cried. But, after they had worshipped the Golden Calf—when God had decided to detach Himself from His people, not to dwell any more in their midst, but to entrust an angel with the task of leading them out of the wilderness to the Promised Land—Moses exclaimed: "If Thou Thyself dost not go with us, take us not out of the wilderness" (Exodus 33:15). This, perhaps, is the secret of our history: *to choose to remain in the wilderness rather than to be abandoned by Him.*

Israel's experience of God has not evolved from search. Israel did not discover God. Israel was discovered by God. Judaism is *God's quest for man.* The Bible is a record of God's approach to His people. More statements are found in the Bible about God's love for Israel than about Israel's love for God.

We have not chosen God; He has chosen us. There is no concept of a chosen God but there is the idea of a chosen people. The idea of a chosen people does not suggest the preference for a people based upon a discrimination among a number of peoples. We do not say that we are a selected people. The "chosen people" means a people approached and chosen by God. The significance of this term is primarily in relation to God rather than in relation to other peoples. It signifies not a quality inherent in the people but a relationship between the people and God.

Our life is beset with difficulties, yet it is never devoid of meaning. The feeling of futility is absent from our souls. Our existence is not in vain. Its meaning may not be explicable to us, yet even when we do not know *what* it is, we know *that* it is. There is a divine earnestness about our life. This is our dignity. To be invested with dignity means to represent something more than oneself. The gravest sin for a Jew is to forget what he represents.

We are God's stake in human history. We are the dawn and the dusk, the challenge and the test. How strange to be a Jew and to go astray on God's perilous errands. We have been offered as a pattern of worship and as a prey for scorn, but there is more still in our destiny. We carry the gold of God in our souls to forge the gate of the kingdom. The time for the kingdom may be far off, but the task is plain: to retain our share in God in spite of peril and contempt. There is a war to wage against the vulgar, against the glorification of the absurd, a war that is incessant, universal. Loyal to the presence of the ultimate in the common, we may be able to make it clear that man is more than man, that in doing the finite he may perceive the infinite.

NOTES ON JEWISH SURVIVAL

By MENAHEM BORAISHA

JUDAISM WAS NEVER meant to be a church. The church is a place for worship. It is a place where believers gather on certain days to witness and partake in some religious rites and offer their prayers. The role of the church in the life of the individual ends the moment he closes its doors behind him. The synagogue, or to be more exact, the *Beth Hamidrash,* was never meant to be exclusively a place of worship or a prayer house for Saturdays and holidays only. It was open every day and night of the week for worshippers, for wayfarers, for itinerant preachers, for students. What we call religion did not end for the layman in the synagogue. The same *mezuzah* which was attached to the portals of the synagogue door was also on the portals of the home. The books that filled the synagogue shelves were also to be found in the home, and the commandments and teachings in those books guided and regulated every action and deed of the individual, whether in the home or in the street, whether at work or at his dinner table or in his personal life. There was no division between one's home, the school of one's children and one's prayer house; they were all integrated into one way of life.

Judaism thus was not "religion." It was a culture, the fullest manifestation of which was *the Jewish individual.* It was not the Book that was the culture. Not the Bible and the Talmud and the later commentaries. Not the myriad of commandments, interpretations, legends, prayers and tales contained in the Book, but the individual who was formed by this vast accumulation of historic memories, ideas, moral concepts, hopes and visions. To the outside

97

world Judaism represents chiefly a library. To ourselves we are the product of the truths and ideas contained in that library. These were carried in the cells of our brains, in the marrow of our bones, in the expression of our eyes, in our aggressiveness and fears, in our laughter and sadness, in the thousand and one ways in which we adapted ourselves to all circumstances. Memories of four thousand years, from the serfdom in Egypt to the slaughterhouses in Poland, are alive in us. Whether a "race" or a "nation" or a "people," *we are a human type, an individuality*. In that we are and must be different, as is every individual who insists on being himself. More so, we are different with the memories of thousands of years of being different.

What then does Jewish continuity mean? It means the preservation of the "differentness." As a specific human type, as a historic individuality, we have a particular place in mankind and in its eternal process of cultivating higher types of the human species. If we preserve the accumulation of wisdom, morals and ideas impregnated in us in the course of four thousand years of struggle with brute power, with prejudices and hatred, we have a contribution to make to mankind. And again, this contribution is not in the library we have accumulated. We are no longer the sole proprietors of the Bible, and the enormous post-biblical literature is gradually becoming the property of every non-Jewish student who wants to make his way through it. We have no specific "mission" in the world. The Book that contains our message is open to everybody. What is exclusively ours and cannot be duplicated by any other people is the personality of the Jew, that mysterious, adored and despised personality which is the creation of the experience of but one people and no other. The only "mission" we have is to preserve the essence to ourselves.

Now, when you ask the brutal question—Does it "pay" to be the constant object of hatreds, discriminations, libels, persecutions and mass slaughters?—the answer is plain. If through this ordeal the historic Jewish personality is to be further crystallized and is to reach higher planes in its identification with the purest ideals of mankind, it "pays." But if being a Jew means just preserving a few miserable crumbs of religion, it certainly does not "pay" to be subjected to all the tortures and pangs that go with it.

It seems that the process of quantitative growth is over and the continuity of Israel must in the future rely not so much on large numbers of Jews whose bonds with their people are loose or questionable, but on smaller numbers who will find a way of integrating themselves with its destiny as deeply and closely as were the Jewish devotees of past centuries. True enough, no single new formula of such integration within the confines of the mighty civilizations in which most of the Jewish people live today has yet been evolved. The search for such a formula among various groups of Jewish survivalists is intense and it is in itself an expression of their awareness of the new turn in our history. But there is one community where the beginning of this new turn has manifested itself in the most positive terms. That community is the Yishuv of Palestine.

In the light of this new turn of our history, the rise of the Yishuv in Palestine assumes the significance not only of a National Home and a political and cultural center but of a great laboratory where a new type of a self-sustaining, creative and integrated Jew is being born. Whatever internal and external forces have contributed and will continue to contribute to the shaping of this new Jew, he and the Yishuv which he has built represent the essence of that toward which the new cycle of our history is turning. Thus the work accomplished by the five decades of political Zionism and the previous decades of the *Hovevei Zion* appears to be a miraculous kind of preparation which Jewish history made for the arrival of this crisis and the new turn. Just as the great migration to the New World and the settling of five million Jews in the Western Hemisphere was designed to save a portion of the people from the oncoming extermination, so the Yishuv in Palestine was designed and destined to become the basis and foundation of a new way of Jewish existence.

The events of recent years have caused some of our younger people to discover their ancestry and what they call their racial affiliation, but only those of the prodigal sons and daughters who have had access to Jewish knowledge and way of life through a Jewish language have actually rediscovered their roots. The others, brought up in an atmosphere where no Jewish language was spoken, are experiencing great difficulties in reaching Jewish self-recognition. Of course, Jewish knowledge acquired in any language is a key to the subconscious feeling of "belonging" as a Jew, but a Jewish language opens the door wide into the individual's conscious and subconscious existence. Pick up a book printed in Hebrew characters and you are instantly surrounded by thousands of years of history into which you step as a rightful heir and full-fledged citizen. No other token of "belonging" is as concretely personal as is language—in this case the Hebrew language.

Hebrew is gradually becoming and will in time develop fully into the most pronounced sign by which one will be able to differentiate between a Jew fully integrated with his people and one who maintains only loose connections with it. Adherents of conflicting theories of Jewishness may go on endlessly discussing their points of view in the abstract, but the Jew familiar with the Hebrew language and the great stores of ancient and modern Jewish knowledge in that language will feel and act like a Jew whatever label the theorists of one or another camp may place on him. The elimination of Hebrew from the prayerbook was the most effective weapon employed by the assimilationists to demolish the concept of an identifiable Jewish culture and to reduce Jewish self-awareness to a minimum. Just as the Reform synagogue made its about-face toward Zionism in defiance of the teachings of its early founders, so it will in time be forced to stage a return to Hebrew if only to save itself from total disintegration in the process of the cultural assimilation which it fosters.

The fear of and escape from belonging to the Jewish group finds its most striking manifestation in the Jewish adoption of the Christmas holiday. It is not merely a compliment paid to Christian neighbors or a concession to children's "happiness." In the real Christian this thoughtless emulation evokes only scorn. And as to the concession to the children, it is the most pronounced demonstration of the individual Jew's disregard for his heritage, for his history, for his identity. It is the fate of the Jew in the Diaspora to function as a minority, religiously and culturally. Only through the recognition of this basic fact can Judaism hope to survive. Only by the introduction of the awareness of this fact can the individual home become Jewish. The escape from it is Jewish self-negation and spiritual suicide.

The difference between the non-Jew and the Jew rests on the fact that the Jew constantly subjects himself to a spiritual and ethical regimen which helped him conquer the evil in himself. The minute the regimen is abolished the Jew is no better and may become worse than others. Being a Jew therefore means perpetual, constant effort in maintaining a trend of thought, an attitude toward the world, a control of a spiritual discipline that help cultivate the good in man. There is no denying that in the course of many generations of such efforts Jews developed certain abilities, inclinations, talents, which provide them with the power to conquer evil in themselves. The former generations did leave us a heritage. But living on that heritage alone without constantly enlarging upon it means, in the first place, to live as parasites and, secondly, to squander the heritage. Were it not for all former generations that worked upon enlarging that heritage, our youth of today would have no chance to boast of Jewish progressivism and to rely upon Jewish perseverance. And if our youth of today has real intention to survive as Jews, chauvinistic boasting will not achieve it. Like all former generations this generation, too, must become active and make itself not only the guardian but also the builder of new values to enrich and enlarge its heritage.

A Jewish civilization which is to be able to withstand the overwhelming cultural pressure of the non-Jewish environment must exploit *every* Jewish value, *every* product of Jewish creativity. If that civilization is to be based on the Diaspora, it must also accept that the Diaspora is creative and can build a culture of its own, as did the Yiddish culture of the last several centuries. Diaspora conditions did not prevent the creation of a Yiddish press, literature, theater, school system, and institutions without number. What is characteristic of this culture is that it grew out of the very elements which guarded Jewish existence in the Diaspora. The Yiddish language had its beginnings in the adaptation of the language of the environment to Jewish religious thought and customs, and Yiddish culture as a whole revolves around the central idea of Jewish peoplehood. As a manifestation of the creativeness of our people within a different cultural environment, modern Yiddish culture is surpassed only by the Babylonian Talmud and the subsequent centuries of religious writing in the Aramaic language. But

the approach to this rich and enriching reservoir of Jewish creativeness is barred by the anti-democratic prejudice and snobbery
still prevailing among wide Jewish circles. Were it not for the
translations of Sholem Asch's *The Nazarene* and *The Apostle*, I. J.
Singer's *Brothers Ashkenazi,* and a few others, the average Jewish
reader would never suspect the existence of a literature which can
hold its own with the literature of many of the countries of the
world.

It is time we unmask the myth which all escapists and apologists
use to cover up their Jewish barrenness and impotence. No American *Jews* have made contributions to the general culture of this
country. There were men of Jewish origin or extraction who contributed to American journalism, letters, science, arts, commerce,
etc. They did not make contributions as American *Jews*. What
have Walter Lippmann, David Lilienthal or for that matter, any
of the magnates, directors, actors and script writers who star in the
Hollywood sky to do with Jewish life in America? What have they
in common with the American-Jewish community? There may be
exceptions like Ernest Bloch in music, recently Marc Chagall in
painting or Ludwig Lewisohn in literature, who function in the
general American culture as Jews. But what have all these writers,
reporters, musical virtuosi, merchant "princes," jurists, Broadway
producers, brought of the Jewish spirit, of the Jewish concept of
the world, of Jewish ethics and inspirations, into American culture? In many cases, particularly in the cases of the "geniuses" of
Hollywood, we often feel like bowing our heads in shame at what
the Jewish "spirit' produces. There was more Jewish thinking
brought into American minds by a single non-Jew, Pierre Van
Paassen, than by dozens of his Jewish colleagues in the same field.

No living body which carries a vacuum within itself can exist.
And no body of Jews has ever suffered from such hollowness as does
this greatest of Jewish communities. The superabundance of organizations, societies, fraternal orders, benevolent groups, etc., is
in itself a result of the attempts of this body to fill in the internal
hollowness. Only some of the organizations fill out the social and
private life of the Jewish man and woman; others merely cover
the emptiness.

Where does this emptiness come from? It comes from a discrepancy between the nature of the Jew as developed during many centuries and the mode of life which is common in this easygoing democracy. Our masses who settled here in the last sixty years came from lands where persecutions, starvation and semi-starvation had been the lot of generations. They experienced hard and bitter beginnings, days of sweatshops and peddler's aching feet, until they achieved prosperity. This point of satiety and prosperity was the critical point in the life of the individual. At this point the inner makeup of the individual had to assert itself. Men in whom the innate Jewish traits of living with the spiritual, social and national interests of their people predominated, remained the leaders and active members of all organizations and movements. The others who for the first time after many generations got the chance to live a full life of freedom and satisfied appetites gave up all spiritual and communal interests for the sake of material success and enjoyment of life. There were many gradations between the two groups, but the impression prevails even among the staunchest defenders of American Jewry that the group of pleasure-seekers still constitutes a large portion of our community.

The transformation of Jews into self-satisfied, life-enjoying and luxury-craving men and women could go on for a generation, for two, for three. It could not go on forever. Tens of thousands could be swept away with the waves of materialism. But thousands were bound to develop a feeling of nausea at their own emptiness and begin seeking for something to fill it with. That was one of the sources of the new search for Jewish content, a source which feeds the restlessness of the upper and lower-middle class.

The interfaith movement is justified as long as it rests on three basic assumptions: (1) that we all believe in one God; (2) that every man has the right to serve God according to the ways of his own faith and in keeping with his ancestral concepts and traditions, and (3) that we must overcome our prejudices against and hatreds of men of other faiths and accept them as brothers under one God. If the interfaith movement carries any promise of progress in relations between groups and men, that promise lies exclusively in fostering the recognition that men of various faiths commune with Divinity in their own ways and it is that differentness that must be respected and recognized as everyone's birthright. Any attempt to sacrifice distinctiveness and differentness for the sake of brotherhood, borders on totalitarianism and abolishes the most sacred principle of human existence—man's liberty to walk with his God in the way of his fathers. The assumption that uniformity makes for brotherhood robs the latter concept of the richness which makes it meaningful. An interfaith movement which makes the merger of religions a prerequisite and condition of brotherly human relations indirectly justifies and enhances the prejudices and hatreds that exist between those who refuse to merge; and these constitute 99 per cent of religious humanity.

The burden that rests on the Jew of today is one of concrete actions. His is the responsibility to effect the rescue of those who are still alive in the European inferno; to guard their status in the countries where they may remain; to work toward a speedy political solution of the Palestine problem; to follow the rebuilding of Palestine and the expansion of the Yishuv to the point where it will no longer require outside assistance. His is the responsibility for joining in the struggle of the progressive and democratic elements toward the safeguarding of complete Jewish political and social equality; for mending the mistakes of former years and saving as much as can still be saved of the new generation for Jewish self-awareness. His is the task of laying the foundation for an integrated structure of communal Jewish life which should become the instrument of Jewish survival as a people. And he also must find the solution to the hardest problem we have ever faced: the problem of spiritual and cultural survival.

During the last years of the nineteenth century, two new types of political thinking developed among Jews. One was Zionism and Diaspora Nationalism which, though influenced by external forces, grew mainly out of Jewish traditions and internal historic processes in the lips of the Jewish people. The other were the various interpretations of socialism and, later, communism, which, though owing something to the prophetic strain in Hebrew thinking, came from beyond the limits of Jewish life and conceived Jewish salvation as exclusively and inevitably a by-product of the universal salvation of humanity.

The basic difference of approach to the Jewish people and its problems persists to this very day. The Zionist, the Jewish nationalist, the Jewish survivalist, recognizes that the Jewish problem does not exist in a vacuum. He knows that the peace and security of the Jewish people are inseparably linked with the peace and security of all mankind. But he also insists that the Jewish problem has many unique and special aspects and therefore requires a unique and special solution. He visualizes the integration of the Jew with the rest of humanity as that of a free people, guarding its identity and contributing its creativity to the family of peoples.

The international Communist, on the other hand, regards himself primarily as a member of an international class. His first loyalty is therefore to his class interests and ideology as formulated by his Party; the solution of the Jewish problem is simply a by-product of the solution of the general social and economic problem of our age. Changes in the Jewish policies of communism are thus dictated invariably by the over-all political strategy of communism and may have no relationship whatever to the internal processes of Jewish life.

When Zionism seeks sameness for Jews *as a people among peoples* it leads toward survival. The tendency toward sameness on the part of individuals, however, leads only to spiritual extinction and the ideal of most of us in this country is to achieve sameness as individuals and not as a people. That the wave of assimilation engulfs millions does not matter, since in their drift toward assimilation these millions do not represent a people but merely masses of individuals.

Safeguarding survival on this continent means, in the first place, creating conditions for the preservation of the historic identity of the Jew. The majority of American Jews, however, have adopted a formula of existence which reads: "I am an American first and foremost, and also a Jew." Jewishness is merely a kind of an appendix to Americanism. By the very fact that an ancient people with a great heritage lowers the loyalty to that heritage to a secondary place in its thinking, it gives up its historic role and commits itself to self-effacement. No honest attempt to survive is possible unless Jewishness and Americanism are placed on a par and Jews regain the courage to declare to themselves and others that European notions which made self-effacement the price of equality is not binding on American democracy.

Those who are trying to rid themselves of Jewishness even as an appendix do not concern us. We are concerned with those who still pray on Yom Kippur, who still make Bar Mitzvah parties, who still listen to sermons in which the latest success novel is analyzed, who still try to serve the people of Israel through interfaith meetings. It is futile to believe that a sudden revolution can be brought about in their thinking. What can be done with them is to attempt to plant more Jewish knowledge in their minds which may in time lead the more sensitive among them to different concepts of Jewishness.

WHEN I THINK OF SERAYE

By MILTON STEINBERG

I HAVE BEEN THINKING a great deal of late about Seraye.

What, you will ask, is Seraye?

Seraye is a village situated in the Lithuanian county of Suwalki, just to the east of the old German frontier.

And what—to paraphrase Hamlet—is Seraye to me or I to Seraye?

Seraye, as it chances, is the town whence my family stems, where my father was born, from which he set forth at the ripe age of ten to continue his Talmudic studies at more conspicuous seats of learning—a venture which ended up, after many wanderings, physical and spiritual, in this land.

I say that I have been thinking about Seraye a great deal of late, and for a compelling reason. I cannot think about all of Europe's Jews: the six million dead, the one and a half millions of walking skeletons. Such numbers are too large for me to embrace, the anguish they represent too vast for my comprehension. And so I think of Seraye instead.

Now since, in all likelihood, there is not another person in this auditorium who has even so much as heard of Seraye, I would not have ventured to speak of it were it not that each of us has a Seraye, some place of origin abroad from which, as the case may be, we or our parents or grandparents or remote forebears set out for the new world.

These Serayes may lie in Germany or France or England or Hungary or Poland rather than Lithuania; they may be large cities rather than villages. In any event they are places toward which we feel some personal bond, and constitute therefore a handle by which we may the more readily and vividly lay hold of the agony of Europe today and of the even deeper agony of Europe's Jews.

Let me then speak to you of Seraye, and do you, as I speak, translate it into its equivalent in your own lives. So we will make real and concrete for ourselves the largest and most terrible tragedy in all recorded time.

Let me confess here and now that, having been born in America, I have never seen Seraye, let alone set foot in it. And yet I am sure I am well acquainted with it. I know it from the tales told me by my father, from descriptions of similar towns in books like Irving Fineman's *Hear, Ye Sons,* and Maurice Samuel's *World of Sholom Aleichem,* from the writings of its inhabitants, and most of all, from the kind of people it produced.

I know for example of Seraye that, though it was a tiny town, it made up in poverty for what it lacked in size. Even in its best days it was so poor that black bread and herring brine often made a full-course dinner.

I suspect, too, that physically Seraye left something to be desired. Its houses were ramshackle, its streets unpaved. It was, all in all, a slum.

It had its limitations, Seraye did; but it had its virtues also, and quite extraordinary virtues.

There was piety in Seraye, intense, pure, and exalted.

There was learning in Seraye, and reverence for learning. Bread might be scarce there, but not books. The village of near beggars supported a system of universal schooling and maintained a scholarship at Volozhin, the great Talmudical Academy of the district.

What is more, the townspeople of Seraye, as befitted disciples of the scriptural prophets and rabbinic sages, had a keen sense of justice, so that, according to an ancient practice, anyone who had been wronged was entitled to interrupt public worship, holding it suspended until the inequity had been righted.

And it was a merciful place. The poorest of Seraye, even those who themselves lived on alms, gave something regularly for sweet charity's sake. Nor was its philanthropy merely formal. It sprang rather from spontaneous compassion, from that sense of *weltschmerz* which created the Hebrew phrase: *tsar baal hayyim,* "the pain of all living things."

And it was a place of a great spiritual earnestness.

Do not smile when I say this, but Seraye was very much like Boston and Concord in the days when New England was in flower.

The Kabbalist of Seraye, probing the mysteries of transcendentalism, what was he but a Hebraic Emerson? And the *Parush*, the scholarly recluse, was he not another Thoreau whose Walden chanced to be a corner of the *yeshiva*?

That is why Jewish immigrants to this country came so quickly to understand Americanism. They needed only to translate the spirit of Seraye into English.

And now Seraye, at least the Jewish part of Seraye, is gone, wiped out, expunged by a ruthless hand almost to its last trace.

To be sure, I have no specific information about its fate. We do not yet know in detail what befell cities like Vilna or Suwalki. How then shall we have heard concerning villages?

And yet it is safe to venture a guess. After all, when evil men went about destroying a whole world, it is unlikely that they spared one tiny and insignificant corner of it, especially evil men so efficient in their wickedness.

Seraye is no more. Of that I am certain.

Its old, old synagogue where my ancesters for uncounted generations worshiped God, is in ruins.

Of its Academy, where my father studied, nothing remains.

The books it composed and treasured, for which it dreamed, scrimped, and saved, are now ashes.

Even its cemetery where my forefathers sleep has, I suppose, been erased.

And as for its Jews, of whom there were about two thousand in all—men, women, and children, some saints, some sinners, some learned, and some untutored, some wise and some foolish, but all eager to live, all undeserving of the fate which overtook them—I do not want to think of them. Especially I do not want to think of how most of them were done to death.

Yet think of them I must.

For some of those Jews still live.

How many?

I do not know, of course. No one knows. Perhaps no one will ever know.

But there are probabilities and presumptions on which one can calculate.

We have learned for example that Jews in small towns fared much worse than those in the cities. They were so much more easily detected and apprehended; their opportunities for concealment were fewer. Besides, the non-Jews of Seraye, long schooled in anti-Semitism, would seem to have helped the Nazis in their job of extermination.

Let us, however, be optimists and say that, of two thousand Jews, as many as twenty came through alive.

These twenty Jews haunt me.

In the first place, I cannot figure out why they are they and I am I. Through what merit of mine am I safe, secure, free, and light in heart whenever I watch my wife going about her household duties or hear my children laugh as they play? And what was their offense that they are cold, naked, hungry, haunted by horror? I simply cannot puzzle out what sin they committed so horrible as to merit the torments meted out to them; to look on while one's wife disappears into a death train or gas chamber, to see one's children spitted on bayonets, or to ponder their slow starvation, their bellies waxing great with bloatedness, their arms and legs turning match-stick thin, their bodies growing feeble with lassitude until life and death can no longer be told apart.

That is what haunts me: the thought that there, but for the grace of God and a capricious decision made by my father, but in any case through no virtue of mine, there go I, there my wife, there my children.

This thought, this morbid vagary if you prefer, takes on further poignancy when I reflect that, though I did not know them, some of those twenty Jews may very well be my remote kin. Who knows? Perhaps they bear the names common in our family—the Samuel to which my father answers, the Shraga Feivel, or Philip of one of my American cousins, the Jonathan of my son. What is more, being kin to me, they may actually resemble members of my family in both appearance and character. Perhaps one of them is short, limpid-eyed, and gentle like my father. Perhaps another, a little girl, is fair-haired, blue-eyed, and delicate as my Aunt Sarah was said to have been in her childhood, as her little American granddaughter, Alice, is today.

That is why these Jews haunt me; I feel that I know them and their lot.

After all, are they not flesh of my flesh, and blood of my blood?

Twenty out of two thousand are still alive—if a word so suggestive of joy, vigor, and hope can be applied to human wreckage.

Twenty out of two thousand, and these scattered to the four winds. A few are in Salzburg in the American zone of occupation, several in Bergen-Belsen in the British, one or two in Italy, a couple in France, one in Siberia, and one, of all places, in Shanghai.

And only yesterday a strange wonder occurred. Two Jews of Seraye wandering the streets of the internment camp at Theresienstadt unexpectedly came face to face with each other and cried out in one voice, "Merciful God, are *you* still alive?"

And then they wept heartbroken with the joy of a familiar face and the inconsolable grief of memory.

But the dispersion of the townspeople of Seraye is the least of their ruin.

Not one of them is sound in body. The starvation, torture, and terror that wasted their frames, have ulcerated their stomachs, poisoned their kidneys, hardened the arteries of their brains and hearts, rotted the teeth out of their mouths, and so crippled and stunted their children that six-year-olds are often incapable of walking and ten-year-olds may be mere babies in structure. Nor is any of them "rosy cheeked"—unless it be with the flush of consumption.

Only one or two among them are actually insane. But everyone of them is at least touched with madness—and some cannot sleep for the terrors that come in dreams by night.

Not one of them has a single garment beyond the rags on his back, the broken shoes and burlap wrappings on his feet.

Not one has a single possession—neither watch, nor fountain pen, nor scarf, nor coin.

Not one has a home, or shop, or a tool of his trade.

Not one has a newspaper to read, a prayerbook from which to worship God, a religious calendar to tell him which days are Sabbaths and Holy Days, a synagogue in which to pray.

Their children are unschooled, their young people untrained in crafts and skills.

Mention anything pertaining to life and its graces and they do not have it.

Of the twenty Jewish survivors of Seraye, three want to go back.

After all, one cannot stay in an internment camp forever.

And who knows, perhaps in Seraye by some miracle one will come upon a dearly loved and long despaired of wife or mother or child or friend.

Perhaps something remains of one's former home, or shop, or library, or synagogue.

Then, too, there is the unfinished fight for freedom in Seraye—including freedom for Jews.

Besides, Seraye is home.

And so they are on the move—a tottering old woman from Switzerland, a young man from Lublin, a girl from a camp in Germany, half labor camp and half brothel.

These three need to be sustained now. Once they set out for home they will need more: provender on the way, protection from anti-Semites as they travel, Polish anti-Semites whom the Polish government has been unable to suppress, and Lithuanian anti-Semites whom not even the Soviet Army has brought to heel.

When they arrive at Seraye, the odds are the husband, wife, brother, friend will not be there. The home will be gone, the shop gone, the synagogue gone.

Then they will begin to require our help in earnest. They will need houses, shops, books, tools, and since not so many as ten Jews are left to form a *minyan*, they will need a synagogue at least in Suwalki, the county seat.

Of all the things they require both for the present and the future, they will have none unless we give it to them.

Which means the fullest support to the Joint Distribution Committee—the first participant in the United Jewish Appeal.

Of Seraye's Jews, seventeen will not go back to Seraye.

They will not go back for any one of many reasons; because they know that nothing remains in Seraye to which to return; because they can never again trust their neighbors who joined with the Nazis against them; because the streets of Seraye cry aloud of rape, murder, and torture; because, despite all the efforts of the Red Army, there is more anti-Semitism in Seraye today than ever; because they are tired of defending themselves and apologizing for themselves; because they want to live normal lives.

Whatever the reason, they will not go back to Seraye.

Of these seventeen Jews, three have set their hearts on America. Though, thanks to the quota system, only one will be so fortunate as ever to get here.

But for that one, American Jewry must be prepared, not only for his own sake but so that other lands may be encouraged also to open up their doors to homeless Jews. Which means the fullest support to the National Refugee Service—the second element in the United Jewish Appeal.

And as for the rest, fourteen out of twenty, they will go to one place, and one place only—to the land of their fathers, the place where refuge was promised to them by the nations of the world, to the Jewish Homeland, Eretz Yisrael.

Some are going to Palestine because there is literally no other place on earth for them; others because that is the only place where they are really wanted; still others, because, long before the World War, most of them had been made Zionists by the Jewish tradition, by the dream of a Judaism reborn and of historic Jewish ideals incarnated in the land which first gave them birth.

Observe, I do not say that they want to go to Palestine; I say they *are* going to Palestine.

They are going and nothing will stop them.

They will not be stopped by broken pledges, whether British or American.

They will not be stopped by force of arms.

They will not be stopped by inane, pointless, time-consuming, and, therefore, life-devouring investigations.

They will not be stopped, these Jews of Seraye.

And I am proud to say they are not being stopped.

One of them, a young vigorous man, is even now on a schooner Palestine bound. An old couple who wondrously have not only survived but remained unseparated, are trudging their way to a Yugoslav port, where, rumor has it, passage can be found. Two orphaned children in France scheme by day and night how they will make contact with the underground railway.

They may not all succeed, these Jews of Seraye. Some may be

drowned when British destroyers overtake their little boats. Others may be shot by British machine guns.

But most of them will get through, and safely. They will get through because they must, because the alternative is slow death. They will get through because the right is on their side. And the right will not forever be denied. They will get through because they are going *home*.

They will get through. And when they do, we shall be able to rest more easily. Not only will they know at last what it means to be welcome and wanted, they will be participants in one of the most brilliant, creative, and idealistic enterprises of modern times, the rebuilding of the Jewish National Home in Palestine, an enterprise which has revived, enriched, cleaned, and modernized, for the benefit of *all* its inhabitants, a land long poverty-stricken, sterile, retarded, and disease-ridden; which has established an outpost of political and economic democracy in the feudal medievalism of the Near East; which has blazed trails toward more equitable and cooperative forms of group life; which has evoked an infinitely rich and colorful revival of Hebraic culture; which has converted Jews like the survivors of Seraye from pauperism to stalwart self-reliance, from a burden to themselves and a problem to the world into a social asset for all mankind.

All these wonderful things can and will come to pass—provided we do our fullest duty by the United Palestine Appeal, the third constituent agency of the United Jewish Appeal.

Let us think, then, on these twenty Jews of Seraye, and on the Jews of your own Serayes, human beings like yourselves, your own kith and kin. Let us reflect on the unspeakability of their present misery, on what they need to return to Seraye, or to come to America, or to go to Palestine. Can we delay for a moment our work of deliverance? Can we give to the United Jewish Appeal calculatingly, stintingly, on any scale less than our resources or their anguish?

We can, of course. It is physically possible for human beings to behave like beasts. But the one who so comports himself, if he has the least intimation of conscience, will not look comfortably into a mirror or ever think happily of the God who made him, singled him out for good fortune, and bestowed on him so many benefits which he merits so little.

The Jews of Seraye, and of ten thousand places like Seraye, look to the United Jewish Appeal, that is to say, to us, for deliverance. That deliverance must be, and I am sure will be speedy and full.

Such are my thoughts of Seraye.

With them and in their wake come all sorts and conditions of feelings.

Sometimes, when I think about Seraye, I am ashamed to be a human being, ashamed to be a member of a species which could perpetrate the evil done to Seraye, and almost as much ashamed of the supposedly good people of the world who stood by when the evil was being perpertated, and who stand idle now.

Sometimes when I think of Seraye and its survivors, I burn with indignation against those British statesmen who, after a war fought for the sanctity of covenants, so pervert their country's promises that the Jewish Homeland is today the one place in the world from which Jews are debarred simply because they are Jews; sometimes I wince for President Truman, who before the last national election felt Jewish needs sufficiently to promise an open door to Palestine, but who, elections over, blandly announced that he had changed his mind—a change in which happily and honorably the United States Congress refused to follow him; sometimes I just turn bitter—bitter against politicians, whether British or American, who fiddle with investigating commissions, looking into facts that are matters of common knowledge, while lives nine-tenths broken are altogether destroyed.

Sometimes, when I think of Seraye, I want to hurl hard words at God, that terrible saying of Abraham: "Shall the Judge of the whole earth not do justice," that soul-searing inquiry of the prophet:

> Thou, too pure of eyes to behold evil,
> Thou that canst not look on oppression,
> Wherefore hast thou looked on when men did treachery
> And did hold Thy peace when the wicked swallowed up the
>   righteous?

Sometimes, on the other hand, I want to slip into some synagogue and say Kaddish, the prayer for the dead, not the familiar Kaddish but the *Kaddish shel-Hasidim*, the Saints' Kaddish, as solemn as the other but with its grief more brightly illuminated by hope. I want to stand up and cry out over Seraye, over its dead, over its handful of living:

Yitgadal v'yitkaddash shmeh rabbah b'olmo di hu atid lehithadata. . . .

Magnified and sanctified be God's great name, in the world which He is to create anew, in which the dead will live, and life be eternal, and Jerusalem be rebuilt, and its shrine restored and heathenism be uprooted and the worship of the true God be set in its place, when the Holy One, blessed be He, will establish His Kingdom. . . .

Baagalah uvizman kariv va-imru amen.

Speedily and at a near time, and say ye, Amen.

Such are the mingled emotions that attend my thoughts of Seraye. But through them all moves a two-fold resolution that is always with me, that never falters nor fails, no matter what else I may be thinking or feeling.

I am resolved that, so far as lies within my power, those Jews of Seraye shall, at long last, have justice done them.

Which means, that those who want to go back to Seraye shall have the right to do so without hindrance, and shall enjoy security, freedom, and equality, when they have come home at last; which means further that those on the other hand who want to go to Palestine shall have *that* right without hindrance and shall enjoy security, freedom, and equality when *they* have come home at last.

This is one resolution.

And the other is that, so far as lies within my power, those Jews shall have everything they require to survive and to rebuild their lives; that at no moment, if I can prevent it, will they lack for food, clothing, shelter, medical and psychiatric care or the things that minister to the spirit.

Shall I attempt to catch in two words, almost two gestures, all the complex, subtle, terrible, and exalted things I think and feel when I think of Seraye and its Jews, living and dead—thoughts and feelings which I know you share since you would not otherwise be worthy to be fashioned in human form or to be called Jews?

We feel together, you and I, the will to *fight* and the will to *give*, to fight until justice is accomplished, to give until mercy is done.

These then are our final and deepest thoughts in all our thinking about Seraye, your Seraye and mine.

FIGHT—and GIVE!

ARE THE JEWS A "RACE"?

By ASHLEY MONTAGU

THE JEWS ARE almost always referred to, in popular parlance, as a "race"; but it is not only the man on the street who does so, for scientists, philosophers, politicians, medical men, and many other types of professional men, likewise speak of the Jews as a "race." When reference is made to the "Jewish race" what is implied is that there exists a definite, though widely scattered group of people, who are physically and behaviorally distinguishable from all other "races," the "Jewish race."

The so-called "Jewish race' is generally held to be characterized by a combination of physical and behavioral traits which renders any member of it recognizable anywhere on earth. The physical traits are held to be short to middling stature, a long hooked nose, greasy skin, dark complexion, black, frequently wavy, hair, thick lips, and a tendency in women to run to fat.

The characteristic behavioral traits are said to be aggressiveness, "loudness," unscrupulousness, considerable brain-power, peculiar gestures both of the hands and face, and a quality of looking Jewish, and behaving in a "Jewish" manner hard to define, but nevertheless real.

There are many persons who claim to be able to distinguish a Jew from all other people simply by the total appearance which he presents, even when his back is all that the observer sees.

It is not only non-Jews who assert these things and who make such claims, but the Jews as a whole have tended to pride themselves on the "fact" that they were God's Chosen People and hence distinguished from all other peoples. Most Jews have insisted that they belong to a distinct "race" of mankind, the "Jewish race." The Jews have, in fact, presented no exception to the general rule, that every human entity, whether it be a real one or only imagined, considers itself just a little better than its neighbors.

Whatever may be generally believed about the Jews, and whatever the latter may think of themselves, it is high time that the facts be dispassionately presented together with an interpretation of their significance. Assertions and denials are of little value when they are based on emotion or when they are based on misinterpreted observation or both. It is only when the actual facts are clearly presented in the light of scientific investigation and correctly interpreted that assertions and denials are in order, but these are of a very different nature from those which are usually made, and they are not of the kind which is likely to appeal to those who prefer to accept what their emotions dictate rather than be persuaded by scientific demonstration.

What then has the anthropologist to say in answer to the question: "Are the Jews a 'race' or any other kind of entity?" Do they possess distinguishable physical and behavioral traits? If they do, why do they? Are any of these alleged traits inborn or acquired? These are some of the questions which, as an anthropologist, I shall try to answer in the following pages.

Since the term "race" is objectionable from many points of view, first because as it is customarily understood it corresponds to no reality whatever, and secondly because it has become so weighed down with emotional meanings that it can no longer serve as a satisfactory scientific term; for these reasons the non-committal neutral term *ethnic group* will here be used instead of "race." By *ethnic group* we may understand here any group of human beings who are held to be distinguishable from other groups of human being in virtue of their possession of a unique combination of physical characters.

Do the Jews possess a community of physical characters which marks them out as a distinct ethnic group among the peoples of mankind? To this question the answer of science is an unequivocal "No." This does not mean that the Jews are not recognizable as a distinct group, but it does mean that they are not distinguishable as such upon the basis of supposed physical characters. If they are not distinguishable as a distinct group upon physical grounds,

upon what basis then are they distinguishable as a group at all?
The answer to that question is: Primarily, and almost entirely,
upon cultural grounds, and upon cultural grounds alone.

We may now proceed to present the evidence for these statements.

Our sole authority for the early physical history of the Jews is,
at present, the Old Testament. The physical anthropology of this
work is far from consistent but from it the following facts may be
pieced together: The ancestors of the early Hebrews lived on the
stretch of land skirting the western bank of the Euphrates. The
home of Terah, Abraham's father, was Ur of Chaldees close to the
Persian Gulf; here, and to the southwest, lived numerous Arab
tribes, all of whom spoke closely related languages which, after the
"brownish" son of Noah, Shem, we customarily term Semitic
(Shemitic). The original converts to the religion which Abraham
had founded were drawn from several of these Arab tribes. Their
physical differences, if any, were probably negligible. But shortly
after they had established themselves as a distinct religious group
intermixture commenced, first with the Canaanites of the low-
lands, with whom they had traded for some time, and then with
the Amorites of the highlands of the southwest. The Amorites were
distinguished by a high frequency of red hair. The Hivites, Ken-
ites, Egyptians, and the Hittites all mixed with the Jews during
this early period of their history, as did many other peoples mentioned in the Old Testament.

There is good reason to believe that the peoples mentioned were
characterized by somewhat different frequencies of one or more
distinctive physical characters. Thus, we know that the Amorites
showed a high frequency of red hair, while the Hittites, who spoke
an Indo-Germanic language, presented two types, a tall, heavy
bearded, hook-nosed type, and a moderately tall, beardless type
with thick lips, a straight nose with wide nostrils, and sunken eyes.

Thus we see that already in the earliest period of their development the people whom we now call Jews were a much mixed group
and while, for classificatory purposes they might all be lumped together as Mediterranean in type, there can be no question that
they were at this period definitely not a people of "pure" ancestry.
Owing to their geographic position and relations we can be
virtually certain that the peoples of the East from whom the Jews

119

originated, and the many others with whom they subsequently mixed, were themselves far from "pure" in ancestry.

During the period of the Exodus (1220 B.C.) there was further intermixture with the peoples with whom they came into contact, principally the types embraced under the term Egyptians, and probably, also, some Hamitic peoples. Some 662 crania recovered from a Jewish cemetery at Lachish, dating back to approximately 750 B.C. show marked resemblances to those of the Dynastic Egyptians. This is not to suggest that all Jews at this period resembled Egyptians, but it does suggest something vastly more significant than that, namely, that already as early as 750 B.C. there existed local groups of Jews who in their physical characters resembled or were identical with the population among whom they were living, and differed from other groups calling themselves Jews. This is, of course, exactly the state of affairs that we encounter today, and there is every reason to believe that it has been increasingly so from the earliest times. In other words, the Jews were never at any time characterized by a community of physical characters, but generally varied as the populations among whom they lived. This would mean either that they originated from these populations or that they had become physically identified with them as a result of intermixture. We shall see that the latter explanation is the one which most nearly agrees with the facts.

During the Diaspora the Jews have been dispersed to practically every part of the earth and have intermixed with numerous peoples. In the sixth century B.C., during the Babylonian captivity there was some intermixture with many Mesopotamian peoples. During the Hellenistic period, in the fourth century B.C., Jews followed Alexander the Great into the Hellenistic world, Egypt, Syria, Asia Minor, and Macedonia, to mention a few of the more important regions into which they penetrated and settled. The pattern followed by these Jews was identical with that which the Jews have always followed with such great success: they took over the language of the Greek-speaking populations, and in general identified themselves with Hellenistic culture.

In the second century B.C., at the time of the Maccabees, there commenced the movement of the Jews into the Roman world which carried them to the furthest corners of the Roman Empire, especially to western Europe and particularly to Spain, Italy,

France, and to the Rhineland of Germany. A very large number of Jews settled along the Rhine in the region of Frankfort, Worms, Cologne, and Trier. The language spoken there during the Middle Ages was acquired by these Jews and preserved, with but little modification, to this day in the form of Yiddish. It is preserved in its purest form practically unchanged to the present day in certain cantons of Switzerland. In its eastern European form it is spoken by many more Jews than those who speak Hebrew or any other single language.

During the eleventh century, at the time of the First Crusade, the plunder and massacre of the Jews by these very Christian knights started a Jewish migration eastward which was accelerated into a mass migration after the thirteenth century. These Rhineland Jews settled in what is now Galicia, Bukovina, and the southern and western Ukraine. Here they met and merged with earlier Jewish settlements and adopted as their common language the speech of the Rhineland group, Yiddish. These came to be known as the Ashkenazim (the Hebrew name for Germany), as distinguished from the Jews of Spanish origin, the Sephardim.

It has been claimed that the modern Sephardim are a very much more homogeneous group physically than the Ashkenazim, and that they "preserve with reasonable fidelity the racial character of their Palestinian ancestors."[1]

That the Sephardic Jews are less variable than the Ashkenazim is possible, since they may be slightly less mixed. It is, however, very greatly to be doubted that they preserve with any fidelity whatsoever the "racial" character of their Palestinian ancestors. This is so for the reason that "their Palestinian ancestors" were themselves of very different types. Indeed, it is doubtful whether anyone is today in a position to say exactly what the Palestinian ancestry of the Jews was; certainly even less can be said concerning the anthropological characters of the groups which entered into that ancestry. At the present time it would be wisest to take the view that if there does exist a significant physical difference between the Sephardim and the Ashkenazim then that difference is due to the somewhat different biological history of the two groups. It must be recalled that during their residence in Spain, from the

[1] C. S. Coon, "Have the Jews a Racial Identity?" in *Jews in a Gentile World* (edited by I. Graeber and S. H. Britt), New York, 1942, p. 31.

beginning of the eleventh to the end of the fifteenth century, the Sephardim certainly underwent some admixture with the Moors and for some three centuries with the non-Moorish populations of Spain and Portugal.

To list the peoples with whom the Jews have at one time or another intermixed would include a very large proportion of the populations of the world. This does not mean that the Jews as a whole have undergone such intermixture, but—and this is the important point—that different populations of Jews have undergone independent and different kinds and degrees of intermixture with differing populations. Now, the result of such differing biological experiences would be, even if the Jews started off as a homogeneous group—which they did not—that a certain amount of diversification in physical characters would eventually be produced between different local groups of Jews. That this is actually what has occurred is proved both by historical facts and the analysis of measurable anthropological characters. Thus, in the Russian department of Mogilev only 4.9 per cent of Jews show light-colored eyes; in Galicia, however, this rises to 23 per cent; and in the city of Vienna it goes up to 30 per cent. It is the same with hair color; Turkish Jews show 3 per cent of blond individuals, Ukrainian Jews show 15 per cent, English Jews 26 per cent, German Jews 32 per cent, and in the city of Riga the proportion is 36 per cent. In Jerusalem Jewish Ashkenazic children showed 40 per cent blonds and 30 per cent blue-eyed, while the Sephardim showed 10 per cent blonds and even fewer blue-eyed.

The census of schoolchildren in Germany taken during the last century under the direction of Virchow, revealed that among 75,-000 Jewish children 32 per cent had light hair and 46 per cent light eyes. In Austria these figures were 28 and 54 per cent respectively, and in England 26 and 41 per cent. As Fishberg[2] long ago pointed out, these figures follow the population trends for blondness as a whole, exemplified by the figures for England, Germany, and Riga, whereas in Italy, where the population is predominantly brunette, less than five per cent of the Jews are blond, while in Bokhara, the Caucasus, and North Africa the percentage is even less.

Even with respect to that unreliable, but beloved child of the

[2] Maurice Fishberg, *The Jews*, New York, 1911.

anthropologist, the cephalic index or shape of the head, the variation as between different local groups of Jews is considerable. Among London Ashkenazim one finds 28.3 per cent longheads (dolichocephals), 28.3 per cent moderately round-heads (mesatycephals) and 47.4 per cent of round-heads (brachycephals); among south Russian Jews these figures are respectively, 1, 18, and 81 per cent; for London Sephardim these figures are 18 per cent dolichocephalic and 34 per cent mesatycephalic; Galician and Lithuanian Jews yield a proportion of 85 per cent brachycephals and only 3.8 per cent dolichocephals.

If, as is customarily done, the mean or average shape of the head is given, a very incorrect idea is obtained of the actual conditions prevailing among the Jews so far as head shape is concerned. It is the percentage distribution of the various head shapes which gives us a true account of these conditions, and these percentage distributions show that head shape or cephalic index (Breadth x 100/ Length), like all other characters, is very variable among the Jews as a whole, the head-shapes of the Jews in various countries being quite different from one another, as is demonstrated by the following table:

	Daghestan, Caucasus Per Cent	Jews in Europe Per Cent	North Africa Per Cent	Yemen, Arabia Per Cent
Hyperdolichocephalic (–76) .	....	2.89	25.97	71.80
Dolichocephalic (76–77)	....	7.36	24.67	14.10
Subdolichocephalic (78–79) .	4.70	15.51	19.48	7.69
Mesocephalic (80–81)	6.10	25.78	13.00	2.56
Subbrachycephalic (82–83) ..	17.37	24.01	9.09	3.85
Brachycephalic (84–85)	23.94	15.97	6.49	....
Hyperbrachycephalic (86+) .	47.89	8.47	1.30	....
Number of Observations	213	2,641	77	78

This table shows that Caucasian Jews are predominantly round-headed, while those in North Africa, and particularly those in Arabia, are predominantly long-headed, while those in Europe are predominantly of intermediate type.

Sufficient, I hope, has been said concerning the origins of the Jews and of the variability of only a small selection of their physical characters to show how very mixed and how very variable the Jews are in both their ancestry and in their physical characters. From the standpoint of scientific classification, from the standpoint of physical anthropology, and from the standpoint of zoology, there is no such thing as a Jewish type, and certainly there is not, nor was there ever anything even remotely resembling, a Jewish "race" or ethnic group.

Are the Jews then constituted of a number of different ethnic groups distinguishable from other non-Jewish ethnic groups? The answer is, no. There are certainly many different types of Jews, but these, in general, do not sufficiently differ from the populations among whom they live to justify their being distinguished from those populations on physical grounds and classified as distinct ethnic groups. It is quite impossible to distinguish Jews from most of the native populations among which they live in the East or the Orient, and in many other localities. Anyone who has lived for any length of time in Italy will know that it is utterly impossible to tell a Jew from an Italian in that country. The same is not, however, true of all lands, for in England, in Germany, and in America, it is certainly possible, with a high degree of accuracy, to pick out many people who are Jews as distinguished from non-Jews of all types. Is the fact that one can do so due to the physical characters of these persons, characters which distinguish them from the rest of the population? Again, the answer is no.

There undoubtedly exists a certain quality of looking Jewish, but this quality is not due to any inherited physical characters of the persons in question, but rather to certain culturally acquired habits of expression, facial, vocal, muscular, and mental. Such habits do, to a very impressive extent, influence the appearance of the individual and determine the impression which he makes upon others.

The fact is that the Jews are neither a "race" or ethnic group nor yet a number of ethnic groups, no more so, indeed, than are Catholics, Protestants, or Moslems. It is, in fact, as incorrect to speak of a Jewish "race" or ethnic group as it is to speak of a Catholic, Protestant, or Moslem ethnic group. What then does the term "Jew" mean?

Strictly speaking a person is a Jew in virtue of his adherence to the Jewish religion. If he is not a member of the Jewish religion then he is not a Jew. There is, however, another sense in which a person who does not subscribe to the tenets of the Jewish religion may nevertheless be correctly described as exhibiting Jewish traits, in just the same way as we say of a person that he behaves like a Frenchman, or a German, or a member of any other national group. The Jews are not a nation, but interestingly enough they have preserved cultural traits, almost everywhere, which we usually associate with differences in national culture; these traits therefore have a quasi-national character. The Jews, wherever they have been, have clung tenaciously to their ancient beliefs and ways of life, more so than any western people of whom we have any knowledge, and they have everywhere preserved a certain community of cultural traits. These traits are social, cultural traits and not biological ones. Any person who is born into or brought up in a Jewish cultural environment will acquire the traits of behavior and certain personality traits peculiar to that culture. These are the traits which make many Jews socially "visible" in almost every community in which they live. These traits, taken collectively, differ sufficiently from those which are the rule in the communities in which Jews generally live, as to distinguish them at once from all other members of each of those communities.

It is extremely difficult to define the "quality of looking Jewish," even though it is doubtful whether anyone could be found who would deny that such a quality exists. This quality is exhibited not only in the facial expression, but in the whole expression of the body, in its movement, and in its gesticulations. No attempt to define this quality will be made here because it defies definition, but that it exists in many Jews, and that it is culturally determined there can be little doubt. The quality is completely lost by persons whose recent ancestors have abandoned Jewish culture for one or more generations and who have themselves been reared in a non-Jewish culture. It is even lost, or is never developed, in Jews who have been predominantly educated in a non-Jewish cultural environment. Such Jews as the latter are Jews by religion alone; culturally they will belong to whatever culture in which they have been reared and educated, be it English, French, German, Italian, or what not.

What makes certain persons or communities of persons visible or distinguishable as Jews is neither their physical appearance, nor the fact of their adherence to the religion of Judaism, but certain cultural traits, which they have acquired in a Jewish cultural environment.

We have then a rather interesting situation: a person is never a Jew in virtue of his belonging to some definite physical type, nor is a person necessarily recognizable as a Jew because he subscribes to the tenets of the Jewish religion; he is a Jew by religion but in every other way he may be culturally non-Jewish; finally, only those persons are recognizable as Jewish who exhibit certain behavioral traits commonly associated with Jews, yet such persons may not subscribe to the Jewish religion, but to some other or none at all.

We see then that it is membership in Jewish culture which makes a person visibly Jewish and nothing else, not even his adherence to Judaism.

It should be clear then that in the same sense in which we speak of a person as a Catholic or a Protestant it is possible to speak of a person as a Jew by religion and something else by culture, say a German, an Englishman, an Italian, or what not. Similarly it is possible for a person to be a Jew by culture and at the same time a member of any other religious group but the Jewish. There are thus two senses in which a person may be described as a Jew. He may be a Jew culturally or he may be a Jew by religion; the one is, however, not necessarily associated with the other in the same person. Thus, in Italy, for example, it is quite impossible to distinguish a person as a Jew by means of his overt cultural behavior. Culturally the Jews have been virtually completely amalgamated with the Italian people for a long time. Such persons are Jews by religion, but not by culture; culturally they are Italians. Those that give up their religion cease to be Jews in any sense whatever. The same is true in the Orient and in many other parts of the world.

It is possible to distinguish many Jews from members of other cultural groups for the same reason that it is possible to distinguish an Englishman from such groups, or an American, a Frenchman, an Italian, or a German. Every cultural group differs in virtue of its difference in culture from every other cultural group, and each cultural group molds the behavior of every one of its members according to its own pattern. Members of one cultural group do not readily fit into the pattern of another. Because of the complexities and subtleties which characterize each separate pattern of culture, persons who have been brought up in one culture—however closely related it may be—cannot, and should not be expected to make a perfect adjustment to a different pattern of culture. Even when persons are anxious to free themselves from one culture and adopt, and become part of, another, such persons rarely, if ever, succeed in making the complete change. Once the pattern has been woven it is generally not possible to unmake it and weave a completely new one. The reason for this is that habits of behavior formed in early life become, in a very real sense, part of one's second nature, and it is notoriously difficult to throw such habits off in later life.

This, of course, explains why persons of Jewish cultural background, or persons of any other cultural background, try as they may, usually fail to succeed in the attempt to free themselves from the conditioning effects of that background.

What, in the case of persons who are recognizable as Jews, are these conditioning effects which render them visible to other cultural groups?

Before we attempt to answer this question it must be emphasized that not all persons who have been brought up in a Jewish cultural environment exhibit Jewish cultural traits. There are many varieties and degrees of Jewish culture, some being much less intense than others, and a large proportion of them being modified in the direction of the culture in which the family or community happens to have lived for some generations. In addition to this, some individuals take rather more readily to the Gentile culture outside the home than they do to that of the home or local community, while still others emancipate themselves very early from the domestic cultural environment.

It will be generally agreed that those persons who are readily identifiable as Jews almost always originate from the lower socio-economic classes of their community. As in all lower socio-economic classes the conditions of life are such as not to be conducive toward the development of gentle manners and refined thoughts. On the other hand, the very opposite is likely to be the case. Good breeding is something one does not expect from any but those who have enjoyed the necessary opportunities. Jews of the lower socio-economic classes are no better bred than the members of the equivalent classes of any other culture, and for the same reasons: because the struggle to keep body and soul together has been a full-time job, while the opportunities for developing into a well-bred person have been rare indeed.

What distinguishes the conduct of those persons who are recognizable as Jews from their behavior is, of course, the addition of a certain cultural quality to that behavior. Thus persons who have lived the greater part of their early life in a lower socio-economic cultural environment generally exhibit a certain coarseness and wildness in the expression of their features. If, as they do, they habitually feel and think in certain culturally common ways, such emotions and thoughts register themselves in the index which is provided by the thirty-two muscles of expression of the face.

Just as there is such a thing as an English, German, French, Italian, and even American cast to the face, so there is a Jewish cast to the face. This cast of face is often taken as biologically determined, but the fact seems to be that it is predominantly culturally determined in precisely that manner which has been indicated.

Add to the culturally determined cast of face, traditionally determined gesticulations of the face and body, together with certain similarly culturally determined preferences for color-combinations in clothes, style and total ensemble of clothes, and we have a powerful association of traits which readily enables one to distinguish certain persons as Jews from non-Jews. That all these traits are culturally determined is readily proved by the fact that every last trace of them is usually completely lost in a single generation following the adoption of a non-Jewish culture.

Now, it should not for a moment be supposed that any of these traits are in themselves objectionable; certainly they are *different*, but they have been labelled "objectionable" by those who see reason to find them so. Many of the traits which non-Jews find objectionable in Jews are the very traits upon which the latter pride themselves; aggressiveness, and the habit of gesticulation with the hands, for example.

Centuries of dispossession, massacre, oppression, and discrimination have forced upon many Jews the absolute necessity of aggressiveness or else the inevitability of perishing. A normal amount of aggressiveness is a quality of great survival value, and it is very fortunate that under the abnormal conditions in which they have generally been forced to live, the Jews have been able to develop the necessary type of aggressiveness to enable them to survive at all. That those who have forced the Jews to develop this quality should find it objectionable is, of course, the usual sad logic by which the wrong-headed conduct themselves in such matters. When discrimination against the Jews will have ceased their peculiar brand of aggressiveness will vanish, but so long as that discrimination continues they will need their aggressiveness in order to make their way in the world. From the standpoint of the scientist objectively evaluating the quality within the framework in which it functions, the aggressiveness of so many Jews is a highly desirable quality, since it enables them to survive in a hostile world. With the disappearance of this hostility the necessity for aggressiveness will disappear. But for those who maintain this hostility to object to the aggressiveness which they have forced upon the Jews is something less than reasonable.

With respect to the gesticulations of Jews, these are often called vulgar by peoples who are not given to expressing themselves in any other way than by speech. Such a judgment is, of course, purely subjective. Many Jews regard their habits of gesticulation as a kind of auxiliary language, without which they are practically tongue-tied, and those who have studied these gestures find them to be very expressive indeed. Nevertheless, those who indulge in them are at once rendered identifiable thereby as Jews.

Interestingly enough the gestures customarily used by many Jews have been asserted to be "racially" determined. Nothing could be farther from the truth. Scientific investigation of the gestural behavior of Eastern Jews and Southern Italians living in New York City, show that the more members of each of these groups become assimilated into the so-called Americanized community the more do they lose the gestural traits associated with the original group.[3] Gesture has no connection whatever with biological factors, but merely represents a mode of expression peculiar to certain cultural groups, being determined by cultural factors and by cultural factors alone.

[3] David Efron, *Gesture and Environment*, New York, King's Crown Press, 1941.

We see then, that it is, indeed, not a difficult matter to distinguish many Jews by means of certain traits which they exhibit, but it should also be clear that those traits are all *culturally* determined, and have no connection whatsoever with inborn biological factors. Neither on physical nor on mental grounds can the Jews be distinguished as an ethnic group. This brings us to the oft-repeated assertion that the Jews have a more considerable amount of brainpower than other peoples.

This statement is, of course, not generally made in order to flatter Jews, but is rather urged as something against them because, it is held, owing to their superior brain-power one is thereby placed at an unfair disadvantage in competition with them!

Science knows of no evidence which would substantiate the claim that Jews or any other people have better brains than any other. This is not to say that slight mental differences may not exist between different peoples; they may; but if they do, science has been unable to demonstrate them. The business acumen, the scholastic, and interpretative musical abilities of Jews, have been specially cultivated. The life of the merchant has been forced upon Jews under the most unfavorable circumstances; under such conditions he has in each generation been forced to develop a sharpness of wit which would enable him to survive. Scholarship has been a revered tradition among Jews for many centuries, furthermore it has, in the modern world, been the one means of raising oneself socially or of escaping from the depressing conditions of life in the ghetto. It has been the case that in order to make their way in the world Jews have had to offer a great deal more than anyone else; they have simply had to do better than anyone else.

It may be owing to the very great variety of intermixture which Jews have undergone that their considerable physical variability is also exhibited in their mental capacities, that there may be a somewhat greater frequency of mentally well-endowed individuals among them. Whether this is so or not we cannot tell, and it would in any event be of no great moment if we could, for the reason that it is not so much biological as cultural factors which, other things being more or less equal, determine what a mind shall be like. As Boas has written: "Our conclusion is that the claim to biologically determined mental qualities of races is not tenable. Much less have we a right to speak of biologically determined superiority of one race over another. Every race contains so many genetically distinct strains, and the social behavior is so entirely dependent upon the life experience to which every individual is exposed, that individuals of the same type when exposed to different surroundings will react quite differently, while individuals of different types when exposed to the same environment may react the same way."[4]

The facts then, lead to the following conclusions:

Owing to the original mixed ancestry of the Jews and their subsequent history of intermixture with every people among whom they have lived, and continue to live, the Jews of different regions are neither genetically nor physically equivalent. In each country the Jews closely resemble the general population in their physical characters, but many Jews may differ from that population in behavioral characters because they have been primarily educated in a Jewish cultural environment rather than in that of the general population. As Huxley and Haddon have said: "The word *Jew* is valid more as a socio-religious or pseudo-national description than as an ethnic term in any genetic sense. Many 'Jewish' characteristics are without doubt much more the product of Jewish tradition and upbringing, and especially of reaction against external pressure and persecution, than of heredity."[5]

It would be better to call the Jews a quasi-national group for there is nothing "pseudo" about their nationalistic cultural traits, even though they may not be definitely recognized as a nation neatly delimited by definite geographic boundaries. It is in virtue of the traits of this quasi-national Jewish culture that a Jewish community may be said to exist, and that any person exhibiting these traits may be recognized as a Jew, whether he is an adherent of the Jewish religion or not. Such traits are not inborn but acquired, and have nothing whatever to do with biological or so-called "racial" conditions. They are conditioned by culture alone.

A Jewish physical type has neither been preserved nor transmitted down to the present day because such a type never existed, and if such a type had existed it would long ago have vanished as a result of the subsequent intermixture of Jews with other peoples. What the Jews have preserved and transmitted have been neither

4 Franz Boaz, "Racial Purity." *Asia,* vol. 40, 1940, p. 234.
5 Julian S. Huxley and Alfred C. Haddon, *We Europeans,* New York, 1936, pp. 73–74.

physical nor mental "racial" traits, but religious and cultural traditions and modes of conduct.

The final conclusion is then that the Jews are not and never have been a "race"or ethnic group, but they are, and always have been, a socio-cultural entity best described as a quasi-national group.

A PARABLE OF ALIENATION

By DANIEL BELL

Woe to him who has no home.—NIETZSCHE

ARTHUR KOESTLER, IN his *Dialogues with Death,* describes the day before his capture by the Spanish Fascists. He is standing on a hill outside the seaport town of Malaga. The Loyalist forces were evacuating the area; Queipo de Llano's army was moving up rapidly. De Llano was eager to capture Koestler because of a book the Hungarian journalist had written exposing Fascist atrocities. Although urged by his friends to flee, Koestler remained rooted to the spot. As he records the sensation, the setting of a brilliant, sunny day was peaceful and real; all else, the distant hub-bub, nearby confusion, the far-off rattling of gunfire, the word *fascism,* all were unreal. The only truth was his presence on the hill, outside a villa owned by a friend. Everything else was a surrealist fantasy. The next day the town was occupied, and Koestler was captured, threatened with a death sentence, and finally jailed for a period of more than four months.

This experience on the hill in Malaga as Koestler described it is no longer symbolic but a tangible actuality. Most living today has that blank awareness that gripped Koestler. The men at war had the constant feeling of: What am I doing here, Where did all this come from? Though it was the panic of war which had brought that feeling for a while to the level of conscious reflection, it is not a transient but a fundamental experience of our time. People move about, in the huge caverns that modern technology has constructed, with little sense of relationship to meaningful events. Life is experienced through the unreality of newspaper headlines or five-

133

minute radio news flashes. We work together, but live as atomized beings, no longer controlling our lives but carried by events.

This quality of being lost is the most pervasive symptom of the alienation of our times. The breakdown of *brotherhood*, the loss of the immediate emotional reward which arises out of the spontaneous actions of work and play—for that is the basic meaning of love—have created a deep tension in the social make-up of modern man. It is a strain which he cannot long endure—under which, in fact, he has already cracked.

The root of this alienation and this strain lies, I believe, in the divorce in our contemporary world between moral and secular conceptions. Our moral world still proclaims the primitive traditionalism of kinship, coherence, personalism; we live in a secular world—dominated by the rationalization of life, the cumulative "division of labor" into minute and diverse specialities, and the resultant impersonality.

In this situation, the Jew plays a special role. His life and his wanderings are, in a sense, the image of the world's destiny. His heightened sense of his own alienation is a prescient tremor of the quake to come, for as Auden has written of Kafka, "It was fit and proper that (he) should have been a Jew, for the Jews have for a long time been placed in the position in which we are now all to be, of having no home."

Our world, as Benjamin Nelson points out in a commentary on Max Weber, is a world of "otherhood." The joining of the Protestant ethic to a rational economic calculation of the ways of life encouraged the growing tendency of men to ignore the relationships of brotherhood, based on personal bonds, in social action, and to act toward all men as "others," linked by impersonal ties. Emerging capitalism found that "brotherhood," or the traditional ways, hindered the rational pursuit of economic ends. Whole areas of living once considered sacred were thus rendered profane.

In the general rationalization of society, the traditionalist ethic which is rooted in the tribalism of the Old Testament had to be abolished. The moral conceptions that ruled economic relations in pre-capitalist society were marked by a dualism in the attitude toward profit. As described by Weber in his *General Economic History*, within the family group there was "attachment to tradition and to the pietistic relations of fellow members of tribe, clan and house-community, with the exclusion of the unrestricted quest of gain within the circle of those bound together by religious ties." Toward the stranger, the "other," there was "absolutely unrestricted play of the gain spirit in economic relations, every foreigner being originally an enemy in relation to whom no ethical restrictions apply; that is, the ethics of internal and external relations are categorically distant." The development of capitalism and the introduction of an impersonal ethic involved "the bringing in of calculation into the traditional brotherhood, displacing the old religious relationship. As soon as accountability is established within the family community, and economic relations are no longer strictly communistic, there is an end of the naïve piety and its repression of the economic impulse." Traditionalist relationships, even that between master and slave, could be judged by ethical rules since persons acting directly were involved, "but the relations between the mortgage creditor and the property which was pledged for debt or between an endorser and the bill of exchange would at least be exceedingly difficult if not impossible to moralize."

The growth of rationalization also meant the increasing separation of men from the immediate experience of the rationale of their work. Marx has emphasized the divorce of the worker from the means of production, arising from concentration of ownership; Veblen has shown that this separation is heightened by the very nature of modern technology, since the planning of work is removed from the shop and centralized in an impersonal organization; Weber has argued finally, that these are cases of an even broader trend which he calls *rationalization*, "the modern soldier being equally separated from the means of violence, the scientist from the means of enquiry, and the civil servant from the means of administration."[1]

This comprehensive *rationalization* of modern living pointed to the inevitable *depersonalization*. The German sociologist Georg Simmel wrote in 1903: "The modern spirit has become more and more a calculating one. . . . Through the calculation of monetary values there has entered into social relationships a precision

[1] From the introduction to *From Max Weber* by H. H. Gerth and C. Wright Mills, Oxford University Press.

and a degree of certainty in the definition of equalities and inequalities and an unambiguousness in agreements and arrangements, just as externally this precision has been brought about through the general diffusion of watches. . . . Punctuality, calculability, and exactness which are required by the complications and extensiveness of metropolitan life are not only most intimately connected with its capitalistic and intellectual character, but also color the content of life and are conducive to the exclusion of those irrational, instinctive, sovereign human traits and impulses which originally seek to determine the form of life within, instead of receiving it from the outside in a general, schematically precise form. . . . It is in the light of this that we can explain the passionate hatred of men like Ruskin and Nietzsche for the metropolis—men who found the value of life only in unschematized individual expressions which cannot be reduced to exact equivalents and in whom, on that account, there flowed from the same source as did that hatred, the hatred of the money economy and of the intellectualism of existence."[2]

Over the past hundred and fifty years, the capitalist economic ethic has been stripped of its religious support. The sanction of the Protestant "calling," the ascetic devotion to work and thrift and gain, has given way to an Epicureanism and glorification of luxury and debauch. The rhythms of factory life and the human relationships it imposes dominate our moods and manners. The result is a life of "otherhood"—where common living has given way to rational exploitation—although our moral precepts still dictate that men should live in brotherhood.

This condition of "otherhood," with its repression of spontaneity and personalist affections between men has created a tremendous strain. Subtly these tensions have fashioned an urge for *belonging*, one of the most compelling needs of our day. That yearning has been skillfully utilized by the Nazis in their call for *Gemeinschaft* and the Communists in their cry for *Comradeship*. However warped, these doctrines are an affirmation of a need for brotherhood which the world has denied.

In this situation, the Jew, forced to assume openly the role of the

2 *The Metropolis and the Mental Life* by Georg Simmel. I have followed, with modifications, the translation by Edward A. Shils, included in the University of Chicago Social Science Readings.

"other," is doubly suspect. He is suspect for what he is and also feared for what he symbolizes. He is a constant reminder of the moral contradiction from which the Gentile is inwardly seeking to flee. A deeper knowledge heightens this fear. The Jew, while alienated in his relation to the Gentile world, is pictured as a *whole* person. The Gentile, however, is estranged from his world, his life is fragmented, his guilt large, and he suffers the torment of not even realizing the source of his estrangement. The estranged Gentile desperately seeks coherence and wants to reconcile himself to this world. The alienated Jew, self-conscious of his position, knows he is irreconcilable, and by his vocation of alienation sits in judgment on the world. This paradox produces an ambivalent attitude in the Gentile's conception of the Jew. On the one hand, he envies the alleged traditionalism of the Jew, sees the family structure as the source of its strength, even exaggerates that strength by charging the Jew with "clannishness." Yet, while envying this cohesiveness, he also regards it as a threat to himself. He sees it as a means of competition which places him at a disadvantage. Further, the Jew, with the perspective of the outsider, can exercise a natural skepticism which, when focused on the Gentile world, reveals the hollowness of its pretensions to community.

The accusation of clannishness is important in understanding the insecurity of the Gentile. For in this charge the Jews are deemed to be the disrupters of the solidarity of the larger society—a spurious one—because they form the most close-knit type of primary group organization which refuses to dissolve within the larger sphere. In this impersonal, atomistic, insecure world, the Jews seem to possess the magic key to mutuality, identification, and unity. One might say that there is the nub of modern anti-Semitism.[3] The Gentile world in its state of psychological crisis cannot brook outsiders or any reminder of the moral contradictions which produce the crisis. Moreover, it sees in the homelessness of the Jew the image of its own estrangement, but the uneasy premonition that this homelessness means a permanent dissolution of its world because of the lack

[3] An unpublished study by the Institute of Social Research at Columbia University on *Antisemitism among American Labor* graphically demonstrates the emotional hunger felt by the workers for brotherhood and the envy and resentment shown toward the Jews for their alleged solidarity. Themselves trapped on the bottom rungs of the ladder of vertical social mobility, they cannot understand how the Jews are able to rise into the middle classes, unless it is because "they stick together."

of any genuine social cohesion. Thus, the very existence of the Jew is the provocation of anti-Semitism.

A personal experience is relevant here. A., a sensitive Gentile boy and close friend of mine, has grown up and revolted against the *anomie* of his shabby, Southern world. Coming to New York, he became active in the radical youth movement and soon occupied some posts of responsibility and leadership. When the war came he enlisted, and a long exchange of letters followed. After a series of discussions, A. wrote me: "I know that the alienation of which you speak is only a temporary, artificial thing, that it dissolves once you find yourself on native grounds again. In a sense there is no America except where men are fighting. All the energy and spirit of our generation has been exported to these shell-pocked beaches. I am with these boys, and I find myself growing like them even as an expatriate melts into a foreign land. . . . There are reasons why the Jew is not in his place at war . . . for one thing he is sensitive enough not to share the casual brutal attitude we have toward the Jap, and his imagination is too lurid to be casual about the approaching horror; war is for the callous, and callousness is one virtue the Jew can never attain . . . the castration of will is so inevitable in the liberalism of our time. The Jews are particularly prone to it because the liberalism of our generation is a Jewish liberalism, combining the language of idealism with the spirit of materialism. . . . You say you have lost your community. I could not have survived this new atmosphere if I had not come to it stripped of pride and confessing myself an expatriate, but it is an unstable community and it will not last out the war. . . ."

This intellectual anti-Semitism is increasingly shared. The charge is accurate, but the gun is pointed the wrong way. Someone, something is keeping the world from brotherhood. The Jew who espouses skepticism toward dominant values seems to be the one. The urge toward personification finds an easy outlet. Yet the deeper forest, the rationalization of society and the divorce from its own moral codes, is lost for the trees.

Arthur Koestler has argued in a recent article on Palestine that "it is time to liquidate this anachronism of a people who are neither nation, community, or religious sect." Koestler's answer is assimilation. But it takes two sides to make a bargain. What are the conditions of assimilation? Are they feasible? The Jews *are* a chosen people, if not by God, then by the rest of the world. A fore-ordained dialectic reinforces this fact. Most Jews grow up casually accepting or ardently seeking cultural assimilation. They find themselves, however, rejected by the dominant culture because of its historical fear of the Jew. This rejection then turns the Jew toward an identification with his past and a vocal assertion of cultural difference; a situation, in turn, which reinforces the Gentile world's historical memory in its suspicion of the Jew. Hence, an impasse.

Historically, the only condition for full Jewish assimilation which the Gentile world will accept is not the negative act of repudiating the identity of Jewishness, but the positive step of embracing the Gentile religions.

But above and beyond the issue whether the Gentile world would permit a fundamental tolerance is the question: Can the Gentiles ever allow the Jews to disown their identity? Do not the Gentiles "need" the Jews, either as a necessary hairshirt for their own conscience, or as a group to be used for a blood sacrifice in an effort to escape the fear of a fall from grace?

Is not this question insoluble as long as the world lives in a state of permanent alienation?

Within his own world, the Jew faces a different problem of defining himself as a personality. Here the focus of his living is the nature of, and his relation to, his family.

American Jewish life, both in the ghetto and in the greater polis, has had a dialectical quality that shapes its basic expressions: the personal environment of the immigration generation was defined by a pervasive love that emerged out of the concreteness of family experience, since ritual and social life were one. As he grew up, the young Jew confronted with the pressure of secularization gradually detached himself from this source. But the secular world, stripping him of his kinship, could offer no other unity or purpose in its place. Today the Jew feels the loss of this concreteness of love so necessary for all moral life. As a result, he turns back into himself, creating either a pride or resentment in an empty status. It is this loss of communal love which is the source of the self-love and the self-hate, the arrogant chauvinism and the cringing sycophancy so characteristic of Jewish life in our time.

The significance of communal family as the source of love in

Jewish living can best be understood by comprehending each individual's need for love and the crucial role of love in Western religious experience. In Catholicism, the Church is an agency for winning love and salvation, its tolerant forgiveness through confessional the healing salve for sin. Among the Protestants, each man can lean upon God directly and through that grace reach love. In Jewish life the cradle of love is the family. It is more primitive and tribal, yet more direct and intimate than any other creed. It is also, in our time, the most painful. For the heritage of each Jew is the loss of home and the destiny of footsore wandering. The story of the Prodigal Son, thus, is ever alive. But it is more meaningful and real today, for the Prodigal Son's Return can rarely be realized. The Jew values the quality of sacrifice which characterized that home, yet he knows that two languages, not one, are spoken, and the sons cannot speak to the elders.

In the Catholic world, one can leave one's home and wander in various fields, but the tents of the Church are large, its compassion great, forgiveness easy. The loss of home in Protestant living is more difficult, yet not shattering, for each man is still part of the entire community of sinners who are bound by an impersonal ethic of love. But in Jewish life, each home is an island unto itself, and the severing of the ties of family and tradition causes a tremor which can never be settled. The position of the Jews through the centuries, a stranger in every land, no voice, no ban their own, deepens this traumatic condition. For not only have they no home as their own as a people, but within each alien culture the strange gods tear away the sons and there is no home in the family.

The young Jew is left helpless, and aware. He is aware of a distance both from the Jewish culture from which he came and the Gentile culture into which he cannot or will not enter. He is helpless, for he cannot find his roots in either. Yet out of this tension of understanding and inhibition has been bred a new kind of Jew, the Jew of alienation, a Jew who consciously accepts this situation and utilizes his alienation to see, as if with a double set of glasses, each blending their perspective into one, the nature of the tragedy of our time.

Jewish writing in America, until recently, has shown a curious insensitivity to this theme. It has dealt with two almost disparate motifs, the experiences of the fathers and the experiences of the sons. And while it has fully told of those experiences, it has rarely explored their meaning or assessed the general position of the Jew in this land.

The immigrant group, Asch, Pinski, Singer, sought to recapture the flavor of the unity of ghetto life in Poland. Where they turned to the American scene, as Cahan in *The Rise of David Levinsky,* or Asch in *The Mother,* or Z. Libin in his short stories, their concern was with the emotional adjustment of the *immigrant* to a strange soil.

The first generation of American-bred writers dealt largely with the *sons* and their efforts to escape the old world by accepting a new. Mike Gold in *Jews Without Money,* Isidore Schneider's *From the Kingdom of Necessity,* Joseph Gollomb's *Unquiet* or Sam Ornitz's *Haunch, Paunch and Jowl* treated the problem of secularization. Their characters sought to flee the miasma of slum life either by accepting the materialist values of the dominant culture or escaping into the radical movement to merge their identities in the larger brotherhood of the deracinated.

A second generation of native Jewish novelists mainly repeated the themes of the first, with the Hemingway imprint in evidence in the hard-boiled approach. Jerome Weidman's Harry Bogen, or Budd Schulberg's Sammy Glick are merely sophisticated versions of Sam Ornitz's Meyer Hirsch. (The real story, parenthetically, in Schulberg's novel is not what makes Sammy run, but the question, Why didn't his brother run?) Albert Halper's "little people" are a more subdued variant of the first generation's radical cardboard figures.

One other representative writer, Clifford Odets, has attempted to approach the nature of Jewish tragedy and has met with a broader response. Odets, like Gold, Weidman, and other etchers of American-Jewish life, has reproduced the nostalgic flavor, the clangor, the rhythms and language, but with a truer and more sympathetic ear. The mother slaves, as Jewish mothers do, and the son does not understand, as Jewish sons don't until it is too late. Actually, though, Odets has given us idiom, not character. The people he projects are true because they are precipitates of the middle-class Jewish family with which we are familiar. But his characters are stock models, with no individual variation; and so, they have no basic dignity, for dignity derives from a sense of the ambiguities

141

of living and the emergence of coherent values from the inner tensions. They are not alive, and the sense of pathos which is the nerve fiber of Jewish life does not flow from their actions; it is breathed into the characters by the audience. This great stimulus toward audience participation is why Odets has been so successful.

Odets has been compared with Chekhov because their methods of revealing character are the same; their people talk out and unfold the pain in their lives on the surface of a heartrending babble. With Chekhov the pathos is clear since the nature of the tragedy is unambiguous. The social structure which produced the tension is part of the setting. With Odets, all we can see is the foreground of frustration, but the source and necessity is never clear. In *Awake and Sing,* why is the Berger family frustrated? Because they are impoverished petit bourgeoisie in a capitalist world, or because they are Jews? The answer is never stated, although the distinction is real and crucial. Odets's answer was that our society does not offer economic security or chances for advancement. "He dreams all night of toilets like a monument," says Grandfather Jacob, sardonically describing the effect of Hollywood on young imaginations. The implication is that Hollywood is a fake because we all do not and cannot have these toilets. That is the crime. Yet is it Odets's answer that "success" or security is the answer? Uncle Morty the dress manufacturer is a success. He has a toilet like a monument, and a Japanese valet and luscious mistress to boot. Is Uncle Morty therefore secure? Are his problems as a Jew less real?

Odets was delineating the frustration of Jewish life, not its alienation, the effect not the source. Consequently, his solution is not understanding, but a muddled aggression. Ralphie Berger, the hero, goes off to mount the barricades. Yet I doubt whether that is the solution of the dilemma. For the etiology of frustration also lies in the special conditions of being Jewish, and this has to be grasped first before one can turn to the more difficult question as to what positive social roles are possible.

As with any cultural situation, the crisis of the Jewish family and individual inevitably finds its reflection in the literature and finds a voice. One of these voices is the novelist and critic, Isaac Rosenfeld.

In his autobiographical novel *Passage from Home,* Isaac Rosenfeld becomes a major interpreter of the perceptions and emotions

of the young Jewish intellectual. Seen as a parable, which I believe
it is, the story recapitulates the phylogeny of a race in its search for
moral independence; and only as a parable does its true poignancy
and anguish appear.

Passage from Home spans the summer of a fourteen-year-old boy
named Bernard. But it is not an attempt to recreate adolescent life.
It is a reflection, a musing, a reordering of crucial meanings which
first become clear at that age. The opening lines of the book remark: "I remember the year in which I first felt respect for human
intelligence. I was fourteen, a precocious child, as sensitive as a
burn."

Some critics found difficulty in accepting such perceptions in a
fourteen-year-old. Yet it is precisely at this age that one does, almost
in a flash, realize the nature of one's destiny. A prefatory inscription, taken from Paul's epistles to the Corinthians, sets the tone of
the book:

When I was a child, I spake as a child, I thought as a child: but
when I became a man, I put away childish things.

For now we see through a glass darkly; but then face to face;
now I know in part; but then shall I know even as also I am known.

Here, then is an attempt to blend two subtle essences: the un-
blinking perceptions of the child, uncorrupted by the regulated
compromises of later living, and the first insights of the adolescent
into the pain of the world.

The plot, if one must indicate the story line as such, deals with
the conflict of father and son; the flight of the son to an estranged
aunt; an attempt to become part of her life by arranging an affair
between her and a Gentile "cousin" with whom the boy identifies
himself; the shoddy nature and break-up of the affair; the return
home in an attempt to regain love; and as foreshadowed from the
start, failure in that attempt.

The story seen in this bare dimension is admittedly thin. But it
gains depth from other considerations; for the quest of the young
adolescent is to find understanding. Missing in the novel are the
sprawling, clangorous sketches of immigrant life, or the other conventional hallmarks of the Jewish novel of American life: the
mawkish *weltschmerz*; the self-pitying torments of growing up in a
hostile world; the *goyishe* gangs waiting at the street-corners to
initiate the young Jew into the realities of metropolitan life.

Rosenfeld is concerned with the inner thread of meaning rather than the outer world of sensation. He treats the young Jew as a sensitive person trying to face the implication of maturation. For most young Jews, racial antagonism is an experience encountered much later in life. Youth and adolescence were spent in the closed confines of a Jewish world. The metropolitan ghettoes were tangible, real, cosmopolitan, and almost self-sufficient. Being a Jew was a simple, undramatic, accepted fact of life. There was a knowledge of being different. But this was taken for granted.

Seen as a search for meaning, Rosenfeld's story becomes a parable, as do all searches for basic truths which define our lives. This one is, in modern setting, the story of the prodigal son. In the original, the prodigal son returns home, his quest revealing to him that home, the concreteness of family love, is the greatest truth.[4] Rosenfeld's retelling of the story has a modern ending. The Jew cannot go home. He can only live in alienation.

Rosenfeld's opening pages are a warm, evocative picture of the Passover ceremony. He has an ear for Jewish rhythms which ring more true than the conventional attempts to reproduce them by stilted ideographs of inverted spelling or neologisms. "Passover," he writes, "has always been my favorite holiday . . . although it never had more than an almost perversely romantic significance." It is, I suspect, the favorite holiday of all Jewish children. The bustle, the warm smells of cooking and the wine, the closeness of the family squeezed about the enlarged dining-room table, the sly attempts of the children to steal the *afikomen,* the competitive recitation of the Haggadah, the singing of *Daiyenu* and the kid bought for two *zuzim*—all this gains meaning as a manifestation of the concreteness of family love as the binding element in Jewish life.

This world, however warm and real as it is in its own moments, is only a mirage within the impersonal Gentile world, and the young adolescent slowly begins to detach himself from it. The family world is one pole, but there is also the world of Minna, the aunt. Her attraction for Bernard, the adolescent, is that she leads her own life, divorced from the commitments and staleness of fam-

4 The son who has remained home resents the fact that he who is true and faithful is not rewarded while the wayward one is greeted with the fatted calf. The moral is perhaps that he who has ventured forth to seek the truth himself is judged wiser than one who has accepted the dominant values uncritically.

ily life; she is emancipated. Bernard thinks he is in love with
Minna. There is also a hint of a quasi-Oedipal relationship which
has bearing on his relations with his father. He goes to her apartment, tries to act grown-up, steals a kiss in some secret hope of
response, but is sharply rebuffed. Bernard seeks to reach Minna by
introducing to her his "cousin" Willy, a Gentile who had been
married to Bernard's cousin, now deceased. In Willy's freedom and
loneliness Bernard sees a kinship, imagines a vision of his own
future. One of Willy's stories creates the symbolic identity. Willy
had run away from home, wandered afar and then retraced his
steps.

"Almost a year had passed, but as he was going home his wandering seemed to him no more than an extension of the first day and
he expected his father to beat him with an anger preserved from
the morning of his departure. . . . (The father) came to the door
saying, 'That you, boy?' and shook hands with him and led him to
the stove. . . . There were no blows, no questions asked. The old
man looked him over, saw he had grown and was satisfied. . . .
Their meeting after nearly a year told Willy that from then on his
father would respect him and regard him as a man. . . . It surprised him to find, after a year's absence, that he should return
not with his mother, not his brothers or his sisters, but with his
father stamped in his heart and driven into his soul, to resemble
above all else the man he had fled."

"Of all the stories I had heard Willy tell," remarks Bernard, "it
was the one which made the deepest impression upon me—perhaps
because its theme suited me so well, expressing my own loneliness
and reassuring me in my fear of my father."

Bernard feels that he will have to leave home, yet he must explore all the threads of attachment. A minor counterpoint in the
story reveals the tension. Bernard goes to live for a weekend with
his grandfather, the family patriarch who lives on the intermittent
gifts of his children. The grandfather's life sums up the nature of
family love. Yet Bernard finds: "I was tired of it, tired of this poor,
overdone figure of an old man, his endless complaints and ironies
—his constant and unalleviated *schlepperei*. Was this, then, that
Jewish spirit from which I had shut myself off?" Later he walks
with the old grandfather through the ghetto section, and the two
enter the home of Reb Feldman, a Hasidic *melamed*. There the

atmosphere is subtly transformed. The rhythm of discussions creates a low hymn of quiet, which, as the murmuring chant rises, suddenly breaks into a rhapsodic dance crescendo. Another side of the grandfather is revealed. "A look of completeness lay on his face, an expression of gratitude, as if for the ecstatic understanding to which Feldman had led him. Though unable to understand, I had shared the experience of that ecstasy, and I, too, felt grateful for it."

Yet Bernard knows that this cannot be his world. This too is a world of moments, an echo of the past. Irresistibly he is drawn to Minna. He hunts out her place of work, watches her from a distance, follows her, seeks to understand those mainsprings which drove her from the family and toward her own way of life. As he stands waiting for her on a street-corner he reflects on the essential loneliness of life, the "empty space, which one might never hope to fill, stretched between person and person . . ." And Bernard knows that loneliness was always with him, "as a token both secret and obvious" of his own existence.

"For as a Jew, I was acquainted, as perhaps a Negro might be, with the alien and divided aspect of life that passed from sight at the open approach, but lingered, available to thought, ready to reveal itself to anyone who would inquire softly. I had come to know a certain homelessness in the world, and took it for granted as a part of nature; had seen in the family, and myself acquired, a sense of sadness from which both assurance and violence had forever vanished. We had accepted it unconsciously and without self-pity, as one might accept a sentence that had been passed generations ago, whose terms were still binding though its occasion had long been forgotten. The world is not entirely yours; and our reply is: very well, then not entirely. There were moments, however, when this minor world was more than universe enough; times as when grandfather would be raised to nobility, or when the family gathered for a holiday, would distill so rare and joyful a spirit that all the assurance which had been lacking would rush back in a flood and one could feel the presence of God in it, and one could cry, 'This is reality, truth, beauty, freedom! What has the rest of the world to compare?' But then, this too would vanish, and I would ask, 'What Am I?' . . . For as a Negro might ponder his outer body, asking himself why it should differ from other men's when inwardly he felt his common humanity, so I would consider my skin, my eyes, my hair and wonder why I should feel an inner difference when outwardly I was the same as other men. . . ."

Bernard leaves home after a quarrel with his father regarding his father's past relationship with Minna—an episode which is still a mystery for Bernard—and goes to live with Minna and Willy. But emancipation was not there; it was merely an empty existence. Minna's life was prosaic, rhythmless, spiritless. She, too, was searching, but never even half-vaguely understanding what she was searching for. Her emancipation was only in the realm of sex, that escape valve of American society. Minna, he finds, had been secretly married to, but had left, Mason, a Jewish cabaret owner, a character stripped of all remnants of Jewish feeling, who had taken on all the grosser aspects of the raw Chicago life about him: the sadistic jokes, the jaded taste of sex, liquor, and glazed sensation for the sake of sensation. Having fled Mason, Minna had whirled through a series of affairs and has now taken up with Willy. Willy, however, with his lazy ways, begins to irk Minna, and unable to rid herself of him directly she recalls Mason and in a cruel, wild party they jeer him out of the house.

Bernard is left with shattered hopes and strong shame; but out of the penitence of shame there emerges a yearning for home, for acceptance by his father, to be the prodigal son and realize the concreteness of family love as the source of grace. Bernard seeks out his father. He wants to confess his deliberate intention of hurting his father in order to receive compassion. He tries to explain. "(My father) looked at me sadly, as if to say, 'Can't you understand that I don't demand an explanation? It is I who have to explain.' I realized then—without being aware of it I had feared this most of all—that our guilt was doubled and shared, and I felt so much the greater need to affirm my own." Bernard concludes in the last passage of the book:

"I had wanted to make an absolute commitment of the truth I had discovered about myself. Our lives contain a secret, hidden from us. It is no more than the recognition of our failing; but to find it is all of courage, and to speak of it the whole of truth. If this was an error of childishness, I was proud to be a child. . . . Now, I thought, it was too late. I had put off declaring myself only to have my father deprive me of my last opportunity. From now on I was bound to accept him without question—and if without fear, also without the knowledge that there lay some truth between us into which we both might enter. My only hope had been to confess that I did not love him, to admit I had never known what love was or what it meant to love, and by that confession to create it. Now it was too late. Now there would only be life as it came and the excuses one made to himself for accepting it."

At this point manhood begins. At this point, in a true Bar Mitzvah, begins the assumption of alienation.

Rosenfeld, as a young Jewish intellectual, has followed a course which many other young Jewish intellectuals have taken.[5] At an early age, a product of Chicago's West Side, he entered the radical movement, was an active Socialist on the University of Chicago campus, joined the Trotskyite movement in the late thirties and left soon after as the general futility, rigidity, and fatal Bolshevist direction of the party was revealed. Today he stands, as many, a homeless, independent radical. Unlike some captious radicals, who, in their fear of Stalinism have identified democracy with capitalism, Rosenfeld still retains a deep critical sense regarding the inequalities, injustice, mechanistic, oppressive nature of an exploitative society. At this juncture, he, with many like him, are in mid-passage.

We reject the basic values of American society as they stand. The increasing centralization of decision, the narrowing of the area of free moral choice, the extension into all domains particularly the cultural, of the rationalized, stilted forms of mass organization and bureaucracy, the rising sense of nationalism as a product of the war, all of these heighten the awareness that the way of life resulting from these pressures—the rawness, vulgarity, mass sadism and senseless sybaritism, the money lust and barbaric extravagances—can only stifle creativity and free living.

The bureaucratic age into which we are moving is an inexorable extension of the rationalism of ethics and economics. Its outline can be glimpsed in the anguished reflections of Kafka, Toller, or

5 While I have written only of Rosenfeld, this discussion can apply generally to such writers as Saul Bellow, Paul Goodman, Delmore Schwartz, Clement Greenberg, whose writings have also dealt largely with the theme of alienation. I have written in detail of Rosenfeld out of admiration for his work and because the thread of his story states the problem so forcefully.

von Horvath. It has been foretold more dispassionately by Burck-hardt and Max Weber. It is an "official" world where art, litera-ture, and culture especially will bloom in pattern under the water-ing hand of the official gardener. For it will require, as it has al-ready begun to practice, a corruption by word and image. Organic in its conception, it can only exist by stimulating a spurious brotherhood, while in practice atomizing man.

What meaningful role can the young Jewish intellectual play in such a world? The problem inheres in the very nature of being a Jew and an intellectual. If, as a primary aim, one seeks to under-stand, the effort by its nature inhibits action. Assuming an activist role involves subordination to a black-and-white judgment. In a world of organized forces each seeking to exact conformities, how can one maintain a critical temper? To join one of the competing interest blocs one must become either a cynic, or a romantic—like my friend A. Yet the intellectual knows too well the ambi-guities of motives and interests which dictate individual and in-stitutional action. He cannot surrender himself wholly to any movement. Nor can he make those completely invidious or utopian judgments regarding the nature and needs of man which the cynic and romantic make. He can only live without dogma and without hope. He can only, as an intellectual, realize his destiny—and by consciously accepting it, rework it—through seeing the world, in Friedrich Schiller's phrase, as disenchanted.

The deepest impulses urge us home. But where are we to go? Our roots are in a Yiddish immigrant world from which we ven-tured forth each day to return at night. It was a home that had, in its best moments, a warmth and quality of selfless sacrifice which shaped our ethics and defined our lives. It is a world that has faded and cannot be recreated. All that is left is the hardness of aliena-tion, the sense of otherness. And with it a special critical faculty, an unwillingness to submerge our values completely into any "cause" because of the germ cells of corruption which are in the seeds of organization.

Superficially, this may seem to be a retreat to personal identifi-cation or nihilism. Yet we cannot accept philosophical nihilism, for if each man's values are exclusively his own, then no universe of discourse is possible, mediation between peoples is inconceiv-able, and the only method of persuasion open is force. The assumption of alienation is a positive value, fostering a critical sense out of a role of detachment; it is, if you will, the assumption of the role of prophet, the one who through an ethical conscience indicts the baseness of the world, the one of whom the Hebrew essayist Ahad Ha-am has written: ". . . He is a man of truth. He sees life as it is with a view unwarped by subjective feelings; and he tells you what he sees just as he sees it, unaffected by irrelevant considerations. He tells the truth not because he wishes to tell the truth, not because he has convinced himself, after inquiry, that such is his duty, but because he needs must, because truth telling is a special characteristic of his genius—a characteristic of which he cannot rid himself, even if he would . . . ."

Alienation does not mean deracination. It means the acceptance of the Jewish tradition—its compulsion to community—and the use of its ethical precepts as a prism to refract the codes and conduct of the world. As long as moral corruption exists, alienation is the only possible response. A dialectic of action accelerates this course; the tragic gesture of the Bundist leader Szmul Zygielbojm is a relevant example. Zygielbojm has been smuggled out of the Nazi-encircled Warsaw Ghetto to plead for help for the doomed Jews. When the world refused to listen, he took his own life. For, as he wrote in his suicide note, he felt he had no right to live while his comrades lay buried in the Warsaw rubble. We are told that it is the mass death of thousands that has failed to stir the world. But precisely because this act had no effect do we recoil even more sharply at the lack of conscience and callousness of the world.

What of the relation of this position to Zionism? The stand outlined is a personal one, fused out of inheritance and experience, creating its own life and destiny. It is not meant as a political program, although it is an attitude, I feel, which is shared by others of the homeless radical generation. This "otherness," for us, is a special role. It cannot exist within a territorial demarcation. It can exist, and with it the special historical quality of being Jewish, the quality of alienation, only as the attitude of an eternal stranger in a foreign land. This does not mean that alienation is a solution for the "Jewish problem." For most people, undoubtedly Zionism is. But for those who like us have grown out of the peculiar radical ghetto soil, it is the only path. Emotionally and morally, we identify ourselves as Jews, the definition being derived from our specific immigrant roots. From this position, Zionism and nationalism, paradoxically, have intellectual not emotional appeal, with no roots in our living. Thorstein Veblen in a prescient essay defined the special quality of being Jewish in our culture, a quality which would disappear in a Zionist world:

". . . In short, he is a skeptic by force of circumstances over which he has no control. . . . Intellectually he is likely to become an alien; spiritually he is more than likely to remain a Jew; for the heartstrings of affection and consuetude are tied early, and they are not readily retied in after life. Nor does the animus with which the community of safe and sane Gentiles is wont to meet him conduce at all to his personal incorporation in that community, whatever may befall the intellectual assets which he brings. Their people need not become his people nor their gods his gods, and indeed the provocation is forever and irritably present all over the place to turn back from following after them. . . . One who goes away from home will come to see many unfamiliar things, and to take note of them; but it does not follow that he will swear by all the strange gods whom he meets along the road."

The plight—and glory—of the alienated Jewish intellectual is that his role is to point to the need of brotherhood, but as he has been bred, he cannot today accept any embodiment of community as final. He can live only in permanent tension and as a permanent critic. The Zionist message is extremely strong. Like migratory terns we need to make our way back and the Zionists offer a haven for prodigal sons. But the whole world is our world; we were born in its ghettoes and have a special place. Each man has his own journey to make and the land we have to travel is barren. Out of this fact emerges the tragic sense of life: that we are destined to waste it.

THE LOST YOUNG INTELLECTUAL

By *IRVING HOWE*

A NEW SOCIAL type has appeared in recent years on the American-Jewish scene: the struggling young author who has published a few stories—perhaps even a novel!—or written a few reviews for obscure magazines; the painter whose pictures seldom reach public view; the leader of a revolutionary political group who has very few followers; and most frequently, the unattached intellectual who can function neither as creator nor politician because he is either frustrated and barren in his cultural pursuits or disillusioned with politics.

In the type we have in mind here we do not include those intellectuals who retain a sense of kinship with Jewish activities, such as the Yiddishist or Zionist, or the semi-intellectual who finds security in the world as a professional. Our special type is the young American Jew whose interests usually fall into two main categories: cultural activity or radical politics. Usually born into an immigrant Jewish family, he teeters between an origin he can no longer accept and a desired status he cannot attain.

He has largely lost his sense of Jewishness, of belonging to a people with a meaningful tradition, and he has not succeeded in finding a place for himself in the American scene or the American tradition. At the same time, his feelings toward the Jews are troubled, indecisive, and conflicting. His attitude to the Jewish cultural tradition in which he was reared is an ambiguous compound of rejection and nostalgia. What these writers, artists, politicals, and others have in common is a *marginal status* and sense of estrangement in their relation and attitude toward both general American society and their own Jewish background.

I doubt if the like of our intellectual was very frequent before the late twenties; before that, Jewish intellectuals were usually anchored in some strong tradition or movement: Zionism or socialism or Yiddish Culture. With the appearance of the depression, and the decline of large sections of the intelligentsia to marginal and often *lumpen* status, our intellectual could no longer feel security or strike roots; he has today become the most atomized member of an increasingly atomized society.

He suffers, of course, from the same sense of alienation that besets Jews as a group. Even when he succeeds in detaching himself fairly completely from Jewish life, he continues to exhibit all of the restless, agonizing rootlessness that is the Jew's birthmark. He feels in his flesh the brand of his people: echoes of the endless trek of a people that could never find a home ring in his ears; the tradition of a people always "living on its wits" and on the precipice of disaster, he finds fulfilled in his own life; the highly literary quality of his religious tradition, with its semantic nuances that produce a thinned-out verbal refinement, he finds characteristic of his own literary activity; and the traditional mock-hero of Jewish life, the *luftmensh,* of whom no one knows how he lives, our intellectual finds recreated in his own being. This very awareness of an inheritance makes for him inexpressibly poignant the double sense of being tied to, and having broken from, the past. *He has inherited the agony of his people; its joy he knows only second-hand.*

Significantly, his problem usually finds its central focus in his relationship to his family. Traditionally, the Jewish family has been an extraordinarily tightly knit group. A people deprived of the sense of nationhood and constantly dissevered by overwhelming enemies could only turn inward toward the family unit as a substitute. If King David was no longer in his temple, if the temple was now merely dust, then the patriarch leading his family in prayer would construct a temple of his own. The family was the last shelter to which the persecuted and miserable Jew could retire. Hence the peculiar poignance of Heine's anecdote about the Jewish peddler who was a miserable beggar all week long, but on Friday night! ah, he was king of his realm in the worship of his God.

Today, however, it is this very shelter that the Jewish intellectual has lost, this shelter which, however he may momentarily yearn for it, he knows he can never find again. Literally homeless, he has become the ultimate wanderer.

Fundamental to the Jewish intellectual's sense of separateness is the simple fact that he is a Jew. The world will not let him forget this. Even if he has succeeded in constructing some uneasy *modus vivendi* with American society in which he can never quite lose his separate identity, contemporary events stir in him reactions he cannot suppress or disown. When Jews are murdered in a Polish pogrom, he feels a sense of communal martyrdom, not merely because "it might happen here too"—that is after all the least of it!—but because in a very real and bitter sense it is he too against whom the pogrom has been committed; it is his blood that stains the streets of Kielce.

Some time ago, *Commentary's* predecessor conducted a symposium (*Contemporary Jewish Record,* February, 1944) in which writers of Jewish descent discussed the significance of their Jewishness for their work. Those who testified that Jewishness meant little to them did so with a profound sense of uneasiness; those who testified that it meant a great deal to them did so with the very same uneasiness. For the kind of contemporary intellectual of whom we write, *it is difficult to be a Jew and just as difficult not to be one.* He is caught in the tension resulting from conflicts between his society and his tradition, his status and his desires; he suffers as man, intellectual, and Jew.

But the compensations he might acquire from a vital tie with his folk-past are also unavailable to him. *He has lost the sense of continuity which was such sustenance to his forefathers.* Who are his spiritual ancestors? The Rambam? Marx? Freud? Thoreau? Kierkegaard (if he keeps up with the literary journals)? Or Sholem Asch's dehydrated Jesus?

Jewishness is no longer a vital part of his life: this is a matter of neither choice nor pique; *it is nothing about which to moralize or judge;* it is, in the circumstances, unavoidable. He rejects religious values in general, as many modern intellectuals do. He cannot convince himself that a transfer of the source of his woes from this world to another is meaningful for him, and his scientific, radical outlook makes him skeptical of any supernatural explanation of either nature or man. Together with his rejection of religion there is often a feeling of irritation toward the observances of its tradition. In many instances, this tradition is still a living part of his family's life; in other instances, the tradition is not so intimately known, for the father himself may no longer observe it. But in either case Jewish tradition gives our intellectual a feeling of uneasiness.

If he has experienced in his own life some of the Jewish folkways, he may recall with some nostalgia, for instance, the beautiful Seder ceremony his family observed each year: the melody of its chants; the vigor and sweep of his father leading the family in Passover songs; the quiet pride of his mother watching the group in its most satisfying and ecstatic fulfillment of the unity for which she constantly yearns. While still a child he felt himself part of this tradition, of its beauty and pride; he loved to watch his father chant; he would wait especially for that part when the family would break off the prayer—always shortly before mealtime—to engage in a semi-serious, semi-humorous disputation on the meaning of the "ten plagues," only to have it resolved by his father's typically ironic remark that whatever the symbolic meaning of the plagues, the Egyptians certainly had the opportunity to discover their earthly meaning!

And now twenty years later, cajoled by his parents into attending another Seder, he observes the decay of his family as it tries again to go through with the ceremony. He watches himself—*that is after all what he is almost always doing*—in relation to "his" family, he whose head may have been buzzing a few hours back with Kafka or Existentialism or the theory of permanent revolution or Chagall's technique, and he wonders: where does he fit in now? The words of the prayer, which he does not understand, and the melodies of the chants, which touch some subterranean source of kinship, stir in him a feeling of continuity that conflicts with his rejection of the ceremony.

So he sits on the sidelines while his father watches him out of the corner of his eye, acutely aware of the existence if not the cause of the son's alienation. . . .

The conflict exists not only on the level of intellectual rejection as against emotional recollection; it functions on another level as well. Our intellectual has in the course of his education developed an interest in the esthetic components of religion, though he may reject its dogmas; his esthetic senses are stirred by the beauties of the prayer and music, which he knows his world has never equalled for depth of feeling or integration. And as he sits at his father's table, he is tempted to allow his senses to succumb to the rhythms of the prayer, though his skeptical intelligence warns him that it is a thing of the past which he neither can, nor wishes to, recall.

I suspect that this conflict between present conviction and past tradition is more painful with those intellectuals whose major concerns are cultural than those absorbed in politics. The writers and artists lack the systematic conviction that the political finds in the revolutionary movement. The political intellectual finds an anchor in his system of ideas, often explicitly anti-religious. And since the literary intellectual approaches tradition with a greater sensitivity to its beauty and possible sustenance for the creative artist, he may more readily succumb to it than the political, whose major interest is in the future rather than the past.

The family quite naturally becomes the center and arena of the struggle between his past and present. For what is, after all, the Jewish world to him but his family?

The primary struggle, I believe, takes place with the father. In most Jewish immigrant families, the father occupies an anomalous position. His education is incomplete, though his wit and sense of irony are not. Quite often he is not really the power in the family, the mother is often much more "practical" and decisive. But the father is still accorded the formal respect that is his traditional due. It is he who is the thinker, he who knows at least something of the mysteries and wisdom of the Torah; and it is he who reads the Yiddish paper after work, when even the most shrewish wife will admonish her children "not to bother papa when he reads the paper."

The father desires in his son the fulfillment of his own undeveloped and frustrated ambitions. "My son shouldn't have to work in a shop"—how often have these words rung out with bitterness and determination in Jewish immigrant homes! The father as one who still feels himself part of a people whose tradition is that of learning (after all, isn't Einstein a Jew?) and who does read a little, if only the *roman* in the *Forward* or *Day,* has an exaggerated reverence for things intellectual; he will literally work himself to death so that his son can go to college. But—and here is where the tragic conflict erupts—to the father intellectual achievement has become wedded to professional success—this he learned in America. Learning is an end in itself—provided it is not an end in itself, provided it helps his son become a teacher or a doctor. But our intellectual who has rebelled against the standards of bourgeois capitalist society cares little about professional success; he wishes to be a great novelist or immerse himself in a great cause, neither of which are particularly remunerative occupations. What is the good, asks the father, of my son's education, his intelligence, his *edelkeit*—if he can't make a living? And what is the good, asks the son, of being a success if it means succumbing to philistine standards of values?

Often enough the father does understand his son's objections to America's commercialized standards, for many immigrant Jews, especially those who are workers or have not themselves been traduced by the money mania, have a certain critical perception of American culture. But often the father deliberately closes his eyes to his son's point of view because of a desire to see him "get ahead."

This climax of the father-son conflict, of course, has its roots in the son's early childhood. As soon as the Jewish child is old enough to go into the streets, he discovers that the Yiddish his parents usually speak represents some kind of difference between his family and the external world.

I recall vividly an incident that took place more than twenty years ago. Like many other Jewish children, I had been brought up in a constricted family environment, especially since I was an only child, and at the age of five really knew Yiddish better than English. I attended my first day of kindergarten as if it were a visit to a new country. The teacher asked the children to identify various common objects. When my turn came she held up a fork and without hesitation I called it by its Yiddish name: "*a goopel.*" The whole class burst out laughing at me with that special cruelty of children. That afternoon I told my parents that I had made up my mind never to speak Yiddish to them again, though I would not give any reasons. It was a shock for them, the first in a series of conflicts between immigrant and America.

A similar incident: When I was a few years older, about eight or nine, my parents had a grocery store in an "Americanized" Jewish neighborhood, the West Bronx. I used to play in an abandoned lot about a block away from the store, and when I'd neglect to come home at supper time, my father would come to call for me. He would shout my name from afar, giving it a Yiddish twist: "Oivee!" I would always feel a sense of shame at hearing my name so mutilated in the presence of amused onlookers, and though I would come home—supper was supper!—I would always run ahead of my father as if to emphasize the existence of a certain distance between us. In later years I often wondered how I would react if my father were again to call "Oivee" at the top of his lungs in, say, Washington Square.

Somewhat similarly, Isaac Rosenfeld in his novel, *Passage from Home,* has described still another aspect of the father-son conflict. In his eagerness to raise the social status of his son, the father makes many sacrifices; one of the signs of that sacrifice is the accumulation of books bought by the son with his father's money. The relationship between them, as Rosenfeld describes it, takes an indirect form: rather than flowing from person to person, it moves through the feelings held toward the books. The father feels the books to be both a reason for pride in his son's intellectual attainments, and at the same time a barrier to free communication with the son. That which he has given to his son out of his own labor marks the cultural differentiation widening the gap between them.

And yet there often is a measure of understanding on the part of the fathers to their wayward intellectual sons. Two of my friends report identical experiences. One of them, a not very successful painter, tells me that when visiting his studio, his father gazes at his abstract paintings directly, sideways, from various angles, and then turns to him with a glance of irony as if to say: And for such madness I sent you to college! Yet, among his own friends, his father speaks with great pride of his son as a promising painter and will even drag out a few review clippings.

My second friend is a leader of a small radical group. His father periodically berates him for wasting his time ("All right, go change the world, but can you make a living from it?") and predicts a "bad end" for him as a jailbird. But let some acquaintance make a disparaging remark about his son, and the father will shout: "Boob! He is an idealist! You think he couldn't make a good living if he weren't an idealist?"

In relation to the mother, the problem involves emotion more than status. Most marriages contracted between two timid and lost immigrants a quarter of a century ago manage to survive if only in order to provide a home for the children, but they seldom survive on the basis of a genuine relationship of love. The mother often seeks in her son's life a vicarious fulfillment for the emotional yearnings her own life could not satisfy, just as the father seeks vicarious fulfillment for his yearnings for status.

From infancy on, the child is spoiled and petted by his mother: she keeps him in the feminine pattern as long as possible, delaying the cutting of his baby curls, and later trying to prevent him from entering street relationships by tying him to her apron strings; she inhibits his normal urges toward athletic activity by her fears that he will be hurt, infecting him with the same fears; and she burdens him with such a variety of tasks (school work, music lessons, Hebrew school, family obligations) that he has little time for normal childhood games. She constantly hovers over him, developing in him—as if with unconscious skill—the sense of dependence on her which he is later to find so difficult to overcome. The psychoanalyst Helene Deutsch, in her book, *Psychology of Women,* notes that "Jewish women show an overstressed oral-motherly giving toward their children . . . the mother develops a special interest in the nutritional process of the objects of her love and shows much solicitude about their food. . . . This overemphasis on eating is especially typical of Jewish women." Even when the son is a grown-up man, the mother will still fuss and fume about his food when he comes to visit her, as if to maintain the same modes of affection and dependence.

In later years, again, the mother will exploit all sorts of desperate devices to maintain her hold on her son. She is constantly appealing, no matter how subtly, to his guilt feelings: "After all I have done for you, now in my old age you are going to leave me!" A few subtly poisonous remarks about the girls whom he brings home "for inspection" are useful in this connection. In many instances, mothers develop neurotic complaints and psychosomatic illnesses as a means of binding the straying son to the family.

These patterns are of course not unique to Jewish families, but one's impression is that they are considerably stronger in Jewish families. For one thing, the family is given a higher valuation among immigrant Jews than among most other groups. For another, the more or less typical parents whom we have sketched live

their lives so vicariously, so without individual purpose or fulfillment, so thoroughly immersed in the lives of their children, that
the urge to hold them to the family hearth is almost irresistible.
And when the son is an "intellectual," the mother especially hates
to lose her control. For then the son is not leaving for respectable
familyhood with a "fine" wife with whom he will call at his folks'
house every Friday night for supper. He is leaving to be a *luftmensh*—a starving poet, a painter without pictures, a radical leader
without followers. He offers little promise for *nachas*—and who
knows, God forbid, in his wanderings in the alien world he may
find a *shiksa* for himself.

And just as the kindness and indulgence of his parents make a
break more difficult, so the son's own understanding of his parents' feelings has the same effect. The son has become sensitized to
human feelings; he is an intellectual who is aware of the complexity of life and the tragedies of its development; he cannot but
realize how painful his behavior, which he considers unavoidable
if he is to maintain his integrity, must be to his parents. And thus
the tragedy of the family relationship persists: largely insoluble, a
clash between two worlds in which even mutual understanding is
of little help. The son must stray and wander along his tortured
path; the parents must watch with bewilderment and anguish an
alienation of the son on whom they have banked their entire lives.

Perhaps the one word that best expresses the emotional complexion of the Jewish "intellectual" is that extraordinarily expressive German word *Angst*. It is a feeling that can be described as one
of total loneliness, of complete rootlessness. It is the feeling of
futility common to all contemporary intellectuals, the "powerless
people"; but it is somehow heightened within the Jewish intellectual because of the special difficulties he faces. What makes *his*
situation more unbearable is that he often cannot take even his
own misery with complete seriousness.

The biting sense of irony he has acquired from his family associations and from the Jewish cultural tradition forces him to
observe his own ridiculousness, his own posturing, his objective in-
significance in relation to his self-preoccupation. *He is a victim of
his own complexity of vision:* even the most harrowing of his feelings, the most intolerable aspects of his alienation, he must still

examine with the same mordant irony he applies to everything else.

This dilemma often takes the form of an internal split in personality. One of the most glaring aspects of our Jewish intellectual's personality is its total lack of spontaneity: his obsessive need to control or at least to understand the situations in which he finds himself makes it impossible for him to react in any way which is not contrived, premeditated, calculated. He cannot surrender himself to events or moods or people, for he is always searching for meanings and examining himself while he acts. And this self-examination, this split into participant and observer—in which he watches his own personality as if it belonged to someone else—is the core of his lack of spontaneity. For spontaneity requires a total reaction, and that the Jewish intellectual cannot find.

Our intellectual suffers further from a very great overvaluation of verbal forms of communication. The word has become his final retreat; it alone has ultimate substantiality for him. *The word becomes a substitute for experience rather than an aspect of it.* And in that way, the word also becomes an obstruction to thought. Who does not know intellectuals who juggle words brilliantly, effortlessly, to such an extent that the process of thought, a process which involves struggle and effort, is often hardly visible? He who cannot act spontaneously finds his refuge in the word.

Together with this excessive verbalism, there is often found a distressing unproductivity among young Jewish intellectuals. A glance through the pages of any serious magazine will show dozens of names of writers who indicate one degree or another of promise. For the most part they write one or two stories, poems, or articles and then are never heard from again. (Little communication with the literate world filters up from the salt mines of publicity work.) This blight on productivity is not of course unique to Jewish intellectuals; it has been the theme of innumerable critical laments on the state of American culture. Yet, whatever the more general causes of the difficulty in sustaining creative talent in America, is it not likely that the problems here described help produce the sterility which withers the early promise and hopes of so many talented young Jewish intellectuals?

For a writer or artist who cannot lift himself out of the pitfalls and swamps of his own ego can hardly expect to reach the plane of

161

objectivity essential to sustained and valuable work. So much of the work of young Jewish writers is the expression of either retribution or nostalgia for their past, the painful record of their painful ascent from adolescence to what they hope is maturity. But once they have chronicled their own pattern of sensitivity, they become barren. Choked by their internal conflicts and pervasive self-consciousness, they lapse into a brooding silence.

In his relation to other people, the Jewish intellectual suffers from similar difficulties. There is a constant conflict between his pervasive need to be with other people, to find a sense of kinship in close relationships, and his trend toward withdrawal. And because withdrawal is often a necessary prerequisite for serious and creative intellectual work, this conflict becomes even sharper. It would not be so sharp if the Jewish intellectual had a sense of belonging, a sense of security in relation to his world and the people with whom he associates. But the lack of external buttresses forces him to turn to his own inner resources for intellectual and emotional sustenance—the more he does so, the more does he withdraw, and the more he feels unhappy about his withdrawal and desires a sense of community.

That all this should affect the more personal aspects of his life, his relationships to women for instance, is inevitable. Hence his ambiguous attitude toward love: his romantic yearning for it as the one possible sustenance in an atomized, crazed world, the one pillar in a world of crumbling dust; and simultaneously, his shyness toward it, his inability to throw himself into it as a total personality.

The social result of this situation can best be measured by recalling the short stories of Jewish life of several decades ago. Thyra Samter Winslow's stories gave the then typical pattern: the partly intellectualized immigrant rising through painful struggle to economic security, only to be disdained by his "Americanized" children who seek an integration into American culture that their father can never have. Today, however, the pattern is different. Actually, the parents, even if they live in a half-ghetto and retain Yiddish for their language and still adhere to Jewish customs, have achieved a better integration into American society than their intellectualized sons. It is the son who is the "outsider," the outcast.

Of course—fortunately!—few individuals suffer from all the

characteristics listed here. What I have attempted has been to abstract a typical pattern that characterizes a certain stratum of Jewish intellectuals; it goes without saying that I have not tried to portray any one individual.

And I suppose that it is necessary to say at least a word about the possible solutions for the Jewish intellectual in his dilemma. Some would suggest Zionism; still others a return to traditional Judaism; others Jewish education; others a reconstruction of a Jewish community and a Jewish culture. I am very skeptical, however, of any familiar pat solution.

My personal opinion is that any conclusion which affirms the necessity of "returning home" to the ways of one's people is—like it or not—unrealistic and unlikely to be effected: the Jewish intellectual cannot, even if he wished to, return to a world no longer his. Possibly he can find some alleviation in individual psychotherapy, but even that can only ease individual problems without touching the cause. Ultimately the problem can only be solved if an American society appears in which both the Jewish intellectual and his people, along with everyone else, can find integration, security, and acceptance.

At the moment he must live in a society providing none of these; he must continue as what he is: the rootless son of a rootless people. He can find consolation and dignity, however, in the consciousness of his vision, in the awareness of his complexity, and in the rejection of self-pity. To each age its own burdens.

PLIGHT OF THE JEWISH INTELLECTUAL

By LESLIE A. FIEDLER

I SHOULD LIKE TO speak in these remarks quite frankly (being
among friends), and only for myself—though with the hope that
my plight may seem relevant to others. I am an Intellectual. I cannot use the word without a little irony, knowing the mockery and
contempt attached to it in certain quarters. I should like to be a
Jew. When anybody else asks me, you understand, I *am* a Jew; when
I question myself, I am not so sure. I hear a lot these days of "negative" and "positive" Jewishness. I prefer to think of a Jewishness
sufficient for others, and a Jewishness satisfactory to oneself. I
know that, given another Hitler, I could qualify to die as a Jew;
for me that is not enough; I must know how to live as one.

The problem is especially pressing for me, because I have chosen
to live among Gentiles. To many urban Jews, surrounded by
neighbors with a common background and descent, the word Exile
is a rather remote metaphor; to me, in a town where a *minyan* cannot be gathered unless someone has a visiting relative, Exile is the
essential fact of my life. No child of a Jewish family in our community has ever married another Jew. I am faced day by day with
the real possibility of losing forever in my own family whatever
Jewishness may be. And what do I have to guide me? A year in
Hebrew school twenty years ago, the dimly remembered stories of
my grandfather—plus what I have been able to read and learn on
my own, my slight Hebrew refreshed with two semesters' study (it
is the final joke!) in the Harvard Divinity School.

The conscious beginnings of my reaching "back" toward
Judaism did not depend upon the successes of Hitler, but on the

164

failures of Stalin. There seemed to be in the thirties answers to nazism superior to a "return" to Judaism; and there was the specially hopeful dream of the Soviet Internationale: the scientific culmination of an Enlightenment which had brought our ancestors out of the ghetto and set us on the road toward a world where all national and ethnic differences would be resolved into a universal humanity. The Moscow Trials (how many Jews, particularly susceptible to the dream, were degraded before death), the betrayals of Spain made clear to me not only how false were the promises of communism, but more important, how we had been seeking in a historical movement a kind of redemption possible only out of time.

It is a difficult thing to have to rediscover God. This, Abraham should have done for us, once and for all. I do not think that the comfortable Jew, who has never left the security of Synagogue or Temple, can quite know how hard it is for some simply to say, "I believe in God." Your closest "intellectual" friends look at you askance, as if you had admitted having some horrible disease, or having voted Republican. Secretly, they are sure you are lying, *playing* with words to be fashionable or different; though at the same time they are condemning you as regressive, sentimental—and even, in encouraging a rebirth of religiosity that could spread to Christian Intellectuals, too—running the risk of unleashing a new wave of anti-Semitism. In your mind, you are uneasy, feeling that, having taken the first step, you may, indeed, be led into denying the whole progressive hope of a united mankind. Is not religion the worst divider of men?

It must be this last consideration that makes many intellectual radical Jews (Simone Weil is a good example) at their moment of conversion, turn to Christianity rather than Judaism. Judaism seems permanently destined to be the belief of a harassed minority, but Christianity proposes the ideal, at least, of a universal Church, in which all men will be brothers. Besides, there is already in the Christian Church a tradition more than two generations old of a radical faith for intellectual converts—at once fiercely loving God and despising the "good" bourgeois believer. Bloy, Claudel, Maritain—Kierkegaard, Eliot, Auden—the new believer feels at home with these men, whose writings gave him pleasure even in the days of his skepticism—and, perhaps, even helped lead to his own change of heart. What corresponds to this tradition among believing Jews in America?

What does the Intellectual, fumbling his way "back" toward a Jewish faith discover in our Jewish institutions? In the Orthodox *shuls,* the *Hasidic* fire, the old unity of devotion are moribund beneath an emphasis on *kashruth,* and the endless *pilpul,* long since turned into a substitute for any moving faith. In the Reform Temples, the glib young rabbi, with his tags from Freud, his sociological jargon, speaks his conviction that God is a "cosmological blur." Like the more debased Protestant Churches, the Temples have tended to substitute "social service" for religion, felt to belong to the unenlightened past. These conditions do not prevail universally, of course, but in general, American Judaism has made everything its center but God: amateur psychoanalysis, collecting money for the Jewish Appeal, hating all Germans, worshiping force, bowing down before a revived nineteenth-century nationalism.

The intellectual refugee from the idolatry of Stalinism, finds the Jewish community making on a hundred fronts what seems to him the very error from which he is fleeing: the error of bowing down before the Golden Calf or the False Messiah—finding in this or that material, historical event the End which can only be in eternity. To the returning Jew, unwilling to accept peace of mind as a sufficient Judaism, the heart of Jewish belief seems to be in the phrase, "The Messiah *will* come," or in the Passover sentence, "This year we are slaves, next year we shall be free!" This sense of the endless futurity of redemption strikes me as the essential beauty and truth of Judaism. Our real spiritual freedom is always "next year," and our aspirations point the way out of time.

But the Intellectual can only *think* this and bite his tongue. Who is he, a newcomer, a snot-nose, to tell his Elders what is the core of their faith! He is regarded with suspicion before he opens his big mouth—a *nudnik* who has neither deep Talmudic learning, nor enough money to make a substantial contribution toward the new community center!

As a believer, the Intellectual is uncomfortable enough coming "home," but as an intellectual he finds himself even more alienated among his own people. From the Jewish Philistine he gets the same hostility as from his Baptist or Knights of Columbus counterpart.

The books he reads or writes are unknown to the congregation into which he comes. They are satisfied with what they have, a middle-brow "Jewish" literature, cheaply reminiscent, sentimental and trite. And the second-rate purveyors of this "literature," who have found it easy or profitable to peddle their Jewishness, turn their scorn on the returning intellectual for his lack of *Yiddishkeit*, his obscurity and his highbrow pretensions.

In what a ridiculous situation the Intellectual who wants to be completely and positively Jewish, without abandoning sincerity or taste, finds himself! The poets and thinkers he most respects, those whose sensibility and piety are most like his own, are likely to be neo-orthodox Christians, with, more often than not, a cruel streak of the higher anti-Semitism. His former comrades, staggering from political faith to political faith, or ending in despair, regard his religious convictions as a betrayal of humanity. Most members of the Jewish community to which he turns distrust intelligence, hate serious literature, fear religious fervor, and believe really only in success and sanitary plumbing. His "return" has only made him more than ever aware of his aloneness.

The situation is my own. Perhaps that is why I live here where I do not have to confront the problem face to face every day. And yet, hoplessness is not my final response. In a few days it will be *Pesach;* my son will rise to ask me the Four Questions, and I will tell him, "This is on account of what the Lord did for me, when I went out from Egypt." Did for *me!* I am forever with all of Israel on the way out of the long bondage that has made slaves of us all.

Saying the sentence, I am one with all who have said it and shall say it forever, one with those that were redeemed, and are even now, in the eternal present tense of God of which the Passover Haggadah reminds us, being redeemed. In that Israel of myth and reality which cannot die, my children and I will always be at home.

TO THE YOUNG JEWISH INTELLECTUALS

By LUDWIG LEWISOHN

IT IS FIVE or six years now that we have been hearing of the plight of the young (now no longer *so* young) Jewish intellectuals. They tell us that they desire to be Jews and that they desire—though this is fainter—to re-ally themselves with the community of Israel. And nothing happens. The nostalgia seems to continue. But it seems also to become frozen. Out of a frozen mood of nostalgia which is more and more tempered by a subconscious gesture of avoidance—a gesture as of one who fancies that he might face a storm of stones —arise literary exercises of the restatement of that mood or of the repetition of that gesture of avoidance. An example of the first is Mr. Alfred Kazin's *A Walker in the City,* of the second Mr. Leslie Fiedler's Introduction to the book *Waiting for God* by Simone Weil. The strange thing about these literary exercises is that they scarcely seem to break an interior silence. The essays are *there* and Mr. Kazin and Mr. Fiedler are both gifted writers and scholars, and the feeling arises from these documents that their souls are mute.

This circumstance, like so many others arising in American Jewry, is new and melancholy. There have been returning young intellectuals before. Surely Mr. Kazin and Mr. Fiedler and Mr. Howe must have read the *Diaries* of Franz Kafka. Did they force themselves not to observe the circumstance that Kafka's most gifted friends and comrades, not only Max Brod but also Hugo Bergmann and Felix Weltsch—now all and for many, many years active in Israel—were "returners" and that these men burst all the bonds of alienation and of an alien world and penetrated not only to the

Zion of the body but also the Zion of the faith and the soul? Kafka himself drew nearer and nearer to a similar liberation. The destiny of genius and self-destruction held him in check.

I do not suppose that Mr. Fiedler or Mr. Kazin or the others in that group have any real acquaintance with that wide return of young Jewish intellectuals which took place in Germany between the two wars under the teaching of Buber and Rosenzweig. I do not suppose either that they are aware of such figures as those of Else Lasker-Schueler or Karl Wolfskehl. For one of the deepest maladies of our younger Americans is that gesture of avoidance— that gesture of seeking cover against a hail of stones and among those stones to be avoided, lest the muteness of their Jewish soul be broken, is Jewish example, Jewish inter-communication and comradeship. In Italy, too, among that indistinguishably assimilated community there were those who were first called *ritornandi,* the returning ones, and later *ritornati,* the returned, and from among these came such figures as that of the heroic, the forever memorable Enzo Sereni.

And here and now? One does not, let it be emphatically said, expect the younger American intellectuals to do what Bergmann and Weltsch or Sereni did. Perhaps that is not even their function. The Jewries of the European Continent were doomed. That is what all the works of Kafka *say.* That and that alone. Here, in America, there exists one half of the Jewish people. Here are life and functioning for Mr. Kazin and Mr. Fiedler and the others. Nor need they give up their writing or their teaching or their participation in American cultural processes. But all that is so clear and there are a few examples to show the way. Yet neither opportunity nor example seem to be of any help. Not one of these younger American intellectuals has yet broken the bonds and thongs and fetters— the interior ones—and come out to participate in the existence of the living Jewish people. They live, as it were, behind a wall which they themselves have built.

Let us go to the groundwork. Mr. Fiedler writes: "When anybody else asks me, you understand, I *am* a Jew; when I question myself, I am not so sure." Mr. Howe tells us that the young Jewish intellectual "has largely lost his sense of Jewishness, of belonging to a people with a meaningful tradition." Mr. Kazin uses almost the same phraseology: "I learned long ago to accept the fact that I am Jewish without being a part of any meaningful Jewish life and culture." Are these not strangely opaque observations? For one's Jewishness is an objective fact. One was born of these parents, these grandparents; one is a link in that unbroken chain—had it been broken one would not be here as a Jew—which extends back into the darkness of the immemorial. Nothing, to the plain common sense of all experience, is less accidental than birth and descent. The objective fact of one's Jewishness, it may well be repeated, is irrefragable. What, subjectively, one does with that fact is another matter.

The young intellectuals want, apparently, to do something, subjectively with that objective fact. Not all of them go so far as Mr. Fiedler who says: "I should like to be a Jew." Now, if they want to do something subjectively with the objective fact of their existence *as* Jews, what do they mean when they say, as both Mr. Kazin and Mr. Howe do say, that they are accustomed to being Jews *meaninglessly?* One would have thought that the whole aim of all they say and feel would be the recovery of the meaningfulness of their Jewishness which is, as all experience teaches, inseparable from their Judaism.

The state of mind portrayed by these writers themselves is not easy even to imagine. By definition they are "intellectuals." One may not like that term. It smacks of the false and vicious classification of the Communists, and in our place and time is almost identical with the concept of a Mandarinate. Let us say that these men are educated men, reflective men, men, too, I am persuaded, of heart. There is a shattering objective fact in their lives which they desire—else what are they talking about—to render meaningful in order to become whole and integrated human beings. Very well. Were the fact any other fact except their Jewishness, what would they do?

An authentic anecdote has it that, during the late war, a young biologist was, by one of those errors said to have been not uncharacteristic of the Army, placed in command of a bridge-building project. He knew that appeals to reason would be in vain. Luckily he knew some mathematics. He bought books. He studied night and day. He built the bridge. To his awe and delight it did not collapse. Were Mr. Fiedler or Mr. Kazin or Mr. Howe faced by an analogous situation they would do the same. But in this matter of the towering fact of their objective Jewishness which they would like to render subjectively meaningful, they act—they will forgive this observation—like undisciplined children. "There was little in the synagogue ritual that was ever explained," Mr. Kazin tells us. Doubtless, and that was a grievous omission and attempts have been made, even since Mr. Kazin's childhood, to remedy this state of affairs. But what has prevented Mr. Kazin in the years since then from studying our sublime and psychologically appropriate liturgy? What has prevented Mr. Fiedler and Mr. Kazin and their fellows from giving an hour a day to Scripture, Talmud, Midrash, history, *responsa*—in *any* language they happened to read with ease, including English—in order to make up for the defects of their early Jewish education? And why—*why* are they not in the forefront of those who fight for the Jewish school in order to save their children and the children of their coevals from the lack of early training which they deplore? The "meaningful tradition" exists; it is there; it is taught and learned and *lived* by thousands. Why does it seem so unapproachable to these scholarly, sensitive men? "How many *melamdim*," a brilliant young Jew who has never had to "return" asks, "have alienated sensitive young Jews in America?" Nonsense! Were Mr. Kazin's and Mr. Fiedler's public-school teachers all experts and sages? Hardly. They did not on that account abandon Shakespeare or Milton—I beg their pardon —Donne, or Matthew Arnold or T. S. Eliot. The majority of foreign-language teachers in our public schools are notoriously neither too expert in the languages they teach nor impassioned communicators of literary values. Has that prevented our younger intellectuals from later expertness on Sartre, Eluard, Kafka or Simone Weil? No, the plea concerning the defects of Jewish education may be dismissed as frivolous and as a plea in avoidance.

Learning, however, when the will to learn is there, need not be exclusively from books. Mr. Fiedler is quietly bitter concerning what he finds in the existing Jewish community. Mr. Kazin gives no evidence of ever having sought to establish a living contact with that community. Now the American-Jewish community exhibits to the eye of authentic Jewish observation many tragic, many horrifying characteristics. But only those—and here I appeal directly to Mr. Fiedler's moral sensibilities, which I know to be delicate and acute—only those have a right to criticize and castigate who are filled with the *ahavat Yisrael,* the love of Israel. If my body hurts, I seek to have it healed. It is my body. It remains mine. That must be clear, so soon as it is uttered, even to the younger intellectuals who feign to desire to return. We read in the Talmud (no closed book any longer) that "he who shares the pain of the community is destined to see its consolation." (*Taanith* 11a.)

But that is not the whole story. On the level on which Mr. Fiedler and Mr. Kazin and their fellows could, if they desired, seek out instruction and examples among Jews, the American community is not poor. Authentic Jews, both lay and rabbinic, *abound on that level.* Nor are these Jews inarticulate. A rapidly growing literature serves to express them and their teachings. "What," Mr. Fiedler asks, "corresponds to the neo-Catholic tradition among believing American Jews?" Well, I would not use the word *corresponds.* The two things have scarcely a common measure. But I know what Mr. Fiedler means. Yet his very asking of the question betrays, I am afraid, an obscure unwillingness to know. For the Hasidic evangels, whether according to Buber or even Rabbi L. I. Newman, have long been accessible, as have the writings of Hayim Greenberg, latterly of Will Herberg, during long years the books of Maurice Samuel and of the present writer. I could mention many others. But I am aware of Mr. Fiedler's and Mr. Kazin's literary sensibilities. I share them keenly. And I do not expect them to overlook the literary defects of men not without both scholarly and saintly qualities. Yet there is visible that gesture of avoidance already described. Mr. Fiedler would not ask his question if he had not, doubtless reading all the trash of the Nihilists, avoided my little book *The Permanent Horizon* in 1934 (but perhaps he was too young) and those very crucial essays by Hayim Greenberg and Will Herberg in the *Jewish Frontier Anthology* in which they inaugurated the great spiritual revision in 1945.

We must, however, go still deeper. And it is not hard, alas; for Mr. Fiedler makes a confession of the full painfulness of which he seems to be unconscious. "The conscious beginnings of my reaching back to Judaism did not depend upon the successes of Hitler but on the failures of Stalin." It is hard for a Jew—a *Jew*—to read that sentence with equanimity. Not the martyrdom of his people, not the destruction of his people's children who might have been his children, nay who *were* his children, not the vast and blazing historic symbolism of that ineffable tragedy had power over Mr. Fiedler's soul, but the foreseeable horrors attendant upon the most sordid, the most lightless theory of "man and nature and human life" that ever darkened the historic horizon.

It is very well for the super-sophisticated today to deprecate the concept of Jewish self-hatred. But all that "red assimilation," all that horrible hopefulness that in the Soviet Union Jews would be permitted to perish *as Jews,* whence did it, whence could it have arisen, save from a hatred of one's Jewishness so intense that anything seemed preferable to it—even the bleak squalor of the Soviet Utopia? No wonder, then, that Mr. Fiedler could bring himself to write almost worshipfully of that dreadful moral psychotic Simone Weil who is *said* to have wished to sacrifice herself for the poor, the oppressed, the disinherited but who, when she and her parents had to flee from France and from Europe in fear of deportation as Jews, had no word of sympathy or grief, no syllable of even a consciousness of her fellowship with the most persecuted, the most innocent, the only *martyrs* of the age. Mr. Fiedler assures us, seeking to explain Simone Weil's pathological Jewish self-hatred, that her father was an agnostic—since when did *that* deter children from a *teshuvah,* a turning or *re*-turn—and that the Jewishness of her kinsmen was "cold, oppressive, and meaninglessly legalistic." It *may* have been. Even so it was in its decay a great and venerable tradition which, in a thousand other aspects and places, was even then revealing its eternally redemptive power. But the report is only through the agnostic, assimilatory father and the self-despising daughter and it is quite possible that these kinsmen were kindly and sincerely devout people, such as were and are not infrequent among French Jews of Alsatian origin. No such suspicion crossed Mr. Fiedler's mind.

Mr. Kazin, who has been very generous to my critical writings, sedulously avoiding (the old gesture!) my Jewish fiction and non-fiction, sums up his case, as Mr. Fiedler summed up his own in that sentence about Hitler and Stalin, as follows: "Ludwig Lewisohn is a Jew who has raised the immemorial loneliness of the Jewish mind to a historical principle." I read and reread that sentence. I ponder it. I did not know that the Jewish mind had ever been lonely. Is it not rather the least lonely of minds through the circumstances that all Jewish tradition and all Jewish lore and history constitute a living simultaneity in every aware and authentic Jewish mind, even as we are bidden in the Pesach Haggadah to know that not our fathers alone but we, here and today, are experiencing the liberation of Israel? My Jewish contemporaries and I, companioned by each other, quote and discuss as living factors in our lives and the governance in our lives, scriptural patriarchs, Talmudic sages, Hasidic *Zadikim*. We live in two concentric living worlds. Vertically through the ages, horizontally through Israel and the lands of the dispersion, we form an intercommunicating group of profound and constant fellowship. Does Mr. Kazin know what he means? For he cannot mean by loneliness detachment from the non-Jewish world. He offers me as an example. But have I not written that history of American literature, of which he is kind enough to think well, and a life of Goethe and sundry other volumes on non-Jewish literature? And I am, of course, not alone or singular in this respect. So it appears to me that the Jewish mind has less chance than any other mind of being "lonely," unless, as in Mr. Kazin (whose chief theme in all his writings is "alienation," both American and Jewish) loneliness, alienation, hovering between two worlds and unable to grasp either or both, has become the structure of the psychical or spiritual economy. It is he who is lonely, imputing that loneliness to another, a process known both to Talmudic sages and Freudian analysts. Some day he may burst these bonds and come home to fellowship in both Israel and the world.

Why are these lines written? I was once—thirty-five years ago—a young returning intellectual. And I didn't stay "returning." I returned. I returned so with my whole soul and heart and mind that today, when somebody reminds me of once having been in a state of alienation and is kind enough to assign to me the merit—*un*merited—which our sages grant to a *Baal Teshuvah*, it seems to me like a legend, like a dream, like something that has no relevance to the man I am. And perhaps these present younger returning intellectuals, who are nearly all scholars and writers, sensitive and gifted, have a faint notion of that peace within Israel which *can* be found today as in every age and yet being, for strange and varied reasons, impotent to approach even the sources whence that peace springs, feel a natural and pardonable and understandable irrita-

174

tion in the presence of a result which is the object of their desire but not within their power to attain.

It is a great pity. The American Jewish community is not too rich in lay leadership. Younger scholars and writers would be a very precious accession to its ranks. But the first quality that is needed for one who desires indeed to return is humility. He must "learn"; he must sit at the feet of the sages and saints of Israel, the living and the dead. And the second prerequisite is a true abjuration of pagan idols—of nihilist Utopias, not because they have failed but because God forbid, they might have succeeded. But even humility and the abjuration of pagan idols will not suffice— I warn my young contemporaries—without the spontaneous love of Israel. They will know that they are Jews again and no more lonely and no more alienated when the humblest Jew and the most recalcitrant Jew is dear and precious to them for the sake of that eternal bond of pain and glory, of aspiration and even of defeat, of service to man and of suffering for that service which constitutes the fellowship of Israel through the ages.

TROUBLED INTELLECTUALS

By CHARLES ANGOFF

O NE OF THE most enduring psychological traumas in history is apparently the one inflicted upon the Jewish people by the Diaspora. The severity of it has varied with individuals and fluctuated with the changing conditions of the 2,000-year-old exile, sometimes becoming almost unbearable and sometimes barely perceptible, but it has never disappeared. Being virtually a perpetual guest of other peoples, across so many centuries, was hardly conducive to collective mental health. A traveler away from home, for no matter how long, may be homesick but he is never homeless. A vagrant is both homesick and homeless.

The homesickness and homelessness of the Jews has little relationship to citizenship or nationality in general. A Jewish citizen of England or France or Italy or the United States may be a perfectly good and loyal national of those countries, and yet, in his innermost being, feel uneasy—not quite wanted, not entirely accepted, with a belligerent defense of his status of equality ever ready to come to the fore. Jews, indeed, are specialists in being, at the same time, superpatriots of the nations they reside in—even those that have persecuted them—and looking upon themselves as in *Golus*. German Jews in all parts of the world still speak with deep emotion of their *Vaterland,* and when a Russian Jew, living in the United States for a half century, speaks of events *in der haim* he refers to the Russia of the Czar.

Precisely what is the nature of this historic Jewish trauma that hardly any Jew, however vague the consciousness of his Jewishness may be, can altogether escape? It is difficult to say. Part of it, undoubtedly, is due to the persistent anti-Semitism of large sections of the Christian world. Alas, this anti-Semitism is not confined to the "lower elements." The recent statement by the Archbishop of York regarding "the pressure of Jewish groups in New York City" which allegedly impedes the settlement of the Israel-Arab issue is the latest startling reminder of this. The defense of the *numerus clausus* in colleges and universities made by American college presidents is another. The Jew has learned not to be surprised by the appearance of anti-Semitism in no matter what exalted places— but he has never learned not to be hurt by it, and he probably never can.

Anti-Semitism, of course, has its religious roots. The Christians have not been able to forgive the Jews for the fact that Judaism is the mother of Christianity, and that the mother disowned the daughter for fraud and ingratitude. No amount of Christian theological casuistry has been able to hide this, and the more honest among the Christian theologians openly admit the ingratitude— for they know that all that is true, good and beautiful in Christianity is basically Jewish; but most of them still haven't it in their heart to question the concept of the divinity and divine mission of Christ.

But there are other roots to anti-Semitism. People, as a rule, are ill at ease with those who are profoundly different in their metaphysical and emotional outlook. Here we are on debatable territory. At the risk of being charged with chauvinism, I hazard the statement that there is such a thing as a Jewish soul or spirit, which is to say, a Jewish attitude toward life. It is as real as the English spirit and the German spirit and the Spanish spirit. The Jewish spirit is a compound of exuberance, spirituality, dedication to moral ideals, lyricism and profound concern with ultimate metaphysical values. Of course, there are many other elements in it, but to list them all would be impossible, for no spirit can be completely defined; it can only be sensed. Why the French, for example, as a group, often feel so strange in the presence of the Jewish spirit, whereas they feel more tolerant toward the English spirit, the Spanish, or the Italian, is not wholly clear, though it may be that here, too, the primordial resentment of Christianity toward Judaism is the determining factor.

But whatever the causes of Jewish homelessness, it has frequently played havoc with the Jew's psychological health. Many Jews throughout the ages have tried to accept this homelessness, finding solace in their religion and traditions. But a large number have not been able to do this, and even the establishment of Israel has not afforded them much help. They naturally wish the new state well and take pride in its progress, but their trauma remains pretty much what it always was. Israel may, and most likely will, do more for their children and grandchildren, in this respect; but for them Israel is still in large part a remote influence.

Jewish intellectuals have always been especially troubled by their homelessness, and perhaps never more so than in the wilderness of the twentieth century. Relatively few of them have sought internal peace in a greater understanding of Judaism. Why they have not turned in this direction is puzzling; this fact in itself may be part of the over-all trauma. Most of them, it seems, have looked elsewhere for spiritual satisfaction and emotional stability. Earlier in this century many Jewish intellectuals decided it was their duty, as "civilized" people, to abandon Judaism completely and devote themselves entirely to working for the welfare of the Common People, the most recent of the Golden Calves of history. They became Socialists, Communists, Anarchists, Trade-unionists, Syndicalists. But many of them eventually realized the coldness and aridity of their new devotion, and were once more in a state of homelessness.

Some of them sought refuge in the all-embracing security promised by such newer religions as Christian Science, Divine Science, Unity. Others returned to Judaism, but with a vengeance, so to speak. Either they became ultra-Orthodox, as they had been ultra-radical before, or they have steeped themselves in the most abstruse of the writings of the most metaphysical of the Talmudists, in a great hurry, of course, so that they have soaked up only the surface fanaticism and missed the inner poetry—and they have blossomed forth as the new mystics of Jewry. They are in a state of delirium that they mistake for peace.

Unfortunately, some of them—one, in America, had been a violent radical whose gibberish stumped even the most dialectical of Marxian dialecticians—are taken seriously by a number of Jewish institutions of learning and American universities and also by the editors of the more pretentious Anglo-Jewish reviews. Now, alas, some of these former Jew-despisers speak for the Jews, and Jews who should know better listen to them and read them with respect. It could yet be—as actually did happen in the case of Simone Weil—that our *ersatz* mystics and the other higher *nudnicks* will end up as adorers of Christ, if not actual members of a Christian church, and as metaphysical anti-Semites—a brand of psychopaths that, while not new in Jewish history, is always troublesome.

The pathology of homelessness among Jewish intellectuals has its pathetic as well as offensive aspects. We can all recall relevant case histories. I knew a lawyer, the son of Orthodox East Side Jewish parents, who vowed in his early 20's to marry only a *shiksa* because "*shiksas* are so much more refined, quieter than Jewish girls, who are so loud and messy." He courted an Episcopalian girl and boasted to me how happy he was. "She's so neat," he said, "and so considerate, not like Jewish girls who push you, who want material things." But then, when she took him to a church, just to hear music, of course, for they were both music lovers, he noticed that she kneeled and mumbled a few prayers. He was appalled and asked her to explain herself. She said, "Oh, that means nothing. It's only habit and I rather like it. It reminds me of my childhood." He was terribly disturbed and soon they parted. He had a similar experience with a Methodist girl. She who had boasted of being "a total non-believer," loved to sing Christmas carols and Easter carols and camp-meeting songs because "Dad loved them and he used to sing them and I like them—but they really don't mean a thing to me, dear."

Not long afterward, he took up with an editor of a liberal New York periodical. She insisted that religion meant so little to her and her family that her people "never, as far as I remember, went to church, and maybe I was baptized, for grandma's sake, my mother's mother, but I honestly don't remember in what church I was baptized. It's all so silly anyway." And this liberal editor's heart—as was true of her magazine—bled for the underprivileged of India on Monday and of Indo-China on Tuesday and of Puerto Rico on Wednesday and of the Malay Peninsula on Thursday, and she went to protest meetings and signed petitions for this and that.

But, then, one evening, after both had had a few drinks—this was in the high, dazzling Coolidge-Hoover days—and they felt romantically inclined, she kissed him tenderly and fingered his hair, and said, "Darling, you know, I was thinking, if you took a haircut more often, you wouldn't look so Jewish." And his heart sank and a long-cherished dream turned rancid and a bitterness entered his soul.

Eventually my lawyer friend married a Jewish girl. To his dismay she quickly embraced the Communist *meshuggaas* in its most bigoted anti-Jewish form, but he went back to the warmth of the customs and stories of his Orthodox boyhood, and such comfort as he enjoyed was found in the affectionate telling and retelling of what his father did and his mother did and their equally *frum* neighbors did. This process of self-discovery took him more than twenty heart-breaking years—and even now he is burdened with their sour memory in the form of a *shlak* for a wife.

Honesty among intellectuals, Jewish or otherwise, is even rarer than among the non-intellectuals. For some of them enlightenment is equivalent to mental blindness, moral snobbishness and spiritual obtuseness. And such powers of logic as they have are especially dangerous, for logic can enslave as well as liberate. With logic one can prove almost everything, as the entire history of bigotry and persecution shows.

The case of the celebrated French-Jewish composer, Darius Milhaud, unhappily, is not as common as it should be. He begins his autobiography, *Notes Without Music,* with the exhilaratingly honest sentence, "I am a Frenchman from Provence, and by religion a Jew." He does it as simply as another would say, "I am an American, and a Protestant." He does not hide behind the apologetic phrase, "I am a Jew by birth." No. He is himself a Jew. And then he goes elaborately into his Jewish ancestry as far back as he could determine, and he does it with directness and pride. And when he reaches the age of thirteen, he says, "I went through the Bar Mitzvah, or initiation into the Jewish religion. What a great day that was!" Still later in the book he says, with obvious sincerity, "I have always regretted not having learned to read Hebrew fluently," and he states as a mere fact that he was married in a synagogue, implying that for him to have done otherwise would have been unthinkable.

The case of Dr. Norbert Wiener, the mathematician, is far different. The son of two Jewish parents, he did not know he was a Jew until he was in college, and even then he learned it by deduction rather than by direct statement. The knowledge came to him "with a profound shock"—as he confesses in his life-story, *Ex-Prodigy*. It was his mother chiefly who had not only flatly denied that he was Jewish, but tried to instill in him a dislike, nay, a feeling of disgust, for Jews and other minority groups. "Scarcely a day went by in which we did not hear some remark about the gluttony of the Jews or the bigotry of the Irish or the laziness of the Negroes." His father, who was a linguist of considerable attainments in the Slavic and Yiddish languages, was not as anti-Semitic as his Jewish wife, but he too was afflicted with an anti-Jewish virus and was only too eager to believe malicious gossip about his own people. He claimed, for instance, that Jewish organizations insisted that "a Jew was a Jew before he was a man, and . . . he owed inalienable allegiance to his own group before humanity itself." No wonder that young Norbert was so disturbed when he learned the truth! No wonder that ever since he has remained an intellectual vagrant, in so far as Judaism is concerned.

He was healthy enough not to want to live a lie, yet he didn't have the resources to discover intellectual and emotional satisfaction in Judaism. Without trying to learn something about the faith of his fathers, in a most unscholarly manner he denied validity to it, and implicitly approved of its death by way of assimilation. Apparently all he now believes in is humanity and its decencies. He does not realize how bogus such a position is. He does not realize how cruelly inhuman it can be, how psychologically diseased it is; for it robs him of vast reservoirs of warmth, sympathy, understanding, and the very humanity he pretends to cling to. He does not realize that one is a better citizen for being a good family man, that one is a better member of mankind for being a loyal member of a segment of it. But not only has this religion of humanity hardened Dr. Wiener's heart, it has also dulled an area of his mind, for how else could he say that "anti-Semitism has ceased to be a really important factor in the environment in which I live, and to a large extent in the country as a whole"?

Perhaps the most bewildered and pathetic of all the lost Jewish intellectuals is he who has embraced the ideas of Christianity on the ground that they are superior to those of Judaism—yet who nevertheless cannot "overcome" even so "irrational" a precept as that forbidding the eating of meat and dairy products at the same time. One of the most verbal spokesmen for this group of Jews is Victor Gollancz, the British publisher. His spiritual adventures are recounted at length in his digressive autobiography, *My Dear Timothy*. He dabbled in socialism and vegetarianism for a spell, at the same time enjoying the creature comforts made possible for him by his well-to-do father, and then he began to find "untold riches" in the gibberish of various Oriental religions. All the while he kept on, so to speak, giving Judaism another trial and still another, and there was a time when he thought that "liberal Judaism" was the religion for him. But he got to "detest" this, too, as he had already learned to "detest' the Orthodox Judaism of his father. He simply couldn't stand the "irrationalities" in all branches of Judaism, neither could he stand the "absence of spirituality." Whereupon he embraced a new *meshuggaas*, "universalism," which doesn't seem to have reached America as yet, thank God, at least not in a very virulent form. A "universalist," according to Mr. Gollancz, is "a person for whom nations don't exist, only persons."

But the pretentious hollowness of "universalism" didn't hold him much longer than did vegetarianism or Hindu philosophy. Whereupon he made the final leap—into the arms of Christ—and he has accepted as wholly rational, beautiful and spiritual, pretty much all the Christian theological and metaphysical baggage. Soon Mr. Gollancz was trying to make others see that, "Isaiah was the forerunner of Christ," that "Christ . . . knew everything . . . [and was] the greatest of the Hebrew prophets." At last he had left behind "everything stuffy and outlandish in my Jewish background." Now he gave his "wholehearted assent, both intellectual and emotional, to the ethics of Christianity." He had been unable to give such assent to the ethics or the philosophy or, indeed, anything else in Judaism. Even liberal Judaism, he now saw, in the light of his new revelation, was "cold" and "flat" and guilty of "impersonal ethicism and moralism." Mr. Gollancz admits that he is somewhat troubled by the doctrines of Trinitarianism and the Atonement, but he leaves the reader with the impression that the Christ, who "knows everything," will clarify these problems for him in the not too distant future. The anomaly is enhanced and complicated by the fact that Mr. Gollancz has refused to join a

Christian church or flatly proclaim himself a Christian.

There are, alas, too many Victor Gollanczes among Jewish intellectuals the world over. I met one of the American variety recently. To my dismay I later learned that he is a professor of Romance languages in one of the largest and oldest Eastern universities. He told me that he was especially pleased that the Nobel Prize Award for peace was given to Dr. Albert Schweitzer. He said, "If I belong to any religious group it is to the Christian group represented by Dr. Schweitzer. I think his concept, which is, of course, basically a Christian concept, of reverence for life, is marvelous, beautiful, suits me just right." I looked at him with incredulity and asked him if he had done much reading in Talmudic lore, in Jewish folklore. He said, "I've read all I'm ever going to read." I told him that Dr. Schweitzer's concept was a strictly Jewish concept, that the rabbinical writings are full of references to it in numberless beautiful variations. I told him that even Jewish folklore could boast of it and had cherished it for centuries. I told him about the common Jewish expression, *tsar baal hayyim,* mercy for all living things. I told him about the rabbinical precept that one must feed a dumb animal before one feeds oneself. My friend hadn't known all this. He hadn't known what is truly an essence of Judaism.

Perhaps the fault is not entirely his. Perhaps the fault in part is also that of much Jewish education. It may well be that our rabbis and *melamdim,* even those recently graduated from seminaries, are not stressing enough the poetry, the unutterable beauty, the relevance to our time, of the Chumesh and the whole Tanach of all our great rabbinical and lay writings and commentaries and glosses —of all our imaginative creations in every literary form. Biblical history and Jewish customs are very important, of course. But poetry in its most inclusive sense is also very important. Too many Jews seem to be ignorant of this magnificent richness of melody in Judaism. Large groups of intellectuals especially seem to be ignorant of it. Perhaps the most effective cure for the great trauma of Judaism, and also the most effective antidote for assimilationism in every guise, is the propagation of the whole truth about Judaism. Even when this truth is presented in stray bits it seems to accomplish miracles of intellectual and moral and psychological regeneration.

REPEAT PERFORMANCE

By MILTON HINDUS

THERE IS ONE thing above all else which the younger generation of Jews in America requires now, and that is perspective. Man as a species has been defined in many ways, and those definitions have not been of much practical help, but it is necessary at the very beginning to add one more to the list of definitions. Man, as he appears to us, is the animal *infinitely resilient* and at the same time *infinitely stubborn,* and in the proper analysis and understanding of that paradox lies the key to the general human problem of which the Jewish problem is only a part—though for Jews it is understandably *the most important part.*

The resiliency of man is a matter of more common understanding perhaps than his stubbornness. No natural catastrophe has ever been observed which could frighten him permanently. The sides of the volcano which erupts and buries whole cities are as densely populated as ever the moment that the lava cools. Earthquakes have devastated regions which in a few short years were more thriving than they were before. In fact, no natural terror is sufficient to keep man away from any area in which he can make a living, no matter how meager or for how short a period of time. The same thing holds true for social catastrophes as well. Wars and revolutions, massacres and proscriptions, no more than volcanic eruptions and earthquakes, have never exercised any permanent effects on the human mind. Hope apparently is the only thing which can spring out of literally nothing.

No better instance of the resiliency of the human race could probably be offered than the history of the Jews for the past two thousand years. If others have made their dwellings on the sides of volcanos, the Jews have made theirs within one. For that is what Christendom has been for them. Inquisition, expulsion, massacre, and pillage—these have set the pattern of the rhythm. In between, there have been periods of enlightenment, rationalism, liberation. But a good case can be made for regarding these interludes as the necessary preparation for the other and more serious business. Why have the Jews been kept alive at all? Possibly only to serve as a living illustration of a Christian biblical text and to go on paying over and over again in terms of self-respect, property, and life itself for the role which they play within it.

In the West, the Jews were almost spoiled by the long respite between the Age of Enlightenment and the Age of Hitler. But Hitler's national socialism made up for all previous neglect. Now the play for the Jew starts again. He sits in the midst of an audience of Gentiles listening to some speech on some impersonal subject— let us say science. And he hears the speaker identify all the members of his audience as parts of a single race—the human one. He looks around him and he sees everyone in the same resplendent full evening dress as himself. Their faces seem to indicate agreement with the speaker, or at least acceptance of his premises for the sake of his argument. And the Jew feels the warmth which human society always gives, and he wonders (if he is sensitive and apprehensive) how long it will last. For he knows by experience that even the tamest and most model volcano—the one that is always being pointed out by guides to peaceful tourists—is capable of going off and making Pompeiis and Herculaneums out of trusting communities. The names of Belsen, Auschwitz, Dachau ring a small bell deep in his primitive mind underneath all the layers of formal dress, civilization, and education with which it is covered up.

But gradually the Jew is beginning to forget the horrors of only a few years ago, just as he has forgotten all previous pogroms, ghettos, Hamans, Tituses, and Nebuchadnezzars. Forgotten is a relative term. No man ever really forgets what has happened to him in life, nor does any nation forget either. And if it does forget, its historians, preachers, poets, and critics are always there to remind it. The unpleasant memory, however, is pushed off to some remote corner of the subconscious, where it can cause no immediate discomfort. And it is only right that it should be so. Otherwise, life would soon become unbearable and impossible to continue. When the whole world is learning to live in what comfort it is able to enjoy in the shadow of the atom bomb, is it any cause for surprise that the Jew learns to live for the thousandth time in the shadow of potential persecution and hatred?

Stubbornness is never given the credit it deserves as a natural prescrvative of ideas and peoples. Usually it is a term of opprobrium. To say that somebody is stubborn is the equivalent of condemning him of inflexibility in the face of truth. It may be that, and it may also be inflexibility in the face of a lie. The stubbornness of a revolutionist may be among his most admirable qualities. There is a third kind of stubbornness which does not have either the clear-cut justification or lack of justification of the other two. That is the stubbornness in defense of an existing condition when neither its truth nor its falsity is especially evident. That is the quality which the Jew requires today, and which should be valued most highly in him.

Persecution can have a number of different effects. It can destroy, it can soften, it can bend, and it can harden. It therefore acts as the most stringent of all sifting processes. Those who remain Jews after Hitler are as different from those who were Jews before him as a political party before and after it has been forced to go underground. A term came into existence in the thirties to denominate the man whose radicalism consisted entirely of talk. The term was *parlor pink*, and it was a useful one. Entire intellectual groupings such as the Oxford poets could conveniently and illuminatingly be designated by it. A term such as *parlor Jew* is now almost an equal necessity to describe a similar phenomenon. In the countries hit by the National Socialist terror, nothing was left of the parlor Jew as nothing was left of the parlor pink, for the reality of each man's being and faith was tested mordantly and infallibly.

Out of that test came a number of new and significant and interesting phenomena. The outstanding one to my mind is exemplified by the case of the philosopher Henri Bergson. He had never thought of himself as a Jew and never been thought of as one by other people. He was a famous philosopher, so famous that the Hitlerites when they conquered France would not have courted

186

world-wide condemnation by subjecting him to the discriminatory laws aimed against all other French Jews. But this thoroughly assimilated philosopher who doubtless thought of himself as a citizen of the world and a child of the human race discovered himself as a Jew. Perhaps his action in identifying himself with the Star of David may be taken by some as the ultimate triumph of liberalism, but I put another interpretation upon it. I prefer to call it by the name of *stubbornness,* which, in the absence of a positive philosophy or a negative one, is the foundation of national group consciousness. And why should we not attribute Bergson's action to an impulse which has nothing to do with intellectual abstractions but is grounded in the most elementary and comprehensible aspects of the nature of man? The Nazis said to people like Bergson—you are a Jew because your grandmother was Jewish, and she might have been Jewish for the same reason. Bergson's reply could have been —very well, I do not understand what being Jewish means in your sense of the word, and since I never thought about the subject before, I certainly do not have my own definition for it, but if it pleases you to call me a Jew, I am happy to accept the designation and I think that it probably is an honor to be one (though I do not know what it is) since at least I am not one of you.

Such a reaction, it seems to me—born of defiance, pride, and indignation—is a credible one, and regardless of how it may appear to others I respect it. The man who exhibits it seems to me to have some very valuable human qualities and to add strength to whatever group he belongs to. He, at least, is no parlor Jew. He was a voluntary martyr, whereas others were involuntary ones, and his *choice* helped to *dramatize* their *plight.*

The positive values of being a Jew were never more evident than they are to the young American Jew today, and that is why all appeals to him that are based upon such positivism must seem meaningless. If—as I hope is not very likely to be the case—he is asked tomorrow to face the trials which young Jews in European countries faced during the last decade, it would appear to him that he was suffering for *nothing at all.* That, then, is precisely the point upon which any adequate contemporary living Jewish philosophy must fasten. The value of *Bergsonism*—if I may use the term to indicate not the philosophy which he consciously developed but the one which he unconsciously illustrated at the

187

close of his life—must be stressed and explained and honored. It is not the first time that people have been called upon to suffer for *nothing at all.* Perhaps it is even true that all suffering is gratuitous and is not to be decried and condemned but glorified instead.

Though the value of Judaism may be without emotional import to the young Jew today, the value of individualism is not without such import. For the non-Jewish intellectual of our time, anti-Semitism has often been an assertion of his individualism. So, for the young Jew, an active awareness of his Jewish nationality may be the last barrier of his individualism. Here, an analogy with military history may be useful in clarifying my meaning. It is a matter of record that the famous battlegrounds of the world—Gettysburg, for example—achieved their unique distinction by accident rather than by intention. Neither one side nor the other intended to give or to receive battle at precisely that point. A collocation of chance circumstances *plus* the original intentions of one side to go as far as possible and of the other to fight rather than to retreat any further determined the choice. The generals of each side might have thought that the clash would occur elsewhere. They were as much surprised at the designation of the actual battlefield as anyone else. That is how it is now with Judaism, the young Jew, and the Gentile. Judaism is the accidental meeting point between the aggression of some Gentiles and the determination of the Jews not to retreat further. And what seems to be at stake is not Judaism itself—which we must grant has become small and meaningless apart from its choice as a place of carnage—but the individuality of the Jew. *The Jew cannot surrender his Jewishness without throwing open the entire country of his soul to the most alien, despotic, and debilitating influences.* The independence and self-respect which are the outward emblems of his individuality will be mercilessly ravaged from him. It is significant that the technique of the concentration camp was aimed at insulting the purely human qualities of its Jewish inmates more often than their characteristically cultural or national ones.

When a young Jew looks at me and asks seriously: "What is there Jewish about me aside from the fact that they call me a Jew?" I feel like saying to him, "Isn't that enough?" What else is necessary in heaven's name? Or have we all gone so far along the road of intellectualization and decadence that if a man came up to us

188

in a public place and for no recognizable reason hit us in the face, we should subject *ourselves* to a psychological analysis to find out what it was about us that irritated him? Before we go in for humanitarianism, science, or philanthropy, we must settle the elementary problems of self-defense. Surely we must not try to rationalize the hatred of our enemies by inventing a real Jew for them to hate, but we must also not rationalize away the necessity for a reaction to that hatred simply on the ground that it is irrational.

Perhaps a confession which will serve as a personal illustration would not be inappropriate at this point. It is a fact well know to each of us, I think, that for an emotion to strike home to us it is not sufficient simply for the proper object of that emotion to be present but rather that a relationship be set up between that object and ourselves. The object may be huge, overwhelming, "hopeless to conceive" in the words of Emily Dickinson—it will not affect us in the least unless such an immediate relationship is present. Thus, when somebody who has been very close to us dies, we may be unable to shed a tear—not through callousness but through *excess of sensitivity*. We believe and yet do not believe in what has happened. The object of emotion exists, and we exist, but as yet there is no connection between us. Only when that connection becomes active—sometimes it may be established by an tangential trifle to the real tragedy—is the spring of adequate feeling unlocked within us. We realize (that is to say, we make *real*) what has happened. That is a common experience, I believe, and if it is not recognizable it is because my description is bad rather than because it does not exist. What I am trying to lead up to is a statement of how I personally became aware as a Jew of what was happening to other Jews in Europe.

For each Jew who has achieved such an awareness, the immediate cause may have been another trifle—certainly my own has no mark of universality whatsoever about it but is related to the fact that I am a literary person of very special, perhaps peculiar, interests. More than all headlines in the newspapers, more than all travelers' tales and political propaganda, the concept of anti-Semitism took on reality for me when a writer with whose literary character I had identified myself sympathetically for a long time turned out to be an anti-Semite. Here was a man who displayed such funds of pity and understanding that he had brought me comfort across half the world, striking at me and all my kind with a sudden inexplicable ferocity. I could have sworn that he was my spiritual brother, as Ernst Toller, Leon Trotsky, and other Jews had already sworn, and without any warning he was printing pamphlets in Paris, thousands of miles away, calling for my death. At first, I firmly refused to believe it; I wanted to talk to him first. I wrote an article intended to disprove the slander—for that is what I thought it was in the absence of proof. But the proof came until I would have had to believe it if he had been my actual brother, and I sat in the Jewish reading room of the New York Public Library (where all anti-Semitic literature is kept) and wept over the pages of his fantastic books. The Nazis, then, I realized emotionally for the first time—intellectually I had realized it a long time ago—were not merely subhuman beasts with whom it was as impossible to conduct a rational conversation as it is with a gorilla, but people such as myself, who for some reason that I was unable to make out hated me and wanted to destroy me. *I realized Hitler imaginatively* for the first time. And my emotion surpassed fear. In that opening moment, I was paralyzed with pity for the whole human race. That it should come to this—to this relief by cutting off one of its own members. It was not until much later—much time had to pass— that I was able to classify the madness of Céline along with the madness of Strindberg. The first blamed all of the world's ills upon Jews just as the latter blamed them all upon women. But regardless of that, I realized that this madness could infect highly civilized and intellectual and sympathetic men. It is one thing to believe that every sensitive, brilliant human being is in the same camp as yourself fighting against "the beasts," and another thing altogether to discover bestiality breaking out in the camp itself among its most stalwart inmates. I saw then that though I might consider myself as a pure intellectual or as a Socialist, or Communist, Thomist, or liberal, or 100 per cent American—the important thing in this time and place was that I was also a Jew, and if a man chose to ignore the other classification in which I put myself and approached me or attacked me as a Jew, I was forced to allow him to do so, to accept his challenge—though my heart might cry out that it was all a mistake, that there was really no necessity for our cutting each other's throats. I felt like Bazarov in Turgenev's *Fathers and Sons* when Pavel challenges him to a duel. He does not believe in duels, and even if he did he sees nothing over which to fight this particular one, but he has to accept or else Pavel will thrash him mercilessly with his walking stick, and it seems to be both more esthetic and pleasant to be an agent and to fight back than it is to be a patient and helplessly to suffer outrage.

If such a triviality were something personal to me only, it would hardly be worth mentioning. But I have seen the same thing happen to others. There is, for example, the prominent *Saturday Evening Post* writer who is a friend of mine and whose profession belies his serious intellectual interests. His icon had been his idea of Henry Adams—who seemed to him the very model of the eighteenth-century rationality he admired and altogether immune to such a thing as anti-Semitism. He sympathized with me because my own icon had turned into my worst enemy until Edward Saveth's article dealing with the anti-Semitism of Adams appeared in *The Contemporary Jewish Record*. I could watch objectively what happened in his case as I could watch subjectively what happened in my own. I could see his liberal intellectual confidence progressively disintegrate under the shock, and it was painful for him to suffer and for me to observe his suffering. The look reappeared on his face (probably for the first time since he was five years old) of a naïve child who is hurt by his discovery of positive evil in the world—the time after which we all find that we are not in Eden and that from now on we are on our own. We are all children in these matters. That is how Ben Hecht discovered his Jewishness and described in it *Guide for the Bedeviled*. That is how many an emancipated Russian Jew must have discovered it when he came to the anti-Semitism in *Journal of an Author* by his favorite writer, Dostoyevsky.

This does not differ materially from the phenomenon I have called Bergsonism. Proust's character Swann discovers himself as a Jew under the impact of the Dreyfus case; perhaps the author discovered his part-Jewishness under the same circumstances. If the actual experience of Hitlerism or of French reactionary injustice may seem to be more worthy as an object of emotion than the literary examples I have given, it must be pointed out that it is not the object which is important but our relationship to it. It is perfectly in order for esthetes to find themselves as Jews through

191

esthetic means, though this is not as likely to happen as it is through some more direct pressures. The literature, however, in my own case was merely an excuse for the realization of the terrors with which my mind had long been assaulted by the cruder means of newspaper reports, etc. The conversion of Céline to anti-Semitism was merely the Sarajevo lighting the carefully laid fuse which exploded me back into intense Jewish consciousness.

If only I felt that every young Jew had gone through an experience similar to any of those I have been describing, I think that I should be less worried about the question as to whether we can trust the anti-Semites again. But unbelievably there are many young Jews in America who were not so fortunate as I—that is, they never did realize imaginatively, either through the impact of a trifle or through some more harrowing experience, what has happened to their kind in Europe. Intellectually, they can't help but realize it of course, but emotionally they remain untouched. Astronomic figures—six million dead—find room in some pigeonhole of their brain, but have as little reality for them as the figures of astronomy. Who has ever *felt* what a light-year signifies as well as *understood* it? Jewish magazines such as *Commentary,* which are concerned with the spread of active Jewish consciousness, would do better in compiling what might be called *A Treasury of Anti-Semitism* than in devoting themselves to the more usual efforts to find a positive meaning in Judaism which is contained in the department called *Cedars of Lebanon.* Among all the Treasuries that have been put out by publishers in recent years, this is the one that is most singularly lacking—*A Treasury of Anti-Semitism.* What a wealth of material is being missed there! The most eminent authors of the West would be amply represented, and maybe one or another of them would have the effect upon some other young Jew which Céline had upon me, Henry Adams had upon my friend who writes for *The Saturday Evening Post,* Voltaire had upon Ben Hecht, or Dostoyevsky had upon my hypothetical emancipated Russian Jew.

But it may be objected (if my suggestion is taken seriously—as I mean it to be) that such a Treasury may find its way into Gentile hands as well as into Jewish ones and help to spread the very thing it seeks to combat. I must answer that this does not seem likely to me, not only because the readers of such a Jewish maga-

zine as *Commentary* are almost exclusively Jews, but because the
Gentile who is minded to anti-Semitism is not likely to wait for a
Jewish magazine to print it before seeking it out. *They know
where to find it.* It must be remembered that the Jew is not likely
to seek out anti-Semitic literature, because it is painful for him to
do so as it was painful for me, but to the anti-Semite it is pleasure-
able, and while men avoid pain they usually do not wait long to
seek out pleasures. For the Gentile who is not already anti-Semitic,
a *Treasury of Anti-Semitism* could hardly serve any purpose except
to make him ashamed of men who call themselves members of his
race. Is it the Jew who has to be ashamed to be the object of abuse
in such an anthology? The subject is unpleasant but deserves to be
dragged out into the light of day, as sex and other subjects have
been dragged into the light. It seems to me that the Jew has
blushed for his enemies long enough. It is time that some of them
be made to blush for themselves.

The advantage of such a diet for the young Jew is an obvious
one. It is related to the principle of immunization, which even
some ancients were aware of. Mithridates drank a little poison at a
time, so that later not even the greatest amounts were able to kill
him. We make ourselves a little ill with smallpox or influenza in
order that later on we may be saved from being very ill of such
diseases.

It is painful for a human being to find that other human beings
hate him, even if their hatred is grounded upon reason. It is even
more painful when it is not grounded upon reason. It is painful
for the Jew to find that he is hated, and it is even more painful
when the enemies turn out to be not only the worst specimens of
non-Jews but some of the best ones as well, some of the most powerful intellectuals and artists, the ones most sensitive to injustice,
those most satiric of prejudice, etc. The old saying is: "It is hard
to be a Jew." But that saying may have negative as well as positive
implications. Not the least part of the tragedy of the present generation is that it is the negative implications of the difficulty in
being a Jew that are most striking. It is hardest to be a Jew, because some of those who hate us are precisely the ones by whom
we would most wish to be loved. The realities of the world will
not yield to our wishes in other things, and they will not yield in

this one either, and the sooner we find out what that reality is the better. We may be able to accomplish more for the revival of Judaism upon such a basis than upon all the positive hopes of Zionism!

THE CONCENTRATION CAMPS

By HANNAH ARENDT

The SS has made the camp the most totalitarian society in existence up to now.—DAVID ROUSSET

THERE ARE THREE possible approaches to the reality of the concentration camp: the inmate's experience of immediate suffering, the recollection of the survivor, and the fearful anticipation of those who dread the concentration camp as a possibility for the future.

Immediate experience is expressed in the reports which "record but do not communicate" things that evade human understanding and human experience—things therefore that, when suffered by men, transform them into "uncomplaining animals" (*The Dark Side of the Moon,* New York, 1947). There are numerous such reports by survivors; only a few have been published, partly because, quite understandably, the world wants to hear no more of these things, but also because they all leave the reader cold, that is, as apathetic and baffled as the writer himself, and fail to inspire those passions of outrage and sympathy through which men have always been mobilized for justice, for "Misery that goes too deep arouses not compassion but repugnance and hatred" (Rousset).

Der SS-Staat by Eugen Kogon and *Les Jours de notre mort* by David Rousset are products of assimilated recollection. Both authors have consciously written for the world of the living, both wish to make themselves understood at any cost, and both have cast off the insane contempt for those "who never went through it," that in the direct reports so often substitutes for communication. This conscious good will is the only guaranty that those who return will not, after a brief period of sullen resentment against humanity in general, adapt themselves to the real world and become once more the exact same unsuspecting fools that they were when they entered the camps. Both books are indispensable for an understanding not only of the concentration camps, but of the totalitarian regime as a whole. They become useless and even dangerous as soon as they attempt a positive interpretation—Kogon because he cites apparent historical precedents and believes that the camps can be understood psychologically, Rousset because he seeks the consolation of an "extreme experience" in a kind of suffering which, strictly speaking, no longer permits of experience, and thus arrives at a meaningless affirmation of life that is extremely dangerous because it romanticizes and transfigures what must never under any circumstances be repeated on this earth.[1] What is really true, on the contrary, was recently remarked by Isaac Rosenfeld in *The New Leader* (February 14, 1948): "We still don't understand what happened to the Jews of Europe, and perhaps we never will. . . . By now we know all there is to know. But it hasn't helped . . . as there is no response great enough to equal the facts that provoked it. There is nothing but numbness, and in the respect of numbness we . . . are no different from the murderers who went ahead and did their business and paid no attention to the screams."

---

[1] That Rousset's purely literary vitalism could survive the years in Buchenwald would seem to be striking proof of Kogon's thesis that "most of the prisoners [left] the concentration camps with exactly the same convictions that they had before; if anything, these convictions became more accentuated" (p. 302). David Rousset concludes 702 pages of horror, which prove many times over that it is possible to kill man's humanity without killing his body, with a short paragraph of "triumph," that sounds as if it had been written by a literary hack who had never set foot outside of Paris. "We never blasphemed against life. Our systems of the world were not alike, but more profoundly, more remotely, our affirmation of the power and creative grandeur of life, our absolute faith in its triumph remained intact. We never believed in the final disaster of humanity. For collectively it is the highest, strongest expression of the vital gesture in the history of the universe." It is not surprising that this "vital gesture" should have appealed to Georges Bataille with his theory of "extreme experience"—yet it is somehow surprising that the proponents of extremity and meaninglessness should not have changed their mind in the face of a reality that surpassed all their dreams. Bataille (*Critique,* October, 1947) writes: "One of Rousset's most unexpected reactions is his exultation, almost to the point of euphoria, before the idea of participating in an experience that made no sense. Nothing could be more virile, more *healthy.*" The translation is quoted from *Instead* (No. 1, 1948); it would seem to be no accident that this pseudo-profound reflection was the first break in the silence that the intellectuals have maintained on this whole matter.

Fearful anticipation is the most widespread and perhaps the only fitting approach to the reality of the concentration camp. It certainly has a great deal to do with the attitudes of men under the totalitarian terror, although it always seems to go hand in hand with a remarkable and very characteristic uncertainty which impedes both rebellion and any clear, articulated understanding of the thing feared. Kogon reports: "Only a very, very few of those who entered a concentration camp for the first time had the slightest idea . . . of what awaited them. [Some] were prepared for the worst. But these ideas were always nebulous; the reality far exceeded them." The reason for the uncertainty was precisely that this reality was utterly incredible and inconceivable. In totalitarian regimes, uncertainty as well as fear is manufactured and fostered by the propagandistic treatment of the institution of terror. "There was hardly anything connected with the SS that was not kept secret. The biggest secret of all was the routine of the concentration camps . . . whose only purpose was to spread an anonymous terror of a general political character" (Kogon). Concentration camps and everything connected with them are systematically publicized and at the same time kept absolutely secret. They are used as a threat, but all actual reports about them are suppressed or denounced as fantastic.

It is not surprising that those who made terror the actual foundation of their power should know how to exploit it through publicity and propaganda. The surprising thing is that the psychological and political effects of this propaganda could survive the collapse of the Nazi regime and the opening up of the concentration camps. One would think that the eye-witness reports and, to an even greater degree, the works of ordered recollection which substantiate one another and speak directly to the reader, in Rousset's case most persuasively, should have punctured the propagandist claim that such things were absurd horror stories. This, as we all know, is not the case. Despite overwhelming proofs, anyone speaking or writing about concentration camps is still regarded as suspect; and if the speaker has resolutely returned to the world of the living, he himself is often assailed by doubts with regard to his own truthfulness, as though he had mistaken a nightmare for reality.

This doubt of people concerning themselves and the reality of their own experience only reveals what the Nazis have always known: that men determined to commit crimes will find it expedient to organize them on the vastest, most improbable scale. Not only because this renders all punishments provided by the legal system inadequate and absurd; but because the very immensity of the crimes guarantees that the murderers who proclaim their innocence with all manner of lies will be more readily believed than the victims who tell the truth. The Nazis did not even consider it necessary to keep this discovery to themselves. Hitler circulated millions of copies of his book in which he stated that to be successful, a lie must be enormous—which did not prevent people from believing him as, similarly, the Nazis' proclamations, repeated ad nauseam, that the Jews would be exterminated like bedbugs (i.e., with poison gas), prevented anybody from *not* believing them.

There is a great temptation to explain away the intrinsically incredible by means of liberal rationalizations. In each one of us, there lurks such a liberal, wheedling us with the voice of common sense. We attempt to understand elements in present or recollected experience that simply surpass our powers of understanding. We attempt to classify as criminal a thing which, as we all feel, no such category was ever intended to cover. What meaning has the concept of murder when we are confronted with the mass production of corpses? We attempt to understand the behavior of concentration camp inmates and SS men psychologically, when the very thing that must be realized is that the psyche (or character) *can* be destroyed even without the destruction of the physical man; that, indeed, as Rousset convincingly shows, psyche, character, or individuality seem under certain circumstances to express themselves only through the rapidity or slowness with which they disintegrate. The end result in any case is inanimate men, i.e., men who can no longer be psychologically understood, whose return to the psychologically or otherwise intelligibly human world closely resembles the resurrection of Lazarus—as Rousset indicates in the title of his book. All statements of common sense, whether of a psychological or sociological nature, serve only to encourage those who think it "superficial" to "dwell on horrors" (Georges Bataille, in *Critique,* January 1948).

If it is true that the concentration camps are the most consequential institution of totalitarian rule, "dwelling on horrors" would seem to be indispensable for the understanding of totalitarianism. But recollection can no more do this than can the uncommunicative eye-witness report. In both these genres there is an inherent tendency to run away from the experience; instinctively or rationally, both types of writer are so much aware of the terrible abyss that separates the world of the living from that of the dead, that they cannot supply anything more than a series of remembered occurrences that must seem just as incredible to those who relate them as to their audience. Only the fearful imagination of those who have been aroused by such reports but have not actually been smitten in their own flesh, of those who are consequently free from the bestial, desperate terror which, when confronted by real, present horror, inexorably paralyzes everything that is not mere reaction, can afford to keep thinking about horrors. Such thoughts are useful only for the perception of political contexts and the mobilization of political passions. A change of personality of any sort whatever can no more be induced by thinking about horrors than by the real experience of horror. The reduction of a man to a bundle of reactions separates him as radically as mental disease from everything within him that is personality or character. When, like Lazarus, he rises from the dead, he finds his personality or character unchanged, just as he had left it.

Nor can horror or thinking about horrors become a basis for a political community or a party in the narrower sense. Attempts have failed to create a European elite with a program of inter-European understanding on the basis of the common experience of the concentration camp, much in the same way that similar attempts after the First World War failed to draw political consequences from the experience of the front-line soldier. In both cases it developed that the experiences themselves could impart only nihilistic platitudes, such as: "Victim and executioner are alike ignoble; the lesson of the camps is the brotherhood of abjection; if you haven't acted with the same degree of ignominy, it's only because you didn't have time . . . but the underlying rot that rises, rises, rises, is absolutely, terrifyingly the same" (Rousset). Political consequences like postwar pacifism followed from the universal fear of war, not from experience of the war. An insight, led and mobilized by fear, into the structure of modern war would have led not to a pacifism without reality, but to the view that the

199

only acceptable ground for modern war is to fight against conditions under which we no longer wish to live—and our knowledge of the camps and torture chambers of totalitarian regimes has convinced us only too well that such conditions are possible. An insight into the nature of totalitarian rule, directed by our fear of the concentration camp, might serve to devaluate all outmoded political shadings from right to left and, beside and above them, to introduce the most essential political criterion for judging the events of our time: Will it lead to totalitarian rule or will it not?

In any case fearful anticipation has the great advantage that it dispels the sophistical-dialectical interpretations of politics, which all rest on the superstition that some good can come out of evil. Such dialectical acrobatics retained at least an appearance of justification as long as the worst evil that man could inflict on man was murder. But murder, as we know today, is still a limited evil. The murderer who kills a man who must die in any event, moves within the familiar realm of life and death, between which there is a necessary relation that is the basis of dialectics, although dialecticians are not always aware of it. The murderer leaves a corpse and does not claim that his victim never existed; he may obscure the traces of his own identity, but he does not efface the memory and grief of those who loved his victim; he destroys a life, but he does not destroy the very fact of its ever having existed.

The horror of the concentration and extermination camps can never be fully embraced by the imagination for the very reason that it stands outside of life and death. The inmates are more effectively cut off from the world of the living than if they were dead, because terror compels oblivion among those who know them or love them. "What extraordinary women you are here," exclaimed the Soviet police when Polish women insisted on knowing the whereabouts of their husbands who had disappeared. "In our country, when the husband is arrested, the wife sues for divorce and looks for another man" (*The Dark Side of the Moon*). Murder in the camps is as impersonal as the squashing of a gnat, a mere technique of management, as when a camp is overcrowded and is liquidated—or an accidental by-product, as when a prisoner succumbs to torture. Systematic torture and systematic starvation create an atmosphere of permanent dying, in which death as well as life is effectively obstructed.

The fear of the absolute Evil which permits of no escape knows that this is the end of dialectical evolutions and developments. It knows that modern politics revolves around a question which, strictly speaking, should never enter into politics, the question of all or nothing: of all, that is, a human society rich with infinite possibilities; or exactly nothing, that is, the end of mankind.

There are no parallels to the life of the concentration camps. All seeming parallels create confusion and distract attention from what is essential. Forced labor in prisons and penal colonies, banishment, slavery, all seem for a moment to offer helpful comparisons, but on closer examination lead nowhere.

Forced labor as a punishment is limited as to time and intensity. The convict retains his rights over his body; he is not absolutely tortured and he is not absolutely dominated. Banishment banishes only from one part of the world to another part of the world, also inhabited by human beings; it does not exclude from the human world altogether. Throughout history slavery has been an institution within a social order; slaves were not, like concentration camp inmates, withdrawn from the sight and hence the protection of their fellow men; as instruments of labor they had a definite price and as property a definite value. The concentration camp inmate has no price, because he can always be replaced and he belongs to no one. From the point of view of normal society he is absolutely superfluous, although in times of acute labor shortage, as in Russia and in Germany during the war, he is used for work.

The concentration camp as an institution was not established for the sake of any possible labor yield; the only permanent economic function of the camps has been the financing of their own supervisory apparatus; thus from the economic point of view the concentration camps exist mostly for their own sake. Any work that has been performed could have been done much better and more cheaply under different conditions.[2] The example of Russia, whose

[2] Kogon has the following to say of working conditions in the Nazi camps, which presumably were better organized from this point of view than those of the Soviet Union: "A large part of the work exacted in the concentration camps was useless; either it was superfluous or it was so miserably planned that it had to be done over two or three times. Buildings often had to be begun several times because the foundations kept caving in" (p. 58). As for Russian conditions, even Dallin (*Forced Labor in Soviet Russia*, p. 105) who has built his whole book on the thesis that the purpose

concentration camps are usually referred to as forced labor camps, because the Soviet bureaucracy has given them this flattering title, shows most clearly that the main point is not forced labor; forced labor is the normal condition of the whole Russian proletariat which has been deprived of freedom of movement and can be mobilized anywhere at any time.

The incredibility of the horrors is closely bound up with their economic uselessness. The Nazis carried this uselessness to the point of open anti-utility when in the midst of the war, despite the shortage of rolling stock, they transported millions of Jews to the east and set up enormous, costly extermination factories. In the midst of a strictly utilitarian world the obvious contradiction between these acts and military expediency gave the whole enterprise an air of mad unreality.

However, such unreality, created by an apparent lack of purpose, is the very basis of all forms of concentration camp. Seen from outside, they and the things that happen in them can be described only in images drawn from a life after death, that is, a life removed from earthly purposes. Concentration camps can very aptly be divided into three types corresponding to three basic Western conceptions of a life after death: Hades, purgatory, and hell. To Hades correspond those relatively mild forms, once popular even in non-totalitarian countries, for getting undesirable elements of all sorts —refugees, stateless persons, the asocial and the unemployed—out of the way; as DP camps, which are nothing other than camps for persons who have become superfluous and bothersome, they have survived the war. Purgatory is represented by the Soviet Union's labor camps, where neglect is combined with chaotic forced labor. Hell in the most literal sense was embodied by those types of camp perfected by the Nazis, in which the whole of life was thoroughly and systematically organized with a view to the greatest possible torment.

All three types have one thing in common: the human masses sealed off in them are treated as if they no longer existed, as if

---

of the Russian camps was to provide cheap labor, is forced to admit: "Actually, the efficiency of forced labor, despite incentives and compulsion, was and is on an extremely low level. The average efficiency of a slave laborer has certainly been below 50 per cent of that of a free Russian worker, whose productivity in turn has never been high."

what happened to them were no longer of any interest to anybody, as if they were already dead and some evil spirit gone mad were amusing himself by stopping them for a while between life and death before admitting them to eternal peace.

It is not so much the barbed wire as the skillfully manufactured unreality of those whom it fences in that provokes such enormous cruelties and ultimately makes extermination look like a perfectly normal measure. Everything that was done in the camps is known to us from the world of perverse, malignant fantasies. The difficult thing to understand is that, like such fantasies, these gruesome crimes took place in a phantom world, in a world in which there were neither consequences nor responsibilities; and finally neither the tormentors nor the tormented, and least of all the outsider, could be aware that what was happening was anything more than a cruel game or an absurd dream.

The films which the Allies circulated in Germany and elsewhere after the war showed clearly that this atmosphere of insanity and unreality is not dispelled by pure reportage. To the unprejudiced observer they are just about as convincing as the pictures of mysterious substances taken at spiritualist séances. Common sense reacted to the horrors of Buchenwald and Auschwitz with the plausible argument: "What crime must these people have committed that such things were done to them!"; or, in Germany and Austria, in the midst of starvation, overpopulation, and general hatred: "Too bad that they've stopped gassing the Jews"; and everywhere with the skeptical shrug that greets ineffectual propaganda.

If the propaganda of truth fails to convince the average Philistine precisely because it is too monstrous, it is positively dangerous to those who know from their own imaginings that they themselves are capable of doing such things and are therefore perfectly willing to believe in the reality of what they have seen. Suddenly it becomes evident that things which for thousands of years the human imagination had banished to a realm beyond human competence, can be manufactured right here on earth. Hell and purgatory, and even a shadow of their perpetual duration, can be established by the most modern methods of destruction and therapy. When people of this sort, who are far more numerous in any large city than we like to think, see these films, or read reports of the same things, the thought that comes to their minds is that the power of man is far greater than they ever dared to think and that men can realize hellish fantasies without making the sky fall or the earth open.

The one thing that cannot be reproduced is what made the traditional conceptions of hell tolerable to man: the Last Judgment, the idea of an absolute standard of justice combined with the infinite possiblity of grace. For in the human estimation there is no crime and no sin commensurable with the everlasting torments of hell. Hence the discomfiture of common sense, which asks: What crime must these people have committed in order to suffer so inhumanly? Hence also the absolute innocence of the victims: no man ever deserved this. Hence finally the grotesque haphazardness with which concentration camp victims were chosen in the perfected terror state: such "punishment" can, with equal justice and injustice, be inflicted on anyone.

In comparison with the insane end-result—concentration camp society—the process by which men are prepared for this end, and the methods by which individuals are adapted to these conditions, are transparent and logical. The insane mass manufacture of corpses is preceded by the historically and politically intelligible preparation of living corpses.

In another connection it might be possible, indeed it would be necessary, to describe this preparatory process as a consequence of the political upheavals of our century. The impetus and, what is more important, the silent consent to such unprecedented conditions in the heart of Europe are the products of those events which in a period of political distintegration suddenly and unexpectedly made hundreds of thousands of human beings homeless, stateless, outlawed and unwanted, while millions of human beings were made economically superfluous and socially burdensome by unemployment. This in turn could only happen because the rights of man, which had never been philosophically established but merely formulated, which had never been politically secured but merely proclaimed, have, in their traditional form, lost all validity.

Meanwhile, however, totalitarian regimes exploited these developments for their own purposes. In order to understand these purposes, we must examine the process of preparing living corpses in its entirety. After all, loss of passport, residence, and the right to work, was only a very provisional, summary preparation, which could hardly have produced adequate results.

The first essential step was to kill the juridical person in man; this was done by placing the concentration camp outside the normal penal system, and by selecting its inmates outside the normal judicial procedure in which a definite crime entails a predictable penalty. Thus criminals, who for other reasons are an essential element in concentration camp society, are ordinarily sent to a camp only on completion of their prison sentence. Deviations from this rule in Russia must be attributed to the catastrophic shortage of prisons and to a desire, so far unrealized, to transform the whole penal system into a system of concentration camps.

The inclusion of criminals is necessary in order to make plausible the propagandistic claim that the institution exists for asocial elements. It is equally essential, as long as there is a penal system in the country, that they should be sent to the camps only on completion of their sentence, that is, when they are actually entitled to their freedom. It is, paradoxically, harder to kill the juridical person in a man who is guilty of some crime than in a totally innocent man. The stateless persons who in all European countries have lost their civil rights along with their nationality have learned this only too well; their legal position improved automatically as soon as they committed a theft: then they were no longer without rights but had the same rights as all other thieves. In order to kill the juridical person in man, the concentration camp must under no circumstances become a calculable punishment for definite offenses. Criminals do not properly belong in the concentration camps; if nevertheless they constitute the sole permanent category among the inmates, it is a concession of the totalitarian state to the prejudices of society which can in this way most readily be accustomed to the existence of the camps. The amalgamation of criminals with all other categories has moreover the advantage of making it shockingly evident to all other arrivals that they have landed in the lowest level of society. It soon turns out, to be sure, that they have every reason to envy the lowest thief and murderer; but meanwhile the lowest level is a good beginning. Moreover it is an effective means of camouflage: this happens only to criminals and nothing worse is happening than what deservedly happens to criminals.[3]

The criminals everywhere constitute the aristocracy of the camps. (In Germany, during the war, they were replaced in the leadership by the Communists, because not even a minimum of rational work could be performed under the chaotic conditions created by a criminal administration. This was merely a temporary transformation of concentration camps into forced labor camps, a thoroughly atypical phenomenon of limited duration. With his limited, wartime experience of Nazi concentration camps, Rousset overestimates the influence and power of the Communists.) What places the criminals in the leadership is not so much the affinity between supervisory personnel and criminal elements—in the Soviet Union apparently the supervisors are not, like the SS, a special elite of criminals—as the fact that only criminals have been sent to the camp in connection with some definite activity and that in them consequently the destruction of the juridical person cannot be fully successful, since they at least know why they are in a concentration camp. For the politicals this is only subjectively true; their actions, in so far as they were actions and not mere opinions or someone else's vague suspicions, or accidental membership in a politically disapproved group, are as a rule not covered by the normal legal system of the country and not juridically defined.

To the amalgam of politicals and criminals, with which concentration camps in Russia and Germany started out, was added at an early date a third element which was soon to constitute the majority of all concentration camp inmates. This largest group has consisted ever since of people who had done nothing whatsoever that, either in their own consciousness or the consciousness of their tormentors, had any rational connection with their arrest. In Germany, after 1938, this element was represented by masses of Jews, in Russia by any groups which, for any reason having nothing to

[3] "Gestapo and SS have always attached great importance to mixing the categories of inmates in the camps. In no camp have the inmates belonged exclusively to one category" (Kogon, p. 19). In Russia it has also been customary from the first to mix political prisoners and criminals. During the first ten years of Soviet power, the leftist political groups enjoyed certain privileges as compared with counter-revolutionaries and criminals. But "after the end of the twenties, the politicals were even officially treated as inferior to the common criminals" (Dallin, 177 ff.).

do with their actions, had incurred the disfavor of the authorities. These groups, innocent in every sense, are the most suitable for thorough experimentation in disfranchisement and destruction of the juridical person, and therefore they are both qualitatively and quantitatively the most essential category of the camp population. This principle was most fully realized in the gas chambers which, if only because of their enormous capacity, could not be intended for individual cases but only for people in general. In this connection, the following dialogue sums up the situation of the individual: "For what purpose, may I ask, do the gas chambers exist?"—"For what purpose were you born?" (Rousset). It is this third group of the totally innocent who in every case fare the worst in the camps. Criminals and politicals are assimilated to this category; thus deprived of the protection distinction that comes of their having done something, they are utterly exposed to the arbitrary.

Contrasting with the complete haphazardness with which the inmates are selected are the categories, meaningless in themselves but useful from the standpoint of organization, into which they are usually divided on their arrival. In the German camps there were criminals, politicals, asocial elements, religious offenders, and Jews, all distinguished by insignia. When the French set up concentration camps after the Spanish civil war, they immediately introduced the typical totalitarian amalgam of politicals with criminals and the innocent (in this case the stateless), and despite their inexperience proved remarkably inventive in devising meaningless categories of inmates. Originally devised in order to prevent any growth of solidarity among the inmates, this technique proved particularly valuable because no one could know whether his own category was better or worse than someone else's. In Germany this eternally shifting though pedantically organized edifice was given an appearance of solidity by the fact that under any and all circumstances the Jews were the lowest category. The gruesome and grotesque part of it was that the inmates identified themselves with these categories, as though they represented a last authentic remnant of their juridical person. It is no wonder that a Communist of 1933 should have come out of the camps more Communistic than he went in, a Jew more Jewish.

While the classification of inmates by categories is only a tactical,

207

organizational measure, the arbitrary selection of victims indicates the essential principle of the institution. If the concentration camps had been dependent on the existence of political adversaries, they would scarcely have survived the first years of the totalitarian regimes. "The camps would have died out if in making its arrests the Gestapo had considered only the principle of opposition" (Kogon). But the existence of a political opposition is for a concentration camp system only a pretext, and the purpose of the system is not achieved even when under the most monstrous terror the population becomes more or less voluntarily coordinated, i.e., relinquishes its political rights. The aim of an arbitrary system is to destroy the civil rights of the whole population, who ultimately become just as outlawed in their own country as the stateless and homeless. The destruction of a man's rights, the killing of the juridical person in him, is a prerequisite for dominating him entirely. For even free consent is an obstacle; and this applies not only to special categories such as criminals, political opponents, Jews, but to every inhabitant of a totalitarian state.

Any, even the most tyrannical, restriction of this arbitrary persecution to certain opinions of a religious or political nature, to certain modes of intellectual or erotic social behavior, to certain freshly invented "crimes," would render the camps superfluous, because in the long run no attitude and no opinion can withstand the threat of so much horror; and above all it would make for a new system of justice, which, given any stability at all, could not fail to produce a new juridical person in man, that would elude the totalitarian domination. The so-called *"Volksnutzen"* of the Nazis, constantly fluctuating (because what is useful today can be injurious tomorrow) and the eternally shifting party line of the Soviet Union which, being retroactive, almost daily makes new groups of people available for the concentration camps, are the only guaranty for the continued existence of the concentration camps and hence for the continued total disfranchisement of man.

The next decisive step in the preparation of living corpses is the murder of the moral person in man. This is done in the main by making martyrdom, for the first time in history, impossible. Rousset writes:

How many people here still believe that a protest has even historic importance? This skepticism is the real masterpiece of the SS. Their great accomplishment. They have corrupted all human solidarity. Here the night has fallen on the future. When no witnesses are left, there can be no testimony. To demonstrate when death can no longer be postponed is an attempt to give death a meaning, to act beyond one's own death. In order to be successful, a gesture must have social meaning. There are hundreds of thousands of us here, all living in absolute solitude. That is why we are subdued no matter what happens.

The camps and the murder of political adversaries are only part of organized oblivion that not only embraces carriers of public opinion such as the spoken and the written word, but extends even to the families and friends of the victim. Grief and remembrance are forbidden. In the Soviet Union a woman will sue for divorce immediately after her husband's arrest in order to save the lives of her children; if her husband chances to come back, she will indignantly turn him out of the house. The Western world has hitherto, even in its darkest periods, granted the slain enemy the right to be remembered as a self-evident acknowledgment of the fact that we are all men (and *only* men). It is only because even Achilles set out for Hector's funeral, only because the Romans allowed the Christians to write their martyrologies, only because the Church kept its heretics alive in the memory of men, that all was not lost and never could be lost. The concentration camps, by making death itself anonymous—in the Soviet Union it is almost impossible even to find out whether a prisoner is dead or alive—robbed death of the meaning which it had always been possible for it to have. In a sense they took away the individual's own death, proving that henceforth nothing belonged to him and he belonged to no one. His death merely set a seal on the fact that he had never really existed.

This attack on the moral person might still have been opposed by man's conscience which tells him that it is better to die a victim than to live as a bureaucrat of murder. The totalitarian governments have cut the moral person off from this individualist escape by making the decisions of conscience absolutely questionable and equivocal.

When a man is faced with the alternative of betraying and thus murdering his friends or of sending his wife and children, for whom he is in every sense responsible, to their death; when even suicide would mean the immediate murder of his own family—how is he to decide? The alternative is no longer between good and evil, but between murder and murder. In perhaps the only article which really gets to the core of this matter, Camus (in *Twice a Year*, 1947) tells of a woman in Greece who was allowed by the Nazis to choose which among her three children should be killed.

Through the creation of conditions under which conscience ceases to be adequate and to do good becomes utterly impossible, the consciously organized complicity of all men in the crimes of totalitarian regimes is extended to the victims and thus made really total. The SS implicated concentration camp inmates—criminals, politicals, Jews—in their crimes by making them responsible for a large part of the administration, thus confronting them with the hopeless dilemma whether to send their friends to their death, or to help murder other men who happened to be strangers.

Once the moral person has been killed, the one thing that still prevents men from being made into living corpses is the differentiation of the individual, his unique identity. In a sterile form such individuality can be preserved through a persistent stoicism, and it is certain that many men under totalitarian rule have taken and are each day still taking refuge in this absolute isolation of a personality without rights or conscience. There is no doubt that this part of the human person, precisely because it depends so essentially on nature and on forces that cannot be controlled by the will, is the hardest to destroy (and when destroyed is most easily repaired).

The methods of dealing with this uniqueness of the human person are numerous and we shall not attempt to list them all. They begin with the monstrous conditions in the transports to the camps, when hundreds of human beings are packed into a cattle car stark naked, glued to each other, and shunted back and forth over the countryside for days on end; they continue upon arrival at the camp, the well-organized shock of the first hours, the shaving of the head, the grotesque camp clothing; and they end in the utterly unimaginable tortures so gauged as not to kill the body, at any event not quickly. The aim of all these methods, in any case, is to manipulate the human body—with its infinite possibilities of suffering—in such a way as to make it destroy the human person as inexorably as certain mental diseases of organic origin.

It is here that the utter lunacy of the entire process becomes most apparent. Torture, to be sure, is an essential feature of the whole totalitarian police and judiciary apparatus; it is used every day to make people talk. This type of torture, since it pursues a definite, rational aim, has certain limitations: either the prisoner talks within a certain time, or he is killed. But to this rationally conducted torture another, irrational, sadistic type was added in the first Nazi concentration camps and in the cellars of the Gestapo. Carried on for the most part by the SA, it pursued no aims and was not systematic, but depended on the initiative of largely abnormal elements. The mortality was so high that only a few concentration camp inmates of 1933 survived these first years. This type of torture seemed to be not so much a calculated political institution as a concession of the regime to its criminal and abnormal elements, who were thus rewarded for services rendered. Behind the blind bestiality of the SA, there often lay a deep hatred and resentment against all those who were socially, intellectually, or physically better off than themselves, and who now, as if in fulfillment of their wildest dreams, were in their power. This resentment, which never died out entirely in the camps, strikes us as a last remnant of humanly understandable feeling.

The real horror began, however, when the SS took over the administration of the camps. The old spontaneous bestiality gave way to an absolutely cold and systematic destruction of human bodies, calculated to destroy human dignity; death was avoided or postponed indefinitely. The camps were no longer amusement parks for beasts in human form, that is, for men who really belonged in mental institutions and prisons; the reverse became true: they were turned into "drill grounds" (Kogon), on which perfectly normal men were trained to be full-fledged members of the SS.

The killing of man's individuality, of the uniqueness shaped in equal parts by nature, will, and destiny, which has become so self-evident a premise for all human relations that even identical twins inspire a certain uneasiness, creates a horror that vastly overshadows the outrage of the juridical-political person and the despair of the moral person. It is this horror that gives rise to the nihilistic generalizations which maintain plausibly enough that essentially all men alike are beasts. Actually the experience of the concentration camps does show that human beings can be transformed into specimens of the human beast, and that man's "nature" is only "human" in so far as it opens up to man the possibility of becoming something highly unnatural, that is, a man.

After murder of the moral person and annihilation of the juridical person, the destruction of the individuality is almost always successful. Conceivably some laws of mass psychology may be found to explain why millions of human beings allowed themselves to be marched unresistingly into the gas chambers, although these laws would explain nothing else but the destruction of individuality. It is more significant that those individually condemned to death very seldom attempted to take one of their executioners with them, that there were scarcely any serious revolts, and that even in the moment of liberation there were very few spontaneous massacres of the SS men. For to destroy individuality is to destroy spontaneity, man's power to begin something new out of his own resources, something new that cannot be explained on the basis of reactions to environment and events. Nothing then remains but ghastly marionettes with human faces, which all behave like the dog in Pavlov's experiments, which all react with perfect reliability even when going to their own death, and which do nothing but react. This is the real triumph of the system:

The triumph of the SS demands that the tortured victim allow himself to be led to the noose without protesting, that he renounce and abandon himself to the point of ceasing to affirm his identity. And it is not for nothing. It is not gratuitously, out of sheer sadism, that the SS men desire this defeat. They know that the system which succeeds in destroying its victim before he mounts the scaffold . . . is incomparably the best for keeping a whole people in slavery. In submission. Nothing is more terrible than these processions of human beings going like dummies to their death. The man who sees this says to himself: "For them to be thus reduced, what power must be concealed in the hands of the masters," and he turns away, full of bitterness but defeated. (Rousset)

It is characteristic of totalitarian terror that it increases as the regime becomes more secured, and accordingly concentration camps are expanded as political opposition decreases.[4] Totalitarian demands do not seem to be satisfied by political success in establishing a one-party state, and it seems as though political opposition were by no means the cause of terror but rather a barrier to its full development. This seems absurd only if we apply to modern totalitarian movements those standards of utility which they themselves expressly reject as obsolete, sentimental, and bourgeois.

If on the contrary we take totalitarian aspirations seriously and refuse to be misled by the common-sense assertion that they are utopian and unrealizable, it develops that the society of the dying established in the camps is the only form of society in which it is possible to dominate man entirely. Those who aspire to total domination must liquidate all spontaneity, such as the mere existence of individuality will always engender, and track it down in its most private forms, regardless of how unpolitical and harmless these may seem. Pavlov's dog, the human specimen reduced to the most elementary reactions, the bundle of reactions that can always be liquidated and replaced by other bundles of reactions that behave in exactly the same way, is the model "citizen" of a totalitarian state; and such a citizen can be produced only imperfectly outside of the camps.

The uselessness of the camps, their cynically admitted antiutility, is only apparent. In reality they are more essential to the preservation of the regime's power than any of its other institutions. Without concentration camps, without the undefined fear they inspire and the very well-defined training they offer in totalitarian domination, which has nowhere else been fully tested with all of its most radical possibilities, a totalitarian state can neither inspire its nuclear troops with fanaticism nor maintain a whole people in complete apathy. The dominating and the dominated would only too quickly sink back into the "old bourgeois routine"; after

4 This is evident in Russia as well as in Germany. In Russia, the concentration camps, which were originally intended for enemies of the regime, began to swell enormously after 1930, i.e., at a time when not only all armed resistance had been quelled, but when all opposition to Stalin within the Party had been liquidated. In the first years there were in Germany at most ten camps with a total of no more than ten thousand inmates. All effective resistance against the Nazis ceased by the end of 1936. But at the outbreak of the war there were more than a hundred concentration camps, which after 1940 seem to have maintained an average population of one million.

early "excesses," they would succumb to everyday life with its human laws; in short, they would develop in the direction which all observers counseled by common sense were so prone to predict. The tragic fallacy of all these prophecies originating in a world that was still safe, was to suppose that there was such a thing as one human nature established for all time, to identify this human nature with history and thus declare that the idea of total domination was not only inhuman but also unrealistic. Meanwhile we have learned that the power of man is so great that he really can be what he wishes to be.

It is in the very nature of totalitarian regimes to demand unlimited power. Such power can only be secured if literally all men, without a single exception, are reliably dominated in every aspect of their lives. In the realm of foreign affairs new neutral territories must constantly be subjugated, and while at home ever-new human groups must be mastered in expanding concentration camps, or, when circumstances require, liquidated to make room for others. Here the question of opposition is unimportant both in foreign and domestic affairs. Any neutrality, indeed any spontaneously given friendship is from the standpoint of totalitarian domination just as dangerous as open hostility, precisely because spontaneity as such, with its incalculability, is the greatest of all obstacles to total domination over man. The Communists of non-Communist countries, who fled or were called to Moscow, learned by bitter experience that they constituted a menace to the Soviet Union. Convinced Communists are in this sense, which alone has any reality today, just as ridiculous and just as menacing to the regime in Russia as for example the convinced Nazis of the Roehm faction were to the Nazis.

What makes conviction and opinion of any sort so ridiculous and dangerous under totalitarian conditions is that totalitarian regimes take the greatest pride in having no need of them, or of any human help of any kind. Men insofar as they are more than animal reaction and fulfillment of functions are entirely superfluous to totalitarian regimes. Totalitarianism strives not toward despotic rule over men, but toward a system in which men are superfluous. Total power can be achieved and safeguarded only in a world of conditioned reflexes, of marionettes without the slightest trace of spontaneity. Precisely because man's resources are so great, he can be fully dominated only when he becomes a specimen of the animal-species man.

Therefore character is a threat and even the most unjust legal rules are an obstacle; but individuality, anything indeed that distinguishes one man from another, is intolerable. As long as all men have not been made equally superfluous—and this has been accomplished only in concentration camps—the ideal of totalitarian domination has not been achieved. Totalitarian states strive constantly, though never with complete success, to establish the superfluity of man—by the arbitrary selection of various groups for concentration camps, by constant purges of the ruling apparatus, by mass liquidations. Common sense protests desperately that the masses are submissive and that all this gigantic apparatus of terror is therefore superfluous; if they were capable of telling the truth, the totalitarian rulers would reply: The apparatus seems superfluous to you only because it serves to make men superfluous.

They will not speak so frankly. But the concentration camps, and even more so the corpse factories invented by the Nazis, speak only too clearly. Today, with population almost everywhere on the increase, masses of people are continuously being rendered superfluous by political, social, and economic events. At such a time the instruments devised for making human beings superfluous are bound to offer a great temptation: why not use these same instruments to liquidate human beings who have already become superfluous?

This side of the matter is only too well understood by the common sense of the mob which in most countries is too desperate to retain much fear of death. The Nazis, who were well aware that their defeat would not solve the problems of Europe, knew exactly what they were doing when, toward the end of the war—which by then they knew they had lost—they set up those factories of annihilation which demonstrated the swiftest possible solution to the problem of superfluous human masses. There is no doubt that this solution will from now on occur to millions of people whenever it seems impossible to alleviate political, or social, or economic misery in a manner worthy of man.

THE JEWS OF THE SOUTH

By HARRY L. GOLDEN

M ORRIS, YOU KNOW where I stand, but let's face it: when I think of Ed Whittington, I think of the Community Chest; when I think of Frank Hendry, I think of the Red Cross; when I think of Morris Steinman, I think of a Jew." The leading banker in one of the larger Southern cities was addressing his friend, the president of the local Jewish Welfare Fund. He was suggesting that the Jewish community accept a "separate group quota" for the coming Community Chest drive, "so that folks may see the full extent of Jewish participation in civic affairs."

The banker did more than make a point. Unwittingly he put his finger on the heart and core of the streams of consciousness which flow through the mind of the Jew of the South—his relentless struggle to become *one* with the population mass which surrounds him, and the equally relentless resistance that renders the struggle futile.

Like the story of the whole section itself, there has been a tendency to oversentimentalize the story of the Jews in the Old South, which includes Virginia, North Carolina, South Carolina, Georgia, Alabama, Mississippi, Louisiana, Arkansas and Tennessee (Florida is an entirely different story). The sagas of Francis Salvador, Judah P. Benjamin and Bernard M. Baruch's father are as interesting as they are heartwarming, but they represent only a tiny fragment of the link between the South of the "old plantation"—and the ebb and flow of Jewish life today.

In such cities as Charleston and Sumter (S.C.), and Columbus and Savannah (Ga.), one may still find on the synagogue rolls a

Mendoza, a Laporte, a Moise, and a Kiralfy; but in the main the descendants of the Sephardic Jews who came to Savannah in 1830 and who built a synagogue in Charleston in 1750, have all but disappeared. Some of them live in other parts of the country, but many of them are now third and fourth generation Christians. Oddly enough, formal conversions to Christianity were few and far between even during the second half of the nineteenth century when Jewish communal life was almost wholly non-existent. In most cases the family drifted into Christianity through the process of "elimination." The Jew married a Christian; the children were raised as Christians; and they in turn married others of their faith. Through all of this the head of the family continued to maintain at least a perfunctory connection with Judaism and the Temple; but upon his death the link was irrevocably broken. Even in our own day, this process is approaching the inevitable climax in five or six of the most outstanding families in the South. When the head of each of these families passes on, all ties with Judaism and the Jewish community will have come to an end.

This "slow" Christianization has its own folklore. Every community in the South has at least one leading Protestant layman of whom it is whispered, "he was once a Jew." Even the names have persisted. You'll find Christians in the South with such names as Herschberger, Mordecai, Salomon, Goodman, Hayman, Hertzinger, Rosenblatt, with particular emphasis on Baumgardner, Jacobs and Isaacs. These are the same names you see on the early nineteenth-century gravestones in the Hebrew cemeteries of Richmond, Charlotte, Charleston and Savannah. Some humorous situations have arisen. In one Southern town the name of the president of the Hebrew congregation (an immigrant from Poland) was Smith; and the name of the local Lutheran pastor was Kohn.

Basically what we have today are approximately 150,000 Jews in the nine states, who are German and Eastern European immigrants or children of immigrants who began to establish themselves in hundreds of Southern cities, towns and hamlets during the first decade of the twentieth century. The textile mills of Massachusetts and Rhode Island had also begun to move southward. The Jews brought with them the new methods of distribution, which helped make the Southeast the greatest textile-producing area in the United States. The early Southern cotton mill situation was af-

217

flicted with chaotic competitive methods and the manufacture of only one type of plaid. The "textile Jews" introduced a diversity of cotton manufactures—flannels and denims—as well as a higher grade of finishing. In their wake came the Jews with smaller capital who established retail stores in every city, county seat and rural way-station in the South. In 1910 there were sixty-three established congregations in the South serving a community of approximately 38,000 Jews. Today there are approximately 150,000 Jews with 213 established congregations. The migration from the northern centers took a sharp upturn in the late 1930's and is at its very peak today.

The South leads the country in the number of congregations in proportion to the number of Jewish residents, with one congregation for each 600 Jews. The national average is one congregation for each 1,300 Jews. There are several reasons for this phenomenon. In the first place there is the natural inclination to conform to the habits of the surrounding society, and the South is the most "church-minded" section in the country. There are, of course, many pious Jews to whom the synagogue is a necessary part of everyday living, but their proportion is no greater than the national average. The difference is explained, at least partly, by this intense religiosity of the Christian majority, and the Jews, "of all people," are "expected" to be members of a religious organization.

In this connection, too, we must not overlook the economic status of the Jew in the South. Basically he is almost wholly "unemployable" in the Southeast. There are no clerks, salesgirls, white collar workers, or civil servants. In cities with as many as 2,000 Jews the only one of their number who is not self-employed is the rabbi. If a man loses his business and lacks the new capital to try again, he will find it necessary to go to one of the metropolitan centers in the North to look for a job. When a young man is ready to embark upon his career, he will go into business with his father or father-in-law; or he may take a job as a salesman, traveling the territory for a (Jewish) manufacturer, wholesaler or mill agent. In effect, approximately 90 per cent of the 40,000 to 45,000 Jewish families in the Southeast represent a single-class society of small capitalists. Their activities center around the manufacture and distribution of textiles; wholesalers, and mill agents for knitting and hosiery mills; operators of retail stores ("soft goods," credit jewelry, pawn shops); manufacturers and distributors of chemicals; dealers in textile machinery, metals, metal scrap, linen service and supply, and cotton waste. There are very few Jews in banking, insurance, publishing, advertising, small loan companies, or in the food, drug, beverage, tobacco, and contracting and construction industries. If we are to accept the yardstick that "successful business is honest business," the Jews of the South have achieved a record that compares favorably with the general community. At least 85 per cent of the establishments, plants, and stores doing business today are operating under their original certificate of ownership or articles of incorporation.

This higher economic status is certainly a weighty factor in the ability to build and maintain religious establishments. It is reflected, too, in the per capita contribution to the United Jewish Appeal which according to official statistics, runs as much as 20 per cent above the national average. The number of contributors in proportion to the population is even greater. It is much easier to contact every individual prospect; his business, social and philanthropic activities are an open book, and the desire to maintain "status" is another stimulus to maximum giving. There are Southern cities of 200 Jewish families with 195 individual pledges. While essentially the giving is motivated by a deep sense of responsibility for the survivors of Hitler's massacre, as well as an almost unanimous devotion to the ideal that is Israel, it is also a fact that the mechanics of organized Jewish philanthropy in the South are more conducive to maximum gifts and a greater proportion of contributors. The higher average of giving and greater proportion of contributors extend also to the campaigns within the general community, such as Community Chest, Red Cross, hospital drives, and all other local projects. There are schools, playgrounds, hospitals and Christian churches throughout the South which bear the imprint of Jewish generosity.

There is yet another major reason for the seemingly closer "religious life" of the Jew in the South. The Temple is in fact the alpha and omega of all Jewish communal life. The attendance at the religious services, Orthodox, Conservative, and Reform, is not one iota greater than the attendance at religious services in the rest of the nation; but the attendance in the recreational hall and banquet room is far beyond that of the other Jewish communities.

The Temple is the center of all "defense," social, philanthropic and cultural activities. The social segregation between the Jew and non-Jew intensifies this, as well as the fact that outside entertainment and cultural activities are fewer than in the northern metropolitan centers. Still it would not be fair to say that the bazaars put on by the Temple Sisterhoods and the card games sponsored by the Temple Brotherhoods bring out capacity crowds, without also stating that a lecture by a Rabbi Mordecai Kaplan or by a Dr. Ludwig Lewisohn will bring out the entire Jewish community too.

In this matter of Temple affiliation it is interesting to watch the reaction of the newcomer to the community (now an everyday occurrence). In his first contacts with the local Jewish community he may be asked to join the Temple. His answer has become a standing joke, because he generally will say one of two things: "I am an agnostic and do not believe in that stuff," or "I never go to *shul* more than once, maybe twice a year." The local residents smile knowingly and there the matter rests. A month later Mr. Newcomer is pulling all sorts of wires to become a director of the Temple, and his wife is knee-deep in rummage sales with the ladies of the auxiliary.

In hundreds of small towns there are two, three, maybe five Jewish families. Paradoxically his very "conspicuousness" gives him a feeling of "relaxation" which would be the envy of his fellow-Jew in the larger centers and even in the great cities of the North. Here his "status' is clearly defined. He is the Jew who runs "the Jew store," and all civic and social relationships with the rest of the community start from this definitive "beginning." On this basis he becomes as permanent a fixture in the consciousness of the general community as the Confederate monument in the square. The society editor of the local weekly records the comings and going of his entire family and visiting relatives. The editor calls on him on his regular rounds and about once a month he'll ask the Jewish merchant for "a wise saying by one of the rabbis" to head up his editorial page. There is an annual Passover story, and during the High Holidays the ladies of the several churches will make a tour of the Jewish homes to examine books and "ceremonial objects," to learn something of the rituals of the occasion. There are, of course, moments of tension and distress—a Klan meeting nearby, or perhaps a "revival" conducted by an itinerant tent evangelist with heavy emphasis on how "the Jews reviled Him," and how "the Jews led Him to the slaughter." However, the Gentile community does not think in terms of their Jewish fellow-townsmen, but rather associates these acts with "those New York and Miami Jews," and lets it go at that.

The political influence of the individual Jew in these small towns on a local, state, and even national level is much greater than that of whole communities of Jews in the large cities. He is often on first-name relationships with the Congressman, the two United State Senators, and the Governor. These men have been to his store many times as they passed through his town in their early political campaigns for Sheriff, County Attorney, and minor state office, and the friendship continues throughout their lives.

The Jew in these towns has been to the home of many of the leading citizens in his community, but his visits are occasioned by meetings of the Polio Committee, the Retail Merchants Association, and the Watch This Town Grow Club. The men gather in the living room of the leading citizen, and there is even a little collation after the session, but it never reaches the level of "let's have the Nathans over tonight."

The intense religious atmosphere of the community is a definite influence toward making him a more "observing" Jew. He closes his business on the leading holidays, and when the Christian ladies have a public dinner for one of their projects, special foods are prepared for the three or four Jewish guests. Sometimes a Protestant Sunday-school teacher, who knows the "Five Books of Moses" by heart, will stop at the store to ask an opinion on some fine point of biblical criticism; and needless to say he goes away with something less than enthusiastic results.

About one out of every three Jewish boys takes a Christian wife. The percentage is only slightly lower in the larger cities. Propinquity and biology are the only motivating factors. Incidentally, the mixed marriages are consistent with the "social segregation" which exists between Jew and non-Jew. The Jew must always bring to the union something more than just himself, and the social cleavage is bridged by the "special advantages" the Jew contributes to the marriage. He will marry the Christian girl who works in his father's store; he'll marry the Christian daughter of his father's competitor. Despite the higher economic level upon which she usually enters, the Christian girl presumably makes the greater sacrifice. These "mixed marriages" have become so common-place that they do not cause a ripple within the Jewish community; on the other hand, a Christian wife of a Jew does not change the status of his application for membership in the country club, or automatically qualify their children for the private school.

It is well to note that in recent years there have been a considerable number of converts to Judaism. In these cases the non-Jewish wife enters upon her duties in maintaining "a Jewish home" with an enthusiasm seldom seen in the Jewish community itself. In one town a convert wife asked her husband why he insists upon maintaining a "kosher home" and why he objects to her having a Christmas tree "when your own two sisters don't keep kosher, and also have their Christmas tree every year." Indeed, hers was the only "kosher home" in town. When the Christian wife does not enter in the Jewish faith (and the great majority of course do not), they each maintain their separate religious affiliations. Many practicing Christian wives attend Friday night and High Holiday services with their husbands. Some of them teach in the Sunday schools of their own churches. In the recent organization of a new Temple in North Carolina, four of the eight charter members had Christian wives.

A mixed marriage involving a Jewish girl, however, is a rarity. Whereas the boy must remain in the locality to establish a means of livelihood, his sister need not stay in the community. Her "departure" is necessitated by two important considerations. First of all, she has little chance of carving out a career for herself in the South as a nurse, a schoolteacher, or in the social welfare services. Practically all that is open to her in the commercial world is a U. S. Civil Service examination or a job in her father's store or office. The other consideration, of course, is marriage. Thus most of the Jews in the small communities send their daughters off to live with relatives in Atlanta, Baltimore, and New York, to give her a chance of meeting Jewish boys, as well as an opportunity to use her education and talent in establishing a career. Sometimes a stroke of genius can reverse the process. One big merchant in a Southern town with six marriageable daughters notified all his suppliers in the North that if they wanted to continue to sell him merchandise they must send salesmen with two qualifications:

(a) he must be a Jew, and (b) he must be single. All six girls, their husbands, and their children are today leading happy and prosperous lives in their respective communities.

In the cities where there are from fifty to five hundred Jewish families the situation is entirely different. In the general community, the country club, the civic club, the downtown luncheon club, and the private school for children are tremendously important. With most of these social "rewards" withheld from the Jews, the incentive to a greater participation in the affairs of the general community is seriously lessened. It is interesting to note that the purely "social" adjuncts of this society—the country club and the private school—have never relaxed their "vigilance." The civic club, however, which presents less "social" implications, has opened the door on occasion. In one city the Rotary Club handled the matter "open and above board." Several of their members indicated that the club was ready to take in a Jew, and they made definite inquiry to determine whom the Jewish community wanted to "represent" them.

Confronted with these pin-pricks and little frustrations, the Jew in the South seeks "relief" in more intensified Jewish work, Jewish country clubs and interfaith activities, which, of course, result in even a greater "exclusiveness." The scramble that follows for *koved* and "little honors" is so far out of proportion to their true value that the question of who shall sit on the dais when the UJA speaker comes to town is now a most weighty and serious problem.

With "exclusiveness" has come a trembling uneasiness. Every little incident of bigotry and bias is magnified out of all proportion. There is a community of fifty "solid" Jewish merchants, with fine records of contributions to their city, living in day-to-day fear of a local semi-illiterate vagrant who writes "letters to the editor" inveighing against "foreigners," "aliens," "New Yorkers" and "Zionists."

This paralysis of fear not only prevents the pursuit of a "normal life," if that is possible at all, but results in a further retreat into "exclusiveness." The real big fear is that one Jew may say or do something that "will involve the whole Jewish community." Thus the socially-conscious Jew hesitates to risk an active participation in the general political and civic life of the community. (The conviction of one Jewish merchant in a tax case plunged an entire community into gloom and deep anxiety.) In one city a Jew inaugurated an educational project patterned after the *New York Herald Tribune* Forum, which was very well received by the general population. The Jewish community, however, fought him tooth and nail; they insisted that he transfer the sponsorship to Christian auspices:—"maybe he'll bring down an unpopular speaker—maybe some day, someone will say something from that platform that will disturb things—let's take no chances." Finally the pressure became so great that the annual event had to be abandoned. In another city, a rabbi, who had acquired considerable stature in the community, signified his intention of entering his name as a candidate for the School Board. The leaders of his congregation quickly "advised" him to put aside all "political" ambitions.

The Jews of the Southern communities live in deadly fear of a "disturber." "Let's do nothing to rock the boat" is the first commandment. This fear has nothing whatever to do with current political tensions. The studied attempt to avoid all debate (except on purely Jewish matters) has been in force so long that it would be hard to find six Jews below the Mason-Dixon line who hold sufficiently strong convictions to be "accused" of anything. When the Hebrew Union College sent word that the term "Reform Judaism" had been officially changed to "Liberal Judaism," the directors of one Temple challenged the idea. They reasoned that the word "liberal" has no place in "religion." The mildest New Deal expression in a "letter to the editor" signed with a Jewish name sends a shiver through the entire Jewish community—("now we've got *someone else* to worry about"). But the greatest fear of all is that the next Jewish newcomer to town may be an "agitator," a "pink," an organizer for the CIO, or even a worker for some Negro cause. One night last year a woman called at the home of the rabbi in a Southern city. Did he know of a Jewish home where she could get room and board for a couple of weeks? The vice-president of his congregation was visiting him at the time. When the woman introduced herself as an organizer for the Textile Workers Union, the vice-president grabbed his wife and ran out the back door. In a big Court House rally for the Scottsboro boys a few years ago (a rally initiated by two Protestant clergymen), not a single Jew made an appearance.

Let us note, however—though their number is very small—that there are liberal, politically aware and socially conscious Jews in every Southern community. Paradoxically these Jewish "non-conformists" are far less "exclusive" than those who try so desperately to "hew to the line." These one or two Jewish liberals in each town find natural allies among the Gentile non-conformists, dissenters, Unitarians, and Humanists. They actually weld themselves into another small minority and pursue all their political, cultural and social activities together.

The basic truth is that in general the Jew is distrusted by the very low income group and disliked by the middle class; and he is powerless to affect the course of this phobia to even the slightest degree. Yet vocal anti-Semitism is much less evident in the South than in Massachusetts and New York. To a great extent the deep concern of the Southerner over "The Negro" serves as a "shock absorber" for the Jewish minority. In addition, the South has in recent years produced many influential liberals, particularly among the Protestant clergy and the editors and publishers of the daily press. Upon the recent resurgence of small Ku Klux Klan elements, three clergymen in one city attacked the hoodlums from their pulpits. This would have been unthinkable twenty-five or thirty years ago. The Methodist-Episcopal Church South (now part of the main Methodist fellowship) was the first major non-Jewish organization in the world officially to condemn Hitler's racial laws (1934). The editors, too, across the South take very little nonsense when overt racial or group hostility is involved. In one town there was an epidemic of chalk markings—"Jew"—on store fronts. The local editor went after the culprits in his editorial columns. The fact that the "teen-agers" turned out to be from "the best families" made no difference at all.

Of course, the "exclusiveness" of the Jewish community in the South is not entirely self-imposed. The Christian population delivers some mighty blows in that direction. Every young Jewish couple waits from day to day for the inevitable crisis. It will come soon enough:—"*Momma, what's a Jew boy?*" There are established periods of Christian Bible study in all the elementary schools (in high schools it is now optional). The Jewish community maintains a respectful silence, primarily because of the tremendous preponderance of the Protestant population. The Jewish children have the option of leaving the room; but it's a difficult decision to make. Some believe it is better to remain seated than to have forty-three children watch one or two others shuffle out. Neither side, of course, can be expected to understand what it's all about. The Christian children wonder why one or two of their number "do not want to hear about God," and the Jewish child is also heart-sick as well as bewildered. In some schools they maintain separate rooms for the daily devotionals, which is little better, because it involves only two or three Jewish children and their absence can be as conspicuous as their walking out. (The Roman Catholics have more or less solved this problem, below the high school level, by the great expansion of their parochial school system in recent years.) The non-Jewish community, in general, in every contact with the individual Jew emphasizes this concept of "separateness." It associates each individual act with the body as a whole, and to most of them "every Jew is the spokesman for all of Israel." In one town a Justice of the Peace held a warrant for the arrest of some itinerant with a Jewish name. When his marshals could not locate the fugitive, the Justice called the rabbi "for cooperation."

Into this great vacuum of Jewish communal life in the South, the benign vacuity of the "interfaith" organization fits like a glove. The popularity of the movement is based on two very pleasant illusions. First is the illusion that here is a "Jewish activity" in which the Jews need make none of the decisions; and second is the illusion that here, at long last, is a "social club" of Jews and Christians. In one state a fund-raising campaign for a new Hillel building on a college campus brought an offer from a Jew to donate the entire $150,000 required, if they changed the name of "Hillel House" to "Interfaith House." His offer was turned down, but the sad thing about it is that the very ends this loyal and generous Jew sought in Christian-Jewish relations would be served better if it remained the "Hillel House," and perhaps better still if it were called "The Jewish House."

Primarily the Jews of the South reflect to a large extent the mores, the hopes, the politics, and even the prejudices of the society around them. The pattern follows an instinctive search for the "security" which comes with some degree of "anonymity," and nothing reflects it more poignantly than the all too common boast that "my son looks like a Georgia Cracker" (or a "Tar Heel," or a "Tennesse Mountaineer").

The observation that *m'ken leben ober m'lust nisht,* could be tragic at times, but more often it is humorous. Recently a wealthy old-timer with a long and honorable record of good works and philanthropies in his community, was appointed to an important secular board in the Christian community. They were making preparations for a fund-raising drive for a new hospital building. He was the first Jew ever to achieve this distinction. It was a great honor. As he left the building after attending his first session he had a look of chagrin on his face, and with the air of a man both very sad and very tired he said, "The *mommzer* gave me all the Jewish cards. . . ."

THE STORY THAT MUST BUILD ITSELF

By MAURICE SAMUEL

WHEN I HEARD some months ago that John Hersey had written a powerful book on the destruction of the Warsaw ghetto, I was filled with something akin to anxiety. For me, as for a great many others, this subject—part of the larger subject which is comprised in the dread episode of the Nazi extermination of European Jewry—is not one for exploitative writing, even of the higher kind. By exploitative writing I mean the kind which is born of the attitude, "That's a wonderful theme for a book." Only dedicated writing can be congruent with this subject. My anticipatory concern was the deeper because Hersey is not an exploitative writer, in spite of his consistent choice of "good ideas." He is a gifted and dependable craftsman, and his book would be a serious one. But its literary merit—which in a general way could be taken for granted—would have to establish itself by extraneous and exacting criteria which are not merely literary. In other words, this could not be regarded simply as a piece of writing; one would have to examine it as an incident.

The fate of the Warsaw ghetto has become the symbol of the fate of European Jewry; and when we speak of fate we think primarily of meaning. We want to know what it has all meant. We might answer that it meant nothing at all; in this episode, as in countless others of its kind, a number of human animals destroyed another number of human animals—part of the process of mutual extermination which has gone on since life appeared on the planet. If this is the case, we must not speak of "fate," with its connotations

228

of meaningful pattern; and we must not pretend that there is any-thing here to hold our interest beyond certain decorative details: this human animal died well, that one badly; this one showed spirit, resourcefulness and endurance, the other was spiritless, shifty and cowardly. The spectacle is everything, and behind the spectacle there is nothing. We might, I say, take up this point of view; or, more accurately, we might pretend to; for merely to assert it is to reveal our susceptibility to the other point of view, which bids us look for meaning. Most of us, except in uncharacteristic moments of exhaustion, will not even make the pretense. We are committed to the search.

The search is conducted on three levels, though the objective we have in mind is a single one. There is the obvious individual level, the raw material of the case history, the almost behavioristic record of what certain persons did and said. Without this raw material we can do nothing, of course. The individual is the starting point, the unit of observation; unless we know what happened to him, unless we can study him attentively in the midst of events, we have no clue to the meaningful pattern.

But the individual is what he is by virtue of at least two major factors: his particular set of endowments, and the form, expression and articulateness which he found in his social group or groups. When we say that a man is a Polish Jew and a left-wing Zionist, or a Polish Jew assimilated into the culture and nationalism of Poland, we do more than give his social coordinates. We are de-fining him internally. It is of the utmost importance to remember that this man is unintelligible to *himself,* as well as to us, without these terms; they are realities of his soul. Therefore the second level of search is national. There was such a thing as Polish Jewry, without a knowledge of which the Polish Jew, the Warsaw Jew, is unrecognizable, and that which happened to him humanly in-describable.

We must know, therefore, the meaning of what happened to Polish Jewry as a Jewry. It exists no more, today, and is to itself beyond meaning. But it was part of world Jewry, and for Jews who live in the affirmation of Jewishness the total destruction of Polish Jewry, and of most of the rest of European Jewry, is an apocalyptic tragedy which the sensitive bystander can respect, but cannot share. I am not speaking here of an intimate feeling of family bereavement, inaccessible to the outsider; that happens, actually, to be the less inaccessible aspect of the anguish, for every human being knows what it means to lose a parent, a brother, or a sister. But few know what it means to lose at a blow, in one all-embracing calamity, the largest single source of their corporate personality, their spiritual identifiability—a source which yesterday flowed with abounding vigor, and today is a dried up well in a waste land.

Therefore on this second level, the national or group level, the search for meaning extends beyond the boundaries of dead Polish Jewry, and also backward and forward in time; backward into the common origins of Polish and world Jewry, forward into the effects on surviving world Jewry, and on American Jewry—the largest group—in particular. The sum of the individual destinies now ascends into the historical.

On the third level we seek a universal meaning in which the other two meanings play their role; and as some of us see it, the first two meanings are illusions unless they are sublimated into the third. The relationship between Nazidom and Jewry was not that between the power-seeker and his victim; it was not the standard, immemorial pattern of group conflicts. It was a unique phenomenon with a unique content; its interpretation can be offered only within the inclusive framework of the interpretation of our civilization. The fact that most Jews are not aware of this large meaning is no argument against it; few people grasp the fulness of the purpose which, with varying degrees of willingness, they serve with their essential selves. Far more decisive is the fact that we cannot explain all the phenomena on the first and second level without an acceptance of what is to be found on the third level.

These are the difficult and exacting criteria with which I approached the reading of John Hersey's *The Wall*.

Perhaps only a sensitive bystander—one who neither shared the experience, nor shares the feeling of national bereavement and diminution—could have produced this chronicle. Piously, with immense and unconfused diligence, John Hersey studied the mountainous dispositions of witnesses, devised a fictitious framework for their presentation, filled it in person by person, incident by incident, for six hundred printed pages. The narrative is crowded with honesty, and this honesty acquires additional density from two contrasts.

The first is the necessary element of invention. The implausible figure of Levinson, the "archivist," who, besides accumulating and burying a vast library of "diaries, novels, notebooks, accountbooks, minutes of meetings, collections of letters, plays, poems, short stories, sketches, musical compositions, as well as a great mass of official records," also *wrote* more than four million words in the three and a half years covered by the book—over three thousand words a day for nearly thirteen hundred consecutive days, in the midst of confusion, displacements, disease, hunger, darknesses, slaughter, crowding and horror—the Levinson without whom *The Wall* could not have been written, is accepted by the reader because he has to be accepted. How else could Hersey have given us such a detailed, continuous, almost day-to-day account of the lives of these men and women? But instead of being troubled by doubt under this compulsion, the reader, won to the story by its irresistible truthfulness, finds himself doubly convinced precisely because the "device" is so transparently inacceptable.

The second contrast which testifies to the reliability and honesty of the book is, rather strangely, the evidence that it is the work of a bystander. This does not refer to the few—the very few—slips (such as the impossible rendition of the Passover Four Questions, or the *Chatos Neurim* as author) which occur here and there. My observation refers to tone and atmospheric effect. Mr. Hersey, in his "Editor's Prologue," acknowledges his indebtedness to the translators, who "had a very difficult task." He continues: "They had to try to convey in English the life of Eastern European Jews without falling into the colloquialisms, word orders, and rhythms which, as taken over and modified by the American-Jewish community, have become part of an entirely different culture; the connotations would have been misleading." Certainly. One would not be conveying the tonality of Polish Jewish conversation by approximating it to East Side English. But, unacquainted with that tonality, Mr. Hersey has given us something equally remote from the original. Thus:

We read that Rutka Mazur, who is carrying on a serious flirtation with Mordecai Apt, comes to the Apt apartment for the weekly contribution of food for "orphans and indigent refugees" in

231

the ghetto. This time it is a teaspoonful of flour from every person in the apartment. Mordecai's sister, Rachel, opens the door.

"Rachel (almost sullenly):—My brother's not in.

"Rutka:—I'm not pursuing Mordecai. I'm scavenging."

Now this is not in the Jewish or Yiddish style of pleasantry. It is sophisticated Anglo-Saxon "witty" back talk. It belongs to Huxley and Evelyn Waugh and Saki, not to a narrative written in Yiddish (though the two girls may have spoken in Polish) as the archivist Levinson's was.

Or again: Reb Yechiel Mazur, the gentle pietist, is returning with his fellow-mourners from the burial of his young son, Schlome, who died in the ghetto typhus epidemic. We read:

"On the way out of the cemetery, Reb Yechiel bent down three or four times and picked some weeds until he had quite a handful —brome, fescue, and devilgrass. Finally he said:

"—And they of the city shall flourish like the grass of the earth."

It is a moving passage, one of scores. It is also noteworthy for its verisimilitude—except for one illuminating detail. It is impossible that Levinson's *Yiddish* narrative should have contained the words for "brome," "fescue" and "devilgrass." It is alien to the spirit of the language (and of Jewish thought and experience) to endow it with the equivalents of such specialized nature terminology. Mr. Hersey may have found brome, fescue and devilgrass among the ruins of the Warsaw ghetto: he (or his translators) could not have found them in Levinson's "Archives."

Now these betrayals do not, in themselves, diminish the trustworthiness of Mr. Hersey. On the contrary, they startle us into appreciation of the care and insight and industry which he brought to the raw material of his book. That the bystander should have learned as much as he did is altogether extraordinary; besides being an act of piety, the book is a spiritual and intellectual *tour de force*. Or, as a Hasid might say, it is a *tour de force* in piety. But its character as such is emphasized by the gulf between the narrator and his subject; and of this gulf more will be said later.

Let us now return to the story. All of us are familiar with it. But we have not had it set down before in this full orderly manner, with this proper, systematic blending of what befell the individual and what happened panoramically. The orderliness is, however,

232

kept decently in check. Whether by instinct, accident or design, Mr. Hersey has introduced a certain superficial confusion of effect, in part through the multiplicity of characters, in part by a technique of cross-reference. The book therefore demands close attention—rightly. I have not the slightest doubt that tens of thousands of readers, members of the Book of the Month Club, or non-members rushed off their feet by prestige-pressure, will skim most of the book or even give up half way. But a smooth, attractive story of the Warsaw ghetto, written for the lazy entertainment-seeker, who will sandwich it in between a mystery thriller and a dreary, pseudo-erotic historical romance, would have been a coarse affront to the subject—exploitative writing at its most indecent. The cooperative effort which the book exacts from the serious reader—something like a religious service—is a necessary element in the story.

I also do not doubt that within a few years only a handful of specialists will remember the book or refer to it. That again is not a reflection on Mr. Hersey's achievement, which is hemmed in by restrictions beyond the scope of conscious literary effort even of the highest order. For actually we are concerned with two stories: the story of the Warsaw ghetto, and the story of how that story is establishing itself in the Jewish people (it is not likely to establish itself anywhere else). In the second story, which is the continuing fate of the first story, Mr. Hersey's book is an incident, and this is in itself a high distinction. But now we will turn once more to the first story, the familiar one which is becoming part of the Jewish historic consciousness.

We know all the people in the narrative, from countless articles, books, and conversations with survivors, if not of the Warsaw ghetto, then of other expunged Jewries. We know them by diffusion, and do not remember when and where we first heard of them. There is Dolyk Berson, who enters as a likable, personable no-one-in-particular, and who in three and a half years is transformed into the powerful man of action. There is Rachel Apt, the timid, homely girl, in whom a spirit lies latent even greater than Berson's: a gentle, loving soul, fumbling and frustrated, but of profound instinctive intelligence (that intelligence itself a function of her goodness), unfolding slowly, revealing successive reserves of endurance and devotion and decision, until she becomes the "mother of the partisans," until she stands with them as they direct their fire against the Germans: "Now Jews; now, my dear ones." There is Fein, the carpenter, *amcho*, of the folk, solid, resourceful, an early activist, who organizes ingeniously the sabotage of the merchandise which has to be delivered to the German autorities, and is a first-class, all-round addition to the resistance. And there is Stefan Mazur (son of the lovable pietist Reb Yechiel Mazur), the young member of the Jewish ghetto police, the decomposition of whose character proceeds in a sort of counterpoint with the upbuilding of the character of his sister, Rutka; till it reaches the point where, bidden to obtain his quota of four persons for deportation from the ghetto (this is toward the end, when the meaning of deportation is half-understood), he demands that his father and mother give themselves up, and meanwhile he himself carries off in his arms the frail, dying Symka Berson, the wife of the partisan leader. There is Mauritzi Apt, the wealthy, assimilated jewelry merchant, a stupefying embodiment of the sheer will to survive, at any cost, at anyone's cost; though drawn convincingly as a human being, and a not indifferent father (Rachel Apt, mother of the partisans, is his daughter! to be sure, not his favorite daughter), he is somehow less a person than a manifestation of blind biologic self-centeredness—blind not only to the horrors about him, but, in a grisly-comical way, to what he is up against. There is Fischel Schpunt, the clowning *mah yofes* Jew, whose persistent, sickening buffoonery before the Germans is an involved stylization, part surrender, part defiance, part insanity (a normal person could not act it out), part fulfilment—one cannot fathom him without becoming slightly mad oneself. There is Yitzhok, the grim young fighter and partisan leader, man of action almost before he is a man (reminiscent of Israeli army officers). There are dozens, scores, hundreds of others; the book swarms with human beings; we have the impression of being in the ghetto, not in the narrative. But though we know all these people, we learn to know them better because we are able, here and now, to contemplate their carefully drawn portraits. Nothing new is told us; the externals of the old are brought back, fixed where we can concentrate on them; our increasing insight into them is our own work, for which Mr. Hersey has dutifully and honorably supplied the material.

We are also familiar with the panoramic projection, and we

brood again over the dark riddles of the Jewish group reaction to the developing strategy of the Nazi destroyers. Here again Mr. Hersey supplies, with fidelity and skill and far-sighted continuity, the technical portrait—this time of a historic phenomenon—in the contemplation of which we are moved to a renewal of our insights. In the portrait of a historic phenomenon we must get the effect of motion, which is its essence. A person too evolves as we watch him, but a person can be "caught" convincingly in a still-life, too. It is otherwise with history, which *is* motion. It has no still-lifes. And here the kinetic effect—magnificently brought out—begins early in the book, when Jewish forced labor is erecting the wall about the ghetto and Levinson, the archivist, the all-seeing eye, is groping for the pattern:

"The occupation authorities are building this wall as they do everything else—section by section, episode after episode, without apparent sequence. Here and there, now and then. Casual looting of Jewish property; kosher slaughter forbidden; *Kehilla* disbanded and *Judenrat* formed; public worship forbidden; census; registration for labor; ghetto decree; ghetto decree called off; armbands; bank accounts frozen; limitations on change of residence; registration of Jew's jewelry; schools closed; restrictions on travel; registration of property; Jews barred from trolleys and buses; restrictions on postal savings; prohibition of purchase of gold; wall sections built. Each episode comes at a different time. And when each group raises a clamor, all the other groups cry:

"—Hush! Do you intend to endanger the majority? Hush, friends!

"Yet I think we are all going to wake up one of these mornings, hear a loud click in the sky, and see all these puzzle parts fall into place around us. I wish I could understand the real meaning of the sections of wall. . . ."

That is in April, 1940. In September, 1941, long after the wall has been completed and the Jews sealed in, Rutka Mazur goes as the underground messenger of Hashomer to Wilno, and brings back a report which is presented to the *Judenrat*. Levinson writes: "The nature of the mass killings in Bialystok and Wilno, the thoroughness, the technique employed—these leave no doubt as to our future. And yet the impossible is happening: people are rejecting this certainty. Influential people. I heard one man very high in the *Judenrat* say: *The Hashomer crowd is exaggerating these things in order to rouse us to their particular political program.* I am a historian, an archivist, I have studied the Mazur documents; there is internal evidence of their authenticity and of their modesty and understatement. I have heard others say: *All right, suppose those killings did take place. They were in the zone that was formerly Russian. The victims were very likely Communists, or suspected of being Communists. We have no such hazard here.*

"Another formula one hears is this: *We all know that the Germans insist on collective responsibility. How do we know what provocations the people in Bialystok and Wilno gave the Germans?* Others simply shrug and say: *Those were local happenings.* As if one could not see all the other awful tiles being prepared for the grand mosaic! . . . So we know: we delude ourselves. We know: we refuse to understand. It is really incredible."

In the summer of 1942 came the orders for the "delivery" of ten thousand Jews daily, to be rounded up by the Jewish police, under the *Judenrat,* for "resettlement." The orders were carried out with considerable efficiency. The figures given are: "July 22— 6,289; July 23—7,815; July 24—7,744"—and so on, a total of 47,343 in the first week. Levinson knows that these Jews are not being resettled; they are being evacuated for slaughter. The typhus epidemic induced by the concentration of 500,000 Jews in a little more than half a square mile had not done its work properly. The victims who are roped in by the Jewish police have their suspicions; they smell death, as cattle smell it approaching the abattoir. They struggle to escape, they dodge the police, they hide, they seek a reprieve in the dwindling category of "favored" workers. They know, and they do not know.

Then a certain Schorr, one of the hated Jewish police, happens to notice that the railway cars which take away the Jews for "resettlement" somewhere in the east, or for work near the Russian front, are returning much too fast. An underground worker, this time a Bund member, Lazar Slonim, goes out to investigate, and brings back—*Treblinka!* The gas chambers: the whole hyena story of mockery and deception, of seemingly purposeful classification of the victims into trades, of kindly reception by a "gentle-looking SS officer": *After the bath and the disinfection, this property will be returned to you in accordance with your receipts:* the mass graves; bulldozers. And now the leaders in the ghetto—or most of them—believe at last. They send a message by underground courier to the Jews of Berne and Istanbul:

"Cousin Israel is sick and is going to live with uncle Mavetski. Any help you can send must hurry." (Mavetski—*Mavet*—death.)

Yet four weeks later Levinson records: "It appears now that the Germans intend to get rid of all of us, it will be just a matter of time, as I see it, though our optimists—and how stubborn they are! —still maintain that part of the population will be spared. The deportations slackened off this week: a total of 31,396 for the week, compared with 56,786 in the preceding week. The optimists say: *See! They are letting up. Only thirty thousand.*"

Thus till the very end! In March of 1943, a month before the open revolt, when about fifty thousand Jews were left of the half million, Levinson must still record: "It is hard to rouse the whole to a pitch of concern over one of its parts."

And while all this went on, the deterioration of most of the survivors went on too: a deterioration manipulated by the destroyer with maniacal cunning: by half-actions and concealments; by delegation of authority; by the law of "corporate responsibility"— corporate responsiblity when the entire community had been condemned to death in advance; by fantastic little concessions—"the Germans allowed us to bring typewriters and office equipment from the Grzybowska building"—in the midst of the deportations; by the classic Machiavellian technique of piecemeal destruction, accompanied by deprecation of the total destruction already irrevocably decreed; by the ingenious encouragement of hope in groups, in persons, in classes, in "useful ones," in "superior types."

"In general," writes Levinson (or Levinson-Hersey), "I feel rather sorry for the Jewish police. Originally most of them enlisted with the sincere conviction that the 'Order Service' might fulfil the sense of that phrase. . . . Even Berson signed up with this conviction. In spite of themselves, and often without knowing what was happening to them, the Jewish police have been driven into becoming executors of German cruelty. Many would have withdrawn, as Berson did, but they felt that their position protected their families. I have seen a couple of them (Dickstein, Brottles) in agonies over this dilemma. In these two cases the decision to stay at a hated job to protect beloved relatives has had two tragic reversals in effect: it has made them hate their relatives and it has made them love their jobs, or at least seem to, so that they have become brutal, Gestapo-like policemen. Two years ago, Dickstein and Brottles were both gentle, respected, intelligent lawyers. Now they are monsters."

The portraits of the individuals stand before us with a certain finality. We suffer with them, we feel pride swelling in us, we shrink from them; but they do not torment us with dreadful questioning. It is otherwise with the panorama in motion, with the evolving mass action. We agonize over possible alternatives. Suppose they had understood quite early, when they were still nearly half a million in number, what had been decreed for them. Suppose the resistance which burst out at the end, and which for all its pitiful smallness—a few hundred guerillas in the warrens of the ghetto, a few hundred rifles and revolvers, a few bottle bombs—caused the process of annihilation to slacken and falter in the last stages—suppose this resistance had flared up wildly at the beginning. Would it have made any difference? Or would it have meant an early, crushing, Rotterdam-Coventry assault on the Warsaw ghetto with—in the end—the same practical result? And even if it had meant the same practical result, would it not have meant quite another result in the important imponderables which are of a high practical order in the long run? We ask these things in the midst of our everlasting lament, and we seek some guidance for the future.

It seems to us that it could not but have made a difference, immediately and remotely practical, if the revolt had been staged in the early days. Before the Jews were concentrated in the ghetto they were not so accessible to complete mass destruction. Also resistance at that stage, compelling the Germans to resort to unmasked savagery on a grand scale, might have embarrassed them in their long-range program for the Poles, the Ukrainians and others. It might also have produced a *tactical* change (the most one could hope for) in the attitude of the Poles toward the Jews. Poland was soaked to the bone in anti-Semitism; not for nothing was it chosen as the principal abattoir for European Jewry—the action could be carried on in congenial surroundings. But early, frantic Jewish resistance might have tempted the Poles to make an alliance with the Jews. . . . All these are considerations of immediate practicality.

But they are the less important ones, and, as I shall show below, calculation along these lines is folly. And this is true even of greater "practical" possibilities which were lost by delay and indecision. One such possibility towers above all others. An immediate revolt would have nullified the whole theory and technique of the Machiavellianism which was the classic foundation of Nazi strategy. It would have demoralized the Nazis by cutting from under their feet the groundwork of their demonic technique for the handling of human beings. The process applied to the Jews was concealed from the outside world; no one knew what was going on; today the exposure of the process still meets with skepticism, or with that momentary acceptance and hasty forgetting which is also a form of skepticism. The thing was too incredibly horrible; such sustained virtuosity in villainy is almost as miraculous as sustained virtuosity in saintliness. Not to have given the Germans a chance to exercise their virtuosity, but instead to have compelled them to wipe out a people openly, grossly, in uncomfortable violation of world opinion—that might have had far-reaching consequences.

But almost until the end (thank God, only until *almost*) the Jews supplied what the Nazis must have longed for in their maddest dreams: a perfect guinea-pig nation. Captive individuals as laboratory specimens are not new things. But a nation segregated, isolated from public view, stretched out on the operating table and delivered up unconditionally to the uninhibited imagination of the outside operator—that is a thing unheard of. Unheard of, and unbelievable.

What Hersey has done, in giving us these individual and panoramic portraits, is, I repeat, to provide the opportunity for reflection. Here is the material, faithful and well-ordered. Consider it at length, and you reach a certain grim calmness; you cease to beat your head against the wall; you understand that it could not have been otherwise. Repining is not only vain and spiritually wasteful; it is an injustice to the victims. "It is incredible!" cries Levinson, when the ghetto refuses to accept the Mazur and Slonim reports. But what is there incredible about people refusing to believe the incredible? This is the very essence of the situation. The Machiavellian tactic, when applied by a genius of the first order—and in evil Hitler cannot be ranked lower—is, at the present stage of our general moral intelligence, irresistible. Nations and individuals are paralyzed by it; if and when they revolt it is still without insight. "We have been fooled!" they cry, furiously, like Nevile Henderson. Of course they have been fooled; the Machiavellian technique is the supreme form of the con game. But that is not the crux of the matter. When the victims complain that it was their good-nature, their kindliness, their trustfulness, which blocked their perception, they are, as in every con game, only half right, and this half-rightness is linked with the essential corruption which marks our present condition. The corruption expresses itself in the amoral evaluation of events, in political expediency, in the deferment of moral judgment to guessed-at practical consequences in the near or remote future. An act is no longer intrinsic.

One tremendous truth issues from this setting: you must fight with uncalculating, instinctive and implacable rage against the *first* infringement of the moral law. You must do it as if it were the *last* and intolerable infringement. And you must do this not as a matter of strategy, in shrewdness and foresight, for that is already an adulteration which approximates you to the attacker. You must not do it because this first injustice has hurt you: the first Machiavellian infringement is designed to be painless, except to a few. You must do it because you will not tolerate evil, because the first manifestation of it affronts the hope of mankind and the purpose of the Creator.

How can we expect human beings in the mass, and even individuals except in inspired instances, to act thus? Were they at that stage, the whole dialectic process of history would be at an end, and humanity would have arrived at the metahistorical condition foretold by the prophets: "I will pour out My spirit on all flesh. . . ." Yet we must understand that this is the only possible direction for us, every other road leading back into the labyrinth.

The Machiavellian technique is the perfectly natural concomitant of our moral defectiveness, which actually begs for Machiavellianism, or, indeed, exhales it. We are not thieves, we are the fences who conjure thieves up. We are not bullies, we are the audience needed by some bullies, or we are the rancorously unresistant victims needed by other bullies; and often we are both. Our pacifism is not a loving saintliness, which might disappoint the lust of the power-seeker; it is prudence and cowardice, which fill him with joy. We are not insulters; we are only the people who "bite" at an insult, providing the insulter with reward and incentive. We are not liars, we are worldly, broadminded, tolerant, fundamentally honest people, who feel that a certain amount of propaganda, rearrangement of facts, soft-pedalling of ugly realities, latitude for the exigencies of "public relations," are unavoidable, are essential to the smooth running of things. And we call it realism, a sense of humor, a feeling for proportion.

The condition is universal; and why should we have expected the Jews of the Warsaw ghetto to have acted differently from England, America, France,—nations with vast political experience? Will it be pleaded that those nations had groups friendly to the social philosophy of nazism? So had the Jews. Those nations were divided on many issues? So were the Jews. The heart sinks with every review of the record in Warsaw: until the last—even during the strategic alliance for the uprising—the divisions dominated: Bund, Communists, Left Poale-Zion, Hashomer, Dror, Akiba, Mizrachi, General Zionists, Orthodox. . . . And all are "guilty." Not that political and religious parties, even a multiplicity of them, are negative things at any time. But it is seen finally that all the parties (are they not made up of individuals?) are steeped in expedience, strategy and the political evaluation of events. Had they differed only with regard to pedagogic method toward the universal moral purpose (should not politics be the school for the moral liberation of social forms?), they would have united at once. But they did not understand at once, and never understood wholly, because they were what they were. The circle cannot be broken.

Incorruptible honesty and not strategy is the answer to Machiavellianism. It is folly, as well as wickedness, to seek to outwit the devil on his own ground: it is just the sort of challenge he is looking for.

The foregoing section is a necessary extension of my subject, not part of it. The general lesson of the meaning of Machiavellianism is contained also in the Jewish episode in Hitler history, with only minor variations. There is no reason why, in these terms, the Jews should be singled out for special study, or why their story should "establish itself"—that is, become a special section of the folklore, part of the minimum area of *Jewish* cultural being.

But when we begin to consider the relation of the story to the Jewish people, we shall discover those exacting, extraneous criteria by which Mr. Hersey's book must ultimately be judged. For its value is as an incident; the extent to which it helps the story to establish itself in the above sense is the measure of its seriousness. Likewise, we must bear in mind the various levels.

Something was taking place in the Warsaw ghetto, in the Yiddish-speaking Jewry of Europe generally, which was visible to certain Jews at the end, and which should have been visible to Levinson, the archivist-historian. A *civilization* was being razed. The Yiddish form of Jewishness, a particular and irreplaceable expression of eternal Jewishness, was a creation *sui generis*. In *The Earth Is the Lord's*, Professor Abraham J. Heschel says that, at its highest, the Yiddish episode "was the golden period in Jewish history, in the history of the Jewish soul." I cannot judge. I can only say that here was a world which achieved one of the most fascinating syntheses in human experience. Rooted spiritually in the old faith and philosophy which we know as Judaism, it had found new and subtle expression for its values in media acquired locally: in the Yiddish language, in Polish dress, in Ukrainian melodies. Essential Judaism was not diluted or deflected thereby; it was enriched, it was confirmed in its direction. From the Yiddish Jewishness of Europe there sprang the Jewish life of America, of Palestine, of most of the Western world (the Jewishness of earlier migrations westward, Sephardic and German, is now vanishing rapidly). An American Judaism, organically interwoven with this country, as European Judaism was with Europe, is yet to be born—and every great regional Jewry (Babylonian, Spanish, European) has needed centuries for its growth. We were still being nourished by European—chiefly Polish—Judaism when the source was cut off suddenly.

Polish Jewry itself was but half of the Yiddish Jewishness which is our origin. Russian Jewry had already been cut off from world Jewry, and was dissolving under applied propagandistic and cultural pressure. But that remaining half was, in spite of large assimilating elements, authentic, energetic, full-blooded. A thousand years had gone into the creation of the Yiddish-speaking sub-civilization; long before the coming of Hitler, before the compulsory assimilation of communism, it had been subjected to corroding forces. It had lost ground, rallied, and reasserted itself through Zionism. On the eve of its extirpation it was still powerful and promising.

We do not get from *The Wall* the overwhelming sensation of a *civilization* being destroyed. Perhaps no single book could convey that effect. We must bring to any book, perhaps, antecedent knowledge, and such antecedent knowledge means—involvement. Now I have spoken of the de-Judaization of the conversation of Hersey's Jews: it is symbol and substance of un-involvement. This is not because the book had to be written in sound idiomatic English. Soma Morgenstern's *Son of the Lost Son* and *In My Father's Pastures* are in sound, idiomatic English, and yet they give the feel of a deep and distinct civilization, that of Polish-Ukrainian-Galician Jewry. (And when Morgenstern writes of nature in terms alien to Yiddish, he does not commit the error of attributing a Yiddish origin to the passage.) I urge the reader to go carefully over at least two passages in the first of these books—*The Son of the Lost Son*—and there are many similar passages in both books. One is the description of Velvel Mohilever at his morning prayers (pp. 8–10), the other the description of the *El mole rach'mim* at the opening of the Agudat Israel Congress (pp. 93–96). Mr. Hersey's reverent and sympathetic "reportage" of, let us say, two of the most Jewishly Jewish characters, Reb Yechiel Mazur and Rabbi Goldflamm, does not get us inside them, and inside Jewishness, in Morgenstern's manner.

Yet there is no inaccuracy in the reportage. We get the material, and we must rework it for ourselves. The question is not, either, one of emotional insight. Some time ago I read in manuscript, and am now re-reading in book form, a Columbia doctorate thesis—*Jewish Schools in Poland, 1919–39,* by Miriam Eisenstein. It is a factual technical study, objective, historical, statistical. There is no attempt at "appeal." But out of the curricula and histories of the Cysho schools, the Tarbut, the Horev, and Wilno Seminary, out of the budgetary reports—the upkeep was provided by voluntary contributions—there issues into being a separate, three-dimensional world. Here too pre-knowledge is necessary, but only a little, and the material need not be reworked by the spirit.

It is overwhelming to think that this powerful, functioning organism, with its tradition, purpose, ingenuities, devotions, should simply have been wiped off the earth. But first one must feel the organism. Then one asks: Is it all gone? Has it no heirs? Is it merely one in a catalogue of issueless civilizations?

Zalman Segalovitch, the poet, who survived the slaughter of Polish Jewry, went to Palestine, could not rest, came to America, and died here recently, cried out despairingly:

> *This was no spectacle, to be seen and forgotten:*
> *It cost us something more than the price of a ticket. . . .*
> *It cost us nothing less than the folkhood of Jewry.*

His words are: *die Yiddishe uhme.* One might say, the Jewish people. The translation would be correct. The implication, however, goes deeper. There is still a Jewish people, as Segalovitch knew. But this Jewish people had lost the source of its folkhood; or at least of its most recently created, most vital form of folkhood —the Yiddish world, almost one might say its *Yiddishkeit.*

It is perhaps not the direct business of the record to convey this annihilative effect: but it must make this effect possible by its recreation of the feel of an old civilization, unitary in its divisiveness, inheritor and transmitter. There are, in fact, a few hints here and there, and I shall refer to them. However, it is not a question of hints, but rather of the suffusion of the whole. I do not find this. And therefore it seems to me that a second bystander, as sensitive as Mr. Hersey, and acquainted only with his record, will not know of the continuing role of the story in Jewish history.

He will not know that in the national consciousness of a still vital people the destruction of European Jewry has entered upon its meaningful existence. He will not be susceptible to the weightiness of the event in still living terms, because he will think that only a group or community was destroyed in Warsaw, in Europe, not a specific sub-civilization, heir and transmitter of a master-civilization, yet in some ways independent. The master-civilization is now struggling to rephrase itself without the folk support of European Jewry. The transmission from Europe has been arrested; American and Israeli Jewries and world Jewry generally must re-order their spiritual strategy. They must learn on their own account how to tap the earlier sources.

They are learning; but the fate of European Jewry is sinking deep, deep into their spiritual make-up. It is coalescing with the vast trajectory of total Jewish history, past and to come, and assimilating toward its legend-symbols. There were about forty thousand Jews in the Warsaw ghetto when the revolt began; it was about forty days before the resistance was crushed and the last survivors fled in the night to join the partisans in the forests. The figures are now folklore. No doubt there will arise intelligent historians who will point out that this mystical number is pure legend-pattern: the forty days of Noah's flood, the forty days of Moses on Sinai, the three times forty years of Moses, the three times forty years of Rabbi Akiba. . . .

The hints which the Hersey narrative contains of a civilization and folk, something more than a group or community, consist of descriptions of ceremonials and transcriptions of prayers. But the descriptions and transcriptions do not fuse with each other, and a background. There is something about them, too, of a sympathetic anthropologist's report; and it would be wrong to ask for more under the circumstances. Yet at one point Mr. Hersey does, in a remarkable way, achieve the fusion. The ceremonial, in this instance, is not formally religious. In the thick of the fighting, a few day before the end, a large group assembles underground to hear Levinson give a talk on—Peretz. Levinson tells us, first:

"What I wanted to evoke in my speech, if I possibly could, was a definition of Jewishness that was at once exact and yet broad enough to cover all ages, all loci, and all conditions of Jewry: a definition embracing Herod's slaves and the great modern bankers of Paris and London, covering alike the rag-decked furrier's needle-women of our prewar Lodz and Warsaw slums and the ladies in the mink coats stepping from their limousines in pre-war Vienna and Rome, going from the *meshummed* who has explicitly forsaken the religion of his forefathers all the way to the Baal Shem Tov and the Great Maggid, taking in the fate-smeared fighters of the Warsaw ghetto and also the very rich and influential men, about whom we have heard, in America, reaching from the lowest pogrom insect to Spinoza and Disraeli and Mendelssohn and Einstein and Christ."

So it is a religious ceremonial after all; and Jewish not only because of its content, but because the Jew must study his Jewishness always, under all circumstances.

And here Hersey, by his description of the meeting, by the short essay on Peretz, by the translation of a few paragraphs, flashes a light into the interior of the structure. We are suddenly aware of the larger lines and spaces. This is not a home; this is not an apartment house; it must be some immense, ancient and famous building. But, in an astounding way, this greatest success in the narrative is its greatest failure; and we are compelled to distribute the blame chiefly between Hersey and Levinson. By Levinson I mean here the composite of the Jews whose depositions Hersey took, who instructed him in Jewish ways and meanings, and supplied him with the material on Peretz. They must be blamed because they could not instruct the sensitive bystander on the ultimate essential values, which I discuss below. Perhaps they lacked the illumination themselves. Hersey must be blamed because he might have deduced these values for himself from the material his deponents gave him. He only had to ask the leading question, the obvious question, which he and they incredibly avoid. Peretz is least to blame because he, in his time, could not have asked the question; it would never have occurred to him.

"—Then what is Jewishness?" Levinson asks in his lecture. The narrative continues:

"And then in the bunker's twilight I gave Peretz's answer:

"*Jewishness is that which makes the Jews, in eras of national independence, feel free and enables them to fashion institutions as embodiments of their national creative will. Jewishness is, in such times, joy, ecstasy, zestful living.*

"*Jewishness is that which creates, in troubled eras, institutions for defense, for prevention of danger, for protecting itself and its members. Jewishness is, in such times, a call to battle and a challenge to heroism.*

"*Jewishness is that which must, in times of dependence and weakness, retreat into its shell, conserve its resources, endure in silence, and wait for better days. Then Jewishness is hope and pain, Messianic dreams, and other-worldliness. Then it demands real sacrifice.*

"It was now almost dark in the bunker, and I went on:

"*—Nomadic blood. A wandering clan in the desert.*
"*Implanted in its blood—honesty and justice. Of these qualities does*

it fashion its God, a God who accompanies it on all its wanderings and is therefore not formed of wood or stone, a God who moves and lives.

"A sublime concept of the deity, a free and breath-taking concept of a boundless, limitless universe. . . .

"We were in blackness. We seemed, indeed, to be in a universal place, not limited by a wall, not bounded by fear and stench. I think we all felt free. I hurried to the words which Peretz himself, writing decades before we were put in our ghetto, entitled *Conclusion:*

"—Now, I am not advocating that we shut ourselves up in a spiritual ghetto. On the contrary, we should get out as Jews, with out own spiritual treasures. We should interchange, give and take, but not beg.

"Ghetto is impotence. Cultural cross-fertilization is the only possibility for human development. Humanity must be the synthesis, the sum, the quintessence of all national cultural forms and philosophies."

The question is well enough chosen. Let us forget the slur on the ghetto—this was an obsession with Peretz: and in those days one fled from the ghetto to *Germany!* The ghetto, by heaven, was not impotence; it was potency under terrible handicaps. The quotation as a whole comes well, however, after references, in the lecture, to Peretz's *Devotion unto Death, The Three Gifts,* and *The Transmigrations of a Melody*—all mystic Hasidic stories, notice, springing from the ghetto, intelligible to the ghetto, meant for it. Let us reread the quotation and ask ourselves: "Is this, indeed, what embraces 'Herod's slaves and the great modern bankers of Paris and London . . . the rag-decked furrier's needlewomen . . . the ladies in the mink coats . . . the *meshummed* . . . the Baal Shem Tov,' etc., etc?" Did they really all have some portion in this version? They, and all assimilated and apostate Jews, all exploiting Jews, including pro-Fascist and pro-Nazi Jews, all Jewish power-seekers and anti-Semitic Jews? One cannot grasp it. With the best will in the world, with the widest latitude to poetic license, it is unacceptable.

Yet there is something which does bind all Jews, as long as they are, for any reason at all, identifiable as Jews, if only by name, or by remote partial derivation. That something lies in the answer to the leading question which neither Levinson nor Hersey asks, and which Peretz could not ask because to him it was an inconceivable as well as unborn monstrosity.

The question lies open before us in Hersey's narrative: August, 1942, Levinson writes: "It appears now that the Germans intend to get rid of all of us . . . though our optimists . . . still maintain that part of the population will be spared."

Yes, it took even Levinson some time to absorb the reality. *"All of us."* But he never asks, and Hersey never asks: "Why?" *Some* of us, *most* of us—that is, God help us, intelligible. Why *"all of us"*? And not in Bialystok, Wilno, Warsaw only, but wherever we are; wherever the Nazis set conquering foot. And if not in America or Australia, only because they did not set conquering foot there. *"All of us"* means all the Jews in the world, the pietists, the saints, the bankers, the needlewomen, the apostates, the good, the bad, and those who had never had a spark of the vision in them, to whom Peretz's words were, and would always be, gibberish.

What is the meaning of this seizure, this annihilative frenzy, planetary in range, yet so particularized in choice? This is not a recognizable historic phenomenon. It is not an incursion of barbarians wild for blood and loot; nor is it the total destruction of a people for its territorial or other possessions. It is not blind hatred, either. It is a seeing, articulate and directed hatred. One might compare it with a fanatical, homicidal crusade against a world-scattered sect: except that no one is given the chance to abjure the heresy; and large numbers of the sectaries have already abjured it, or never shared it, never even heard of it. No mitigation is recognized, no possibility of redemption, conversion, partial salvation; no penitence and expiation in slavery. It is death for all, everywhere.

To have been a Jew, to be identifiably descended from Jews, is the unforgivable blasphemy. There is nothing in the human historic record to compare with the position which the Jew occupied in Nazidom. And if we refuse to recognize the implications, we simply do not understand what nazism meant.

That which binds all recognizable Jews, whether they will it or not, deserve it or not, is their inexpungeable symbolic character. They are the everlasting flesh and blood reminder. As long as Christendom chokes on Christian principles, as long as the civilized world desires war, and knows war to be wrong, it will nurture a deep, annihilative resentment of the supreme anti-war tradition which torments it, and of those who are personally connected in

any way whatsoever with the accepted source of the tradition—
the Bible. And Jews who imagine that they can escape this resentment by disowning all connection with the tradition do not understand how inexorably the resentment will reject the disassociation
—and perhaps find in it something additionally infuriating, if that
is conceivable. They have no escape except in the salvation of the
world. Their position will undergo the great change only if mankind wholly accepts or wholly forgets the anti-war tradition and its
source; and in the second case the world will destroy itself.

There is a third alternative: the world may destroy itself while
still in the convulsive confusion between paganism and Christianity. European Jewry was destroyed in an imperfect rehearsal
of the third alternative; and some day the meaning of the episode
will be understood on this level, too. Those Jews who perished in
the demonstration are—whatever the moral deterioration they underwent in the demonstration—*k'doshim,* martyrs; even if they
were reluctant or apostate witnesses. When a just government
requisitions the property of citizens, it sets a fair price on it, to be
paid whether or not the citizen agrees to the requisitioning,
whether or not he recognizes its purpose. Certainly those who try to
swindle or evade are punished; but the principle of compensation
is not affected by the views of the citizens. In this episode lives were
requisitioned by Jewish destiny, and the compensation is in principle the attribution of martyrdom. *Zichronam l'vrachah.*

RELIGIOUS TRENDS IN AMERICAN JEWRY

By WILL HERBERG

THE PAST TWENTY years have witnessed a remarkable change in the religious situation of the Jews in America. Trends that had prevailed since the earlier days of immigration and that seemed to be part of the very "nature" of American Jewry have been reversed, and new tendencies have emerged that are shaping the American-Jewish community in ways undreamed of a generation ago. There can be no doubt that we have entered a significantly new period in the history of American Jewry. It is the purpose of this paper to examine the new situation in its major aspects and to assess the significance of the new trends for Jewish life in America.

The outstanding fact defining the new situation is the reversal of the two major trends that characterized the pattern of American-Jewish life well through the 1920's—the trend toward the dissolution of Jewishness and the trend toward the abandonment of the Jewish religious tradition and of all religious concern whatsoever. Assimilation and secularism marked the pattern of American-Jewish life from the beginning of the great immigration at the end of the last century, although for decades these tendencies, particularly the former, were masked by the continuous influx of new immigrants. When large-scale immigration came to an end during the First World War, the logic of the underlying social and cultural pattern became evident: American Jews were abandoning their Jewishness and losing all interest in their religious heritage. There were not wanting those who were already sounding the knell of American Jewry and confidently relegating the synagogue, along with the church, to the limbo of obsolescent institutions.

The situation is obviously very different today. The trend toward dissolution and secularism, so marked through the twenties, has been halted, even reversed. Among all sections of American Jewry, but particularly among the younger generation, there is a movement of "return." "Return" to what? It is hard to say exactly: return to a new sense of Jewishness, return to the synagogue, return to personal religious concern. These various aspects are often fused and compounded in the movement of "return"; yet they sometimes also exhibit a certain tension, which shows that the underlying forces and motives are not of one piece but reflect different facets of the experience of the American Jew in mid-twentieth-century America.

The return to Jewishness, to self-affirmation as a Jew and to self-identification with Jewry, is perhaps the most obvious sign of the times. The young people in the colleges—who, let us remember, make up the next generation of American Jews—as well as those out of school, who are setting up homes for themselves, recognize and affirm their Jewishness in a way that would have seemed unbelievable some thirty years ago, and to a greater or less degree this is also true of other sections of American Jewry. In a manner that is difficult to define but which can hardly be denied, the events of the thirties and forties—the upsurge of anti-Semitism in Europe on the one hand and the struggle for the establishment of a "Jewish state" in Palestine, on the other—served to heighten the sense of Jewish identification and self-affirmation among American Jews, as among Jews everywhere. This underlying factor of contemporary history cannot be denied; its influence has been wide and pervasive. But it is well to recognize that, in the United States at least, it has fallen in with a significant sociological trend, which has not yet been sufficiently studied or appreciated. This trend is signalized by the emergence of the "third generation" of American Jewry. The first generation, the immigrant generation, came with their Jewishness as part of their immigrant heritage; it was embedded in their life and culture. The younger members of that generation, and of the next, revolted against this heritage, and in the process of establishing their independence and adjusting themselves to their new environment, they strove to cast off their Jewishness as part of the immigrant baggage they were so eager to abandon. They were intent—quite naturally and properly intent

—upon becoming Americans, and to become Americans they had to cease to be foreigners, which to them only too often meant to cease to be Jews. The third generation is in a very different position; it is secure in its Americanness and does not have an immigrant burden which it is anxious to throw off. It can therefore face the problem of its Jewishness in a new and creative manner, free from many of the anxieties and compulsions that afflicted the earlier generations. How it is coping with the problems of its Jewishness we are only just beginning to discern in vague outline.

But here a question arises that leads us to the heart of the matter. This phenomenon of the "third generation" is common to all of the many immigrant groups that came to these shores in the past century and that have entered into the making of the American people. But in every other case, the emergence of the "third generation"—I refer here to the sociological category; in some cases, it may actually be a fourth or a fifth generation—in every other case, I say, the emergence of the "third generation" has meant the dissolution of the ethnic-immigrant group from which it came and its absorption into the developing mainstream of American life; that is precisely how the American people and American culture have come into being. With the Jews it has been different. The first and second generations of Jews in America repeated the common immigrant pattern: immigrant foreignness followed by an anxious effort to get rid of that foreignness and become American. But the "third generation" of American Jews, instead of somehow finally getting rid of their separateness and dissolving completely into the general community, which is what all other "third generations" have done or are doing, the "third generation" of American Jews are actually returning to Jewishness. How are we to account for this strange anomaly which distinguishes Jews from all other immigrant groups that have gone into the making of America?

We can account for this anomaly only by recognizing that American Jewry cannot be understood if it is taken to be merely one of the many ethnic groups that left the old world for the new in the course of the great migrations of the past century. The Jews who came to America did of course constitute an immigrant group, but their Jewishness was apparently something that transcended their immigrant character in a way that was not true of the merely ethnic or national character of the other immigrant groups. Their Jewishness was apparently something very different from the kind of ethnic or cultural foreignness that tends to disappear with the emergence of the third generation. Had it not been something very different, we would not now be witnessing a return of the "third generation" to Jewishness.

The fact of the matter seems to be that just when the immigrant-cultural basis of American-Jewish existence was beginning to disappear with the emergence of a thoroughly American "third generation," American Jewry was becoming transformed into what sociologists call a "religious community." The religious community has, in fact, become the primary context of social location in contemporary American life. When an American asks of a new family in town, "What does he do?" he means the occupation or profession of the head of the family; when he asks, "What are they?" he means to what religious community do they belong— Protestant, Catholic, or Jewish. A century ago, the question, "What are they?" would have been answered in terms of immigrant-ethnic origin, and today it is still answered in some such terms for Negroes as well as for Americans of Oriental or recent Latin-American origin. But increasingly, the great mass of Americans understand themselves and their place in America society in terms of the religious community with which they are identified. And "religious community" in this usage refers not so much to the particular denomination, of which there are scores in this country, but to the three great divisions, Catholics, Protestants, and Jews. America is the land of the "triple melting pot," for it is within these three religious communities that the process of ethnic and cultural integration so characteristic of American life takes place.

We can restate all this by saying that while the unity of American life is indeed a unity in multiplicity, the pluralism that this implies is of a very special kind. America recognizes no permanent national or cultural minorities; what Europe knows under this head are in this country regarded as "foreign language" or "foreign culture" groups, whose separateness is merely temporary, the consequence of recent immigration, destined to be overcome with increasing integration into American life. America does indeed know and acknowledge the separateness of so-called minority "races," but such separateness has always involved some degree of segregation and consequent relegation to an inferior status in the social hierarchy. The only kind of separateness or diversity that America recognizes as permanent and yet also as involving no status of inferiority is the diversity or separateness of religious communities. In short, while America knows no national or cultural minorities except as temporary, transitional phenomena, it does know a free variety and plurality of religions, and it is as a member of a religious group that the great mass of Americans understand the status of the Jew in this country and that the American Jew understands himself. This is particularly true of the younger generation of Jews. When they are moved to affirm their Jewishness, and they must do so if only to identify themselves to themselves and to others, they can conceive of no way of doing so except in religious terms. The many substitutes for Jewish religious identification, which were open to earlier generations, are no longer viable to them. It is simply a fact that the average American Jew—I mean the Jew who is acculturated to America—if he thinks of himself as a Jew at all, tends almost automatically to think of himself as belonging to a religious community, even if he himself does not have personal faith. In the Vilna of the 1920's, it was possible for a militantly anti-religious Jewish doctor to assert himself as a Jew by sending his children to a secular Yiddish school, and for a time this pattern was familiar among Jewish immigrants in this country. For some time, too, one could "be a Jew" simply by being a Zionist or by identifying oneself with some Jewish philanthropic cause. All this is becoming increasingly untenable. Today, if the American Jew is to regard himself as a Jew, and if he is to be so regarded by his non-Jewish neighbors and friends, some religious association, however vague, is necessary. The only way in which the Jew can integrate himself into American society is in terms of a religious community.

That is one reason why the "return" to Jewishness of which I have spoken has also meant a return to the synagogue. It is beyond dispute that synagogue construction, synagogue membership, and even synagogue attendance are growing at an unprecedented rate in this country. This is part of a larger movement characterizing the entire American people today, for the growth of religious bodies and the increase in religious affiliation on the part of the American people is one of the most striking facts about the present situation in the United States. In 1900, 36 per cent of the American people were reported as religiously affiliated; by 1930, the figure had risen to 47 per cent; and by 1950, to 57 per cent. In the quarter of a century from 1926 to 1950, the population of the United States rose 28.6 per cent; church membership, however, jumped nearly 60 per cent. There are no comparable figures applying specifically to the Jews, but all evidence goes to show that the movement of American Jews into the synagogue in recent years has been at least as sweeping and as vigorous as the movement of Americans generally into the church. Many of the older people, who had once broken away and had never thought of the possibility of returning are back again, but it is primarily the trend of the younger generation that is decisive. For them, the "return" to Jewishness which we are witnessing is in great measure a return to the synagogue, for not only is the synagogue the one enduring and representative Jewish institution; not only is it the unique embodiment through the ages of Jewish spirituality: it is also the characteristically American vehicle of Jewish self-identification. When a young Jewish couple in New York get married and move out to Westchester or Long Island, the first thing they do is to join the synagogue; quite naturally—for how else are they to express and signalize their Jewishness? The revival of the synagogue in the past fifteen years would have stunned the social prognosticators of a generation ago, who saw in it a culturally moribund institution as well as a remnant of immigrant foreignness. It has turned out to be neither: it has become a thoroughly American institution whose growth is reflecting the current "return" to religion in America.

It is worth noting that the movement back to religion has involved a considerable number of old-line secularist Jews. Indeed, militant secularism in the sense of anti-religion is almost entirely gone; today's secularists are no longer so sure they possess the key to the riddle of the universe, nor are they so certain that religion is the source of all evil and the primary obstacle to man's advancement. Even in Jewish labor circles, once the stronghold of radical anti-religion, there is taking place a notable change of heart, reflecting not only the spirit of the times, but also the new status of labor in the American-Jewish community. In all sections of American Jewry, there are those who, without seriously modifying their own religious indifference, have come to adopt what may be called a pro-religious attitude because they recognize that religion possesses a strong "survivalist" potential. I recall the words of a distinguish Jewish scholar of pronounced secularist views: "Jewish religion [he maintained] has proved itself the most stormproof aspect of Jewish life. It is the only force that can preserve the Jews as a group, in America at least." Such people are often ready to associate themselves with the synagogue, give their children a "Jewish education," perhaps even adopt certain of the traditional ritual observances in the home, without thereby implying any religious commitment. With some, as with the scholar I have mentioned, this attitude is a conscious and well-articulated ideology; for the most part, however, it is little more than a vague sentiment, though surely an influential one. In either case, it finds a strong appeal in Reconstructionism, with its combination of a secularist humanistic philosophy in matters of belief and an emphasis on external forms for the sake of "survival" in matters of observance.

But this rather sophisticated pro-religionism without religion is by no means characteristic of all those who are today turning to the synagogue. On the contrary, by and large, those who are "returning" feel themselves sincerely religious, though they are not oblivious to the utility of the synagogue and its educational institutions in keeping their children Jewish. Their religion, however, is generally very far, at least in content, from the faith embodied in Jewish religious tradition. In fact, it often consists of little more than "belief in God," a high regard for Jewish moral teachings, and a feeling that attending synagogue occasionally, giving one's children a "Jewish education," and some ritual observances are necessary for Jewishness. An increasing proportion of younger Jews, it is true, especially those in the colleges, are beginning to look for something more authentically religious and more authentically Jewish; about them I will have something to say in a little while. But by and large, the religion of the average American Jew is, as I have described it, a "liberal Judaism" not very far removed from the "liberal Protestantism" of the church around the corner. This is about equally true of the American Orthodox and Conservative groups as of the Reform group, despite important secondary differences among them. Nothing is perhaps more American than this kind of religion, sincere but without content.

And yet one should not leave it on this note. The superficiality of religious content may not be a fair measure of the depth and reality of the religious concern. It is the concern that is crucial, for it is tht concern that opens the heart to God. And I think it can be said that for all the shallowness that characterizes so much of contemporary American Judaism, the concern is there to an increasing degree, particularly among the younger generation of American Jews.

Let me, before carrying the argument off in another direction, summarize what I have so far said about the present religious situation in American Jewry. Largely in response to basic influences affecting the entire body of the American people, American Jewry is returning to a renewed sense of its Jewishness, to a renewed affiliation with the synagogue, and to a renewed awareness of religion. This is a reversal of trend of really historical significance. Within this general movement, there is under way another movement, if movement it can be called—a new and growing concern with religion as personal faith and commitment. In such matters, it is difficult to supply "objective" documentation, but I feel that I can with some confidence draw upon my own experience as well as upon the conclusions of other observers. During the past seven years, I have lectured at scores of colleges and universities in all parts of the country, usually in interdepartmental programs that have brought me in touch with either the entire academic community or else a sizable section of it. In the course of these campus programs, I must have had discussions with thousands of Jewish students, in classes, seminars, and lectures, as well as in personal conferences and bull sessions. And, of course, these days, discussions, no matter how they begin, always end up with religion. I think I can say without qualification that interest in, and concern with, religion as manifested by the present student generation, Jewish and non-Jewish alike, is something really extraordinary, and is constantly growing. I have no hesitation whatever in confirming the testimony of Professor Stuart Hughes of Harvard, who states with some surprise: "The avant-garde [of students] is becoming old-fashioned; religion is now the latest thing" (*Saturday Review*, March 3, 1951). It is to this "avant-garde" that we now turn.

The new concern with religion as personal faith is much harder to define or describe than the larger movement of return to the synagogue of which it is part; it is, however, just as real, and in the last analysis may prove to be even more important. In varying degrees, this new concern is to be found among all sections of American Jewry, but, as I have just indicated, it is most pronounced and perhaps most vital among the younger people, particularly those in the colleges, for it is the younger people who are most open to new influences and most accessible to rapid shifts in the intellectual and spiritual climate. Within the framework of the social and ideological reorientation of American-Jewish life I have described, there is undoubtedly taking place among many of the "returning" generation a real, though by no means clearly defined, shift in fundamental outlook, a change of "mind" and "heart" that sometimes means a radical restructuring of existence. Unsympathetic observers may sometimes find it difficult to detect the conventional marks of religion in this new spirituality, but that does not change the fact that it is truly and profoundly religious, perhaps closer to the enduring tradition of faith than the "liberalized," "modernized," denatured versions of religion that have conventional standing. It is in a basic sense a reflection of the new world that has suddenly emerged in the course of the past generation, a world of total insecurity, a world in which the easy hopes and reliances of earlier decades seem grotesquely unreal and in which some deeper foundation of existence must be found if life is to be livable at all. Professor H. Richard Niebuhr of Yale has well indicated the nature, as well as some of the deeper sources, of the new spirituality in a study of what he calls "Our Conservative Youth" (*Seventy-Five*, anniversary publication of the *Yale Daily News*, 1953, p. 90).

Present-day youth [he writes] has to rest its large-scale security on deeper foundations, and this is probably the source of its religious interest. Some of it is finding no greater security than what an Epicurean philosophy of life affords; but much of it is getting down to the bedrock and finding a foundation on which life can rest unmoved, if not unshaken, in stormy times. There is a venturesomeness in this quest, but it is a hidden thing. . . .

The best of American-Jewish youth is also engaged in this quest, but because it is a "hidden thing" it is often overlooked by the outsider. Yet it is of decisive importance, for it is that which gives the "returning" generation its characteristic outlook and temper.

How shall we define this outlook and temper? It is difficult to give any clear account of it because it varies so widely in its personal expression, and in the nature of the case, it can have no official formulation. But I think the following characterization is fairly borne out by the facts, at least as I have come upon them in recent years.

It seems to me that the first, and perhaps basic, aspect of the outlook of the "returning" generation is a thirst for the "metaphysical" that marks it off distinctly from its immediate predecessors. There is wide dissatisfaction with the naturalistic and humanistic philosophies that only yesterday were the mark of the "modern" mind; there is a demand for something deeper, for a philosophy that takes account of the full dimensions of human existence. There is a new feeling for depth and a new sense of realism. The old-fashioned "liberalism," that saw only the surface of things and was therefore totally unprepared for Hitler or Stalin seems quite unintelligible to many of the younger generation, who can hardly fail to be aware of the spiritual "underworld" lurking in the depths. The "returning" generation is hard-boiled and worldly wise; yet for all its realism, perhaps precisely because of that realism, it reveals an inwardness that stands in striking contrast to the busy activism of the college generations of the thirties and early forties. For this reason, some observers have accused it of apathy, inertia, and unconcern with the issues of the day, but this indictment, though in part perhaps well-founded, overlooks the possibility that the apparent inertia on the surface may, as Richard Niebuhr suggests, hide a venturesomeness and activity in essence much more serious than the externalism of other times. The turn to inwardness reflects a deep need for personal appropriation, and it often expresses itself in a marked distrust of conventional standards and beliefs, in an almost biological allergy to the pat, prefabricated catchwords that are so frequently made to do service as answers to the problems of life. To some people, this attitude may seem to verge on utter skepticism and disbelief, but in this attitude there is also a readiness to listen, an openness to the new, that makes this generation (in Ludwig Lewisohn's words) so "accessible to good." There is above all a genuine desire to recapture, or perhaps better, to recreate for oneself, the substance of Jewishness. As a consequence, there results that surprising interest in, and regard for, tradition that distinguishes this otherwise skeptical generation. "A generation without creeds and Scriptures," notes H. Richard Niebuhr, "has none to reject, but looks with respect on historic affirmations and revelations, orients itself toward them, and seeks to understand their meaning and power. . . . Youth is seeking, fumblingly often, to reclaim the ancestral ground on which previous generations were nurtured, but which they abandoned."

I am well aware that this description is too schematic to be accurate; it applies fully only to the most advanced of the "returning" generation, and even to them only in a general way. And yet it has its truth, and that truth seems to me important. For it is a fact that the generation now in college or recently out of it are beginning to think and feel and be concerned religiously in a way that is startlingly new, yet also everlastingly old. The newness is obvious, often too obvious; but the other side should be emphasized as well. For it is a paradox, yet also a truism, that the thoroughly American, modern "returning" generation often feels itself closer spiritually to its grandparents than to its parents. More than once, I've heard a young man or woman on some college campus tell me in a puzzled way, "You know, I'm really beginning to understand my grandfather; I'm beginning to understand how he feels about things, especially about religion." And I shall never forget the dedication which a young man from New York in a select New England college inscribed on his honor thesis: "To my grandfather, who had the courage to bear witness to the living God in a new world." Here again, but in a much deeper sense, the "third generation" is returning to the first.

This new concern with Jewishness and Jewish faith leads the "returning" generation to the synagogue, and the statistics of institutional affiliation and membership bear witness to this "return." They enter the synagogue with eager anticipation, especially if it is for the first time; what they find there is often such as to disconcert and dishearten them in their search for a deeper understanding of their Jewish existence.

I do not want to be unfair to the present-day American synagogue. Under pressure of its environment, it is called upon to perform a thousand and one tasks of which the old-time synagogue knew nothing, and it does most of them well; but in the one task of providing a significant and creative environment for the "returning" generation, it is failing most deplorably. It may plausibly be argued that the expectations of the younger people are perverse and unrealistic and that no synagogue can afford to be diverted from its more important purposes in order to meet them. But it remains a fact that only too frequently the first contact with the synagogue since childhood on the part of these "returning" young men and women is a deeply disillusioning experience which many of them never really get over. Whether they are married couples making their first uncertain venture in synagogue affiliation, or students coming home with vague anticipations, their disappointment is often quite profound. This may come as a shock to many who see people attend services and take their part in various synagogue activities, but one should not be misled by surface appearances. Of course, the "returning" young people, or at least most of them, sooner or later get accustomed to the routine of synagogue life, and some of them even get to like it, but the initial ardency is quenched, the eager anticipation repressed, and whatever remains of the original venture in faith is largely dissociated from the synagogue and its activities and driven to assume what are often questionable forms.

What is wrong with the contemporary synagogue from the point of view of the "returning" generation? To put the whole case in a nutshell, it is the essential secularism, the externalism, and the ingrained mediocrity of the contemporary synagogue, Orthodox, Conservative, and Reform alike, that render it so inadequate in meeting the needs of those who come to it with high, though often vague and ill-defined, anticipations. What is the religion to be found in the present-day American synagogue? The religion of the present-day American synagogue is not one but many. It may be a religion of "Jewish values," and that means either ethical culture plus social service or an idealized version of ritual observance. Or it may be a religion of Jewish scholarship, in which acquaintance with texts becomes the vehicle of Jewish identification. It may be a religion of Zionist nationalism or a religion of Jewish folk-culture; a religion of "religious experience," cultivating inspiration and uplift, or a religion of nostalgic sentimentality, feeding on "quaint" little Hasidic tales. Or it may be all of these combined in varying measure. But whichever or whatever it may be, it is equally remote from the kind of faith the "returning" generation is seeking, a faith that will yield some glimpse of the meaning of life in its ultimate terms and some way of living on the level of really significant existence. In a poignant statement (*Congress Weekly*, April 9, 1951), Leslie Fiedler expressed the plight of the "returning" Jewish intellectual confronted with the realities of contemporary synagogue Judaism.

In the Orthodox *shuls* [Mr. Fiedler wrote], the Hasidic fire, the old unity of devotion, are moribund beneath an emphasis on *kashrut* and the endless *pilpul*, long since turned into a substitute for any moving faith. In the Reform temples, the glib young rabbi, with his tags from Freud, his sociological jargon, speaks his conviction that God is a "cosmological blur." Like the more debased Protestant churches, the temples have tended to substitute "social service" for religion. . . . These conditions do not prevail universally, of course, but in general, American Judaism has made everything its center but God: amateur psychoanalysis, collecting money for the Jewish Appeal, hating all Germans, worshiping force, bowing down before a revived nineteenth-century nationalism. . . .

What Mr. Fiedler expresses here so vigorously, many young men and women have tried to communicate to me, stumblingly and inarticulately, perhaps, but with quite as much urgency. The language and ideas of the present-day American synagogue strike the intelligent young people of the "returning" generation as something strangely obsolete and utterly remote from the real problems of life. The spiritual atmosphere of the present-day American synagogue proves even more perplexing. I recall a medical student, with a deep religious concern, who had some interesting things to say about the liturgy and form of service of the synagogue he occasionally attended. He found it all very unsatisfactory, primarily because it was not (as he thought it should be) an act of corporate worship in which all are involved, but rather a religious performance put on by the rabbi and *hazan* and "appreciated" or "enjoyed" by the congregation as audience. Besides, he found that the rabbi "talked too much"; and, in fact, the rabbi was always talking, introducing this and explaining that, turning the entire service into a sort of inspirational adult education program. As a result, this young man, and some other young people I know, have more than once decided that they would go to some old-style Orthodox synagogue where, as they put it, "there is less talking and more praying." But of course, in most cases, that won't work either; the cultural barriers are too great, not to speak of their inadequate knowledge of the Hebrew liturgy. So there seems to be no direction in which they can turn to find the "religious substance" they are seeking.

This "religious substance" is but rarely to be found in the present-day American synagogue; the present-day American synagogue is basically an extrovert institution, caught up in an endless round of institutional externalities. It is this externalism that the young people who come in search of faith find it hard to take. Perhaps, as I have suggested, the present generation is reacting excessively against the mindless activism of their predecessors. Perhaps; but the fact remains that the present generation is distinctly organization-shy; it is suspicious of "movements" and cannot work up any real enthusiasm for busy programs and bustling activities. But the present-day American synagogue is almost always a big institution that lives by programs and projects and campaigns, and the present-day American rabbi is eminently organization-conscious. The young man or woman who comes to the synagogue with grandiose, perhaps overly romantic notions of a House of Prayer and a House of Study actually finds a big community center in which the synagogue is almost lost. The shock is sometimes one that leaves a deep and lasting imprint.

There is something in the cultural atmosphere of the present-day American synagogue that has a depressing effect on many of the "returning" generation. I have in mind a certain commonplaceness of thought and sentiment, a certain self-satisfied mediocrity, a certain slackness of spiritual tone and stodginess of feeling that cannot but embarrass young people who come to the synagogue with the passion of faith or with the hope of finding it. What they have heard and read, what they have come to feel, has led them to believe that authentic religion may be anything in the world, but it cannot be dull or mediocre. The very stirrings that brought them to the point of "return" render them particularly sensitive, perhaps unduly so, to the dull, philistine atmosphere that so often pervades the synagogue and renders suspect every sign of intellectual or spiritual ferment. The rabbi, especially if he is a younger man, may attempt to resist the wave of mediocrity, but he too is usually engulfed in it along with the others.

What happens to the "returning" generation when it comes to the synagogue and finds it as I have described? It is hard to say exactly because the development is still too new to draw conclusions. But by and large I should say that however disappointed in their expectations, most of them settle down to a kind of passive synagogue connection, which they feel necessary to satisfy their own need for "belonging" as well as to provide their children with a "Jewish education." As time goes on, many of them, altogether too many unfortunately, become routinized and fall in with the conventional mediocrity of the environment, though generally something of the old longing still remains. At the other extreme are those who never become reconciled, whose disillusionment leads to conscious alienation from the synagogue, even to a certain aversion to it. But it is not a total alienation, for it does not lead to active hostility, least of all to anti-religion. What it leads to is a kind of resentfully private "inner religion" which on occasion takes on extravagant forms, uncontrolled as it is by the regulative forces of tradition and community experience. It is not a healthy development, but sometimes it is perhaps the only way out.

There are, of course, mitigating influences. In the first place, the description I have given of the present-day American synagogue, if taken literally, is altogether too sweeping. There are synagogues in which sensitive young people can find themselves at home and even be moved to an interest in institutional affairs. There are rabbis—I know some of them myself—who show a real understanding of, and sympathy with, the "returning" generation and are able to speak to them in their own terms. There is the widely influential Hillel organization on the campuses, which has shown a remarkable sensitivity to the religious needs and capacities of the Jewish student. And there are the growing intellectual resources at the disposal of the serious-minded American Jew. The writings of Martin Buber are now widely available, and something of Franz Rosenzweig has recently become accessible. There is also the new religious thinking in America, the writings of A. J. Heschel, Emil Fackenheim, and others, as well as a growing accumulation of translations of basic texts. And the writings of outstanding Christian thinkers of the post-"liberal" school—the two Niebuhrs, Tillich, Kierkegaard—can prove useful in developing an intellectual armature of faith. In any case, the "returning" young Jew need not feel alone even when he can find no real place for himself in the synagogue he has joined. Of course, he will be rebuked for succumbing to "mysticism" and "existentialism," the current bogeymen of the philistines. But he need not mind that, for he can see himself part of a new spiritual movement with wide perspectives, corresponding to the deeper realities of human existence and the real needs of the time. In this conviction, he can keep alive the stirrings of faith and thought, the new sense of his Jewishness, that brought him to the point of "return."

There is indeed, I seem to feel, a new type of Jew emerging in America, a Jew to whom the beliefs and traditions of Judaism are not merely inherited routine, but something new, personal, and exciting. To this type of Jew—and he is represented very considerably in the "returning" generation—the old shibboleths and institutional loyalties, the old catchwords and platitudes, have little meaning. He is looking for something deeper and more basic. What he is looking for, I am convinced, can be found in the authentic tradition of Jewish faith. There is only one question: Is the present-day American synagogue in the position to communicate that tradition to him in a way that he can understand and appropriate? Can the present-day American synagogue provide him with a spiritual home adequate to his needs and, in a measure at least, to his expectations? These questions cannot be answered with any assurance at the present time, but upon the answer will depend a good deal of the future of Judaism in America.

There is always something rash and presumptuous in speaking about the "religious situation." The religious situation is indeed, in one sense, a part of the total social and cultural situation, and therefore subject to human scrutiny and analysis. But in another sense, it is something that transcends the social and cultural framework in which it is embedded and takes on a dimension that relates it to the divine-human encounter to which it refers. Analysis, forecasts, and programs become dubious, if not altogether irrelevant, for man's faith in response to God's call is not something that can be charted or reduced to plan. When we deal with the religious situation, we are brought up short before the final mystery in a way that is even more immediate than in the ordinary affairs of life. In the end, we know so little, and hope and trust for so much. What I have said about contemporary religious trends in American Jewry must be taken in this spirit and within these limitations. New forces are at work among American Jews, revealing new possibilities of religious life and thought. But we must not fall into the delusion that we have these forces at our disposal and these developments under our control. They remain hidden in the unfathomable reaches of divine providence and human action. We discern, or think we discern, what is happening, but it is not in what we discern that our confidence can be placed. It is rather in the knowledge that God has His purpose with the world and that shall prevail, and in the conviction that in the fulfilment of that purpose, Jewry, including American Jewry, has its part to play. Just what that part is, or will turn out to be in our time, we do not know, but we do know that we have a function to fulfil, in this time as in any other. In this assurance, we can face the present without illusions and the future without fear or misgiving. In this assurance, too, we may permit ourselves to see in the contemporary religious situation signs of promise opening new perspectives of Jewish faith and Jewish existence in America.

BUILDING OUR FUTURE IN AMERICA

By JACOB B. AGUS

CAN IT BE doubted that, in the past generation, the collective energy of American Jewry was centered in the vision of itself as simply an embattled minority? Our religious and cultural characteristics receded into the background. To be sure, not one of our religious spokesmen would have defined the Jewish group thus baldly, without qualification, as just a minority, like other minorities within the American people, struggling for sheer survival. On the conscious level of ideas, the old ideologies, together with some new ones, provided the shifting official façade for the conflicting doctrines and interpretations of "Jewish life." But none of the ideological trends within Judaism could possibly command the depth of emotion that attached to the character and problems of Jewry as a whole. For the most part the conscious "Jewish community" thought of itself as an encircled and besieged minority, battling for sheer existence against the pervasive and hostile power of the majority population.

Among the masses of immigrants the conception of a minority was modeled chiefly after the pattern of the minority-nationalities of Europe, that staged so remarkable a renaissance in the first two decades of the twentieth century, particularly as a result of the Treaty of Versailles. It was through the insistence of the American Jewish Congress, which was brought into being for the purpose of articulating the opinion of the Jewish masses, that the Jewish representatives to the Versailles Conference—including, be it remembered, the leaders of the American Jewish Committee—pressed for the status of a minority-nationality for the Jews of Central Europe.

Nor was the category of a minority-nationality given up even when it became apparent that, on the American scene, immigrant nationalities slowly merge into the general population, with the residual loyalties fading out of sight in two or three generations. The peculiar and complex character of the Jewish heritage made possible a variety of different and even conflicting comparisons. Thus, we were a minority like the Swedes of Minnesota or the Dutch of Pennsylvania, preserving our quaint customs; or like the Irish, fighting for our homeland against the British from the security of the American base; or like the Catholics, cherishing an all-embracing faith that shaded off by degrees into a variety of cultural areas; or we were like the Negroes, scorned as men of lesser breed. But the adjectival modification was not as important as the substantive concept. The basic, ineluctable fact of our Jewish being was our status as a marked and numerically inferior group. Thus it was generally held. Hence our susceptibility to the bias and hostility of the majority population, the need of our being permanently mobilized to fight against discrimination, and the obvious logic of joining other "minorities" in the battle for fairness and equality.

Two factors combined to produce this collective fixation of the past generation, extending into the present. First, the insidious malice of anti-Semitism attained overwhelming proportions in our day, threatening the utter annihilation of world Jewry, so that all motives other than sheer survival were rendered mainly academic and relatively unimportant. Second, the force of religious conviction was weakened by a tidal wave of skepticism and indifference to the point where the "eternal verities" of the Jewish faith no longer seemed worth living for. With the inner content of Judaism reduced to the vanishing point, and the need of battling for sheer physical survival becoming paramount, American Jewry settled down to live and work with the vision of itself as a "minority," expecting prejudice as a matter of course, and fighting against it doggedly, in routine fashion, virtually as the "way of life" of our collective existence.

It was not in financial terms alone that the two fundamental motivations of Jewish collective activity were Zionism and Antidefamation. These two fields provided psychical outlets for the fevered emotions of "Jewish life," serving to compensate for the distressing consciousness of minority existence. In the varied activities of Anti-defamation, Jews articulated their frustration and indignation, erecting and ceaselessly mending the protective walls of the inner ghetto, even as they fended the attacks of bigots and fanatics. Through the far-flung efforts of Zionism, the self-assertive instincts of our people were channeled, the sense of oneness of "Jewish fate" was cultivated, bonds were forged with the glory of the past and the promise of the future. While expression was thus afforded to humanitarian activity within the Jewish community, scope was given as well to feelings of despair and cynicism, of resentment and militancy toward the non-Jewish world in the Diaspora and in Zion itself. The practical activities in both domains may or may not have been justified in all instances. Quite apart, however, from any pragmatic or utilitarian considerations, those activities functioned as mass-media for the release of psychical energy, certainly as expressions of the poignant pathos of "Jewishness," possibly also as religious rites—rites reflecting the attitude of the Jew toward his own destiny in particular and toward human life in general.

For many Jewish men and women, thus, either Zionist work or Anti-defamation work, or both, have constituted the sum and substance of Judaism. The entire burden of their self-awareness as Jews has revolved around the painful focus of a trapped and hapless minority. How unrealistic, then, how superficial it is for those of us who urge the diminution, rationalization and even partial liquidation of the Zionist Organization and the "defense agencies," not to realize that their activities have become psychical necessities —sacred rites, as it were—for their innumerable votaries and followers.

In the field of Jewish education, too, the dominant motivation in the past generation has been the need of building up the "defense-mechanism" of our young, As a minority—it is still being contended—we must provide our young with the spiritual equivalent of an all-covering coat of mail, for protection against the slings of hate and the arrows of malice that are certain to be hurled at them. A study of the texts in our Hebrew and religious schools, and of the aids provided by the Bureaus of Jewish Education, reveals a conspicuous shyness in religious affirmations and a loud emphasis on the "armor theory," in all its variations. There are plenty of other evidences. That a world assembly of top-level Hebrew educators in Jerusalem should seriously debate whether the purpose of Jewish education was *solely* to prepare the young for emigration to Israel, or whether that purpose was only its *major concern,* is itself proof of the extent to which the keen awareness of minority-status had become the most potent factor in Jewish consciousness.

The echoes of this awareness in the literature of the past two decades are too various and wide-ranging to describe here. It is enough to mention the works of Franz Kafka, for whom the Jewish sense of insecurity has become transmuted into a universal judgment concerning the "existential" tragedy of the human race. Who can read *The Castle,* in which the tragic hero is a man without home and status and the outcasts are those who rejected the love of the Master when it was offered, and fail to see the travail of mankind reflected through the prism of Jewish experience? In Jo Sinclair's portrayal, in *Wasteland,* of the young Jew who is cured of self-hatred by psychoanalysis, religious convictions play no role at all: the "hero" is perplexed by the meaning of Jewish identification, his spirit tossed about in stormy upheaval from the crest of self-acceptance to the trough of self-rejection.

Perhaps the keenest expression of this mood is to be found in Norman Katkov's *Eagle at My Eyes,* precisely because it is more a stirring social document than a literary work. Dealing with the question of intermarriage, it ignores religious considerations, makes light of all the positive elements in the Jewish heritage, and reveals the painful reality of Jewish consciousness in all its stark horror when it is reduced to the sheer awareness of belonging to a hunted pack, pursued by implacable and crafty foes, neither expecting nor giving quarter. Even so coarse a work of genius as James Jones's *From Here to Eternity* captures the essence of its one Jewish character in a bullying aggressiveness that is intended to cover up the agonizing sense of being "different" and "set apart."

The point to remember about all these floating straws in the stormy intellectual sea is the almost complete disappearance of the voice of faith or idealism from the consciousness of so many Jews, leaving only the dregs of minority-feeling—messy, unsightly, insipid.

When your finger is caught in the door, remarked Bialik, you forget about all your other organs and interests, and your whole life seems to be concentrated in the finger. The Hitlerite challenge to our very existence made us all overly and painfully conscious of our numerical weakness and our helplessness—to the sad detriment of the healthy, positive factors in our spiritual makeup. Now that the finger is released from the door—at any rate in Western countries—we must not permit the impetus of the immediate past to prevent us from taking a fresh look at ourselves, so that we may see our life whole and see it truly.

Does the term "minority," then, do justice to the character of our Jewish being in America?

The other minorities with which we automatically classify ourselves are either ethnic groups or religious alignments. But we are both of these *plus—plus* an indeterminate factor that makes our situation quite unique. Alike in the consciousness of most Jews and in the lingering tradition of most of the Christian population there is an undeniable feeling that the gulf between Jew and Gentile is somehow deeper and more significant than the national dividing lines in the European family or the denomination differences within the same nation. This felt difference is not a matter of race, as is still sometimes supposed, erroneously; for, as has been demonstrated times without number, the Jewish people of Europe and America are biologically of much the same racial strain as the rest of the population. Rather, it is in the dichotomy of *religious traditions* that this profound sense of difference lingers—a dichotomy which persists even when the dogmatic substructures of the two traditions crumble and merge into the general background of Western culture.

In fact, we are a special kind of minority, not to be classified with either the Catholics or the Negroes. While our existence is dependent mostly on our conscious and collective "will to live," there is also a large measure of compulsion in our being. This union of the "must" and the "will," the fate and the faith, seems as ultimate in the long run as the mystery of Providence in the chaotic confusion of human affairs. One thing is certain. If we continue to operate on the basis of an ordinary "minority concept," we undermine the "will to live," the positive spiritual force, of our people. The natural course of a merely physical minority is progressive disappearance. At the same time, however, the compulsive factors in our Jewish being render "the will to die" illusory and self-defeating.

Only the intellectual and moral underworld, and those among us who have lost the last traces of faith, can subscribe to a designation that reflects merely the sheer compulsiveness of our existence. Yet the conception of a religious community, for all its aptness, still fails to capture the full truth of the situation of the Jewish group within the American nation as a whole. We cannot escape the fact that we constitute a minority set off by something deeper than the grooves of purely denominational differences.

What, then, shall we make of our awareness of minority-existence?

Upon the answer to this question may well depend the continued allegiance of our young intellectuals. For to most of the enlightened, to most liberals, the ceremonies and rites of different faiths constitute just so many varied expressions of the one basic truth (if they believe in religious truth at all). What is to prevent a light-hearted change of the language of piety, in the interest of convenience and integration, even as we normally exchange an inherited tongue for the language of the majority? Only the realization that the Jewish tradition, which characterizes our being, possesses unique and non-expendable values, not only for ourselves but for the American nation as a whole. Ours is more than a creed, more than a so-called "way of life," more even than the ethnic-cultural ties of a people. *We are the living bearers of a tradition that both supplements and corrects the onesidedness of the Christian tradition.*

By the attractions of the merely psychical virtues of piety we can lose as many of our searching souls as we might gain, unless the specific quality of Jewish piety is understood and appreciated.

In our tradition it is as a consecrated people that we emerged upon the stage of history—"a people of priests and a holy nation." We were to be, unto all the nations of the world, prophets and priests, perhaps also "the suffering servants" in behalf of God and man. This stirring conception was a prophetic development and interpretation of the earlier doctrine of the "Chosen People": that doctrine insisted that our ancestors were selected for their own sake, not as instruments for the salvation of mankind. "The Lord did not set His love upon you, nor choose you, because you were

272

more in number than any people; for ye were the fewest of all people. But because the Lord loved you, and because He would keep the oath which He had sworn unto your fathers. . . ." (*Deuteronomy* VII:7, 8) Love is selective, arbitrary, evoked only by the sheer being of the beloved, not by any act of hers. But the prophets transmuted this doctrine of an inscrutable divine fiat into a magnificent dedication to the enlightenment and salvation of all the nations of the earth.

Through all the long tribulant centuries of the pre-modern era the Jewish people thought of themselves as the custodians of truth and salvation, their own tragedy serving only to accentuate the arduousness and supreme importance of their divinely appointed task. We are even as the seed rotting in the ground, said Judah Halevi; the proud branches waving in the sun are powerful domains of Christianity and Islam; but when the fruit on those branches ripen in the end of time, it is we who shall reappear as the seed in the core of the ripe fruit. The biblical designation of Israel as "my eldest son," and the talmudic reference to "the sons of kings," corresponded to the mass-feeling of our people, even in periods of darkest persecution. Said the Chief Rabbi of Vienna in the seventeenth century, Yom-Tov Lipman Heller, when the threat of expulsion was held over the hapless community he headed: "A king had two brothers. The beloved elder brother and true heir was banished from his father's good graces for his sins. Now the younger brother sits proudly at the table, while the elder one gathers the crumbs. If the younger brother in his arrogance take the crumbs away from the elder, would not the father resent this effrontery and punish the younger brother still more severely than ever the elder was chastised? We, the people of Israel, are the older brothers. Beware, lest you take even the crumbs from us." (*Megilath Aivoh*) Thus, proudly, did the rabbis of old carry on the work of "Anti-defamation," conscious as they were of being "the elder brother," to whom belonged the Promise and through whom was to come the Redemption.

With the advent of the Age of Reason and the revolutionary upheaval of Emancipation, only the dwindling remnant of naïve Orthodoxy was able to hold on to the belief that, as a people, we had been chosen and consecrated and charged with the task of treasuring "Torah and Mitzvot." Yet, after a brief period of hesitation and confusion, the ancient doctrine reappeared in modern garb, with its vital and sustaining power hardly impaired. In the proud ideology of Classical Reform, the Jews were declared to be a Specially Endowed People, gifted with the genius for religion. As the ancient Greeks had a genius for beauty and systematic reasoning, and the ancient Romans a native bent for law and organization, so the Jews—according to the faith of Classical Reform—were historically the people of pure ethical monotheism. Today the Classical Reformers continue to stand for a healthy and rational, humanist and liberal, life-centered and life-affirming type of piety, in conscious opposition to the various popular distortions of the meaning of faith.

Though the Reform doctrine of a "Jewish mission" to the nations was the favorite target of contemptuous sarcasm on the part of Zionists, the ideology of Cultural Zionism retained the principle of the Jewish people as a Specially Endowed Nation. To Ahad Ha-am the unique genius of Israel consisted not in its religious faith but rather in its profoundly ethical bent. The ideas of Judaism, he held, are not of decisive importance, since ideas quickly become the property of the entire educated world. To survive, or at all events to live worthily, the Jewish people must find the way of re-establishing itself as a healthy nation, on its own land, where it might evolve new ideals and original forms of living. It is the recreation of the national base in the ancient homeland that will make possible the rebirth of the native "genius" of Israel. So ran the argument. As for Jewish life in the Diaspora, we may hope to become again a Specially Endowed Minority—through our very labors for the reconstitution of the Jewish homeland and through the spiritual production of a renascent Israel entering into the stream of universal civilization.

These two conceptions still linger in the varying ideological trends within American Judaism today. But if we now seek to activate the community as a whole we cannot take, as its philosophical cornerstone, either the claim of a divine act of consecration in the dawn of history or the equally dogmatic assertion of a unique "genius" in the domain of the spirit. Today these conceptions belong to what might be termed the vertical dimension of spiritual "over-belief," out of which particular groups in the community draw the material for their own specific ideologies. No dogma either of a literalistic belief or of an ethnic pride can serve as foundation for the program of the all-embracing community.

Does it follow, then, that the Jewish community as a whole, as an interdenominational structure, is inevitably condemned to deal only with the negative phases of Jewish existence, and thus exalt negativism—or the defense-psychology—to the rank of a predominant philosophy?

By no means. It is possible for the community as a whole to think and act in terms of a *creative minority*. This the community can do without identifying itself with any particular interpretation of Jewish life. It need repudiate only such groups as negate the value of our continued existence in the Diaspora—whether in the name of a totalitarian Zionism or in the name of a totalitarian Americanism. And, as a *creative minority*, the Jewish community must be neither "past-centered," devoting itself to the preservation of a sacred tradition for its own sake, nor "Zion-centered," seeking its inspiration in the culture that might one day spring up in Israel. For thus to place the vital focus of its being outward is lethal—as devastating for the spirit of a community as it is debilitating for an individual to live only in the past or hang on the approval of others. The emphasis rather an autonomy, on creativeness, will cherish and foster whatever cultural and spiritual values are generated by every individual interpretation, every aspiration, within the community.

In his massive work, *A Study of History*, Toynbee points to the fact that new cultural creations are virtually always the achievement of minorities that, through a variety of historical events, get set off from the general population. To be sure, Toynbee regards contemporary Jewry as hardly more than "a fossil of Syriac civilization," unaware as he is of the evolution of ideas and institutions within Judaism, unaware of the continuous interplay of challenge and response in the making of the modern Jew. Furthermore, as a Christian theologian, Toynbee can hardly extol the function of the Christian as the perennial savior of civilization, through fresh acts of surrender to God, without writing *finis* to the Jew's history.

Actually, it is the ideal Jew who lives both in the world and above the world at the same time, never so fully enmeshed in the web and coils of immediate narrow loyalties as not to sense the challenge and charm of the more universal values. Thus, even in the Middle Ages, in defiance of the ghetto walls, it was out of the Jewish community that the pattern of municipal democracy arose; and the challenge was issued for a return to the original springs of faith in the Hebrew Scriptures; and even the idea was fostered of non-conformity in matters of creed; and the liberal doctrines of human goodness and divine rationality were treasured. Later, in Germany and Austria before the Nazi flood, Jews were among the foremost creators and patrons of literature and art; for, aloof as they felt in Central European society, they clung all the more tenaciously to their roots in the universal homeland of the spirit.

Now what are the characteristics of a "creative minority"?

A "creative minority" is, first, a minority that senses its underlying and essential unity with the general population, even as it is conscious of its own distinguishing attributes. We are not as a lonely island, battered by the endless waves of the encircling ocean, but one of a chain of islands which form a solid continuous range beneath the raging, restless surface. Distinctive as our history and tradition are, they yet constitute a vital part of the realm of ideas and experience upon which American civilization is based. Thus we are part of Christian culture, though apart from it; and, even as we cherish and cultivate our own specific heritage, we must not ignore the massive historical reality, the "Judeo-Christian tradition," which forms the spiritual substratum of Western civilization.

Secondly, a "creative minority" evolves new values for the general community, of which it is a part, out of the peculiar circumstances which set it apart. While not officiously seeking to lead or teach or preach, it expands the cultural horizons of the whole community by developing the implication of its unique position. In this sense the Jewish community, by faithfully tracing out the inner logic of its traditions and developing the implicit truths of its peculiar status, might unfold fresh insights for the guidance of the entire American nation.

Thirdly, a "creative minority" is value-centered and oriented to the future. Neither exhausted by the elemental struggle for bare survival nor overcome by the great glory of the past, its face is turned toward the sunlight of spiritual growth. It refuses either to chafe vainly against the boundaries that enclose it or to look above them with olympian detachment as if they did not exist.

The unique features of our status within the all-embracing American community are thus fashioned through the impetus of our specific religio-cultural tradition in continuous interaction with the Christian tradition. It is also this dichotomy of traditions that sets the stage for the role we must play as a "creative minority" in the achievement of higher rungs on the ladder of progress. However, before we can profitably study the relationship of the Jewish to the Christian tradition, we must first envisage clearly the nature of the challenge that religion in general is now facing.

For long now the unifying function of a religious tradition in the total complex of culture has been a truth forgotten. So that our century has witnessed a crescendo of disasters, resulting largely from the inability of modern man to achieve inner unity and harmony. In the Western world the classic ideal of a well-rounded culture, embracing all the interests and values of man, was given up stage by stage through the course of the nineteenth century. Principally, the "split" in the soul of modern man was occasioned by the failure of philosophy to relate successfully the values and aspirations of human nature with the hard facts and iron necessities of the physical universe. At his most human levels, man became a stranger in the universe, while increasingly able to handle its physical forces. It was significantly, a German, Immanuel Kant, who first delineated this bifurcation of the human personality, in his meticulously elaborated distinction between the "pure reason" and the "practical reason," the one formulating the laws of comprehension, the other setting forth the laws of action.

The amazing proliferation of genius that is known as the German Romantic Movement took the Kantian analysis for granted, widened the breach between faith and reason to catastrophic proportions, and exhibited the seeds of all the follies that were to become the popular fads of the next century. If the comprehensible and the spiritual are essentially unrelated, the flood-gates are thrown open for the cynical exaltation of cleverness above wisdom, for the deprecation of the higher reaches of the human spirit, for the reduction of all ideals to impulses and needs, for the downgrading of all that is human and divine and the upgrading of the necessitous, the beastly, and the unconscious.

The romantic flight from reason led to Fichte's thesis of un-

277

conscious genius in chosen individuals and in chosen peoples, thereby launching the wave of auto-intoxicated nationalist "crusades." The yawning gulf between reason and faith made possible both the Hegelian adoration of the all-encompassing Prussian State and the Marxist worship of the inevitable and cataclysmic emergence of the Proletarian Revolution. That gulf made possible the Nietzschean vision of the "superman" rising "beyond good and evil" to the apex of a laughing ruthless "blond beast," and induced the conviction of Sorel that violence is the dynamic expression of the subconscious current of life, hence the source of all progress. That gulf brought about the willingness of modern man to subordinate his soul and conscience to a totalitarian State or Movement, thus driving out religion from the spheres of cultural orchestration and social idealism in the Western democracies. The cult of the irrational in literature and art as well as in politics; the substitution of training in technical skills for the classic goals of education in our big universities; the demise of the "gentleman and scholar" and the rise of the "common man" in all his natural ruggedness and utilitarian standards and vulgar tastes—these things too have resulted from the fission between the "pure" and the "practical" reason.

All these distressing developments of the past century flowed inevitably from the ineluctable fact that the classic synthesis of the age of faith had broken down. Now it is idle to attempt to turn the clock back, to pretend that the failure of all the substitutes for the old religion proves the truth of the old religion. Idle to exhort our contemporaries to repudiate modernism so as to regain the pristine purity and healing balm of the pre-modern world-view, securely founded as it was on authority and mightily raftered by firm dogmas. A healthy synthesis today cannot be achieved by flight from one extreme to the other. It is not faith against reason, nor reason against faith, that we must pursue. We must rather seek to develop a fresh comprehensive philosophy in which all the expressions of human nobility are harmonized, set free, invigorated.

This central quest of our age is now moving toward the orbit of our grasp. The mighty achievements of the physical and social sciences are combining to make possible once again the ancient classical ideal of all-inclusive wisdom. Strange as it may seem, the very advance of science has brought it into the realm of the incomprehensible, and that is where the spiritual nature of man has long resided.

Ponder the impact of the following summation by a leading physicist, Professor Percy Bridgman of Harvard University: "The physicist finds himself in a world from which the bottom has dropped clean out; as he penetrates deeper and deeper, it eludes him by the highly unsportsmanlike device of just becoming meaningless. No refinement of measurement will avail to carry him beyond the portals of this shadowy domain which we cannot even mention without logical inconsistency. A bound is thus forever set to the curiosity of the physicist. What is more, the mere existence of this bound means that he must give up his most cherished faith and convictions. The world is not a world of reason, understandable by the intellect of man, but, as we penetrate ever deeper, the very law of cause and effect, which he had thought to be a formula to which we could force God Himself to subscribe, ceases to have any meaning." (From "The New Version of Science," in *Harper's Magazine* for March, 1929.)

As the disastrous split in the human personality was engendered by the dichotomy between the brightly comprehensible physical universe and the hidden non-rational springs of man's nature, so now the way back to the harmony of wisdom is opened up by the growing realization that the physical universe about us is equally incomprehensible. We now realize that both faith and reason derive from the same fundamental mystery. While only a short while ago the ultimate source of knowledge appeared to be split clean down the middle, we now see it as one, dynamic and all-embracing, a challenge for the construction of a magnificent new synthesis of ideas and ideals, deserving of the old function and title of "Wisdom."

It is in the light of this central goal of our time that we may obtain a fresh appreciation of the relative merits and functions of the two traditions that constitute the spiritual sub-structure of Western civilization.

In our society a religious tradition constitutes the social instrument whereby the meaning of life, in all its scope and depth, is interpreted and mediated. Now a philosophical synthesis of reason and faith, however inconsistent in theory, is powerless if it is not embraced in a living tradition and channeled into the religious

279

experience of a social group. While philosophy provides the principles of construction and the engineering blueprints, so to speak, the religious tradition furnishes the bricks and mortar for the ideal structure of wisdom in every generation. For wisdom, we must remember, is a social as well as an individual reality; and it is rooted in personal experience and the cultural momentum of history as well as in the realm of abstract ideas and convictions.

Religious experience is generated at the outer boundary of human capacity—the plane where our physical power ends, reason fails, and the will for self-aggrandizement changes direction and turns into the vertical growth of the spirit. At this hair-line juncture of the temporal and the eternal, the human and the more than human phases merge into the experience of holiness, though in varying proportions. At this apex of the spirit all the fragmentary values of life are led back to their source. Wisdom rises to piety.

In the Christian tradition and its resulting pattern of piety, it is the super-human, or divine, quality of religious experience that is emphasized and fostered. Reason is defied in the awareness of the totally "other," and in the dogmas of the trinity and the incarnation "that are a stumbling-block to the Jews and folly to the Greeks"; the objective rule of conscience is negated in the dogmas of "original sin," of predestination and justification by faith, and of salvation coming as a free and unearned act of Grace from the Deity; the multiple feelings of self-assertion, echoing the natural "love of the world," are turned into the pale frost of asceticism, the inverted pleasure of total surrender, the "creaturely" feeling of unreserved submission.

In the Jewish tradition, on the other hand, what predominates is the human phase of experience of the ultimate. It is the advancing might of reason that carries us to the brink of what is humanly knowable, so that the Oneness of God is our fundamental conviction, as the one all-encompassing formula is the ultimate goal of reason; the principles of conscience, as we know them, are extended to the Infinite and applied to Him, in their double connotation of Justice and Mercy; the feeling of piety is that of active participation in the upbuilding of the Kingdom of God. Hence it is through the perception of law in the universe, order in history, unvarying norms in the life of the individual and firm standards of decency and dignity in group life, that Jewish tradition leads the worshiper to "the mountain of the Lord." Hence, also, in the cultivation of these virtues Jewish piety is concretized, as it descends from the ecstatic heights of Sinai to the varying levels of mundane reality.

For the Christian, religion enters into life as a continual protest against the "pride" of the self expanding in the direction of either reason or will or feeling. The negating, meta-human phase of the experience of holiness is propelled into every situation—as in rejecting the aspiration to solve social problems through the humanist insights of intelligence and conscience; or in repudiating the "pharisaic" faith in laws, norms and deeds. Here is the negation of the varied "feelings of this world" in behalf of the "feeling of the other."

It would take volumes to show in detail how the two phases of the same fundamental experience are developed differently in the two traditions, each unfolding according to its historical impetus. The important point to remember is that the initial difference of emphasis is magnified into an all-inclusive tradition that touches upon every aspect of life—from the music and mysticism of Wagner to the sociology of Toynbee and the penitent philosophy of the ex-Communist Whittaker Chambers. Even when the central focus of the Christian faith is negated, the characteristic emphasis deriving from its tradition continues to be felt. Similarly in Judaism, the impetus of this-worldly idealism may continue to function, at least for a while, even when the central experience of faith is neglected or disavowed. In each case the experience of transcendence is the vital center of an organic and wide-ranging pattern of life that is founded upon a living tradition.

Which tradition, Jewish or Christian, is truer to the nature of things, yielding a more adequate philosophy of life? Let us hope that we have by now outgrown the impulse to indulge in such idle questions. Be it admitted that both the Jewish and Christian traditions are liable to abuse, if uncorrected by their reciprocal influences upon one another. The Jewish tradition, it is true, tends to develop among the orthodox into a one-sided emphasis on the sheer legalism of piety; and among the non-orthodox it tends to pass into a naïve and uninspired kind of humanism. On the other hand, the Christian tradition is perennially in danger, on the orthodox level, of separating faith from morals and the intellect;

and of degenerating among the neo-orthodox into a sterile anti-intellectualism, unrestrained romanticism and social reaction. The Unitarians and the Universalists, for their part, lean so far over into the domain of Jewish rationalism as to lose the support and impetus of their own historic traditions. With varying effectiveness these liberal groups mediate between the Jewish and Christian faiths, keeping the two streams in continuous contact and interaction. However, they can no more replace the historic faiths than philosophy can take the place of religion.

In continual mutual criticism, even as they challenge and stimulate each other, the two traditions, Jewish and Christian, develop each its own genius best.

But—and here is the rub—how are the two traditions to stimulate each other without allowing their essential opposition to degenerate into mutual contempt and recrimination? The Christian emphasis can hardly be developed without coming perilously close to a wholesale condemnation, or at least a systematic deprecation, of the Jewish tradition. This emphasis enters indeed into every phase of culture, permeating the study of history, philosophy and literature, and affecting the general climate of opinion. It was thus that modern anti-Semitism maintained its momentum in the last century, though its source in Christian Orthodoxy weakened and waned—attesting to the power and pervasiveness of the Christian tradition. Franz Rosenzweig, in his mystical view of history, declared that anti-Semitism was foreordained and inevitable, since it flowed necessarily from the basic dichotomy of the Jewish and Christian traditions. The perpetual likelihood of this opposition turning into hate and contempt loomed to him as inescapable doom, living as he did under the balefully rising shadow of nazism.

In fact, this danger can be averted only if the mutual interaction of the two traditions is maintained on the highest levels of thought and scholarship. Suffice it to recall the association of "Higher Criticism" of the Bible with "Higher Anti-Semitism," and the faith of the Pharisees with a mean and narrow-minded legalism, so long as authentic Jewish scholarship in this field was in its early stages, unrecognized by the outside world.

It is the relationship of the Christian and Jewish traditions that sets the stage for the spiritual challenge which the thoughtful Jew senses in the American environment. At the same time it is the mutually supplementary roles of the two traditions within the context of Western civilization that offers to the modern Jew a vision of the unique significance of his faith and culture. Thus the healthy orientation and inner peace and spiritual productiveness of the American Jew depend upon the continuous unfolding of the values implicit in his own tradition. Through this creative process the modern Jew will be enabled to integrate into his life the spiritual values of the Jewish faith, and provide a counterbalance to the Christian emphasis in Western civilization.

Thus we can help to achieve a new all-embracing wisdom, adequate for our time. And thus we can aid Christian students and scholars to recognize the place of Judaism in the over-all pattern of human culture.

We have become rather shy about our "mission" to teach other people, and sensitive about the age-old claim to the possession of the "eternal verities" in their purity. There is indeed no justification for any people to lay claim to the possession of unique faculties, or to the exclusive possession of a set of true ideas. Still, we are no worse than our Christian neighbors, even if we are no better. Does the disavowal of any pretensions to superiority involve the concession of inferiority? We do have a cultural heritage and a religious tradition, a pattern of piety shading into a secular philosophy of wisdom, which is as essential for the balance of Western thought as is the piety and wisdom of the Christian. It is the primary function of our cultural tradition to help achieve the classical synthesis of wisdom in our lives. The function of a cultural tradition consists not so much in the ideas it propounds as in the total impact it directs upon the personalities of its sons. To build spiritually healthy, well-balanced Jewish individuals, who will in their turn contribute to the spiritual health of the whole American community—that is our basic concern.

Our young people are inevitably exposed to the impact of the Christian tradition in literature and philosophy, living as we do in a predominantly Christian civilization. Without the counterbalancing influence of the Jewish tradition, they cannot but move step by step to the point of sensing Judaism as a strange and incongruous phenomenon, ultimately even as an anachronistic "fossil" that has somehow cheated the Angel of Death. In such yielding to the dominance of the Christian tradition they not only plant the seeds of self-hatred within their own souls; they deprive the Judeo-Christian cultural pattern of the balancing and healing effects of the Jewish contribution.

The Zionist "negators of the Diaspora" may almost be forgiven their contention that only in Israel can the Jew acquire a solid cultural base for the development of the insights in his rich tradition. Yet, though we can understand and even excuse this widespread mood of retreat and defeat, if we concur in its pessimistic estimate of the potency and charm of Jewish tradition we in effect submit an abject application for spiritual bankruptcy. For if Judaism is of universal value and significance, it need not be sheltered by the walls of a national sovereignty from the free interplay of ideas and sentiments in the Western world. It is here in the Western world that Judaism faces its greatest challenge: here that its right to function as a basic cultural factor must be tested and proved true.

Furthermore, five million Jews in America can no more find spiritual sustenance as "Israeli colonials" than they can afford to assume this status in social or political terms. Israeli culture, whatever forms it may take in the future, will necessarily develop the values of our tradition along nationalist lines. Hence, as time goes on, its reflected influence on the American scene will differ less and less from that of the other national sub-cultures in this country.

As American Jews, we are called upon to rise to a far greater challenge—that of unfolding the values of our tradition in the free and open spaces of a non-parochial universal culture. Thus we may render our contribution to the achievement of that synthesis of wisdom which our age is trying so desperately to attain.

From all the foregoing considerations it follows that we should seek to foster the development of the Jewish tradition on all levels —but especially on the highest academic level, in the colleges and universities. The prime importance of concentrating in the collegiate level is obvious, if we are to win and hold the allegiance of our rising intelligentsia. Having lost one generation of intellectuals, we must assign top priority to the task of infusing the hundreds of thousands of Jewish students on the campuses with the light of Jewish knowledge and the fire of Jewish idealism. Is this task being effectively done today?

There is a huge network across the country of Hillel Foundations, carrying on "Jewish activities" at over two hundred colleges and universities. Do they still reflect the negativist mentality of the past generation, setting up campus-ghettoes, or are they geared for the task of projecting the ideals of Judaism onto the American scene? The university campus is potentially the place where a renaissance of Judaism might begin. Certainly the impact of Judaism on the cultural life of America should be felt primarily on the campus and in the university faculties. Is it then the purpose and function of the Hillel Foundations to expound the Jewish heritage on the campus? Are their directors so chosen as to qualify for high academic posts? Do the students esteem their scholarship and wisdom as of equal standing with that of their professors? Or is the whole context of the Hillel Foundation social in character, segregationist at worst, "armor-building" at best, reverberating with the negativist undertones of the Anti-defamation mentality? Are the budgets and limited framework of the Foundations adequate for the tasks they are meant to perform?

In any case, we need Departments of Judaism in the great American universities, or at least a series of Chairs of Jewish Literature and Philosophy, together with a system of liberal Fellowships in this field. It is not enough to offer courses in the Hebrew language or ancient Hebrew texts in the Oriental Departments, for Judaism is no longer an Oriental factor but a vital ingredient in Western culture. Nor should we permit the transformation of an existing Hebrew course into a Department of Israeli Culture, on the pattern of other language courses. The Jewish tradition must be presented as a cultural factor vitally relevant to our own time and place, not merely as a relic from the past or as a foreign national development.

High time indeed for us to envisage the challenge and true function of Judaism on the American scene, and not allow ourselves to be deflected from our purpose by "defense" hysteria, or by the tinsel-substitute of a resurgent nationalism, or by the "fossil mentality" of seeking refuge in the Orient and the Past.

Those who do not believe in the creative potentialities of American Jewish life are willing enough to spend millions in behalf of a *halutziut* program of emigration to Israel. Are those of us who envision a Golden Age of Judaism in America equally willing to provide the necessary means for such a glorious consummation?

CULTURE

Culture, being an extraordinarily broad term, includes, in this section, an essay on the revival of Hebrew by one of the great Hebraists of the era; a delightful description of a form of Yiddish literature which entranced generations of Jewish women; a definition of what constitutes a Jewish book; a symposium on the Jewish novel; a lugubrious depiction of the plight of the Jewish writer; a critical analysis of anti-Semitism and the contemporary Jewish novelist; and an examination of the portrayal of Jewish gangsters as characters in the popular reprint editions of recent fiction.

In addition, Marvin Lowenthal, a precise and clever essayist, offers an eye-opening discussion of Jewish attitudes and legends which, according to him, can scarcely be defended. Culture is seldom presented in so entertaining a form. Sidney Hook, in a detailed analysis of Jean-Paul Sartre's *Anti-Semite and Jew,* writes a sharp essay on anti-Semitism and on the role and the attitude of American Jews today. Also within the province of culture are penetrating studies of the musician Ernest Bloch and of Jewish sobriety and humor.

The twelve essays in this section also appeared in a variety of publications, ranging from *Partisan Review,* to *Commentary,* to *Congress Weekly,* to *Judaism,* to *The Chicago Jewish Forum,* and several Zionist periodicals.

HEBREW: REVIVAL AND REDEMPTION

By MENACHEM RIBALOW

THE LOVE OF the Jew for the Hebrew language, popularly called "the sacred tongue," is one of the most precious national possessions of the Jewish people. This love is woven, like a golden thread, throughout Jewish history for the Jew knows that "the sacred tongue" is the eternal tongue of his people. One generation passeth away and another generation cometh; and the Hebrew language abideth forever. Exile may end and redemption come and the root-language of the land of Israel stands firm.

Although the Jewish people made use of many different languages, corresponding with the many lands into which it was driven by its fate of exile, it never—even for a day—betrayed or rejected its language. The Jew would use Hebrew in his prayers, his lamentations, his liturgical poetry; in its accents he would pour forth his heart to God in stirring and plaintive psalms. Week in and week out he would review the weekly biblical portion according to the traditional practice, twice in the Hebrew original, once in the Aramaic translation, and the entire ancient history of his people would pass before his mind's eye.

"The universe was created by means of the holy tongue—" thus spoke the Jewish sages because to them the universe was revealed in Hebrew. They felt, and many feel with them today, that through the Hebrew language the Jewish national and cultural character are most truly revealed. Actually, the reasoning is simple. There live in this language historic Jewish concepts and Hebrew expressions that are peculiar and unique and find their like in no other language. There are words, phrases and verses whose roots go so deep that they touch the limits of time and thus can have their comparison in no other tongue. Every word bears the scent of ancient eras and has the savor of old wines that stir up longings that transcend the boundaries of language.

Therefore the man who speaks or writes such a language becomes a partner with the great of distant epochs and enters a mystical enclosure with those noblemen of spirit who lived most richly and draws sustenance from their fountain. He feels that a great and majestic hand casts him—in the phrase of Hayim Nahman Bialik—into "an unexplored height, an unknown remoteness."

For it was through the Hebrew language that the God of Israel revealed Himself to His people and it was in this language that the covenant was sealed between them. This is the language of the Jewish people's past—as it is the language of its future—in Israel.

The Hebrew language is the language of the Jewish beginnings, for it was in Hebrew that God revealed Himself in a vision to Abram, before he became the patriarch Abraham, when He commanded him to gaze heavenward and to count the stars, even before he had made his covenant with Him.

It was in Hebrew that God disclosed Himself to Moses, out of the bush that burned with flame, yet was not consumed.

It was in Hebrew that Moses and the people of Israel burst forth into song at the Red Sea, a song of national glory and rebirth, after their departure from Egypt.

It was in Hebrew, too, that Moses spoke from Sinai's peak and "God answered him by a voice"—and the Torah was given to Israel.

All the statutes and ordinances of the Torah, by which the Jewish people has lived for thousands of years, were written in Hebrew. Similarly, the Hebrew language has been warp and woof of the Jewish fabric from the conquest of Canaan, to the destruction of the first Temple and the Babylonian captivity; from the first King to the last Prophet; from the return from Babylonian exile to the destruction of the second Temple. Hebrew has been branch and root of the Jewish creations of spirit from Ezra and the men of the Great Synagogue to the days of the writing of the Mishnah and the Gemara; from the Halachic literature to the literature of mysticism; from the Gaonic literature and that of the Middle Ages through the Kabbalah and Hasidism and the Haskalah—up to our own time, up to the restoration of the Jewish State.

The entire Jewish approach to life, in which are united the earthly and the heavenly, the material and the spiritual, finds full and exact expression in the Hebrew language. Abstract and lofty concepts are blended together with the concrete and simple. Symbolic images of the completely incorporeal divine dwell honorably side by side with very human descriptions, converting the spirit into matter and the godly into human. The anthropomorphic element is characteristic of the Bible and, therefore, of Hebrew.

The Jew is fond of concreteness, of the figure of bas-relief, the definiteness of the idol—the forbidden idol. He ascribes even to God human characteristics. God is not only *the God of hosts;* He is also *the man of hosts.* He can wax angry at His people. Light is His garment; His tent—the heavens. He rides upon the thick clouds and flies upon the wings of the wind. He speaks and remembers, loves and hates. He is jealous and avenging, merciful and compassionate.

These are human qualities and it is these human qualities which philosophers and theologians have labored so hard to explain, qualities which the Jewish people have illustrated so perceptively in the Bible. These qualities are safeguarded in the Hebrew language, for in Hebrew there are retained the naïveté of the folk in its childhood and something of the strength of primeval man whose flesh yearned for the living God.

Yes, the Jewish generations come and go, language and culture enter the world and pass on, but the Hebrew tongue remains, it stands forever. Actually, the word "stands" is inaccurate, for Hebrew moves; it is alive, constantly developing and rejuvenating itself with new vitality.

This is an inner vitality, one of the soul, for Hebrew has lived within the Jewish people, in all periods and ages, in all lands and in all exiles. In Babylonia and Persia, in Greece and Egypt, in Spain and Africa, in Germany and Poland, in Italy and France, in Lithuania and Rumania and now in North and South America, the Hebrew language, like a good and faithful angel, accompanied the people it loved.

In every age and in every land, there arose redeemers for Hebrew in the shape of poets and scholars and codifiers and grammarians.

291

They played upon the harp of the language so that the chords of the people vibrated. Not all Jews knew or spoke Hebrew, for a people's fate in exile is a harsh one—exile is like a stepmother with an ill-tempered face—but the majority of the people, if not all of them, used Hebrew in prayers and hymns, in psalms and lamentations and, for that matter, in daily affairs. Legal documents and accounts, memoirs and family records of births and deaths, letters and wills—these were all written in Hebrew. For the people knew for a certainty that the tongues they used in the lands of exile were alien tongues and that these languages, acquired during the long exile, were not as important or as sacred as their first and national language—Hebrew.

The most Jewish of the alien tongues, one used a great deal for a long period of time, was Aramaic. Most of the Talmud was written in Aramaic, as was the sacred book the Zohar. The Kaddish and Kol Nidre are recited in Aramaic and the wedding ketubah is written in that language. But Aramaic remains in the treasure-house of Jewry because of the precious books written in it, and not because of the language's own intrinsic value. It cannot be imagined that at some future time a movement will arise for the revival of Aramaic because it is the language of the Talmud and the Zohar. These vast works are studied in their original language by students and by scholars, but they are gradually being translated into Hebrew. But Aramaic itself belongs to the past; it can have no future.

Arabic, too, has left Jewish life, never to return, although Jews like Saadya Gaon, Judah Halevi, Solomon ibn Gabirol, Maimonides and others created in Arabic. Yet some of their greatest works, those that plumbed the profoundest depths, were written in Hebrew. These, and the works they wrote in Arabic which were translated into Hebrew, remain. Maimonides made this point when he said to his son, "My son, I know the sin I have sinned against my people and I pray to God that I may be found worthy to return the stolen article to its rightful owners and to translate my books into the sacred tongue."

The language that has stood the test of time, that has overcome the tempests of history and the waves of wrath that threatened to swallow it and its people, has been the Hebrew language.

When the Yiddish language encompassed millions of Jews, some centuries back, what did the Hebrew language do then? It found for itself a dwelling place in the concealed depths of the Yiddish language. More than three thousand Hebrew words, expressions and concepts were assimilated into Yiddish. These filled the language with charm and with Jewish flavor. Religious and sacred concepts thus entered Yiddish in their original tongue. Expressions like: *Hakodesh baruch-hu; Ribbono shel olam; Yom Tov; Chuppah, Mazal Tov, Torah, Tefilah,* these and hundreds and hundreds more were gathered together and absorbed by the Yiddish language. Similarly, the "salt and pepper" of Yiddish comes from Hebrew, including words like *efshar* and *afilu* and *ad'raba* and *chalila* and *halvai* and *mayla.*

Thus Yiddish was filled with the scent of Hebrew expressions and the flavor of Hebrew verses. The sayings of the sages would hover on every lip and out of both casual and serious conversation there would flow a stream of the wisdom of the ages. The splendor of the Hebrew language shone through the life of the Jewish people.

It is because of the Jew's great and enduring love for the Hebrew language that there has came to pass the great marvel of the renaissance of the Hebrew language in our generation. And through this revival has come, in part, the rebirth of the Jewish state, for it was the Hebrew language that was a powerful force in the revival and redemption both of the people and of the land.

It was the Hebrew language that, through all the vagaries of time, was the fortress of strength in which the Jew, cleaving to the rock whence he was hewn, entrenched himself. Through the language of the prayers and hymns, the lamentations and penitential psalms, his heart would cleave not only to his Father in heaven but also to the desolate land for which he yearned and to whose redemption he looked forward. This land would live in his heart through the poetic descriptions of the Bible that were included in the prayer book and that became the daily bread of the Jew. The distant Palestinian landscapes would overshadow the landscape of the country in which he dwelt. When he recalled the wonders of God, the Creator of the Universe, he would remember the Exodus from Egypt and *his* wandering in the desert and *his* war with the kings of old until *he* finally entered the land given by God as "an inheritance to Israel His servant." The rains, the early rains and the later rains, the grain, the wine and the oil of far-off days in a geographically distant land became real entities and influential factors in his life in the Diaspora. On Passover the Jew would pray for dew and on Sukkot for rain.

Even the incense of spice of the Temple and the various sacrifices brought upon its altar accompanied him upon the path he trod. As he sang the Hallelujah psalms, he would recall the servants of the Lord "who stand in the house of the Lord, in the courts of the house of our God." And how did his prayers conclude? With the entreaty that "May the Temple be rebuilt speedily and in our days" and with the hope that "May our eyes behold Thy return to Zion in mercy" and with "A redeemer shall come to Zion."

All of these desires and yearnings formed such an integral part of the Hebrew language that it became impossible to distinguish between the two. It is possible to say without exaggeration that the essence of the chant of the prayers in their gentle and soulful language would quiet the sighing of the heart and calm the storm of longing. Thus the uttering of the Hebrew words of the prayers was not only a means to an end but in no small measure an end in itself. It became a great individual and national achievement. Because of it, Zionist sentiment lived in the heart of every Jew through all the years of the Exile.

Is it any wonder, then, that with the Haskalah period, the period of enlightenment, and after it, the age of the renaissance, the Hebrew language became so precious and powerful an instrument for revival and redemption? All of modern Hebrew literature was born and grew with this concept of the redemption of the people and the land. From Abraham's Mapu's *The Love of Zion* up to the latest story of the new Israel, and from the Zionist and biblical poems of Micah Joseph Lebensohn to the biblical and pastoral poems of the contemporary young Hebrew poets, there can be felt the yearning for the motherland that helped create the Zionist movement and cleared the way for the State of Israel.

Now that Israel has been established, great days lie in store for the Hebrew language, days of creativity and development, the like of which has not been experienced in many generations.

Thus a generation goeth and a generation cometh, a language goeth and a language cometh, exile goeth and redemption cometh —and the Hebrew language endureth forever.

LITERATURE OF A VANISHED WORLD

By NAOMI BEN-ASHER

WHEN THE JEWRIES of Eastern Europe were wiped out, a unique culture was destroyed with them. The sights and sounds, smell and taste, shape and color of that world will be preserved to some extent in the mainstream of its literature. Some of the tributaries and streamlets which fed the folk mind and influenced its mental climate will be lost, or buried in books accessible only to the linguist and scholar. Much of the folk literature and many of the folkways have already become unintelligible to the average American-Jewish reader; ignorance and sentiment have already wrought a distortion in the popular conception of the East European Jew.

A certain type of writing and painting has established the sterotype of the Jew as a scholar exclusively. He is inevitably a man with a furrowed brow, peering from under his *shtreimel* into a large folio of the Talmud, completely surrounded by an assortment of commentaries. Thus a fixed image of universal Jewish scholarship has been created and has remained almost undisturbed by the type of Jew best described in the works of Sholom Aleichem, Mendele and Peretz. Singularly little has been written in English about the folk literature of the *kleine mentschelach*—the semi-literate folk of the teeming Jewries of fifty years ago.

The ghetto did abound in scholars, but it also swarmed with those who were too poor to take full advantage of the prevailing safeguard against illiteracy—the Talmud Torah, which provided a free elementary education. The hewer of wood and the drawer of water, the tailor's apprentice, the shoemaker's helper, and that symbol of all ignorance—the *baal agoleh* (the teamster)—were usually compelled to leave the *cheder* at the age of ten or eleven to earn a daily crust of bread and a pair of shoes for Pesach. Then there were the women—half of the ghetto population. Not obligated to study the Law, they frequently remained semi-literate.

What about the morality books of these people? What about their reading matter? And what fed the starved imaginations of the little *cheder* boys, who began their study of the *aleph beth* at the age of three or four, went on to Chumash at five, and Talmud at six?

It is this body of folk literature, read and loved by these people, which is well on the way toward being forgotten. This product of a vanished world is not merely the poor relation of the great body of Hebrew and Yiddish literature. It should be recognized as a rich repository of folk imagination and humor. In it are to be found, alongside areas of semi-literacy and an encrustation of superstition, attributes which demonstrate how deeply the people were permeated with the great spiritual and ethical qualities of the Hebraic record.

It may not be amiss to start with the mothers of that vanished race. There was always among them a sprinkling of "aristocracy"— the daughters and sisters of scholars, whose native endowment combined with opportunity enabled them to escape the semi-literacy of the average woman. The average woman, however, was taught to read Hebrew mechanically, to read and write Yiddish, and little else. It was therefore natural for her to seek out the folk literature for recreation and to satisfy her spiritual needs with several books of sacred character, some of them written especially for her.

First among these was the *Tzenah Urenah* (Go Forth and See), a Yiddish paraphrase of the Bible with homiletic commentaries, written early in the seventeenth century by Rabbi Jacob Ben Isaac. *Tzenah Urenah* went with her every Sabbath to the synagogue, and to it she turned in her free moments at home. Very appropriately it begins with a *techinah* (a supplication) for such basic needs as the daily bread. An even more passionate plea is the *techinah* "that her children might not forget what they were learning."

The homiletic character of the *Tzenah Urenah* can be savored immediately with its explanation of why the Lord departed from the strict dictates of logic and began the Torah—"*Bereshit . . .*"

(in the beginning)—with the second letter of the *aleph beth*. *Aleph*, the first letter of the alphabet, runs the explanation, is also the first letter of the word *arrur* (cursed), while *beth* begins the word *baruch* (blessed)! As a compensation to the complaining *aleph*, however, the Almighty permitted her to form the first letter of the Ten Commandments: "*Anochi . . .*" (I am the Lord.)

Most beloved of all the devotional books was the *Reshit Chochma*, which derives its name from *reshit chochmah yirat Adonai* (the beginning of wisdom is fear of the Lord). Side by side with instruction for resisting the *yetzer horah* (the evil inclination) is a complete inventory of hell, describing in great detail the punishments for every variety of sin which await souls after death. As a rule the offending member of the body is punished. For example: A tongue that speaks evil of friend or neighbor will be pulled out by the roots with red hot pincers. Similarly, "Eating without washing the hands is punished in the hereafter by grinding those hands between millstones for a long time." A more severe punishment for the same crime is the transmigration of the soul into a frog that is continually submerged in water.

Another interesting aspect of this book is its concept of individual human responsibility. The number of parts of the body corresponds to the number of commandments, each member being responsible for obedience to a specific *mitzvah*. The reckoning is quite exact. There are 248 positive commandments and exactly that many parts of the body. There are 365 veins and just such a number of negative commandments; the sum total of parts of the body, as well as commandments is, of course, *taryag* (613). When a given commandment is broken, the responsible part of the body suffers *ferderben* or deterioration—hence each human being is responsible for his own sickness. Moreover, during sleep each soul ascends to heaven and enters its own daily record of transgressions and good deeds in the proper ledger. In this sense each soul sits in judgment upon itself. Personal salvation, however, is not the only objective to be gained by fear of the Almighty and fear of punishment for sins. Among the four reasons for guarding against sin, number one is the assertion that transgression prolongs the *galut*—the exile.

Reshit Chochmah was highly esteemed by men as well as women. During the long winter evenings after the children had been put to bed, husband and wife sat close to the oven for warmth, she pluck-ing feathers for a new feather bed, he reading aloud from this holy book. The description of the agonies visited upon sinful souls was punctuated by deep sighs from the couple and by the complaining sound of each feather being stripped from its quill. In families where the husband was the illiterate one, the wife read aloud from *Reshit Chochmah* on Sabbath afternoons, the only time her hands were idle.

Highly regarded, but more limited in its appeal, was the *Kav Hayashar* (The Straight Path). A book described as "wonderful for the purposes of the spirit, the body, and the soul," it was rigidly ascetic, renouncing all earthly joys and filling the mind with dread of the consequences of transgressions.

The *M'norat Hamaor* (The Candelabrum of Light) was in a class of its own. Widely read by women, it was revered by men and loved by both. Written by Rabbi Isaac Aboab of Spain in the twelfth century, it is mainly a collection of talmudic *hagadot,* ar-ranged in seven major sections representing the seven branches of the menorah. The author remains modestly in the background, permitting the imaginative quality and the pungent flavor of the short talmudic tales and parables to envelop and charm the reader.

All these Yiddish morality books had far more color and drama than their Hebrew prototypes. They aroused interest through story and parables and illustrated each moral with an allegory. The mys-ticism of the Kabbalah flavored them all.

Nourished by these books, the woman translated their precepts into the stuff of daily life. Schooled in their attitude toward Torah-learning as the highest form of worship, she cherished and re-spected her scholarly husband even when he could not provide for his family. As compensation there was always the hope that in the life to come she would be permitted to serve as her learned hus-band's footstool in paradise. With their midrashic excerpts and concepts she taught and admonished her children. The biblical concept of pity she had absorbed made her cry out when her small son pulled the cat's tail: "Don't do that—the cat too suffers the *tzaar baal hachayim* (the pain of all living things)."

There were some women who could not read at all, but even these unfortunates were not condemned to complete ignorance. Their parched souls were refreshed by the *forezogerin* (she who "read before them") in *shul*. They clustered about her during the *oisnemen* (the "taking out" of the Torah) for the reading of the weekly portion. The Book of Supplications, from which she read during this interval between morning *shacharith* and noon *musaf* prayers, was very thick, and it contained a large variety of specialized *techinot*. There was a *techinah* for the mother in childbed, for the critically ill, in remembrance of the dead, for Mondays and Thursdays, for Sabbaths and holidays, and of course for the Days of Awe.

On the night of *Selichot*, two days before Yom Kippur, when "God is near to those that seek him," men and women went to synagogue before dawn to recite *Selichot* and *Tochachot* (penitential prayers) and obtain forgiveness for their sins. The *forezogerin* was then burdened with a great responsibility. In the small hours of the night, before the coming of dawn, the women assembled in *shul* for the ceremony of *kneitlach legen*. The myriads of waxen tapers which filled the synagogue on Kol Nidre eve with light, heat, and the smell of melting tallow were no ordinary "bought" candles; they were made by the women in a prescribed ritual, each dedicated to a member of the family, to the health and welfare of the living ones, and to the souls of those who had gone on to life eternal. The first step in this ceremony was the *kneitlach legen*. Over the ritual presided the *forezogerin* and as each woman formed a wick, it was dedicated with the chanting of an appropriate *techinah*. The crying of the women as they remembered their dead in prayer pierced the dark silence outside and quickened the steps of the belated penitent.

Throughout the Days of Awe the *forzogerin* chanted and the women wept. They wept with good cause. Their poverty was crushing, their children were numerous, their sense of security was nonexistent. And so they repeated the prayers after the *forezogerin* and cried out to God from the fullness of their hearts. The *forezogerin* and her weeping flock were particularly active during the Ten Penitential Days. On Rosh Hashonah, when the fate of mankind for the coming year is inscribed in the Heavenly Books, they prayed with all their might. To cleave the heavens with prayer and to reach the Throne of Judgment during the *Eth Ratzon* (the very moment of graciousness) was of utmost urgency. During the solemnity of the services, they strained every fiber to catch each familiar word as it was intoned by the *baal tefillah;* and during the *oisnemen* they repeated the prayers after the *forezogerin.*

A *maskil* (follower of the Enlightenment Movement) once offered an explanation for the *forezogerin's* lack of efficacy in breaking through to the Gates of Mercy and achieving a more prosperous year for her flock. It was not due to a lack of piety or of contrite hearts, or to an insufficiency of *techinot* or of fears. Not at all; it was just inherent in the nature of things. When the Great Books were opened on Yom Kippur, and it was necessary to place the seal upon the inscription of "who should prosper and who should become impoverished," the first ones to come under consideration were, quite naturally, the Rothschilds, the de Hirsches, and their like. While these were few in number, their affairs were complicated and important, and by the time their accounts were straightened and their fate determined, the morning was gone. Then came those next in rank whose affairs were simpler but whose number was greater. By the time their merits were evaluated, their affairs considered, and their fate decided and sealed, the afternoon was gone. The great majority of the people—the poor— still remained to be reviewed. In the waning daylight, just before the *N'eelah* and the closing of the Gates, the pages had to be stamped rapidly, one after the other, so that the Books might be closed in time for the final blowing of the *shofar.* Of course, without an individual evaluation, heavenly justice could not alter the lot of everyone. And so the fate of the poor for the New Year was always stamped "the same as last year." This state of affairs insured the continued use of the *techinot* and a steady occupation for the *forezogerin* which to her everlasting credit she performed gratis.

Many members of the *forezogerin's* flock—and their children as well—were devoted to yet another form of literature: the *maaseh bichelach* (story books). The subject matter of the *maaseh bichel* was a large variety of folklore unified by a moral purpose. The talmudic *hagadot,* the legends which originated in the German towns along the Rhine and were written down perhaps in the fifteenth and sixteenth centuries, the mystic stories derived from the Kabbalah, the endless Hasidic stories, the tales based on life in the ghetto—all these are only a few of the *maaseh bichel* categories. Dr. A. A. Roback, in his book, *The Story of Yiddish Literature,* traces the origin of the *maaseh buch* back to the sixteenth century, when one famous collection of 250 stories established a pattern and served as a source for centuries to come.

These books were all purveyed by the *packen traeger* (literally, the pack-carrier), who traveled from region to region, made his headquarters in a given townlet, covered the surrounding territory in a month and then moved on to the next locality. His arrival was eagerly awaited, and pennies were carefully hoarded toward the agonizing pleasure of making a selection from his pack.

Little boys who spent their days pondering the vital problems engendered by "the ox who had gored a cow" and "the two who grasped the same *talith*," and older boys, far more advanced in their talmudic studies—all saved up the pennies intended for the purchase of a bun to still the mid-day hunger, and used them instead to buy a *maaseh buch* from the *packen traeger*. Sometimes it took the combined savings of two friends to buy a coveted story. This transaction could not take place in the open where the stern eye of parent or teacher might observe the iniquity. Nor could these stories be read openly.

The only ones who could really revel in the practice of *maaseh* reading were the servant girls. The mistresses encouraged them tacitly, for under the guise of humoring the servants they too could indulge with impunity. Mistress and servant alike shivered in delicious anticipation at the sight of a title page that proclaimed the story of "A Murderer with an Ax, or Stop Repeating the 'Confession Before Death,' Your Time to Die Has Arrived," and in smaller letters: "From this title itself it is possible to understand that it is a frightening, interesting story. And so it is. A murderous tale about a magnate with a lot of money who was lured into a forest. . . ."

With an equal degree but a different quality of delight, they read such stories as *G'dulath Mosheh Un'shikath Mosheh* (The Greatness of Moses and the Kiss of Moses), subtitled "What Moses Saw in Heaven and on Earth, in Gehenna, and in Paradise, and We Transposed It into Ivri Teitch So That People Should Be Able to Read and Understand."

On Friday nights, when the Sabbath meal was ended and the men folk lingered at the table over "a *shtikel* Torah," the little ones clustered around Freide Perl or Yachneh Dvosie in the kitchen and gave her no peace until she sat down and told them the stories she had read in the *maaseh bichelach.* She told of robbers, blood accusations, and miraculous rescues, the forcible partings of *choson* and *kaleh* and the dire results of these separations. She poured out tales of conversion, forcible or voluntary, tales of the pious poor miraculously endowed with riches by Elijah the Prophet.

As the night grew older, the Torah talk at the table became more abstruse, and the twelve-year-old "man," who had scorned the very thought of joining the children in the kitchen, gradually edged away from the table. After all, he could instruct the little ones in something loftier than could the ignorant servant girl. Somehow, he found himself in the kitchen listening to tales of the *shedim* (*"die nit-gute"*), male and female, some of whom had special power over brides and mothers in childbed.

Out of his own reading he contributed stories of the *Lamed Vav Zadikim,* the thirty-six righteous men whose existence is a secret hidden from all save the Lord. Their number never varies: before one dies, another is born; else this iniquitous world, upheld only by their righteousness, would go down to destruction and disappear.

As the lights of the guttering Sabbath candles flickered in their brass sconces and shadows took possession of the kitchen, Yachneh Dvosie usually had trouble putting the children to bed. Only the promise of more stories on the morrow, before the *Havdalah* terminated the Sabbath, would get them to sleep.

The young man of twelve also looked forward to the end of the Sabbath day when, between *mincha* and *maariv,* he and his friends would gather in a corner of the synagogue with full intentions of using the time between the afternoon and evening prayers to discuss "a *shtikel* Torah." Yet they usually ended by telling tales.

Of course their tales were different from Yachneh Dvosie's kitchen *maasehs.* Some of them had begun to dabble in the Kabbalah, and they were interested in the stories that dealt with the transmigration of souls that became *dybbukim* or *gilgulim,* and in those condemned to wander about in the world of *Olam Hatohu.*

By a natural transition, the stories went on to the great Hasidic *Zadikim,* the saints who in the most miraculous way stopped in the middle of ordinary occupations and went off on unexpected journeys that resulted in restoring lost souls to peace and eternal rest. The mysterious, special wisdom of the *Zadikim,* who bridged heaven and earth by means of a purity undefiled by earthly considerations, was a constant theme for their stories.

It must not be assumed, however that these young people never deviated from such serious matters. With the approach of Purim they might be found reading the tale of "Koppel the Cymbals Player, or the Dead Who Came to Shul to Celebrate Purim," subtitled "The Gay Ghosts—A Remarkable Story for Old and Young." With Purim-licensed frivolity they might also dip into a volume of "Beautiful Short Stories, Humorous and Comical."

The most intellectual fare among this humorous Purim literature was a parody entitled "The Folio on Purim from the Talmud of Drunkards, with Many Learned Commentaries, Composed by One Who Had Gained Fame in the Science of Imbibing—a Precious Limb Sprung from the Root of the Vine."

During the frivolous Purim season the *yeshiva* students indulged in a pastime which required considerable mathematical skill. Armed with *goral* or fortune books, they labored to fathom the future.

The *goral* book or chart was a very complicated affair, requiring an accurate knowledge of one's name and those of one's parents, the date and the very hour of birth, and the signs of the zodiac. The combination of specific verses from the Bible related to one's name, the numerical value of each letter of these verses, plus acrostic combinations of name and verses placed in the proper boxes, gave the exact information on what was destined to transpire at a particular time of one's life. Many a young man labored to discover, for instance, whether the bride selected for him by his father, and whom he had met only once if at all, was his *basherter zivug* (his predestined mate). He strove to arm himself with such foreknowledge so that he might avoid disaster in later life.

His more ascetic and learned comrade, who secretly dabbled in the Kabbalah, looked with a patronizing eye upon these efforts. Should he desire to stoop to mere personal matters, he could completely alter the course of his life by means of the Kabbalah. Instead, he was seriously considering abandoning the theoretical Kabbalah for the forbidden practical Kabbalah, so that he might force the hand of the Almighty and bring about the redemption of Israel before the appointed messianic time.

Thus the people sought at both poles—the personal and the national—to foresee and influence the course of future events. The *kleine menshelach* prayed and wept and turned to their books for solace. The idealistic mystics, deeply concerned with the fate of the whole people and largely unaware of the new movement, political Zionism, sought in their own way to put an end to the *galut*. For them the instrument for hastening the coming of the Messiah was the Kabbalah, and they therefore sought to master its hidden mysteries.

These seekers of hidden knowledge never determined what fate had in store for them. And this was just as well. They might otherwise have recognized the internal dissolution, already begun in Jewish life, which was to make survival for them and for their kind more difficult with each passing day. They might otherwise have foreseen the final cataclysm in which a psychopathic Austrian corporal would one day unleash the forces that would destroy them, their children, and their whole remarkale world.

THE JEWISH BOOK

By JACOB S. MINKIN

FOR SOME TIME past, those interested in the dissemination of Jewish culture have been thinking, wondering, and worrying, not a little sadly, about the Jewish book. This Jewish book we hear so much about, what shall be its quality and character, its mark of identification, as it were, to stamp it as Jewish? Shall we regard as Jewish all books written by Jews, no matter the language and the choice of literary material, or only such books as display some sense of Jewish awareness on the part of their writers? There are writers of Jewish descent who disdain to write as Jews, whose hearts are not lacerated by Jewish doubts and problems, who, indeed, would resent it if rumors of their Jewish identity were to be circulated—are their works to be considered part of the creative Jewish genius? Ahad Ha-am raised this issue nearly a generation ago, and he decided the question in his own way. But the matter has become more complicated in recent years since the literary sphere of Jewish men of letters has been enlarged and they now figure prominently in almost all the literatures of the world.

At the outset it must be remarked that no such question could be raised with regard to books written by non-Jewish authors. In the case of other literatures the problem is comparatively simple. Language is the index of a people's literature. The language in which a book is written gives it a stamp, a character, a sense of belonging as it were. Thus, there will be little dispute that books written in English are English, no matter the choice of the writer's material. Shakespeare, for instance, has drawn his material from a variety of sources, but because he wrote in the English language, his work is indisputably English. And the same may be said of the literary pro-

305

ductions of writers in other languages. In other words, language is the barometer of a nation's literature, the unfailing, exquisite, sensitive test by which it naturally and spontaneously lives and has its being.

There was a time when the same was true of the Jewish book. Hebrew was the natural expression of the Jew; its roots lay deep in his inner life; it was his superb, his only medium of communication. What he thought and wrote, he poured into the vessel of this language. There was no question then about the authenticity of the Jewish book. Even when the content was foreign, the form, the very vocabulary in which it was written, stamped it as Jewish. There is a wealth of material in Jewish literature which came from non-Jewish sources, but because it was clothed in the garments of Hebrew speech, no one ever disputed that it was authentically Jewish. There are scholars who maintain that Job is a Greek drama, and so it may be; but because it came down to us in Hebrew form, it became part of the Jewish genius and was included in the Bible.

When the Jews went into exile—indeed, long before then—and Hebrew ceased to be fully alive, they adopted an Aramaic idiom for their national tongue. But because of its close resemblance to the Hebrew language and its Hebrew characters, it became the folk-language of the Jews in which the Talmud was written. The Zohar, indeed a goodly portion of the Kabbalistic literature, contains thoughts, ideas, and doctrines many of which are more pagan than Jewish, but having been composed in the Jewish vernacular, who will suspect the piety and devotion good and pure-hearted Jews lavish upon it?

Language ceased to be the test of the Jewish book after the first century or so, when Jews, coming under the influence of Hellenic culture and civilization, began to write in Greek. A great and rich literature tapping almost every form of literary and philosophic expression, was the result of this period. Anonymous writers almost without number rivaled one another in transforming and translating the genius of their people into the new garb. Hebrew was no longer the vocabulary of these men, but the quality of their work was nevertheless Jewish because it was rooted in the national Jewish memories and consciousness. In other words, the exigencies of their times and experience brought about a new test of the Jewish book. Without regard to language, it was now the writer's point of view, his Jewish slant, as it were, which determined the quality of his book.

The same was true when, centuries later, Arabic became the spoken and written language of the Jews. After the rise of Mohammedanism, during a span of time longer than the Hellenic period, Jewish thinkers, writers, and liturgical poets composed their works in the current Arabic tongue. A brilliant literature arose which in scope and influence is unparalleled in Jewish history. But although not written in Hebrew, it is Hebraic in tone and substance, down to the very Hebrew characters in which many a writer composed his Arabic works.

When, during the Middle Ages, in addition to the national Hebrew language, a popular folk vernacular, Yiddish, came into use and Jews began to write in this dialect, the character and identity of the Jewish book did not change. Written in Hebrew characters and wholly by Jews, one will not hesitate to classify books written in this language as Jewish. From the *maaseh buch* in the sixteenth century and Nahman Bratzlav's fairy tales in the nineteenth century down to the latest Yiddish literary production, books composed in this tongue indubitably belong to the cultural and spiritual wealth of the Jewish people.

Indeed, the Jewish book is never so truly and characteristically Jewish as when it is written in Yiddish. From this language, more so than from any other, one can build up a picture of Jewish life both in the old and in the new world. Do we want to know the pain and struggle of the Jewish masses, Rosenfeld and Yehoash sing of them in touching and tender verses; are we interested in the humor and bitterness of the Jewish world that passed, we need but resort to the volumes of Mendele and Sholom Aleichem; have we a taste for Hasidic stories, few told them more beautifully than J. L. Peretz and Sholem Asch. The pathos of Jewish life as well as its peculiar romance and charm have been caught up by a host of writers who, with skill and understanding, made the Yiddish book genuinely and characteristically Jewish.

Until comparatively recently, therefore, the Jewish book presented no problem. Its identity could not be mistaken, the stamp of belonging was plainly upon it. It was written by Jews and in the language of the Jews. It had character, identity, one might almost say a personality all its own. Until the eighteenth century, books written by Jews were Jewish; no one else but Jews would write about Jews. Books written by other hands, were either to attack the Jews or to lampoon them. Of the latter there was quite an extensive literature during the Middle Ages, some, unfortunately, the work of Jewish renegades; but by no stretch of the imagination could they be classified as Jewish books.

But the French Revolution and its consequent emancipation of the Jews changed all that. The fall of the Bastille did more than merely crash the ghetto walls; it set the Jews flying in all directions, mentally and spiritually as well as politically and economically. A compact body became a universal organism; a people living in isolation became citizens of the world. The Jews took the declarations of liberalism literally and lost no time in implementing them by engaging freely in all the trades and professions as well as in all the arts and sciences. They made all the alphabets and vocabularies of Europe their own, and rivaled their fellow-countrymen as journalists, poets, dramatists, and novelists. They changed roles quickly and with eagle-like agility. From passive and indifferent spectators, they became eager and even aggressive participants. It did not matter that their benefactors were irked by this sudden intrusion and that dire consequences might result. Nor had they stopped to consider the price they were paying, that in the new intellectual atmosphere their old Jewish culture was dissolving, and that their alien books and ideas were supplanting a tradition of proven strength and durability. To these things they gave little heed; all they knew was that the tide was set in their favor and they were resolved to take full advantage of the opportunity while it lasted.

It was at this point that the Jewish book became a problem. As pointed out, a people's literature is either written in its own language, or, as in the case of the Jews, on subjects closely related to them. But who would presume to call Jewish the large number of books that were written by Jews in the years following their emancipation? Indeed, as if with spiteful and malicious intent, they emasculated their Jewishness, so that in their brilliant salons and in their artistic life not the vaguest reference to it remained. With their own hands they melted down the ore of which the pillars of their life were cast; they took without paying back; they recognized no obligation to the community from which their genius borrowed, so that, no matter how much others rejoiced in their work, as far as the Jews are concerned, it lacked unity, harmony, and a deepening sense of power. For no man can forsake his camp, be false to his origin, without paying the price.

Heinrich Heine, Ludwig Boerne, Ferdinand Lassalle, and to a lesser degree, Karl Marx who ended by abusing and lampooning his erstwhile brethren—all born and nurtured in the bosom of Israel—are perhaps the most famous illustrations of the point we wish to make. No other men so closely approached the social vision of the ancient Hebrew prophets as they. Their work was uniquely and characteristically Jewish. There was a spirit of rebellion in these men. They looked forward to a new world order of which we are still at the beginning. They charged against political oppression; they assailed class and social distinctions, and delivered mighty thrusts at the entrenched power of wealth and economic injustice with the same fervor and passion as did their forebears of old, and like them, they suffered for their ideals. Nonetheless, who would think of regarding Heine's poems, Boerne's *Letters from Paris,* or Karl Marx's *Kapital* as Jewish books? They cannot be said to have been peculiarly sensitive on the subject of their Jewish extraction. The men, who themselves remind one of the Old Testament prophets, never so much as made allusion to the prophets in their writings. When they wrote they did not descend into the inner sanctuary of their Jewish life, if they had one; they did not probe for the spiritual threads of the Jewish future; the national life of their people with their tragedies, hopes, and aspirations played no part in their work. They looked beyond their people toward a dream and vision they imagined greater and richer than those in which they were born. Heine loved and enthusiastically admired the Old Testament, but his admiration was more romantic than real. His writings abound in bitter thrusts at the Jews with Semitic noses walking about vulgarly with large crucifixes upon their chests while he himself was baptized not once, but twice. Ludwig Boerne railed against the sunless street of the ghetto in which he was born and weakly advocated its abolition, but he never systematically and persistently contemplated the conditions that created it or the means which would nullify it. Jews inspired Karl Marx with a feeling of aversion and contempt because of the commercialism with which he naïvely charged them. And as for Ferdinand Lassalle, the flaming torch and avenging sword of the

German working classes, and, had he willed to become so, the savior of his own people, he suffered persecution and imprisonment for one woman and death for another.

A moral and spiritual bankruptcy unknown among the nations had been visited upon the Jews. As a rule, men of talent or genius do not cut themselves off from their people, make no attempt to destroy the roots which gave them sustenance, never intentionally obscure anything that is characteristic of their origin. On the contrary, they do everything to emphasize it so that all the world may admire the rock from which they were hewn. Jewish writers and artists alone are the exception. They not only take no pride in the people which nourished their creative power, but boast of the success with which they erased the ancient landmarks. Georg Brandes explored the intellectual wealth of all nations, wrote on all literatures, took up and defended all causes, and protested against all wrongs; but the wrongs that were committed against the people into which he was born he left discreetly alone. The man who hailed the creative spirits of almost all peoples in thousands of pages, ignored or was ignorant of the spiritual and intellectual heritage of the people of which, as a Jew, he might have been expected to write with authority.

The same might be said of many others, whose names, alas, are legion. They enriched the literatures of all the world while impoverishing their own; they shared the pride and boast of almost every nation while the heroes and thinkers of their own people left them cold and indifferent. And this, in large measure, is the reason why many a writer has failed to reach the highest level of development and why his work is stamped more or less with the seal of untruth. A man cannot empty himself of what is best and truest within him, scorn what he alone knows at first hand, and produce lasting work. Stefan Zweig is dead barely more than a year and what does the world remember of the more than forty books he had written? They are all but forgotten. One ventures the prediction that if his name shall at all be rescued from oblivion, it will be among the people he spurned and rejected, those he remembered only in his one book, *Jeremiah*. There Zweig is uniquely and singularly Jewish, the tone and color of his race and ancestors adorn its pages, harking back to a tradition that is spangled with kings and prophets, with altars, temples, and the rich guttural of the Hebrew speech.

Franz Werfel is at present the most widely known "Jewish" writer in this country, although he himself has done his utmost to dispel this allegation. He has proved that he is not allergic to Jewish themes, and when one comes to his hand, he masters it with exceptional insight and depth of understanding. Among his youthful dramas is a play, *Paul Among the Jews,* in which Rabbi Gamaliel, the teacher of Paul, is handled with considerable clarity and sympathy. Like Stefan Zweig, he is also author of a book, *Hearken Unto the Voice,* which one might call a narrative poem based on the life of the Prophet Jeremiah, a work of delicate texture and precision, one might almost say of sensuous beauty, in which everything lives and glows and is splashed with the dazzling sunshine of the Palestine sky. The cumulative effect of the book is well-nigh overpowering. Jeremiah at the king's court, at the gates of the Temple, the stern prophet, the tender and compassionate lover of his people who prophesies evil, yet soothes and comforts them when the evil descends upon them, the man who sits and mourns in the ruins of their fallen glory, yet his gaze directed upon an ideal far beyond the ken of the despairing multitudes—all these things are depicted against a background that is majestic and stupendous.

Yet this man, who in a mood of self-illumination, writes, "I am therefore one of the people of the covenant, and although I did not know my father, yet he is in me, and his fathers and their fathers are in me too, back to the first and the last father. . . . And it is this first and last father, the God of my fathers, who sets me in opposition to all the others and has allotted me a fate for which there is no solution" (*Hearken Unto the Voice,* p. 29), as if to belie his own words, makes his American debut with two Catholic books, *Embezzled Heaven* and *The Song of Bernadette!* Are these hollow and empty words without meaning or substance, or are they the voicing of a conflict, an inner rage going on in the soul of the artist perpetually at odds with himself? This writer believes the latter to be the case. For underneath his veils and masks, there is in every true artist an inner spirit which will not be destroyed— the innate spirit of his people which is an avenging spirit, exacting terrible punishment from those who sin against it.

It would, of course, be absurd to suggest that the artist must be limited in his choice of material to the people from which he stems. But if he is a true artist, true to the Holy Ghost of his craft, so to say, there must be some inner unity between the writer and his subject, an instinctive feeling, a depth of sympathy and understanding. Werfel's education and upbringing may have been different, but what is closer to Jewish sympathy and experience than the subject of *Embezzled Heaven?* He must have heard in his childhood any number of stories of pious Jewish women who, for the good of their souls, had literally denied themselves and their families their last crust of bread to support a student of the Torah that he might one day become a great rabbi and they thereby reap their reward in heaven, only to discover to their chagrin that, instead of the Torah he was believed to be studying, he was clandestinely preparing himself for examinations in some secular school. These is no parallel in Jewish experience to the story of *The Song of Bernadette,* but Werfel the mystic might have found ample opportunity for his imaginative faculty in the wonder tales of the Hasidic saints and teachers which Martin Buber so poetically recorded in his *Chassidische Buecher.*

His lofty mind, noble idealism, ethical outlook, and his keen and sensitive sympathy have given Franz Werfel a position as one of the greatest world humanitarians. When during the last World War, the Armenians were persecuted by the Turks, who had robbed, decimated, and driven them from their homes, Werfel voiced his blazing protest in *The Forty Days of Musa Dagh.* We do not begrudge the Armenians the flaming sword a Jew had raised in their behalf. A man of genius owes an obligation to the world besides the community in which he was born. But where was that avenging sword when right outside his window Werfel heard the moans of thousands of stricken Jewish victims, indeed, when he himself suffered the cruelties and barbarities committed against his people?

A questionnaire directed by a Jewish periodical to eleven writers of Jewish descent "under forty" as to what place, if any, their Jewish heritage played in their creative literary work, is revealing. When the question is not dismissed entirely as irrelevant, it is treated sometimes with disdain, sometimes with superior, snobbish aloofness, and by some with frank and unconcealed contempt. Only three or four confess to some sort of Jewish awareness in their writing. Thus one of the "emancipated" delivers himself: "When I write, I make no attempt to see things through the eyes of a Jew. It seems to me that too many Jews fall into a sort of soul-sickness, whereby they become the center of a universe—a dark universe where forces are pro-Jewish or anti-Jewish, where Jews are hated or persecuted or tolerated or loved—and so on ad infinitum. The logical end of this sort of thing is on one hand the dark and neurotic world of Ludwig Lewisohn or on the other the savage, irrational semi-fascistic world of a Ben Hecht. . . . For me, the Jew is a man. He is persecuted; so are other minorities. He is libeled, so are others. There is discrimination against him; is there none against the Negroes? He has been murdered, tortured, driven across the face of the earth, but isn't that the fate of millions who are not Jews?" Some regret the imputation of a Jewish slant in their work and feel that its presence is a hindrance rather than help to them.

We do not blame them as individuals for such feeling, for a thousand tragic factors in the Jewish position in the world produced these results. But who, indeed, will maintain that by deploring our losses, we are committing treason against the world? Who will pretend that by delving into the obscure corners of our people and their history, humanity thereby suffers a loss? What man or woman with a correct feeling and understanding of art and literature will say that Rembrandt, by filling his canvases with Dutch figures or Tolstoy by peopling his pages with Russian characters, have betrayed the art and literature of the world? How has the cause of art and literature suffered by the enrichment of these countries? The contrary seems to us to be the case. By interpreting their national types, they shed light and understanding on lands and cultures which otherwise might have remained obscure and unknown.

Likewise, how would the world suffer if our Brandeses and Zweigs and Werfels and a host of others, gave their talent, or a small portion of it, to the service of their people; if they revealed to the world that which is at present unfamiliar; if they gave life and form and warmth to men and incidents which to an unfriendly world seem strange and grotesque? Ludwig Lewisohn, to cite but one example, "wallowing in his Jewishness," might have followed the easy course and gone on creating Methodist types of the Southern variety, duplicating the work of many others. But he chose for himself the harder course, wrote *Up-Stream, The Island Within, Israel,* and *Mid-Channel* and became the teacher and guide of a generation. It is for others to judge the literary quality of his work, but as a torch to his people, as an awakener and summoner of minds that were perplexed and bewildered, he permanently affected thousands of lives.

After this long detour, the question, What is a Jewish book? almost answers itself. We have seen that the test of language, important as it is under other conditions, is not for us, at least not in our present dispersed and scattered life. There will come a time, and for a considerable portion of our people the time has already come in Palestine, when our national literature will be written in the only language which is the symbol of our national unity—Hebrew. But for us, children of the *galut,* the criterion of language no longer suffices, and we must therefore look for some other quality which might make our books Jewish. Nor is Jewish authorship alone enough to give a writer's work Jewish value, for, as we have seen, many a Jewish writer has so de-Judaized his work as to make it belong to the language in which it was written without even a suggestion that it stems from Jewish craftsmanship. Content and point of view are something; but here, too, large reservations must be made, for many a non-Jew has written with sympathy and understanding on Jewish subjects, yet one wonders whether their books may legitimately be called Jewish.

One, therefore, roughly speaking, is compelled to define the Jewish book as one written by Jews in a manner to reveal the national spirit and Jewish consciousness of the writer. Mere meandering in the Jewish field is not enough, nor scrupulous detailing of facts and incidents. These things are necessary in order to give one's work character and authenticity, but they are the scaffolding as it were; the inner spirit does not depend upon them. What gives a book Jewish value is when, in spirit and content, it is recognizably Jewish, in other words, the product of the author's authentic and uniquely conscious Jewish life.

If this definition of the Jewish book be correct, then to our shame and humiliation it must be admitted that, at least in the English language, there are not many books to answer to this description, although there are notable examples of it in other languages. But although the harvest is scant, there is no reason for discouragement. The national Jewish revival which is making itself felt everywhere, holds out the promise of restoring to us the talents of which we have long been deprived. Under a quickened tempo of Jewish life, our creative thinkers and writers will realize that to produce true and lasting work, they must return to the source of their nourishment, instead of scattering their energies to all the winds. Then we shall have a Jewish literature worthy of its name—alive, dignified, and vocal with the quickening impulse of a living people.

WHY I WROTE A JEWISH NOVEL

By NINE CONTEMPORARY NOVELISTS

During the past year there have been an extraordinarily large number of novels of Jewish interest published in the United States by Jewish authors sensitively aware of their Jewish material. *Congress Weekly,* in an attempt to discover from the novelists themselves some of the factors of importance involved in the writing of their books, asked nine contemporary novelists the following questions:

1. Why did you, in writing your book, select a Jewish theme or a major Jewish character?

2. What was the critical and public reaction to your book?

3. What opinion do you have about the book's reception?

4. Do you plan to continue to write on Jewish themes, or to project Jewish characters in your future work? If so, why? If not, why not?

The editors of *Congress Weekly* believe that the following statements offer an important insight into the thinking, as Jews and as creative artists, of some of the most prominent and promising Jewish writers in America.

ZELDA POPKIN

I have written not one "Jewish theme" novel but two. *Small Victory* was published in 1947. It was a novel about the survivors of the concentration camps and the anti-Semitism of American Military Government in Germany. It was based upon an actual, unpublicized and significant episode of the postwar period, the reopening of the German universities with a *numerus clausus,* and it was in a sense a documentary novel. I wrote it out of profound feeling, aware that by using the fictional form, one can blow hot and cold upon events and give them emotional impact. My publishers thought it was a good book and so did I. Although my previous novel, *The Journey Home,* had been a best-seller, we lost money on this one. It was ignored by both Gentile reviewers and the Jewish audience.

With that experience, since I earn my living by my typewriter, it was with trepidation that I tackled another "Jewish theme" book and then I wrote it for the only reason that a novelist goes through the long drudgery and creative agony—because this was what I most wished to write. *Small Victory* was a product of anger and pain; *Quiet Street* is a gift of love.

I am not a Johnny-come-lately in discovering my Jewishness and it has never been a source of conflict, self-hatred or even minor trouble to me. I was reared in Orthodoxy and I liked it. The festive spirit of the Holy Days and the Shabbat are part of the richness of my childhood. I went to *cheder;* I wrote Purim and Hanukkah plays and childish poems of religious content. Perhaps because my Jewishness was affirmative, or perhaps because I grew up in American small towns, or perhaps, too, because I have long been a writer, no door has ever been closed to me and I have personally never known the frustrations and cruelties of anti-Semitism. Yet, when I went to Germany in 1945, in the uniform of the American Red Cross, I found a complete identification with the survivors of nazism, and when I first went to Israel in 1948, there, too, I belonged.

I wrote about the siege of Jerusalem because it was one of the great stories of all time and it moved me deeply. But I found I was writing of the men, women and children who went through that siege not as strange and exotic creatures, but as people at home, as much at home as white Protestants in Plainfield, N.J.

The book is still recent and I shall not be surprised at whatever happens. But some things I know, and know emphatically about the "Jewish audience," and these are not pleasant ones. One is that the "Jewish audience" prefers to read books written by Gentiles about Jews; another that it will not support a "Jewish theme" book unless that book has earned the accolades of the Gentile world. Whether this is shyness or snobbery, I am not sure, but by and large, American Jews, like American Gentiles, limit their reading to the sex and sensationalism which tops the best-seller lists. The writer who tackles a Jewish theme may be a happier man for having returned to his times a bit of understanding and compassion or having cleansed his own emotional closets, but the chances are that, financially, he will be a poorer man.

I do not know whether I shall write another "Jewish theme" novel. I have at the moment no plans for future creative work. But I do know that when I undertake another work of fiction I shall write about people, and naturally, Jews are among them.

ETHEL ROSENBERG

The simplest precept for the new writer is perhaps the easiest to follow and in writing *Go Fight City Hall* and subsequently *Uncle Julius and the Angel with Heartburn* I stayed more or less within the bounds of the rule—write about what you know best. In the creation of the character of Uncle Julius I limited myself to an American-Jewish background, since Uncle Julius was the product of that exciting mixture of Europe and America which created that colorful world. There was still another reason. It seemed to me there was room for a book to present the Jews without problems, other than the every-day garden variety, and with their capacity for joy and humor and warmth shown—in other words, one more side of the picture that we don't get to see often enough. Judging from the response of both the critics and the reading public, I should say there was general agreement on this point. I was, naturally, most gratified.

At this moment, I cannot say in which direction any future work will take. I have nothing planned. If such stories or ideas evolve needing a Jewish background, I shall continue along the same lines; if not, then I may go on to something else. I am entirely in the hands of my characters.

YURI SUHL

I have selected a Jewish theme for my novel *One Foot in America* because it is a theme I am most at home with. I say "at home with" and not "familiar with" because a writer can, with the aid of painstaking research, become thoroughly familiar with his material and yet not be sufficiently at home with it to justify his choice of this material for his literary theme. It takes more than an intellectual understanding of the subject matter to shape it into a successful literary product.

The author's subjective attitude to and emotional involvement with his theme and characters are vital components of the creative process. It is these elements that imbue his work with that living, pulsating quality without which his finished product may sound factually authentic but emotionally unconvincing. And without the ring of conviction permeating the atmosphere of his story there can be no genuine reader-character identification.

If I have restated here what to most creative writers is common knowledge it is only because the Jewish theme in American literature has, to a considerable degree, suffered from a grievous lack of the above-mentioned two components. Many writers were attracted to the Jewish theme, nibbled at it and, after the first bite, fled from it never to return again. The reason for this, it seems to me, lies in the fact that their initial interest was an external one and did not stem from a deep personal need for this theme. They went slumming to the Jewish theme and wrote as outsiders looking in. And what usually strikes the eye of the outsider first is the quaint, the bizarre and the negative.

With some the choice of a Jewish theme was motivated by box-office opportunism. Others came to it with an air of charitable condescension, easing their conscience by throwing the Jewish theme a few crumbs of their creative talents. And of the few who took to the Jewish theme out of an honest groping for self-identification some were *a priori* headed for failure because their premise was unsound and befogged by mysticisms.

It is easy to see, therefore, why the end products of some of these writers have done us more harm than good. Let me give a few illustrations. It is a known fact that Budd Schulberg's *What Makes Sammy Run?* was incorporated in Hitler's anti-Semitic arsenal in the form of a German translation. Various Jewish organizations at one time found it necessary to campaign for the withdrawal of some of Jerome Weidman's books from circulation for similar reasons. And, in my opinion, Norman Katkov's *Eagle at My Eyes* attained best-seller status only because of its sensational thesis that

Jews hate Gentiles even more than Gentiles hate Jews. This must certainly have come as a soothing revelation to many an anti-Semite who now had it on no less an authority than Norman Katkov that his anti-Semitism was practically nothing more than self-defense.

But to return to the original question. For me the selection of a Jewish theme for my first novel, for the second one that is now in progress and for those that will follow, is a natural one. As an immigrant who came to this country in his early teens the process of my Americanization was not accompanied (as so frequently happens) by a process of alienation from my cultural heritage of the past and the American Jewish community. Quite the contrary. It was here, in America, that I came to know the secular face of this heritage. Side by side with my discovery of Jack London, George Eliot, Edgar Allen Poe and Walt Whitman, came the discovery of Mendele, Peretz, Sholom Aleichem, Bergelson, Asch, Kobrin, Rosenfeld and Edelstadt. This dual process is still going on with me and I do not find it in any way contradictory or conflicting. Rather, I find it broadening and enriching.

I believe, therefore, that the choice of the Jewish theme does not constitute a limitation of the writer's literary range. I consider a work of fiction on the Jewish theme as integral a part of the broad stream of American literature as the American-Jewish community is of the American scene generally.

Unfortunately, many editors and publishers in this country do not share this view. They persist in treating the Jewish theme as a second-class citizen in the community of literature. And since they wield the tremendous power of either bringing the book to the public or preventing it from ever seeing the light of day, they must be held largely responsible for the lack of growth of American-Jewish culture. I would like to cite two instances from my own personal experience. The editor of a well-known literary prestige magazine in which a short story of mine on a Jewish theme had been printed, a half year later rejected another story of mine on the grounds that, "I have done more than my share in printing Jewish stories." One publisher rejected *One Foot in America* because he had recently published a book on a Jewish theme and did not want his firm to be "stigmatized as a Jewish house." In his introduction to his anthology *This Land, These People,* Harold U.

Ribalow cites some startlingly revealing statistics about short stories on Jewish themes that support my contention.

But despite the difficulties confronting the writer on the Jewish theme, books do manage to appear and it is heartening to note that a new crop of talented American writers like Louis Falstein, Saul Levitt, Miriam Bruce and others are writing on the Jewish theme and treating it with a sense of honesty and dignity that justifies the hope that more works on Jewish themes will be forthcoming from these writers.

The critical and public reaction to my book was both gratifying and encouraging. It was reviewed in many publications throughout the country and practically all reviews were on the plus side.

I am now at work on my second novel dealing with contemporary Jewish life in America. After I finish that I intend to write a fictionalized biography of the Yiddish poet Morris Rosenfeld.

DAVID MILLER

1. The selection of a Jewish theme was a process of growth stemming out of a long absorption of details concerning my own background and that of my family. It was not my original intention to make use of the milieu that later provided the framework of *The Chain and the Link.* The first plan was to deal with a narrative concerning an immigrant family in the American Middle West.

From the beginning it became apparent that a greater familiarity with cultural background and roots was in order. A search began for a starting point. It was found in the Lithuanian-White Russian provinces of the nineteenth-century tsarist empire. The life of that period and locale became the literary vehicle which could carry the cultural "load" absorbed through training and environment.

So much for the question of "milieu"—"framework"—"culture." For at this point another factor intervened. It was the need to extract meaning from the accumulated material in terms of human aspirations that went beyond the period and the locale selected. The retreat into the cultural past became joined with the necessity to break forth toward the future. Out of the implications of such a withdrawal, coupled with such a drive toward moving forward, there ensued the development of the theme presented in *The Chain and the Link*. The characters were chiefly Jewish, the background was chiefly Jewish, and yet there was an effort—not always deliberate—to extract a significance applicable to the non-Jewish as well.

The situation is here intellectually stated—divested of the emotional implications. But it will suffice to present a thumbnail sketch of what took place.

This, as accurately as it can be given at the moment, is the answer to the "why" of your question.

2. The critical reaction has been highly encouraging. The same is true of the public reaction. During the period of writing and of editing there was concern that the theme, background, treatment would prove too esoteric for the reviewers and critics in the general press. Juding by the response of critics writing for *The Saturday Review of Literature, The New York Times, The New York Herald Tribune,* and a Catholic periodical, among others, the concern was groundless. Where the critics made adverse comment, the points raised did not have reference to the use of Jewish background or theme. Interestingly enough, the sole objection—to my knowledge—directed against the use of a Jewish historical period, not specifically modern in locale and plot development, appeared in a periodical belonging to the English-Jewish press.

3. Considering the level of fiction sales in general at the present time, the fact that this was a first novel, together with the nature of the background, the reception of *The Chain and the Link* has not been discouraging. It is probable that had the book not been Jewish in theme, particularly had it not been historical in time and remote in locale, the public reception would have been greater. This applies to the Jewish as well as to the non-Jewish public.

The full extent to which this is true is difficult to gauge for the reason that another factor must be considered apart from the Jewish theme—and that is the use of what might be described as an analytical-philosophical approach. Background, era, locale, theme, approach—all presented handicaps. Inherent in such handicaps, however, there is a challenge that can best be met through the achievement of quality. Yet the entire task of surmounting the handicap cannot be laid upon the writer. It is also necessary to develop receptiveness on the part of the public. Here the task must be shared with the critic, with periodicals such as yours, and with all those—including the public itself—who are genuinely interested in literature as a statement of experience.

4. I wish to continue writing on Jewish themes and to develop Jewish characters. This does not mean that I wish to devote myself exclusively to them. There are many other themes that interest me—drawn from American life, and from modern life in general. The world is large and multiform, the potential scope of canvas attracts, the desire to grow as much as possible in depth and breadth exists. But having begun with Jewish themes, for the reasons already given, there is a desire to grow out of them—without spurning them—in an ever-widening and deepening search for the directing values of human living. The preference is to do so without sudden wrenches and abrupt departures. That is why public and critical acceptance is important. If that is unfavorable, because of Jewish theme or treatment, the relinquishment of such materials becomes inevitable. The table cannot be set if too few come to dine.

If the response remains favorable, and continues to grow, then a more natural, unforced development can ensue. It is not always necessary to state a Jewish thought or theme in terms of a specifically Jewish background. It is possible, even advisable, to distil meaning out of Jewish themes, thoughts, values, approaches, and apply them to the general non-Jewish scene—even through narratives that contain no Jewish characters or incidents. It is in brief a process of universalization whereby the total human values of Jewish life—ethnic, religious, philosophic—can be projected and broadened for the ultimate enrichment of Jewish and non-Jewish life both.

But in order to accomplish all this, the writer must be given the opportunity to develop without being pressed or discouraged by a reluctant reception. The avoidance of such an unpleasant development is, as previously indicated, the combined task of writer, critic, community, and publisher.

CHARLES ANGOFF

What happened to me in the case of *Journey to the Dawn*, I imagine, is what happens to most fiction writers. The theme selected me more than I selected the theme. The world of its people and situations became more and more a part of me across the years.

The people grew and developed almost through a power of their own. In time they became so much a part of me that I had little more to do, in a sense, than to organize them—make them presentable, so to speak, for human society. The people and situations are rooted in my personal past. But for years they were wholly or largely absent from my mind. Only in the past fifteen years have they come back to me. . . . As for the relationship of the characters in *Journey to the Dawn* to actual people in my own life, all I can say is that, as in all fictional works, my *fictional* people are, at most, only the remotest cousins to whatever "real" people they may, now and then, bring to mind to those who lived in the same world I lived in. They bear the same relation to the "real" people as does the memory of a scent to a rose of yesteryear. My fiction, to quote a beautiful phrase of Willa Cather's, is my "cremated youth."

The public reaction to *Journey to the Dawn* (and also to my previous collection of short stories, *When I Was a Boy in Boston*), so far as I know, has been uniformly good, heartening, and occasionally thrilling. I have found that on the whole, the "ordinary" reader has responded to and appreciated the lyricism I have tried to get into my fiction better than the professional critic. I always begin writing with an obsessive song in my heart and distant music-box hum in my head, which I try to put into such words that the reader, God willing, will experience the same or a similar song and hum. One evening last spring, as I was roaming the campus of the University of Kansas City, a woman in her middle thirties approached me and introduced herself. She said she wanted to tell me how she felt about the opening chapter in *Journey to the Dawn,* and also about several other chapters, but particularly the opening one. She said: "You write like an oboe." I'm afraid she exaggerated, but I shall always remember her tribute.

The critical reception? I shouldn't have grounds for complaint. Fully 99 per cent of the reviews were friendly and favorable, and some were both intelligent and exuberant. Perhaps two of the critics understood what I was trying to do, which is not at all a poor percentage in the critical world as a whole, *goyish* or otherwise. The level of comprehending, sensitive, and well-informed criticism these days is low enough in American literature, and all in all, it is not much worse in the realm of English-Jewish literature.

However, I was amazed by some of the remarks of the reviewers in the English-Jewish press. Three of them objected to my theme on the apparent ground that immigrant life was unworthy of the attention of the writer; yet these same critics went on to say that my book held their attention and to point out some of the "memorable" characters in it. I still don't understand why immigrant life is "unworthy" of the writer. I had thought everything of human interest was worthy of the artist. Can it be that the critics want to forget the past? But why? Then I was surprised by the fact that several of the English-Jewish papers couldn't find room for reviews of *Journey to the Dawn*. Plenty of room for society news, but very little for the discussion of literature. Is this in line with the tradition of the "People of the Book"? One of the most important of these journals had decided to ignore *Journey to the Dawn,* completely, as it had decided to ignore many other works of fiction, but the editor was badgered so persistently by one who admired the book that he finally did print a review of it—a very good one, but several months after publication date. I met the editor later, and he boasted of his heroic efforts in behalf of Jewish-American culture. I congratulated him. . . . As the result of the publication of *When I Was a Boy in Boston* and *Journey to the Dawn* I got to know the English-Jewish press fairly well. I am astounded by the shabbiness of so much of this press—its snobbishness, its poor taste, its immersion in petty politics, its editorial vacillation, its subservience to the social arbiters in its midst, and its abominable character from a journalistic technical point of view. Some of the papers and periodicals are on a high level, but the others—*zoll Gott ophitten!*

Journey to the Dawn is the first of a trilogy—and the trilogy made turn out to be a tetralogy. Hence the next three, four, and possible five years I shall devote, in large part, to writing about Jewish folk and situations. But at the same time I shall also write about others subjects. I have a longish anthology and critical study of George Jean Nathan in the works. I am also making notes for a study of the Mencken-Nathan-*American Mercury* period. A short novel, a fantasy, is now being polished for the third time. A sonnet sequence has begun to *boozhe* me. . . . In short, I am an Amerian and a human being as well as a Jew—and as in the past I shall continue to write of people and things in all forms of the literary art, from these various points of view. I imagine, though, that more Jews will appear in my imaginative writing hereafter than hereto-fore. My distant past, which was steeped in Jewishness, as is made evident in *Journey to the Dawn,* is becoming more "real" to me than my immediate past or the present. I believe Willa Cather—I refer to her again because I have the highest respect for her fiction and her critical essays—was right when she said that the first twenty-one years of a writer's life form the total of his fruitful ex-perience from the imaginative standpoint.

HERMAN WOUK

Characters and themes are not always consciously "selected." Lieutenant Barney Greenwald, the fighter pilot who is defense counsel in the courtmartial scene of *The Caine Mutiny,* simply walked into the book, so to speak, and stayed. He has the intelli-gence to see the events aboard the *Caine* in true perspective, and the wit to express his views; that is probably why he is in the book. Also, he has the legal skill to make a lost case into a very tight con-test.

In the future, as Jewish characters and themes occur to me, I will certainly use them. I know of no reason to avoid them. Per-haps an author, in the context of existing events, has an obligation to exercise common sense selection of such themes and characters; that is, to refrain from excoriating, mocking, or burlesquing Jew-ish people—on the theory that the task has been ably executed once for all in our century.

Regarding the reception of the novel, I can only say that I have been as fortunate as possible. The press liked it, and the readers have made a best-seller of it.

STEPHEN LONGSTREET

As my novel *The Pedlocks* is soon to be translated into Yiddish and German in Europe your letter interests me, as I did not write a book for Jews, or anyone else, but readers. I have always felt any writer who limits himself as either an American writer, or a Jew-ish writer, or for that matter any kind of a writer but as a writer of literature, is not a person who could be called a writer at all today. I have written about Jews before in my books, but *The Ped-locks* is the first book I have done in which the major section of the book is about Jewish family life.

Why did I write the book? I could have told you when I was writing it, but now I am on another book and the mood and method of *The Pedlocks* are far away. I saw a great deal of Jewish life as a boy. It interested me. My family had a Jewish base going back to my great-grandfather whose name was Weiner-Longstrasse. My grandfather called himself Longstreet and by that time the Jewish strain was getting thinner, and of the ritual and the dogma and the race very little was left. However, looking back I began to collect material of a family and a way of life that I had never lived but which somehow was of value to me in a world falling apart at the seams. Of course, little of this got into *The Pedlocks,* but some of it found a little space here and there.

Who are the Pedlocks? I didn't invent them and they were once living people. Most of them are dead. They died as Jews, or Christians, or as men without a godhead. They are a great many people and many families that I once knew and I have put them into this huge Jewish novel, but of course as fiction, which means I have changed here and there, colored, moved around, redated, invented an action, but in the main I think they are real and are the people I once knew.

I must confess they are not like the usual Jews in novels, but then I've never cared much for Jews in novels; the portable wailing walls, the dramatic laments, the grin and poverty, the theater of ghetto and ritual, the painful humor and the feeble desires to live up to the idea that they are the Chosen People. In real life I didn't find many such Jews. I will tell you a secret: Jews are just like other people. There is no racial type that colors all Jews, there is not even, I have found, a godhead that most of them follow. Not any more. But in the novel in the past, the Jew has been used as a type and a character that I never found.

You can't put a label on a person and that is what novels about Jews have been doing. I hate self-pity and most Jewish writers roll in it. I dislike black and white in any thing and the relationship of Jews and Gentiles is almost always presented in black and white. My Jews are human beings first. That certain people dislike Jews or tennis players or actors is too bad, but I don't think the Jew can solve anti-Semitism, because it's not a Jewish problem at all. It's a Christian problem. The Christian world, having invented it, must solve it or perish.

This doesn't mean I am for accepting anti-Semitism, but rather for seeing it for what it is: a perverted form of the Christian ideal and something the Jew must face and understand. My novel I think says a little clearer what I mean because I put a great deal of time into it.

The critics have liked my book. A few, I must admit, seemed to dislike Jews and avoided reviewing the book properly.

The public reaction has been fine, at least from my viewpoint. When I wrote "The Jolson Story," the people liked its picture of one facet of Jewish life, but they accepted it as comedy. *The Pedlocks* is accepted as a deeply thought-out book and one that has a lot to say, but always remember it is a story. Anyway it is as deep as I could make it. People write to me about the book, and people buy it and give it to their friends and relatives. Not just Jews. Being a writer who likes people this pleases me. There are, of course, those people who find fault with certain minor details of Hebrew ritual. The book was read in manuscript by two learned rabbis and if they disagreed I don't see much hope of making it perfect from a ritual point of view.

The readers want to know what I was trying to say. I think I was only trying to say, here is a good story worth telling and I hope worth reading. I did not expect the book to be such a success. I did not expect it to become a banner for Jewish culture and Jewish history, which it has become among certain Jewish groups. I worried about putting real Jews into the novel, people like Zangwill and Herzl and others, but it seems to have come off.

Yes, I am pleased by the reaction to the book, and I hope people keep letting me know how they feel about it. I don't like it to be called a Jewish book, or an American-Jewish book, or a book that pleases just one section of the nation. It certainly means as much to the non-Jew who feels a feeling for mankind as it does to the Jew. If I were writing just for Jews I would not write at all. My nature, my outlook, is fixed on the human being, the world, and our short time spent here on earth. I plead no special cause, creed or hope.

Do I intend to go on writing about Jews? Or on Jewish themes? Yes, if they fit the story; no, if I have to be labeled as a writer of this kind of story. I am now writing a novel about Southern California—one of the characters is a Hollywood movie producer. He's a Jew but only because most producers are. Would I make a violin player a Christian, or the Pope a Jew? Certain things are right for certain kinds of stories. But my producer is facing problems not as a Jew but a creative artist in an industry that destroys artists. It isn't other Jews or banks or bigotry that wreck my hero. It's just that there is no place today in a mass entertainment group for the true creative artist. If I can make this point clear you will understand how I use Jews in my books, as human beings not as folk heroes or symbols of a culture.

It seems to me, as a critic, that Jewish writers do the most harm to the Jews. Irwin Shaw, or in such a book as *The Naked and the Dead,* the Jews are dreadful figures of self-pity, inviting blows or acting in a way to arouse the fist or the dirty word. Perhaps these authors have found the world reacting to them in this way—but from what I have seen, most Jews of sense, of courage, of hope, walk the earth free men, honest men and proudly with an understanding that they are no better than the Negro, or the serf, or the masses or people any place. Bigots and evil men are against mankind and not just against Jews.

The wise Jew is not hurt by the country club, the bathing beach, the school that keeps him out. He is a free man in a free country and there is lots of room for him elsewhere. Besides he knows too that the Jew is not one color, one blend, one type and that the objectionable human being, the crude, vulgar, evil person, could just as well be a Jew, as a Baptist, Holy Roller, American Indian or Elk. Once the Jew knows he is no better than the next man, he will be sure he is no worse.

As for the Jew in American literature, he almost doesn't exist. As a Marxist he appears in certain minor novels not as a real person but as a symbol. As a businessman he is hinted at in certain books but never made clear. As a human being he is treated like smallpox or Chanel No. Five to solve a problem, point a moral or shake a finger. But full-grown as Huck Finn or Arrowsmith or Captain Hornblower he has yet to appear. Milt Gross, I think, came closer to catching on paper the vital human living of the Jewish family, its fables, tears and joys. The rest of the young Jews have been only bright and flip about the salesman who can get it wholesale, about the Jewish intellectual or the left-winger, about the Jewish banker or the smart young playwright or doctor. In glib comedy he has helped debase the American theater (but he didn't start that). As the writer of radio and TV wit the Jewish gag man is far from the healthy humor of the great Yiddish wits.

Where the Jewish artist has failed he has failed because he has lost the true Jewish hope, the true Jewish desire to serve art rather than money or Marx; perversion rather than the morals of the Torah. The smart Jewish publisher, the limp-wristed Jewish art dealer, the Bronx gag-writer, the Hebrew intellectual with his glass of tea is no worse than his Christian brother, but nevertheless he has failed to see in America the solid sheets for his talent. I don't mean that he should write of Jewish or Yiddish or Hebrew themes. But I do say he has failed to bring over from the vast treasure-chest of his blood those honest forces that made the Old Testament, the Laws, The Torah, the Chants real and important. That made Freud and Einstein and the great minds true to life and facts because they stood on solid ground. The American-Jewish writer and artist stand on shifting values of popular success, money in the bank, hope in class wars, dreamlands and fears and libidos that do him little credit.

I go into all this because I had to know all this before I wrote *The Pedlocks*. I had to avoid the faults of the others who tried to write of Jews in America. The job in the past has been badly done. I do not say I have done it well; I have only tried and I appear to have some success. But I do not intend to write novels about Jews and would never think of setting myself up as expert, even a close observer of the whole subject.

JAMES YAFFE

I am certainly glad to give what answers I can to your questions about my book. Please keep in mind, however, that this is my first book, I am very new to the whole publishing field, and therefore I can't really express a terribly authoritative opinion about my book's reception. Nevertheless, to take your questions one by one.

1. I wrote my stories about Jewish characters and a Jewish environment for no other reason than that these are the characters and environment that I know best. I believe that this is what a

writer ought to write about—especially when he is just starting out. I had no particular sociological axe to grind in picking Jewish characters. I do not think Jews are more (or less) interesting than other people—a good writer ought to make whatever he writes about interesting. Also I do not think my book is about "Jewish themes." I have written, I hope, about "universal" themes—which is a fancy way for saying that I have tried to show ordinary human beings going through ordinary human activities and dealing with human problems. The fact that these people are Jews gives a special flavor and atmosphere to the stories, but does not, I think, affect the basic themes.

2. The book enjoyed an excellent critical reception, but a small public reception.

3. I don't see how I can arrive at any valid general conclusions from the above facts. The enthusiastic response of the critics does seem to indicate that non-Jews are willing to take a book about Jews seriously, without thinking of it as a "specialized" sort of book. On the other hand, the meager public response does not for a minute indicate to me that the public will necessarily shy away from books about Jews, out of anti-Semitism or indifference or what-have you. The fact that I am a young unknown writer, and that this is a book of short stories (always bad sellers), has as much to do with the public response as the subject matter of the book.

4. Yes, I certainly do plan to go on writing about Jewish characters. I also plan—and have already done so in several short stories, and the novel that I'm working on now—to broaden my canvas to include other kinds of people that I'm familiar with. But I don't suppose I'll ever stop writing about Jews completely—you don't get away from your childhood that easily. Besides, Jews are fun to write about.

MIRIAM BRUCE

First of all, as to why I chose a Jewish theme: I think the answer to that is the same one you'd get if you asked any seriously intentioned writer why he chose any theme. I write about things that move me and make my life. My theme was not chosen intellectually and certainly not with deliberation, but emotionally, compulsively, if you like. I started with an emotional proposition of enormous importance to myself: that the American Jew is in constant danger of contracting anti-Semitism himself and dying of a sort of quiet soul-rot which so far nobody seems to have thought it worthwhile to discuss. Like most writers (I think), I started page one with more questions than answers, and I wasn't quite sure what I'd meant until I'd said it. In other words, *Linden Road* was not a tidy bit of construction laid down all ship-shape according to a well-drawn blueprint, nor even a polemic delivered because I thought it would "do people good," but simply the resolution of a private argument and what we would have referred to in the Innocent Thirties as a declaration of faith. I dare say there are writers whose motives are altruistic, but I am not among them.

So far as my experience has been concerned, your second and third questions are one. In the light of the pre-publication reaction to *Linden Road* I found the critical reception exceedingly curious. Before the book came out it had generated an astonishing amount of heat among people who'd seen it: a leading "Jewish" publishing house took violent objection to its ideological content, and I had the pleasure of being called a "dangerous woman" by a fashionable Jewish novelist who maintained that I was trying to push the Jews back into the ghetto. Once out, however, the book was received with a species of tame respect which, I admit, surprised me. The reviewers made my publishers very happy but, in the main, ignored the ideological implications of the book in favor of pointing out that I seemed able to tell a subject from a predicate. One of the few exceptions to this rule was your own reviewer, Mr. Charles Angoff, who, less favorably disposed than most of the other critics, nevertheless discussed the problem I was writing about as though it really existed elsewhere besides in my mind. In general, however, I have been left with the feeling that the subject of Jewish anti-Semitism is still taboo, particularly among Jews, and that most of my fellow-Jews would be grateful if next time I would confine myself to writing a nice clean love story.

As to your last question: I think I shall undoubtedly write more on Jewish themes. However, since besides being a Jew I am also a woman, an American, a human being, and probably half a dozen other things as well, I hope and intend to write on other themes, too.

THE DILEMMA OF THE JEWISH WRITER

By ABRAHAM ROTHBERG

To DISCUSS THE "Jewish writer" is to employ a linguistic con-venience; to deal with the problems of the "Jewish writer," one must deal with the problems of the Jew as well as of the writer, not to speak of that combined and different entity, "the Jewish writer." To write of the place of the Jew in America life in a short space would be presumptuous in the extreme, and what comments I make are therefore only prefatory. And what is a "Jewish writer"? Is he a writer who by accident of birth is Jewish, and must therefore have his work treated as "Jewish" writing? Is he a man who writes only of problems generally acknowledged to be "specifically Jewish" or origin or nature? Is he a writer whose native language is Yiddish and who writes in Yiddish? Or is he a man who accepts Judaism as a religion? And what of that more complicated genus, the "American-Jewish" writer, to use an attributive adjective far more appropriate to restaurant cuisines and Catskill hotels?

The Jewish writer I shall deal with was born a Jew, deals specifi-cally, although not necessarily solely, with Jewish characters, ma-terials, and problems, and whose Jewishness somehow subsumes his work. I think it is generally agreed that "Jewish writers" are not only those who write in Yiddish or in Hebrew, for if that were the case there would be very few "Jewish writers" indeed. I shall consider "American-Jewish" writers as those who live in the United States, and who write in English. But the "Jewish writer" is *not* unavoidably a religious Jew, nor is he devoted to writing for an all-Jewish audience. The difficulties that face the American writer who is a Jew are of two kinds then: first, he is a writer, and second, he is a Jew. It seems to me that the problems of the former condition, difficult enough at best, are multiplied by the problems of the latter.

The writer in America is faced with a public that is, by and large, distinterested in quality literature. They are in search of escape and the mass media—radio, moving pictures, television—are willing purveyors to their craving. The book publishing industry, and this includes the magazines, have since the beginning of the twentieth century tried to become mass media and have achieved an almost utter success. The few quality magazines and publishers that have persisted have done so either by catering to a relatively small audience, or by scaling down the general level of most of their materials for the general audience and continuing to publish a few worthwhile books for the rest. America is probably the most semi-literate nation in the world, and with the continued incursions of radio, cinema, and television, will in all likelihood become virtually illiterate in the future. Felicity of language, complexity of thought, or intensity of feeling are all things to be avoided in material that the writer—Jewish or Gentile—would present to this audience—Jewish or Gentile—through the editorial and publishing world—Jewish or Gentile. Publishing is a business, and publishers are in business to make money, and apparently they cannot make money with quality writing or even masterpieces. Some of the best writers of our time, James Joyce, for example, were denied the blessings of commercial publication, and often for what was their best work.

The writer is then faced with the choice of writing what the publishers can sell and will take, if he will be heard and if he would eat, or of writing what he would like and making his living in some other way. Then he may hope for publication in the literary quarterlies or, more formidable, he may hope for that strange miracle whereby every now and then some publisher, genuinely in love with literature, or out of *noblesse oblige,* or drunk or mad, decides to publish a "prestige" book and lose money by it. If the writer makes the first choice, he inevitably depletes his creativity, debases his style and thought, and eventually reaches the level of those writers who "might have" achieved something. If the writer makes the second choice, he must devote his prime energies to making a living, and his writing suffers because he does not have enough time to write, read, and think. Further, if he counts on publication in the "little" magazines, then he is caught up in the web of cliques that envelope the literary quarterly world as much as he is caught in the taboos, "contacts," and commercialism of mass media publishing. It must seem more sensible to most that if they must write what editors want, they ought to do it for "slick" magazines and appreciable pay, rather than for the pittance the quarterlies pay, when they pay at all.

If the writer is a Jew, his problems are thornier. There are always the hints from agents, editors, and publishers, that it might be wise, well, you know, to change one's name to something, well, you know, not quite so Semitic. And there is the ruder reminder that Jews are only a 2 per cent minority of the population, and people want to read about the other 98 per cent. Or there is the half-ashamed, half-regretful rejection that says this is beautiful but we cannot use it because we used one Jewish theme story six months ago and we don't want to be typed a "Jewish house" or a "Jewish magazine." Always the fact that the author and his material are Jewish makes publication complicated.

There was a time when Jews had a common background of custom, language, and God, but that time is long past. Its literary heritage is almost dead, and names like Mendele, Peretz, Reisen, Sholom Aleichem, Singer, Pinski, and all the rest—names once to be conjured with—are now merely words in the mouths of grandfathers, or footnotes to the history of European literature. Those names and the works that belonged to them were fortunate in having common customs, language, and religion, but it gave them an exclusive and closed-in audience to write for, so that, combined with the trick of history that they committed their best efforts to a dying language, their reputations and their work are now moribund.

The modern tendency among Jews and Gentiles is to say that Jews are *not* "different," but this is only the other pendulum extreme from having said that Jews were irretrievably strange. Neither is true, and both are true. Jews are different and not different. In a world of diverse cultures, individuals brought up in variant cultures will differ from one another. They will have much in common with members of other cultures and traditions, but they will have been shaped somewhat differently by the forces of their own particular physical and cultural environment. Like all other people, Jews want to "belong" and "stand out" simultaneously, and depending on which, they will emphasize either the factors in common or those that are unique. From these urges stem in part the problems of "self-hatred" or Jewish anti-Semitism, and anti-Gentilism. The strange is often the unpleasant, and may in part account for Gentile reactions to Jewish customs and modes of behavior but can it account also for Jewish shame about the caftan, the earlock, or the Yiddish accent? The Jew *is different* because he comes from another cultural stream, and this, of course, applies to the Jewish writer. All too frequently, the Jewish writer wants to "belong" so much that he denies his Jewishness in one way or another; often, he wants so much to "stand out" that he is deliberately and "professionally" the Jew to the point of insane insistence and parochial poisoning.

• As both writer and Jew, he never quite "belongs," and this can be as much of an advantage as a disadvantage. His sense of being beyond the pale may help the writer to perceive more sensitively and truthfully, or he may—and all too frequently does—mistake his own individual problems, as Jew or writer, for the problems of the whole society, and this may warp his work. However, as a Jew, he should also have a cultural, literary, and religious background that will help him shape and interpret his experience more richly and accurately, if he will use it, and not only as a Jew and for Jews, but as an artist and for all mankind. In this respect, his best example is the Old Testament. Are Job, Kings, Amos, Ecclesiastes, or Isaiah merely Jewish books for Jews? They are that, but they are far more; they are books for all men everywhere, and it is sufficient evidence to point out that the entire Western world, Jew and Gentile, has adopted the Old Testament for its own. And so must any genuine and important "American-Jewish" writing be books for all men. The universal in literature is always achieved by the most particular. Raskolnikov, Lear, Rastignac, and Huckleberry Finn are as indubitably Russian, English, French, and American as they are also human beings without national boundaries, dealing with problems that vex humankind throughout the whole world.

• In this sense then, paradoxically perhaps, the Jewish writer will plumb the depths of his unique and individual "American-Jewish" world, and, if he is blessed with good fortune and genius, his work will be not particular but general, not parochial but universal, and always human and important. Out of a Jewish tradition that is essentially concerned *with this world* and *with human beings* and *their conduct,* there will arise a vision of life that speaks of the urge for social justice that was Amos's, of the love of Ruth, of the dignity and honesty of Job, of the intellectual candor of Ecclesiastes, and which will transfigure the writer's work. •

Like Jonah, the American-Jewish writer must go to Nineveh to preach the truth of that vision, that highly personal and individual vision that belongs in the Jewish tradition and that is a broadly human and general vision for all peoples and traditions. Nor must the writer hide in the belly of the whale, or flee to Tarshish, nor may he despise the gourd. He must continue to feel deeply, think clearly, and write truly so that all of Nineveh will understand. And if, at first, they do not understand, he must not despise his own heritage, nor despair of them, but remember the old rabbinical saying, "It is not for us to complete the task, nor may we desist from it."

And how then does he survive as a writer? Jack London once wrote that a writer must choose between bread and glory. If he chooses bread, his work dies; if he chooses glory, he dies. What then? I do not know. The writer keeps writing because he must, and the fact that he perseveres is an almost equal miracle with his act of creation. He keeps hoping for the change, for the fluke, for the miracle, for whatever comes his way, for he must keep hoping to keep writing. And, if he would be great, he keeps writing, writing, writing! Melville's despairing cry for time, patience, and cash will ring in the hollow of his brain, but most important, he must remember in the face of the difficulty, even of the impossibility, of achieving acceptance or status in life, or of making a reasonable living, that if he has written truly, the truth of his writing will endure beyond diatribe or accolade, beyond brass or stone.

ANTI-SEMITISM AND THE JEWISH NOVELIST

By CHARLES I. GLICKSBERG

A<small>N ANOMALOUS AND</small> enigmatic figure, the Jew in fiction is generally represented as either a victim of harrowing injustice or a mysterious compound of ideal spirituality and prophetic power, a staunch fighter against inequality and injustice, a seeker after salvation. In novels written by Jews that deal with the perplexing and perennial Jewish problem, the protagonist is seldom or never an upholder of the *status quo,* a defender of entrenched conservatism, supporting the aristocratic principle or hierarchical privilege. And the reason for this is quite simple: the Jew is not like other men. He both feels himself to be, and is made to feel, *different.* Is it strange that in his extreme plight he should make an honorific badge out of this sense of being different? A cultural hybrid, the eternal Don Quixote of Western civilization, a dreamer and a rebel, liberal in his sympathies and idealistic in his aspirations, he is a bundle of contradictions, but he knows what it is to suffer and he is consistent in his feeling of profound compassion for the underdog, the poor and the oppressed of the earth. If he is so often at war with himself, it is because in all lands (except Israel) he remains the alien, never fully assimilated, unconverted to the dominant religion of the country he dwells in, full of intense anxieties generated by the malevolent forces of anti-Semitism.

The central preoccupation of contemporary Jewish fiction with the problem of anti-Semitism reflects, in part at least, a crusading desire to wrestle with the evil contradictions of life, to slay the dragon of iniquity in his den, to make love and justice and brotherhood prevail. When contemporary Jewish novels are serious in content, they are necessarily reformist in tone and intention; their object, primarily, is to expose an ugly condition, to study an aberration with objective understanding, to denounce evil in high places. And no matter how objectively the writer treats his complex material, the indictment is implicit in his interpretation. It is the impulse of sympathy, however, when carried to extremes, which sometimes leads him to tamper with his creative *élan* and to work out a resolution of the problem which is not inherent in the dynamics of the situation that he presents. The problem of anti-Semitism, however, is not a minor or local problem; world-wide in scope, it has implications that embrace the whole of collective life. It is certainly not enough to compose a bitter diatribe demonstrating that anti-Semitism is a pernicious social phenomenon, for an essay on the subject could achieve substantially the same effect. But an honest, intense, imaginatively penetrating confrontation of the problem of anti-Semitism in fiction does help to bring about a catharsis, an emotionally illuminating realization, that is not within the compass of sociological analysis. The Jew, victim of multiple injustices in our society, is not only in conflict with his environment but passes judgment on it.

The problem of anti-Semitism thus cuts to the heart of social existence in our time. In *The Jew in Our Day*, Waldo Frank makes the discovery that the Jews are truly different but not for the reasons usually assigned. They are different because they stem from a religious-prophetic cultural tradition which makes them the articulate conscience, the embattled messianic leaders, of mankind, the impassioned apostles of democracy the world over. This tradition is grounded in the knowledge "that life has meaning, and that every man, woman and nation can discover life's meaning—which is, to win the world, under God, through justice, mercy and love, for the brotherhood of man." Whether the Jew consciously accepts or rejects this tradition, he is nevertheless an integral part of it. Hence it is the responsible task of the Jews to usher in the millennium of the brotherhood of man.

In *The Death and Birth of David Markand,* written in 1934, at the height of the depression, when Waldo Frank was torn between his metaphysical devotion to Spinoza and his attraction to Marxism, the chief character is unquestionably a sublimated portrait of the author himself. Middle-class in outlook and in sympathies, he is driven by the desire to find himself—a desire that can be consummated only in the act of renunciation. Only in hunger and privation, in identification with the working class, can David Markand find hope for ultimate salvation; at the end he awakens to a new life, spiritually reborn, mystically inspired by the Marxist eschatology. This is how Waldo Frank states the Marxist thesis which he then accepted: "There is a class, hardly born, which struggles with the world to live. By its struggle for life the whole world may be reborn alive again." In the lofty tones of a convert to a new religion, the hero of the novel aligns himself wholeheartedly with the proletariat. "All men who want to live today must embrace it. My own life needs it to live. I have only the body of a class that dies: I need, that I may live, the living body of the class which now is life." A triumphant credo which reminds one of the message Clifford Odets sounded in his play, *Awake and Sing*. In short, Christ and Jehovah are dead; long live Marx and the Revolution!

More typical, more revealing, as a study of Jews in America, is *The Old Bunch*, by Meyer Levin, a novel about the children of immigrants in Chicago. In essence, he tells us in *In Search*—his full realization of his potentialities—he wanted to justify his own spiritual autobiography as a Jew born in America who seeks the character, his own past, to say: "See how all the ties of family and tradition were shattered by the impact of American civilization, see how we could not honor the way of life of our parents when they themselves held their way of dubious value, see how we had to stumble into life." That was the emotional genesis and ideological import of the work. In *The Old Bunch*, Meyer Levin sought to portray the destructive forces of assimilation at work, the disturbing pull of the new culture in conflict with the parental mores. The novel pictures the life of a section of Chicago from 1921 to 1934, particularly as seen through the temperaments of a group of Jewish boys and girls. The camera shifts swiftly from scene to scene, character to character, and we behold how some retain their fundamental integrity as Jews while others succumb to temptation and break down under the strain. Illuminating is the skill with which the author, in this composite sociological study in fictional terms, reveals how the sensitive, the idealistic, and the talented are crushed, since there is no room for them in this materialistic, industrialized country. The younger Jewish generation, ashamed of their forebears, their religious traditions, their foreign ancestry, repudiate their parents, commit cultural suicide, and adopt with enthusiasm the spurious slogans and shibboleths of their day.

The reception of this novel among Jews was curious and extremely revealing. Why, it was asked in high dudgeon, were Jews described in this disgraceful fashion, as in *I Can Get It for You Wholesale*, by Jerome Weidman? Here is a striking illustration of the moral difficulty in which the scrupulous Jewish writer in America finds himself. On the one hand, he is committed to the ideal of imaginatively delineating people and situations with as much honesty as he can command, holding nothing back. On the other hand, as a Jew he is expected to take into consideration the probable effect a book or a situation or character in a book will have in spreading and intensifying anti-Semitic prejudice. The result, of course, and a similar reaction took place among cultured Negroes when *Native Son* was first published, is that the Jewish writer cannot write freely and spontaneously about Jews. Now Levin denies categorically that in *The Old Bunch* he caricatured or falsified his material. There was no character in his novel, he believes, which could be regarded as a discredit to the Jewish people. The real question, as Levin sees it, is "whether freedom of expression should be permitted when it is socially destructive. And who shall judge, and how is one to judge whether a piece of writing is eventually destructive?" Exactly! No fast and binding rules can be formulated. Each case is, in a sense, exceptional and unique. The author must simply be careful to apply the best wisdom that he possesses, and be faithful to the imaginative truth of his vision. Even at that, Levin felt that he had sinned, unconsciously, on the side of evasion, since he had stressed the American rather than the Jewish aspects of experience. He had failed in not making it sufficiently clear that this was preeminently a Jewish novel. The American taboo against fiction about Jews must be overcome, not by evasion but by focusing the spotlight more determinedly on the Jews. Levin protests against the tendency of the Jewish community in America to play down the role of the Jews, to be circumspect and apologetic. The Jewish writer must integrate himself in the life of his people if he wishes to solve his creative problem, though this does not, of course, mean that the Jew cannot or should not write about anything but Jews.

During the thirties, when many writers turned Communist,

Levin remained a sincere and steadfast progressive, convinced that the shibboleths of the class struggle were not applicable to the American scene. In the novel, *Citizens*, he wrote about the Little Steel strike and the Memorial Day massacre. His participation in the strike, his first-hand observation of the massacre, his attempt to help the victims, his efforts to punish the guilty, all this went into the making of the novel. Dr. Wilner, the Jewish doctor who attends to the wounded, perceives that the Communists are not animated by idealistic considerations and is left to puzzle out his problem without benefit of doctrinaire solutions. He realizes that there is an irreconcilable conflict taking place in the world and that everyone has to play his part. Should he content himself with fighting for the liberalization of his profession or should he escape from his intolerable position by fighting the war against fascism openly?

Citizens ends on a note of affirmation; the people are not indifferent and apathetic; the anniversary parade calls forth a huge response, and this is a covenant of hope for the future. And Dr. Wilner thinks he had found the missing clue: economic democracy is essential, but in addition all the people must take upon themselves directly a feeling of responsibility for whatever happens. Not only the workers, not only those immediately affected by a crisis, but all the citizens. It is interesting, in this connection, to compare Dr. Wilner's resolution of his problem with that which the author describes for us in his autobiography, *In Search*. Levin's whole life was embodied in his effort to give voice to the Jewishness in him. He does not feel that there is a contradiction in his being an American and a Jew. He had to discover and articulate the Jewish sources in his being and to identify himself with the Jewish people. After thus transcending his early rejection of his Jewish past, he has come home, restored his severed roots, come out of the stifling dark of the ghetto of alienation. The search has ended in a triumphant reaffirmation of his Jewishness.

That is how Meyer Levin solved his personal creative problem, the dilemma that troubled him as a writer and as a man. Unlike Ludwig Lewisohn, he does not feel an irreconcilable dichotomy between his being an American and a Jew. The writer in America can function, as he says, as a "multicultural" personality, but he must first steep himself in the life of his people and reject the falsely simplified notion implicit in the doctrine of assimilation. Lewisohn takes another view. The Jewish contribution to American literature has been undistinguished, Lewisohn believes, because Jewish writers in America are without roots, without metaphysical depth or organic religious convictions. Jewish literature or art which is not distinctively Jewish in character constitutes no genuine contribution to American culture. Jewish intellectuals, according to Lewisohn, by cutting themselves off from the profound sources of Jewish life, have become alienated. "Out of a great mass of apparent productivity," he asks in *The American Jew,* "what have we that is authentically our own and is therefore an authentically Jewish contribution to the American cultural scene?" He mentions the books by Maurice Samuel, a single book by Marie Syrkin, a book by Abraham Joshua Heschel (*The Earth Is the Lord's*), and that is all. He does not include or desire to include such figures as Norman Mailer and Irwin Shaw.

For these younger Jewish novelists are animated by no such messianic folk-ideal, no such religious vision and creed, as Lewisohn recommends to us. Mailer's *The Naked and the Dead,* a war novel, is not primarily concerned with Jewishness or anti-Semitism. Instead, it seeks to show that modern man is afraid, that failure and not success is his portion, that the end, no matter how bravely we labor and struggle, is bound to be tragic. The individual in the armed forces in the Pacific is reduced to impotence, surrounded by nameless fears, victimized by forces beyond his comprehension and control. Life is full of ironic twists of circumstances, crushing paradoxes, destructive contradictions. A naturalistic picture of a platoon of men on an island in the Pacific, *The Naked and the Dead* portrays how these men are the product of their early conditioning, their environment, their social milieu. Each of the men in the platoon—Red, Gallagher, Toglio, Polack, Brown, Croft, Roth, Goldstein, Wyman, Ridge, Heenan, and Wilson—is a distinct personality, and each one knows that he is a failure. There is Red with his yearning for freedom and his determination not to be caught in the trap of marriage; there is Goldstein with his choking resentment of anti-Semitism; there is Roth who repudiates Judaism and announces that he is not a Jew by virtue of religion or nationalism or race; there is Gallagher with his multiple frustrations, his search for a scapegoat, his feeling that life has dealt him a raw deal. Anti-Semitism is shown to be a rankling traumatic experience, but it serves only as an incidental part of the total picture.

A novel of an entirely different kind dealing with the plight of the modern Jew is *Thieves in the Night* by Arthur Koestler, an attempt to justify the use of force and terror in seeking to establish a homeland in Palestine. With impassioned earnestness, Koestler paints the historical condition from 1938 to 1939—the flow of Jewish immigrants to Palestine in the hope of building a Jewish State, the imprisonment and fiendish persecution of Jews in Germany, the deliberate betrayal of the Jewish dream by perfidious Albion, the heroic sacrifices and achievements of the Jewish settlers in the collectives, the criss-crossing conflicts of ideologies and ideals, the collectivist ideal standing in marked opposition to the nationalist aspiration. We get a vivid picture of the land, the collectives, the political and religious sects, the personalities drawn to Palestine, the past which they are trying to escape, the vision they nourish of creating a new organic community in which everything will be shared in common. The Jewish refugees are nervous, restless, inwardly scarred and damaged, yet willing to make any sacrifices in order to take root in this historic soil, but their children are creatures of a different species: hardy, self-reliant, self-assured, free from neurotic complications and the crippling sense of inferiority. They "belong!"

The argument about force and terror goes on all the time. Joseph, the leading character in *Thieves of the Night*, half-Jewish and half-Gentile, has, because of a painful experience in his past, allied himself with the Jews, though he cannot overcome his tendency to brood, doubt, speculate. He sees the essential futility of both pacifism and the Marxist incitement to revolutionary violence. And he feels that the Jews are a sick race, a people with a history but no background, still carrying about with them wherever they go the vestigial traces of the ghetto. If he remains in the collective and subordinates himself, he is afraid of contracting the specific Jewish ailment, stomach ulcers. A point is reached, he thinks to himself, where violence is the only source of relief. "If I can't bite, my wrath will bite in my bowels. That's why our whole race is ulcerated in the bloodiest literal sense. Fifteen hundred years of impotent anger has gnawed our intestines, sharpened our features and twisted down the corners of our lips." But Joseph still suspects that this is a rationalization, an evasion of the central issue. "Our ethics are but an elaborate form of schizophrenia." The Jews, he thinks bitterly, "were the slum race of the world: their slums were ghettoes, whether the walls were made of stone or prejudice." Just as Joseph became a Socialist because he hated the poor, so he became a Hebrew because he hated the Yid. His major problem, as in the case of Meyer Levin, was to get rid of his split personality, his tormenting frustrations, his feeling of misery and impotence.

Impassioned, profoundly in earnest, brilliant in its handling of situations and in its interpretation of character, *Thieves in the Night* is spoiled by its strident and angry propagandistic message; it is a tract for the times. It is true that Koestler tries hard to be objective and to present other perspectives. When Joseph is converted to the cause of terrorism, it is not without painful heart-searching and agonized crises of conscience. Nevertheless, the preponderant emphasis is on the use of violence and terror. That is the only way the stricken remnants of Israel, fleeing from the scourge of the modern Pharaoh, can be saved.

Brooding on all this, Joseph is convinced that if the Jews are tolerated in the West, it is because their spiritual substance in the *galut* had become dissipated and enfeebled; they were partially assimilated. The novel ends as another collective is to be established. As the truck rumbles into the night, Joseph reflects on the condition of the modern Jew, and in his thoughts we hear the reflection and echo of the author's own convictions:

For Jews were not an accident of race, but simply man's condition carried to its extreme—a branch of the species touched on the raw. Exiled in Egypt, in Babylon, and now over the whole globe, exposed to strange and hostile surroundings, they had to develop peculiar traits; they had no time nor chance to grow the hide of complacency, of a specious security, which makes man insensitive to and forgetful of the tragic essence of his condition. They were the natural target of all malcontents, because they were so exasperatingly and abnormally human. . . .

Since they were homeless, their vision was turned inward, increasing both their cunning and their spiritual arrogance. As they lived in bondage, they were forced to cringe beneath the whip, with the result that only the superior could hope to assert themselves. The urge that drove the Jews to Palestine was not nationalistic craving but a terrible longing to arrive at a state of normality. And Joseph repeats to himself hypnotically: "We are homesick for a Canaan which was never truly ours. That is why we are always foremost in the race for utopias and messianic revolutions, always chasing after a lost Paradise. . . . A country is the shadow which a nation throws, and for two thousand years we were a nation without a shadow. . . ."

Koestler's portrait of the Jew as debilitated, crushed, the scum of the ghetto, is not one which the younger generation of Jewish novelists in America would recognize. These novelists do not feel themselves to be either abjectly inferior or messianically superior. In *The Young Lions* by Irwin Shaw, the problem of Jewishness looms large, so large in fact that Aldridge, commenting on the work in *After the Lost Generation,* feels that this quality distorts the author's perspective and forces the character to act in a manner inconsistent with reality and human nature. This is a serious and sweeping indictment, and it must be met on its own grounds, for it brings up again the vexed problem of how anti-Semitism can most effectively be presented in fiction. Aldridge takes particular umbrage at the way in which Noah Ackerman is delineated as a symbol of Jewish loyalty and fortitude. Shaw has so colored the picture as to make Noah into a shining example of these virtues in action. The result, we are given to understand, is a caricature of idealistic devotion and saintly suffering. By being made to endure incredible ordeals of persecution because of his Jewishness, Noah is transformed into a mythic hero of his oppressed people, a noble champion of Israel. Noah, in short, is but a puppet designed to mouth the author's sentiments and support his allegorical intention. Aldridge's main point is that it is a mistake for the novelist to overemphasize the problem of "racial" conflict, since it is a relatively minor issue. Let us see how much truth there is in this arraignment.

Though *The Young Lions* is structurally weak, the author does succeed in giving us a panoramic view of the war: the life going on in Austria immediately before the outbreak of the Second World War, the rise of the Nazi spirit, the spreading infection of hatred against the Jews. As a Jew, Shaw is naturally deeply interested in tracing the psychological, historical, and sociological ramifications of the violent animus against the Jews. What are the roots of anti-Semitism? How and why does it spread like a plague? Who are its carriers and its victims, and what does it do to both? All this, of course, Shaw attempts to translate in terms of character and action, without overt preachment. It is Noah Ackerman who enables Shaw to bring to a focus all his ideals and beliefs bearing on the problem of anti-Semitism. When his father is dying, Noah hears his moans of guilt for the brothers who perished in Nazi Germany. On his deathbed, and only then, does he feel a sense of community with the Jews of Germany. Everyone who is a Jew must feel this bond of brotherhood, for the Jew is being hunted down throughout the world. As Noah later watches beside the still form of his dead father, he thinks of the fate of the Jews who came to America from Russia and settled in New York. Thus the problem of Jewishness and anti-Semitism emerges challengingly from the beginning, and forms an integral part of the plot.

When the United States is dragged into the war, Noah feels that "as an honorable citizen, as a believer in the war, as an enemy of fascism, as a Jew," he must play his part. (This need on the part of the Jew to demonstrate his loyalty, to prove his patriotism, crops up as a motif in the work of other Jewish writers.) When he arrives at camp, anti-Semitic persecution begins, a persecution that is brutal, irrational, relentless. Noah's Jewishness is now a source of suffering, a veritable curse. In the army, he learns that prejudice is rampant not only against Jews but also against Negroes and Mexicans and Chinese. He hears the slimy lies and rumors the men in his bunk spread and seem to believe. When ten dollars are stolen from his barracks bag, he publicly challenges to fight anyone who took it. The ten tallest and strongest men take up his challenge. He is cruelly beaten up, his teeth knocked out, but he desperately goes ahead with his mad plan, until he suceeds in knocking out the tenth man. But those who had come to witness his physical humiliation, give him no sign of acknowledgment. Noah will listen to no advice, not even from Fein, the other Jew in his company, who points out the insane folly of striking out aggressively every time someone calls him a "Jew bastard." After all, if all the Jews in the past had reacted in that crazy manner, the Jews would long ago have been wiped out. But Noah will not give in. When in his last fight against Brailsford, he feels the other man's fear, he keeps swinging with all his might. "All his enemies, all the men who had stolen his money, cursed him on the march, driven his wife away, were standing there, broken in nerve, bleeding before him." Thus the enemy, anti-Semitism, is not one man, not even one class of men. Noah symbolizes the Jew who is fighting against all forms of injustice and privilege, all cruelty and discrimination and bigotry.

After winning this moral victory, Noah deserts, writes down his reasons for doing so, and then gives himself up. The immediate cause of his action is that he is a Jew; he could not live with these intolerant men from the South, but since he believes in the war he must help to win it. This time, when he goes back, he is determined to stand for no nonsense; he has come prepared. When a "welcoming committee" of three arrives to beat him up, he takes out the six-inch knife he has bought and grimly warns them that he will kill any man who touches him. From then on, he is left alone. When the soldiers arrive in Europe and come closer to the fighting front, conditions for Noah become a bit more bearable. He is wounded in action. Later, when his company liberates the prisoners in a concentration camp in Germany, he sees the emaciated bodies, bony and ulcerated, the dying survivors, the ghastly heaps of the dead. Beholding all this, Noah wonders: Why go on living in such a diabolical world? But when he sees how Captain Green, the commander of his company, restores order and metes out justice, his faith in human beings is restored, for there must be millions of men like Captain Green. The world is full of them. This is the affirmation Shaw makes, the note on which he ends his novel.

It is clearly not the function of the novelist to provide a solution, happy or otherwise, and yet in struggling with the baffling problem of anti-Semitism, in trying to understand it and to present it objectively, he seeks to resolve a problem that rages in his own breast. He knows, as Koestler and Shaw must know, that it is useless to fight, to use violence against anti-Semitism. The moral law, the injunction of the Torah, is his most powerful weapon, the only one he can hope to wield with any chance of success, but he also knows that he must not compromise with evil, he must not keep silent in the presence of iniquity. His is the voice of eternal protest, the immemorial voice of conscience, the cry for justice that cannot be silenced. He must keep his integrity clean and whole.

In speaking out in the name of the universal moral law that is the heart of Judaism, he helps to redeem not only the persecuted Jew but all men who are oppressed and who are made to suffer unjustly.

If the Jewish novelist of our time is drawn to the problem of anti-Semitism, it is because he cannot help himself. Here is a dybbuk of irrationality that must be exorcised, an injustice that must be denounced, a grievous evil that must be fought. Carried away by his sense of outrage, his hatred and horror, he may be led, as is true in part of the fiction by Koestler and Shaw, to exaggerate, so that the theme overshadows the rest of the world and blots out all other problems. He is thus tempted to falsify the picture, to make the Jewish character too heroic and the Gentile foe altogether vicious and despicable. But if he damages his work artistically, his intention is still to show that the problem of anti-Semitism is world-wide in scope, that it affects all people, all groups, and that it inflicts incalculable damage upon the persecutor as well as his victim. However wide he may be of the mark he aims at, his purpose is still "to win the world, under God, through justice, mercy and love, for the brotherhood of man."

THE EAST SIDE GANGSTERS OF THE PAPER-BACKS

By MEYER LEVIN

REMEMBER THAT JEWISH boy in the Fannie Hurst era, that sensitive son of the unworldly Talmudist? He wanted to become a great violinist, a great surgeon, a great lawyer. His breed has vanished from today's fiction about the East Side. We are more "realistic" now and our typical Jewish lads become prizefighters, hoodlums, gangsters, and what not. "Typical," that is, if quantity of print means anything. For the Jewish gangster has become a dominant figure in the most widely read form of fiction of our time, the paper-back novel. If this literature reflects and by the same token perpetuates folk beliefs, then it faces Jews with a public-relations question. That it is a delicate one, particularly in these days when censorship is shouted from all directions, should not prevent us from making a critical examination of the material involved.

During the past six years a tremendous change has taken place in American reading habits. Paper-back fiction reprints and original novels in soft covers now sell over 200,000,000 copies a year. For every novel read in hard covers, at least five are read in paper-backs. And this new situation has begun to determine, in many cases, the kind of novel written for hard-cover publication. Paper-back sales of a single title may reach millions, in contrast to the few thousand copies of the same book that will be sold in standard form.

The paper-back novel, then, could well play a most important part in projecting, and even in forming, certain essential popular images. Among these is that of the Jew.

By far the largest-selling titles in paper-backs are the so-called realistic novels, replete with violence and the more "sporty" forms of sex. Thus the popular image of the Southerner is derived from the indolent and inverted characters of Erskine Caldwell's and William Faulkner's books, the image of the city Irishman from James Farrell's novels. The fact that all three have literary status is fortuitous in this case. Talents of lesser stature, however, are responsible for the image of the Jew found in such "realistic" books as *The Hoods, A Stone for Danny Fisher,* and *The Big Brokers.* In these and other current novels, all the principal characters are gangsters, and almost all the gangsters are Jews. The paper-back reader may find out there are other kinds of Jews only when he encounters a few soldiers in *The Naked and the Dead* and *The Young Lions.* There is also the portrait, not very readable, of an honorable Jewish merchant family in *The Pedlocks,* but this can scarcely offset the influence of the big-selling novels of violence.

The Jewish gang boss is usually named "Maxie." His boys may be "Spit," "Danny," "Noodles the Shiv," "Cockeye Hymie," "Fat Dovel," "Jake the Goniff," "Nutchy," "Solly." After all, there was an authentic "Bugsy" Siegel.

Maxie and his friends are preferably written about in the first person. As any old *True Confessions* hack knows, this makes a story more believable. And so we have Danny Fisher talking from his grave in Mt. Zion Cemetery, to tell us how Maxie put him there.

Danny's Maxie is Maxie Fields in *A Stone for Danny Fisher,* by Harold Robbins, which was originally presented by the house of Knopf between hard covers as literature. It went to two editions, but the paper-back reprint by Cardinal Press at thirty-five cents a copy is expected to sell millions. For this, as the cover tells us, is "a violent novel of a lonely guy, his girls and his enemies in New York's toughest slum."

Before meeting Maxie, Danny is a nice bright boy whose father, a drugstore owner, has just bought a new home in Brooklyn. Moving in, Danny gets a hazing from the neighborhood Jew-hitters. So when he is Bar Mitzvah'd, he tells us, "Deep inside me I knew I had never wanted to be a Jew. I remembered the first time I had thought about it: the time Paul and his kid brother Eddie had pushed me into the pit at Clarendon and Troy. I remembered asking Mama the next day if we couldn't be something other than Jews." This is the last we hear of the Jewish question. It seems as though Mr. Robbins had started to write a serious novel, and then been deflected by the paper-back possibilities. The change to a novel of sex and violence comes after the first fifty pages.

With the depression, Papa loses his store and the house; the family moves back to Delancey Street. Papa gets a dismal job in a chain drugstore. Danny meets Spit and Sollie and "the gang," shows them he can use his fists, takes part in robbing a five-and-ten, and in robbing and beating Papa's boss.

Danny is also the protégé of his high-school gym teacher, Sam Gottkin, an ex-pug who has a basement handy for training—and for girls. Danny is, needless to say, on the way to winning the Golden Gloves.

The moment has come for Maxie Fields, who runs a check-cashing service for a front. He summons Danny. "I followed Spit into the store and through a small room with cages like a bank. . . . We passed through a horse room, where a few men were standing idly studying a blackboard. . . . I followed Spit up to the first landing, where he stopped in front of a door and walked in. I stopped dead in my tracks, blinking my eyes. I had heard about this but I never really believed it. This room was out of the moving pictures, it didn't belong in a partly condemned old dump like this.

"A big man with a red face, a fat stomach, and the largest shoes I ever saw came toward us. Nobody had to tell me: this was Maxie Fields. . . ."

Maxie wants him to throw the Golden Gloves fight so Maxie can make some real money betting on it. When Danny balks, Maxie calls in his cocktail-serving girl, tells her to take off her dress, and offers Danny her twenty-dollar-an-hour charms as inducement. Later, just to make sure that the reader doesn't imagine things get out of the family, we are informed that Ronnie's real name is Sara Dorfman. This typically Jewish East Side beauty is in thrall to Maxie because she needs money to care for her crippled brother.

Danny collects in advance for throwing the fight, but inadvertently wins. He flees Maxie's "Collector," and Spit with his vengeful knife. But he leaves the bribe money for Papa to buy a new drugstore with. Papa, a true Jewish parent, declares that this "son of the devil is no son of ours," and that "fighting is a murderer's business."

In a few years Danny returns to Delancey Street to find his true love, Nellie, a Catholic girl he met on his first heist, still waiting behind the frankfurter counter at the five-and-ten. He marries her. They go on relief. Their baby dies.

Danny muscles his way into the office of his one-time coach, Sam Gottkin, now a big concessionaire. Sam has married Danny's sister, Miriam, who found him repulsive but wanted to help the family, and—being no boxer—had to sell her body in the only way a good Jewish girl knows.

Danny catches his lecherous brother-in-law in the act with a secretary, and blackmails him into giving him a job. He rises fast. The war is on—none of these athletic Jews are bothered by the army—and Danny becomes a big-time black-marketeer on his own. But Sam, in a friendly Jewish brother-in-law way, hijacks $100,000 worth of Danny's merchandise, so Danny goes back to the all-powerful Maxie, who will rub out the brother-in-law. Cocktail-serving Ronnie, too, has come back from flight, and in that gilded back room Maxie rubs his hands, gloating, "Nobody can keep away from Maxie Fields, baby, that's what I always said."

Meanwhile Nellie is having another baby. Danny has bought back the old family mansion in Brooklyn, and put Nellie in it, and Nellie falls down the stairs for joy, and a transfusion is needed to save the baby, and whose blood is the only blood that will do? Jewish gangster blood always sticks together. So it is brother-in-law Sam who gives it. After all, a small retribution for $100,000 worth of cigarettes. Now Danny remembers that Maxie and his boys, with the "chopper," are waiting in their souped-up car for Sam to appear on the street. So Danny runs out and gets into Sam's car, and the burp-gun speaks, because with Maxie, as with Shylock, a deal is a deal.

Mr. Robbins' portrait of what really goes on in those same East Side streets where Fannie Hurst could only find fiddlers is confirmed by another first-person narrator who signs himself "Harry Grey." Under the slogan "Good Reading for the Millions," Signet offers us this thirty-five-cent "Giant" with a plug by none other than the great Mickey Spillane. "This book by Harry Grey—an ex-hood himself—will shock you, but you must read it. He dares to tell the truth about cold-blooded killer mobs and how they work." We are offered blurbs from *The New York Times* and the *Wichita Eagle,* who seem to take the fact-pitch seriously. "One of the most terrific fact stories to come out of New York in a century," says the *Eagle.* And "the reader . . . will recognize many of the criminal world's top-drawer figures, past and present," says the *Times.*

Thus *The Hoods* sells "authenticity" in competition with the "literary quality" of Pocketbooks' *Danny Fisher.* And instead of being a nice boy misled by a murderous Maxie, Grey's hero, "Noodles the Shiv," is a Robin Hood who provides escape angles for his boss-pal, Maxie the murderer.

Good old Delancey Street is again the locale, and the dropping of Yiddishisms begins on page six with Noodles and Maxie in grammar school. Maxie loudly advises the lady teacher to *"kish mir"* you know where.

Mr. Grey's Maxie is "Big Maxie"; he has an uncle who is an undertaker, and the embalming parlor becomes a hangout for the boys, whose specialty is to make embarrassing bodies disappear. They pose as rug-cleaners, wrap up any corpses lying around, and walk out of anywhere. Their services are soon in demand by "The Combination," and as the boys rise in the world their rugs rise in quality, until they are using orientals to wrap up high politicos who have met sudden death.

For authentic Jewish atmosphere, we have "deals" plotted in Yonah Schimmel's knisherie. And we have poor Noodles, as a youth, watching his family evicted because his sick father can't work. Noodles gets a four-dollar-a-week job on a laundry truck, and gets beaten up by thugs when he joins a strike. So who wouldn't become a crook?

The boys are caught in a "small-time drugstore heist." "In the getaway in Cockeye Hymie's brother's cab, with the police after us, we ran out of gas on Delancey Street." One lad gets knocked off, two "take the rap," with Noodles sent to a Jewish Home, Cedar Knolls—incidentally, the name of a well-known Jewish institution for delinquent girls. He enjoys it, reading *Don Quixote.* "The day I was to be dismissed, the rabbi called me to his study and gave me his final sermon. How a good Jewish boy should behave. It went in one ear and out the other. . . ."

So our Robin Hoods are sitting around their morgue one morning. "Cockeye went over to Ratner's for a couple of dozen hot bagels. . . . The rabbi from the shul around the corner came in. In Yiddish he told us a pathetic story about an unexpected death in a very poor family. 'No burial plot and no money for the funeral.' Maxie called the cemetery and told them to charge the plot to us. He gave the rabbi permission to use our funeral parlor and to help himself to a pine box from our storeroom. The rabbi's story reminded me of the like predicament my family was in years ago. I included the hearse and two funeral cars."

In reward, the rabbi tells Noodles something he hadn't known about his own sickly father. "In the ghettos of Odessa your father was called Srulick the Shtarker. He was a well-known horse thief and smuggler. . . ." The proud son proceeds to outdo his old man. We have rapes, murders, pulp-beatings galore. A jewel robbery scene includes the requisite masochistic nymphomaniac who begs to be tied and beaten. The taking over of a rival operation includes the requisite homosexual incidents. "Authenticity" is provided by casual mention of conferences with Capone. The "Combination" tenderly instructs Noodles to help a striking group of elevator operators, so he invades the strike-breaker agency, poses as the boss and feeds knockout drops to the bruisers as they report for work. Soon a representative of the bosses arrives. "Moritz was a 'white Jew' all right . . . the type that uses any means for self gain. He used his Jewishness, his Masonry, anything, like a whore. Yes, you find guys like this Moritz everywhere. . . . The gist of his spiel was, 'We Jews got to stick together. We're an abused minority; we got to do things for each other. Come over on our side of the fence, we'll pay you well.' "

Says Robin Hood Noodles, " 'Sure I agree with you. We're in a minority, and we're oppressed. But you stupid sonofabitch, what has that got to do with this situation? I'll bet fifty percent of the elevator pickets walking in the street are Jewish. But you, as a Jew, don't give a damn.' " Ergo, even gangster Jews are better than Jewish businessmen.

Noodles, Maxie's brain, provides clever alibis such as having the boys officially listed as in jail when they slip out to do a rat-tat-tat job for the "Combination." Finally Big Maxie gets really big: he starts sitting in a throne chair at their meetings, and planning how to stick up the Federal Reserve Bank. Noodles, realizing this is suicidal, again seeks the safety of jail for Maxie by tipping off the Feds when Maxie is on a routine liquor-running job. But alas, in the ensuing shooting fray Maxie is killed, and consequently our Noodles is almost dipped in a bath of cement for stooling. However, he fights his way out, and escapes to a life of literary leisure. Moral: the clever Jewish crook gets away with murder.

Equally "authentic" is Avon's fifty-cent double-decker, *The Big Brokers* by Irving Shulman, whose novels are usually presented as not only authentic but "sociological." This one is supposed to reflect the Kefauver investigation findings. It also includes some of the surviving characters from the street-gang boys of *The Amboy Dukes* and *Cry Tough*. Brooklyn slums instead of Delancey Street provide the atmosphere. But now, the boys have arrived in the big time, and the action swings from New York to Hollywood, and to a plush gambling hotel in Las Vegas.

Maxie appears this time under the name of Itzik Yanowitz who got his start as a strike-breaker for clothing manufacturers and rose to be one of the three top men in a "Combination." Itzak is given to heart-rending confidences about how his wife divorced him, and wouldn't let him see his son. How he had to stand at the back of the *shul* to see the boy's Bar Mitzvah. This drove him into an alcoholic breakdown, and only the devotion of his friend "Fat Dovel" Apfelschpein brought him back to health. Fat Dovel, a kind of minor partner, produces bright little side ideas for Itzik like forcing their protected clothing manufacturers to buy ads in a trade journal founded for no other purpose but that.

Itzik and Fat Dovel are David and Jonathan, having their laughs together, eating good Jewish meals together. But this doesn't prevent Itzik, with a heavy heart, from having Fat Dovel rubbed out when it looks like he might spill too much about their bank-fronted horse room at a government investigation. "Dovel was his enemy, and because Dovel had to die Itzik went into his bathroom and wept . . . and Charley . . . hurried to the bathroom off the master bedroom and saw his boss hunched on the seat, crying with heavy sobs into his knuckles." As a last tender gesture, Itzik includes Dovel's wife Sadie in their permanent disappearance. Then he buys two mourning candles.

Itzik is a man of principle, however, and when the empire is toppling and the boys suggest going to Detroit to muscle in on the union racket, he says "no." "Itzik looked pained. 'You know I don't like to touch what belongs to someone else. But we could study their methods. The plant gambling in Detroit,' he ruminated, 'is worth about thirty million a year.' "

His scruples do not prevent him from ordering and enjoying many a murder, and from being proud of the kids he picked up and trained for this work. There is "Mitch" Wolf, of the Amboy Dukes. When Mitch was trying to go straight as an assistant cutter for Sam Rappaport, Itzik, who was Sam's protection man, took the boy along on a party and fixed him up with one-hundred-dollar-a-night Joyce. Soon Mitch threw over his nice Jewish girl and went out to roll a few drunks in order to collect enough for another night.

So we find Mitch and Joyce out in Las Vegas, with a couple of other ex-Dukes, "Bull" Benson and Larry Tone (*né* Tunafish), with the assignment of running Itzik's gambling hotel. But first they have to rub out the previous incumbent, who didn't do well enough for Itzik.

They also rub out a "bookmaker's bookie" named Brodsky, and a "Bitsy" Kznowsky, etc. Bull gets hurt on one of these forays, and nearly loses the use of one arm. This inspires author Shulman to inject some more Jewish background stuff. Bull gets remorse, and going religious, prevails upon one of the showgirls in Las Vegas, who is likewise Jewish, to slip over to Los Angeles and buy him a Hebrew prayerbook and an authentic *yarmelke*. He even tries to hold a Passover service in his hotel room. And when one of the boys remarks that "The malachhamoves doesn't cut his price," Bull has hallucinations that the *malachhamoves* is coming into his room after him. He goes berserk, and when last heard from is in an asylum in Vera Cruz, whither he has been conveyed by the last of the Dukes, Larry, who will doubtless become the subject of another Shulman gangster epic.

True, there are Irish and Italian and Anglo-Saxon gangsters mixed in with the Jews in all these novels. In *The Big Brokers*, Itzik and his Irish partner walk on either side of their Italian colleague, putting him on the spot to be mowed down by Itzik's hoods. But the central figures in all these books are Jews, and the atmosphere is slum-Jewish.

Of course one can argue that all this material should be dismissed as mere entertainment, without lasting effect on the psyche of the reader. I don't agree. I think that it leaves an impress. And it happens that serious writers are presenting similar images of the Jew in a way that may leave a deeper impress.

Take Leonard Bishop's double-decker, *Down All Your Streets*. A genuinely talented writer, Bishop has been tempted, apparently, by the high sales in this sensationalized field. His East Side portrait deals with one "Boxie" Lewis and family. Boxie, an ex-pug, is a thieving dope addict who ends up peddling drugs to high-school kids. While the family milieu is pictured in a more "positive" vein, and while the portrait of Boxie's wife Lil has high merit, the novel nevertheless adds to the Jewish rogues' gallery on the stands.

And Mr. Bishop's second novel, *Days of My Love*, which is certain to appear in paper-backs next season, shows what a deleterious influence the paper-back novel can have upon a talented writer. Again the story is about a Jewish family. The father operates a telephone solicitation racket, using a Catholic charity as a front. There are scenes of sex, perversion, and violence that seem obviously injected to catch the paper-back buyer—for a "hot" novel can draw as high as $35,000 in advance royalties from these reprint sources.

Quite gratuitously, Bishop inserts a scene in which a "high executive in the UJA" becomes friendly with the charity racketeer. "I know promotions like yours backwards, because that's my business," says the UJA man. . . . "A man like you, Dave, with your business sense and reputation, can be an invaluable asset to my organization." And at the end of the book, Dave is actually recruited into the UJA!

Thus even the main financial resort of the Jewish people in distress, an organization that, outside Mr. Bishop's book, is the symbol and vehicle of a humanitarianism unrivaled in history, become part of the background of Jewish gangsterdom. To the uninformed reader, the UJA and the Combination can look as though cut on the same pattern.

It seems to me that fictional episodes of this kind, and novels of this kind, have their source in classic impulses of Jewish self-hatred. Nor is this a new tendency in American fiction. The first notable example was Jerome Weidman's story of a business cheat, *I Can Get It for You Wholesale*, which was followed by a story of similar character in Budd Schulberg's *What Makes Sammy Run?* Such novels are socio-critical, yes, but their emphasis on negative characters is not accidental. Sammy Glick and Harry Bogen have become synonyms for Jewish perfidy: minor Shylocks and Fagins.

But there is an even deeper tradition to which these characters may be linked. The fundamental image of the "Maxie" character is that of a secret power operating in a secret room, handing down decisions that mean life and death for other people. Big Maxie, in *The Hoods,* becomes a devil-king in his undertaking parlor. Maxie Fields, in *A Stone for Danny Fisher,* presides in a palace behind a slum façade, with a girl slave in attendance. Itzik telephones across a continent, ordering death.

These gang bosses call to mind a powerful image. Is not this modern Jew-gangster psychologically linked to the all-powerful Jew of secret world conspiracy, the archetypal Jew of *Der Stürmer* and the *Protocols of the Elders of Zion,* who from some hidden chamber pulls the strings of world intrigue? Is not the Jew as gang-boss simply a new version of an old anti-Semitic stereotype?

Do we not find him, for example, in *The Great Gatsby,* an elegant *goyish* predecessor of today's Delancey Street gangster novels? To confront the gang-boss who pulled the strings on Gatsby, Fitzgerald's narrator seeks him out in an obscure office. "A lovely Jewess appeared at an interior door, and scrutinized me with black hostile eyes. . . ." (Jewesses are always "lovely" because the sinister and the attractive go together.) And presently, behind the partition, the narrator meets Meyer Wolfsheim himself, the boss killer who wasn't loyal enough to his *goyish* minion to go to Gatsby's funeral.

"I raised him up out of nothing, right out of the gutter. I saw right away he was a fine-appearing, gentlemanly young man, and when he told me was an Oggsford, I knew I could use him good. I got him to join up in the American Legion and he used to stand high there. Right off he did work for a client of mine in Albany—"

But Meyer (the "Maxie") Wolfsheim won't go to Gatsby's funeral. "When a man gets killed I never like to get mixed up in it in any way. I keep out."

Thus a cardinal anti-Semitic accusation, that of cold-hearted disloyalty, is embodied in Meyer Wolfsheim, as it is in Mitch Wolf when he turns state's evidence against the "Big Brokers," and in Danny Fisher when he hires Maxie to kill his brother-in-law.

Scott Fitzgerald, I assume, carelessly perpetuated a Jew-image he had absorbed from myth; our own Jewish writers may be perpetuating the same image by compulsive self-hatred. They may imagine they are showing the myth up, to be destroyed; but in actuality they are confirming a sinister image of the typical Jew for the mass-reader.

For it seems to me that in the public's consciousness the Maxies fuse with the Shylocks and the Prague "world-Jewish-Zionist" conspirators, and the ritual slaughterers.

It may be argued that Maxie is not supposed to possess international power, or to be an agent of a worldwide Jewish cabal, and that Maxie therefore does not conform to the legendary image in its essentially terrifying aspect, and therefore cannot be "harmful." If identification with this international-Jew image is the only criterion for the anti-Semitic stereotype, then Fagin and Shylock, too, are innocent figures. Yet they have become hate-words used against the Jew.

There need be no absolutes in propaganda. The evil Jew is a composite of hatred characteristics. Every repetition of a propaganda point recalls the whole image, as the Nazis well knew. A Jew shown as murderer, lecher, cheat, confirms the whole. The millions who were destroyed in Europe were not supposed each to be members of the secret inner cabal, but they were all supposed to be carriers of vile "typical" Jewish characteristics.

Must we therefore object to the slightest presentation of a Jew in anything but a favorable light? Of course not! Jews, I think, have traditionally shown a remarkable willingness to pay the price of truth, including the bitter, and including the falsehoods that are sometimes inextricably mingled in truths. And every writer must feel free to present the truth as he sees it. But this specific problem relating to the image of the Jew must make the writer all the more sensitive, all the more conscientious in testing his truth. Nor does freedom of expression for the writer demand that the reader should be intimidated from showing him meanings of which he may have been unaware. Nor does everything written and promoted in response to sales opportunity have to be accepted as the free expression of a writer's spirit.

The writer should want to understand the source of his image. What is influencing him? Does he write from within himself, or is he merely producing a facsimile of other current images? Is he writing under the distortion of hatred? from motives of revenge? for mere gain? from irresponsible prankishness?

In the whole context of the Jewish image, distortions and exaggerations of emphasis can constitute dangers which fully aware writers might themselves not want to produce. And I feel that this applies to the current crop of gangster portraits.

It may be argued that the gangster Jew in himself refutes the anti-Semitic stereotype of the Jew as a physical coward. The mythical Jews gets others to do his murdering for him. And he does not have them kill fellow Jews. Only Gentiles. In the present crop of gangster novels, Jews have no hesitation about killing other Jews. We might therefore conclude that these novels have a "wholesome" effect insofar as they show Jews to be like any other gangsters, and engaged only in business killings, not in international plots.

All this may be true, particularly of the rank and file of the mobs. But the Maxies, like Fitzgerald's Meyer Wolfsheim, do not soil their hands with weapons. Maxie Fields and Itzik Yanowitz are still Jews who get others to do their killing for them. The last we see of Maxie Fields is the glow of his cigar as he sits back in his car while a minion pulls the trigger on Danny Fisher.

As for the international-plot link, it is true this has been absent from gangster fiction, though the reader may supply intimations of internationalism from his well of crime-reading about opium rings and such. The direct plot is only one step further, when we read about "Combinations" and manipulations in labor fields.

The fact that Jews may also be victims, in these novels, can again be argued in both directions. To the academic student of anti-Semitism, it may mean that the image is broken. But to the anti-Semite, it may simply mean that the Jew is even lower, viler than he had ever thought, since the hitherto alleviating characteristic of loyalty at least to his own kind is now disproven: in these novels he will sacrifice his own people for personal gain.

And the point that some Jews in these books are shown as exponents of physical violence need not be looked upon as necessarily erasing the stereotype of the cunning or cowardly Jew. The reader susceptible to anti-Semitic suggestion may simply pick up the violence as one more evil trait, and not worry about consistency. Since when, in any case, has anti-Semitism been logically coherent?

Indeed, the anti-Semitic image of the Jew has never been clean of blood, for the blood-ritual accusation has been part of it, and the recent Moscow "doctors' plot," though repudiated, served as evidence that the legend has not died, and that a modern, "scientific" version of it can be offered to the world.

How does it happen that Jewish writers and Jewish publishers are just now supplying these Jewish gangsters in such fictional quantity? Because there is a market for them. The high market in paper-backs, as has been pointed out, is for "realism." The buyers seem to be stimulated by the notion that they will truly find out about "life," about areas of life that have been kept taboo—sex, and crime, and secret influences. Indeed, the books offer themselves, to a degree, as sociology and psychology for the average man —presumably "informational," even scientific.

Thus the books that sound most "true" are the ones most popular. The use of the confessional tone, and of recognizable local color, provides this illusion of truth. And Jewish local color is convincing. (And Jews are also, perhaps, part of the "mystery" of life.) Moreover, it "comes natural" to Jewish writers who remember that it's easiest to write about what one knows about. They may not know too much about inner gang life, but they know the names of the East Side streets, they know lots of Yiddish locutions. The same trick could be done with Polish or Italian background, and it would be equally distasteful to Polish or Italian Americans. But there is an added appeal in the Jewish gangster story; it has novelty, and it contains the implicit promise of the revelation of something more, of something occult and secret that pertains to the "mysterious" Jews. Thus, Bull Benson, seized by remorse, reverting to religion, may be behaving in a fashion that would be a cliché if he were a Catholic, but clothed in a *tallis,* he gives the reader the sensation of having a peep into inner truth.

Whether or not they reason the matter out in this way, publishers who generally shy away from fiction about Jews have no resistance to this kind of fiction, for they know that it sells. Perhaps not to the literati—but it sells. Dial Press exploited the formula with *The Amboy Dukes,* and have found a new provider in Leonard Bishop. Three of the large paper-back publishers are pushing their separate items in the field, each perhaps convinced he ought to have one since his competitors have a similar article.

Should "something be done"? This raises first of all the question of literary truth. Are we being presented here with works that contain an amount of such truth? Is the Jewishness of these hoodlums a determinant of their behavior?

An answer may be found in a recent revision of Irving Shulman's "sociological" *Amboy Dukes*. The new edition bears few Jewish references, Yiddishisms are rare, Bar Mitzvah has become a vague confirmation, and Frank Goldfarb has become "Frank Abbott." What has this done to the book? It has merely revealed *The Amboy Dukes* to be a routine little crime novel. It would appear, then, that the use of Jewish atmosphere gave this story a "smear of realism," the Jewish background being exploited to provide an illusion of depth for an essentially shallow set of characters. The same effect, I think, would result if the identifying Jewish touch were removed from *The Hoods* and *A Stone for Danny Fisher*.

Shulman's revisions seem to be an admission that nothing literary was to be gained from the Jewishness of the book, and that some harm might result. "Something was done," and in a way that recognized the public-relations aspects of paper-back circulation.

What, are hard-cover readers to be treated as a superior species? Is there to be a kind of censorship for paper-backs? Even if it is self-censorship by some voluntary agency set up within the paper-back industry, I would advocate nothing of the kind.

I would prefer rather to have the paper-backs' potential for harm serve to make some writers, and publishers, aware of factors that apply just as strongly to hard-cover books. An uneasiness over the effect of a book's contents would be seen to mean that the book was never true in depth, never true in representative quality, and the realization that it may give some wrong ideas to the less discriminating in a vast body of readers would thus alert writers and publishers to a responsibility they should have felt in the first place.

Basically, the question becomes one of literary judgment—and conscience, both applicable alike to hard-cover and paper-back books. A book about Jewish gangsters that was completely penetrating, that awakened *rachmones*, would be a matter for praise. But literary judgments are always personal. And repression, even of trash, by any form of censorship, is out of the question. Organized opinion-pressure is just as dangerous, as one may see from the effect of the McCarthy campaigns on the U.S. Information Service libraries.

And I can speak from personal experience with the oversensitive Jewish reader, for when my own novel, *The Old Bunch,* appeared in the thirties, there were some who objected to my having presented, in a minor character, a Jew who was a venal politician.

Yet it is precisely because I have written fiction in the same field that I feel I am in a position to argue that Jewish writers must recognize a particular responsibility in regard to the image of the Jew. And I believe we as Jews do have a special problem. The Irish, the Italians, or any other group do not have to deal with anything as dangerous to themselves as the anti-Semitic myth. For this reason, the prevalence of these books about Jewish gangsters is to me a matter for concern. I think it is a matter that can be remedied by awareness on the part of writers, publishers, critics, and public. Such an awareness might cause the writer more often to ask himself, "Is this true in depth? Am I merely perpetuating a myth without showing that it is a myth? Am I tailoring my writing to hot sales? Am I perhaps working out some self-hating impulses, or am I truly trying to make my characters understood?"

What is today being published about Jews in America, particularly in the paper-backs, provides a fantastically lopsided picture of Jewish lift and character. Here we have several huge novels about Jews as gangsters, with virtually nothing about any other kind of Jews at all. The paper-back reader would have to conclude that gangsterism was the chief, if not only, occupation of Jews.

In the absence of other images, these novels cannot leave the undiscriminating reader merely with the casual feeling that "Jews are like everybody else." I rather think they leave readers with the feeling that "Jews are cheats, gangsters, murders. They admit it themselves."

Lest I fall victim to the misinterpretation that comes so readily in questions of this kind, I should like categorically to repeat that I hold for no form of censorship. Nor do I want to suggest that Jews, or others, should abstain from writing about Jews in an unpleasant light. I want rather to suggest an appeal to integrity and responsibility on the part of writers and publishers, and that, on the part of us all, we should encourage a whole and representative literature about Jewish life.

DON'T YOU BELIEVE IT!

By MARVIN LOWENTHAL

ABOUT THREE HUNDRED years ago, 1646 to be exact, Sir Thomas Browne—physician, antiquarian, skeptic, religionist, and a master of symphonic prose—published a work in several volumes, entitled *Enquiries into Vulgar and Common Errors*. It is a compendium of popular misconceptions and superstitions as well as a mine of curious information, the whole seasoned with conceits and sonorous with verbal melodies. One of the current errors he exposed was that "Jews stink." I cannot recall how he disposed of it, but like many errors it contains a modicum of truth.

All peoples who maintain a distinctive way of life exude, if not individually at least in the mass, a distinctive odor. It arises in part from their diet, hygiene, clothing, and habitual surroundings, and generally strikes an outsider as pungent when not downright obnoxious. Every sensitive traveler recognizes the characteristic smell of a land or a city, a smell easily though not always rightly confounded with that of its inhabitants. More vividly than from photographs or paintings, California is evoked from my memory of the eucalyptus-and-orange scent that stirs the nostrils as one glides by train or car down the western slopes of the San Bernardino range—a delectable perfume not to be confused with a stench, and not to be associated either, except by Hollywood star worshippers with Los Angelenos. On the other hand there is the unmistakable odor of Paris—a sweet-sour compound of bakeries, perfume-shops, stale wine, damp aging stones, and an imperfect sewage-system, a blend of the exquisite and the rotten, of mustiness and splendor, which might plausibly be identified with the physical and moral qualities of the Parisians.

The urine of Rouen; the garlic of Siren Land (smell Naples and die!); the thick acrid fumes of a Moroccan village, retchy evidence of the animality of mankind; the attar of roses-and-camels which carries the nose in one comprehensive whiff from Bucharest to Mecca when you step inside a Levantine home; the mud, goat, onion, and gaberdine *combinatzie* of a Polish-Jewish *shtetel;* the joss-stick and wash-boiler reek of a Chinese laundry which—overland with the prickly titillation of kumquats and the sticky fetor of opium, the cool fragrance of bronze and a bouquet of sandalwood and teak—make up our olfactory impression of a Far Easterner: these manifold exhalations indicate that all races of men stand in good or bad odor. Moreover, every individual (including you and me) is "high" with a smell peculiarly his own; it hangs in the air he has tainted for hours and days after his presence has vanished—as any hunting-dog knows.

Individually and in groups, men exude a psychic aroma as well. Their thoughts and convictions, their attitudes toward themselves and their judgment of the world, are redolent with predilections— with what people who do not approve call prejudices, and sympathizers call insights. Out of the miasma of our likes and dislikes rise, like a marsh-damp, most of our more tenuous or untenable beliefs. In and by themselves such beliefs can hardly be judged benign or harmful. The one indisputably bad thing about them is that, as with physical odors, the people who breathe them constantly become hardened to their existence; they cannot smell them out for what they are. We take these airy opinions for granted, neither questioning their substance nor realizing that they are vapors which emanate from "desires of minor absurdity"—as Sir Thomas Browne would say. And like everyone else, Jews too sometimes gas themselves with their own beliefs.

Accordingly, my purpose in the following casual notes is not so much to correct sundry dubious or mistaken views as to bring them to attention. If only for a moment, let us try to clear the air.

1. That East European Jews Are the "Real" Jews

My earliest memorable encounter with this erroneous notion enlivened my first visit to Palestine—in 1925. The *halutzim* and old settlers, largely from Russia, Rumania, and Poland, looked upon me, though with all kindliness, as some sort of diluted, alien, and inferior Jew—in any case, not the real article. They assumed this attitude not because I was living in *galut*—for in those days who wasn't?—but because Yiddish was not my mother-tongue, *tzimis* and *gefilte* fish were not my culinary ideals, and no little because I preferred coffee to tea, having in fact a mild distaste for that "genuinely" Jewish beverage. I was not a real Jew, either, because to me Sholom Aleichem and Peretz were foreign authors, however gifted, describing a foreign life in lands where my ancestors had never set foot; because my knowledge of Russian folk melodies, then being assiduously mated to Hebrew words, was meager and without nostalgia; and my appreciation of Rumanian dancing under the name of the Hora was dim. Altogether and obviously I did not belong to the "real" Jewish people. I can't say I resented this superior pose, with its overtone of lordly patronage— it amused me then as it does today; but, unlike some of my American fellow-travelers whose perverted snobbism led them to enjoy being put in their place, I didn't quite take it lying down. In such circumstances I am tempted to adopt Job's line: "No doubt but ye are the people, and wisdom shall die with you."

The pose still exists over here in America. In a witty ribbing of some of our current pseudo-Jewish novels, Charles Angoff lays down the criterion of "real" Jewishness, at least as of November 13, 1950 (*Congress Weekly*). Real Jews, we are instructed, are those "you and I meet in the Bronx and on Seventh Avenue." The characters portrayed by Delmore Schwartz, for example, are completely un-Jewish because "no herring, no black bread, no real *lokshen*" ever passes their lips. Reading about them is "just like being in an ultra-Reform temple." "If that is Judaism," Angoff declares, "if these people are Jews, then I'm Father Divine." A veritable Jewish life, he concludes, is as honest as cream cheese or *lox;* and veritable Jews say *Sukkes* instead of Sukkot. (About 3,112 years ago the Gileadites applied the latter test, using the word shibboleth, with fatal results to those who couldn't pass it.)

There is no end to these tests and claims of reality. *Yahudim!*— the intonation of the epithet was something to remember as it used to be heard in my boyhood when the members of the *shul* referred to the members of the temple; and *Pollakim!* when the temple pew-holders retorted in kind. Professor Harry A. Wolfson, in his salad days, published an extensive thesis which proved to his own sardonic satisfaction that East European Jews—*Yids* was the technical expression—were not Jews at all, and *Yiddishkeit* a culture to be radically distinguished from traditional *Judenthum.* Lately, a group of youngsters in Israel have come up with still another definition of what constitutes a real Jew. They are banded together in a society called the *Tenuat Ha-ivrim* (Hebrew Movement), and I quote from their periodical, *Alef:*

"The genuinely Hebrew youth of our land are not a continuation of preceding generations. The literary values taught in our schools ring alien to us; they provide no food for our spirit and prevent the development of a pure Hebrew genius. The present native-born generation of Israel youth feels itself in far closer kinship with the ancient Hebrews, with the life reflected in the books of Judges and Kings, before a world-Jewry existed. The entire system of *Yahadut*"—that is, Yiddishkeit *and* Judenthum, Eastern *and* Western Jewishness alike—"with all its ideas and achievements is foreign to us, root and branch. The social reality from which our youth has sprung finds itself in direct conflict with the realities of world-wide Jewry." And the invidious conclusion is reached that "no healthy nation can evolve in Israel if it remains bound to *Yiddishkeit*—whether of the religious, socialist, or Zionist variety." This is what is known as telling them off.

What the Yemenites, who *nebbich* have regarded themselves as simon-pure Jews for time out of mind, say to these claims and counterclaims I am unable to report, for they are not given to scribbling; but I can guess. The Iraqis, Moroccans, Tunisians, Libyans, Iranians, Kurds, Afghanis, Hindis, and the Jews of Hadhramaut (bearded giants, these! veritable Anakim) have likewise not been heard from; yet among themselves, and being Jews, they are undoubtedly vocal. The Israel authorities, I know, find it a headache to furnish what a real Jew east of Suez is prepared to call real Jewish food. *Lox* has no savor of reality for people dedicated to *cous-cous;* and all Oriental Jews regard cream cheese, even with a *baigel,* as the abomination of desolation.

These claims, one and all, are of course provincial—both in a geographic and temporal sense. Still, an element of historic truth lies behind their interplay of vanity and ignorance. At stated times, in the course of empires and whirligig of events, certain Jewries have played a formative role in the evolution of Jewish destiny, while the remaining Jewries lolled in quiescence. During the moment they ride the crest, such creative Jewries may be granted the courtesy to deem themselves superior to the passive communities. In this respect East European Jewry might be called "real" in the latter half of the nineteenth century and the first quarter of the twentieth. But throughout this period—the precise dates are of no account—it had no monopoly of "reality." German, Bohemian, and Austrian Jewries were, to say the least, its peers in creativity. German Jewry, indeed, has been a "real" Jewry intermittently ever since the year one thousand. When we survey the range of Diaspora history we discern many of these "real" Jewries—in Babylonia, Alexandria, North Africa, Spain, Persia, France, Italy, Holland—each flourishing for a proud creative hour.

But the hour passes. Even while the Palestine *Yishuv* was smiling down at me from the throne of East European "reality," the scepter was crossing the Atlantic, Coca-Cola was supplanting tea as the characteristic beverage of the world's largest Jewry. Apple-pie was ousting *tzimis,* as *tzimis* had pushed Heine's *schalet* off the plate, and as *schalet* in its turn had succeeded the *adafina* of Spanish Jewry, and *adafina* had done to whatever had been the "real" Sabbath dish of the Babylonians.

The heart of the error, and the point at which it betrays the man who holds to it, lies in the bland assumption that quiescent Jewries are somehow not "genuine." Yet in their own terms and for their own people they comprise whatever Jewishness there is. They exist—which, I take it, is a sound definition of reality.

Incidentally and as a corollary of the basic error, I have noticed that Jewries in the decline of their creative powers seem to hold a special grievance against any Jewry on its way up. They can respect a rival, but they resent a successor. Thus, the Spanish Jews of the eighteenth century, when their great days were vanishing, spurned the German Jews, whose greatest days were about to be renewed; and during the late nineteenth century the German Jews despised the *Ostjuden*—and all three, till recently, the *Amerikaner.*

It may be hoped that the time is far off when American Jewry will similarly feel its oats—a fairly sure sign that the bottom of the feed bag is reached.

2. That the Enemies of the Jews Always Perish

The heartening assurance that all of Israel's foes eventually bite the dust is a common theme in prophetic literature. A typical example is Isaiah's judgment on Damascus: "Behold, Damascus is taken from being a city, and it shall be a ruinous heap." Chapter 18, which opens with this minatory note, concludes by declaring: "This is the portion of them that spoil us, and the lot of them that rob us."

When Jews repeat and believe such assurances at their face value they generally advance by way of proof the fate of Moab, Edom, Nineveh, Tyre, Babylon, Egypt, Rome, and even Spain: the list, it would seem, depends more on their recollection of geography than history. For what are the facts? Moab indeed has vanished, together with other semi-desert enemies of ancient Israel. So have Nineveh and Babylon—though the latter took its time, a good thousand years, to bow to the prophetic verdict. But if we include a few other peoples whom it hardly warrants the trouble to recall, the roll is complete. Moreover, it signifies little or nothing.

Of the ancient world, Tyre, to begin with, was no enemy; and yet it has disappeared. Other city-states, such as Carthage, Nabatea, Greek Alexandria, Cyrene, Palmyra, whether friendly or not, have sunk into oblivion. Peoples have a way of perishing regardless of their relation to the Jews, and nothing further can be deduced from that relationship.

On the other hand, what is called the disappearance of Egypt and Rome, two of Israel's arch-foes, is a more complicated affair. The kingdom and culture of the Pharaohs have gone with the desert wind; new Egypts—Greek, Christian, Moslem—have supplanted one another. But in its latest incarnation, Mizraim by all accounts has preserved unabated by age its ancestral enmity toward Israel. Much the same holds true for Persia, Syria and the Bedouin Amalekite, all of whom have undergone in varying degree the alteration that is synonymous with mortality. Rome, however, still flourishes in its fresh guise as Italy; transformation is hardly the equivalent of extinction.

For that matter, Israel and the ancient Jews have likewise "perished" in the sense that their culture has been transmuted into forms that neither Abraham, David, or Isaiah would recognize.

Many traits of the early culture have, to be sure, survived among modern Jewries, but analogous survivals are also to be seen among modern Romans and Greeks. Latin tongues are still spoken in vast areas of the former Roman Empire, Greek is still the language of Hellas; Graeco-Roman ideals molded European art and survive as its classic norm; Greek canons of thought still dictate how Western man must think; Roman law, modified to meet changing conditions, governs the major part if Western Europe, and many a pagan god receives his customary homage under the halo of a local saint. Titus might have a difficult moment reading the *Osservatore Romano,* but no greater than Johannan ben Zakkai confronted with a copy of *Haaretz.*

Nevertheless, the Jews, it can be urged, have maintained an approximate identity across a welter of time and events that must be measured in millenniums. Yet the Greeks and the riverains of the Tiber can proffer a similar claim. To Jewry alone can be credited a continuity of aims and ideals, of spiritual personality, which has outlived the vicissitudes of time—provided, of course, we eliminate from consideration several hundreds of millions of people east of Bombay, and another several hundred millions north of Hong Kong.

Of the more recent and contiguous world, wicked Spain has patently not perished, and what is rather disconcerting, her most prosperous and creative period followed immediately upon her expulsion of the Jews. From Yemen to Morocco the Moslem states have intermittently persecuted Jewry since their inception, some fourteen hundred years ago; they have had their ups and downs, but they remain altogether extant and seem to run no foreseeable danger of fading away. The German Third Reich has collapsed, if only for the nonce, but Germany keeps her place on the map and among the powers to be courted.

Damascus, to return to our starting point, has not become a ruinous heap. In company with Aram (alias Syria), nations too numerous for comfort have spoiled and robbed the Jews, and lived happily ever after.

3. THAT JEWISH SURVIVAL IS UNIQUE

Many of us like to flatter ourselves that the Jews are the only people who, despite smallness of number, deprivation of statehood and homeland, and in the teeth of recurrent persecution, have survived centuries on end—"a piece of stubborn antiquity." This strange fortune is considered unique.

The Jews are of a surety unique. The history of no other people furnishes an exact or approximate parallel; their qualities are singular, their achievements distinctive, and their mode of life cannot be duplicated. But in these respects every people is unique.

However, merely in the matter of survival under oppression and without the benefit of statehood, and ignoring what I consider to be Jewry's more remarkable points, other examples immediately spring to mind. The Samaritans have hung on for nearly 2,400 years, in the face of alternate contumely and attack. Granted, they were never expelled from their stony home-acres, but on the other hand their numbers have been so pitifully few and their lot so wretched, it would seem that unless they enjoyed the advantage of a miracle, they could not have outlasted the centuries. The Armenians have unhappily matched the Jews in political and social misfortune; no independence, no let-up in obloquy, harrassment, and depredation—and, again and again, singled out for genocide. The Gypsies have suffered a congruous experience, and in addition they have been compelled, as were the Jews, to dispense with a homeland—what is stranger, ages ago they reached the point of no return, literally forgetting where their homeland had been. Yet both peoples continue to trudge, battered but intact, down the aisles of time, the Romany folk without even the support of a religious ideal.

Of all comparisons, that of misery is most odious, and of diuturnity most puerile. Except for mummies existence is no endurance test. The Jews, in common with other peoples, live by their works and not by their calendar. They are to be remarked for what they have thought and done (and may still think and do), and not for being always on hand.

4. That the Diaspora Is Unnatural and Reprehensible

Largely based on a misreading of history, the notion has prevailed that the dispersion of the Jewish people (or Diaspora) represents exclusively a compulsory exile from the ancient homeland. Consequently, life in the Diaspora, regardless of the presence or absence of a Jewish State, has been deemed an evil—unnatural, sterile, and reprehensible. Today this view assumes the form, among circles in Israel and elsewhere, of "negating" the Diaspora, that is, of morally and philosophically wiping it off as a loss, once immigrants and money enough are secured from it to ensure the stability of the new state.

As is too often the case with current notions, the facts run otherwise. A good portion of the Diaspora originated not in mass expulsions but voluntary migration. The contrary illusion rises from an obsession (for doctrinal purposes) with two series of undeniable expulsions: the first at the hands of Babylon, and the second engineered by Rome. Yet on the face of it these two major catastrophes cannot account for the wide and populous dispersion of the Jews in ancient times.

There are no precise data on the total number of captives deported to Babylon or of the refugees who fled to Egypt when the Jewish kingdom fell at the beginning of the sixth century (B.C.E.). All but the tillers of the soil, "the poorest sort of the people," had been carried or driven away. When the state was re-established, at the end of the same century, some fifty thousand returned. A considerable but unknown number declined to exchange the waters of Babylon for the Jordan; they dried their tears and were content to contribute funds, temple furniture, and experts (such as Ezra and Nehemiah) to the renascent homeland—and elicit for it grants-in-aid from the Persian government.

During the next six hundred years—until the destruction of Jerusalem in 70 C.E.—there existed a Jewish State, more or less self-governing and fairly prosperous, to which any Jew dwelling in a foreign land could return. Yet we find that after a lapse of six centuries in which to come back, nearly three-quarters of world Jewry lived in the Diaspora, outside the Jewish State—on the whole, evidently, as a matter of free choice. A recent authority estimates the world's Jewish population on the eve of the Roman conquest as eight million. Only two and one-half million of them lived in Palestine; the remainder were settled across the globe, from the confines of India in the east to Spain in the west, one million in Babylonia alone. Writing some fifty years before the destruction of the Jewish State, Strabo reports that "it is hard to find a spot in the inhabited world where this race [the Jews] does not dwell and traffic."

Where did these huge numbers come from? Nothing certain can be said in answer, except that there had been no sizable deportations from Judea in over eighteen generations. Many of the Diaspora Jews were converts to Judaism, or their descendants. Others were descendants of the first bands of exiles, with six hundred years in which to change their minds about staying where they were. Finally, large numbers must have been emigrants, or their offspring, who in the course of these ample years voluntarily left the homeland to seek their fortune abroad.

In any case, until 70 c.e. all of them were virtually free to return —but didn't. Many of the dispersed communities maintained intimate, indeed religiously profound, ties with Judea. Their members contributed to the upkeep of the Temple, pilgrimaged to Jerusalem, and toured the sacred land. But, obviously, millions of them did not find it unnatural to stay in the Diaspora, nor did it seem reprehensible, nor their life sterile.

Then, with the Roman devastation of the homeland and wave upon wave of expulsions, the night of exile, replete with nightmare, again enveloped the Jewish people.

After nearly two thousand years of deprivation, banishment, and dispersal, the present restoration of homeland and state has compelled the Jews to undergo a conscience-racking examination of the concepts of Diaspora and *galut* (exile).

Addressing the recent Zionist Congress, Yitzhak Gruenbaum conceives that all of the ten million Jews who still remain outside the borders of Israel "are living exiled from their country," and although persecution may not be their lot, "their position is one of subjugation as long as they do not live their own life in their own land." Expressing another typical view, Meir Grossman draws the logical conclusion that the entire Jewish people should be transferred to Israel. Not so, explains Rose Halprin, and advances an ingenious distinction between the Diaspora, which embraces the Jewries (such as the American and British) who live happily in freedom, and the *galut,* which comprises the Jews who live miserably under duress. Only the latter must perforce be ingathered to the homeland; the former are free to stay or go as they desire. To which Nahum Goldmann replies: "*Galut* does not cease being *galut* because Jews are happy and well-treated there. *Galut* is not measured by good or bad treatment. *Galut* is a mystical concept. If one denies that America is *galut,* one may as well deny the necessity for Israel."

The debate can be simplified and perhaps dissipated by sticking to historical realities. When a Jewish homeland and state did not in fact exist—as during the Babylonian Captivity, and throughout the past seventeen centuries—the Jewish people lived in exile. But whenever homeland and state are existent—as during the six centuries which preceded the Roman conquest and as again today—there is no such thing as exile. The confusion, the contradictory views, the ingenuities arise from failing to distinguish between the Jewish people and individual Jews or communities. It is a distinction cardinal to Zionist thought. The Jewish people taken as a whole, *Am Israel,* was in exile so long as it possessed no land or state of its own. Possessing these essentials today, it is not and can not be in exile—or language is fatuous.

Furthermore, ever since the first Jew emigrated from the land of Israel, possibly in the days of Solomon, Jews have lived in dispersion—like scores of other peoples, from the ancient Phoenicians and Hellenes to the modern Englishmen and Italians. And their Diaspora, while a Jewish State exists, does not cease to be a natural, normal, and affirmative status because it has its bad times as well as good. The Jews of Soviet Russia who wish to go to Israel and can't, are not exiles but prisoners. The Jews of America and elsewhere who can go to Israel but don't, are not exiles but Jewish settlers of one or many generations in the world at large—as much justified in their choice of flag and country as any other human being. *Herut Zion*—the freedom of Zion—will not be freedom unless, as during the ancient Diaspora, it includes the freedom to come or go, to remain or stay away.

As matters stand, the freedom of Zion is a reality, the exile is over, and to the Diaspora falls the sacred and obligatory task of seeing to it, through the strengthening of Zion, that the exile has vanished forever.

5. That Jewish and American Ideals Are Identical

Recently a prominent Boston lawyer was quoted as saying, in a public address, that "the Jewish way of life is the American way," and calling for "more conscious awareness" of the "close and actual affinity between the ideals of Americanism and Judaism." The phrases have a familiar ring and echo the genuine sentiments of countless American Jews—sentiments no one would controvert. But they bring to mind other sentiments that other Jews have from time to time entertained with similar conviction.

"The character of the Jewish people always had a strong affinity to the character of the German race"—the statement is Heine's, and thousands of his fellow German-Jews heartily agreed with it. The emotional warmth of the Germans, their religious fervor, moral earnestness, and intellectual *Gründlichkeit* were felt—in pre-Nazi days—to be in singular accord with the Jewish spirit. They ordered this matter better in France (as Sterne would remark)—or, at any rate, differently. The French Revolution, wrote James Darmesteter (in 1880), brought into being "an order of ideas which Judaism had no need to combat, for it recognized in the Revolution its own instincts and traditions." Recasting the thought of Joseph Salvador—the latter an extraordinary figure worth meditating by our contemporary Jewish theologues and seers—Darmesteter found the bond between Paris and Jerusalem "as good as indestructible," for it expresses "the eternal human instinct for all that is noble." Salvador, it is piquant and instructive to note, held that the principles of the eighteenth-century Age of Reason were virtually identical with those enunciated by the God of Israel; that Revelation spoke the same language on the summit of Sinai as in the salons of the *philosophes;* and that Moses was, in spirit and intent, a member of the National Assembly, orating from a top bench of the "Mountain" in 1789. All in all, a colorful anthology could be compiled in illustration of the satisfaction French Jews have derived from the intimate *rapport* between the *esprit français* and the *esprit juif.*

On the other hand, the affinity said to exist between Britain and Jewry is notorious. For a while it amounted to a literal identity, at least in the minds of that considerable section of the English people who looked upon themselves as descendants of the ancient Israelites and claimed that the word *British* was in reality the Hebrew *brit ish,* or "man of the covenant." In the late nineteenth century a British-Israel World Federation boasted that it embraced some five million members. On the Jewish side, Weizmann found that British statesmen of the old school readily understood the concept of Zionism, because "it appealed to their tradition and their faith." Nor was it all a matter of Puritan enthusiasm for the Old Testament or a democratic philosophy common to England and Israel. Quite the contrary! An older Jewish statesman, Disraeli, felt a different kinship. Speaking through the mouth of Sidonia, the Jewish character in his novel *Coningsby*, Disraeli explains at length that, being themselves the aristocracy of nature, "the Jews are a race essentially monarchical, deeply religious, and essentially Tories." Speaking in his own voice (in the *Life of Lord George Bentinck*) he declares that "the native tendency of the Jewish race is against the doctrine of the equality of man. They have also another characteristic—the faculty of acquisition. Thus it will be seen that all the tendencies of the Jewish race are conservative. Their bias is to religion, property, and natural aristocracy." Needless to recall, Disraeli stood for an enlightened Toryism, a "partnership of peers and people"—a view he transferred from his own person to the Jewish people. It is human to treat our views in a fashion contrary to our money—to lend to others whatever we possess.

The spiritual and cultural kinship between Islam and Judaism, between our "Semitic cousins" and ourselves, was a beloved Jewish theme—until our cousins lately proved themselves "a little more than kin, and less than kind." Analogous themes, I venture to believe, have been conterminous with the Diaspora. No doubt the Falashas, gathering nights around their white-washed huts, still listen with grunts of assent to discourses on the basic unity of Jewry and Abyssinia—is not Haile Selassie the Lion of Judah? This much is certain: from land to land and age to age Jewish philosophers have argued learnedly and cogently that Judaism is in tenor, and often in tenets, fairly identical with theocracy, monarchy, and democracy; with nationalism and internationalism, capitalism and socialism, individualism and cooperation, conservatism and progressivism, mysticism and rationalism, racism and universalism; with Platonism, Aristotelianism, Stoicism, Deism, Hegelianism, Evolutionism, and the single tax. The latest identification seems to be with Existentionalism—and behind the iron curtain, I should not doubt, with communism.

If, as these various proponents sincerely believed, the spirit of Judaism is at one with such a diversity, indeed self-contradictory assembly, of spirits, what kind of a spirit must it be when it is

377

taken simply by itself? Off-hand, one might suspect, there hangs about many of these assertions, claims, and philosophic or historical arguments, no matter how erudite, an unpleasant air of "me too" Judaism.

In most cases, thankfully, the suspicion is groundless. The fact is that these identifications belong to a category of human expressions which are neither true nor false, right nor wrong, good nor bad. Such expressions are not rare. Most adjectives, most nouns, and many propositions fall into this class. To say that the Jewish way of life is the American way is much like saying "green" or "nail" or "so long!"—words from which nothing true or false is to be adduced. As Captain Jack Bunsby liked to remark, "the bearings of the observation lays in the application on it." The Jewish way of life has been a long and complex way, with numerous meanderings and detours; it has been paved with everything from the tablets of Sinai to good intentions. Even in its short run, the American way is likewise no simple straight lane. The two coincide for a stretch; and to give a statement of their common direction any significance, we must set side by side only those Jewish and American ideals which are in agreement. This means leaving great segments of the Jewish and American experience out of account.

Important as our common course may be, I happen to think that America (as other lands and civilizations in the past) has given its Jewry many valuable ideals and ways hitherto unknown to them; and Jewry, in turn, possesses valuable ideals and ways of which America is ignorant or heedless. Whenever we demonstrate the latter (and not merely write about it, as I am doing), thereby showing how Judaism differs from Americanism in the things that count toward a richer life, we add perhaps to our discomfort—but also to our stature.

6. On the Preservative Quality of Hebrew

From time to time it is asserted that only such Jewish books as are written in Hebrew or receive a Hebrew translation will endure through the centuries. "Some important works were written in Arabic and other languages," says William Chomsky (*Reconstructionist,* Dec. 1, 1950), reflecting this not uncommon view, "but in order to survive, they had to be incorporated into a Hebrew text." Speaking of Saadia, one of the most important of these

Arabic-writing Jews, Abraham S. Halkin laments that "so little of his contributions to Halaka has been preserved, probably because it was not translated into Hebrew" (*The Jews*, Ed. L. Finkelstein, III, 799). The Jews, so runs the notion, faithfully guard and transmit Hebrew literature down the generations; whereas books written in other languages are often lost as the Jewish people, in their wanderings, adopt a new vernacular and neglect or forget the tongues they no longer use. I have heard Ludwig Lewisohn lecture eloquently on the thesis. It is used, of course, as an argument for the cultivation of the Hebrew tongue. There are numerous forcible and attractive reasons for learning and employing Hebrew, but its preservative quality is not among them. This is fortunate, for the quality does not exist.

Only a few of the more conspicuous facts need be recalled. One of the masterpieces of Jewish thought, the philosophic works of Philo, was written in Greek and safely transmitted in Greek across the stretch of two thousand years—thanks, one should add, not to the Jews but the Christians. The same good fortune holds true for the collection of writings now to be read in the Apocrypha. Some of its capital works, such as the Wisdom of Ben Sirach, the First Book of the Maccabees, and the First Book of Esdras, were composed in Hebrew. Much good it did their authors or posterity!— for the Jews proceeded to mislay the Hebrew texts. Luckily, they had been translated into Greek, and were kept extant by Christian piety. (About half of the Hebrew text of Ben Sirach was dug out of the rubbish of a Cairo *genizah* some fifty years ago.) The Hebrew originals of the *Psalms of Solomon,* the *Book of Jubilees,* the *Testaments of the Twelve Patriarchs,* and the *Book of Adam and Eve,* to name but few of the more important writings now embraced in the Pseudepigrapha, have vanished into oblivion. These works are called "pseudo" because they were written in the name of venerable worthies from the past or falsely ascribed to the famous dead—much as modern opinion believes that the Song of Songs is falsely ascribed to Solomon and most of the Psalms to David. They can now be read only in Greek or modern languages. Moreover we should have virtually no knowledge of the epic struggle involved in the second destruction of the Jewish State if Josephus had not found it good politics to have his *Jewish Wars* turned into Greek. Of the original Hebrew (or possibly Aramaic) text not a word has survived.

In short, not only precious works of literature but invaluable accounts of two of the epoch-making events of Jewish history—the revolt of the Maccabees and the fall of the Jewish State—have been transmitted to us *via* Greek and not Hebrew, though they were originally written in the holy and eternal tongue.

The risks accompanying a reliance on Hebrew do not end here. Works once existed in Hebrew and were subsequently lost, which the world would give fortunes to recover. I refer to the books or writings mentioned in the Bible, of which nothing or barely a line remains to us. My own rough and probably incomplete count runs to twenty-one titles. The contents suggested by many of them make the mouth water. What, we wonder, happened to the Book of the Wars of the Lord? A casual reference and a snatch of cryptic song are left to tease us (Num. 21:14). Of the Book of Jashar two shards, like opalescent bits of an ancient glass vase, gleam in the account of the sun standing still for Joshua, and in David's lament over Saul and Jonathan. Samuel, we are told, wrote a treatise or screed on the "manner" (the constitution?) of the kingdom he and Saul were about to found, and deposited it at a holy shrine for safe-keeping (I. Sam. 10:25). It has vanished—together with the Book of the Acts of Solomon, and all the chapters from the Chronicles of the Kings of Israel and the Chronicles of the Kings of Judah which the writer or editor of our extant books of Kings alludes to but saw fit to omit. Where, too, are the Thousand and Five Songs of Solomon and his Three Thousand Proverbs? It is tantalizing to learn that Solomon wrote of beasts, birds, snakes, fishes, trees, herbs, and flowers, and not even to know whether this lost work was a volume of fables or a cyclopedia on natural science (I. Kings 4:32–33).

Conceivably the above-mentioned writings were destroyed in the wrecking of Jerusalem by the Babylonians. Carelessness and wilful neglect may have had no hand in it. But the writer of the chronicles, which were compiled after the safe return from exile, had under his eyes at least a dozen other books, for he cites them, which have crumbled into nothingness. With what confidence he assures us, "now the rest of the acts of Solomon, first and last, are they not written in the book of Nathan the prophet, and in the prophecy of Ahijah the Shilonite, and in the visions of Iddo the seer?" Little did he dream that there is no end not only to the making of books—but the losing of them. Gad, who campaigned with David, and Nathan, who was a statesman-prophet in David's court, likewise wrote biographies of this incomparable monarch—which the author of Chronicles explicitly distinguishes from our present books of Samuel. For my part, I should gladly dispense with the genealogies upon which the Chronicler dotes if he had given their space (and more besides) to those perished first-hand accounts of "the acts of David the king, first and last . . . with all his reign and his might, and the times that went over him, and over Israel, and over all the kingdoms of the countries" (I. Chron. 29:29–30).

Alas, Hebrew offers no better guarantee of immortality than any other civilized tongue. Time and chance. . . .

7. That Israel Specialized in Religion and Greece in Art

Books, essays, and sermons have been devoted to the notion that the ancient Jews were mainly absorbed in religion, and the ancient Greeks in art—and, it is generally added for good measure, the ancient Romans were given predominantly to law and government. The source of this misconception is evident. It lies in a confusion of *post hoc* with *propter hoc*. Due to the accidents of history, as well as the merits of the case, the Occident derived its basic legal principles from Rome, its standards of art from Greece, and its religious faiths from Judea. Accordingly, it assumes that it took over these concepts on law, art, and religion because they were about the only things the donors had to give. Because the Western world was won over to—or had imposed upon them— Roman law, Greek art, and a Judaistic religion, it tends to believe that the Romans concentrated on political science, the Greeks on esthetics, and the Jews on worship.

The lives of these ancient peoples are cut and dried and compartmented because they lived so long ago. Yet we ought to learn to suspect our conventional notions about them from observing how readily we employ similar stereotypes in characterizing modern peoples with whose lives we have ample means—books, periodicals, motion-pictures, travel—of real acquaintance. For no other reason than the fact that French cooking has the virtue and prestige of excellence, too many of us are wont to believe that most Frenchmen spend most of their lives cooking and eating. Because Italian opera holds the highest score for popularity, Italians do little else than thrum and sing on street-corners. A couple of generations ago German philosophy swept the boards, and the quaint idea prevailed that the German people passed their time smoking over the problems of metaphysics . . . a notion, however, that was exploded in 1914.

Actually and in direct contradiction to our conventional ideas, the ancient Greeks and Romans were wrapped up in religion. The ancient Jews and Greeks were adept in law. And all three peoples, being human and gifted, were highly appreciative of beauty. It is bizarre to think that a people like the Jews, whose fundamental religious documents embraced minute and finely-nuanced laws on property, equity, criminality, and personal relations, were not legal-minded. Or that a people like the Greeks, who were assiduous in ritual observance, engrossed in divine mysteries, and dominated by their sacred cults, were not essentially religious. Roman piety was, of course, a by-word.

"Oh that my soul might lead me in the path of holy innocence of thought and deed, the path which august laws ordain, laws which in the highest heaven had their birth, neither did the race of mortal men beget them, nor shall oblivion ever put them to sleep; the power of God is mighty in them and groweth not old!" No, this is not a passage from one of the lost psalms of David, or from an unfamiliar *piyyut;* it is from *Oedipus Rex,* a prayer composed by the esthetic Sophocles. Perhaps the sentiment has too lofty a ring. Sophocles, however, can sound the same homely note, touching the heart and conscience, as the author of Deuteronomy: "I know that God is ever such as this, darkly disclosing counsel to the wise; but to the simple, speaking fewest words, a plain teacher."

If anyone will take the trouble to read, for example, Jane Ellen Harrison's *Themis,* a sympathetic and richly illustrated study of the Greeks' underlying beliefs on the relation between divinity and humanity, he will write off whatever conventional ideas he had previously hugged on Greek religiosity. If he will read Alfred E. Zimmern's *Greek Commonwealth,* written with the eye of a top-rank journalist and the knowledge of a scholar, he will comprehend the Greek genius for law and statecraft. Any general survey of the Talmud, such as Strack's, will of course obliterate the fancy that the Jews were disinterested or inferior in jurisprudence.

But no Jew believes that ancient Israel had little interest or ability in the realm of lawmaking; anyone who has the slightest knowledge of the subject ought to know better. Ah, but that is exactly the point with respect to the Greeks, not only in the realm of law—but religion.

As for the Jewish appreciation of beauty, we stand, I confess, badly in need of a fresh modern appraisal and interpretation of the literary art of the Bible. But it will have to be undertaken by someone who understands that, as an art, literature rests on the same plane as painting or sculpture, neither above nor below. The word, like paint or stone, is used to express perceptions, feelings, and judgments—not of the reality, but only the appearance, of things. Words, too, grasp nothing but the *lebendiges Kleid der Gottheit*. The word too can become an idol—worse, a fetish. If a Jewish writer and Hebraic scholar, sensitive to beauty, and understanding how it is wrought—and we have a number of them—but likewise a writer and scholar who is as humble before Rembrandt as he is before a Psalm—and we have, to my limited knowledge, none—were to reveal anew the esthetic splendors of the Bible, we would stop talking about beauty as an ancient monopoly of the Greeks.

With respect to all three peoples, Jews, Greeks, and Romans, we would, in fine, stop—just talking.

8. On the "Unprecedented" Hardships in Israel Today

There are many sound reasons for ascribing most of the prophetic passages dealing with the restoration of Israel to a period either before the return from Babylon, or long after it. One of the soundest derives from the joy they attribute to the people and the conditions following that marvelous event. Their enchanting picture of everyone sitting under his own vine and fig-tree, or of the law going forth from Zion, is fairly clear proof that they had no picture whatever of the realities of the Return. Either the event had not yet taken place; or, as in the case of supplementary passages, it had occurred so long ago that the actualities were forgotten, and had been supplanted by romantic reconstructions.

At the beginning of the exile, Ezechiel, for example, foresees that, upon its end, Israel "shall feed in a good pasture" and "the tree of the field shall yield its fruit, and the earth shall yield her increase, and they shall be safe in their land" (34:14, 28). A post-exilic psalm, which bears about the same factual relation to the return as William Morris' visions to the real Middle Ages, does not hesitate to imagine that when the Lord turned again the captivity of Zion

> We were like them that dream;
> Then was our mouth filled with laughter,
> And our tongue with singing.

The tenor and promise of that dream sustained, as little else, the Jewish people in the well-nigh two thousand years of their second captivity. In our own days these prophetic and psalmist visions were the positive inspiration of the men and women who rebuilt the Jewish State.

Now they have awakened—not in the sense that the Return has been invalidated, but in the realization of the tremendous gap between dreams and life, between striving and getting what one strives for. It is, however, an old story. In contrast to their visionary predecessors, two of the prophets spoke of the restoration out of personal experience. They knew and reported the face of reality, with its hardships and heart-strains. Haggai and Zechariah sound as though they were writing in 1952 c.e. instead of 520 b.c.e.

"Ye have sown much," says Haggai to his contemporaries, "but bring in little. You eat, but you have not enough. You drink, but you do not drink your fill. You clothe, but there is none warm. And he who earns wages, earns wages for a pocket with holes in it" (1:6). Although it was all on a smaller scale, the consequences of a comparatively large immigration, equipped with little experience and skill, trying to revive quickly a land of limited resources, were the same 2,500 years ago as today: shortages, austerity, and inflation. But there was humor, too, then as now—as in Haggai's definition of inflation. And Haggai, moreover, has the right and pointed word for those of us who stay comfortably in the Diaspora: "Is it time for you to dwell in your snug houses? . . . Consider your ways!"

Zechariah, who wrote within a year or two of Haggai and whose messages (ch. 7–8) are dated to the day, month, and year, does not dwell on the hardships but on their cure. His remedies are as contemporary as a speech by Ben Gurion. "Let your hands be strong, ye who hear these words," he writes, speaking by prophetic privilege in God's name, "and I will save my people from the east country and from the west country." Besides courage and hard work, further essentials are required: "These are the things that ye shall do—execute the judgment of truth and peace in your gates . . . show mercy and compassion every man to his brother; oppress not the widow, nor the fatherless, the stranger nor the poor." With uncanny timeliness, Zechariah directs a warning to all parties concerned, one might say to all parties, from Right to Left, with a seat in the Knesset: "Let none of you imagine evil against his brother in your heart."

We hear something too much of prophetic idealism. Perhaps it would sound less remote and unsubstantial if heard as the echo or counterpoint to prophetic realism. When men like Haggai and Zechariah show themselves as hard as nails in fastening upon reality, we can trust their vision of what lies behind and beyond the work at hand. The present scene in Israel has had an anguishing precedent; and yet, if the precedent holds, one fraught with fulfillment. A stout heart, an industrious hand, and a regime of social justice, which Israel is manifesting today, will bring, as once before, the promised results: "For the seed shall be prosperous, the vine shall give her fruit, and the heavens shall give dew; and I will cause the remnant of this people to possess all these things. And it shall come to pass, that as ye were a curse among the nations . . . ye shall be a blessing."

This takes care of everyone according to precedent, except, as hard-headed Haggai would insist, those of us who still dwell in our snug houses and need to consider our ways.

REFLECTIONS ON THE JEWISH QUESTION

By SIDNEY HOOK

WHATEVER SARTRE'S MERIT as a philosopher—not very consider-able, in my opinion—his writings reveal a depth of psycho-logical insight more rewarding than a library of tomes on scientific psychology. Why, despite these psychological gifts, Sartre writes such bad novels perhaps others can explain. Psychology, however, has its limitations when applied to historical themes, and all Jew-ish questions, except definitions of what constitutes a Jew, are his-torical. Sartre's "anti-Semite" and "Jew," authentic and inau-thentic, are ideal psychological types based not on what most Jews and anti-Semites are but on the kind of Jews and anti-Semites literary people are interested in. In virtue of his phenomenological approach, all Sartre needs is just a few specimens to construct a timeless *essence* of Jewishness and anti-Semitism.

For all its historical limitations, Sartre's book, *Anti-Semite and Jew,* is unquestionably one of the most brilliant psychological analyses of the marginal Jew and the fanatical anti-Semite which has ever been published. That he has independently discovered conclusions which Kurt Lewin and Horace Kallen, who know in-finitely more about the subject than he, reached many years ago, only adds to the measure of his achievement. Would only that he had kept to psychology. For when Sartre does discuss social and po-litical matters he lapses into the most vulgar and sentimental kind of orthodox Marxism. Anti-Semitism is a "bourgeois" phenome-non—as if it were not found among peasants, in feudal society, among the nobility. It is a mythical representation of the class struggle. "It could not (*sic!*) exist in a classless society"—presum-ably by definition. Its presence in the Soviet Union (legally forbidden—to be sure) Sartre would probably explain as the result of capitalist encirclement and the existence of those terrible "cartels" which he regards as also responsible for the Marshall plan.[1]

In a curious way Sartre's book supplements the politically acute and psychologically obtuse study Marx wrote on the Jews a century ago. Marx argues against Bruno Bauer's demand that the German Jews give up their Jewishness as a precondition of being regarded as German citizens. Sartre argues against French anti-Semites who insist that the Jews can never really become French because they can never cease being Jews. His answer is that the Jew can be just as good a Frenchman as the Gentile, and that after the social revolution, the Jews may assimilate themselves willingly, and become authentic Frenchmen. The naïveté of Marx's solution—"The emancipation of the Jews is the emancipation of society from Judaism" (which is commerce)—is mitigated by his assumption that what distinguished the Jews would automatically evaporate in the strong sun of the political enlightenment.[2] A century later, and after Hitler, too, this naïveté is a little too much.

Economic competition or distress exacerbates oppositions. It intensifies anti-Semitism but it does not create it. It explains why a scapegoat is sought but not why one particular group is *always* the scapegoat in the West whenever any profound social change or affliction takes place. Is capitalism the common causal factor in Russian, Polish, English and Spanish anti-Semitism?

Even the radical movement is infected with anti-Semitism—conscious and unconscious. At the time of the Stalin-Trotsky feud most non-Jewish Stalinists used anti-Semitic arguments against the Trotskyists. On the West Coast I was asked by a Stalinist why all the Trotskyists were Jewish intellectuals. In the East during the period when Malcolm Cowley was writing literary criticism for

---

[1] The two countries of the world Sartre is most ignorant of are the U.S. and the U.S.S.R. For the position of the Jews in the Soviet Union, cf. two noteworthy articles, "The Soviet Partisans and the Jews" by Solomon M. Schwartz, *Modern Review*, Jan. 1949 and "Has Russia Solved the Jewish Problem?" by Harry Schwartz, *Commentary*, Feb. 1948.

[2] Marx did not understand that Jewish capitalism was what Max Weber called "pariah" capitalism and that the Jews played no important role as a group in capitalism *as a process of production* whose study became his life work. He never returned to the theme of his essay "On the Jewish Question" written when he was a young man of twenty-seven. In that essay he argues for the emancipation of society not only from Judaism but from Christianity and all other religions.

the Stalinists in the pages of *The New Republic,* Communist Party fellow-travelers made no secret of their belief that the Trotskyists were a bunch of "neurotic New York Jews." Just about two years ago, Pierre Hervé wrote in *l'Humanité:* "It is not by accident that three quarters of the Trotskyist leaders are Jews."

I once asked a leading Communist who had broken with the Stalinists to explain as objectively as he could the source of this anti-Semitism. He groped haltingly for an explanation. "It's a matter of superficial cultural differences." He then exclaimed in a burst of honest confession: "I must admit that even I become irritated when I see people in the subway pull Jewish newspapers from their pockets. I feel that if they are living here they really ought to become part of the culture." "Do you feel the same way," I asked him, "when people draw Greek, Russian, German or Italian newspapers from their pockets?" "Why, no," he replied wonderingly. "That's odd," he added, "I never thought about that before." He is still mystified.

Sartre is aware, however, that the causes of anti-Semitism are not to be found in the behavior of the Jews. That is why the theme of his book is more topical today than it was when it originally appeared. For since then, the actions and thought-ways, to some extent even the psychology, of many Jewish groups seem to be changing without any noticeable decrease in anti-Semitism.

Any careful observer of Jewish affairs is conscious of these transformations among the Jews since the end of the war. To a large extent they are attributable to the profound shock which followed the discovery that almost six million fellow Jews had been slaughtered by Hitler. That they died was one blow; how they died another; the way the rest of the world reacted to the news a third. It is safe to say that the Jews as a whole will never be the same again. As a historical event, the extermination of the greater part of European Jewry will take its place with the Exodus and the destruction of the Temple. Even if the brotherhood of man had followed hard upon the fall of Hitler, it would have taken a long time for the wounds to heal. As it is, these wounds are torn open afresh by every sign that the world does not feel it owes the pitiful survivors anything, and by the multiplying evidences that anti-Semitism has now reached an intensity in some Western countries almost equal to that observed in Germany a few years before the Nazis came to power.

Some liberals and friends of the Jews are puzzled. After all, they point out, this is not the first time in recent history that millions of innocent human beings have been destroyed by despots. Without making comparisons between degrees of infamy and differences in the techniques of murder, Stalin has probably killed more people from the time of the man-made Ukrainian famine in 1932 to the present than even Hitler. When these events happened, and similar ones in China and India, the Jews were no more and no less indignant than anyone else. Why do they seem so "hysterical" now?

The answer is simple. When six million Jews are slaughtered, the remaining Jews cannot but feel uneasy about their own position; when six million Gentiles are slaughtered, the remaining Gentiles do not feel uneasy. Whether the feeling in the case of the Jews is justified—and I believe it is not—is hardly the point. That it exists is a sufficient explanation of the great differences in attitude, speech, and behavior of many Jews throughout the world, and not least in the United States.

In certain respects these differences are not desirable even from the standpoint of Jewish survival and the quality of Jewish life. A people that has, by and large, been rational and pacific now seeks by an act of resolution to be belligerent and to cultivate the *mystique* of action. The desperate courage and will-to-death-through-resistance which would have been appropriate throughout Europe—and not only in the last days of the Warsaw ghetto—in combating the Nazi extermination squads, is now on tap to meet difficulties that are honorably negotiable. It was not Hitler who was assassinated but Bernadotte. And the Jews have now created their own non-Jewish D.P.'s, more numerous than the remaining Jewish D.P.'s in Europe. Because the Nazis fooled them again and again, they have become overly suspicious of those who kept the Nazis at bay. Goebbels used to assert that the Jews were not as intelligent as they or the world believed because they persisted in misreading Hitler's clearly expressed intentions with respect to them. To prove their intelligence now, many read Clement Attlee's words in such a way that only a Nazi could have uttered them. And as for Bevin!

It is as if the Jews were out to prove that they are like everyone else—inconsistent, fanatical, atavistic. Even those Jews who are distressed by these changes, who prefer to look at Jews as Sartre sees them, "mild," endowed with "a sense of justice and reason," "spontaneous and warm," full of "obstinate sweetness which they conserve in the midst of the most atrocious persecution"—even such Jews, despite themselves, feel a throb of satisfaction at the feat of Jewish arms in a world that has cast slurs over Jewish willingness or ability to fight. Some Jews—fortunately a minority—judge all issues of foreign policy not by their bearings on the preservation of democracy throughout the world but by the way in which the fortunes of the State of Israel are affected. And not unlike the fellow-traveling Christian clergyman, there has emerged the disingenuous Jewish rabbi who permits his name to be used by Communist Front organizations.

All this is reflected in cultural and theoretical matters. The same liberal Jewish periodical which denounces in unmeasured terms— "undemocratic," "unconstitutional," "utterly indecent"—the Mundt-Nixon Bill calling for the registration of subversive organizations plotting the overthrow of the U.S. government by force and violence grows lyrical over the Israeli Constitution that condemns as criminal any propaganda against democracy—a provision which in effect makes Plato's *Republic* seditious literature. Opposition to any official Zionist measure, condemnation even of the Irgun, is sure to bring a raft of scabrous anonymous letters. A people of dissenters have become impatient of their own dissenters and have almost succeeded in cowing them. There has been an upsurge in religious orthodoxy in many Jewish communities outside of Palestine—an orthodoxy not a whit less superstitious than that of other religions. And as if to add a comic touch, the "new failure of nerve" is observable among some young literary Jewish intellectuals, who, looking enviously at the Church, are prepared to join the Synagogue if only Kafka is added to the Apocryphal Books of the Old Testament. One is tempted to characterize them, modifying a phrase of Horace Kallen's, as "amateur Catholics."

If Sartre is right, all this is in vain. It is a matter of profound unconcern to the anti-Semite what the Jews believe and how they behave—whether they are Communists or democrats, pious or agnostic, aggressive or shy. The anti-Semite hates them all. The existence of the State of Israel will not diminish anti-Semitism. It will merely furnish the anti-Semites with another charge. We can expect to hear references to Jews as "hyphenated Americans." Sartre here sees truly and sees what some Jews themselves do not see. It is pathetic to observe how many Jews seek to pin on other Jews, those who differ in some perceptible manner from themselves, the blame for a discrimination whose explanation lies not in them, save in the tautologous sense that if there were no Jews there would be no anti-Semitism, but in the beliefs and habits and culture of the non-Jews. A whole volume can be written about the illusions Jews harbor concerning the disabilities imposed upon them by public disapproval of *other Jews*—non-believing Jews or rich Jews or radical Jews or second-generation Jews or what not—and the resistance they set up to recognizing the truth that in the eyes of those who "don't like Jews" these differences are utterly irrelevant.

What, then, is anti-Semitism? This is Sartre's first question. What is a Jew? is his second. What is an authentic Jew? is his third. Sartre's metaphysics muddies all his answers but he has something psychologically illuminating to say about each question.

Anti-Semitism is not so much an opinion as a *passion*. This passion is not a result of a personal or direct experience with Jews but is a "predisposition" which lies in the psyche of the anti-Semite, his uneasiness about himself, his mediocrity. The idea that the anti-Semite has about the Jew is not explained by "any social fact." "It precedes the facts that are supposed to call it forth." Although Sartre contradicts this by his Marxist derivations of anti-Semitism, this is his deeper, underlying thought. He even goes so far as to say that, "If the Jew did not exist (today), the anti-Semite would invent him."

But why would he invent the *Jew* and not someone else? One would imagine that some historical answer to this question is necessary. Sartre boldly denies it. The *idea* of the Jew as a special and detestable creature must first be present in the anti-Semite before he lets historical facts influence him. Consequently "no external factor can induce anti-Semitism in the anti-Semite." It is an idea or passion that has no adequate cause in its object. *Whence,* then, does it spring?

Instead of answering this question Sartre gives us a phenomenology of the anti-Semitic consciousness. And here he is at his best. He pictures the anti-Semite as a man who is afraid of the human estate, as a sadist with a "pure heart" who justifies infamies in a good cause, a coward and malcontent, a would-be murderer, who glories in his mediocrity, and legitimizes his right to belong to the world by assimilating himself "to the permanence and impenetrability of stone."

Brilliant as all this is, it is overdrawn. It is too narrow. It does not recognize distinctions and degrees in an appropriate way. This is the psychology of the active anti-Semite who has either harmed Jews by act or libelous word or is aware that under favorable circumstances he would be happy to do it. But what of the much more numerous group who are aware that they have no use for Jews, who desire neither to buy from, nor sell nor rent to Jews, to hire them or compete with them, who at most can only be taxed with participation in a cold pogrom, and yet are free of the vicious traits detailed above? Sartre lets them off lightly. They are really not anti-Semites but mindless nonentities who unconsciously serve as the medium through which the active anti-Semites exercise power. Sartre falters at the point. His eloquence, as well as his insight, stops short. For there are so many of them. To account for *their* moral culpability, comparatively minor as it may be, he would have to face the question he evades all the time (except in a few hasty lines): Why are the Jews, of all possible pretexts, of all possible scapegoats, selected as the sacrificial objects of Western culture?

Before considering this question, let us note that in its fullness Sartre's psychological analysis applies only to the professional anti-Semite, to those who in a sense make a political and social career of anti-Semitism. But there is a significant group of anti-Semites to whom it does not apply.

It is true that in any competitive situation, where inner security or assured social status is lacking, *mediocrity* generates fear of personal failure and hatred of the successful competitor. Where Jew and Gentile are involved, the greater the fear, the more likely it is that the non-mediocre Jew will become the object of embittered hatred by the mediocre Gentile. The latter solidarizes himself with all the Gentiles in a contrived defense of their common interests against the insidious "plot" of the Jew, all the more insidious for being invisible, in order that probing concern about his own failure of achievement be averted from him. Mediocrity, a hopeless, fuming, nervous mediocrity, particularly when it burns with ambition for power or fame, is almost invariably anti-Semitic.

But there is still another type of anti-Semite who is barely touched by Sartre's psychological analysis. This is the anti-Semite who, far from being mediocre, has a touch of genius. He is not a sadist or moral degenerate in the sense of Sartre's active anti-Semite. Nor does he belong among the mindless ones who constitute the latter's mass base. Yet he has provided a great deal of the ammunition for the vulgar advocates of extermination and made anti-Semitism a respectable sentiment in the salons, and among the literary hangers-on of the genteel tradition, who fancy themselves liberal because they make exceptions for one "white-haired boy" among the Jews they know.

What Sartre says applies to creatures like Hitler, Goebbels, Rosenberg and their corresponding type in other countries, Drumont, Mosley, Gerald Smith, but not to figures like Schopenhauer, Wagner, Dühring, Houston Chamberlain, Proudhon, Bourget, Maurras, Sorel, Dostoyevsky, Henry Adams, Dreiser, Chesterton and Belloc—who, for all their gifts, have helped poison the little minds of Europe and America, and prepared the way for the easy credulities which, while dismissing the *Protocols of Zion* and the charge of ritual blood-murder, murmur: "After all, there must be something in it." The sensibilities of the Ezra Pounds are finer than those of the Himmlers, the stomachs of the Célines are weaker than those of the Streichers but is the objective meaning of their statement about the Jews so fundamentally different? Yet their psychology is certainly not the same. Every anti-Semitic "genius" has a unique psychology. Even as social psychologies the anti-Semitisms of Central European clericalism, anti-Dreyfus French nationalism, German racialism, English snobbism, must be distinguished. Perhaps the psychology is not so important as that it has a common object.

A study of the literary history of the West reinforces the same point, to be sure, in a gentler and much more indirect way. The reasons are complex and vary somewhat from country to country but it is undeniable that the role assigned to Jewish characters in literature has been unedifying when not actually odious. What seems to me more telling is that despite their tremendously rich imaginative power, the depths of their compassion, and the range

393

of their understanding, the great creative spirits in poetry, novel and drama have never treated the tragic theme of Jewish experience in the modern world in a manner befitting its universal human significance.

Time and again Sartre tries to bring his analysis into line with what he conceives the Marxist position to be by pressing into use a series of sociological banalities. Having read in Communist literature that the intellectual is more undisciplined (i.e. more inclined to question Party Dogma) than the worker because he has not been educated by the compulsions of the processes of production, Sartre believes he can show why anti-Semitism is present in some classes and absent in others. "Shaped by the daily influence of the materials he works with, the workman sees society as the product of real forces acting in accordance with rigorous laws." That is why workers and engineers are not anti-Semites. One wonders how many workers and engineers Sartre knows. In Germany and the United States the engineering profession was probably the most anti-Semitic of all. And it is a myth that the workers are more "disciplined" than the intellectuals. It is only when the Communists have established job control that they can keep the workers in line. If the behavior of the intellectuals in Western Europe and the U.S. during the last fifteen years is studied, it will be found that an amazingly large number of them jump to the crack of the Communist whip on matters of belief with far greater enthusiam than the workers.

There is ample evidence to show that anti-Semitism is present in every class in Western society from top to bottom. There are, to be sure, variations in the intensity of its expression but they perhaps are more significantly correlated with *the number* of Jews which a given group encounters than with the degree to which it deals directly with the "material" world. Professor Philip Frank, a shrewd observer, tells us that the German students who put up the greatest resistance to Hitler were drawn from the faculties of pure science and philosophy which specialize in "abstractions," and were not disciplined by direct contact with the material world.

There is no cause of anti-Semitism, or of any other mass movement, but it is possible to find certain constant factors which are present, in all its manifestations in diverse countries, conditions and times. These indicate that anti-Semitism is not so much a bourgeois phenomenon as a Christian phenomenon, that it is endemic to every Christian culture, whose religions made the Jews the eternal villain in the Christian drama of salvation. Sartre mentions this only to dismiss it. It was once true but is no longer true. Again his psychology is better than his history. "Have we ever stopped to consider the intolerable situation of men condemned to live in a society that adores the God they have killed? Originally, the Jew was a murderer or a son of a murderer—which in the eyes of a community with a pre-logical concept of responsibility amounts inevitably to the same thing—it was as such that he was taboo. It is evident that we cannot find the explanation of modern anti-Semitism here. . . ."

No, not *the* explanation but one which goes a long way to explain the *persistence* of anti-Semitism in a world that recognizes the difference between Jew and non-Jew, and in which the Christian dogma—Sartre rightly calls it a legend—that the Jews killed Christ is still taught at some time or other to almost every non-Jewish child. And it is the child who conspicuously lives by the pre-logical concept of responsibility. Even when the legend fades out of the focus of consciousness or belief, the natural horror and resentment, the curl of repulsion and hateful rejection, leave scar-tissue deep in the unconscious which bursts into angry infection later in adult life often to the surprise of the carrier. This does not have to be universally true to be generally true. There are exceptions. The community, too, has its cultural scar-tissue—e.g., the use of the term "Jew" as an epithet of disparagement—which may act as host to any passing evil germ. And there obviously cannot be a germ-free life. This is not past history but present history, and its meaning is reinforced by the findings of modern psychiatry.

There is, of course, an anti-Semitism which precedes Christianity; and there is, and probably will continue to be, an anti-Semitism in Moslem countries. But these anti-Semitisms are of the same kind as oppositions between Moslem and Christian, Christian and pagans, or between Christians of different sects. They are not so integral to one another as anti-Semitism is to the Christian epic.

That is why it is safe to predict that anti-Semitism will endure as long as orthodox Christian religious education which pictures the Jew as a deicide. That is why, for genuine democrats, religion must be a private matter in fact as well as profession, why secular humanism and not Christian humanism is a safer, as well as truer, philosophy for democratic life. That is why every revival of religious orthodoxy, every manifestation of intense *public* concern with the *truth* of religious dogma—to which some foolish literary Jewish sophisticates seem eager to contribute—churns up the already troubled waters of secular liberalism with dangerous historical sediment. That is why it becomes necessary to distinguish between kinds and degrees of anti-Semitism, and avoid the generous illusions of Sartre that everyone's life is at stake when any Jew is threatened in any way anywhere. The Jews, I am sure, would be willing to settle for much less than this Utopian universal brotherhood—for security and justice under a common law for free men. They do not ask to be loved, nor even that people cease feeling prejudices which in a free society everyone is entitled to—including Jews. Legislation against certain discriminatory practices is legitimate but one can no more legislate against social and personal prejudice than one can make all lies actionable at law.

"Anti-Semitism leads straight to National Socialism," declares Sartre. This is preposterously and dangerously false, else all the Jews would by now have long since been dead.

The second question: What is a Jew? is one which Sartre answers correctly but for the wrong reasons—correctly, insofar as he says "a Jew is one whom other men consider a Jew"; wrong, because he suggests that there are distinctive Jewish traits, physical and psychical and cultural, which are created by the pejorative consideration. The problem deserves some independent analysis. Nothing is to be gained from that pose of profundity which affects a deep metaphysical approach to the question of what is a Jew, illustrated in the procedure of one Jewish philosopher, not noted for his modesty, who, with unctuous cheek, writes: "No one is a Jew who is not ethical, reflective and modest."[3]

What definition of the Jew is most adequate to the various usages of the term "Jew" in current life? There are approximately five million Jews in America. Nothing is so absurd as the attempt to find some one trait, or combination of traits, which will explain the usage of the term "Jew" or which marks off Jews from non-Jews.

[3] *Commentary*, October, 1946.

Whether it be religion, history, culture, language or political aspiration, every criterion breaks down in the face of the multiplicity
of facts concerning the beliefs and behavior of those who call themselves Jews or are called such by others.

Religion, for example, is not a differentiating factor. Those who
subscribe to a particular form of Jewish religion still regard those
in the Jewish community who reject this form—or any form of religion—as Jews. What is even more to the point, the non-Jewish
community does not regard religion as a differentiating factor. It
does not distinguish between religious and irreligious Jews or believe that "Jewishness" is washed away in the waters of baptism. I
recall being asked, during the thirties, to join an organization
which called itself, "The Society for the Help of Non-Aryan (!)
Christian Refugees."

What is true for religion is true for any other trait of differentiation—physical appearance, psychology, culture, language, political faith. This may be roughly established as follows. Take any
trait "x" or combination of traits, "x^s" which is presented as *the*
mark of Jewishness. Classify all those who are regarded or who regard themselves as Jews, East or West, North or South, in an order
ranging from those who manifest the least amount of x, or x^s, to
those who display the most. It will then be found that the difference between Jews who possess the least and the most amount of x,
or x^s, is greater than the difference between most Jews and most
non-Jews in respect to this trait. This is clearly so in the United
States, and if on a world-scale we include Jews in the fastness of
Yemen, the Caucasus, and Abyssinia it is even clearer.

Some think that they can define the Jew in terms of origin as one
whose ancestors were of the Hebraic religious faith. The difficulty
with this is twofold. There are some who are not regarded as Jews,
and who do not regard themselves as Jews, whose ancestors many
years ago were of the Hebraic faith. Second, how many ancestors
professing the Jewish faith does one need—one grandparent, two
or three, one great-grandparent, two or three? Every decision is
purely arbitrary. No wonder an anti-Semitic mayor of Vienna,
when taxed with close friendship with Jews retorted: *"Wer Jude
ist, dass bestimme ich."*

Paradoxical as it may sound, the only formal definition of a
Jew that can be given which will do justice to the various ways in

which the term "Jew" is used is this: *A Jew is anyone who for any reason calls himself such or is called such in any community whose practices take note of the distinction.*" Let any Catholic Irishman or Boston Brahmin or Southern aristocrat move into a community in which he is unknown and pretend he is Jewish only to the extent of *saying* he is Jewish, and he will be treated like all other Jews including those who do not *say* they are Jewish but whom the Gentile community regards as Jews.

One may quarrel with the adequacy of the definition but not with the facts which suggest it. There is no trait or dogma or practice common to all Jews who recognize themselves as such or who are recognized as such by others. What they have in common is a condition or situation of exclusion from one or another pattern of social life, an exclusion which ranges from minor annoying restrictions in good historical weather to major discriminations in bad. What unifies them is nothing positive but, by and large, a common historical condition which, whether they like it or not or whether they like each other or not, cancels out in the eyes of others their not inconsiderable differences.

But what nonsense to say with Sartre that the Jew has been "poisoned" by these restrictions and pressures to the point that he lacks "a metaphysical sense" (would it were so!) and a feeling for "the vital values." The leaders of positivism from Hume to Mach, from Russell and Poincaré to Carnap, have not been Jews, and not a single great pragmatist—Peirce, Dewey, James and Schiller—is Jewish. Sartre has to convert Bergson's anti-intellectualism into rationalism, and the intuitionism of Spinoza and Husserl into intellectualism to make them fit his scheme. Yet every Jewish thinker of note in Western Europe owes more to his non-Jewish contemporaries and predecessors for his ideas than to his status, willing or unwilling, as a Jew. And as for movements that are distinctively Jewish like Hasidism and Zionism, which *can* be explained by the social and cultural pressures of Western Christendom, they are as far removed from rationalism as anything can be. Sartre is almost ready to agree with the anti-Semite that the Jew as such has certain obnoxious traits but mitigates the charge with the counter-impeachment: "You made him so." No group of people so heterogeneously constituted, who have so many assorted reasons for affirmatively or negatively expressing their "Jewishness," can be pressed into one characterological type.

There are many kinds of escape which individual Jews try to make from the common situation of loose negative togetherness which the Christian culture of the West imposes upon them. It is in his account of the psychology of these Jews that Sartre writes his most powerful and poignant pages. But his psychological insight is obscured by an untenable distinction he makes between the "authentic" and "inauthentic" Jew—which I wish to discard in order to use these terms in a different sense. For Sartre "authenticity consists in having a true and lucid consciousness of the situation, in assuming the responsibilities and risks that it involves, in accepting it in pride or humiliation, sometimes in horror and hate." Although he pretends that no normative connotation is attached to "authentic living," he quite clearly indicates that the person who lives inauthentically lacks courage and dignity. Whatever else a man should be, he should be authentic! But this is obviously wrong. "A true and lucid consciousness of the situation"—by all means and in all situations. But whether one should *accept* the situation—why, that depends upon the situation. If one is a thief, a sadist, an anti-Semite, or a Communist Party functionary—it would be far better if he lived inauthentically. And if in any situation, one carries out the responsibilities and risks it involves with "humiliation" or "with horror," this is *prima facie* evidence that he has not accepted it.

The "authentic Jew" for Sartre is one "who lives to the full his condition as Jew"; the "inauthentic Jew" is one who denies it or attempts to escape from it. But to live to the full his condition as a Jew, according to Sartre, is "quite simply to lay claim to and live in the situation of a martyr." Now one may praise an individual for living like a hero or martyr; but one cannot condemn a human being for not living like a hero or martyr. More important, there are many ways in which a Jew can affirm his Jewishness without being a martyr. Sartre says nothing about this because he does not recognize the plural ways in which those who are recognized as Jews by Gentiles *can* live as Jews. What he is really concerned with is the Jew who is recognized as such by the Gentile community but who refuses to admit to himself, and sometimes to others, that he is so recognized and that consequences flow from that recognition. As

I use the term "inauthentic" it applies only to the Jew who imagines that he can identify himself with non-Jewish experiences so completely that he can avoid the pains and penalties and discriminatory regard suffered by other Jews whose affirmations and behavior seem to him to be the main source of disabilities imposed upon Jews. According to Sartre, the Jew who is a Socialist or liberal or anything else that a Gentile can be is an inauthentic Jew—a fantastic assumption which can only make sense on the notion that there is a metaphysical Jewish essence irreducibly different from a non-Jewish essence, so that the Jew appears to be another *kind* of human being, perhaps not a human being but something above or below him.

In describing the psychology of what he calls the "inauthentic Jew" among Gentiles, Sartre does not distinguish between the psychology of what I call the "inauthentic" Jew—the Jew who desires, so to speak, to pass himself off as a Gentile, and the psychology of what I call "the authentic Jew" who accepts himself as a Jew for any reason whatsoever. *La mauvaise foi* or inverted self-consciousness, as Sartre describes it in the few illuminating pages of his turgid and boring *L'être et le néant,* is different in both cases.

The "inauthentic Jew," in my sense, is afflicted with an additional dimension of self-consciousness. No matter how impeccable his conduct, he is always on guard in predominantly non-Jewish company, exquisitely conscious of the possibility that at any moment something he says or does will be regarded as a telltale sign. He feels that there are some things that are appropriate for him to do, and others which are not appropriate, *merely* because he is regarded as a Jew. Whether he is active in public life or in the professions, wherever his words or deeds affect his fellowmen, he is pursued by a nagging consciousness of the specific effect activity as a Jew has on others. In his utterances he must think not only of whether what he says is true or false, but of how, as coming from *him,* it will be received. He finds that he is bothered by what Jews do or leave undone in a way his own attempted escape makes it difficult for him to understand. He develops a guilty sense of Jewish responsibility despite the absence of any consciousness of Jewish loyalty. When he is pretty far down in the scale of creation, he does not overhear anti-Semitic remarks, and touches bottom when he regales the company with anti-Semitic jokes, told with an air that suggests the difference between himself and other Jews, usually too subtle for others to see. Sometimes, without any religious faith, he embraces another religious faith. There are very few inauthentic Jews of this kind. They are really inauthentic people. The main problem of the authentic Jews is to find some rational basis or ideal fulfillment of their authenticity. Sartre is no guide here.

The genuine problem which confronts those who are regarded as Jews in the modern world is whether they should regard themselves as Jews, and what meaning they can give to their lives as Jews once they acknowledge, as elementary decency and dignity demand, that in some sense they accept themselves as Jews. This is a problem of tremendous complexity just because there is no one thing that constitutes Jewishness and because of the ideological imperialism of so many different Jewish groups which seek to impose their own particular conception of Jewish life upon all other Jews. Before discussing this question, I wish to indicate how the problem arises.

Perhaps the best way to do this is to relate one of my experiences with Jewish and Gentile youth in many institutions of learning. Plato's *Republic* is an ideal introductory text in philosophy and I have always read it with my classes. In the concluding book of the *Republic*, and as a profound commentary on his Utopia, Plato relates an interesting myth about a Greek, named Er, who was left for dead on the field of battle. Er is transported to the meadows of the other world where he observes how the souls of those about to be born anew pick out their future lots on earth before they drink of the waters of forgetfulness from the river Lethe. After a discussion of the significance of this myth in Plato's *Republic* and an analysis of the idea of immortality, I would invite (I no longer do so) the students to partake in a kind of extra-philosophical homework exercise to motivate the next assignment. They were asked to list on one side of a card their sex, place of birth, religious origins, vocational interests and other information they considered relevant to the kind of person they were. On the other side, they were asked to indicate under corresponding heads, what they would choose, if, like the souls in the Platonic myth, they could determine their lot in a future reincarnation on earth. The entries were anonymous, and all students entered into the spirit of it although the results were never disclosed. The results, however, were very instructive. For example, all students want to be born again with the same sex in their next reincarnation. The only exceptions were those girls whose vocational choices indicated that they hoped to become physicians or engineers. They wanted to be reborn men. But more significant for present purposes was the fact that the overwhelming majority of Jewish students did not want to be born again as Jews but as something else—"no religion," "agnostic," "pagan," "Protestant" (mostly Unitarians with a few scattered Episcopalians), "nothing that would be a burden or be discriminated against"— were some of the typical responses. Not a single Gentile student ever wanted to be born Jewish.

This is no more an expression of "inauthenticity" in Sartre's sense than the desire to be born in a better age. But it does indicate a profound *malaise* on the part of Jewish youth. Sometimes it takes an acute form. Over the years I have met numbers of young Jewish men and women who wanted to know why they shouldn't change their name, why, if a job or life career was at stake, they shouldn't deny their origins. "After all," they complain, "we don't conform to, or believe in, anything distinctively Jewish." They wanted to know from me as a professor of ethics why it was wrong for them to seek to escape punishment for a condition for which they have no responsibility. It was not hard to point out that for most of them escape was practically impossible, that where it was possible the psychological costs were usually too burdensome, and that morally it was intrinsically degrading to capitulate to irrational prejudice and deny kinship with their own fathers and mothers who, often against heroic odds, had courageously kept their integrity and faith whatever it was. Except for one or two cases it turned out that these young men and women were content to remain Jews because they were fundamentally decent, not because they had any clear conception of what made them Jews.

This feeling of ambiguity and negation toward Jewish existence is characteristic not only of certain sections of Jewish youth but even of greater numbers of their elders, particularly in the United States. Many American Jews have acknowledged themselves as Jews for the sake of their Jewish brethren in distress. Many more have become concerned with their Jewishness for the sake of their children in hopes of providing them with psychological security and a sense of historical belonging with which they can meet the shocks of discrimination and rejection without neurosis. The Jewish child as a rule experiences the impact of scorn, hostility and opprobrious rejection during his tender years. Sartre has some remarkable passages on this theme. It is difficult for any one not acquainted with specific cases to appreciate how deep the bewildered hurt goes into the psyche of the child, and how often these frustrations express themselves in tensions toward his parents, the innocent cause of the child's plight, or in a tortured silence that gives rise to self-doubt, and sometimes self-hatred. Most parents find it much easier to carry their own burdens of suffering than to stand by helplessly in the presence of their children's agony. That is why so many Jewish parents, especially in this neurotic-conscious age, seek eagerly to supply some consciousness of historic or contemporary Jewish association. But they avoid facing frankly the question of what their own Jewishness consists in, and how it is related to the Jewish and world scene.

It is at this point, usually, that a quest for definitions begins and Jews cast around desperately for some conception or clear formula which will express "the essence" of their Jewishness. The quest is not only fruitless but foolish. It is a capitulation to the muddy metaphysics of the anti-Semite.

Far wiser, it seems to me, is to recognize the historic fact of Jewish existence, the plural sources of Jewish life, and its plural possibilities. No philosophy of Jewish life is required except one—identical with the democratic way of life—which enables Jews who for any reason at all accept their existence as Jews to lead a dignified and significant life, a life in which together with their fellow-men they strive collectively to improve the quality of democratic, secular cultures and thus encourage a maximum of cultural diversity, both Jewish and non-Jewish. Such a philosophy recognizes that there is no dignity in denying one's origins or in living as if they were something to be apologetic about. It recognizes that morally, even more significant than acceptance of one's origins are the *fruits* of such acceptance, what one does with it, what one makes it mean, what comes out of it.

This is not the place to discuss the various "positive solutions" that have been offered as a basis for Jewish life. I shall return to them on another occasion. Meanwhile I permit myself a preliminary comment.

One solution, very unpopular among Jews today, is the universalist solution in which the individual thinks of himself as a Jew by unfortunate accident but as a human being by enlightened choice. He usually looks to some form of universal democratic socialism in the future where the differences between Jew and non-Jew will forever disappear. This dream has its noble features, but it overlooks the fact that human beings live as Jews and non-Jews here and now and will continue to do so for a long time to come; that the dream itself is based upon the acceptance of differences among men and not on the hope of an undifferentiated unity; and that the microbes of anti-Semitism infect even movements which do not officially allow for its existence. The dream still has its uses as a guide in some ways but not as a home.

If it is pruned of its Utopianism and its failure to understand that the ethics of democracy presupposes not an equality of sameness or identity but an equality of differences, much of the universalist view still has a large measure of validity which Sartre, for one, completely ignores in his caricature of the attitude of the liberal and democrat toward the Jews.

According to Sartre the man of democratic principle, although a better person than the anti-Semite, is just as hostile to the Jew as a Jew. He wants him to disappear into the abstract universal, *man*, and annihilate himself as a concrete, historical individual. Whereas the anti-Semite "wishes to destroy the Jew as a man and leave nothing in him but the Jew, the pariah, the untouchable," the democrat "wishes to destroy him as a Jew and leave nothing in him but the man, the abstract and universal subject of the rights of man and the rights of the citizen." To the Jew, therefore, Sartre concludes, "there may not be so much difference between the anti-Semite and democrat."

No, not much difference except between death and life, between *Mein Kampf* and the Statute of Virginia for Religious Liberty. Now we know what surrealism in logic is! Because *the man* does not exist, Sartre tells us with a gesture of rigorous thinking, therefore only particular kinds of men exist. But the sense in which *the man* does not exist is precisely the sense in which *the French-man; the Ger-man, the* Jew, and *the* anti-Semite do not exist either. A sub-class is just as much of an abstraction as a class. Only individuals exist. But whether they should exist as Jews or Gentiles, as Catholics or Protestants or humanists, as Italians or Americans, as existentialists or as philosophers (in the etymological sense), should be, according to the democratic philosophy, *a matter of voluntary choice*. If individuals exist, they must exist as something. This is an analytic statement. But that they must continue to exist in the same social and cultural status in which they are born is a piece of anti-democratic presumption. The democrat wants to give all individuals the right to freely determine themselves as Jews or Gentiles, as citizens of one country or another, as cultural heirs of Socrates or Aquinas or Dewey. He no more wants to destroy the individual Gentile. He wants only to destroy those individuals and social institutions which seek to deprive human beings of their power of uncoerced choice. This is what is perennially valid in the liberating ideas of the French and Anglo-American Enlightenment which Sartre has renounced for a noisome mess of Heideggerian anguish and neo-Marxist historicism. He is a better man than his doctrine because he lacks the courage of his confusions.

THE PROBLEM OF ERNEST BLOCH

By LEON STEIN

It is not my purpose, not my desire to attempt a reconstitution of Jewish music, or to base my work on melodies more or less authentic. It is rather the Jewish soul that interests me—the complex, ardent, agitated soul that vibrates for me in the Bible. —ERNEST BLOCH

—and when Jews are spoken of, I would add "ancient." Bloch seems descended, not from the tribes of Israel dispersed throughout the world, despised and neglected, who are silently perfecting their terrible weapons, patience, persistency, and astuteness, but from the free sons of Judah—. Nowadays, such a race is inconceivable.—GUIDO M. GATTI

There is, indeed, more of Judaism than Hebraism in Bloch; the spirit of the ghetto frustrates that of the promised land.—LAZARE SAMINSKY

At best, Bloch's music may be said to have a touch of Orientalism—. Not through composers without Jewish background, and without being imbued with their people's folk song has Jewish music left any impress upon general art music. For the Jew, his lore and his faith, substitute national atmosphere. —A. Z. IDELSOHN

IN THE SENSE that Debussy is *the* French musician, and Moussorgsky *the* Russian musician, so Ernest Bloch is universally regarded as *the* Jewish musician. Some composers of Jewish birth have written one or more compositions which stem from their racial background, but such works are aside and apart from their characteristic style and output. In Bloch's case, on the other hand, his "Jewish Cycle," the series of compositions inspired by Hebrew lore or the Jewish spirit, comprises the essential core of his work. His other compositions, numerous and important as they are, remain, nevertheless, peripheral to this central core. There is, generally speaking, a consensus of critical opinion as to the importance and distinction of his works; yet, as the quoted opinions reveal, there is no uniformity of judgment as to the kind and degree of their Jewish or Hebrew content.

While Idelsohn's viewpoint (which at best would admit Bloch's music to have "a touch of Orientalism") is an exceptional and isolated one, it nevertheless merits serious consideration, for Idelsohn was the foremost historian of Jewish music, and most intimately acquainted with its various types and expressions. Should his judgment in this instance be correct, then neither the intent of Bloch, nor the opinions of Gatti or Saminsky, have any validity. But if he is in error, there still remains the question posed by the conflicting statements of Gatti and Saminsky. The assertion of the former is quoted from a prophetic article, written in 1920, in which the genius of Bloch was proclaimed before a Europe which up to then had ignored and neglected him. The writer's penetrating appraisal of Bloch's work still stands as one of the most brilliant critiques on this composer. It may seem that the phrase "despised and neglected, who are silently perfecting their terrible weapons—" is irrelevant to the present discussion. Undoubtedly, however, the prejudice which these words reveal, influenced Gatti's feeling that Bloch's music stems from a heroic but ancient Hebraism, rather than from a despised and rejected modern Judaism. With his admiration for Bloch's works he found it difficult to reconcile that admiration and those works with a people toward whom he was not too sympathetically disposed. So firmly is his mind set against admitting any contemporary Jewish influence, that he states a race like that of the ancient Hebrews is today inconceivable.

Both Gatti and Saminsky agree in assuming a cultural and spiritual disjunction between ancient Hebraism and modern Judaism. But where the former derives the spirit and inspiration of Bloch's Jewish works from biblical Hebraism, Saminsky finds more of Judaism and "the spirit of the ghetto" in these compositions.

We are confronted then with these factors: on one hand we have the avowed intention of the composer; on the other, we have three conflicting interpretations as to the realization of that intention. Before attempting to evaluate or reconcile these conflicting opinions, it will be helpful to consider a few relevant facts of Bloch's life, and list the works of the "Jewish Cycle."

Ernest Bloch was born of Jewish parents at Geneva, Switzerland, July 24, 1880. His father was an orthodox and deeply religious individual, faithfully observing all the rituals. At the age of eleven, the youth made a vow to dedicate his life to composition, solemnizing that vow by writing it on a slip of paper, and in the tradition of the ancient offering, burning the paper on an altar of stones. After studies and travels in Europe, Bloch came to America in 1916, eventually gaining the recognition that had been denied him in the Old World. His compositions won important awards: the $3,000 first prize offered by *Musical America,* for his epic rhapsody "America"; the $5,000 prize offered by the Victor Company, for "Helvetia"; and the Coolidge prize for $1,000, for his Viola Suite. It was not until the composition of his "Psalms" in 1912 and the "Three Jewish Poems" the following year that he consciously essayed an utterance and an idiom deliberately Hebraic. The "Three Poems" he later wrote "are the first works of a new period." Though the "Jewish Cycle" does not contain more than half his major works, it includes his most personal and characteristic compositions. Important works in this cycle are: "Psalms for Voice and Orchestra" (1912–14); "Three Jewish Poems" (1913); "Prelude for Soprano and Orchestra;" "Israel Symphony" (1912–15); "Jeremiah," poem for Piano; "Schelomo," a Rhapsody for Cello and Orchestra; the opera "Jezebel," begun in 1918; "Baal-Shem Suite" for Violin and Piano; "Meditation Hebraique" for Cello and Piano; "Jewish Life" for Cello and Piano; "Abodah" for Violin and Piano; "String Quartette in B Minor"; the Sabbath Service, "Avodath Hakodesh" (1934); "Voice in the Wilderness" for Orchestra with Cello Obbligato (1936); and several smaller works.

Bloch is recognized as one of the incontrovertibly great creators of today. His works are distinguished by an uncompromising sense of conviction, a characteristic tension and passion, a mastery of an integrated form, and a personal harmonic and melodic structure that has never catered to any "ism." In these days of so much fabricated music, his work has never been formulated according to some antecedent and premeditated dogma, nor has it ever exploited novelty, dissonance, or sheer orchestral color for their own sakes.

His compositions in general, and the Jewish works in particular, exploit the dark, violent, and dynamic aspects of emotion. One may find the key to their content in Bloch's own selection of words to describe the source of his inspiration: "—the *violence* that is evident in the Prophetic Books; the Jew's *savage* love of justice; the *despair* of the preacher in Jerusalem; the *sorrow* of the Book of Job; the *passion* and the *violence* that I believe to be the characteristics of my own nature." He describes the first movement of his "String Quartet in B Minor" as "a lament of purely Hebraic inspiration, a blending of *bitterness,* of *impassioned violence* and of *anguish.*" There is a certain limitation in these shrill lamentations, hieratic ceremonials, and impassioned invocations, but a more serene phase, a phase of greater calm, is implied in such later works as the "Sabbath Service" and the "Violin Concerto." In Bloch's own development these compositions may well represent a "third period" wherein the anguish and bitterness of his earlier works are transfigured and refined into a more tranquil, though none the less profound, expression.

The assertion of Bloch that he has no desire to base his work "on melodies more or less authentic" may well have been one of the reasons for Idelsohn's attitude toward his music. The gist of the historian's objection is implicit in the phrase "—without being imbued with their people's folk song." Superficially, this may be taken to mean that unless the composer deliberately and recognizably utilizes folk songs, his music is not really Jewish. More fundamentally, it means that unless the composer has adopted or been imbued with the melodic, rhythmic, and harmonic character and spirit of Jewish folk song his work is not racial in character.

Despite national differences, folk songs have a common physiognomy from an analytic viewpoint. I establish this similarity here because, for purposes of comparison, I intend to discuss not only Jewish folk songs; hence, it is important to emphasize this basic likeness. From the standpoint of structure, folk songs have comparatively simple forms: Symmetrical four measure phrases, eight measure periods, small two-part forms of twelve or sixteen measures, or elementary three-part patterns. The music structure resembles the simple rhymed metrical verse with balanced phrases. Melodically, there is a basic simplicity both in line and in rhythm. These songs are primarily the work of folk singers, and are consequently unsophisticated; afterward they have been sung and often refashioned by an ingenuous populace, further reducing the music to a kind of common denominator. Though there may be a wide emotional range and a great variety of types, a folk song is characterized by a certain impersonality. Even when cast in the first person singular and having to do with an isolated personal experience, it is in what one may call the universalized first person; when the word "I" is used, it is immediately transferred into a kind of abstract, universalized expression in the consciousness of both singer and audience. To summarize these conclusions, folk songs generally have a simple symmetrical form, ingenuous melodies, and regular rhythms, and since they are a mass expression, a certain kind of impersonality.

Let us compare these characteristics with Bloch's own style. Bloch's rhetoric is that of free verse, or sometimes a sweeping, poetic prose. Rarely do we find a Mendelssohnian symmetry, the balanced four-measure phrases, the regular thesis and antithesis similar to regular or alternate rhymed verse. In its larger aspects his forms similarly eschew the regular symmetry of song or sonata patterns, and are often rhapsodic in character. His original melodies often exploit wide leaps, difficult (but not essentially unvocal) intervals, and complex rhythms. In contrast to the impersonality of folk songs, his expression is one of the most highly personalized in all music. No folk song, no matter how intense or passionate, approaches the drive and sheer "bite" of his melody. It is evident that the structural, melodic, and emotional characteristics of folk-song are negated by the essential traits of Bloch's own style.

Unless it is employed as a theme with variations, a folk song is most effectively used if its form and content are consistent with the individuality of both the composer and the particular work in which it is incorporated. Brahms, whose style, too, was subjective and highly personal, could and did effectively incorporate folk songs in his compositions because his own melodic, harmonic, and structural style had a definite affinity with the folk *melos*. One has but to recall such melodies (not exceptional, but typical) as the theme of the finale of the "First Symphony," of the slow movement of the "Third Symphony," or the slow movement of the "Violin Concerto." It is significant that the passion, the violence, and the sensuousness which Bloch finds in the Bible and which he projects as Hebraic expressions are those self-same qualities which he finds in himself.

How inconsistent his own style is with that of the folk song is shown by his anthem which closes his epic rhapsody "America." Bloch had deliberately written this anthem in the hope that it would supplant the "Star Spangled Banner." ("Why should an English drinking song be the national anthem of this great country?" he had asked.) The writing of this anthem was no mere catering to expediency or opportunism. His earnest *endeavor* to feel this music deeply and sincerely is indicated by the careful dynamic and tempo markings which he provided. It was the hope of the composer that at the moment of its occurrence in the finale, the audience would arise and lift their voices in this new hymn. At its premiere in 1928, six major orchestras performed the work simultaneously in Chicago, New York, Philadelphia, Boston, Cincinnati, and Los Angeles; in none of these cities did the audience participate in the singing of the anthem. One reason may be the natural reticence of American audiences. The most important reason, however, may be found in the anthem itself: it is a very mediocre composition. Any hymn book will yield dozens of hymns superior to Bloch's anthem.

Bloch, of course, is not the only great composer who has *not* written his country's anthem. Somehow, serious composers do not write songs which become national airs. (Three exceptions may be noted: Haydn's "Kaiser Hymn," Shostakovitch's "United Nations," and John Alden Carpenter's "Home Road.") But what is important in this instance is that Bloch's failure is not merely incidental, it is symptomatic of a nature to which rhymed and balanced couplets, and an impersonal-universal expression is foreign.

There are several instances in which Bloch has used traditional chants or folk songs in his works. In "Abodah" for Violin and Piano, a Yom Kippur melody is used; though the arrangement is skillful, there is an inescapable feeling for those who know the real Bloch that he is merely "quoting." In the third of the "Three Pictures from Hasidic Life," "Simchas Torah," Bloch uses the melody of the wedding song "Die Mezinke Oisgegebn," which, incidentally, is not really a Hasidic tune. The "Simcha" in this composition is somewhat forced, and its character, despite the inclusion of a Jewish folk song, is not Jewish. There is a greater melodic and emotional kinship with the "Pastorale" movement of the

"Concerto Grosso" than with the spirit of Hasidism—and the "Concerto Grosso" utilizes Swiss folk songs.

In "America" Bloch uses a Chippewa War Song; the hymn "Old Hundred"; a Southern ballad; the Negro song, "Row After Row"; "Old Folks at Home"; "Pop Goes the Weasel"; "Hail Columbia"; a Creole folk song; "Dixie"; "John Brown's Body"; "The Battle Cry of Freedom"; "Tramp, Tramp, Tramp"; "I Went to the Hop Joint"; and "Yankee Doodle." In contrast, as Roger Sessions, a former student of his has written, Bloch uses actual Jewish melodies but rarely and incidentally, and not as the result of a desire to reproduce folklore. One reason for this is that "He regards the authenticity of the greater part of traditional Jewish music as doubtful."

An interesting question presents itself at this point. Why does Bloch, in his multitude of Jewish works, use presumable folk tunes "but rarely and incidentally," whereas in the one American work he has written, there are over a dozen American folk melodies. Certainly, Bloch was aware that the American melodies he quoted were no more "authentic" from a musical standpoint than were the many Jewish melodies which he renounced. If one answers that the former are authentic by association, the same, of course, could be said for the Jewish melodies.

The answer is that the authenticity of the American melodies did not mean as much musically as the authenticity of the Hebraic melodies. This is, of course, a purely musical question, and casts no doubt or reflection on the sincere and passionate patriotism of Bloch, who is an American citizen. But he had identified an important part of his own ego with a Judaic musical expression; he was consequently more critical of that material which concerned and was bound up with the very essence of his being, than he was with the folk songs used in "America." For these folk songs, despite his evident sincerity and exalted intention, were approached and used externally; he could not utilize them with the same burning intensity of his own original themes.

Bloch may "quote" a melody for the sake of local color, but as a quotation it ceases to express the man. For, as truly as Whitman, he could say, "I sing myself," and that self could never find utterance in an externally derived quotation.

On the other hand, the impassioned "Nigun" from the "Baal-

Shem Suite," unlike the "Simchas Torah," quotes no traditional melody; nevertheless, it captures the essence of Hasidic emotion— its mystic brooding, its meditation, and its yearning ecstasy. If one relates this music to the first four steps of elevation in the tenets of Habad Hasidism, how truly and beautifully these stages are expressed: *histapchuth hannefesh,* the outpouring of the soul; *hithoveruth,* spiritual awakening; *hithpaaluth,* enraptured meditation; and *dveikuth,* communion with God.

The answer to Idelsohn is that Bloch does have both "faith and lore," a religious quality and an ethical concept which are at once Hebraic and universal. As for the use of folk songs, we have seen that whenever Bloch does use such borrowed material, his own style and content are diluted. Bloch does not need to borrow Jewish folk songs to revitalize his output, for the same reason that Moussorgsky did not need to bolster his racial expression with props borrowed from Russian folk literature. As did Moussorgsky, so does Bloch have a native, indigenous potential which is rooted in the same spiritual soil from which national and folk expressions take their own nourishment and growth. This potential is, however, an intangible factor; its concrete manifestation may be observed in the nuclei of melodies, figures, and rhythms which are similar to, or identical with, Hebraic materials: the use of shofar-like calls, the modal scales which are also to be found in the ancient cantillations, and the augmented intervals of post-biblical Jewish music. These are, of course, transfigured by Bloch's own expression, recast in the fire of his own passionate inspiration, but still recognizable as to their origins.

These are the tangible musical derivations and relationships that refute Idelsohn. We are still left, however, with the dilemma posed by the conflicting opinions of Gatti and Saminsky. The question of whether there is a cultural and chronological-historical cleavage between biblical Hebraism and *galut*-Judaism is too broad to be considered here. We will be concerned with this question only as it applies to Bloch and his music.

In asserting that Bloch's music expresses more of latter-day Judaism than ancient Hebraism, Saminsky continues with the remark that Bloch "studiously wails over his own and the world's misfortunes; he exhibits his wounds even in such priestly music as 'Schelomo.'" The implication is that such wailing is only in the later tradition of Judaism. But the lamentations of Jeremiah, the despair of Job, the disillusionment of Ecclesiastes would contradict such a belief. As we have noted before, Bloch has inevitably gravitated toward those elements in the Old Testament which coincided with, and corroborated, his own feelings. Certainly there is a keen awareness of "his own and the world's misfortunes," an awareness that stems from contemporary life and experience, but that awareness is not expressed in any mere mood of isolated self-pity. Where his music writhes and agonizes, its intensity might have stemmed from the injustices of the ghetto, but its breadth is surely inspired by the magnificent scope of the prophetic writings. There is an indubitable seriousness of utterance, a consciousness of high purpose reflected in the works of the "Jewish Cycle" that lend themselves naturally to an association with the style and spirit of the Old Testament. Those characteristics which Saminsky points out as being Judaic rather than Hebraic are also part of the older tradition of Jewry.

That Bloch, man of today, finds in the biblical writings the text for his expression is an indication of the vital aliveness of those writings, and the continuity, rather than the disjunction, of biblical Hebraism and modern Judaism. In setting up the distinction between the former and the latter, Gatti does so entirely to the detriment of contemporary Jewry, assuring us that from it Bloch's music could not have been derived. But the very title of Bloch's compositions, such as the "Baal-Shem Suite," the sketches from "Jewish Life," belie the exclusive derivation from, and dependence on, biblical sources. However, it may be countered, these are not his really great and representative works; consider "Schelomo," the "Psalms," "Israel." Some may go further, arguing that, despite the titles, the music in the "Baal-Shem" and "Jewish Life" is biblical, Hebraic rather than Judaic.

Such a supposition is not borne out if we examine the music itself. The "Poco meno lento" of the "Nigun," the previously referred to folk song in "Simchas Torah" are definitely Ashkenazic in origin. More important—and this concerns not only the Jewish works—the use of the augmented second, and the other augmented intervals deriving therefrom is a post-biblical phenomenon. It is most characteristically found in the *Ahavoh-Rabboh* mode based on the tetrachords e-f-g#-a+b-c-d-e, or their transpositions. Not only the "Jewish Cycle," but such works as the "Violin Sonata" and the "String Quartette" similarly exploit the augmented intervals which we have come to associate with Jewish music. As Idelsohn has pointed out, "The augmented second step of this scale does *not* exist in the scales of the biblical modes and of their derivations in the prayer modes . . . The fact that this mode is not used for the Bible and the ancient prayers, nor in the ancient communities in the Near East for the prayers or for the old *piyyut*, created in the period 800–1000 C.E. leads us to the opinion that this mode was originally unknown to the Jewish people, and that only later was it adopted as a result of the influx of the Mongolian and Tartarian tribes into Asia Minor, Syria, Palestine, and Egypt, as well as in the Balkans, *beginning with the thirteenth century*."

From a sheer musical-idiomatic standpoint there are, consequently, too many post-biblical materials to justify Gatti's conclusions. Would it not be possible to maintain, however, that, granting the use of post-biblical idioms, the feeling is nevertheless predominantly Hebraic rather than modern-Judaic? Bloch himself inferentially refutes this when, after describing the emotions associated with the various books of the Bible, he writes, "All this is in us; all this is in me and it is the better part of me." The "us" to which he refers is the Jewish race, not the race of 3,000 years ago, but the Jewish people of today.

It is the realization of the continuity of Hebraism into Judaism, of those things that are *still* in us, that led the noted English critic Eric Blom to write of Bloch that "It was reserved for him to find a modern musical medium that conveys something akin to the poetry and passion, the turbulent sorrow and noble exaltation of Judaism *as it is transmitted by the Old Testament, and still survives in its strongest modern representatives*."

The term "Jewish Cycle," then, is no misnomer. Not only in text or in title, but in idiom and in spirit, these works are truly a racial expression. Many are biblical in their inspiration, but any attempt to dissociate Bloch from modern Jewry is founded on an untenable premise. A music that is as alive and vital as Bloch's, that has found as understanding a racial-national audience as has his, such a music is no museum specimen that has resurrected from between the covers of dusty centuries an ancient emotion and outlook that no longer exist. It has the vitality that springs only from a contemporary first-hand emotion and experience, an experience and emotion that one knows is shared by myriads of fellow men. Bloch's "Jewish Cycle" is racially important not only because of its musical values, which by now are universally recognized, but because of its corroborative content, because it brings back to the Jew, as a Jew, part of his unique experience, its beauty and its ugliness, its aspiration and its degradation, its hopes, its fears, its "turbulent sorrow and noble exaltation."

WHY JEWS STAY SOBER

By NATHAN GLAZER

A Lithuanian Jew had given himself up to drink; he spent his days in the local inn swallowing brandy while his wife and children starved. One day, his wife came to the inn determined to drag him out and force him to become an honest provider. He wheedled her into sitting down, and had a glass of brandy set before her, too. She tasted it cautiously, then spat it out, crying, "Pfui! What vile stuff!" "Well, what do you think?" said the husband. "You think I sit here lapping honey?"

A Yid a shikker, zoll er geharget ver'n [A Jew who's a drunkard—hanging's too good for him!].

IN ONE RESPECT, at least, the American Jews are not very different from the Israeli Jews who contemptuously dismiss them as assimilated *goyim*: neither have much use for hard liquor. And therein is wrapped one of the most persistent mysteries of a mysterious people.

The historic soberness of the Jews would not be so mysterious if Jews, like Mohammedans, simply had no use for drink in general. But as a matter of fact, the Jews have been fairly respectable drinkers since Noah's discovery of the vine (Gen. 9:20). Of course, they had a special prayer required before drinking wine; but this did not mean they had any notion of religious restraint in drinking it, aside from the general rabbinic emphasis on moderation. There are a good number of lushes scattered through the pages of the Bible. Ben Sirah, the great Jewish moralist of the third century B.C.E., took his drinking seriously, and one of his maxims, addressed to the wise man, reads, "In a place for wine, pour not forth talk." The rabbis of the talmudic period were against drunkenness but they were properly appreciative of the effects of wine: one rabbi, who gave a dinner to his pupils and found them shy and hesitant to begin discussion, ordered his servant: "Give wine to the young men that they may break their silence." And in Spain, Jewish scholars seem to have been as thirsty as their Christian fellows across the Pyrenees (see translations of some of their songs by Allen Mandelbaum, in *Commentary*, "The Cedars of Lebanon," February 1951).

But then something happened, and it's hard to say whether it was that the Jews began drinking less, or the rest of the world began drinking more. Possibly it was only that the rest of the world began drinking more; in any case, the Jews fell rapidly behind, and Jewish sobriety was for the first time added to the catalogue of traits that annoyed the Gentiles.

In the Middle Ages, the process of distillation, known in Scotland and Ireland from earliest times, spread through Europe, and Western man, who up to then had had to be satisfied with naturally fermented wine (with a top alcoholic content of about 16 per cent) and beer (which may sometimes get as strong), was now able to drink pure alcohol, if he dared. Fortified wines—port and sherry—and brandy and whiskey entered history, and it seems we have not recovered yet. It became easier and cheaper to get drunk than ever before in history. When we consider that the Homeric heroes could become roaring drunk on wine, and the Germans on beer, we must conclude they had heroic capacities indeed—for classical antiquity knew nothing about distilling alcohol to fortify wine or make spirits. Instead, the ancients added spices, resin, pitch, lime, sea water, salt, and all sorts of unlikely ingredients to their wines— whether to improve or cover up the taste of wine in an unperfected state, or to stretch it, or for medicinal reasons, or to increase its potency, or for all of these and other reasons, is still a matter for dispute among classical scholars. These achievements of classical antiquity in the field of alcoholic beverages are lost to us but it would not seem we are missing much. The Middle Ages and modern times gave birth to most of the varieties of wines and liquors we drink today.

About the time that distillation was introduced with explosive effects into Western Europe, the Jews fell behind. They continued to drink wine, and they enjoyed the new hard liquors—but with a moderation foreign to the other nations of Europe. One country after another went off on a tremendous spree—Germany in the sixteenth century and England in the eighteenth century seemed to contemporary observers on the verge of floating off on a sea of alcohol. The diseases produced by excess of alcohol were first discovered and described in these centuries; as for the Jewish contribution to medical pathology, it was not cirrhosis of the liver or Korsakoff's syndrome but diabetes. While the Catholic Church encouraged four cups of wine as a maximum, the Jews—at least at the Seder meal of the Passover holiday—demanded four cups as a minimum (and at one time, it was required that a mourner drink ten); but despite the absence of theological injunction and regulation, Jews managed to resist the temptations of distilled liquor.

In the East European Pale, temperance, along with chastity, was one of the virtues that was taken for granted. The strangest part of all this was that the Jews were not only habituated to the drinking of wine from earliest childhood by their religion but also spent their adult lives producing and selling spirits. The liquor trade in Eastern Europe was a Jewish monopoly: it had originally been granted to the landowners by the Polish monarchy in the fifteenth century, and Jews, as agents of the nobility, became the producers and sellers of hard liquor. When Russia fell heir to the mass of Polish Jewry at the beginning of the nineteenth century, that trade was the chief source of livelihood of the village Jews. All through the nineteenth century tsarist bureaucrats urged the elimination of the Jews from the liquor traffic, and at various times in various places Jews were driven from the trade. Finally, in 1892, liquor became a government monopoly, and 200,000 Jews lost their livelihood. (The story is scattered through Dubnow's *History of the Jews in Russia and Poland*.)

Again, the monotonous conclusion: while the miserable peasant escaped into alcohol, and drunkenness became one of the great problems of nineteenth-century Russia, the equally miserable Jewish artisan and *luftmensh*, it seemed, never gave it a thought.

But after all, no virtues in the East European Jews are very surprising to contemporary minds. They still lived under a moral code more rigorous and more detailed than anything known of elsewhere; and while the code had nothing to say about temperance, presumably the habits of control built up by the observance of the 613 precepts carried over into the realm of alcohol.

419

This is an easy and perfectly satisfactory explanation—up to the end of the nineteenth century. By then, great communities of Jews were growing up in Western Europe and overseas, with less and less attachment to the traditional Law. The Jews shaved their beards, abandoned their traditional dress, began to eat pork and mix meat and milk, deserted the synagogue—presumably their temperance should have gone along with the rest. After all, do Jews have fewer troubles to drown than other people?

But even in America, where it was customary for the unhappy immigrants to drink more and with worse effects than at home, and where Jews were probably less controlled by their traditional laws and observances than anywhere else in history, the ancient pattern held up. No matter what kind of ill effect from excessive indulgence we consider—alcoholic psychoses, alcoholism without psychoses, arrest for drunkenness, broken homes or marital unhappiness because of drink—we will not find many Jews affected.

For example: In 1929–31, Benjamin Maltzberg studied admissions to New York state hospitals for alcoholic psychoses, and calculated that the rate of first admissions for various foreign-born groups (per 100,000 in the population) was as follows: for the Irish, 25.6; Scandinavians, 7.8; Italians, 4.8; English, 4.3; Germans, 3.8; Jews, 0.5.

In 1951, Robert Straus published a study of the religion of persons coming to clinics for treatment for alcoholism in eight cities; 1.6 per cent were Jews, though they formed about 7.5 per cent of the population of these cities.

In 1941, a study was made of arrests for drunkenness in San Francisco; the rate for persons of Irish descent was calculated at no less than 7,876 per 100,000 in the population; for Jews, 27 per 100,000 in the population.

Admissions to a veterans' hospital in Northport, Long Island, were studied for 1936–39; of 111 first- and second-generation Jewish admissions, one was alcoholic; of 113 first- and second-generation Italian admissions, 5 were alcoholic; of 222 first- and second-generation Irish admissions, 36 were alcoholic; of 302 undifferentiated third-generation whites, 40 were alcoholic.

The figures could be repeated ad infinitum. They give a fuller picture for foreign-born Jews than for the native-born; but from whatever evidence we have, it would appear that second- and third-generation American Jews have, by and large, not kicked over the traces. Besides these figures, there is the testimony of doctors, judges, social workers, and welfare departments, all of whom agree that Jewish cases do not, in any large measure, suffer from alcohol.

Presumably, alcohol strips off the outer layers of the personality laid on by convention and conscience, and reveals the true man underneath—or, if we follow the Elizabethan Thomas Nashe, who divided drunkards into those who get ape-drunk, pig-drunk, sheep-drunk, and so on, the true animal underneath. In any case, the same should hold for nations, and their patterns of drunkenness should reveal something about their inner and buried life. The question is, what?

It has been suggested that when Protestantism forced each man to face his God alone without the intermediary of priest and community, the strain was too great, and we had the great binges that followed the Reformation in Protestant countries; perhaps. Except that on that basis we can't explain the intemperance of Catholic Ireland and Poland. And then, too, the Jews have theoretically been in this religious position since their priesthood lost its functions. Many people believe that in northern climates men drink distilled liquor, in southern wine, and this explains the national differences. This holds well enough for Europe; but Central America and Mexico and the Caribbean combine tropic climates with a passion for strong distilled liquor. Another explanation is that in those countries where sexual repression is severe alcoholism serves as an outlet. That helps explain Ireland but then what about Sweden, the freest country in Europe sexually, which also has one of the highest rates of alcoholism? And what too about the Jews, with their stringent code of sexual behavior? One extensive study of addiction to alcohol among primitive peoples proves decisively that it is closely correlated with anxiety over the means of subsistence, and the most secure peoples drink the least. Except that America, one of the most favored of countries, has one of the most serious problems of alcoholic excess. Then, too, Sweden is said to be, materially speaking, one of the pleasantest countries of Europe.

There is no question that a people's relation to alcohol represents something very deep about it; so deep, however, that it is not easy to find a very good explanation of just what it is.

Americans, however, as Tocqueville wrote, "entertain . . . a very lofty and often exaggerated opinion of human understanding." At Yale University an institute exists for the sole purpose of studying alcohol and its varied effects, and a journal is published, the *Quarterly Journal of Studies on Alcohol,* which is already in its twelfth volume, and contains in its approximately 8,000 pages a vast number of studies on all aspects of alcohol—all the statistics, and a good part of the other information in this article, are taken from it. The Yale institute is now engaged in a major effort to crack the problem of Jewish temperance, under a grant from I. Rogosin. At the same time, the somewhat less extreme resistance of the Italians to alcoholic excess and disorder—in its own way, however, as startling as that of the Jews, because they drink much more on the average than Jews do—is being attacked by another research team.

In the September 1951 issue of the *Journal,* Charles R. Snyder and Ruth H. Landman present a "Prospectus for Sociological Research on Jewish Drinking Patterns," carefully culling the literature for explanations of the alcoholic aspect of the Jewish mystery. Now an "explanation" is a complicated thing. And what is an explanation for one age and one person is not for another. At one time, about one hundred and fifty years ago, the greatest philosopher of the age addressed himself to our problem. Immanuel Kant observed that the Jews were a temperate people; he observed too that ministers and women also stayed sober. And he wrote in his *Anthropologie:*

"Women, ministers, and Jews do not get drunk, as a rule, at least they carefully avoid all appearance of it, because their civic position is weak and they need to be reserved. Their outward worth is based merely on the belief of others in their chastity, piousness, and separatistic lore. All separatists, that is those who subject themselves not only to the general law of the country but also to a special sectarian law, are exposed through their eccentricity and alleged chosenness to the attention and criticism of the community and thus cannot relax in their self-control, for intoxication, which deprives one of cautiousness, would be a scandal for them."[1]

[1] This passage was translated by E. M. Jellinek, together with other passages dealing with drink, and published in the first volume of the *Quarterly Journal of Studies on Alcohol.*

Initially, this explanation suggests, Jews remained sober, at any rate in the presence of non-Jews, for reasons of self-preservation; and as a matter of fact, Jews of Eastern Europe often got high on appropriate occasions—but it was unthinkable for a Jew to get drunk with non-Jews. But American social scientists are very cool to the idea that man's reason can play any great role in the way social groups act, and neither to Mr. Snyder and Miss Landman, nor to Robert F. Bales and Donald D. Glad (the last two have written doctoral theses on the problem of Jewish temperance), does Kant's explanation seem very plausible.

Mr. Snyder and Miss Landman look with greater favor on another theory, stemming from the work of the French sociologist Emile Durkheim, who constantly emphasized that the motives of specific individuals, whether rational or irrational, could not very well explain differences between groups—only the nature of the group itself could. Durkheim believed that modern society was suffering from a breakdown of the ties of religion and custom that bound together people in small rural and primitive communities. Suicide, he believed, was an excellent measure of the extent of the breakdown of the moral law among different groups. While men lived in communities closely regulated by custom, under the eyes of their neighbors, they did not commit suicide; when they moved to cities, freeing themselves in increasing measure from the ties that bound them to their fellow men, they tended to commit suicide in ever large numbers. The figures bore him out. According to Durkheim, furthermore, the Jews, to a greater extent than either Protestants or Catholics in the countries of nineteenth-century Europe, still constituted a close moral community. And indeed, their suicide rates were much lower than those of the Catholics.

Not long after Durkheim presented his theory of suicide, L. Cheinisse suggested that Jewish resistance to alcoholic excess could be similarly explained; if Jews formed enough of a cohesive community to prevent people from falling into the despair that resulted in suicide, perhaps their community was also strong enough to keep them from the less drastic despair that found an outlet in alcohol.

In sum, then, this theory argues that despite the breakup of the ghetto and the abandonment of the traditional Law on the part of the majority of Jews, they still form, more than other peoples, a rather close community which is able to supply psychological and material support to its members, and saves them from alcoholism and suicide.[2]

The Durkheim-Cheinisse hypothesis, however, is not by itself very satisfying. Why should a close, "organic" community not get drunk as often as any other? As a matter of fact they do, with the difference only that they all get drunk together on festive occasions. (Sometimes, as with Moi of Indo-China, and the Indians of Chamula in Mexico, these festive occasions seem to be almost continual, and everyone is at least half drunk most of the time.) But that is just the point. The organic community gets drunk all together, at regular fixed occasions, for specific purposes. Drinking is a ritual, and indeed in primitive communities and in all ancient societies drinking had a religious character. (The Moi actually killed an early French explorer who, by refusing to drink with them, threatened to bring down the vengeance of the gods.) It is this ritual element characteristic of the life of organic communities that prevents alcoholism from becoming perverted to individual uses and the solution of individual unhappiness.

That, according to Mr. Bales, to whom we have referred earlier, is the explanation of Jewish temperance. The Jews drink wine on fixed religious occasions: the Friday night *kiddush,* the four cups at the Seder meal, the annual Purim and Simchas Torah sprees, the cup drunk by bride and groom under the marriage canopy—wine even plays a role in the circumcision rite. Of course, Mr. Bales does not argue that Jews, like the Moi, drink only on religious occasions: but these occasions color their attitude to drinking, and prevent them from taking what he calls a "utilitarian" attitude toward alcohol—drinking it quite consciously for psychological effects.

One wonders if this "ritual" interpretation of Jewish drinking will hold even for the Orthodox; one thinks of the Hasidim who got drunk on wine and God together (their enemies, naturally, did not think God had anything to do with it), and there is the talmudic sage referred to at the beginning of the article who knew

[2] Unfortunately for this theory, Jewish suicide rates began to leap upward at the beginning of the twentieth century: indeed, the Jews of pre-Hitler Germany had some of the highest suicide rates ever recorded for any group. But at the same time, as we have seen, Jews did not show any greater propensity for drunkenness and its consequences.

quite well that wine loosens tongues and was quite willing to use it for this "utilitarian" purpose.

If Mr. Bales, however, is right, it follows that we would not expect the American Jews, who have already wandered far indeed from the paths of their ancestors, and are more likely to begin their festive meals with martinis than with the benediction pronounced over wine, to keep out of the alcoholic wards much longer. And Mr. Bales, firmly stepping out on a limb, predicts just this. Perhaps he is right. The great majority of American Jews today, however, are still immigrants and the sons of immigrants. (One study in a representative city showed only 10 per cent of the Jewish population was third generation.) We are all closer to the ghetto than we think; and, even if we drink martinis, most of us were raised in homes where the benediction was pronounced. Perhaps when we are third and fourth generation rather than first and second, we shall not be very different from other Americans in the way we take, and respond to, our liquor.

But perhaps, too, the sociologists have been too hasty in disposing of Kant's explanation. The Jews have been under siege for a long time, and have had to move cautiously for the last thousand years at least. It is revealing to me that when they had no need to move cautiously they minded the number of their cups less: in ancient Palestine, in the days of the First Commonwealth, when the prophets denounced them for leaving the simple ways of the desert; in the days of the Second Commonwealth, when the disputations of Jewish scholars seemed suspiciously close to the drinking sessions of Greek philosophers; in the early centuries of Jewish prosperity in Spain. Christian Europe seems first to have tightened the lips of the Jews; when we think of how our forefathers lived in medieval Europe, it is not hard to understand how it was that Jews began to feel that *they* had to have their wits about them, whatever the Gentiles did. Perhaps the siege has been raised here in America, but most Jews as yet are not, very deep down, sure that it has been.

Of course the siege is only the beginning of an explanation, not the whole explanation. Because of the siege, the traditional Jewish emphasis (traditional, that is, for the post-biblical era) on reason, on logic, on consciousness, has been reinforced, as has the traditional distaste for violence and irrationality. It is revealing that even when Jews get drunk, they are not violent drunks, as, for ex-

ample, Scandinavians are supposed to be—if alcohol permits the
return of the inhibited, then we must conclude that irrational violence has been so deeply inhibited among the Jews that it does
not rise to the surface even when alcohol dulls the higher centers
of the brain.

It is not the consciousness of the siege that prevents any individual Jew from taking one more drink—motivation is more complicated than that. But it is the consequences of the siege, passed
down from generation to generation, and including such elements
as the desire to hold on to one's senses and a distaste for the irrational, that sets a limit to Jewish drinking. So that it is indeed true
that the Jew does not restrain himself because he thinks of the
surrounding non-Jewish world: he is as temperate in all-Jewish
company, or in an all-Jewish state. Rather, his restraint has become
automatic—by what mechanisms, we may perhaps learn from the
Yale study now in progress—in the course of hundreds of years.

But this is only one effect of the Jewish consciousness of difference. Here in America, where the Jews are not another nation, as
they were in Eastern Europe, they wish intensely to overcome the
difference; and so the Jew may very often take a drink in non-Jewish company, or even in Jewish, just to show he is "one of the
boys." But even here the hand of reason shows itself: the Jew
drinks—or he does not drink—from "reasons of state." And the
non-Jews are made as uncomfortable by the Jewish drinker as by
the Jewish non-drinker. As Jake and his pals say, in effect, of
Robert Cohn, the fighting and drinking Jew of *The Sun Also Rises*
—he "drinks by the book."

Drinking, after all, strips us down to the natural man. And, for
better or for worse, there does not seem to be much natural man
left in the Jews to strip down to.

In the *Quarterly Journal of Studies on Alcohol* for 1947 one may
read an interview with a Jewish high-school senior on the subject
of alcohol conducted by Mr. Glad in the course of his studies. "I've
never been drunk myself," the boy told Mr. Glad. "I should try it
though—a fellow should know how it affects him. . . ." He understands well enough why other people drink: "They're trying to
drown their sorrows, and it may give them a false happiness." What
would you say is bad about excessive drinking, Mr. Glad asked.
"It affects the mind—dulls the brain." What's good about drinking

in moderation? the interviewer continued. "When you're at a party it makes you feel like you're one of the gang. If you don't, people feel you're not a regular fellow. . . . It's also a business help . . . it's kind of a social custom . . . you don't want people to get the impression that you're different."

Of course there is a lot here that many non-Jewish Americans might have said. And yet, centuries ago, the Jewish innkeeper very likely also thought, as he saw the pointless gaiety and pointless tears aroused by his liquor, "It affects the mind—dulls the brain." Had he come across these same words, Kant might have used them to illustrate his explanation of why the Jews stay sober.

IS JEWISH HUMOR DEAD?

By IRVING KRISTOL

IT IS KNOWN THAT the surest way of killing a joke is to explain it, and humor has, in self-defense, made an especially comic figure of the man who would earnestly analyze it. Thus humor and seriousness contest the field, with all arbitration or appeasement ruled out, and with the possibility of rising above the battle simply unimaginable; one rises above the battle either through seriousness or humor—and then one is right back in the fight. It is an unequal struggle: humor is more aggressive, more mobile, and has the more penetrating weapons. But in the end, humor loses and seriousness wins. Humorists die and dead men tell no jokes, and this, it must be admitted, is a serious matter.

Jewish humor died with its humorists when the Nazis killed off the Jews of Eastern Europe, though it seems likely that even without the intervention of Hitler this humor would not long have survived the disintegration of the ghetto community from which it drew its inspiration. This opinion is certain to be challenged, especially by those who, though willing to concede that persecution can wound the flesh, are reluctant to believe that it can murder the spirit or that the spirit can, by the erosion of time, simply wither and die. They will ask: does not this humor still flourish in the Jewish communities of America and Israel? is not Jewish humor a treasure in the perpetual custody of the Jewish people? The answer to both questions is, I think, no, and in the course of this essay I hope to show why. But first I would like to illustrate the defeat of humor with an anecdote that some will find amusing but that is really not a Jewish joke so much as the dying echo of one.

A group of Jewish refugees from Poland, recently arrived in the

United States, visited one evening with their American-born relatives. One of the latter thought to lighten the conversation by telling an old Jewish joke:

A Jew in tsarist Russia wished to buy a ticket that would permit him to enter the platform of a railroad station, and he was referred to a vending machine where such tickets were sold at ten kopecks each. The Jew eyed the machine curiously and mused, "Maybe you'll take five kopecks?" He inserted five kopecks and pressed the lever. No ticket came out. The Jew shrugged his shoulders and said, "Well, there was no harm in trying." He inserted another five kopecks, and pulled the lever. Nothing happened. As he stood there, bewildered, a Cossack brushed past him, inserted ten kopecks into the machine, pulled the lever, and got his ticket. The Jew flew into a rage, spat at the machine, and yelled: "Filthy anti-Semite! For a Cossack you give tickets, but for a Jew's ten kopecks you don't bother!"

To the narrator's pleasure, the newcomers laughed heartily at the joke though it is but an inferior specimen of the familiar genre of Jewish humor that pokes fun at the Jews for their propensity to gloss over their own shortcomings and blame the always available anti-Semite for their misfortunes.

Some weeks later there was another family gathering, this time to welcome some still newer arrivals from the D.P. camps. One of the refugees who had been present at the earlier meeting volunteered to tell the "very funny joke" that the *Amerikaner* had related. He told it as follows:

A Jew in tsarist Russia wished to buy a ticket that would permit him to enter the platform of a railroad station, and he was referred to a vending machine where such tickets were sold at ten kopecks each. The Jew inserted his ten kopecks, but nothing happened. As he stood there, bewildered, a Cossack brushed past him, inserted ten kopecks into the machine, pulled the lever, and got his ticket. The Jew flew into a rage, spat at the machine, and yelled: "Filthy anti-Semite! For a Cossack you give tickets, but for a Jew's ten kopecks you don't bother!"

The laughter was every bit as hearty at this version of the joke, though the original point had been blunted and what had been a joke had really become a parable. Actually, these Jews from Poland were not laughing at any joke at all, but only at the way the story summarized their sense of a senseless persecution. The seriousness of the concentration camps had conquered.

It is true that in my telling of this incident the original point has been in part regained, for the butts of my story are Jews so sensitive to anti-Semitism that they have lost the detachment that is at the root of true humor. But it is a point that barely reaches the mark, and whatever smile it arouses is the mere shadow of a shadow. Too many corpses obstruct the comic perspective.

One recent anthologist of Jewish humor, doubtless expressing the sentiments of many, sees in the Jewish joke a victory gained by the Jewish spirit over centuries of adversity, an exultant defiance of persecution and harassment, an affirmation of the will to survival in the face of an ever-impending doom. It would surely be to the glory of the entire human race, and of the Jews in particular, if this were the case. And it is agreeable to note that there is some truth in this description. But not the whole truth.

Though the records are scanty, it seems safe to assert that the kind of humor we know came late to Jewish history, gaining ground in the seventeenth and eighteenth centuries and reaching its apogee in the nineteenth and early twentieth centuries. It is, then, a preeminently *modern* phenomenon. The Jews of an earlier day were rich in proverbs (some of them witty), parables, moralistic anecdotes—but not, it seems, in humor. This fact is no occasion for surprise if we cast a glance at the development of humor in the various Western Christian nations of the Middle Ages. There we see that humor could exist only in the interstices of a religious civilization (just as the Purim parodies existed within Orthodox Judaism), that the religious authorities frowned upon it, and that it won popular affection to the extent that the dominion of religion became questionable, and that, indeed, one of its functions was to challenge this dominion. Humor needs to breathe the air of skepticism, and prior to the modern epoch the Jews were men of faith, piety, and hence sobriety. When one believes that this life on earth is implicated in eternal salvation or eternal damnation, there is little motive for levity.

Take, for example, the matter of *Galgen-humor* (gallows humor), which was elevated to such a fine art in the writings of the man who gaily signed himself Sholom Aleichem. Here is how Sholom Aleichem has one of his characters, Yisrolik of Kishenev, write to his friend Yankel in America after the Kishenev pogrom of 1903 (I use the version given by Maurice Samuel in his fine book, *The World of Sholom Aleichem*):

"Dear Yankel: You ask me to write at length, and I'd like to oblige, but there's really nothing to write about. The rich are still rich and the poor are dying of hunger, as they always do. What's new about that? And as far as the pogroms are concerned, thank God we have nothing more to fear, as we've already had ours—two of them, in fact, and a third wouldn't be worth while. . . . All our family got through it safely, except for Lippi, who was killed with his two sons, Noah and Mordecai; first-class artisans, all three of them. Oh yes, and except Hersh. Perel was found dead in the cellar together with the baby at her breast. But as Getzi used to say: 'It might have been worse; don't think of the better, because there's no limit to that.' You ask about Heshel. He's been out of work now for over half a year. The fact is they won't let him work in prison. . . . Mendel did a clever thing; he up and died. Some say of hunger, others of consumption. Personally, I think he died of both. I really don't know what else there is to write about, except the cholera, which is going great guns. . . ."

This is Sholom Aleichem at his best, which means that it is at the top rung of the world's literature of irony. Yet it is most improbable that a pious Jew who had, say, undergone the expulsion from Spain in 1492 would have found this letter as entertaining as did his descendants, or that he would have found it as "cathartic" as his own Kabbalistic speculations. For him, death at the hands of persecutors was *kiddush ha-shem,* the sanctification of the Name. It was an affair in the realm of the sacred, and jesting was unthinkable. But for Sholom Aleichem death in a pogrom was a somewhat more ambiguous event. It might be *kiddush ha-shem*—Sholom Aleichem nowhere states that it is not. Or it might be nothing but bad luck ornamented with a high-sounding title. In this equivocation between the sacred and the profane, the eternal and the finite, the spark of humor is fanned.

It is interesting to note that fifty Jews were killed in the Kishenev pogrom and that the civilized world was shocked and horrified. Sholom Aleichem's irony was a harmonic counterpoint to this shock and horror. But when some six million Jews were slaughtered during World War II, the world was numbed by the enormity of the crime, and the victims themselves could not respond with the esthetic freedom of Sholom Aleichem. The kind of jokes that Jews brought forth from the concentration camps were mainly bitter thrusts at the idiocy of their oppressors. For just as humor cannot mature in life of utter religious faith, so it cannot survive a life of sheer nihilism.

No pranks, no slapstick, no practical jokes—nothing that reduces the spiritual and human to the mechanical. It is a humor of the spirit, not against the spirit.

What we call Jewish humor is Yiddish humor. It is the humor that was conceived and expressed in the Yiddish language, in a secular language of the market place that had as part of its everyday idiom a multitude of Hebrew phrases having to do with modes of talmudic exegesis or with such non-secular affairs as the world-to-come, the after-life, and reincarnation; a language full of the chanting and inflections that accompanied the translation of holy texts and their memorization: a "knowing language," in Maurice Samuel's phrase, full of internal hints and esoteric references. It is the humor of a folk community of garrulous intellectuals and hair-splitters cut off from nature and animal life, intrigued only by the oddities of the human and the divine, taking as its frame of reference the complex structure of ghetto society, ghetto life, and Jewish tradition. It is, supremely, the humor of an intelligence running amok in the household of the gods without ever daring, or wanting, to set foot outside the open door.

Many of the specific jokes, of course, were borrowed from other peoples and other tongues, and have since been reclaimed with interest. Others have survived the long voyage to America or Israel and translation into English or modern Hebrew. But, with the wiping out of the Yiddish-speaking communities, the creative source of this humor is gone. To the extent that old habits and folkways persist among Jews in America, Europe, and Israel— especially insofar as they involve the family and the hazards of earning a living—slices of Yiddish humor will be appreciated (mother-in-law jokes, marriage-broker jokes, *luftmensh* jokes). However, it is clear that a good part of the pleasure these jokes provide results from the warm nostalgia of merely hearing them. The old folkways are disappearing and Yiddish itself is on its way to becoming a dead language. The Jews of Israel prefer not to think of the ghetto, and their humor seems to be content with variations on Viennese café wit. (Example: Ben Gurion offers a friend the post of minister of colonies. "But we have no colonies," the friend protests. "So what?" replies Ben Gurion. "Isn't Kaplan minister of finance?") American Jews are not so pressed to forget the ghetto, and Yiddish humor has for them a sentimental as well as comic value. But, though parts of the body have been preserved, even adorned and dressed as new, the soul is gone. The Jewish joke is no longer *important*. We are no longer in that world, and of that epoch, where the greatest of all Jewish writers was—one can even say, had to be—a humorist.

The "Jewish situation" that brought forth a humor unique in man's history has altered. What was that situation?

Stated briefly, the situation was one of God-forsaken religiosity. And the humor of this situation is a humor of pious blasphemy, in which the religious emotion is siphoned off into explosive wit.

In one of Sholom Aleichem's stories, Tevye the dairyman, riding home hungry after a day's work, with one ruble in his pocket with which to sustain his nagging wife and seven thriving daughters, addresses God as follows:

"Thou hast made us a little lower than the angels. It depends upon what you call a little, isn't it? Lord, what is life, and what are we, and to what may a man be likened? A man may be likened to a carpenter; for a carpenter lives, and lives and lives, and finally dies. And so does a man."

The form of this speech is that of an edifying rabbinic discourse. The content is impudent and sophistical. But—and this is what is most significant—Sholom Aleichem is loyal at one and the same time to both the form and the content that controverts it. The Jews in their ages of faith had experienced the contradictions of life and the cosmos as revelation, as theophany; now they are only contradictions, existing side by side with a faith that cannot comprehend them.

The conflict between form and content can be seen in innumerable jokes, of which the following is a rather good representative:

If I have the right to take money out of my pocket, from which the other man has no right to take money, then is not my right all the greater to take money from *his* pocket, from which even he has the right to take money?

This "joke" is chanted in the melody usually reserved for talmudic study, and the parody is further stressed by the fact that in the original Yiddish the two clauses are joined by the technical Hebrew phrase, *kal v'chomer,* which is the talmudic counterpart to the logician's *a fortiori.* Indeed, the form is impeccably orthodox; only the content negates the purpose of this form, which in the Talmud aims at establishing the immutable principles of justice and piety. But though the form is negated it is not denied, for the jokester—assuming him to have been an average ghetto Jew—had no intention of substituting other and novel laws of thought: these laws were as good as any, it just happened that reality made an absurdity of them, and that was what was funny.

Ernst Simon has shown how the method of argument in the Talmud, and the singsong incantation of the unpunctuated text, lent itself to the uses of humor.[1] But before such use could be made, a measure of detachment had to be gained; the mind had to be able to stand apart from the sacred text, and to see itself as standing apart. The affective power of faith had to be stilled, replaced by what Bergson has called "a momentary anesthesia of the heart," and the world given over to pure intelligence. The life of faith is then seen as something absurd.

But, after that, Jewish humor takes another, a bold, step: the world of non-faith, of pure intelligence, is seen to be equally absurd.

Jewish humor is the humor of a rebellious rationalism. It is also the *reductio ad absurdum* of rationalism. Thus there is produced a distinctive quality of Jewish wit: its circularity.

Immanuel Olsvanger has recorded three versions—Arabic, Russian, and Jewish—of the same joke, which purports to reveal the "secret of Telegraphy":

Arabic—"Imagine a huge dog having its head in Beirut and its tail in Damascus. Pull the dog's tail in Damascus and the bark will be heard in Beirut."

Russian—First Russian: "Imagine a horse, its head in Moscow and its tail in Tula. Pinch the horse's nose in Moscow and it will wag its tail in Tula. And so it is with telegraphy." Second Russian: "Yes, but how do they telegraph from Tula to Moscow?"

Jewish—First Jew: "Imagine, instead of the wire, a dog, whose

[1] In his article "Notes on Jewish Wit," in the *Jewish Frontier,* October 1948.

head is in Kovno and whose tail is in Vilna. Pull the tail in Vilna and the bark will be heard in Kovo." Second Jew: "But how does wireless telegraphy work?" First Jew: "The same way but without the dog."

Here, rational explanation ends up by being identical with the original confession of ignorance, yet is offered as a proof. Now this circularity is partly a sardonic and sophisticated mimicry of the naïve circularity that is intrinsic to religious faith and that, for instance, permits the pious commentator to prove that Abraham wore a hat when he invited the angels into his tent—for would the patriarch Abraham *not* wear a hat? In the nineteenth century this mimicry was directed in particular against the "wonder-working" rabbis of Hasidism, as in the following:

Rabbi A., in Cracow, while praying, saw in a vision that Rabbi B., in Lemberg, had just died. He and his congregation went into mourning. Later, travelers from Lemberg reported that Rabbi B. was still alive and in good health. The critics of Rabbi A. took this opportunity to scoff at his supposed supernatural powers. To these the disciples of Rabbi A. retorted: "And isn't it miracle enough for you that our rabbi could see all the way from Cracow to Lemberg?"[2]

But if the reasoning of the devout is absurd, it is not ridiculous, for there is always one bit of evidence that makes sense out of the nonsense of faith: the pious man, who by his presence converts what is rationally absurd into something real. One must bear in mind to what extent the fullness of Jewish life was, for almost two millennia, devoted to what is rationally absurd, to what extent it was a dream-life, a sane type of madness. Jewish existence was grounded in a series of fantastic "make-believes." The Jews, seemingly the lowliest of the low, were God's chosen people. The Temple was destroyed but the routine of sacrifice was studied. On the last day of the Feast of Booths all Jews prayed for rain so that the non-existent crops of Palestine's non-existent Jewish settlements might prosper.

And here the Jewish jokester is in a dilemma. He is the child of a later age, and he believes that what is rationally absurd should be really absurd. He is, however, also close enough to the vitality

2 This is taken from Freud's *Wit in Its Relation to the Unconscious,* which is still one of the best books on Jewish humor ever written.

of Jewish faith to be profoundly aware that the absurd can, through faith, become real. He *knows,* uncontrollably, and in every fiber of his being, that the Jew is the son of the covenant, even if such an idea is an outrage to enlightened intelligence. He becomes the victim of an exhilarating paranoia. Truth and reality diverge: what is true is rational, but what is real is the absurd. His reason finds itself impotent, and in the circular joke it proceeds to outwit itself.

A Jew, whose life had been one long trial and who was sustained only by the hope of compensation in the after-life, lay dying. With his remaining breath he told his children, assembled round his bed, how he had suffered and with what joy he looked forward to the world-to-come. "But," he concluded, "what a joke it would be if there were nothing over there!"

The joke comes about if one ardently believes in a God who does not—and one secretly fears it—exist.

Jewish humor dances along a knife-edge that separates religious faith from sheer nihilism. It "knows" that the material world is the only true reality, but it also finds that this world makes no sense in its own terms and is impossible to live in, while the absurd world of Jewish faith, the one into which it was born and whose air it is accustomed to breathe, is no longer true. Then intensity of Jewish humor derives from this double loyalty to incompatibles, to the sacred and the profane. Bergson has said that "a situation is invariably comic when it belongs simultaneously to two altogether independent series of events and is capable of being interpreted in two entirely different meanings at the same time." So it is that the European Jew, achieving self-consciousness in the Enlightenment, found himself at the point of intersection of faith and reason, in a comic situation he could only master with a joke.

Jewish humor is, consequently, also nostalgic. It looks backward to a state where the Jew did not know the comic, was incapable of wit, and did not need humor to make him laugh. Occasionally, its nostalgia is so acute that, as Theodor Reik has demonstrated, Jewish humor, especially in its self-aggression, strongly resembles psychopathic melancholia.

What is this but to say that Jewish humor is of the essence of modernity? Sholom Aleichem is a truly modern writer in the same sense that Dostoyevsky and Nietzsche are modern writers. He has eaten of the fruit of the tree of rational knowledge but he hungers for the fruit of the tree of religious life. And Sholom Aleichem's true heir is Franz Kafka, who used to laugh until the tears came to his eyes when he read his work aloud to friends. But Kafka doesn't make *us* laugh. That is a measure of the extent to which the modern situation, dissolving into murderous nihilism, robs Jewish humor of its victory.

ZION

Some of the most thoughtful and learned Jewish writings of the past decade have dealt, quite naturally, with Zionism, Israel, the Diaspora, and the problem of dual loyalties. Outstanding Jewish theologians, statesmen, philosophers, and journalists have written on what is here called "Zion."

The essays by Mordecai M. Kaplan and the late Hayim Greenberg were originally delivered as addresses. For that matter, Milton Steinberg's essay, "When I Think of Seraye," which appears in the section on "Belonging and Survival," was also originally delivered as an address and is already considered a classic statement of special Jewish pleading. The papers read by Dr. Kaplan and Hayim Greenberg have been reprinted and remembered by all who heard and read them.

Many of the pieces included in this section are in direct contradiction one to another. Dr. Trude Weiss-Rosmarin's "America Is Not Babylonia" is based on an approach diametrically opposed, for example, to that taken by Dr. Kaplan. On the other hand, Hayim Greenberg's analysis of Diaspora Jewry is quite different from both Dr. Kaplan's and Dr. Weiss-Rosmarin's, although all three have their validity and their significance. Hayim Greenberg and Johan J. Smertenko both discuss dual loyalties; again, from quite different viewpoints. Benno Weiser's survey of the disagreement between David Ben Gurion and American Zionists is far more than a topical piece on the subject, because, as the reader will become aware, it touches the nerve of Zionism itself and the disagreements are not only topical but they will apparently remain deep for generations to come. In Mr. Weiser's attempt to report both sides of the problem, we better understand the gulf that is widening between the Jews of Israel and the Jews elsewhere, between the "we" and the "they." Eliezer Whartman's strong essay negating Jewish life anywhere outside of Israel is offered here as an eloquent statement of that radical point of view, not because it is necessarily a true statement. Dr. Horace Kallen, in his long, scholarly essay, offers a lucid survey of the recent history of Zionism and Israel, while the articles on painting and fiction survey related fields in Zion.

Because all ten contributions to this section are so deeply Jewish in approach, all, with one exception (Mr. Smertenko's "Have Jews a Divided Loyalty?"), were first published in Jewish periodicals, including *The Reconstructionist, The Jewish Frontier, The Jewish Spectator, The Zionist Quarterly, Commentary,* and *The Menorah Journal.*

THE NEED FOR DIASPORA ZIONISM

By MORDECAI M. KAPLAN

O N TWO OCCASIONS in our long history as Jews was the sentiment that it is hard to be a Jew sharply articulated. The first occasion was when, at some time during the third or fourth century, the question arose as to how a person who wanted to become a proselyte should be received. The answer then in effect was: He should be warned that it is hard to be a Jew. The second occasion was in our own century; when Sholom Aleichem wished to dramatize the handicaps to which a Jew was subjected, and wrote a play on the theme, "It's Hard to Be a Jew."

The striking fact, however, is that, although throughout the centuries being a Jew was hard to the point of martyrdom, it always seemed to make sense. Indeed, how could Jewish life be other than hard in a world in which to do the right thing has always meant to live in the line of greatest resistance? From the time, however, that Jews began to be emancipated from their medieval disabilities, and were permitted, or expected, to become part of the nations which granted them civic rights, being a Jew has not only been hard, but has ceased to make sense. That is what Heine meant when in the twenties of the last century, he coined the aphorism: "Judaism is not a religion; it is a misfortune." Likewise in our own day, when the goal of Zionism was on the verge of attainment, Arthur Koestler proclaimed that for Jews to maintain their distinctive group life outside Eretz Yisrael was an anachronism, and that Jewish parents had no right to place upon their children's shoulders the burdensome knapsack of Judaism. That is Koestler's way of saying that being a Jew in the Diaspora no longer makes any sense.

What Heine and Koestler put in words is what increasing numbers of Jews actually feel. Even if they dare not think it, it certainly agitates their unconscious or subconscious. The more the average Jew tries to suppress his suspicion that being a Jew in *golah* makes no sense, the more compulsive a force that suspicion becomes. It gives rise to a sense of inferiority, and to all kinds of escapist tendencies like the dejudaization of names, the taking of protective coloration, the fear of being too conspicuous. In extreme cases it leads to destructive self-hate, and reaches its climax in Jewish anti-Semitism.

Is it not high time that, for the sake of our own inner health and happiness, we try to get to the bottom of this affliction and take the appropriate measures to put a halt to it? Why with all the hardships and dangers that being a Jew incurred throughout the centuries prior to the Emancipation did Jewish life seem to make good sense?

The answer is not far to seek. Jews and non-Jews lived during those centuries in the same climate of opinion. Jews and non-Jews alike drew upon the Bible for their fundamental ideas about God, the world, human nature and its destiny. Jews and non-Jews, however hostile in their feeling toward one another, had life made meaningful to them through the stories of Creation, of the Garden of Eden, of Abraham, Isaac and Jacob, of the election of Israel and so on to the end of the Scriptures. To both Jews and non-Jews human history was a divine drama in which the Jews played a central role. The fact that the Christians and the Moslems substituted a different ending to that drama from the one which the Jews took for granted, all the more fortified the Jews in their own conviction that for them to persist in their faith at all costs was consistent with the entire development of the divine drama and its denouement; in other words, the only thing that made sense.

This consensus with regard to the central role of the Jews in the divine drama, a consensus once common to Jews, Christians and Moslems, is now a thing of the past. First the Renaissance and then the Enlightenment upset the applecart. Whatever consensus exists in the modern man's thought-world is due to scientific observation, to experiment and technology. This revolution in man's thinking happens to be the most important link in the chain of circumstances that led to the Jewish emancipation. We Jews, being indebted to this psychological revolution for our freedom from bondage, no longer look to the traditional view of human history in which we played a central role to give meaning to our being Jews. On the other hand, we have not found as yet our own role in the new world order. That is the main reason we have the feeling that we are out of step with the rest of the world in wishing to remain Jews.

It would be untrue to say that we have not tried to redefine our role in the new world order. On the contrary, we have made strenuous efforts. As a result of those efforts there arose four distinct versions or conceptions of what it means to be a Jew, three synagogue versions: the Reform, the Neo-Orthodox and the Conservative, and one secularist or culturist version. All these four groups have tried, each in its own way, to prove that being a Jew made sense. They have each reinterpreted and reconstructed the tradition so as to fit somehow into the modern world outlook or thought pattern.

It is doubtful, however, whether any of the four groups would have gotten very far in its efforts to have Jews accept themselves, if it were not for the Zionist movement. Zionism gave Jews the feeling that, if they wish to be in step with the rest of the world, they should give up waiting for a miracle-working Messiah who would restore the Jews to Eretz Yisrael and should achieve their redemption through their own efforts by retrieving their ancient homeland. Long before this objective of Zionism could be attained the very prospect of it was enough to infuse new life and vigor in all the four modern versions of Jewish life. Without it the three synagogue movements and the one culturist movement would soon have lost their initial impulse and enthusiasm and would have remained sterile and empty of content. Zionism exercised this vitalizing influence on Reform, Orthodoxy, Conservatism and Culturism, because it operated with the modern assumption that groups as well as individuals had the inalienable right to independence, dignity and self-realization. This realistic version of the right of Jews to maintain their group identity helped to fit Jewish life into the pattern of contemporary notions of human society. The moral effect of this new approach to the Jewish situation was to reawaken the feeling that being a Jew made sense, no matter where one lived as a Jew. Once a Jew was a Zionist, he had a purpose to live for, a purpose that gave meaning and content to his life as a Jew.

Now that the immediate goal of Zionism has been attained through the establishment of the state, the Jews in Israel keep on telling us Jews in the Diaspora that the only place where being a Jew makes sense is in Israel. An American-born Jew who migrated to Israel reports the following: "With Israel's growing importance as a place where Jewish life can be lived maximally, the role of American Jewry becomes increasingly unsatisfying. Whether we like to admit it or not, the root, trunk, bough and flower of Jewish life is now in Israel." American-Jewish life, the same writer argues, is bound to grow sterile, contentless and purposeless and completely impotent in its struggle to live amid the disintegrative influences of the American environment. The more imbued with the will to live as a Jew an American becomes, the more likely is he to gravitate to Israel, and thus leave American Jewry orphaned of enlightened or inspired leadership.

Does that mean that we should write off the five million American Jews, and that we should stake the future of our entire people upon the prospective three or four million who will be in Eretz Yisrael by fifty years from now? If Zionism has taught us anything, it has taught us to face realities. With all the small states being drawn into the orbit of one or the other of the rival world powers, with the Arab nations being forced into a unity that seldom bodes well for Israel, there could be nothing more ominous or fatal to the State of Israel than to be left without an influential world Jewry that has a stake in its survival. *But if such an influential world Jewry is to exist, being a Jew will have to make sense wherever Jews happen to live.* Zionism has done a good obstetric job in delivering Diaspora Jewry of its baby, Israel. But if it wants the baby to live, it cannot afford to let the mother die. Zionism has to nurse Diaspora Jewry back to health.

Let us heed the warning sounded recently by the British Zionist Federation at its annual conference: "The State of Israel has solved the problem of Jewish homelessness. . . . On the other hand, instead of uniting and consolidating the Jewish people all over the world, there is real danger that the existence of the State may split them into two camps—Israeli and Diaspora Jews—each speaking a different language, thinking along different lines, living in a different atmosphere and absorbing a different culture. Zionism would then have created the Jewish state but lost the Jewish people." No less imperative, therefore, than making secure the foundations of the new state is the task of uniting and consolidating the Jewish people. That is not the task of the State. That is the task of the Zionist movement.

What is involved in the process of uniting and consolidating the Jewish people? This time the aim is not merely to create a *political state* but something much more difficult, though in the end much more significant—a *state of mind*. That state of mind is one in which being a Jew makes sense.

If being a Jew is to make sense, the basic requirement is the existence of some clearly identifiable and nameable corporate entity to which one can belong as a Jew. It is as absurd to try to be a Jew without a corporate entity to belong to as to be a soldier without an army to enlist in. The Jews were a nation for three thousand years in the truest and most profound sense of the term. They continued to be a nation even when they were exiled from their land and had no state. During those centuries they were a nation in captivity. But, as soon as they accepted citizenship in other nations, they began to disband as a Jewish nation.

If the Jews had been willing to become absorbed completely by the general population, there would have been an end to Jews and Judaism. But in insisting on remaining Jews, they became a riddle or an enigma to themselves and to the rest of the world, because the Jewish nation was in the process of disbanding, while no new social status was emerging to take the place of the status of nationhood. Napoleon I in 1806 was the first to attempt to resolve the enigma. He summoned a group of Jewish notables, named them a "Sanhedrin," and had them sign on the dotted line that the Jews were nothing more than a religious communion. His formula was officially adopted some forty years later by the founders of the Reform movement in Germany. Though Neo-Orthodoxy and Conservatism retained the vocabulary of traditional Jewish nationhood, they eviscerated its substance. The conduct of the synagogue Jews in modern times is like that of veterans of a disbanded army. Veterans, as a rule, get into their uniforms and hold parades with some of the old armor and battle flags on national holidays. Likewise, synagogue Jews, as veterans of the disbanded Jewish nation, get into their best clothes a few times during the year and parade as Jews.

446

The Zionist movement, in concentrating on the establishment of a publicly recognized homeland for the Jews, gave no thought to what would be the status of Jews who wished to retain their Jewish identity without migrating to Eretz Yisrael. Such Jews cannot form part of a Jewish nation, since they belong to non-Jewish nations. For that same reason they cannot belong to the Jewish State of Israel. Neither can they constitute a religious communion, in the conventional sense of the term, because of the wide diversity of religious beliefs and practices, to say nothing of the marked absence of either in the case of many Jews who take an active part in Jewish life. The fact must be faced that the main body of Jews, particularly those outside Israel, is at present a mere conglomerate without a name, a kind of human hodgepodge.

A group that has no name or status is without individuality or character. To belong to such a group cannot add in the slightest to one's self-respect or morale. It is almost like being born outside of wedlock. Pinsker's warning that, as long as the Jews had no home of their own, they were a ghost people that only inspired fear and suspicion still applies to present-day Diaspora Jewries. That is the main cause of the escapist psychology of the overwhelming majority of our key people, of those who play a prominent role in worldly affairs and of those who achieve distinction in the arts and the sciences.

Zionism is the only movement that is capable of undertaking the task of uniting and consolidating the Jewish people. That task is no less difficult than the re-establishment of the State of Israel, and by all counts just as important for all Jews. Jewish unity will have to be redefined in terms that would render it compatible with dispersion as a permanent fact as well as with the wide range of diversity in religious belief and practice. To be sure, religion, too, will have to be reckoned with, since it has constituted the main uniting bond throughout our entire past. But if it is to serve that purpose henceforth, it will have to be freed from the traditional authoritarianism.

The most vexing and difficult problem of all, which is beyond the scope of any individual, or segment of world Jewry to solve, is how to win recognition for the new status of the Jews as a people, which is to embrace so variegated and so far-flung a mass of human beings. The status of peoplehood will have to acquire the rich connotation of psychological unity which is based on historical continuity made possible through a dynamic religious civilization. Only a Jewish world council or synod, representative of all sections of Jewry and of all shades of Jewish belief and practice, meeting in Jerusalem for a considerable period of time, can win recognition for whatever group status it would see fit to assign to world Jewry. Such a convocation should culminate in some written instrument that would have the force of a covenant by which Jews from all parts of the world would mutually pledge one another to foster a sense of oneness through mutual help in times of need and through cooperation in the furtherance of Judaism as a religious civilization at all times.

This is not a plea for just another conference. It is a plea for an awakening on the part of our people to a realization that without a definite basis for Jewish unity and solidarity, which can be accorded publicly recognized status, being a Jew can make no sense. It is a plea to the Zionist organization to make preparations for the necessary demonstrative and dramatic action on a world-scale to close the gap between Israeli Jewry and Diaspora Jewry and the chasm that divides the Jews of one country from those in other countries. This newly achieved solidarity will yield the necessary ethical and spiritual motivation for being a Jew as well as keep alive the permanent values in our age-long tradition.

Nothing less than this ambitious program for world Jewry can qualify Zionist leaders for the new task which some of them are considering, namely the formation of organic Jewish communities. Zionism cannot better employ its energies and resources than to engage in the perpetuation and enhancement of Jewish life in the Diaspora. If our Zionist leaders possess the imagination and the vision to embark on a world-wide endeavor for Jewish unity, they will realize that the most practical way to proceed is to begin by immediately translating that envisioned unity into functioning organic Jewish communities wherever Jews happen to live in considerable numbers.

While, logically, the reaffirmation of Jewish world unity and the establishment of a new Jewish covenant should precede the establishment of local organic communities, psychologically it is necessary to proceed with the formation of those communities as though the new world Jewish covenant had already been drawn up. We

Jews have a precedent for that in the way we lived for centuries on the assumption that ultimately we would retrieve our ancient home. Likewise, we now have to re-order our communal structure on the assumption that we shall succeed in retrieving our lost solidarity and achieving publicly recognized status as a people.

The prospect of re-establishing the House of Israel should impel Zionism to proceed at once with the establishment, in the Diaspora, of a network of local organic communities that would translate into concrete experience for every individual man, woman and child the meaning of Jewish peoplehood.

Zionism should now undertake to revise our present haphazard methods in the conduct of our social, cultural and spiritual affairs. All our cooperation is at present being conducted on an *ad hoc* basis. Each objective, whether temporary or permanent, is planned without relation to every other. Religious activities, welfare services, overseas relief, educational and cultural undertakings, are the responsibilities of self-appointed groups, each group trying to go over the top and regarding as its rival every other which tries to do the same. They are all conducted fundamentally as money-raising campaigns, in which meeting the budget is the first consideration, that of accomplishing what the budget is for, the second consideration, and enhancing Jewish life as a whole is no consideration whatever.

What is chiefly lacking in all our Jewish activities is psychological Jewish unity, which can come only from the will to perpetuate Jewish life. Our fate as American Jews depends upon our ability to maintain our organic unity voluntarily, just as we had to maintain it in the past at the behest of non-Jewish governments. Hence Zionism's second line of action should be the reconstruction of the present local Jewish organizations and institutions into a network of organic Jewish communities.

To be organic they have to meet the following requirements: a) Those in charge of public Jewish activities should relate them integrally to the will of the Jewish people to perpetuate and enhance its life; b) All those activities should be carried on as departments of the entire local community, functioning democratically through its authorized representatives; c) Every individual Jew who wishes to identify himself with Jewish life should be made to feel at home in it, and d) All Jewish creative talent should be given

449

an opportunity for self-expression within the framework of the community.

The fate of American Judaism is now in the balance. Its future depends upon the ability of American Jewry to transform itself from an anonymous miscellany into a branch of the historic people of Israel. American Jews have not yet discovered what they should do to be authentic Jews. An authentic human being, we are told, is one who assumes the responsibilities, and risks of the situation in which fate places him.

We need Zionism in the Diaspora to motivate the Jew "to live to the full his condition as a Jew." To do that Zionism has to inaugurate simultaneously a two-pronged movement: one to retrieve the unity and solidarity of the Jewish people through the acceptance of a covenant which would define our status in relation to the rest of the world, and the other to infuse into the disparate regional aggregates of Jews the purposeful will to be transformed into healthily functioning organs of the living body of the Jewish people.

JEWISH CULTURE AND EDUCATION IN THE DIASPORA

By HAYIM GREENBERG

M Y SUBJECT TODAY is the problem of Jewish culture and education in the Diaspora. The Department I have conducted for the past two years[1] does not include the State of Israel in the scope of its activities. Our area of operations lies in the *galut* countries, and accordingly I must begin with a few remarks about the conception *galut* or exile.

In a sense, *galut* is an algebraic expression. Concretely, over the two thousand years of our dispersion, we have had varying types of exile. Our sense of living in exile was not one and the same in all periods and in all countries. The acuteness and intensity of that feeling depended upon the particular environments and civilizations in which we lived. Jews everywhere might believe the old Midrashic saying: "Exile is hard, for it is equal to the weight of all the curses set forth in the Anathema," but in their concrete historical perspective, Jews differentiated between one exile and another. There were exiles that were worse, and others that were "better," so to speak; exiles in which Jews sensed their foreignness, helplessness, and state of outlawry with every fiber of their being, and other exiles in which they felt themselves partially rooted, or at least enjoyed the illusion of relative integration or adjustment.

Any country outside the dreamed-of land of Israel was exile for the Jew, yet over a period of generations Jews came to regard some of the lands of their dispersion with a sort of "at-homeness" in an alien environment. If it is a paradox, it is not one I have invented. History and social fact create their own paradoxes and ambi-

1 The Culture and Education Department of the World Zionist Organization.

451

valences. Portugal and the Netherlands, Spain and Turkey in the fifteenth and sixteenth centuries were all, in principle, exiles. Yet it was not mere accident that refugees fled from the Iberian peninsula to the Low Countries or to the Ottoman Empire. One exile offered the Inquisition and *autos da fe,* the other—tolerance and relative hospitality. In one exile were Marranos, in the other exile a process of "de-Marranization" took place, if such an expression may be permitted. In our time, too, every country of the Diaspora —every one without exception!—is *galut.* Even Israel itself was for many, many centuries, in essence, *galut.* Wherever Jews live as a minority, where they are not politically or socially independent and are subject to the everyday pressures of its civilization and mode of life, but rely on the good graces of the non-Jewish majority, such a place is *galut.* In this respect, the United States today and, let us say, Iraq, are both "exiles," in the broad psycho-historical sense. But the concrete difference between the two is unspeakably great. Jews are compelled to flee from Iraq; no one drives them out of any part of America. If, in a general sense, exile may be conceived of symbolically as night, then there are some exiles of pitch black night, and some where the night is moonlit.

In rough generalities, the exile complex of our day may be divided into three main areas.

The first zone of *galut* is that to which we have no access whatever and from which no one can emerge. Expulsion is a calamity in the life of a people; but in some situations it is a still greater torture to be incarcerated without any visible prospect of ever being freed. It would be a bitter jest if I were to pretend to outline any principles or methods for cultural activities among the Jews in the vastness of the hermetically sealed Soviet prison.

The second zone includes countries of a feudal and Islamic social structure and way of life. Jews are among the oldest inhabitants of those countries, but in none of them does any Jew today have a sense of security, and the roots they have struck there may be torn out by brutal hands at any moment. The Jews of those countries must depart as soon as possible from their step-motherlands and settle in Israel. Indeed, they are doing it before our very eyes, and we may hope that in a relatively short time they will break free from the intolerable situation to which they are doomed in that part of the world.

The United States and England are typical countries of the third zone of the *galut*. A very substantial part of our people today resides in Western countries with traditions of liberty, with a high order of civilization and technological development, with progressive economies creating sound opportunities for achieving in time modern standards of social justice. Those countries do not constitute for Jews the best of all possible worlds. But it would be wrong to say that Jews have not struck roots there, that they are totally unintegrated, or that they are faced with immediate threats to their existence. Jews have already attained there a degree of relative well-being economically, and though they are *socially* segregated to no small extent, still they are not regarded by the majority as "aliens" in the sense they are so branded in backward countries or countries experiencing the convulsions of a perverse nationalism.

As I have already remarked, I have no remedy for the Jewish communities in Russia and the Soviet satellite countries. They can neither appeal to us, nor can we bring them consolation and encouragement. The way is barred, and who knows when or how it will be reopened.

In the second zone—the Arabic-speaking countries, the Moslem area generally—our cultural tasks are not easy, but they are not too complex either. Our educational aims in that zone must be concentrated upon preparation for resettlement in Israel—language training, ideological, and also technical and professional readjustment. In that zone there are hardly any differences of opinion among Jews as to their situation and prospects. The State of Israel is their only aspiration.

However, we cannot apply the same simple approach to the third zone—the Jewish communities in the democratic West, and particularly the five million Jews of the United States. Mass emigration is not on the current agenda of American Jewry. You may adopt here as many resolutions as you please concerning the "ingathering of the exiles," asserting that it applies to the Western communities too, including American Jewry—Congress resolutions are not effective in creating either pressure or active will toward migration. American Jewry especially is far from a panic situation. There are Diaspora communities in a state of "self-liquidation," without benefit of Congress resolutions, "Jerusalem

Programs," or other exhortation. The Jewish community in the American *galut* is not today prepared to "liquidate" itself through migration to Israel. This does not mean that American Jews will never settle in Israel at all. It should not be interpreted as an assertion that a time can never arrive when a massive number of American Jews will become full participants in the drama of redemption which is unfolding in Israel. But it is not something to be achieved simply by adding a new paragraph to the Zionist *vade-mecum*.

I have heard this argument in the past few days: "You, American Jews, are an alien body in the organism of the American people; you are cherishing vain illusions; you forget that other Jews had the same illusions in other countries, and you know what happened to them." May I say here that such prognostications make no great impression on the average American Jew. He has no reason to consider his position as ideal, but he has become conditioned to believe that "It can't happen here." Not without justification, he regards the American Revolution as the most successful revolution in world history. He is prepared "to boast" that, even though political shifts occur in American affairs and occasionally threatening omens of reaction appear on the horizon, there never was an American counter-revolution, nor does any prospect of one appear in the future, at least as indicated in present realities. He persuades himself that America shows a rational patriotism, but none of that nationalistic mythology that led Germany astray, making it drunk and toxic with political idolatry.

Such a typical American Jew may be wrong, unrealistic, and you may say that in his blindness he fails to note the handwriting on the wall. Others may be convinced that their prognosis is the correct one, that Western Jewry generally, and American Jewry in particular, face more or less the same dangers that befell so large a part of European Jewry, but no one can make him feel these threats as actual. May I add one thing more? It is difficult to refute the argument that if America is doomed in time to become a land of Fascist anti-Semitism, a Gehenna for its millions of Jews, then there may be no safety even in timely flight to the Jewish State. If we should ever see a bestialized America, how long could the State of Israel exist in a world which could produce such a monster, even should Israel's population be increased by several million Jews? There is no room for redemption in a monstrous world, amidst universal wickedness. If the time ever comes, as I believe it will, when considerable numbers of American Jews will go to live in Israel, they will do so not because America will have ejected them, but out of Israel's attraction and inspiration. Not in fear, but in love. At the present time, I can see no such trend in American-Jewish life. Zionism has not become a matter of direct personal bearing for the bulk of American Jewry, nor will it become such a matter unless the younger generation receives a deeper and more organic Jewish education in coming years. The same may be said, with certain modifications, concerning the Jews in a number of other countries of the democratic West, where a flow of Aliya may be hoped for, but where propaganda for mass *flight* would be utterly meaningless.

Whoever enjoys futile gestures may adopt a tone of simple, very simple, Zionist "consistency" and address American Jews in such terms as these: "Have no fond illusions that you are Americans; the genuine Americans regard you as *strangers;* you are not an organic part of the American scene, and your citizenship, in the final analysis, hardly amounts to anything; better make up your minds to leave America as soon as possible, and if you can not arrange your transport to Israel at once, seriously consider yourselves in the meantime as potential Israelis, and educate your children toward the objective of migration." This would be an appeal for the mental "denaturalization" of American Jews. If anyone feels entitled to demand this of American Jews, or even only of American Zionists, then let him take consistency a step further and say: "Be honest with yourselves and with your non-Jewish neighbors, and do not keep a double set of accounts. You are not, and can never hope to be, an accepted part of America, and therefore you ought to act already as 'temporary sojourners' in the country. Accept no nominations to Congress or the State legislatures. Occupy no governorships, Supreme Court seats, or other magistracies. Accept no professorships in American colleges and universities. Recall from their posts the thousands of Jewish men and women teaching in municipal schools and sharing, whether for good or ill, in molding the character of American youth. Do no service on the police force, accept no commissions in the American army, refrain from participating in American journalism and literature, in art, theater and music. Take no stand on political questions. In short, become denaturalized yourself, if not technically, then at least morally, socially, and intellectually." This, at least, would be complete doctrinal consistency, but I have yet to see a delegate at this Congress with "courage" enough to make such a demand on American Jewry, and we can all learn something from that lack of courage. . . .

It is an easy transition for me to pass to another proposition which should not arouse controversy among us, if we do not adhere to fruitless dogmatism. The American Jew (and wherever I use the word "American," my remarks might equally well be applied to a number of other Western countries) is bound by objective circumstances to live in a certain cultural dualism which must naturally be reflected in his educational processes. Culturally, he is at one and the same time both an American and a Jew. Whoever wishes may argue that such a dualism is unhealthy, "abnormal." Cultural monism may be regarded as a much more normal condition than a person's living in the spheres of two cultures. But none of us has the power to create monistic wholeness by decree. A certain degree of cultural integration with the milieu is inevitable for Jews wherever they live as a minority in a country of high civilization, and criteria of "normality" and "abnormality" are irrelevant when applied to situations of objective inevitability. A restricted monotonous diet is, generally speaking, "abnormal"; but it becomes "normal" for people with disorders that require them to abstain from certain foods, or to take certain foods in concentrated amounts. Of course, the degree of cultural integration I have referred to involves considerable danger of assimilation, but in a *galut* situation there is always such danger, and we already agreed to classify the West (including America) as *galut,* though of a different sort than the one of Morocco or Iran. Now, in order to avoid harmful complexes as well as conflicts with their environment, Jews in the West must clearly and boldly declare their cultural dualism and uphold its legitimacy. If some see in this a "double set of accounts," we need not argue over terms and expressions. I am prepared to accept this description. What causes friction and trouble are not so much "double" or parallel accounts, as the keeping of *secret* accounts. The American Jew has the right to identify himself as a Jew, to live a Jewish cultural life (if he possesses the necessary vitality and content), to preserve and, if he can, revitalize his own cultural values, all on one condition: if he does it openly, if he makes no secret of it, if he tells his non-Jewish fellow-citizens about it in all honesty. I would deplore the spiritual and moral fate of any country that imposed among the duties of citizenship an obligation of "amnesia," of becoming oblivious of oneself, of erasing one's memories, one's past, one's intimate group relationships. I know that no man of sense in America demands from American Jews such a spiritual suicide, a self-abduction from the Jewish folk from which he stems.

In the West we face no problem of combating assimilation as a dictum imposed from above or from "around," nor even as a formal ideology among Jews. The chief danger is that of plain indifference to the whole matter of being a Jew. Zionism as such, or rather merely platonic Zionism—which is no less platonic even when it takes the form of helping Israel from a distance—is not enough to stimulate the will in Jews outside Israel to live as Jews, to have a taste for Jewish life and sense a meaning in it. If one is not to be indifferent to Jewish survival and to one's own belonging to Jewry, one must be imbued with the content and values of Jewish culture and Jewish spirit. This cannot be achieved by propaganda. It demands a more fundamental and organic Jewish education than is given to a great portion of Western Jewry in our time. From the standpoint of Jewish survival in the West, consequently, education to "Jewishness" is far more vital than what we call specifically "Zionist education." One can never be a "Zionist by will" (in contrast to a merely sentimental Zionist) if one is not a "Jew by will," if one lacks the awareness of participating in the long, dramatic history of being a Jew.

The living Israel is, naturally, a far more effective stimulus for Diaspora Jews in strengthening the will to maintain and cultivate their Jewish identity than is Zionism as a doctrine or a *Weltanschauung*. But the influence of present-day Israel can be a fertilizing factor for Jewish cultural life in the Diaspora only on one condition: if the civilization of Israel should lean on certain, so to speak, *extra-geographical* elements in traditional Jewish culture, elements that have shown their ability to survive without the support and nourishment of a national soil.

I find it hard to express this point clearly, and I should like as far as possible to avoid using abstract or philosophical terms. In a

457

sense one may say that the Jews have for many centuries—throughout the so-called *galut* period—lived more in the sphere of *time* than in the sphere of *space,* or perhaps more in the sphere of "music" than in the sphere of the "plastic." Plastic art is quite inconceivable apart from space. A painting, a sculptural or architectural work, must occupy room or ground; a melody is spaceless. Basically, it has no way of grasping what space is; it exists, moves, and makes its way in the dimension of time. In a symbolic sense, Jewish culture was more of the historical and musical type than of the geographic and plastic type, and from this point of view, until a few generations ago, the *galut* was perhaps the only example in history (at any rate, the most prominent example) of an ex-territorial civilization. Undoubtedly, a civilization without a soil of its own, without territorial bounds, is from many angles an abnormal phenomenon. But Jews were successful in *sublimating* this abnormality. They brought something with them into exile which I might seek to compare, if I were a poet, to Father Jacob's visionary (yet still real) ladder, which requires no more space than a ladder needs for its support in order to reach heaven ("a ladder set up on the earth and the top of it reached to heaven"). And who can say today, looking backwards, that the almost fantastic history of the Jew was without significance, or dull or fruitless? Upon vast expanses of time and out of nothing more apparently than memories, strivings and aspirations, our people created such grand structures as the Babylonian Talmud, the palaces of Kabbalah and Hasidism, the gardens of medieval philosophy and poetry, the self-discipline and inspirational ritualism of the *Shulchan Aruch,* the color and aroma of Sabbaths and holidays. All these to a great extent are creations of the *galut,* ex-territorial conquests, and however onerous was our isolation from the world we lived in, still it gave us a sense of aristocratic exclusiveness, of lineage, of superiority. We were without territory—yet possessed of clear and fixed boundaries that Jews devotedly guarded; without armies—and yet so much heroism; without a Temple—and yet so much sanctity; without priesthood—and yet each Jew, in effect, a priest; without kingship—and yet with such unexcelled spiritual "sovereignty." Should we be ashamed of the exile? I am proud of it, and if *galut* was a calamity (who can pretend it was not?), I am proud of what we were able to perform in that calamity. Let others be ashamed of what they did to us in exile. We have every reason to consider our exilic past with heads proudly lifted. None of us would idealize a prison; but let those be ashamed who torment in prisons the better representatives of mankind, not those captives who in the darkness of their prison cell were inspired to compose paeans to freedom and truth.

True, the *galut* in which Jews live today is no longer that in which they lived so many generations in the past. The Jewish capacity for living creatively, as a people, in the sphere of time alone has been sadly depleted. This is not the place nor the time to analyze the historical causes that deprived us of that rather unique capacity. But we know—and this is one of the most important elements of the Zionist idea—that not only our political and socio-economic position in many countries of the Diaspora, but also our spiritual and cultural situation everywhere demand that we resume national life in the sphere of space, of territorial rootedness, and of political independence. It is needless to explain to a Zionist Congress that without such a return to the soil, without building anew a Jewish "landscape," we face a general withering of our spiritual life. The spiritual "Jewish problem" was by no means the least among the factors that gave force and momentum to the Zionist movement and to the actual building of Zion.

I would be less than honest with you if I failed to note in a few words a new spiritual danger which may arise from the accentuation—or rather, the hyper-emphasis—of our new *orientation toward space*. In some circles one no longer talks of *Jewish culture* but of *Israeli culture*. This term is used (perhaps only in restricted circles) with clear reference to the State, as though in the three and a half years of its existence there has already arisen a characteristic or original culture of the State of Israel. I do not intend now to discuss the general relations between State and culture. A state can stir and quicken a people's spirit and establish a sound environment for its cultural development; but sometimes a state can also throttle, degrade, and stultify a people's spiritual life. It depends on what sort of state it is, what it does with its citizens, or, more properly perhaps, what its citizens do with it. But the best of states, even the ideal one, has no power to produce an original or characteristic culture of its own in a few years' time. Least of all does it possess this power if it regards itself as an end in itself, if it apotheosizes itself and cuts itself off from the spiritual history of its people, from its past, and from the values created in the past. When I hear so frequently the verse "For from Zion shall go forth the Torah" reverently quoted with reference to the Zion of our day, to the present State in Zion, I too believe, as others do, that new and lofty cultural values will in time be created here—values of universal scope and significance. But for the present I should rather rephrase it to say "For from Zion *went forth* the Torah"; a Torah once came forth from this land, and in virtue of that Torah later Jews, generation upon generation, in one exile after another, created spiritual values which bear the stamp of creative effort and achievement. Those values and the psychic energies embodied in them must continue to be cultivated on the soil of the State of Israel, no doubt in new forms, with new stresses, and by different methods; they must be the foundation of that new civilization that is beginning—with much severer birth-pangs than many of us preferred to imagine—to emerge in the State of Israel. There will be no culture of tomorrow without a culture of yesterday and of the remoter past, unless we want to reconcile ourselves to a shallow pseudo-cultural style attuned to the local ethnography and narrow horizons of a small irritably nationalistic state.

But our cultural history of the recent and remote past is stocked with elements bearing the stamp "Made in *galut*." Should we refuse to recognize them because of this stamp? I pose this question not because I attach great weight to such a pathological phenomenon as the small group of "Canaanites" with their *penchant* for a "Blood and Soil" nationalism, for a futurism that pretends to find support in ancient Semitic paganism. A trace of this lunatic "Canaanitism" is to be found among other, far broader and by no means clinical groups, and its presence is enough to indicate certain perils. It is from these quarters that arises a contempt for the recent Jewish past in the *galut*, for the so-called ghetto Jew, his style, his values, his way of life; that contempt to which not long ago an Israeli Hebrew writer devoted a pamphlet of such signal brilliance. I refer to Kariv and to his book—*Adabera Ve-Yirvah Li* ("Let me speak out and I will be eased"). At bottom, it's an appeal for renewed Hebrew humanism, failing which the civilization of the State of Israel may be led into false and sterile paths and prove incapable of exercising any significant cultural influence upon Jewish life abroad.

During these few days of the Congress we have heard several times the slogan of "Hebraizing the *galut*." I need hardly declare here that such a slogan is far from strange to me and my like. I accept it with all my heart, but what is its substantial content and aim? Simply to diffuse knowledge of the Hebrew language in Diaspora countries, primarily because it is today the official language of a Jewish state? This, too, is certainly a worthy aim toward which we must all strive. But Hebrew has credentials that antedate the reborn Jewish State, and, as we all know, it is neither an accident nor the result of an individual's perseverance that Hebrew has won the position it enjoys, and today still displays such vigor and *élan,* such dynamic force and elasticity.

In our time, almost simultaneously with the Jewish State, one of the oldest and noblest nations in the world, India, also experienced its national rebirth. I am revealing nothing everyone here did not already know when I note that the official language of the Indian Union is still *English,* the language of the former occupying power, the invader, from whose yoke the great country has just been freed. India still lacks a common national language that could bind together all its provinces and ethnic components, even though the Indians—let us remember—lived continuously in their own land for the whole extent of their long history. Take a second example: Ireland. Nominally, independent Eire has its own official language, Gaelic. But, in fact, how many of the Irish can speak Gaelic? How large and how widely distributed is their Gaelic literature? In what language are their newspapers and journals published? What language is chiefly used in their Parliament? If there exists a "Friends of Gaelic" society, it cannot boast of any great accomplishments even in the period of full political independence, and English, the language of the historic "foe," is still actually the language of Ireland. The Irish, like the Jews, have their own Diaspora, and by no means a small one, but the several million Irishmen who live in their homeland have always lived there, have never emigrated, have been continuously rooted in their own soil and milieu. Why then were they unable to do for Gaelic what we did for Hebrew? We succeeded not because we are more skilled than they, but because Hebrew in all generations was our *sacred*

461

tongue, while Gaelic was never more for the Irish than a folk tongue, part of a local ethnographic culture. For many centuries, since the days of St. Patrick, the Irish sacred tongue was the same as in all Roman Catholic countries, the universal, denationalized Latin language, not their own tongue. Hebrew was able to exist for two thousand years, and not as a museum exhibit but as a functional organ, without state or territory, because the language itself was a kind of "territory," a spiritual *home,* and because the *pathos* of Jewish life and creativity, of inner Jewish struggles and victories was chiefly expressed in the Hebrew language. Hebrew in our own time has the power of becoming a secular vernacular—*not in spite* of, but *because* of the fact that for so many generations it was our sacred tongue. If Hebrew (together with its sister language, Aramaic, in certain periods) had not been the organ of sublimation in Jewish life, it would long have become a dead language. If one takes the modern Hebrew of Israel, of which we are so justly proud, it is not simply a fresh new growth sprouted "from the soil" in a few decades. Modern Hebrew would have been impossible if it had not sprung from the stock of *"galut* Hebrew"—the prose of Mendele Mocher Sforim the essay style of Ahad Ha-am, the poetry of Bialik, and the recreation of Sholom Aleichem by Berkovitz. But this *"galut* Hebrew" itself drew its sustenance from the depths of traditional Hebrew, from the *lingua sancta,* from a spiritual stream which contained much more than nationalism, from the Jewish reservoir of great collective and individual spiritual endeavors. Without that background—without the background of *Judaism* in the broad historical sense—Hebrew in Israel today, if it existed at all, would be a kind of Esperanto for immigrants bringing a Babel of tongues, perhaps no more than pidgin Hebrew. But, of course, without that background Zionism itself would probably not exist.

If my observations are generally correct, then they apply both to Israel and the Diaspora, and with particular force to the latter. The fundamental objective of Jewish education in the Diaspora is thus, in my view, not *Zionism,* in the specific or programmatic sense of the word, but *Jewishness.* Zionism should be the natural product of an organic education to Jewishness, the culmination, not the point of departure. Without such education, Zionism may be a doctrine, a convincing theory, a program, a plan, an undertaking of desperate urgency, an appeal to sentiment, a noble humanitarian enterprise, but not a profound creative experience. Hebrew is naturally a very, very important element in this sort of education, but I should prefer to use the term "Hebraism" rather than "Hebrew." I use the word *Hebraism* here not in that polemical sense which in our time signifies an extreme language preference, a purely linguistic shibboleth, but in the same way that I should use such a term, for example, as *Hellenism*. Hellenism is more than the Greek language, more than ancient Grecian mythology or religion, more than the art of Greek antiquity. It is a current in the infinite ocean of mankind's searchings, of humanity's passionate will to find security within itself, an anchorage in the cosmos of its striving toward truth, beauty, and harmony. Judaism, too, is such a mighty current. All civilizations, even the greatest and most sumptuous, are more experiment than consummation. But a viable civilization, one that has not reached exhaustion in its experimenting with itself and still contains potentialities of self-renewal, rejuvenation, and new modulations, should rather be compared to a melody than to a sculpture. Ancient Egyptian civilization, for instance, has long been no more than statuary which can produce no new life. It has more archeological than historical significance. We have every reason to regard Judaism not in terms of a completed plastic "petrification" but in terms of melody, and melody—precisely because the "area" of its existence is time—has in principle an unending continuity. There is always room for possible variations, even for creative mutations, deviations, and complementary contrasts, for new experiments upon itself, but such experiments as do not lose their link (their "memory") with the past, and with those forces that created the past.

That brings us, willingly or not, to the question of religion and religious tradition in Judaism. The tribune from which I speak today is not the safest nor the most detached forum for discussing questions of religion. But religion is not something sealed away somewhere in private seclusion, without relation to a people's, or to humanity's culture. Religion is itself culture, and I am inclined to believe that, potentially, it is indeed the peak of all possible cultural achievement. I should not wish to speak at length on the subject, but it has so transpired that Judaism, Jewish culture, was chiefly religious in its most significant manifestations. In other words, the archetypal motivation of the Jewish people, its struggles with itself, with the "despotism" of nature, and the pressures of "the peoples of the world," sought religious channels, religious implements, and religious forms for their expression. The chief tensions of the Jewish collective psyche were religious, its energies spoke to themselves and to the world of their ethical-religious drama, a sacred tongue. Abstract from the skein of our fate the strand of religious drama, especially in our long, martyred exile, and any attempt to interpret Jewish history becomes senseless. Jewish life over the past two thousand years was either a mystery (and a mystery has meaning and destination) or a misunderstanding. I assume that it was a mystery, and I would be sorry for Zionism, for the whole idea of Jewish renaissance, if it could be regarded as the product of something incongruous, of an historical *faux pas*. I have compared Judaism to a melody. If I should be held to this analogy, the Genesis is the prelude to that melody, the Messianic era (in the striving toward it, not in achieved historical reality) its epilogue, while "Let there be!" is its recurrent refrain. Thus it is quite unnecessary to be religious in a dogmatic or institutional sense of the word, to be orthodox—if I were to use American parlance, I should say it is unnecessary to be a fundamentalist—in order to recognize the inseparable significance in our future folk education of the cultural embodiments of the Jewish religious genius.

I am far from being unappreciative of the importance of diffusing in the Diaspora, not to speak in Israel itself, the knowledge of Hebrew, modern, spoken, so to say, practical Hebrew. I see in this, first of all, a sort of "social cement," a bridge or social medium of contact between Jews in Israel and Jews abroad, as well as between Israeli Jews themselves, speaking as they do such a multitude of languages brought over from their old homes. But may I be permitted to say that a Jew who can name all the plants in Israel in Hebrew, or call all the parts of a tractor or some other complicated machine by their correct designations (in new Hebrew coinages) possesses one qualification for useful service in the State of Israel. And who among us could fail to see in this not merely a technical or utilitarian but a cultural value as well? But if he does not know to their deepest sounding, and in their context of spiritual tensions, such Hebrew expressions as *mitzvah, averah, Geulah, tikkun, tum'ah, taharah, yirah, ahavah, tzedakah, hesed, mesirut nefesh, kiddush Ha-shem, d'vekut, teshuvah,* he cannot carry a part in that choir that gives voice, consciously or not, to what I have called "the Jewish melody." Even so-called secular Jewish education in Israel and the *galut* as well, if it is not to be drained of those powers that build a Jewish personality, must therefore be nourished from sources which are regarded, at least formally, as religious.

I do not propose a detailed practical program, nor a curriculum for Jewish schools. It is much to be doubted whether I am the man for such a task. I have simply tried today, perhaps too abstractly, to sketch the lines along which our thought should be directed. The Hebrew language must naturally occupy a central place in our whole folk pedagogy; there can be no "Hebraism" without a sound background in Hebrew. This does not mean, however, that in my opinion we should use in our educational processes Hebrew exclusively, or that we must wait until the bulk of the people will wish, and be able, to learn Hebrew in such a measure that the language becomes a source of "enjoyment," without which genuine spiritual experience is impossible. In conveying the values of what I call "Hebraism," at various stages and to various strata of our people in *galut,* we shall have to use other languages, too. Regardless of what fate may hold in store for it in the future, we shall have to use Yiddish, too, for those Jews to whom the language still has an organic intimate relation, making them receptive to cultural influences. We shall also have to use non-Jewish languages, foreign to Jews as a collectivity but native to or fully acquired by millions of individual Jews who live and grow spiritually through them.

Such earnest, deep plowing, cultural work permeated with Jewish individuality will in time, I am certain, bring forth a profounder Zionism, an appreciation of our historic drama, and an active will to play a role in it. It will lead even to *halutzism* which will draw its strength from the depths of Jewish being. Only such an organic and wide-ranging educational program can create in the *galut* the inner resolution to identify oneself in full, in act, with the grand process of Jewish revival, which has begun to unfold in our time on the soil of Israel.

Such a program is not easy. It cannot be accomplished or even adequately prepared overnight. No one in this hall, perhaps, knows better than I how great are the difficulties of carrying out such a task in the Diaspora. More than once in the course of the work one feels as if pouring wine into a broken cask. But I believe that without this work Zionism is doomed, especially in the advanced and free lands of the West, to become ever drabber, duller, more anemic and withered. With such a program, Zionism has every chance to open a new, grand chapter in its history.

In the final historical analysis, the State of Israel should be interested in the spiritual growth of Diaspora Jewry, no less than the Jews of the *galut* themselves. All Jewish roads—sooner or later, directly or indirectly, with landmarks or without them—lead to the same destination: to Eretz Yisrael.

AMERICA IS NOT BABYLONIA

By TRUDE WEISS-ROSMARIN

NEXT YEAR THE American-Jewish community will mark its three hundreth anniversary. Appropriately, advance planning and preparations for the observance of this milestone are already under way. According to the American Jewish Tercentenary Committee, there will be concerted efforts made to acquaint American Jews with the history of their community, while simultaneously impressing upon all the people of the United States what Jews have contributed to the greatness of this country.

One need not be a prophet to foretell that at the many hundreds of American-Jewish tercentenary celebrations, which will be held in communities large and small, the festival orators will hail the American-Jewish community as the successor to the great Jewish centers of the past. Once again, the lecturers will wax eloquent comparing Babylonia, during the talmudic period, to the American-Jewish community. Again the thesis will be advanced that just as, fifteen hundred years ago, the Babylonian-Jewish community produced the *Babylonian* Talmud, simultaneous with the analogous effort of the Eretz Yisrael community, which created the *Jerusalemian* Talmud, so in our day, too, there is room and scope for *two* creative Jewries, Israel and American Jewry, almost six million strong and thus the largest and most powerful Diaspora Jewry thus far.

At first blush the postulation of Jewishly creative centers in the Diaspora seems incontrovertible. It certainly is a fact that the bulk of Jewish culture and literature was created on foreign soil, as it were. There is no denying that the *Babylonian* Talmud is more extensive than its *Jerusalemian* counterpart and plays the domi-

467

nant role. As for the contribution of the Spanish center and its outposts, which reached as far as Egypt, where Maimonides among others found refuge, the fame of its poetry and philosophy, to say nothing of its contribution to biblical and talmudic exegesis, Hebrew grammar and philology, Jewish historiography and lexicography provides a rewarding topic for students of any of the many fields cultivated by the choice spirits of the medieval Golden Era of Hebrew literature. Last in the chronological order but by no means least in importance, there was the great Eastern European Jewish center, which was destroyed by the Nazis and the Communists. It was there that the many trends and legacies of the past became fused into the organically integrated *Yiddishkeit* from which the Zionist renaissance of Hebrew letters drew, and still draws, its sustenance.

More than two-thirds of Jewish history has been enacted in the Diaspora. For two thousand years, and more, Jewish communities have flourished and prospered in all the many countries which successively starred in the limelight of the world's stage. Virtually all of these Jewish communities wrote *their* pages into the book of creative Jewish survival—pages which will retain their succinct importance for all Jewish generations to come. One and all these Jewish centers of gravity were eventually annihilated, but the pages they wrote survive—and will live amidst our people.

American Jewry—almost six million strong—is the largest and most prosperous Diaspora community thus far. It would be gratuitous to stress that if not for the political and financial aid of American Jewry, there would be no State of Israel. There is no need either to point out that, despite the emphasis on philanthropy and community relations, American Jewry is alert to the claims of the Jewish cultural legacy and is aware of the obligation to the heritage from the past. American-Jewish education has come a long way since the days of the *melamed* and the *cheder*. There are over 150 Jewish day schools and many hundreds of good afternoon Hebrew schools. There are seminaries training rabbis and teachers—and there are even a handful of "American-born" scholars and writers who produce scholarly and popular books in all fields of Jewish scholarship and on all facets of the Jewish question. In a word, the American-Jewish community is astir and throbbing with activities aiming at creating a Jewish Cultural Center on American soil.

But what about the future? Does the American-Jewish community possess those traits and characteristics which, as we know from the experience of a dozen Diaspora communities over two thousand years, are indispensable for the growth of the kind of Jewish integration and the stamina that gave rise to the Babylonian Talmud, the Hebrew literature in Spain, the Eastern European culture of Hasidism, the Gaon of Vilna, Peretz, Mendele and Sholom Aleichem, and Bialik, Ahad Ha-am, and the galaxy of the writers of the Modern Hebrew Renaissance? Is the situation of the American-Jewish community such that it provides *reasonable* grounds for the expectation that in due time American Jewry will create a Jewish culture of its own, which will form another link in the golden chain of creative Jewish eternity?

The three centuries of American-Jewish history have been marked by three waves of Jewish immigration: the Sephardic group, in the first third of this span, the German group, in the second third, principally, and the Polish-Russian flood-tide, starting with 1882. Of course, there was a trickle of German-Jewish immigrants to these shores also before 1848 and small numbers of Jews from Russia and Poland had settled here before 1882, and Jews from many European countries arrived after the rise of the Nazis in 1933. But for the diagnostic aim of the student of American-Jewish survival prospects it suffices to focus the investigation upon the three major and clearly marked waves of Jewish settlers in this country.

Together with the American-Jewish tercentenary, the oldest synagogue in this country, Congregation Shearit Israel, will mark its three hundreth anniversary. The twenty-three Jews who arrived in New Amsterdam, in 1654, were not only the Founding Fathers of American Jewry but also the organizers of Congregation Shearit Israel. Established by Sephardic Jews, Congregation Shearit Israel is still a Sephardic synagogue adhering to the Sephardic ritual. But the members of Shearit Israel with the exception of a mere handful, are not Sephardic Jews, descendants of those who founded the congregation and those who joined it in the first century of its existence. In other parts of this country, too, there are synagogues of Sephardic antecedents and histories of two centuries and more. The rosters of those congregations, too, no longer contain the

Spanish and Portuguese names which figured so prominently in their early records.

What, then, has become of the Jews of Spanish and Portuguese origin who settled here in the second half of the seventeenth century and the first half of the eighteenth century? They intermarried and left the ancestral community, either by the formal step of baptism or by the no less effective step of unidentification—and thus they left no trace and no memory, except tombstones in a few old cemeteries and some entries in the vital statistics records of a few congregations.

The failure of the German revolution of 1848 and the wave of anti-Semitism which followed it was fortuitously timed for American-Jewish survival. For, by the middle of the nineteenth century, the fortunes of the American-Jewish community were at a low ebb. The Sephardic group had become virtually extinct and there were none to take their places—when unexpected help came from the "German Reaction."

The German Jews—the *Yahudim*—took over where the *Sephardim* had defaulted. But in the nineteenth century life moved at a quicker pace than in the seventeenth and in the eighteenth centuries. The steamboat had supplanted the sailship and the railroad had taken the place of the stage-coach. Traveling time was cut in half, or less. In tune with the new tempo, the German Jews required but decades for achieving the kind of assimilation, which it had taken the Sephardic Jews a century, and more, to attain. By the end of the century, the children and grandchildren of the 1848'ers had already strayed too far from the Jewish community to keep it alive.

And again Jewish tragedy in Europe infused new life into the American-Jewish community. The Russian pogroms and persecutions of 1881 released a flood-tide of refugees. The mass immigration from Eastern Europe began and continued up to the First World War. The Eastern European Jews took over, although some strongholds of power remained in the hands of a small élite of the *Yahudim*.

"The Americanization" of the Eastern European Jews took place so close to our own day and there are so many records of how the process was affected that we have an excellent insight into what occured. Unlike the Sephardic and German Jews, the Eastern

European Jews came here with their own Jewish language—Yiddish. And unlike the Sephardic and German Jews, who came from Jewishly attenuated climates, the Eastern European Jew arrived here with all the riches of a Jewishly integrated community. It is no accident that the beginnings of virtually all Jewish cultural endeavors in this country coincide with the arrival of the Eastern European Jews. They established Yiddish papers and laid the foundations for Hebrew publishing efforts in this country. They organized schools and seminaries, established political and cultural organizations; they created the variegated institutions of American-Jewish life as a projection of their own strong and integrated Jewishness.

Less than half a century has passed since the Eastern European wave of Jewish immigration approached its crest. The bulk of American Jewry are either children or grandchildren of those who came here between 1882 and 1922.

Compared to their Sephardic and German-Jewish predecessors, the Eastern European Jews have done valiantly in creating here a vital Jewish atmosphere. But, then, they came much better equipped, Jewishly speaking. They actually transferred here a center of Jewish survival strength and did not have to grope their way toward developing forms and institutions of Jewish living. They brought here what they had created in Europe.

America is "a country that consumes" its Jews, annihilating their distinctiveness in the great melting pot. Little by little the huge Jewish capital of the Eastern European Jewish immigration was frittered away. First to go was their Jewish language—Yiddish. The second generation still could speak Yiddish, although not read and write it. The third generation understands but a few Yiddish catch phrases. It is for them that such travesties as "Bagels and Yox" and the "Jewish humor" of a Sam Levenson are made to order. Next to go was Jewish religious observance. "This is America," where an Orthodox congregation lays title to Orthodoxy because its rabbi is Orthodox. As for the members, they desecrate the Sabbath and violate the dietary laws with the conviction that they may do so because "this is America," where a Jew is Orthodox if he is a member of a congregation that has an Orthodox rabbi.

Together with the Yiddish language and religious observance went the ideal of Torah study. "This is America," where when a boy doesn't do well at his Jewish studies, Father tells Mother, "It doesn't matter—after all, he won't be a rabbi."

And so the aim of Jewish education is to be able to recite the *haftarah* and the Bar Mitzvah speech. Although statistics show that about 60 per cent of all American-Jewish children attend a Jewish school at some time during their public career, this figure is misleading because the majority attend Sunday schools, where no Hebrew is taught, and all but 3 per cent of those who come into contact with Jewish education, at one time or other, do not attend sufficiently long to graduate. The vast majority of Jewish children who attend the afternoon and Sunday congregational schools never progress beyond the English retelling of Genesis and Exodus. The Jewish publishing field reflects this situation tellingly. There are scores of textbooks for the most elementary level but almost none for the junior high- and high-school level. The same applies to Jewish children's books. They are mostly geared to the kindergarten and first- and second-grade level. The writers of Jewish children books and their publishers have been chastened by experience and so they concentrate their efforts on the pre-school child or on the first-grader who is still being read to.

There are the Jewish day schools as an oasis in the great desert of American-Jewish education. These schools give their pupils a sound foundation in biblical and modern Hebrew, as well as a taste of the Talmud. But when all is said for the Jewish day schools —and everything speaks in their favor—there yet remains the fact that their graduates, with the exception of the few who enter rabbinical and teachers training schools, lay aside their Hebrew books. Despite the truly sacrificial efforts of the Histadruth Ivrith of raising a new generation of Hebrew readers by getting them used to Hebrew periodicals, through special magazines and books for young children and older students as well, there are no indications that the graduates of the Jewish day schools graduate *into* the living stream of Hebrew culture. The difficulty with which publishers of Hebrew books have to contend—and the lack of support of the Israeli Hebrew-book market on the part of American Jews—seem to prove that, thus far, the results achieved by the Jewish day schools, the Hebrew summer camps and kindred efforts are but skin deep—and this is in no way a reflection on the great dedication and sacrificial devotion of those who direct and guide these efforts.

What about the works of Jewish scholarship and expositions of Jewish thought produced in this country? Many of these works set standards which favorably compare with the choicest fruits of the *Wissenschaft des Judentums,* in the German language, and the *Hochmath Yisroel* literature in Hebrew. Written by specialists and for specialists, most of these books, particularly those in Hebrew and Yiddish, are not even known by name to the rank and file of American Jews. As for popular expositions of Jewish history and thought, the fact that there is not one Jewish publishing house in this country which can exist on the proceeds of publishing, not suplemented by the selling of textbooks and ritual articles, proves eloquently that, thus far, the Jewish book has made no impact on the Jewish masses.

As for the scholars and writers who produce American-Jewish books for the adult audience, most of them are products of the Eastern European Jewish center. They came to this country after completing their education in Europe. Most of them merely continued to pursue here the scholarly and literary careers that had been cut short for them in Europe. But there are also a few American-born Jewish scholars, some of whom write Hebrew with ease. So perhaps America can produce Jewish culture, after all? Upon investigating the backgrounds of the few American-born Jewish scholars and writers one discovers that virtually all of them grew up in a home environment that was completely Eastern European. Yiddish was their first language, they attended either an East Side *yeshiva* or a Talmud Torah of the intensive type. They were born *in* America but the environment in which they were nurtured was not *of* America.

And it is here that the crux of the problem lies. All "Jewish Centers of Gravity" of the past were self-contained. Jews lived *in* Babylonia, but although they flourished there for almost a thousand years they never became integrated into the Babylonian, or later the Persian, fabric to the extent where they were actually *of* the woof and warp of the country's spiritual pattern. In point of fact, even politically the Babylonian-Jewish community was not integrated with the rest of the population. They always remained "strangers in a land not theirs." They had their own Jewish self-

473

government under the sway of the "Head of the Dispersion." And they had their own courts of law, where the judges ruled according to Jewish law, not the law of the land. The much-quoted and much-misunderstood principle of *dina demalchutha dina*—the law of the land is binding for the Jew—only applies to general government decrees compulsory for all inhabitants, including the Jews. And, of course, the Jews of Babylonia spoke their own language. They were *in* Babylonia but never *of* Babylonia—and so they created a Jewish cultural center.

It was the same in all other Jewish cultural centers. Everywhere the Jews lived *in* the respective country of their *exile,* but were not *of* it. To be sure, in the Spanish-Jewish setting the impact of Moslem culture and thought was so powerful that a Judah Halevi and a Maimonides had to write in Arabic in order to "Guide the Perplexed" of their time who no longer understood Hebrew. We do not know to what an extent their efforts of stemming assimilation were successful, but it is a fact that only those books of the Arabic-Jewish center have survived which were translated into Hebrew and thus were lifted out of their state of being part *of* the general cultural medium of expression into the sphere of Jewish separateness *in* Moslem Spain but not *of* Moslem Spain.

And it was the same in Eastern Europe, too. Indeed, Rabbi Israel Baal Shem Tov came to Hasidism in the forests of Russia. He was *in* the Russian countryside, but never *of* it. The Eastern European Jewish center was self-contained. Vilna was the Jerusalem of Lithuania not only figuratively speaking but factually. The Gaon of Vilna happened to be exiled to that corner, but it was never home to him—he never became part of it. He lived in Jerusalem. . . . The physical-geographic setting of his career was indeed Vilna, but he lived in Vilna the life of Jerusalem—and so did all Jews of Vilna, of Kovno, of Lublin, and of all the many cities, towns and villages of Eastern Europe where the Jews refused to become, or could not become, part of the general population and life pattern.

American Jews are proud of being fully and unconditionally part *of* America. They support "cultural pluralism," which makes it possible for the cultures of the minority groups to contribute their distinctive notes to the great American symphony. They side with those who stress that "another language," in *addition* to English, and "another culture," in *addition* to our common and shared

American culture, bring personal enrichment while guarding the American cultural climate against provincialism.

The theoory of "cultural pluralism" is sound, but well-reasoned theories do not always conform with the unpredictable realities of life. Notwithstanding the tacit acceptance of "cultural pluralism," American culture is such a jealous mistress that she will not tolerate any claims by another culture upon those under her sway. Moreover, American culture is so bewitchingly attractive that she need not even fight the would-be rivals put into the field by "cultural pluralism." She conquers and holds sway without effort.

The thesis of the possibility of "creative Jewish survival" in America is predicated on the *uncritical* acceptance of the universal validity of the principle of "cultural pluralism." But the histories of *all* cultural minorities on American soil prove that "dual cultural loyalties" persist only in the first generation of the immigrants for whom the American culture and the English language are an *acquired* culture and an *acquired* language learned in adulthood. For the second generation, born in America and trained in American schools, the American culture and the English language are the natural cultural habitat, whose bonds are so strong that a "minority culture" and a "second language" have simply no chance of *co*-existence.

The progressive attenuation of Jewishness and all areas of Jewish expression in this country over the past twenty-five years, during which the American-born group has increasingly taken over, proves conclusively that the chances for "creative Jewish survival" in America are nil. If *intelligent* Jewish identification, as distinguished from community relations and charitable identification, is at such a low ebb already now when but one generation has passed since the height of the immigration from Eastern Europe, what hopes dare we entertain for *sound* Jewishness and *adequate* Jewish literacy in the future?

Unlike the Jews of Babylonia, Moslem Spain, Eastern Europe and some other creative centers of Jewish gravity, American Jews do not wish to be apart and separate from their fellow Americans. The Jews of all previous creative centers of Jewish gravity were mindful of the fact that they must guard their Jewish separateness in order to survive. There is profound wisdom in the Jewish laws which justify their provisions with the formula *mipney hukkos hagoyim*—because the Gentiles do thus and thus, Jews must do differently, just to be different, just to be apart, just to be marked off in their Jewish individuality.

American Jews have neither an understanding nor sympathy for the frame of mind of the *mipney hukkos hagoyim* legislation. They want to be like all Americans, even at the cost of sacrificing fundamentals of Jewishness. It is characteristic of the orientation of the American-Jewish mind, that even such ardent Jewish survivalists as the Reconstructionists have excised the affirmation of "Jewish Chosenness" from their prayers because the doctrine of "Jewish Chosenness" is incompatible with American democracy, as they understand it.

In attempting an analogy between American Jewry and Jewish groups of the past, the Jewries of Babylonia, Moslem Spain and Eastern Europe do not satisfy the standards of resemblance and likeness on which such a comparison must be based. Those Jewries never attrained full and equal citizenship; they never regarded themselves, or were regarded, as part and parcel of the body politic of their respective countries. They were strangers in strange lands. Indeed, they prayed for the welfare of the countries that sheltered them, but they did not *love* them as their own countries; they did not love the countries of their sojourn as the American Jew *loves* with all his heart and soul his cherished country, America.

There is, then, no resemblance at all between American Jewry and the "centers of Jewish gravity" of the past. But there is a close resemblance between American Jewry and Alexandrian Jewry, of two thousand years ago, and German Jewry of the post-Mendelssohnian period.

Like American Jewry, which is not merely *in* America but fully a part *of* America, Alexandrian Jewry and German Jewry were unreservedly integrated with their respective majority groups and their cultures. *They had relinquished their own language,* even as American Jewry has. The bulk of Alexandrian Jews read the Bible, if they read it at all, in Greek—even as the German Jews read it in German, and American Jews read it in English, at best. Jewish scholarships in Alexandria, exemplified by Philo, was couched in the Greek language and had as its principle objective apologetic motives. The same was true of the German *Wissenschaft des Judentums,* whose medium was the German language and which

476

aimed at demonstrating that Jewish scholarship, properly presented, can hold its own in the company of other humanistic disciplines.

It is characteristic of the trend-and-direction of the creative Jewish genius that the works of Philo and of the scholars of the *Wissenschaft des Judentums,* in so far as they were not critical editions of Hebrew texts, did not become part of what is generally defined as "the Jewish legacy." If not for the Church and Christian scholars that preserved his books, it is doubtful whether Philo's works would have come down to us. The Jews ignored Philo, for his books had no relevance for the issues, problems and concerns that agitated integrated Jewish communities living their own lives, separate from the peoples in whose midst they experienced *exile.* Philo was at home in Alexandria, and because of this he could not bring a message to Jews who remained strangers in their many *exiles.*

The same was largely true of the representatives of the *Wissenschaft des Judentums,* especially of the second and third generation of scholars after Zunz. Even a Hermann Cohen, staunch upholder of Jewish tradition, was firmly convinced that Judaism and Germanism are so closely akin that they are virtually identical. Cohen, like Graetz, Steinschneider and Berliner, was a German patriot, glowing with love for the Fatherland. He anticipated by decades the current American-Jewish refrain that because of the kinship of the Hebrew democratic impulse and American democracy, one becomes a better American by being a loyal Jew—only he phrased it that one becomes a better German by being a loyal Jew. . . .

Students of Jewish demography know that if not for a constant influx from Eastern Europe, German Jewry would have become extinct long before the Nazis took over. Intermarriage and apostasy took a frightful toll of German Jewry in the post-Mendelssohnian century and a half. To be sure, there was a remarkable efflorescence of Jewish scholarship of the modern scientific orientation but, like the analogous efforts of American-Jewish scholars, the works of the *Wissenschaft des Judentums* were meant for specialists. The vast majority of German Jews felt bound to the Jewish community by a tenuous religious identification—the three days a year attendance at synagogue—by charitable endeavors and, of course, by the fight against anti-Semitism. Obviously, German Jewry was not a viable group, from the time of Mendelssohn on. It survived by the grace of constant blood transfusions from the strong and vital centers of Eastern Europe, which supplied the spiritual leadership of German Jewry and always mustered a new generation when intermarriage and apostasy had written impending doom on the wall.

American Zionists insist that "America is not *galut*"—and they are right. We do not know what tomorrow will bring, but certainly today America is home, genuine and beloved home, of close to six million Jews. They are *of* America as all Americans and resent, and justly so, any intimation that they are not like all Americans. For they are—they really are Americans, even in their unconcern about the future, *their* future in America.

Theories of "*galut* negation" sound nonsensical to American Jews. The reality—*their own reality*—is a living refutation of the thesis of "*galut* negation." As to the evidence adduced from the fate of other Jewish communities, American Jews react like every normal individual responds to the warning that others came to grief on the hazardous road he intends to take. *We shall succeed where others failed!* American Jews are convinced that they shall succeed in keeping America as their home, for ever and ever. And they are convinced that another Babylonian Talmud will be composed on American soil.

The massive evidence of Jewish history controverts this blithely optimistic view. Everything points to it that American Jewry will write a modern version of the Alexandrian Jewish chapter and add another page to the German chapter, as far as loss of Jewishness is concerned.

America is *not* Babylonia! American Jewry will not be able to survive creatively now that Jewish reinforcement from other parts can no longer be expected. Even "the bridge between American Jewry and Israel," should it *ever* be constructed, will not be able to turn New York into another Sura and Chicago into another Pumbeditha.

American Jewry is *American*—American through and through. Babylonian Jewry was never *Babylonian*. This is the difference—and this difference will determine the future of American Jewry.

WHITHER ISRAEL?

By HORACE M. KALLEN

WHAT JEW, BELIEVER or not, has not once in his life heard, or himself recited, either the 126th or the 137th Psalm, or both? Let me repeat them here, in a version somewhat different from the traditional one. First, Psalm 137:

By the rivers of Babylon, there we sat down.
  Yea, we wept when we remembered Zion.
We hanged our harps on the willows in their midst.
For there our captors required of us a new song.
Our ravishers demanded of us mirth.
They said: "Sing us one of the songs of Zion."

But how shall we sing the Lord's song in an alien land?
O, if I forget thee, Jerusalem, let my right hand forget her cunning;
If I fail to remember thee, let my tongue cleave to the roof of my mouth.
If I prefer not Jerusalem above my chief joy.

Rember Edom, God, that said "Raze it, raze Jerusalem to its very foundations."
O Babylon, destined to destruction, he will be happy who serves thee as thou hast served us,
Taking thy little ones, dashing them against the stones!

Turn from the helpless anger and bitterness of this poem to Psalm 126:

When God brought the exiles back to Zion, we were like men dreaming.
Then laughter filled our mouths and song came from our tongues.
Then it was said among the peoples, "Greatly hath God worked with this folk."

Greatly indeed hath God worked with us! and we rejoiced.
O Jehovah, bring back all our exiles as streams of water to the
Negeb!
Those who are sowing in tears shall reap in song,
He who weeping goes to the field, bearing the trailing seed,
Shall return thence, singing, carrying his sheaves.

Both poems are remembrances, set to music, and passed on from generation of Jews to generation, to be chanted again as tradition ordains, yet with never unvarying tone and accent. Psalm 126 is intoned at a dramatic point in the Seder ceremony. Together with Psalm 137 it fixes the poles of that axis of desire and frustration upon which revolves the enduring legend of the Jewish people. Whoever wrote Psalm 137 had obviously been an enforced exile from his homeland, victim and survivor of a war that destroyed the Jewish State and was followed by spiritual disruption in the community of exiles to whom the State was the force and form of the Jewish psyche. The author and his comrades were remembering a life that was no more. Their song was an endeavor so to reanimate a past as to nullify a present they could not accept. For the neighbor who had desired their dispersion, the foe who had worked it, they craved a fate as bitter.

Their song, together with Psalm 126, suggests something of the mood also of the Jews of our own time. There is, I think, a true analogy between the sentiment common to many twentieth-century Jewish communities and that of the exiles of close to six hundred years before the present era. In many lands of the globe, of which Israel is not the least, men and women of Jewish derivation are remembering an existence long dead, yearning to resurrect it, struggling with pitiful and ridiculous ardor to re-establish it as if it were not over and done with—as if recollection were event and event recollection.

Such quixotism is inveterate in the human psyche. It imparts its own singularity to the tragi-comedy of the human enterprise, whatever direction that take. Often noble, it is always regressive, like the wish to evade the responsibilities of the mature by assuming the ways of the child. But living beings cannot go back to infancy; at most they can live out adult years childishly. Indeed, there are schools of human psychology which argue that childish ways are the prevalent ways among the majority of mankind.

We need not, however, heed the sectarian fantasies of this or that school of psychology. It is enough to regard the activities and life-patterns of any human being, of any age in any place, as they come before us. They impress us firmly enough as events of a struggle to survive and grow, with its winning daily battles, suffering perennial defeat, never doing what is done once only, but ever again and again and again. We note continual searching and seeking to still the same wants by the same satisfactions, both changing as they repeat; both altering simply because they repeat, within and without. Only with death does this self-annulling victory come to its term.

Only the dead have no need to repeat, and to alter as they repeat. Only the dead don't change and can't change; that is, don't die; and only as dead are immortal.

The living are mortal. Their mortality lives in the circumstance that their present passes into their past and stays alive as their memories, which their future transforms. They are able to grow up and grow old because their past is a living past which the future enriches and reforms by entering. Remembering and living are not separate doings but a continuing activity seen now as image, and now as action. When any part of the living past is segregated and used for a mold which the future shall fill, it is experienced as an arrested movement, an image that on-going life leaves behind; it alters from a power into a burden, from a process of passage into a retaining wall.

The natural spontaneity of vital recollection has its variations. There are those which a student evinces when he is trying to repeat for his professor what the professor has said. There are those of the witness testifying, responding to lawyers who press him to remember this and not that. There are those of the painter painting from a model or projecting a remembered pattern on his canvas for himself alone. And there are many others—echoes, conformations, transpositions, projections, recreations and creations, together with all the yet unidentified spontaneous variations of which authentic, vital recollection consists. The most familiar occur as separations and isolations, dammings and rechannelings in momentary abstractions from the vital process whose topmost turn is the stream of consciousness.

When this process is healthy and whole, the future digests and contains the past as the sound body digests and contains its food and drink, rendering them living flesh of its flesh and bone of its bone. Isolation, segregation, abstraction have the effect, among others, of stoppage. They replace the natural multi-dimensional moving image with an unnatural mono-dimensional still.

Theologians and philosophers create and adore such stills. They appraise those abstractions as mankind's ultimate safety and certainty, by definition always and everywhere the same, which is to say, eternal, universal, supreme, ideal and—absolute. So defined, these reworkings from remembrances of things past are assigned another locus than the life process whence they are drawn, thence by grace to guarantee present safety and assurance. Their faithful invest them with values and meanings incommensurable alike to their derivation and their use. The investiture renders them objects of worship—fetishes, idols, gods, emptied of life by being exalted into immortal potencies.

Whatever the provocation, these are the reflections that the question, *Whither Israel?* first leads me to. Throughout the years that Israel has been the name of a historic people with a biography singular to itself, the image "Israel" that the psalmist mourned in Babylon, and the Zionist invokes in New York, has been little a living process, all too much a memory isolated and abstracted into an ideal, a vision of being, happy and high and noble, once possessed, never yet recovered, yet ever to be so recovered that the ideal might be fact again, and vision event.

Students of philosophy know, of course, even more than students of history, that ideals enacted are ideals corrupted, conceptions implemented are conceptions maculated, visions realized are visions disrupted. To keep your conceptions immaculate, don't employ them; to hold your vision intact, don't realize it; to retain your ideals, don't live up to them. Reality and its actualizations transform. They bring unforeseeable distortions and shocking shapes and colors. Their touch contaminates the eternal and universal with protean singularities of time and place. It impregnates their immaculacy with the vital corruption which alone can breed existence from conception. Whatever renders the ideal potent and fruitful deflowers it. To stay ideal is to stay sterile; and any ideal consolations and values must stay those intrinsic to sterility.

The ideal which "Israel" came predominantly to signalize was distilled out of the experiences of the exile. It was abstracted, isolated and established in Babylon, amid the lifeways and thoughtways composing the singularity of a victorious empire worshipping its victory-giving gods. The Hebraism of the prophets' urging was digested in the Judaism of Ezra's ordination, Nehemiah's enforcement, with its invidious distinctions, among others, between the people of the Ingathering and the people of the Dispersion.

Before that alteration, the lifeways and thoughtways of the Judean people had been a process shaped to a program consciously accepted and more or less successfully enacted—mostly less, otherwise there would have been no occasion for the prophets. What else was the word of any of them to the tribes of Judah and Israel, if not that they were failing to accomplish a plan of life and establish it as a life's way, and that dire consequences follow failure? What else do the deliverances of the best and greatest of the prophets whom we read in the Bible communicate?

And how do we think the record they assume and the program they prescribe, as the Bible records them? Certainly not in their totality as complete remembrance of things past directed toward the future. The totality enfolds much that, regarded in and by itself, would be unspeakable, unprintable. We think those data selectively, choosing from the compenetrated melange those which we feel most viable for our times, our places, our vital intention and personal integrity. The monotheism, the moralism, the divine election and the other stressed items of the Law and the Prophets are only portions of the record, and not the most comprehensive portions. There are also the priesthoods and their ways, the tribal customs and folkways and their prescriptions and taboos, the lusts and treacheries and cruelties of kings and nobles, the sufferings of the righteous and the prosperings of the wicked, the reciprocally contradictory claims of all to gratify the desires and obey the will of Jehovah. There is the aggregation of data which ethnologists, archeologists and sociologists study and appraise, which together with the Judaists' own diverse selection compose into that variegated assemblage of the record, and are further continued and varied as the Judaisms of Ezra and Nehemiah, of the Apocrypha and the Talmud, of Philo and Josephus, Judah Halevi and Maimonides, Crescas and Baal Shem Tov, Moses Mendelssohn and Theodor Herzl and Mordecai Kaplan.

The process consists in an indefinite, diverse, and diversifying coming together and compenetration of ideals and events, of faiths and things and forces. "Jew," "Israel," receive their manifoldly conflicting meanings from the fluid constellation of lifeways and thoughtways which this ingathering presents.

Thus, although some form of the word *together* here carries, for me, the meaning nuclear to "Jew," "Israel," it does not for the leaders or spokesmen of any sect or faction within the constellation which elects to monopolize those names for its own intentions. Claiming a mission, each for itself, they use the names both invidiously and tendenciously, as designations of a chosen cluster of memories and events, which they have abstracted from the moving aggregate, arrested and isolated. In the name of that cluster they then assume to signalize themselves as the chosen ones of the Chosen People, and for the entirety of the Jewish past to substitute their selections by which to shape a Jewish future. What Christians or Moslems or Nazis or Communists choose from that entirety to denote by the words "Jew," "Israel," is notoriously something else again.

Grounds of choice are as diverse, as manifold, as their times and occasions. Modernly, they are distinguishable into two not altogether exclusive groups. They may be called, without prejudice, "supernaturalist" and "humanist." There are also "supernaturalistic humanists" and "humanistic supernaturalists" in increasing numbers. But the gradient differences are signalized by the simpler divisions.

The supernaturalists form the Judaist variant of the pre-scientific tradition of Western culture. They sustain the organization and practice in Rabbinic Judaism which are intrinsic to a vital economy ordered to flattering, cajoling, coercing, bargaining, bribing or persuading supernatural power to preserve this economy and its members and to prosper their growth. The typical codex of this economy has long been the *Shulchan Aruch*, the compendium of prescriptions and prohibitions conforming behavior to supernatural requirements. To meet them is to merit salvation, to fail is to merit damnation, in the life to come.

As a lifeway, Judaism is in this of one fellowship with the world's other supernaturalisms. It is called "religion" because of this supernaturalism, not because of the act of faith which asserts the supernaturalism. When the act of faith is considered, it has no more claim on being appraised religious than man's attribution of saving power to any other object or idea.

Those who choose meanings for "Jew," "Israel," on humanist grounds appraise the supernaturalist orientation as one Jewish mode of man's adjustment to the changes and chances of a world no more made for him than for any other living thing. They set the supernaturalist doctrines and disciplines in the perspectives of human history and judge them by the consequences they in fact lead to. They understand the otherworldly providences which the supernaturalists postulate, the magic their ritual purports, the miracles they describe, as fear-created defenses against dangers felt to be insuperable, as lasting compensations in imagination for needs and hungers never in fact lastingly satisfied. Humanists apprehend supernaturalist realities as such stuff as dreams are made of, to be accounted for by the methods of the natural and social scientist, employing the insights of scientific psychology and the other sciences of man.

The numbers and kinds of Jews who have consciously chosen so to envisage and appraise the singularity of Israel are not very great, though perhaps proportionally greater than among others of the globe's peoples who look upon, remember and judge themselves.

That "perhaps," I suspect, is a very large "perhaps." Not alone during the pre-scientific ages of Western history, but also during the scientific nineteenth century the Jewish multitudes believed with a firm faith that Divine Providence had guaranteed the miraculous return of Israel to the Promised Land under the leadership of a Messiah, son of David, who in God's good time would, without force, without might, but by His spirit responding to magical rites, gather the exiles from all lands of their dispersion, into the land of Israel. Like these true believers, the humanistic idealists, of whom Theodor Herzl became the spokesman and the Zionist movement the instrument, also aspired to an ingathering of the exiles. But their ends and means of gathering followed from their humanism, and were as incommensurable with Messiah and miracle as humanism is with supernaturalism.

To the believing Judaists restoration could be nothing else than the repetition of a Judaistic past, hypostatized into what they variously interpreted as the eternal and universal Torah. In daily living it would consist of selections from accumulated precedents and practices, with sanctions from the Talmud and other carriers of Jewry's pre- and anti-scientific traditions, woven into a way of life. Restored Israel would thus be a theocracy, in principle committed to obeying all the commandments and performing all the *Mitzvot*, in practice doing what the folkways and mores approved. A Jew's existence would, perhaps, be regulated and policed by a Sanhedrin, and judged by a rabbinate. Whatever might be said, done, or taught would be conformed thus to that hypostatic Torah, its design for living infallibly defined by the power-holders of the theocracy. Could restoration be perfect, it might perhaps raise the Temple again and serve the Lord with blood-offerings and burnt offerings, first fruits and gifts of money, as well as with confession, song and praise.

But also without this consummation social control would have to be hieratic. For if Divinity were to communicate the intent of its Torah democratically, by direct inspiration of each believer, Torah would be a babel of interpretations, not the one true instruction in the best life here, and sole propaedeutic for the good life to come.

Before Herzl these idealistic Judaists traveled to their Holy Land to die, and in large numbers lived on, making self-righteous claims on the pious charity of the communities of the dispersion. Nor have they quieted their godly clamor since Herzl.

The humanists responded to it, and keep on responding. But the ingathering their vision projects has other grounds and refers to quite other conditions.

Westerners of diverse cultures and disciplines, those humanistic Jews were all poignantly aware of anti-Semitism as a principle of Christian faith and a corollary of party conflicts, economic competition and cultural pretension in political and social practice. In their own persons, or through their observations of such obscenities as the Dreyfus Affair, the Damascus horror, the Beyliss persecution, the massacres of Kishenev and Gomel, they had come to understand that anti-Semitism suffused the entire religio-political outlook of the European peoples. Their reading of history gave added force to the evidence of their eyes. They knew from direct experience how Europe's nationalisms. Europe's racisms, and Europe's socialisms took over and cherished and used, for the benefit of their own power and influence, the intrinsic anti-Semitism of

Europe's religion. From Moscow to Paris and Madrid, from Berlin to Rome and Stambul, "Jew" was a ready-made name any spokesman for a reactionary cult or party could give the scapegoat it needed, and win instant response. The spokesman might be a Sebastian Brunner, a Chateaubriand, a Drumont, a Maurras, a Jaime Balmez, a Dostoyevsky, a Houston Stewart Chamberlain, a G. K. Chesterton, a Franz von Papen, a Karl Marx, an Arab of the Husseini, an Ilya Ehrenbourg, an Adolph Stöcker or an Alfred Rosenberg. His employment of the word "Jew" would make it denotative of danger to whatever social interest he was soliciting.

The humanistic proponents of the Ingathering of the Exiles became convinced that reassembling enough Jews to form a Jewish State in Palestine would immensely weaken this groundless but potent aggression; and would in the course of time alter the anti-Semitic animus of its use of the word "Jew" to secular humanistic attitudes common between peoples not Jewish.

Such a correction of the age-old injustice might, however, be achieved anywhere; and a philosophy of territorialism, postulated on the assumption that an Ingathering in Palestine would forever be blocked by churchly and imperial interests, was proposed as an alternative to Zionism.

This philosophy—even though voiced by dedicated men of noble mind, such as Israel Zangwill, and for an interlude accepted by Herzl—found as little response among the Jews to whom it was addressed as do its expressions having currency today. It received symbolic renunciation in Herzl's dramatic recitation of the verse from Psalm 137: "If I forget thee, Jerusalem, let my right hand forget her cunning." Nor he, nor the congregation of his faith, could yet have the will to sing the Lord's song in an anti-Semitic land. But they knew also that in the land of the fathers, if ever they return to it, the Lord's song could not be the old but must needs be a new song, drawing for spirit upon the old, but prompted, not merely by a renewed, but rather by a *new* vision, wherein all the powers and virtues of the new time might enter and animate into growing new life the old Jewish vision.

These Jews' remembrance of things past elected, hence, to fasten upon the positive intent of the prophets of Israel. Their purpose became to give the admonitions of Amos and Micah and Hosea, as they abstracted, isolated and generalized them, a local habitation and a name in today's Judea.

One imaginative conception of this purpose is Herzl's *Altneuland;* a philosophical exposition and practical projection of it are A. D. Gordon's essays. Its concrete enactment was the initiation, in what was still a vassaldom of the Ottoman Empire, of a cooperative settlement which has become the model for what is now known as the *kvutzah*. Beside the communities of the supernaturalists who had come to the land to die, because they believed that they could therefore live a better after-life, the humanistic sons of the prophets established communities of the faithful who came to the land so to live that their commune would transpose the supernatural holiness of recall and worship into the natural holiness of the works and ways of daily living. They were for the most part intellectuals and romantics, not craftsmen, artisans, or manual workers of any sort. Their strengths were verbal, their skills pilpulistic. But their Judaism had assimilated the wisdoms of humanism, and their feeling for prophetic righteousness had been diversified into Socialist sentiment. They were strong in pity for the servile lot of the human multitudes; they reappraised the thankless labor which was their all of life as liberty and independence, and the leisure their lives lacked as parasitism and helplessness.

Those young Jews freely assumed a discipline that should make them over into authentic proletarians. It was their chosen way to the secular holiness which alone could establish naturalist fact in the place of supernaturalist fantasy. It was their religion, the Hebraism of the prophets in modern dress.

Their vision of it took them into the desert and swamp of Palestine to work them over into fertile acres. They began their labors as soft-bodied, tender-minded specialists of the intellect. Hungering, sweating, sickening, bleeding and dying, they builded that wasteland into their homeland as their toil transformed them into freer spirits, hard in body and tough in mind. Their communes became a fissionable nucleus of social reconstruction on a vital gradient of vision for growth. Willy-nilly, the institutions and enterprises of the Zionist movement bent to their pattern: the National Fund, the Keren Hayesod, the agencies and the colonization which the Funds financed with calculated—often not wisely calculated—risks.

Soon after Balfour published his releasing declaration, American Zionists set the singularities of the Jewish enterprise in Palestine in the perspectives of a more general democracy by means of a group of "Resolutions Bearing on Palestine Policy." These were resolutions adopted by the Zionist Organization of America at a convention it held in Pittsburgh in July of 1918. This was the American organization of what are now called "General Zionists." Their leader at the time was Louis D. Brandeis.

The resolutions became known as the Pittsburgh Program. They begin with an imaginative preamble which transposes into the terms of a natural democratic humanism the supernaturalism in the Jewish tradition. Thus:

In 1897 the first Zionist Congress at Basle defined the object of Zionism to be "the establishment of a publicly recognized and legally secured homeland for the Jewish people in Palestine." The recent Declaration of Great Britain, France, Italy, and others of the allied democratic States have established this public recognition of the Jewish National Home as an international fact.

Therefore we desire to affirm anew the principles which have guided the Zionist Movement since its inception, and which were the foundations laid down by our lawgivers and prophets for the ancient Jewish State, and the inspiration of the living Jewish law embodied in the traditions of two thousand years of exile.

Then follows the realistic program:

First: Political and civil equality, irrespective of race, sex or faith, for all the inhabitants of the land.

Second: To insure in the Jewish National Home equality of opportunity, we favor a policy which, with due regard for existing rights, shall establish the ownership and control of the land and of all natural resources and of all public utilities by the whole people.

Third: All land owned and controlled by the whole people should be leased on such conditions as will insure the fullest opportunity for development and continuity of possession.

Fourth: The cooperative principle should be applied as far as feasible in the organization of all agricultural, industrial, commercial, and financial undertakings.

Fifth: The fiscal policy shall be framed so as to protect the people from the evils of land speculation and from every other form of financial oppression.

Sixth: The system of free public instruction which is to be established should embrace all grades and departments of education.

Seventh: The medium of public instruction should be Hebrew, the national language of the Jewish people.

Far as fulfillment still is from fact, neither the First World War, nor the rule of the British as the agents of the League of Nations after the Balfour Declaration, nor the factional rancors of the Zionists, much deflected Jewish Palestine from forming along this humanistic ethical gradient. Here a little, there a little, the figure of vision became the flesh of fact, right alongside the communities of supernaturalist intention whose members were aspiring only to fear the Lord and obey his commandments. Fearing the Lord consisted, indeed, in following today's version of yesterday's commandments, as tradition had carried them from yesterday into today's meanings. Its substance was the aggregation of *minhagim* (customs), composing the diversities of "traditional Judaism," whose observance the elder required of the younger generation, no matter what the cost, nor who paid it.

The British, who took the rule of Palestine from the Turks for the greater security of their colonial empire, had long experience, alike in Asia and in Africa, in governing submissive communities of supernaturalism. Colonial empires are possible only among such communities; the communities of humanism exact commonwealth. But the British were without precedent for right relations with the Jewish communes, whose humanism rendered them recalcitrant to both their paternalism and their snobbistic bureaucratism. The men and women of the settlements believed with a firm belief that they owed Caesar nothing, that all the land was the Lord's land, and the fruit thereof belonged to the workers who produced it. As their numbers increased and they settled towns even more abundantly than *kvutzot* and *moshavim,* they gathered into a union whose organizational pattern was an adjustment of a compenetration of Hebraic prophetism and European syndicalism to Palestine's primitive, frontier-like economy.

This union is today's Histadruth Ovdim. It was the dynamic of that government within a government which under the Charter consistently challenged and checked the Mandatory bureaucracy, not failing to develop, in the process, bureaucratic ways of their own, which only the behaviors of the ill-disposed, third-rate British civil servants estopped from growing into the full flower of the bureaucratic art.

For a long time almost three-quarters of the Histadruth's membership came from the settlements. Its enterprises added, to typical trades unionism and agricultural cooperation, building trades, transportation and other service cooperatives, cooperatives in banking and finance, in health and hospitalization, in consumer goods, in "culture," and in schooling infants and youth according to the doctrines and disciplines of their humanistically envisaged faith. Where the supernaturalists employed Yiddish or some other vernacular as the speech of man to man and reserved Hebrew as the *loshon hakodesh* (holy tongue) for addressing only Deity, the humanists consecrated Hebrew to the uses of daily life, and became aggressive suppressors of other languages. They even produced for their schoolchildren Hebrew versions of such Yiddish writers as Peretz and Mendele. Of course, they cultivated ideological enmities and political faction: some were leftist radicals like Hashomer Hazair; others radically rightists like the Revisionists, or the later Mapam and Herut splinter groups. But during the always uneasy and intermittently violent and bloody operation of the Mandate, they all learned something of the cooperative discipline of self-government.

British colonialism, skilled in the inertias which keep administration of "lesser peoples" relatively peaceful as well as profitable, favored, among the Arabs, the effendi over the fellah; among Jews, the supernaturalist over the humanist. The Colonial Office knew how, by keeping Arab divided from Jew, to rule with least effort, intellectual or moral, and to make sure of serving the interest of empire elsewhere.

This was not without its benefits, however. If the Mandatory's administration did not consistently keep the peace between Arabs and Jews, it did discourage major clashes between the Jewish supernaturalists and humanists. Over the years numbers of such clashes had occurred, the violent initiative having always been the supernaturalists'. The *Shomrei-Shabbat*, for example, being sure that not to compel an absolute observance of *Shabbat* would draw divine vengeance on Sabbath-breakers, went about, as they still do, beating shopkeepers, destroying goods, and otherwise guaranteeing that such as do not share their views about God's desires with respect to the seventh day should know how painful and costly such heresy must be.

Under the British these aggressions of the "truly righteous" could be simply a bit of disorderly conduct that an Arab policeman could attend to. Today they signalize a confrontation of faithways and lifeways from whose antagonisms will follow whatever future meaning Israel may have for freedom-loving mankind. The Orthodox faction of Mandatory Palestine has become the "religious bloc" of independent Israel. Disorderly conduct of a small band of fanatics has become the symbol of the purposes and policies of a conspirational Judaist clericalism which looks for support to the great majority of the new Israel, ingathered from the degradations and exactions of exile among anti-Semites to the austerities and disciplines of a homeland all embattled frontier. Frontier within, because each immigrant *landsmanschaft* brings the language, folkways and mores of its country of origin, which unite their members to one another and make a boundary between them and the other peoples of Israel. Frontier without, because of political delimitation and military need, also where Israel faces the sea.

If the miscellany of Israel have anything in common, other than being victims of anti-Semitism, it is the Judaist supernaturalism, although this, too, is diversified by suffusions from the cults and cultures of the lands of origin as well as by inner variations of belief and rite. But the Judaist aggregation is the central mass from which the other groups and factions—Israel has nineteen political parties alone—are deviants, as the factions of the prophets were deviants from the factions of the priests in Bible times. Each is a minority of beliefs and programs.

The position of Israel as an integral and solidary polity is inescapably a function of the relations of these groupings to one another. How each lives and works together with all presents a more fundamental problem than the foreign relations of the State. The domestic configuration cannot, in the nature of such things, fail to be an issue, as well as a determinant, of the foreign relations.

For, given the clericalist conception of the Jewish role in the divinely directed course of history, it could very well have happened that, had the Judaist majority of Palestine been as purposefully organized as the Jewish minority, the State of Israel would never have been created. Indeed, when its first war for survival was imposed upon it by the aggression of Egypt and the other states of the Arab League, numbers of Judaists, certain that the creation of the State was rebellion to God, fought with the League against the Jews. And in truth, the decision to make the diverse Palestinian Jewish communities into the independent and sovereign State of Israel was a decision to bet life, liberty and sacred honor on an endeavor which neither the prudent nor the politic could see as having the slightest promise of success, and which the supernaturalist viewed as sin.

The Jews who made this bet undertook to overrule the expediencies of "statesmanship" and the timidities which are often synonyms for "practicality." They bypassed what seemed to men of experience the more hopeful way of meeting the needs of the Jewish multitudes *in extremis*. This was, for Palestine, an international trusteeship under the United Nations that would administer the trust in spirit and in truth, and would thus establish the Jewish homeland by a gradual but speedy development at a minimum cost in life, in suffering, in treasure. This was, to other lands, easement of immigration and settlement. These were held the least hazardous, the least unlikely to succeed. Statehood was regarded as too precarious a gamble.

Making that gamble postulated an idealism of a different order from both the "realism" and the idealism it bet against. It was an act of faith, far beyond any that Jews of the supernaturalist persuasion were capable of exercising. It sprang from the bettors' readiness to stake their existence on an action with no guarantees, with odds against it greater than could be measured. They launched their undertaking in full awareness of the circumstances it defied, the forces it challenged, the hazards it ran. It brought to the ultimate trial the courage which is wisdom concerning dangers.

The critical event of the trial was the war immediately launched by the Arab states. These had early formed a League, not in order to help and strengthen one another, but in order to destroy the Jews of Palestine. The word "Arab," as those fighting Jews had come to employ it, thus tended to express a feeling rather than knowledge and understanding. Usage made it a term of anxiety and aversion, deprecation and antagonism. And there are many causes—in the sinister story of the notorious double-dealer whom Britain's Sir Herbert Samuel had promoted from German-paid traitor to Britain-subsidized "Mufti of Jerusalem" (he later took service with Hitler), as well as in the course of Jewish-Arab relations—why this should be so. Whatever the causes, their effect is reflex of feeling, not wisdom of life. Even the rightly aspiring *Ihud* movement, with Judah Magnes for avatar, was impelled by sentiment rather than guided by insight.

"Arab," it is helpful to remember, is a term no less ambiguous than "Jew," and, like "Jew," denotes many aggregations of conflicting needs, interests and wishes, voiced by many dialects of the Arab tongue. The peoples of the Arab League, from Syria to Egypt and from Iraq to Yemen, have lived a thousand years but as tools with life in them, of less worth to the power-holders of those lands than their camels and oxen. For the standard of living permitted them is below the level of subsistence. In skill, health, literacy and self-rule they have been among the world's most retarded, as in an older time they had been among its most forward, peoples. I say retarded, not backward. They are no less able to advance, to grow in freedom, self-help and fellowship, than their forebears of old, or the most progressive peoples of our own day. But they have been held back. Authoritarian supernaturalism and feudal rule subdue them to the credulous service of masters often absentee, who reap because *they* sow, consume because *they* produce, and live at leisure because *they* labor.

These masters, called "effendi"—the word shares a common derivation with such terms as "authentic," "authority," and suggests "power-filled"—have a vital stake in the fellah's condition. Its continuation became, as elsewhere in Britain's colonial empire, synonymous with the law-and-order which government preserves. Jewish settlement in Palestine carried, both as faith and as works, a vital threat to that order and a challenge to Christian missionary enterprise. It embraced, for the very interests that hate it, a model to emulate, a mode of life to imitate. It set a precedent for such *bonafide* "Arab nationalism" as was permitted to develop, and it stimulated initiatives in farming and trade whose entrepreneurs were inhibited from making common cause with Jewish business by the factitious isolationism of cultist, racist or nationalist ideologies in Arab dress. In effect they served as rationalizations of the interdependence of British colonialism with vested effendi interests. They frustrated all attempts of Jewish labor organizations to unionize Arab workers more than superficially. They constricted the cooperation of citrus growers. They contributed to keeping Arabs and Jews apart on the levels of learning, art and science. They are the postulates of the aggression with which the Arab League blooded the new State of Israel. The appeal to them set off the fantastic exodus from Israel of the hundreds of thousands of Arabs, which is one of the critical chances of that War of Liberation. The ideologies crystallize the animus which the effendi élite, who control the Arab League, invoke in their unyielding aggression against the survival of Israel.

The masters of Egypt, Syria, Iraq, Lebanon, Jordan and Yemen could readily enough find a *modus vivendi* with an Israel whose ways and works were not by their instant presence a judgment in the eyes of their subjects upon the entire economy, political and spiritual, of those countries. Their own Jewries, oriented toward otherworldliness, were not such judgments; nor were the Judaist communities of Palestine; nor are Israel's *Neturei-Karta,* nor the major groups in Israel's "religious bloc." A clericalist Israel administered under the talmudic canon could without great difficulty find a *modus vivendi* with Arab feudalism, the cultural distance between the two being small indeed.

This is not the case with that remnant in Israel who are oriented toward the humanistic freedoms of modernity, who look to the Hebrew prophets for vision rather than to Judaist Torah for rules. Humanistic Israel—the Israel of the Kibbutz and the Histadruth— was seen as more than ever a judgment when Arab lands were found to be richest of all in oil; and after the exploitation of that natural resource by alien knowhow for alien interests has brought the Arabs' effendi overlords wealth and pleasures beyond their greediest dreams, whilst the generations of the fellaheen are continued as poor, as hungry, as ignorant, sickly and servile as their fathers.

Inasmuch as the Arab folk of Jewish Palestine had long been noticeably healthier, wealthier, freer and more literate than their kin in the Arab League, the judgment is of long standing. Inasmuch as the Arabs of the State of Israel are, like its Jews, automatically citizens of the State, equal in rights and freedoms, the social impact of this judgment for the millions of the Arab League is inescapable. Their unrest will keep alert the effendi consciousness that an Israel with a political economy and spiritual outlook like Egypt's or Yemen's is an ethical impossibility as well as a historical anachronism.

How aware the power-holders of those lands have become of the moral challenge of Israel is evidenced by their effort to shut Israelis out and cut them off from all communication with their subjects. They impose and enforce an economic and cultural isolationism by means of barriers against all trade, whether in thoughts or things. It is their unannounced aim not only to quarantine their positions against Israel's democratic contagion, but to destroy that nearest vital source by starving if not beating Israel to death.

Moreover, the event that Israel, poorly armed and outnumbered as it was, could yet hold its own against the Arab League's collective might and win the uneasy armistice under which it since struggles, had unexpected consequences in the Moslem world. The 661,000,000 adherents of that cult are spread from Morocco to Egypt, from Arabia to China and the islands of the Pacific. They constitute majorities or powerful minorities in upward of thirty-six states. Israel's victory over the Arab and Egyptian oligarchies aroused the fanatics among them. They initiated a "back to Mohammed" movement, a new pan-Islamism that might offset Catholic Judaism and Catholic Christianism and Catholic Communism with a Catholic Mohammedanism. They organized a World Moslem Conference, whose principles and policies are conceived in ardent remembrance of the faithfuls' "days of glory," when military victory and imperial rule went with devotion unto death to the Koran.

The potentials of this Catholic Moslemism must needs be counted in any calculation of Israel's existential hazard.

The states of the Arab League comprise the closest external conditions of Israel's survival. Almost wholly inimical, they enclose it in a ring of hate, whose disposition and interests had largely determined the policies of Britain's mandatory role. In the widening circle of the powers, the states spiritually more intimate, societally similar, the states more friendly than unfriendly and the positively friendly, are the most geographically distant. Without the cooperation of the latter, the State of Israel would have been only a brief and bloody interlude between despair and impotence. Without their approval and support, Israel's existence as a nation among

496

nations would be far, far more precarious than it is, and Israel's survival would be a risk challenging all calculation.

However, that friendly disposition of the democratic powers is in no way unconditional. Common ideals aside, it expresses the confluence of two motives. One is a consideration of advantage made by partisan politicians competing for rule within a state, and the other is a similar consideration by statesmen responsible for advancing national self-interest in the struggle for power between states. The ambiguities in American policy toward Israel follow from both those considerations. Soviet recognition of Israel followed from the latter—the Politburo's purpose to hurt Britain, not any will to save Jews.

On the other hand, the procedures of the United Nations Organization, which culminated in the recognition of Israel as a sovereign and independent state and its admission to equal membership in that organization, were due not alone to the initiatives of the United States and Russia. The choices which those actions consummated were shaped as well by another motive. That one is intrinsic to the nature of the World Organization. It is set forth in its Charter and presumably expressed by its agencies and operations. It is especially signalized by the Universal Declaration of Human Rights which the Assembly of the United Nations Organization adopted on December 10, 1948, and which various commissions have since been endeavoring to implement via "conventions."

Charter and Declaration make statements about human relations. They lay down rules which the different peoples of the world can follow when they honestly seek to live together with each other on equal terms of peace and freedom. They embody agreements between all the states to cooperate in establishing "the four freedoms" for each, and insuring for each its inner liberties and outer safety. Although much of the history of numbers of the "high contracting parties" to these global agreements has been one of evasions and nullifications designed to save only their singular and exclusive interests, and to heighten and spread their own powers, the great majority have been as faithful as they dared to the principle of collective security, laboring as they could to apply it practically. The smaller and weaker sovereign states among them recognize that the principle is the one salvation of their freedom and

497

independence; those which have been reduced to satellites are aware that it is their best hope of liberation from servitude. The role of all in admitting Israel to equal fellowship in the United Nations signalizes thus a common understanding of the global nature of the faith which the articles of the Charter and of the Declaration affirm, and of the obligations which the signatories to those documents contract.

Perhaps we do not recognize as loyally as we might that those obligations do somewhat modify the brutalities of power politics, do clothe their corruptions with a little decency, and do promise much more. They are the hope of the world.

And they are certainly the chief hope, almost the sole hope, of Israel—that tiny state assembling a citizenry of many peoples who are far indeed from being orchestrated into a nation, upon a land barren of natural resources, with enemies for neighbors on every side, who could, if their masters win them to such aggression, overwhelm Israel by numbers alone. Although their governments have been stopped in their war upon Israel, they have not abandoned it. Members of the United Nations though those governments be, and vowed to its principles, they know that to embody the principles in practice at home would be to divest themselves of all their inequitable advantages. They hence invoke the principles abroad in order to shut out their application at home. They claim for their internal affairs immunity from those principles on the ground of those very principles, that they may preserve their privileges intact. Since they see in Israel's plans and policies the concrete challenge to these privileges, they wage unceasing war, shifting from hot war to cold, and keeping the renewal of the hot war imminent. Not merely have they failed to make peace; they give every indication that they will agree only to an enforced peace.

And it may be true that no other is possible. For the ultimate issue between them and humanistic Israel is a way of realizing human relations. Whatever be the dogmas of a totalitarian religion —sacerdotal, Nazi, Fascist, Communist, or Communazi—they are closer than the teachings of democracy to the beliefs and conduct of the power-holders of the Arab League. Spiritually and practically the latter belong with Franco and Peron and Malan and Rankin and Mao and Chiang Kai-shek. They impose on Israel a war economy to which all its institutions must needs be conformed, and for which too many of the utterances of Israel's leaders and missioners are anxious rationalizations.

One such rationalization is the oft-repeated and much-resented doctrine that for a Jew not to live in Israel is to live in exile; that the program of the Ingathering is a program of return from exile, regardless of whether they are survivors of the Warsaw ghetto, or Auschwitz or Buchenwald, or are victims of Moslem or Marxist totalitarianism, or livers of the life of Riley in France or England or the United States. Even if it had five million persons on whom it could draw for armed service, Israel would still be surrounded by an enemy that could call upon forty million, and no superiority of organization or firepower (assuming this would be had) could in the long run offset that discrepancy in manpower.

As a rationalization, the idea of a total Ingathering of the exiles is a secular projection of a religious fantasy, which the leaders of the returning remnants from the Babylonian exile likewise had failed to render efficacious. Psychologically, it is a cry out of the depths for help, not a utopian execution of a supernatural design. Its spring is a will to believe, similar to that which established Israel, and in no way less hazardous.

For the European majority among the actually ingathered come from lands at best long immeasurably behind the democratic countries of the West. And those who are "returned" from the Moslem states are taken from lands of a neolithic economy anointed with petroleum, of feudal rule and rotted culture, practicing a faith-sanctioned anti-Semitism of which Yemen probably maintains the most obscene forms. Those ingathered bring habits of submission and evasion which have become, not a price, but a penalty of survival. Those from the concentration camps of Europe have suffered regressions of personality signalized by broken bodies not only, but by confused hearts, inert wills and lax minds. Their penalty for survival has been animalization. All groups nevertheless retain, at least vestigially, cultural singularities from their countries of origin, singularities of folkways, mores, speech, song, diet, dress, tradition and legend. These suffuse and divide whatever is common in their heritage of Judaism.

Inescapably, the State of Israel postulates its own survival as an equal member of the family of nations on converting these many, mutually foreign Judaist communions into a united Israel of soldiers and workers, all equally loyal citizens of the State, all heart and soul committed to its defenses and growth.

But the institutional form which such a conversion calls for is itself a hazard regarding which all calculations are perforce hazardous. The State of Israel had to found itself from the start on a war economy, based on gifts and loans first, and on investments only secondarily. Its rule of life has had to be a rule of austerity, even as measured by the low standard of living of the Near East; and the burdens which sovereignty and independence impose on the people of Israel outweigh the heaviest they were required to bear under the British.

Of these burdens perhaps the most ominous is the menace to the vitality and moral influence of the cooperative economy of the *kvutzot*. It was natural for these fellowships to avert from the dilemma of, on the one hand, choosing between protecting their corporate economy from dilution by unaffiliable newcomers and, on the other hand, the swift conversion of discoordinated, unproductive consumers into eager and disciplined producers, or at least into manpower able to learn producer arts.

Another burden is the governmental dilemma between, on the one hand, a solidarity to be created by appeasing protagonists of religious intolerance and coercion and, on the other hand, remaining loyal to the principle of equal liberty for the different to which Israel's membership in the United Nations commits the State. The exigencies of survival imposed by the Arab League may lead to shaping Israel into a twentieth-century Sparta, with war as its paramount concern, with military service as the over-all duty of every citizen, regardless of sex, faith, occupation or age, and with every other function of this common culture subordinated to its militarism. To acquiesce in militarism as the form and condition of survival might be to require developing Israel into a corporative state with freedom at best but a word for a pretension, democracy a way of talking and not of living. A continuing war economy might require coordinating Histadruth Ovdim and its institutions with the "religious bloc" and its supernaturalist prescriptions and taboos, on at least the same terms as the concordat which Fascist militarism led to between the Italian State and Roman Catholic power.

One item in such a *gleichschaltung* would be the complete surrender of the critical intimacies of human existence such as birth, puberty, marriage, divorce, diet, and burial, and, above all, the education of youth, to clericalist regulation and management. Even if state and church were not completely unified, schooling would be unified, standardized and militarized. Today's control by sect or party would be replaced by an authoritarian central authority. The effort to educate as modernity understands education would be abandoned or forbidden. Instead there would be indoctrination. Guidance in the free use of reason in the arts and sciences and the faith underlying them would be rejected on behalf of inculcation of unquestioning assent to dogmatic repetition of certain principles and practices.

Still another consequence of spartanization for survival would be the projection of what is now a contingent mood among Israelis into a driving demand upon Jews and Judaists who are not Israelis. The truly representative appeal for the latter's moral and material support rests on the scientific spirit and the democratic faith. Their personal involvement is a voluntary act sanctioned by the ethics of universal human brotherhood as well as familial, cultural and cultist belongingness. The statesmen among Israelis so recognize it.

But there sounds in the anxious summons to Ingathering also another tone. This conveys compulsive demand. It asserts claims upon the Jews of the world, even where not Judaists, resembling the claims of the papacy upon Roman Catholics and its pretensions upon all Christians. Hitler's hierarchy made similar claims upon all Germans everywhere. Stalin's makes such claims and gets them served wherever there are Communists. To make good such claims upon the Jews of the world would require the organization of a "Catholic Israel," with headquarters in Israel's Jerusalem, after the manner of Catholic Christianity with its headquarters in Italy's Vatican City, or of Catholic communism, with its headquarters in Russia's Moscow.

"Catholic Israel," so intended, is a fantasy of helplessness bred in the weak by fear of their own weakness. It is a compensation in idea for strength and security lacking in fact. Though entirely unrepresentative, the idea has been seized upon by Christian alarmists and frightened Judaists, as well as by anti-Semites, to charge Israel and non-Israeli Zionists with demanding of Jews everywhere a dual political allegiance. In the United States a certain sect of

Judaists employs the charge to condemn all support or giving by Americans to the Israeli enterprise, even though these be either goodwill offerings freely made, or actions to serve the national interest.

Ironically enough, this traditional argument of the anti-Semite against Jews—the charge of dual allegiance—is addressed to a world-community endeavoring to organize itself for collective security and equal liberty through the United Nations and for the system of international relations it is struggling to realize. The argument implies that recognizing and serving America's interest in the socio-political character of Israel is somehow disloyalty to the United States. That is to say, an American, be he Jew or Gentile, is held disloyal to his country if he cares whether Israel is a democracy, whether its institutions are the institutions of a free society of free men, and if he does what he can to enable Israel to grow solidly into such a society.

The argument obviously disregards precisely that which in fact makes a person an American, and that which Americanism implies for his attitude toward other states—such little weak states as Greece, for example, or Korea, or Turkey, or, for that matter, Israel. I say nothing of the parties to the North Atlantic Pact.

Now, to be an American is not an accident of birth but an act of faith. Although nationality accrues automatically to persons born in the United States, the responsibilities and privileges of citizenship do not. They are not functions of nativity. They come alive and actual when any person, wherever born or brought up, publicly commits himself to the faith and works of a certain way of life. The native is admitted to those duties and liberties at the age of twenty-one, when he becomes a voter and formally responsible for decisions, which his vote registers, regarding the officers, the policies, the entire political life and destiny, of his community, of his State, of the Federal Republic—and he may have been carrying economic and cultural responsibilities long before then. An immigrant makes his commitment when he of his own free will publicly and solemnly abandons all allegiance to any other nation and takes the oath of allegiance to the United States. Thereby he becomes a "naturalized" citizen. There are not very many Americans without "naturalized" forebears; there are millions who are themselves "naturalized."

Being "naturalized," rejecting allegiance to other sovereignties, becoming an American, does not mean committing oneself to any organization of party and power existing at the time. Such organizations keep forming and dissolving; they are formations in the American way, changeable and to be changed. What the American commits himself to is the rules of human association which are to guide these changes. He vows a fighting faith in freedom whose fundamentals are written down in the Declaration of Independence and the Constitution of the United States. These first books of the Bible of America express certain principles and ideals by which the nation endeavors to shape its life. They are the articles of its faith. American history is the history of the struggle of the American people to embody its faith in works as the American way.

True, many who oppose the effort at embodiment are also called Americans. Some want to convert the country into an oligarchic republic. Others would like to reconstruct it into a Fascistic corporative state; others to work it over, from Southern models, into a Nazi-like racist state; others seek over-ruling power and privilege for a sacerdotal hierarchy; others conspire to turn it into a hierarchical soviet. Some make up a "Liberty League," others are "constitutionalists," others "Dixiecrats," others clericalists, others Communists. And unhappily, although perhaps inevitably, each such organization of passion and interest has its echoes and its imitators, for whatever reasons, among the nation's Jews.

Americanism, as the Bill of Rights defines it, protects all of them alike in their rights to believe and to implement their beliefs in policies and programs which, in the frame of reference of that very Bill of Rights and of the Declaration of Independence, do not fit with Americanism. It is the American way for every person who is not an idiot to be a "joiner," to enroll himself in many associations, to each and every one of which he gives allegiance but none of which may claim his exclusive allegiance. That they are many liberates him from servitude to any. Their numbers give efficacy to the assurance of the Bill of Rights that he shall be free to believe, to think, to speak, and to associate with others in multiple and diverse ways: that he shall not be deprived of that spiritual, physical and social mobility which signalizes free society.

Americanism envisages "life, liberty and the pursuit of happiness" as individual ends whose common means are the multiple religious, political, economic, cultural and recreational associations which individuals enter and leave, and the multiple activities they together carry on. Americanism envisages the Federal Union as this communion of the different—one country, of upward of fifty diverse states and territories, with their countless communities, each cherishing, and pooling, its own ways, its own characteristic economy and culture, with those of the others. The American Idea is the national faith in democracy as the religion of religions which guarantees equal liberty to each of upward three hundred sects and denominations. It hence requires of them that they should be united in common loyalty to this democratic faith. The American Idea designs the national economy as the free coming together of men and managements in common enterprises, moved by a common concern so to raise the national standard of living that all may live their lives in ever greater abundance because of the ever-widening knowledge and truer skills wherewith they earn their livings.

Similarly, Americanism in foreign relations is postulated on the idea of an international peace built on the equality of the different nations who have freely come together in order that all might assure to each on equal terms its sovereignty, independence, and well-being. This was the idea that led to American initiative in forming the betrayed League of Nations, and that led to the renewal of the initiative in creating the United Nations Organization, and this time sharing the international tasks and responsibilities.

In sum, Americanism envisages the entire human enterprise in America as one civilization created by the communion of its many cultures, a self-orchestration of all the diverse works and ways of the spirit of man into the singularity of the American way of life. This way of life America wants its arts and sciences to express, to symbolize and to fulfil, and its schools to teach and develop. It locates any American who has become aware of the nature, the ideals, the powers, and the relationships of his country, in a consciously realized network of connections and belongings which centers in his family and joins him to all the peoples of the globe. The network gives substance to the American credo, and direction to the believer's commitments who would live by the credo. It is intrinsically a commitment to a struggle aiming to conform fact to faith, to Americanize existence in America, and by works to communicate the faith to the world. From the battle for the Bill of Rights in Washington's time to the fight for the program of President Truman's Commission on Civil Rights, and for the propositions of the Universal Declaration of Human Rights adopted by the Assembly of the United Nations, the struggle has been unremitting. Its one aim has been, and remains, to free the different from penalties for being different; to unite them as equals in free association so that they might work out and maintain together equal liberty for each.

This religion of equal liberty has never been an easy one. Its faithful have always been confronting entrenched and greatly preponderant power, fear, inertia. They have always sweated, suffered and bled for their belief. Violence has been thrust on them, as in the American Civil War, as in the two World Wars, as in the Korean betrayal.

Recurrent violence is a fact of the history of liberty which Jews can least afford to ignore. Penalized for being Jews on the basis of a religious dogma which demoted them from God's Chosen to God's Rejected People, they were in many ways more conspicuous beneficiaries of the struggle for equal liberty than women or the darker peoples. For they had been excommunicated from the natural fellowship of mankind on the basis of supernatural revelation. The Democratic Idea is the ground of their release from this segregation, of their full restoration as Jews to human fellowship. Not unnaturally many of them took freedom to be a Jew without penalty to be the same as ceasing to be a Jew at all. They interpreted defeating anti-Semitism into liquidating Judaism.

This was both a sociological error and a subversion of the Democratic Idea. Anti-Semitic aggression changes its forms but gives no sign of dissolving its powers or abandoning its purposes. The Democratic Idea affirms the equal right of the Jew, fully as Jew, to "life, liberty and the pursuit of happiness," not as fleeing Jewishness but as achieving it more abundantly.

Morally, the Jewish Americans' commitment to the Democratic Idea is double. It is both American and Jewish, and Jewish as American. This twentieth-century world he lives in is one everywhere of a life-and-death struggle for democracy. Totalitarianisms threaten wherever a free man turns. It is not so long that one such, with horrible cruelty, exacted from Jews six million lives for being Jews. It is still the case that in much of the world where Jews survive they are at the mercy of a ruthless power which nullifies the very idea of freedom on the grounds of an economic myth exalted into an infallible religious dogma—which may similarly penalize them.

That nullification of freedom is not the first, since 1776. In 1820 there was the Holy Alliance. When its plans of aggression came to the knowledge of the Government of the United States, it declared: *You shall not pass*. It declared that since the rule and program of the powers of tyranny were antipathetic to American liberty, they should not be imposed in the Americas, and pledged itself to resist such imposition. The pledge is called the Monroe Doctrine. A century and a quarter later the Nazi totalitarian aggressor turned all his resources of force and fraud against the ongoing struggle for equal liberty. The President of the United States called upon all Americans and all free men everywhere to *quarantine* the aggressor. Little more than a decade later this call was developed, on the precedent of the Monroe Doctrine, into the Truman Doctrine, which tells Stalin's imperialist tyranny: *You shall not pass*.

This Truman Doctrine is at once a weapon in the nation's war for survival as a free society of free men, and an aspect of the nation's commitment as a member of the United Nations. It accepts the American people's partnership in the reconstruction of free Europe. It implements their commitments as one of the insurers of free society in Greece, in Turkey, in all the Near East, and particularly in Israel.

Not in their own right only did the American people acknowledge the claim of the Israelis to sovereignty and indepedence. They did it also as a member of the United Nations Organization of which they are both among the prime sponsors and the sincerest supporters. They voted hence for admitting the new State to that international fellowship with its rights and duties. The action was based not alone on the usual motives joined to lagging humanitarian sentiment, but in no small degree also upon the democratic pattern given the Jewish homeland in the past, upon the new State's avowed design to extend and fortify democratic ways in the future. The American action assumed Israel's integral commitment to liberty and democracy as the American Declaration of Independence affirms them, and as the Universal Declaration of Human Rights, for which Israel voted in the Assembly of the United Nations, extensively defines them.

That Americans have a vital stake in this commitment of Israel's goes without saying. National interest is joined to disinterested devotion to liberty in the requirement that Americans shall, as in China and elsewhere, challenge totalitarian tendencies in the Land of Promise and nullify or avert their causes. Americans have a moral obligation to do whatever they freely can to nourish the springs of liberty in Israel and enable its peoples' growth to self-reliant strength and cooperative union with other free societies.

For Americans who are Jews or Judaists, the stake in Israel has additional, psychologically and socially deeper, older, motivations. And, for that matter, so it has for Judaists wherever they make their homes. They may not forget, and most certainly may not forget in Israel, that the chief, not uncommonly the sole, difference for which Jews have been penalized is religious; that to lay this sort of penalty on any one, Jew or non-Jew, in a land dominated by Jews is a blasphemy beyond pardon. Their leaders might well emulate the example of Purshottamdas Tandon, the orthodox Brahmin recently elected President of the Indian Congress Party.

Tandon was the candidate of Hindu fanatics who stood intransigeant against the rule of equal liberty for all faiths which the Hindu government was endeavoring to apply. But in his presidential address Tandon declared: "The administration of this country cannot be run from the communal standpoint or on the authority of any fixed religious book. Even thinking on these lines will increase internal dissensions and weaken our administration." The Congress accepted this view, and by resolutions affirmed the principle and policy of toleration.

What holds for India holds far more momentously for Israel. It is inadmissible that the spirit of equal liberty and equal responsibility, which initiated Dagania and created the *kvutzot* and the city communities, shall not inform and shape into a free society of free Jews the diverse Jewries of Israel. It is inadmissible that the cultural economy and educational establishments of Israel shall, on the score of exigencies of national survival, be made instruments of a Sparta-like totalitarianism. To permit this to happen at all would be to forfeit all claim on the United Nations' support, without which survival would be forfeited anyhow. But more, it would be a betrayal of the integrity of the humanist freedom from which Judaist supernaturalism has everywhere drawn so many benefits. It would be a moral nihilism. For the action undertaken to realize ideal as fact would nullify the ideal in the name of the ideal.

A consequence inadmissible to faith or reason may readily find admission in perception and fact. The logic of discourse is congruent with the logic of life only by a happy chance; the dialectic of belief can lay down hardly any gradient for the succession of events. Things happen. One leads to another, but not as reason ordains or the heart demands. They move on with a blind contingency which only the retrospective look of some philosophical historian composes into a logical pattern that he then attributes to God's providence or Nature's laws. Beliefs and reasonings are also happenings. Once in a while, they find other happenings from which they receive vindication of their own certainties and confirmations of their own foregone conclusions. At their functional best, they fuse into the form of calculated risks. Supernaturalism verifies the calculations by superseding the experienced with the desired, thus feeding invincible hope on ineluctable illusion. Humanism verifies the calculations by proving the desired on the hazards of experience, forging the valor of idealism on the contingencies of events in such wise as to toughen hope without invoking illusion.

The humanist and the supernaturalist modes of religion span the life of man and together give it shape. Their synergy compounds into the predicament which is human existence in every age, in every culture. It is conspicuously the predicament of free societies. For these, events every so often move to a climax of options which are both momentous and forced, between irreconcilable alternatives and self-defeating programs. The movements follow from the fact that the rule of equal liberty, by which free societies live as free, protects also enemies of liberty who employ their freedoms in order to destroy freedom. Since their ways of living together are ways of toleration, also of the intolerant who aim to put an end to tolerance, the ways could be the murder of tolerance at the hands of the intolerant; while if free societies themselves were not to tolerate the intolerant, they would bring death to toleration at their own hands. When men in the predicament of the free are confronted also by unappeasable aggression from without, what they must needs do to resist and vanquish the aggressor may often involve such a regimentation of all the people, such limitations upon thinking, communication, movement, and assembly, as first to contain, then to suppress, ultimately to destroy, the liberties in whose defense the regimentation has been devised.

The condition is endemic to free societies. Between World War I and World War II, thinking men have become radically conscious of it, again and again and again, in the United States, in Great Britain, in France, in all lands that affirm freedom as their rule of thought and life. The pressure is constant, within and upon them, toward either moral abdication or enemy victory.

These are the horns of the dilemma between which the people of Israel are placed by the being of the State of Israel. The alternatives are to accept the murder of freedom at the hands of its foe or to kill freedom in order to save it from the foe. They shape up a predicament which is no news in the Jewish tradition. Jeremiah could understand it; the second Isaiah could interpret its global import; the author of Job could characterize the strength that can overcome and dissipate it and free the state to form itself into a free society of free men.

The precise way to that fundamental liberation is neither clear nor easy. It cannot be other than one which will both defeat the enemy and preserve freedom as alike the end and the means of Israel's continuing as a different and equal member of the international community. It cannot be mapped as other than the enduring strategy of a discipline of freedom whose tactic and logistic shall be willingly fitted by all whom it engages into the configuration of the common enterprise.

This is not now the case. The record shows a polarity, as well as cross-purposes, among the ingathered of Israel and among Zionists elsewhere. It shows too ready a disposition to lose the design of the whole in the daily round of dirt and drill and disputation, with their habits, their hazards, their aggressions, their evasions and their impatience. It shows too prompt a willingness to ignore the long run for the short run, and to import fabrications instead of cultivating a greater growth of the freedoms already sprung from the soil.

In the communities of free agreement which Dagania initiated, in the primary associative structure of Haganah and Palmach, there may be data of experience from which an economy of free men in arms, loyal to freedom and dedicated to a just peace, can be designed. Made confluent with the Pittsburgh Program of the American Zionists, they may provide a base in thought for a strategy and tactic of Israel's indispensable discipline of freedom.

Israel's logistic, however, is conditional upon investments and loans and gifts from the free world, particularly investments, since investment brings with it a lasting concern of the investor that his venture shall prosper and grow. He knows now that his best risks are those conditioned upon the human freedoms. The free world, certainly the American variety of it, no longer cares to hazard either material or spiritual capital save in the safeguarding of freedom. To win its cooperation, professions with no practice to confirm them are no longer enough, as the Kuomintang has discovered. Unkept or broken promises by Chinese rulers have lost the free world the whole of China.

Not one Israeli sect or party by itself, but all the people of Israel must set themselves the arduous task of learning how, in the day's work and the day's fight, "to perform justly, skilfully, thoughtfully and magnanimously, all the offices, both private and public, of peace and war."

The words are John Milton's. They are his definition of education. But they also signalize the discipline of freedom. If the people of Israel can freely perfect themselves in this discipline, they have more than a fighting chance to achieve the definitive victory over freedom's foes, which a just peace could crown by agreements under the United Nations, of mutual cooperation and support with the Arab States. Or, if Israel's God wills that the foe should prove too strong, Israel will have held fast to its integrity and not paid for some form of physical survival with moral suicide.

ON DUAL LOYALTIES

By HAYIM GREENBERG

THE AMERICAN JEW is not faced with any fundamental conflict between his duties to America and his bond with the Jewish community in Israel. Not even in time of war could there arise any earnest clash of loyalties. There are some, however, who feel that American Jews are confronted with a moral and political dilemma when they are asked to contribute to Israel not only funds but also human resources, volunteers who should go to Israel "for good" and merge their personal destinies with those of the Land of Israel. You would not ask non-Jews to emigrate to Israel—thus runs the argument—nor would you appeal to non-Jewish Americans to return to the countries from which they or their forebears came. There are millions of such Americans, yet you would not proclaim a general slogan that all those Americans who are not of Anglo-Saxon extraction or of "pure" American descent should go back to their erstwhile fatherlands. It is therefore obvious that you believe that American Jews as a group possess specific traits and interests, not shared by any other group in the country. Does not that imply an assumption that American Jews are not truly American— that they are hyphenated Americans, citizens with mental reservations of which other ethnic groups in the country are free? Don't you think that stressing this exceptionalism of the American Jew might place him in an unenviable and equivocal position?

Though I doubt that I can provide a formula that will satisfy everybody in answer to the above arguments, I would like to offer my personal approach to these matters.

I do not believe that Jews living in America are not genuine

Americans. Instead of hyphenated Americanism we should rather speak of uniqueness. *We are unique.*

Everyone, Jew or non-Jew, is different, and possesses a certain degree of distinctiveness if only he or she represents something specific and is not totally lacking in individuality. A true democracy rests on the differences between its citizens, as individuals or as groups. The day these differences disappear will also mark the end of the still imperfect democracy which we now enjoy.

It is not the function of democracy to obliterate or suppress these differences which, whether one like them or not, stem from historic and cultural developments and are also based to some extent on factors which may be classified for lack of a better term as biological. It is democracy's task to harmonize them. Education must strive neither to destroy nor to ignore these differences but to sublimate them, to find the fruitful elements within them and to raise these to a higher level so that they may make their unique contribution to the general civilization of the country.

In America we are blessed (and I say *blessed* advisedly) with a number of group differences which do not generally stem from ethnic descent. Quakers are not distinguishable in any respect from the basic American racial stock (assuming that "basic American racial stock" is a fact and not a myth). They are a native Anglo-American phenomenon, yet one cannot say of them that they are "as American as baked beans." They stand out by reason of some essential differences, yet it will not occur to anyone to question their Americanism.

Or, let us consider another group, less "respectable" than the Quakers and lacking the spiritual aristocratic background which characterizes the Quakers in England as well as in America. I am referring to the sect known as Jehovah's Witnesses. The nonconformist character of this group has in recent years gained a certain notoriety. They do not, for instance, recognize the sanctity of the flag and their children have refused to salute the national colors on certain festive observances in the public schools. Were it up to me I would advise the parents of these children not to bring them up in a spirit of such rigid dogmatism. But Jehovah's Witnesses consider saluting the American flag—any national flag—as a form of idol worship, an infringement on the prerogatives of God's Kingdom on Earth, a fetishist rite. It may be true that their extremism in refusing acts of respect for symbols of American solidarity, such as the national flag, is in itself a form of taboo of which they should rid themselves. I realize my inability to dissuade them from their extremism; nevertheless, I would not question their Americanism, especially when I recall that they are a native growth of the American soil, not transplanted from any foreign land. They do occasionally cause some inconvenience, but it seems to me that with all the rigidity of their concepts of what is right and what is wrong they are more valuable for America than millions of others who ask no questions and take indiscriminately all the elements of our status quo for granted. I was therefore shocked some years ago Felix Frankfurter concurred with other Justices of the Supreme Court in ruling that the children of this sect should be excluded from the public schools—in other words, robbed of their constitutional rights to free education.

I know the objections that will be raised against these analogies. Both Quakers and Jehovah's Witnesses, it will be said, are religious sects, and toleration of religious differences is an organic part of our American heritage. But I have noticed that the concept of religious tolerance as understood by the average American is based on an incorrect appraisal of what constitutes religious differences. The usual idea on the subject is that differences between religions are of a purely metaphysical character and express themselves in varied rituals. It is therefore easy to maintain that it is nobody's business what holy days are privately practiced by citizens in their houses of worship. The State, organized society in general, has no interest in such "private" affairs of the citizenry, and these have no relation to the citizen's duties and responsibilities.

While maintaining such a point of view, we overlook that there exist religious minorities whose difference from the rest of the community is not merely of a metaphysical nature, but manifests itself in definite attitudes toward political, economic and social problems. Thus the political differences that divide Quakers from the rest of the American community are far more earnest than those between Lutherans and Episcopalians or even than the differences between Jews and Christians.

The United States does not impose any civic obligations on its citizens which both Jews and Christians cannot meet equally without violating their religious conscience, but there are civic duties

513

which, though acceptable to Jews and most Christian denominations, are not acceptable to Quakers and Jehovah's Witnesses (military service, specific oaths of loyalty, etc.). Here we are confronted with a case of difference affecting social and political attitudes and not only with variations in the mode of worship. A democracy that wishes to remain true to itself makes allowances for such differences. It may even value them highly, despite the inconveniences which they cause from time to time.

So far as American Jews are concerned, we, too, are characterized by certain differences with whose existence American democracy must reckon and for which allowances must be made. Our differences are not the same as those of other nonconformist groups. But it is in the nature of differences that they *differ* from each other, that they are dissimilar.

The unique mentality of the Jewish people (also of Jews in America) contains a potentiality of emigration, especially emigration to the Land of Israel. This is a potentiality and not an inevitability.

In this respect Jews may not be so unique after all. Judging from my observations, such a mental tendency toward repatriation exists also among Italo-Americans, although objective conditions do not permit such a development. Italy cannot accept any appreciable number of its sons and daughters from abroad. Because of its economic situation, Italy today is a land of emigration, not of immigration. The same is also true more or less of the Irish. Subjectively, a considerable number of Irish in America were in a mood to return to Ireland, especially after that country achieved independence. This is so despite the fact that the Irish have no reason to feel uncomfortable in America. In this instance, too, objective conditions in Ireland preclude such a return. The economy of Ireland, even after its liberation, is not of a sort that can attract immigrants or repatriates. To this day thousands of young people in Ireland dream of lands overseas, especially of America. Gaelic, the Irish national language, has made little progress despite its official status in Ireland and the efforts on its behalf by the government and the public schools. One of the causes for this failure is the fact that a large part of the youth in Ireland still thinks in terms of emigration and therefore feels that the English language would be of greater benefit to them than Gaelic, which no one abroad understands and whose position in the Free State itself is still conspicuously weak.

It is true that, for American Jews, migration to Israel would not be a repatriation in the strict, etymological sense of the word. Such migration would rather be in the nature of the fulfillment of an old traditional sentiment, a longing which in a certain social climate can easily lose its impetus but which can also, under definite conditions, be rearoused and gain new strength.

This potential revitalization of an old dream is part of the Jews' being "different." It is part of the heritage which Jews brought with themselves to America from other lands and which they possessed consciously or subconsciously, even when some of them felt compelled to deny its existence for ideological and other reasons.

Jews need not feel apologetic because of this element in their heritage. It never interfered with the conscientious fulfillment of their duties as citizens of the United States or with their love for the country and its civilization, nor did it hinder the growth of bonds of intimacy between them and the land of their adoption. The unrealized longing, often subconscious, did not lessen their contribution to American life, well-being and civilization.

In any case, that is the way Jews are. Whether this is a perfectly normal phenomenon, I do not know. I have long since given up trying to apply exact measurements to normalcy, and though I realize that the following analogy is far from being a perfect one, I would nevertheless like to point out that while a horse with a hump on its back is definitely a monstrosity, the same deformity on a camel's back is quite normal and may even be esthetically pleasing.

Will American Jews go to Israel in coming years? And in what numbers? I have already stated that there exists a subjective potentiality for such migration. How, when and under what conditions this potentiality may be realized I cannot say.

In any case I rule out the element of catastrophe. I do not care to presuppose a migration of Jews from America to Israel on the basis of prophecies of social cataclysms which will force Jews to flee. Despite our tragic experiences in the old world, I believe that "it can't happen here!" And were I not to believe so, I would have no reason to look to Israel as a haven of refuge. Should the sun be blotted out in America, I could not then see any light anywhere

515

on this planet. A Fascist America would mean a Fascist world; a viciously anti-Semitic America would mean a viciously anti-Semitic world. Should America betray herself, it would mean a moral eclipse on a global scale from which there could be no escape—not even to Israel.

I do not care to share the defiance of that Jewish woman in the popular anecdote who went to the synagogue on the Day of Atonement and presented an ultimatum to the Almighty: "Either You grant me a prosperous year, or I will go to live with my aunt in the country." The aunt in the country is also subject to the jurisdiction of the Lord from whose wrath one cannot escape. The State of Israel can exist and endure only if a certain measure of justice and fair play prevails in the world. Should the world descend below that standard (and we all know how low that standard is at present), Israel could not exist for even a day.

When I think of migration of American Jews to Israel I think in terms of Aliya (ascent) not of flight, in terms of Jews departing from America with a blessing on their lips, with love and gratitude in their hearts, and even with homesickness for America at the very moment when they wish it farewell. For, we must not assume that all situations call for a choice between love and hatred. Sometimes, it is a choice between two loves, one of which transcends the other.

I have already remarked that I cannot prophesy when, how and in what numbers American Jews might migrate to Israel. I recognize the right of being different in some respects not only as between Jews and non-Jews, but also as between Jews themselves. I am not inclined to stereotype the Jewish community in any country and especially not the one in the United States.

I can easily visualize a more or less organic differentiation of American Jewry in our era into three probably unequal groups. One of these groups may in time entirely dissolve in the American melting-pot. Though assimilation is no longer preached as an ideology and a social doctrine, we must not conclude that objective as well as subjective factors working toward group dissolution have ceased to operate. Not all Jews are equally gifted with a will to persevere as Jews, and I am willing to concede that some elements in the American-Jewish community would welcome some form of "kiss of death." I would not like to see those Jews lost to the body of the community, but if they yearn after complete assimilation and the non-Jewish environment does not hinder them, my preferences in the matter will not avail.

I also visualize another segment of the Jewish community, possessing more vitality and a stronger will to continued existence. These elements will seek to survive as American Jews and will draw the strength to endure as a distinct ethnic group from the well-springs of Jewish tradition, as well as from the emergent Jewish civilization in Israel. I do not know what the shape and the essence of such continuity of Jewish life in America will be like. However, we must not rule out possibilities of creative energy to be displayed in the future, even though symptoms of such creativeness are still invisible to the naked eye.

I also foresee a third element, with still greater Jewish vitality, that will orient itself toward a full, dynamic, Jewish life in Israel. It was this element I had in mind when I spoke above concerning two loves, one of which transcends the other.

Assuming that my prognosis is correct, we should not delude ourselves into believing that it is already possible to classify individual American Jews into these three categories. In this respect we should be prepared for many paradoxes, surprises and disappointments. Pilgrims and pioneers for Israel may come from elements which are today non-Zionist or indifferent. Similarly, it is possible that some Zionists of today and their children will seek and find their place in the other two categories. Today, we can only point out those Jews who are ideologically pro-Israel, but it is not at all easy to discover which of them have "a talent for Israel"; talents so often smolder in the depths.

The size of the migration from America to Israel will depend on many factors, some of which cannot even be listed today. The economic situation and the development of Israel on one hand, and socio-economic changes in America on the other hand, will contribute their share. Whether a significant economic restratification will take place in the United States, will be a factor, since persons who have to change their occupations or status are more prone to migration than those whose economic routine remains unbroken. The cultural and moral shape of Israel will also determine its power of attraction. The degree of Jewish isolation or integration in America, as well as the type of education young Jews receive in America in coming years, will also exert their influence.

It is impossible today to weigh these factors, nor was it my intention to do so. I only wished to point out that the migration of certain elements of the American-Jewish community to Israel must be considered by Jews and non-Jews alike as a legitimate process.

In closing, it may not be irrelevent to stress one other point. American law and American political thought has long recognized the possibilities of the type of repatriation which I consider as justifiable. As early as 1779 Thomas Jefferson sponsored a resolution in the Legislature of Virginia defining the rights and duties of a citizen. One of the most significant paragraphs in that resolution outlines *"the natural right which all men have of relinquishing the country in which birth or other accident may have thrown them and seeking subsistence and happiness wheresoever they may be able, or may hope to find them."*

Professor Lauterpacht (in his "International Bill of the Rights of Man") recalls that the same principle was again formulated in 1868 in a joint resolution of both Houses of Congress which recognized *"the right of expatriation as a natural and inherent right of all people, indispensable to the enjoyment of the right of life, liberty and the pursuit of happiness."*

In our own day the spokesman of the American delegation to the Hague Conference on Codification of International Law made the following declaration: *"For a century past it has been the policy of my country that the right to expatriation is an inherent and natural right of all persons. True it is that allegiance is a duty, but it is not a chain that holds one in bondage. . . . This principle is not a little thing. It is not a question of language, or of formulas, or of phrases. It is a principle of the rights of man and of the liberty of the human race."*

HAVE JEWS A DIVIDED LOYALTY?

By JOHAN J. SMERTENKO

FOR MORE THAN fifty years, an increasing number of Jews in America have been engaged in a foreign affair. With ever-growing interest and intensity they have participated in the effort to create a Jewish State in Palestine. Today, with the admission of Israel to the United Nations and the establishment of a minute and menaced country of indefinite boundaries and uncertain future, this effort—known as Zionism—has achieved a measure of success. But this has served rather to increase than to diminish the sense of responsibility and involvement of Jewish Americans in the new State. And it has brought to the point of decision a question which has vexed and perplexed them through all these years but which they were under no compulsion to answer so long as the Jewish State was a prophetic ideal rather than a political reality.

The essential part of the question is whether American Jews are now liable to a dual allegiance. But around this nub are layers of social and political issues, some hoary with age and others of recent formation, some affecting only the Jew and others touching basic American concepts of assimilation and nationality. Actually, the relationship of Jewish Americans to Israel will be determined neither by themselves nor by the new State, but by America. It is necessary, therefore, that all Americans understand the affiliation of Jews outside Palestine to Israel, the difference in position and attitude between Jewish Americans and Jews elsewhere, the effect of an independent Jewish State on the national status of the Jew in the United States and in other countries, and, most important, the role and responsibility of the American people in determining the final decision of the American Jew.

To many dispossessed and declassed Jews in Eastern Europe and in the Near East, to the Jews who lead an uncertain and uneasy existence in the anti-Semitic atmosphere of countries like South Africa where nationalist elements exploit prejudice against the Jew, Argentina where Nazi doctrines are still prevalent, or the Soviet Union where the Jew is persecuted as a "cosmopolitan," the land of Israel represents a hospitable haven for themselves and an inalienable home for their descendants. Their resolve to return to Palestine is motivated by a conscious and practical desire to escape the status of second-class citizenship and the stigma of alienness, to live unashamed and uninhibited by such characteristics of national peculiarity as accents, features, and gestures, to establish their own mores and determine their own destiny—in brief, to be equal, normal, and independent.

But it is also actuated by what I call instinctive nationalism. This is not at all a political phenomenon. It is, rather, the subconscious urge of any people with an intrinsic and sustained tradition to survive as a distinct entity, developing and demonstrating its particular genius in its own particular way. This national longing, as Mazzini put it, "to elaborate and express their idea, to contribute their brick also to the pyramid of history," is intuitively associated by all expatriated peoples with a yearning for their homeland. It is a sound instinct. For only on the soil where the original pattern and rhythm of its life were evolved, where endemic factors and forces have molded its character, and where both tangible and intangible influences have engendered its culture, does a people's genius burgeon into fullest and finest flower. Though segregated in physical and psychological ghettoes, the Jews of the Eastern Hemisphere have been nationally sterile throughout the two thousand years of their exile. The urge to express themselves now operates with tremendous albeit subconscious power.

Moreover, the cataclysm of the Second World War and the recent Arab conflict have added an emotional compulsion to the rational and instinctive motives that impel the persecuted Jews to Palestine. The survivors of Nazi extermination camps, the hounded Jews of Moslem countries, and all their oppressed kith and kin were forged into a nation both by Hitler's furnaces and by the ardent defense of the Israelis against the Arabs. The Jews experienced the profound difference between the roles of helpless victims and heroic patriots. A sense of patriotism as well as of security makes them feel that in Israel they can offer effective resistance to the threat of extermination. With a fervor that is born of emotional conviction rather than intellectual certainty, they believe that their future is inseparably linked with their ancient past and that their only hope for happiness lies in their ancient land.

Most of the Jews in the United States, however, do not share this conviction any more than they shared the martyrdom of European Jewry. They do not believe that life, liberty, and the pursuit of happiness are attainable only in Israel; nor do they feel the urge to seek expression for their Jewish personality. On the contrary, from Colonial days on, the majority of Jews who came to America bent every conscious effort to suppress their instinctive nationalism and to conform to the mores, traditions, and attitudes of their adopted land.

This drive toward assimilation was given great impetus by the fact that in the middle of the nineteenth century Jewish immigration was welcomed. While Irish Catholics and, to a certain extent, German and Scandinavian immigrants were being attacked by the Know-Nothing party, Jewish immigrants found that the good-will and acceptance won by Colonial Jews had been extended to include them. Their appreciation of this welcome took the form of a phenomenally rapid adjustment to American life. They learned the language more readily and spoke it more fluently than other aliens. They adopted citizenship at the earliest opportunity. They discarded their traditional social customs and abandoned their cultural heritage as being out of tune with the young, materialistic civilization of which they so ardently desired to be a part. They even made fundamental changes in their religion to sanction the new mode of life.

If this process of assimilation had progressed unchecked to its natural consummation, there would be no question of Jewish allegiance today—nor even a "Jewish question." But two complementary factors arrested the process and created a situation that must be resolved before the question can be finally answered. The first is the growth of anti-Semitism in the United States; the second stems from it—the Jewish attitude toward America.

In this country, anti-Semitism is not a political movement like nazism, but a prevalent attitude with wide social and economic ramifications. While the reasons for this phenomenon were many and various, the basic cause lay in the fact that the First World War brought an end to the American epoch of limitless resources and expanding frontiers. The postwar depression frightened old-stock Americans and centered their fears on the hordes of immigrants who had risen from their place as menials and laborers in undesirable fields to the rank of competitors in all of the many phases of American economic life.

Now the fear-engendered antagonism was directed chiefly against the Jews. They were the latest and most numerous immigrants; they were the immemorial scapegoat of Christian society for the discontents and hatreds provoked by our competitive civilization. The average American was unconscious of these underlying causes and of the fact that his antagonism, rooted in the prejudice inherited from our medieval past, was being stimulated and exploited for mercenary gain and political advantage by anti-Semitic organizations. He declared that the Jew was a disagreeable and irritating fellow, objectionable as a competitor or a colleague or a neighbor. And he had his reasons. They were grounded as much in Jewish virtues as in Jewish vices; they were attributable no less to the temporary and superficial qualities of the Jewish immigrant's condition than to his inherent and unalterable traits.

Like all mass migrations, the Jewish exodus to America at the turn of the century was composed chiefly of the lowest social and economic class but, unlike others, these immigrants immediately sought to rise to a higher level. For they brought with them that consciousness of persecution which has for centuries stimulated Jews to great achievement. Americans, though more aggressive and energetic than most peoples, could not feel that urge, compounded of physical necessity and psychic impulse. They quickened the tempo of their economic life to meet the competition, but they resented the additional effort and disliked the Jew for increasing the pace.

Similarly, Americans resented social intrusion on the part of the Jews. Sensitive to the point of an inferiority complex about their own social status, since with few exceptions they were of lower-middle-class origin, they were provoked by the problem which the Jew presented. For the Jews rose unnaturally into the class of the socially eligible, as measured by standards of wealth, occupation, and education. Within one generation, the lowly peddler, tailor, junkman, or sweatshop worker wondrously won a place among the leading merchants, lawyers, physicians, and manufacturers of his community. But though he, or his children, had acquired the knowledge and means to admit him to the highest ranks of our commercial and professional life, this strenuous effort left neither time nor energy for the acquisition of social graces. He retained the manners and concepts that characterize the lower classes the world over. He was plebeian, coarse, and aggressive.

Obviously, the difference between Jewish parvenus and others who sought—and received—admission to our upper classes was due to the difference in speed with which the Jews emerged from the lower depths. The children of English tradesmen, Scandinavian peasants, German artisans, or Irish navvies climbed more slowly the rungs of the social ladder and acquired the polish time puts on things and men.

The "successful" Jews leaped the entire distance and arrived bristling with rough edges. To be sure, the Jews had the normal immigrant quota of people of culture and good breeding. However, by and large these were neither financially successful nor socially ambitious, lacking the aggressive, competitive, and mercenary qualities that America demands from nine to five and deplores after office hours. But the arbiters of American "society" were not interested in the whys and the howevers. They decided that Jews were repugnant and undesirable, and their verdict was reflected in the popular attitude.

In the intellectual realm, too, there were grounds for antagonism. A temperamental difference irritated even those who are not normally susceptible to the prejudices of the masses. The American is liberal only in his traditions and principles; he is conservative in habits and attitudes. The immigrant Jew was orthodox in his traditions and beliefs; undisciplined in habits and attitudes. The American mind is the product of freedom, security and contentment; the Jewish mind was the issue of persecution, insecurity, and unhappiness. The American is essentially pragmatic, interested solely in the specific issues that affect his well-being, and intolerant of general criticism; the Jew was a dialectician, concerned about everything that affects the social order, and neurotically critical.

I have dwelt on these irritating differences, not because they are important in themselves but because they served to rationalize anti-Jewish prejudice in America and thus operated as a brake on the process of assimilation. Actually, due to the formative force of our environment, the second generation of white immigrants reaches the American norm in every social characteristic and motive habit. So, at the same time that this antagonism was being implemented in the social and economic life of the country, the very reasons adduced for it were vanishing from the American scene. Both relatively, by comparison with other nationalities, or absolutely, by drawing a balance sheet of vices and virtues, it could be proved that most of the Jews in the United States conformed to the manners and traits of the average American. Such proof, poured forth in interminable protests, apologies, and rebuttals, had no effect whatsoever on the growth of anti-Semitism. As the American historian Bancroft observed long ago, "The prejudices of ignorance are more easily removed than the prejudices of interest. The first are blindly adopted, the second willfully preferred."

Sixteen years ago, in an article on anti-Semitism published in this magazine [*Harper's*], I traced the development and effects of this prejudice "of interest" up to that time. It will be seen from the following quotation that virtually the same situation exists today:

At first its manifestations were so trivial that it seemed absurd to take them seriously, much less to combat them. That some exclusion was practiced against the Jew was deemed a ridiculous and un-American bit of snobbery more derogatory to the institutions which indulged in it than to the Jews. But gradually the blot of discrimination spread into an ever-widening stain of ostracism—from society to the school, from schools to offices, to shops and factories. And there followed, as a matter of course, exclusion from common privileges and communal enterprises. Today, it is no secret that Jews have great difficulty in gaining admission to the institutions of higher learning and that their opportunities for legal and medical training are limited to a minimum. It is equally well known that the professions of banking, engineering, and teaching are closed to all but a few and that the quasi-public-service corporations rigorously exclude them. In the mechanical trades the discrimination is almost as widespread as in the professions, and in clerical work it is worst of all.

Inevitably, these conditions influenced the Jewish attitude to America, and this reaction constitutes the second factor retarding assimilation.

The apparent paradox that the more Americanized a Jew became, the more conscious he grew of his lower-caste status is no paradox at all. Native in our country for two or more generations, conditioned by our environment, taught in our schools the fundamental equality of citizenship, he was more sensitive to the discrepancy between American ideals and practices, more resentful of race discrimination, more jealous of his rights and dignity than the ghetto-timid Jew of the Old World.

Automatically, and without realizing all the implications of their action, Jewish Americans took steps to meet the challenge of prejudice. Jewish clubs, fraternities, veterans' groups, etc., were the obvious answer to exclusion; so was voluntary segregation at vacation resorts or in sections of town and city. Increasing emphasis on Jewish education—a striking instance of which is the study of Hebrew in such uncompromising citadels of assimilation as Reform temples—was a conscious effort to intensify the Jewishness of the younger generation as a form of defiance to those who branded such Jewishness inferior. The renascence, through new members and fresh funds, of purely Jewish organizations, which had come into being to aid the immigrant and were dying as a result of his rapid Americanization, was a defense measure against the threat to Jewish civil rights.

But the most significant element in the Jewish reaction to anti-Semitism was the adherence of many Jewish native Americans to the Zionist movement. At the beginning of the century, Zionism in America was limited to the recent immigrants from Eastern Europe. It was at first ignored and later vituperously condemned and combated by the leaders of American Jewry who feared, even then, that an interest in Jewish nationalism would cast doubts on their loyalty and allegiance to the United States. Slowly and reluctantly, most of them were brought around to accept the philanthropic aspect of the movement, and this gave point to the sarcastic aphorism that the Zionist was a Jew who got money from another Jew to send a third Jew to Palestine.

However, the next generation of Jewish Americans, who returned from the first world war to see the Ku Klux Klan, the Dearborn *Independent,* and other anti-Semitic manifestations rampant in the land, found something besides a charitable institution in the Zionist movement. It became a compensatory substitute for the social activities from which they were excluded. Membership in Avukah (intercollegiate Zionist organization) offered some consolation to the youths who felt unwelcome in college societies; by joining Junior Hadassah, young Jewish matrons could engage in the same sort of ball-room charity as the members of the Junior League; and young and old found an outlet for communal enterprise in the annual drives for millions of dollars, with all the perquisites of organized philanthropy in the form of honors and offices, testimonial dinners, and pictures in the newspapers. Thus, although less than 10 per cent of American Jewry was affiliated with the Zionist organization, it became the yeast-like nucleus of the Jewish community in almost every city and town.

Affiliation with Zionism, no matter how slight and superficial, established a pattern in Jewish-American life. By virtue of it, thousands found meaning and satisfaction in their daily experience. Its compensatory character strengthened its hold upon them. Almost imperceptibly, American Jews became involved in the problems and politics of the Zionist movement. Pride in the American contribution to the establishment of the Jewish State, both in funds and in political influence, added a sense of responsibility for the welfare of the persecuted Jew to what was once merely sympathy for his plight. Even without sharing the latter's nationalism, American Jews began to think of Palestine as the place where they had a particular interest and a personal stake. When Arab armies invaded Israel, thousands of Jewish Americans offered to enlist in the Israeli forces, and hundreds actually joined in the fighting at the risk of forfeiting their American citizenship and sacrificing their lives.

Taken in the aggregate, these actions constitute a definite departure from the American Jews' earlier ardent efforts at assimilation. They indicate a tendency toward separateness in individual interests and communal activities. The Zionists have exploited this tendency for their own laudable purposes. But the temptation to perpetuate it has given rise to the idea that American Jewry can be developed and crystalized as a cultural minority in this country.

"We American Zionists glory in our citizenship in the American nation and in our fellowship in the Jewish nationality," states a pamphlet issued by the Zionist Organization of America six years ago. "As we develop in this country an essentially Jewish life, with Jewish spiritual and cultural values, we shall to that extent also fulfill our obligation as citizens of America. American democracy confers the right, imposes the duty, upon every nationality to be loyal to its own heritage, to be true to its own best and noblest self." This idea is extended to its maximum in a report submitted at the recent national convention of the organization by a commission which devoted an entire year to a study of the question:

The Jews of Israel and the Jews out of Israel are bound together as one people with a common heritage of religion and culture. Jews everywhere have therefore a special concern for the unimpeded flowering of Jewish civilization in Israel and for the tranquillity and happiness of the Jews in their ancient home. Moreover Jews everywhere anticipate the enrichment of their spiritual lives from the renaissance of Jewish culture in Israel.

Israel is a sovereign State. Only the citizens of Israel owe it allegiance. The establishment of Israel has in no-wise affected the citizenship of Jews of other lands. . . .

The existence and unity of the Jewish people have been and are basic postulates of the Zionist movement. An invariant aspect of the Jewish people, throughout its tri-millennial history, has been its attachment to the land of Israel. . . . The modern Zionist movement is an instrumentality fashioned by the Jewish people for the preservation of Jewish existence and the perpetuation of its unity by the re-creation of the Jewish State in Israel, the revival of Jewish culture, and the revivification of its creative forces. These aims are, in their very nature, as eternal as the Jewish people; and the responsibility for their pursuit and furtherance can never be fully discharged. . . .

(1) To safeguard the integrity and independence of the State of Israel as a free and democratic commonwealth by means consistent with the laws of the several countries whereof Zionists are nationals or inhabitants. . . .

(2) To assist in the organization of all Jewry for the above-stated purposes by means of local and general institutions in conformity with local law.

(3) To strengthen Jewish sentiment and consciousness as a people and promote its cultural creativity.

Now this bombastic definition of the relationship between world Jewry and Israel may be accepted as it stands, or may be interpreted simply as a desire to ensure a reservoir of money and manpower outside of Israel. In either case, the Zionist pronouncements are invalidated by two fundamental fallacies where they are intended to apply to America.

Unlike the ethnic states of Europe and the Near East, where national minorities are an accepted characteristic of the political structure, the United States has no place for even ethno-cultural minorities as distinct elements of the nation. The concept of cultural pluralism has been advocated in this country by such distinguished thinkers as Charles W. Eliot and John Dewey, but it is contrary to our traditions and incompatible with our way of life. Our formative concept is based on the principles that "all men are created equal," that we are a nation of many origins in which none has priority, that the new immigrant can and will merge with the old. "America has indicated her desire," wrote Woodrow Wilson, "to be made up of all the stocks and influenced by all the thoughts of the wide world. She has seemed to realize that she could be fertile only if every great impulse were planted among her. And she has set for herself . . . the problem of making disparate things live together in peace and accommodation and harmony."

Because this concept is also an ideal of human relationships, it remains an "unfinished process" imperfectly realized. In practice, most old-stock Americans think that they fulfill their duty to the Melting Pot by heating it with occasional Americanization tracts and night-school interpretations of the Constitution. At the same time, they expect the Jew or Irishman, the Slav or German or Italian, to leap into the crucible and by mysterious alchemy get himself transmuted into the Anglo-Scot-Dutch-Huguenot hybrid whom they consider the proper American type. They fail to take their own proper place in the crucible, though they know that only the positive action—intermarriage—of both the group to be assimilated and the nation that wants to absorb it can achieve the complete transformation of racial traits which makes one type out of two or more.

Yet notwithstanding these and other failings of the flesh and despite the relatively unsolved problems of the Negro, the Jew, the Nisei, the Mexican, and the Catholic, the fundamental idea has remained unimpaired. It is incorporated in our traditions, propagated in our schools, ineradicable from the American spirit. It is manifested every day and everywhere in myriad forms. It is stronger than ancient prejudices and temporary separatist tendencies. For it is a way of life that in itself demands a homologous and mutually interdependent relation between individual citizens.

Moreover, the Zionist conclusion that the stimulus derived from Israel and the tendencies I have discussed above would induce Jewish Americans to accept the abnormal status of a cultural minority is entirely erroneous. Already we have seen that the creation of a Jewish State has tended to normalize the position of the Jew everywhere. It has given him a place of reference, a place in which his right to live is taken for granted. For the first time in two thousand years he is like other men in this respect. He "belongs." He is thus a free agent whose deliberate choice of a land is in itself a token of his desire to belong to it. When Israel is fully established, it will free the Jew in another and more significant manner. He will no longer feel that in making his choice he may be deserting his people in the midst of their battle for existence. Like the Englishman, Frenchman, Italian, and others who leave their native soil to plant their roots elsewhere, he will know that this personal action has no bearing on the survival of his people and their culture. This sense of freedom, both conscious and subconscious, may well be the determining factor in his complete assimilation.

As for anti-Semitism and the Jewish reaction to prejudice, these are but ephemeral digressions in an automatic and inexorable process. Against their influence, there is the far more powerful force of cultural assimilation which is proceeding at a constantly accelerated pace. In the United States, the Jew—no less than any other individual—is incessantly bombarded by the customs, habits, attitudes, and ideas that constitute the American environment. We have no ghetto here imposed by official decree. There is no limit on contacts with all types of Americans who together form a synthesis of the American type. In fact, like an atom in the cyclotron, the individual cannot avoid these contacts or escape the bombardment. Given the natural desire of the average man to be "normal" —that is, like the people who surround him—the effect of this bombardment is inevitable, fundamental, and permanent. It is the making of an American. The Jewish immigrant wanted this normalcy consciously and eagerly. His children and his children's children have been conditioned by it and molded in its form. They cannot change their behavior patterns now without violating their American personality, without destroying themselves.

It is only in the light of all these facts that the question of the Jewish American's loyalty to the United States can be seen clearly. The issue of dual allegiance has been raised many times here in connection with citizens of various nationalities. The Pilgrim Fathers protested against the Scotch and Scotch-Irish on the grounds that their corporate affiliation with institutions across the Atlantic constituted a menace to the new way of life that "may well prove fatal in the end." Benjamin Franklin feared that if the influx of Germans into pre-Revolutionary Pennsylvania were not diverted to other colonies, the original settlers would "be not able to preserve our language, and even our government will become precarious." One hundred and sixty years later, Theodore Roosevelt called the Germans "hyphenated Americans" and charged that their presence threatened the security of our country. When Al Smith ran for the Presidency, there was serious as well as intemperate discussion on whether a Catholic's allegiance to the Pope disqualified him for this high office.

More analogous to the present situation are the instances that followed the First World War, when Czechoslovakia and Poland were reconstituted and Ireland won her freedom. It is undeniable that the independence of these states was in a great measure due to the political, financial, and even military support given to their mother countries by Americans of Irish, Czech, Polish, and Slovak descent. The Irish, especially, opened a front here in their war against England, and behind this front established their headquarters for propaganda and fund-raising, for economic boycott and political pressure through candid and concerted activity in Congress. Dire conclusions were drawn from these exhibitions of "divided loyalty." But the prophecies proved as untrue as the charges. What actually happened when these states were re-established was that a substantial number of their people gave up American citizenship and went back. The rest remained here and retained a normal interest and concern in the affairs of their countries of origin, no more and no less than do Americans of English, Dutch, French, and every other stock.

Naturally, the first to raise the cry of "dual allegiance" against *all* Jewish Americans were the very anti-Semites who have persistently denied the Jew an equal place in our body politic. Zionist leaders promptly denied the charge and again proclaimed the loyalty of *all* Jewish citizens. Their denial was supplemented by the statement of Foreign Minister Sharett, on taking Israel's seat at the UN Assembly, that "the State of Israel claims no allegiance from Jews in other lands." On the other hand, the anti-Semitic accusation was echoed by a small though vociferous group of self-styled "assimilated" Jews, who hastened to dissociate *all* such Jews from "the fanatic Zionists." Haunted by the fear that the long-delayed establishment of a Jewish State will affect adversely their status as citizens, they rushed into print to testify to their 110 per cent patriotism and Americanism and to deny sharing the sentiments and efforts in support of Israel.

No one can speak for *all* the Jews in the United States. At most, one can only predicate their ultimate action on the basis of known factors and conditions. The crisis, compounded of the tragedy of European Jewry and the conflict for survival and independence of Israel, evoked the interest and participation of a large number of Jewish Americans in a foreign affair. When the crisis has passed, Jewish Americans will make their decision. Israel, which is swamped today by the thousands who must go there or perish and which seeks no immigration from the United States except for a few highly skilled technicians, will invite all Jews to return. I believe that of the estimated six million Jews no more than 15 per cent—and no less than 10—will answer that call. Two classes will compose the bulk of this emigration: Zionists whose participation in the movement has been based on nationalist ideas rather than philanthropic activities; and strictly Orthodox Jews who cannot reconcile their way of life with a dominantly Christian environment and who have held the belief through the ages that their hope of salvation lies in the Holy Land. There will be the usual small percentage of those who, having failed to make their way in one country, are anxious to seek their fortune in another. And there will be a small but significant number of impatient souls who go not because they feel less American than those who remain, but because they will no longer suffer the petty indignities and profound injustice of prejudice and discrimination.

The vast majority will stay in the United States. It is here they are at home; alien in Israel. Here are the graves of their fathers, the uniforms of their husbands, brothers, and sons; the birthplaces of their children. Proud of their background, conscious of their Americanism, certain of their loyalty, they will not feel the need to swear allegiance every time a cur barks at their heels. Their very decision will be sufficient proof of it.

But America will have the last word. She will determine whether this is their own, their native land. For assimilation is a dual and reciprocal process. Each individual is incorporated and digested by the surrounding mass much in the same way that a particle of food is absorbed by the amoeba. At the end, both the individual and the environment are mutually changed. When the United States is 4 per cent Jewish—not in population statistics only, but in the warp and woof of her character—then she will make her Jews 100 per cent American.

BEN GURION'S DISPUTE WITH AMERICAN ZIONISTS

By BENNO WEISER

A WOMAN FROM London told me of a visit that a British WIZO group paid to Israel's first prime minister. With a feeling of awe the ladies looked at him. "A head of fire," whispered one. "And his white mane is like a glacier to cool it off!" David Ben Gurion looked at his visitors, his eyes moving from one face to another. Then he said with a rather sad smile: "I wish you were younger!"

It might be safely presumed that the ladies wished so, too, but some minded the remark, though they understood that Ben Gurion meant to say: where are the youth? who will do the job when you are gone?

With some similarly blunt remark, Ben Gurion started the controversy, still running, over the failure of Zionists to settle in Israel. Israel needs immigration from the West; Zionists in the West want to help Israel by all means *short of their own migration*—this conflict of positions has developed as inexorably as in a Greek tragedy.

The first dart was hurled from a banquet dais of New York's Waldorf-Astoria in June, 1951. Prime Minister Ben Gurion, incensed, or perhaps only bored, by some remarks from Zionist leaders who had engaged him in a discussion, stated that so far as he was concerned "a Zionist is a person who settles in Israel."

The issue reached full expression later in the year, at the Zionist Congress of 1951 in the appropriate setting of Jersusalem. There, the discussion revolved around philosophy of history rather than ideology. Some Israeli delegates said that what had happened to German Jewry could happen everywhere: Herzl had prophesied, Nordau had warned, but European Jewry had been deaf and blind;

what was Western Jewry waiting for? Mapam's speakers trod another line: the Jews were no longer needed by the countries of the *golah;* whatever their original functions, they had outlived them; there was no future for them outside Israel. The American delegates disagreed. Hadassah's Rose Halprin distinguished between *galut,* meaning exile, and *golah,* meaning dispersion; America was Diaspora, but not exile. This was countered by the late Hayim Greenberg, who stated that "every country of the Diaspora . . . is *galut.* . . . If exile may be conceived of symbolically as night, then there are some exiles of pitch-black night, and somewhere the night is moonlit." But he told the Israeli prophets of *golah's* doom that, should America really "become a land of fascist anti-Semitism, then there may be no safety even in a timely flight to the Jewish State. If we should ever see a bestialized America, how long could the State of Israel exist in a world capable of producing such a monster?" Dr. Nahum Goldmann went further: addressing himself to the "it can happen everywhere" party, he said that "even Hitler was not inevitable"; had the German Social Democratic leaders had "a little more guts" the whole catastrophe might never have occurred.

The controversy lingered on after the Congress, but Aliya, halutzic and otherwise, from the United States continued its downward trend to a low of one hundred thirty in 1953.[1] After a while even the discussion, purely academic or dialectical as it was, faded away.

It was revived in the last days of 1953 by Ben Gurion again, who in the meantime had become a private citizen. In a letter to the Zionist General Council date-lined from Sdeh Boker, he asked the session convening in Jerusalem to clarify whether "a Zionist movement, particularly after the establishment of the State [is] feasible without the duty of personal immigration, and if so, what is the difference . . . between Zionism without the duty to immigrate and between a love for the State of Israel which is common to almost every Jew wherever he be? What is the ideological content and the special mission of Zionism without immigration and what personal duty is imposed upon a Zionist by the movement, by which one may differentiate between a Zionist and between a Jew who assists the State of Israel?" This challenge was repudiated by

[1] The halutzic Aliya (the body of emigrants who settle on the land) from the United States alone was 325 in 1949, 438 in 1950, 375 in 1951, 190 in 1952, and 110 in 1953.

most of the delegates. Even Ben Gurion had to admit that "undoubtedly, many Zionist workers, and the Zionist Organization abroad, have much credit for the work in the past. But as far as I am concerned, Zionism is a movement that faces the future."

As far as the Zionist workers themselves were concerned, however, that past could not be brushed aside so lightly. In it lay the best years of their lives. There were some bitter answers. If an Aliya from America was desired, said Rose Halprin, "you in Israel must become that ethical force which youth [in the Diaspora] can look up to." The accent was on *become*. Another Hadassah delegate, Judith Epstein, stating that most American Jews, Zionists included, "feel themselves part and parcel of the United States," found that American youth cannot be trained to anticipate spending their lives "elsewhere." A new chord was struck by Israel's Berl Locker, co-chairman of the Jewish Agency, who said: "We must stop saying to American youth that they should come to Israel because they need it. We must start saying to them that they should come because we need them."

Winding up, Dr. Nahum Goldmann said that if Ben Gurion's definition of Zionism were adopted, Zionist organizations abroad would dwindle to nothing. But effort should still be made to persuade some American Jews to come to Israel—not by stressing negative aspects, like anti-Semitism or Jewish social inferiority in the *golah,* but by educating them to feel that "you cannot live a 100-per cent Jewish life in America."[2]

Ben Gurion, writing in *Davar,* was still dissatisfied. Asserting that he had been rebuked but not answered, he continued to heckle the Zionist Organization and Zionists. He did not know, he stated, a single Zionist leader from the West who had settled in Israel since the state had been established. Sadly, he wrote: "The essence of the Jewish question in the days of Pinsker and Herzl was the prob-

[2] I cannot believe that this definition accurately expresses the thinking of Dr. Goldmann, who, besides being the acknowledged leader of world Zionism, is also a citizen of the world. Some people in the Williamsburg section of Brooklyn live, in their way, a life as 100 per cent Jewish as their brethren in Mea Shearim. On the other hand, unhappy connotations have accreted in the last two decades to national hundred-per-centisms. Our generation saw chauvinism lead to two world wars. It saw the Nazi mania of German racial purity, and the Soviet persecution of "cosmopolitans." As a part of his Jewish heritage, the young Jew carries along a basic liberalism and cosmopolitanism. Why should Jews be attracted by a 100 per cent life of any sort?

lem of a people without a country and a state. It never even entered their minds that there might once be a Jewish state without a people [to settle it]."

As could be expected, the American Zionist press did not side with Ben Gurion. *The American Zionist*, published by the Zionist Organization of America, stated editorially: "The truth is that the number of Jews . . . who have immigrated to Palestine from any land since the inception of the Zionist movement has been small. . . . Voluntary immigration to the Yishuv first became feasible on an organized scale in 1904. After 1932, with the rise of Hitler, such immigration became for the most part compulsory. During the intervening twenty-nine years . . . the mean number of Jews living in Europe was seven and one-half million. . . . The pressure on European Jewry to abandon their native lands was enormous and persistent. . . . And immigrate they did. While 155,000 European Jews took the road to Zion, nearly two million European Jews immigrated elsewhere—chiefly to the Americas. . . . Not enough American Jews settle today in Israel, it is true, but virtually no American Jews settle elsewhere abroad."

There were exceptions, though. *The Jewish Spectator* agreed with Ben Gurion. In a book review-editorial, its publisher, Dr. Trude Weiss-Rosmarin, took Maurice Samuel to task for the unorthodox views which that lifelong Zionist expressed in his latest book, *Level Sunlight*. Mr. Samuel had written: "More than once I felt the inclination to settle in Palestine, perhaps to throw in my lot with the pioneers on the land. Reflection showed that it was not for me"—the reason being that he was a writer, and English was his tool. Dr. Weiss-Rosmarin comments: "*We* Zionists know, *all of us know* . . . that our place is in Israel. . . . But, like Mr. Samuel, we have reached the conclusion that 'life in Israel is not for us.' Let us admit it, the real reason that keeps us here are the flesh-pots of America." But, though Dr. Weiss-Rosmarin *knows* where her place is, she does not go there, so her disagreement with Mr. Samuel remains one of rhetoric. "We have no quarrel," she continues, "with Mr. Samuel's conclusion that life in Israel is not for him. . . . We Zionists who stay on in the Diaspora live in the same glass house, and so it would be dangerous to hurl stones against a fellow-boarder."

Evidently, the critic herself is not free from the guilt she senses in the criticized. Perhaps no sensitive Diaspora Zionist is. Undoubtedly, no single person has done, by word or deed, as much to bring that guilt out as Ben Gurion has. If his aim was to make Zionists feel uneasy and remorseful, he has succeeded. But if his aim was also to put them on the move, he has failed so far.

I know of a Zionist leader from Germany who, during my boyhood days, was an idol and inspiration to many a Zionist youngster. He is now living in this country and his speeches and talks still glow with the same spirit as of old. But he confessed to me the other day that he had dropped out of the Zionist Organization. Not so young any more, the provider of a family, and tied down to a profession, he has his own reasons why Israel is not for him. But he agrees with Ben Gurion's definition and, to be consistent, he left a movement to which his heart will always belong. . . .

A paradoxical situation has arisen. Unaffected by remorse, many a non-Zionist, who perhaps was even an anti-Zionist once, has made pro-Israel work a cheerful part of his social routine. All the enthusiasm he did not invest in the Zionism dream is now being poured into the endeavor to keep the dream-come-true alive. He readily finds everything connected with Israel wonderful. On the other hand, many a long-time Zionist has now lost his Zionist enthusiasm. His Jewish *Weltschmerz,* cured by the existence of Israel, has been replaced by Zionist *Weltschmerz.* Made to feel guilty and projecting his guilt, he is prone to find fault with Israel and even to experience incidental *Schadenfreud* over the shortcomings of its leadership.

Nor has his guilt feeling proved to be constructive. There is the anecdote of Ben Gurion's asking an immigrant from Germany whether he was not ashamed of not speaking Hebrew, to which the man replied, "It is easier to be ashamed than to speak Hebrew." Similarly, it is still easier to feel guilty than to settle in pioneering Israel.

For all practical purposes, it is beside the point whether Ben Gurion is correct or not. If one delves into Zionist doctrine, Ben Gurion is certainly right. But how many Socialists have really read Marx, and how many Zionists, Hess, Pinsker, Herzl, and Borochov? For the great majority, Zionism was a sentiment rather than a doctrine. What Nathan Birnbaum meant when he coined the term "Zionism" some sixty years ago may be of interest to scholars.

Whether Herzl said "the Zionist movement is the Jewish State on the way," as is generally presumed, or "the Jewish *people* on the way," as Ben Gurion quotes him, is an academic question. But if today's Zionists are being blamed for inconsistency, from a practical point of view it might be more useful to understand what Zionism used to mean to the average Diaspora Zionist who is now the target of Ben Gurion's challenge

It was not *just* the fight for a Jewish State. Zionism used to be a *Weltanschauung,* a way of life, and an expression of Jewish pride —a flight into Jewishness, the opposite of many a Jew's flight away from it. While others were frequently tempted to find a tangible explanation for anti-Semitism in Jewish characteristics and often ended in self-hatred, the Zionist would not blame the Jews, but the Gentiles, because it was their anti-Semitism which had created the ghetto that was responsible for the unhealthy traits of Jewish life in exile. Whereas others looked for a "cure" for being Jewish, Zionism meant honorable adjustment to Jewishness and transcendence of the ghetto. It was a way of love, love of something inescapable which he did not want to escape from—love of everything Jewish, the unseen persecuted brother, whether near or far.

The difficulties and complexities of living as a Jew became, through Zionist ideology, as stimulating as a voluntary handicap in a game of chess or a foot race. It averted undignified Jewish mimicry of Gentiles. Even the shock of catastrophe was partially absorbed by the consolation found in the fact that Zionist literature had foretold it. There were German Jews who committed suicide because of the blow Hitler had administered their dream world, but there was no shattering of illusions for Zionists.

The Zionist had heard Herzl's saying that the Zionist movement was the "Jewish State on the way." The utopian state was a means of going through life with head erect, and not so much an end in itself. Maurice Samuel speaks for a whole generation, perhaps, when he writes in his *Level Sunlight:* "How much of the Zionist program did I hope to see completed? . . . I did not think I would live to see the proclamation of a Jewish State."

World War II, the plight of its Jewish survivors, and their concrete homelessness changed this attitude, and the Jewish State became a question of now or never. But the Zionist still did not see the Jewish State only as an end in itself. By then ideology had been replaced by propaganda, and the thinkers had lost out to the fund-raisers. The latter's *Reader's Digest*-like condensation of Zionism read as follows: At the bottom of the Jewish problem was Jewish homelessness. There were millions of Irish, Swiss, Italians, *et al.* who lived unmolested outside their states. Similarly, the Jewish State was not supposed to take in all the Jews of the world, but it would eliminate the handicap a Jew had in comparison with an Irishman. There were some ingenuous, though sincere, conceptions about the miracles a Jewish ambassador could perform by the sheer magic of his title; but this idea implied enjoying the ambassador's splendor *in* the Diaspora. Not that the possibility of one day settling in, or retiring to, the Jewish State was deliberately, or knowingly, ruled out. But it was not a necessary part of the scheme.

Ben Gurion is right when he says that these Zionists did not create Israel. But no single factor did, and Israel could not have been created without them. These non-immigrating Zionists were a dynamic force in every Jewish community, and they mobilized financial and political support for the Yishuv. True, they brought up the rear, and the real heroes were the halutzim, who were glorified by them and looked up at with a mixture of pride, admiration, and uneasiness. Yes, the man who could tear himself away from those things which to them—the non-immigrating Zionists—made life pleasurable, to go and fight swamps, malaria, and the desert, brought out that discomfort which the average man will always feel in the presence of idealists.

There have, in fact, always been two threads in Zionism: that of "self-fulfillment," embodied in the halutz, and that embodied in those other, non-pioneering Zionists whom Ben Gurion is now criticizing. Ben Gurion's attitude is an outgrowth of that basic contempt which the halutz has always felt for the other kind of Zionist. With the miraculous establishment of the state, this contempt was legitimized. But soon other elements were added. Bitterness, because those who had fought and made the sacrifices had thought of a state for the Jewish people and not of a dumping ground for wretched and destitute Jews alone; impatience, because the country desperately needed sturdy and "modernized" immigrants from the West; jealousy, because moral superiority was rewarded with depressing economic inferiority; and finally, frustration, because idealism in the country itself could do with a boost from abroad.

Some of this resentment found its escape in prophecies of the Diaspora's doom. If catastrophe alone could move the Jewish people, then catastrophe might become desirable. Some of the resentment went into Ben Gurion's outcry from Sdeh Boker. But if Ben Gurion was right in his affirmation that non-immigrating Zionists should settle for the title "friends of Israel," then he would have been equally right if, years ago, he had told them to call themselves "friends of the Yishuv." Though immigration was not free under the Mandatory regime, "capitalists" could immigrate, and one thousand British pounds made one a "capitalist." Nobody hinted then that Zionists who possessed that sum and did not settle in Palestine were not Zionists.

If it was only a question of proving that the moral biceps of the halutz, and the Zionist complexion of the builders of Israel, were superior to those of Diaspora Zionists, there probably would be no argument. But if something more than the expression of an Israeli grudge against the Jews of Western Europe and the Americas is involved, it might be more useful to consider what it was that created Zionist pioneers like Ben Gurion, and what has changed since then.

According to Jacob Lestchinsky, "virtually all the old Jewish population centers which enjoyed traditions between one and two thousand years old . . . have now disappeared." On the eve of the First World War "more than 75 per cent of the Jews dwelt amid peoples who had only slight assimilative capacity. . . . Now, however, more than 80 per cent of the Jews live in surroundings which favor assimilation to a very marked degree. . . . At the beginning of the twentieth century, about 70 per cent of all Jewry resided in Eastern Europe. . . . Thanks to an entire set of auxiliary conditions it came about that this section of the Jewish people gave birth to almost all its social and national movements." But whereas in 1900, 80.9 per cent of the Jewish people lived in Europe, in 1951 only 23.8 per cent did, and only 9 per cent in non-Communist Europe. Today 80 per cent of the Jews outside Israel and the Soviet orbit live in the Americas.

The difference between the psycho-political climate in which the American Zionist lives and that in which the bulk of European Zionists lived might be illuminated by a remark which a veteran

Zionist from Germany made to me the other day. "Could you imagine a Zionist meeting in Berlin, even in pre-Hitler days, where the audience would sing both 'Hatikvah' and 'Deutschland, Deutschland ueber alles'?" By contrast, without the slightest tinge of hypocrisy, the "Star Spangled Banner" is sung alongside "Hatikvah" in the country. A whole Jewish world has disappeared, an entire epoch has come to an end. Gone is the revolutionary spirit endemic in the Russia of the beginning of the century; gone that creative frustration which made young Jews run away from the ghettoes of Eastern Europe. Whatever the future for American Jewry, it is not *shver tsu zein a Yid* in America today.

True, among those who went to Palestine in the old days were many who left comfortable homes and academic careers because they preferred the unleavened bread of freedom to the "fleshpots." But the hateful feature of Egypt's fleshpots was that they could be enjoyed only in bondage. America's steaks are eaten in freedom. Revolutionary Zionism was a catalyst which converted discontent with one's surroundings into action, and made young Jews break away from their European environment and the economic system in which their parents made their living. But there was nothing artificial in their discontent: the environment gave it plenty of cause. And the discontent was fruitful in terms of Zionism.[3]

In a restlessly shifting European Jewry, Jewish Palestine was the idealist's way out of the dead-end street in which many a young Jew looking for a liberal profession found himself. Nor was the temptation of "business" so great. Life in Palestine was hard, but it was also so in Eastern Europe. The alternative was frequently between a *luftmensh* existence in a more or less squalid ghetto, and fresh air in Palestine.

Too, socialism was still young, shiny, untested. Against the background of *luftmenshentum,* prevailing "business" conditions, and the anti-Semitic charge of Jewish parasitism, the Marxist contempt for the man who did not live from his handiwork, as well as

[3] It is symptomatic that the most successful halutz movement today belongs to Mapam. Of the 1,438 halutzim who went from the United States between 1949 and 1953, 450 came from the ranks of Hashomer Hatzair. Adding 83 from other groups, Mapam's share reached 37 per cent of the halutzic Aliya from the United States over that period. In other countries, Mapam's proportion is still higher. Aside from the question of a better recruiting technique, it is the ideological ingredient of this very leftish movement that provides the necessary discontent with the Western environment that one's being a Jew alone apparently fails to build up nowadays.

its mystic sublimation in Gordon's religion of labor, could fall on fertile ground. The dream of national redemption, Jewish renascence, and Socialist utopia, set the course to Palestine. The early halutz was a daring, revolutionary, and heroic product of his time.

And what a different time it was! I know only by hearsay about revolutionary Russia fifty years ago. But when I think back to the post-1918 Europe in which I grew up, as did the greater number of Israel's younger officials, diplomats, and politicians—many of whom went through the halutz movement and the kibbutz—it seems to have fairly swarmed with ideals and ideologies. All kinds of self-effacing, abstemious, and ascetic movements were in vogue. There were vegetarians (for ethical, not for dietary reasons) and sandal-wearing nature boys, esperantoists and pacifists; Gandhi's passive resistance made people starry-eyed. There were Social Democrats deeply convinced of the infallibility of their doctrines, and ingenuous Communists still dreaming those dreams which the harsh reality of Stalinism has since wiped out. I remember how unhappy a writer friend of mine felt in those days because he had been referred to in a review as a "liberal poet." To be a liberal then meant to be stamped, by the sheer weight of relativity, as a reactionary. *Halutziut* was one of the answers of young Jews to this idealistic whirlpool.

Things have changed quite a bit in the meantime, and if they have not changed completely in Europe, Jewish geography has changed. Two world wars have shaken faith and idealism. According to Abram L. Sachar, president of the Brandeis University, "a whole generation of liberals has swung from high ideals to the ugliest forms of cynicism and escapism. In political life the passion for relaxed living has created a formidable neo-isolationism. . . ."

In a world that has lost its ideals, Israel, which is founded on ideals, has stood up remarkably and even astonishingly well. Social ideals, which remained blueprints almost everywhere else, have made a deep and lasting impact there. On the other hand, there has been much talk since 1948 of the "moral crisis" which the country is undergoing, and whose symptoms are supposedly black-marketeering, nepotism, petty careerism, etc., etc. Israelis try to explain this to themselves by blaming it on eighteen years of almost uninterrupted tension and hardship in Palestine itself. But is it not also, to a degree, the subconscious adjustment of a society of high-pitched idealism to this present world of ours? And isn't Israel, even in this relative crisis, which ought not be exaggerated, still out of tune with a world in which private self-interest is increasingly taken for granted?

Meanwhile the creation of Israel has brought about a paradoxical change in the Diaspora Zionist's outlook not dreamed of in his or Ben Gurion's philosophy. It has become easier to be a Jew. After all the doom and melancholy of the Hitler period, jubilation, happiness, and pride have again entered his life. Organized anti-Semitism decreased as a result of the defeat of Nazi Germany —and also because of the liquidation of some of Europe's worst centers of anti-Semitic infection in the wake, alas, of the disappearance of their corresponding Jewries. The world has probably not become better, but it has become more livable for the Jew in Western Europe and the Americas. Besides, Israel has removed anti-Semitism from his list of incurable diseases, for it promises him a refuge, or at least an ally, in duress. It has also felt good to hear, after a decade of Jewish victims, of Jewish heroes. Whether or not his Gentile neighbor now looked at him differently—and most probably some did—his self-respect increased.

Thus the birth of Israel helped eliminate to a degree one of the most important allies of Zionism, namely the frustration that had become part of the Jewish fate, the Jewish *Weltschmerz*. Since the relief was felt by other Jews than Zionists alone, Israel won many a friend in new quarters. But while this broadened the new state's basis of support, it was not conducive to Aliya. To leave the Diaspora, which suddenly had become much cosier, precisely now would have been like abandoning the ground where one had searched for gold for many years at the very moment when the first nuggets turned up. Hence Israel's first dividend to West European and American Zionists—a new sense of security, relative, of course, in a world which had become insecure—has helped them find a new ease in the Diaspora.

In 1947 and 1948, with the exception of a small fringe, American Jewry at large started to talk in terms which a few years ago would have been the exclusive prerogative of the Zionists. In return—as Dr. Siegfried Kanowitz, a very sensitive Israeli psychologist, noticed on a recent visit here—there has been an assimilation of the Zionists. According to him, the "post-Zionist assimilationist" does not quote prophets at every opportunity, nor does he speak of the Jewish "mission." he simply identifies himself with Israel, celebrates her festivals, applauds her victories, and laments her defeats. He becomes angry when her citizens descend from their moral heights. He contributes to Zionist funds, visits Israel, and even affiliates ideologically with Mapai, the General Zionists, or Mizrachi.

Also, he keeps his Jewish pride before his Gentile neighbors, does not crawl on his stomach, stresses his Jewishness, and his Jewish ties, including those to Israel. At a housewarming of his new country home he might even hint to an Israeli guest of a certain sadness at the fact that he did not build it on Mount Carmel. *But he feels perfectly at home where he is.*

Dr. Kanowitz is not a bit superior about all this. Himself a lifelong Zionist and for a time president of the Zionist Organization of Berlin, it required Hitler's advent to move *him* to Israel. "We look into ourselves," he writes, "and ask ourselves if . . . in all fairness it was not under rather unique conditions that we became Zionists, remained Zionists, and went to Israel. . . . The post-Zionist assimilationist is an expression not less perfect of his time, than we were of ours. . . ."

The sterility of the present dispute about the nature of Diaspora Zionism stems from the fact that problems were broached polemically, and the battle fought in the field of dialectics. What makes one a Zionist in Ben Gurion's eyes is, after all, not the real question, and whether a Zionist nowadays should be called a Zionist or a "friend of Israel" is a matter of semantics. The two genuine issues that emerge from Ben Gurion's challenge are, first: how bring Western Jews to Israel? And second but less important: what is Zionism today?

In connection with the first question, it might be worth rereading what Theodor Herzl wrote in his *Judenstaat,* sixty years ago. Unlike Borochov and Gordon, who have left more of a mark than he on the social composition of Israel, Herzl thought in terms of a bourgeois society basically like that present American one to which Ben Gurion's call is now directed. Speaking in his introduction of the exodus to the Jewish State that would occur one day, he wrote: "We shall not revert to a lower stage, we shall rise to a higher one. . . . We shall surrender our well-earned rights only for better ones. We shall not sacrifice our beloved customs; we shall find them again. We shall not leave our old home before the new one is prepared for us. Those only will depart who are sure to improve their position thereby; those who are now desperate will go first, after them the poor; next the well off, and, last of all, the wealthy. Those who go in advance will raise themselves to a higher grade, equal to those whose representatives will shortly follow. Thus the exodus will be at the same time an ascent of the class."

After fifty-eight years, much in the passage just quoted sounds more realistic than a great deal being said at present by Zionist and Israeli leaders. Though most Israelis would shudder at the very concepts embodied in them, these lines do prove that Herzl, the idealist, knew how to think in terms of those Jews whom *he*—and now Israel—wanted to attract. The bitterness of Ben Gurion, who helped win a beachhead for the Jews that most Jews still won't follow him to, is understandable. But a beachhead society cannot afford to think only in its own terms.

"If the facts are against Israel," said Ben Gurion in a speech in 1951, "we must change the facts." There are some facts about present-day Diaspora Jewry which, I suppose, even Ben Gurion would not want to change. If, therefore, "pull" has to replace "push and pull," "pull" must change.

Though Israel needs Western immigrants *now,* she may not be able to get them in appreciable numbers until conditions in the new state have greatly improved. Until then, Israel may have to go to special lengths if she wants more Western, middle-class immigrants. Up to now no real effort has been made in this respect. As things now stand, many a middle-class immigrant to Israel, after selling his belongings, buying his ticket, then paying customs and even luxury taxes on some of the things he brings into Israel with him, and exchanging his money and paying key money for an apartment, ceases to belong to the middle class.

Also, Israel's government has been blamed for not really knowing how to handle immigrants or prospective immigrants from the West. The number of the latter has not been negligible, and Ben Gurion's attack on Diaspora Zionists may be in a way a projection of unconscious guilt, because there is no question but that the dominance of Socialist ideas in Israel has worked against her own present desire for settlers with money, or at least investors. The country still remains better geared for the absorption of penniless immigrants than of those who can pay their own way, and when Ben Gurion speaks of immigration he continues to think of it as halutzic. Dr. Nahum Goldmann has a broader approach, but he still sticks to the term. *"Halutziut* may have to change its form," he has said. Agricultural life in collective settlements is no longer the only "legitimate form of halutzic effort," but also investment in industry and commerce, and almost any kind of immigration to Israel, even if merely temporary. But the question is whether *halutziut* with its connotation of self-sacrifice really appeals to a businessman.

What is Zionism today? Are definitions really so important? While other Zionist organizations spend their time discussing why they are dying, America's Hadassah, with its membership of 300,-000 suffers no crisis, because it is *doing*. Six years of discussion having now proved futile, the time might be ripe for a moratorium on ideology and theory, and for more concentration on immediate activity. Tasks are not lacking. First, there is the material support that Israel needs, as she does also the Diaspora Jew's identification with her in one way or another; second, the establishment of a *symbiotic relation* of *mutual* helpfulness, between the Jewish homeland and the Diaspora. Now that assimilationism presents itself less as a flight than as a drifting away, Zionism's national and cultural conception of Jewishness can become an important factor in Jewish survival. Zionism might again mean Aliya for some, help to Israel for others, a way of Jewishness for many—and for others again, a social need, a sentiment or even sentimentality. Israel has nothing to gain by repelling any of those Zionisms. They will either be Zionist on their terms or not Zionist at all.

Zionism has survived many a defeat. Now it has to survive victory. It faces the problems of how to replace *Weltschmerz* on the one hand and superficial jingoism on the other, and how to adjust an audience created by the dramatic events attendant upon Israel's birth to the prosaic routine of growth. No single *ad hoc* assignment can provide a program. And certainly the Zionist movement cannot insist on including, in the Jewish prayerbook, a special prayer for our daily slice of anti-Semitism so that more Jews will be drawn to immigrate to Israel. A two-thousand-years-old nostalgia must be able to forego that "sinister ally."

History is written by deeds rather than by words, and however controversial the words that come out of Sdeh Boker, Ben Gurion's settling in the Negev is in itself a challenge. The image of the white-haired, stocky man working day in, day out, under the desert sun has an appeal which does not require the persepective of time to become a prophetic legend. Israel's prophets used bitter words in their anger, but they were often right. So, basically, may Ben Gurion be when he cries for Western Jews to come and help build the Land of Israel. But his challenge is stronger in terms of idealism or need, without ideology and dialectics.

YOU CAN'T GO HOME AGAIN

By ELIEZER WHARTMAN

I AM AN AMERICAN Jew—American born of parents American born—who finds he "can't go home again." Israel has "ruined" me. After a four-year stay in that country, I find that there is no coming back—a permanent coming back—to "the old country." There can be no return to the *galut* for one who has once left it to live in the Land of Israel. Even when he leaves Israel to revisit the country where his fathers died, the memory of the Holy Land haunts him tantalizingly in his wakefulness until he casts aside the hollow forms of life to which he has become accustomed and takes himself back to the source. Try as he may, he simply cannot go home again.

People have asked me what it feels like to be coming "home" again. And they are surprised and offended when I ask them how they think a Jew would feel coming back to *golah*. Wanting to tell them my emotions and yet unable to communicate with them because there simply is not the same background, I feel somewhat like the man in Wells's *The Land of the Blind* who, having had his sight restored, tried to describe the heavens to his blind companions and who was rebuffed by them for being a liar—and a blind one at that!

Actually, before my return here, I did not know how I would feel coming back to America. It was in Italy, *en route* to the United States, that I began to sense a bit of the emptiness I would later feel, when I bought a *Time* magazine and read how a spokesman for American Judaism had expressed what appeared to me to be some of the most incredible ideas as to what makes for a meaningful Jewish life. For the spokesman the days of fear were over. For

548

me they were just beginning. The uneasiness deepened as I passed through France and England and saw the same old attitudes to Jewish life that I recalled from my pre-Israel days. Judaism to the Frenchman and the Englishman, as it is to the overwhelming mass of American Jewry, consisted of a nostalgia for the Jewish past as recalled by the memory of a bewigged *bobeh* blessing the Sabbath candles or the recollection of the corner delicatessen where one could feast his eyes on the various Jewish foods temptingly displayed on the counter. The old memory of Judaism consisting of little more than *kashrut* in the home and an occasional Sabbath attendance in the synagogue arose to gag me. The possibility that such a rich Jewish culture as I had lived in during the last four years was now behind me and I was coming back to anti-defamation societies, bingo-luncheons, *Yizkor* services and Sunday schools was an almost unbearable realization. After tasting the full richness of Jewish life in Israel, one can never happily adjust himself to the dull, insipid, artificially inspired existence that Jewish life is in the Diaspora, and I began to feel the full impact of the words "you can't go home again." Home? More like an institution.

In modern Israel, Judaism is assuming normal and healthy operation (with several exceptions with which I will deal later). If the definition of Judaism as a "way of life" is accepted, it naturally follows that Judaism can be lived most satisfyingly in an environment where it can be lived most intensively. Judaism consists of many ingredients: there is a Jewish culture, a Jewish past, a Jewish sense of destiny, a Hebrew language, a Jewish ritual, etc. It is too complex to be boiled down to any one ingredient. Yet throughout the centuries there has been a constant reduction of the implications of Judaism because of the necessity of adjusting Jewish life to a non-Jewish, non-sympathetic Gentile environment, until in America today the term stands for little more than a particular religious belief. In practice, Judaism has degenerated into little more than a shell of what it once was. In the time when the entire Jewish people lived on its own soil, it developed its own set of customs and values which sprang from the normal way of life by which any people produces a distinctive culture. Each religious ritual in ancient Israel had actually a dual significance: on the one hand, it conveyed some metaphysical meaning; on the other, it had national significance. Thus the rites associated with the ingathering of the harvest, beside conveying a religious idea, provided the people with some tangible way of celebrating the holiday. To have had the one aspect without the other, was a patent absurdity, for the one was directly related to the other: the one provided the underlying idea of the holiday; the other provided the form.

In the Diaspora today the once rich celebrations have lost almost all of their pageantry. Severance from the soil cut deeply into the enthusiasm felt by the people for customs they had formrly practiced differently in their own land. But the compactness and unity of the pre-American Diaspora community provided in its day a satisfying framework in which the customs and holidays could be enjoyed. With the break-down of the ghetto walls, however, and with the reckless eruption into freedom, Jewish life has been irrevocably shattered and grows progressively sterile. For living in an alien atmosphere which dominates and colors all the life around them, Jews are paying a heavy toll. Hanukkah, the Feast of Lights, has almost been overlooked in the Christmas shuffle. Santa Claus, the Christmas trees, the Christmas legend, the carols, the Christmas gifts, the Christmas vacation are all very vital for the Jewish child exposed to the Christmas clamor for the better part of a month each year. At best, Hanukkah is simply the lighting of a few candles and the exchange of a few gifts, largely done, one suspects, to counteract the dominating Christmas spirit. Hanukkah will never, despite all the exhortations of rabbis and teachers, become as meaningful to the American-Jewish child separated from the land of the Maccabees as Christmas is to the Gentile child. And the same holds true of Pesach, Shavuot, Lag B'omer, etc. The little enthusiasm left is growing weaker from generation to generation.

Not so, I discovered, in Israel where the festivals are not only being rejuvenated but given new and dynamic interpretations. Hanukkah there, strictly from the point of view of mass participation, is the counterpoint of Christmas here, with all its pageantry, color, symbolism, infectiousness and life. Torchlight parades, the kindling of vast and innumerable menorahs, the parading of a victorious Jewish army, the government pronouncements, the press, radio and theater, all vividly recalling the struggle of the ancient (and modern) Maccabees—this is the celebration of Hanukkah there. It is a spontaneous outburst, not something assiduously cultivated by rabbis and teachers.

Similarly with every other phase of Jewish life: Hebrew, the language of the people, is not something to be studied painfully for two or three years prior to Bar Mitzvah, but the living language of the populace. Jewish history is studied as a matter of course by all school children, as is geography, Bible and in many cases Talmud. There is no such animal as "Jewish Book Month," for it is not needed. And anti-defamation activity may be considered necessary in America (I think it a colossal waste of funds), but would be ridiculous in Israel. Judaism is literally bursting its bounds in Israel today in a rich and riotous outpouring.

With Israel's growing importance as a place where Jewish life can be lived maximally, the role of American Jewry becomes increasingly unsatisfying. Whether we like to admit it or not, the root, trunk, bough and flower of Jewish life is now in Israel. We are a secondary center, a tributary, a satellite moon. It is only in the sphere of religion that American Jewry still has something to offer, for in this area Israel lags a good thirty years behind America in development. It is this tragic lack of growth that has estranged many a *sabra* (native-born Israeli) from the faith of his fathers. But although he lacks the religious interpretation of life that his forefathers had, he still has much left: he is on intimate terms with the Torah, though he may not believe in its divine origin; he is familiar with his history and literature and, in his own way, observes the holidays and customs. His everyday life, no matter how far away he thinks he is from traditional Jewish life, brings him into contact with some aspects of it. Even an *epicuros* can sense when it is the Sabbath day in Israel. He may not believe in the Divine intervention which in the faith of his fathers gave religious significance to Purim, but he certainly is very much aware of Purim when it rolls around. And although God does not figure for him in the ancient *yetziat mitzraim*, exodus from Egypt, he celebrates Pesach joyfully, recalling the modern *yetziat mitzraim*, the enforced going out of the Egyptian army from his country.

In America this daily contact is missing. The only symbol of Jewishness in most Jewish homes is—if it does exist—the observance of *kashrut*. Aside from this there is almost no sign of meaningful Jewish content to be found. Study, learning, piety, once the heart of Jewish life, have all but disappeared. Study was once the very kernel of Judaism, and customs like *kashrut* were the *seyag*

551

latorah, the fence which safeguarded everything connected with study. A Jew once lived in order to study. His working hours were regarded as necessary to provide him with the means to study in his leisure time. A life without study was regarded as an empty one. Synagogue attendance, ritual observance, etc., were all secondary to learning.

But now only a few empty observances remain. Ritual observance in America, by and large, is only a protective shell, protecting nothing inside. The kernel, the essence, the heart is gone.

There is the rub. That is why the Jew who has lived in Israel finds that he "can't go home again." To what? To the shell? To the outward forms? To the abysmal ignorance of which the shell is at once the symbol and cause? We are engaged in a vast operation of self-deception: we are heaping philanthropy upon philanthropy, building a dizzy pyramid of charity erected on a wobbly base of Jewish illiteracy, and by busily engaging in the raising of funds which will enable others in a distant land to live Jewishly, we imagine that we are discharging our duties to ourselves and our Jewish civilization here. One cannot live Judaism vicariously. The raising of funds certainly is commendable and necessary, but it is not the substitute we would like to think it is. If nothing else, the constant giving of funds ultimately debases the giver as well as the receiver. It cannot go on indefinitely, and when the need no longer exists (may the time not be too far distant!) what will remain when we remove the mask and realize that, although we have helped build a dynamic Jewish culture elsewhere, we are destitute of Jewish culture here?

And yet, ironically enough, a revival of Jewish learning in America would carry within it the seeds of its own destruction. I believe that the sensitive, literate, articulate Jew will, of a certainty, gravitate toward a milieu where he will find himself completely at home, where he will discover kindred spirits. Such a place will be Israel. We will raise a group of leaders who will find happiness elsewhere. To raise them is dangerous. Not to raise them is foolhardy. So where do we go from here?

True, some aspects of life in Israel are discouraging. People there do not have the same background of democratic living that we have here. Their smugness is at times unbearable; their high-handed attitude toward values cherished by the Western world is

YOU CAN'T GO HOME AGAIN

harmful. In terms of democracy, in a man's relations with his neighbor, they have ever so much to learn from us, and living with them can, at times, be distinctly unpleasant.

But these are attitudes and they can be changed. Time and circumstance will force the change. But the general overall framework of a population daringly experimenting with all possible forms of social organization remains. That, I feel, will not come here. Aside from the feeling that I was living in a Jewishly creative world, I had also the sensation of living in a society that had not yet been permanently molded and was seeking to find a political and social way of salvation that had as yet been undiscovered by older and supposedly wiser countries. Here one has the feeling that he is only a very insignificant part of a vast, imponderable machine which was there before he appeared on the scene and will be there long after he has passed away. His contribution is, at best, negligible. The forms have already been set, the mold cast.

Not so in Israel. There new ways of life are being constantly tried out. No experiment is shrugged off without a trial. The fluidity of life has not yet congealed into a mold. There is not the tired cynicism there that one finds here. The country is united by the magnitude of the task before it, and the terrible specter of what failure might bring. Witch hunts are not capable of being passed off as national goals. Anti-Communist hysteria, though Israel lies closer to the Soviet bloc, has not stopped all liberal and progressive thinking there. Lobbies are as yet something unheard of in Israel politics. The individual is not robbed of his sense of being able to influence legislation as he is here, where he knows that blocs and trusts and behind-the-scenes-men play a far greater role in determining what laws are to be passed than he will ever be able to.

One has the feeling here at times that his fate is linked with the fate of one hundred and fifty million others "going nowhere very fast." The life of each man seems detached and dissociated from the next man's and none of the lives seem to have any relation to a national goal. Only the feeling that we are fighting *against* something binds one American to the next. A national goal, something to shoot *for*, seems lacking, each one being wrapped up in his own private dream. This attitude is especially hard for the American returning home from Israel to accept. The still fresh remembrance of a people that is going through frightful times, reducing itself to the bone, going without basic necessities simply for the national goal is something almost incommunicable to the American Jew. While he will sympathize with Israel, he will never experience the deep pain or pleasure. Not only is the apparent aimlessness of American life frightening, but even more so is the fact that, even if Jews should attempt to influence the course of the country in an organized fashion, their votes and voices would always be regarded not as those of impassioned citizens, but as "the Jewish vote"—as if there is something unique and different about a Jewish approach! *The essence of the tragedy is that we have become so accustomed to more delicate dealings with the Gentile, and to being accepted as "the Jewish vote" that we fail to see anything wrong or unusual about it.*

Probably the most immediate sensation I felt upon return, and it grows daily, is the fact that I am no longer one of the majority but a member of a tolerated minority. True, we have as many rights as the next man, but we feel constantly obliged to remind the others that these rights are due us—something that a Jew in Israel would never dream about. And while in this country we have the right to express ourselves as we please when we please, we exercise considerable restraint in doing so because of our peculiar and unhappy status. A word in anger dropped in a bus in Kansas City has ominous connotations for the Jewish passenger. The same word would be laughed off by a bus passenger in Tel Aviv. The simple, overwhelmingly satisfying feeling of normality, of unrestraint, of being unashamed because of the actions of others is gone here. Here I must be "normal," alike, not different from the other gray-faced passengers. A full-throated laugh would bring a hundred staring eyes, some of them conveying the unstated dislike of "that boisterous people."

The sense of belonging to "that people" is overwhelming. The realization that one is Jewish lies just under the surface of consciousness and colors all relationships. One is just a little more careful, just a little more polite, just a little more apprehensive when dealing with non-Jews. (And the same holds true, of course, of the non-Jew in his dealings with Jews.) It is a mask that is terribly trying to the wearer, that leaves him furious with having to wear it, that makes him want to go somewhere where he can throw it away and be completely and unashamedly himself. A Jewish wit has pungently summed up the difference between Israel and American Jewry. "One," he said, "is conscious, the other self-conscious."

It is hard to accept the idea that one is leaving his old home to strike out for a new and strange land. Yet it was that spirit which made America great, indeed that led to the founding of this great land. Leaving the land of one's boyhood, one's friends, is hard. The idea that one no longer belongs to a world power but is throwing in his lot with a small undeveloped country is at first hard to swallow. Jefferson, Lincoln, Paine all come swimming out of the mist. But one does not have to leave these giants behind. One can take them with him.

I remember that just before leaving Israel I went to visit an army camp to look up some old friends of mine who were in training. A little discouraged with things and a bit soured at the attitude of the *sabra,* I felt apprehensive as to whether I would ever return to Israel and I said so. One of the soldiers thought a while and then turned to me and said, "You'll return, Eliezer. You'll return weeping that you have to live among Jews. Yes, you'll literally weep. But you'll return."

And I shall.

PAINTING IN ISRAEL

By ALFRED WERNER

ART LIBRARIANS HAVE had a difficult time with the label, "Art, Jewish." It created special problems, requiring as it did a second, separate listing of such names as Chagall, Liebermann, Modigliani, Soutine, and so on. In 1948, a new question turned up to confuse the cataloguers still further: the new State of Israel had come into existence, and it was logical to revise the category, "Art, Palestine," as well as to add another label, "Art, Israel"—comprising the works coming from this brand-new republic in the Middle East. At this point some librarians (and with them a few critics) asked: "Is there such a thing as a specifically Israel art? On what basis are the artists of that country to be regarded as a group *sui generis?* Have they produced an art which is 'characteristic,' as French art is characteristically French?"

But how "French" is the French art of *today?* Art has become one of the most international forces in modern life, bridging the gulfs between ethnic and racial groups. While a Foujita retains Japanese qualities in his canvases, his studies in Paris have made his essentially a Parisian or European artist. The *Ecole de Paris* owes as much to artists from the Netherlands, Germany, Italy, Spain, Eastern Europe, and even Asia, as to those of Gallic ancestry. Tolerant France has made no attempt to impose upon foreign-born artists (or its native creators, for that matter) a "French" view of life. As a result, the art produced in France in our time is a blending of many strains; it is in many respects universal.

It will be readily seen that a pedantic approach to "national" labels in art can produce great confusion. For example, the term "Jewish art" could be questioned as follows: Should the works of

Camille Pissarro, who had no Hebraic background, be included in this category together with the frescoes of the ancient Dura Europos synagogue—which may have been the work of Greeks or Persians? Chaim Soutine was a typical *Ostjude,* but his portraits, landscapes and still lifes are "French." The "racial" origin of his "distortions" has been the subject of some interesting essays, but this is still a matter of speculation.

Strictly speaking, there have been very few major artists deeply imbued with Jewish lore and capable of translating it into the language of esthetics—for example, our contemporary, Marc Chagall or the late Jankel Adler.

In other times, frontiers could serve to create distinct artistic, as well as political, characteristics; in the fifteenth century, for example, there existed different regional schools in Sienna, Florence and Venice, each of these an independent republic. But an unmistakably and wholly "national" art cannot be launched in an era of airplanes, when distances and frontiers have lost their former importance, except where countries isolate themselves for political reasons. Non-religious "Jewish" art developed in the age of the railroad among a people something more and something less than a nation; and if it showed—apart from subject matter—any "national" traits, these were an *international* mixture of French, German, Italian, Russian, etc. "National literature," Goethe remarked to Eckermann at the beginning of the nineteenth century, "is now rather a meaningless term; the epoch of world literature is at hand, and everyone must strive to hasten its approach." This dictum could also be applied to music or the fine arts. Ironically, it was Goethe's compatriots who, a century after he had made his grand utterances, tried to turn the clock back and to create a "Teutonic" art, entirely stripped of foreign influences.

Artists have generally had a habit of creating art without reference to the fixed notions of the scholars. We would therefore achieve more by examining their works than by seeking to define the precise meanings of labels. The fact is that for a century and a half men and women of Jewish origin have been creating works of art in many countries, in many styles and in different media—although one may be understandably reluctant to include in a history of Jewish art individuals whom the late Joseph Kastein characterized as *Randjuden,* those who lived as far removed from the core of Jewry and Judaism as possible, and those who had decided upon a formal break with their brethren. In Israel, of course, such an issue does not exist. Whatever questions—ideological, political or religious—there may be among the 300-odd members of the *Agudath Hatzayarim V'Hapassalim* (the Israel Association of Painters and Sculptors), "being a Jew" need not—and does not—represent a problem to them.

There are already striking indications that excellent art can develop in Israel, freely and democratically. Many sources of inspiration exist for the artist in this little country—in the colors and shapes of the land and sky, in the excitement of its present and the mystery of its past.

That past was not as devoid of an artistic life as is commonly believed. The old notion, held by the nineteenth-century archeologist Felicien de Saulcy, that Jewish art never existed in antiquity (*"L'art judaique n'existe pas, il n'a jamais existé"*) is being revised owing to discoveries made during the past few decades. For about thirteen centuries (600–1900 C.E.), however, Palestine was, from the viewpoint of art lovers, largely a desert. The works of Christian architecture in Old Jerusalem, Nazareth and elsewhere are the creations of non-Palestinians who built replicas of Byzantine or Western European churches and castles; as for "Moslem" architecture, the famous Omar Mosque in Jerusalem was built by Greek architects.

When Theodor Herzl visited the country in 1898 he encountered, not art, but poverty, misery, and "heat in sportive colors." There was deep dust on the roads, and very little vegetation. While Herzl deplored the preponderance of dirt and rubbish, he was profoundly impressed by the beauty of Jerusalem in the moonlight:

"If ever we possess Jerusalem," he vowed, "and if at that time I am still active, I will have it cleansed. I will have everything that is not holy removed, erect workmen's dwellings outside the Old City, empty the dens of dirt, destroy them, burn the non-holy rubbish and move all bizarre trappings elsewhere. Then, following as far as possible the architectural style of the city, I will erect a comfortable, ventilated, canalized new city around the holy sites."

When he and his associates visited the Wailing Wall, all but

Herzl wept. Asked for an explanation, he said with a disarming smile: "I am thinking of the beauty that can be created here."

In 1906, two years after Herzl's death, the sculptor Boris Schatz moved to Palestine; he, too, was thinking of the beauty that could be created there. At Jerusalem he founded the Bezalel School of Arts and Crafts, and 1906 has been accepted by many people as the year that Art in Israel began. Boris Schatz founded his school in a virgin land at a time when most of the relics of ancient Hebrew arts were still waiting to be excavated. The aims of his school were impressive: he wanted "not merely to teach arts and crafts in Eretz Yisrael, but to create Jewish art: to gather together the threads not only in Palestine, but from the whole world, threads that have been spread and diffused these 2,000 years." As long as he confined himself to teaching the Bezalel pupils to imitate the silver filigree work and carved olive wood objects of Yemenite craftsmen who had trekked to Palestine around 1900, he was on safe ground. But as soon as he became bold enough to attempt the creation of a "new Jewish art," he failed abysmally.

We cannot ignore the fact that Schatz was not an outstanding artist. In Paris he chose to follow, not the great Rodin, but the academician, Falguière. The Tel Aviv critic, Karl Schwarz, for example, has dismissed Schatz's well-known *Maccabi* statue as a "pathetic knick-knack." Curiously, neither Schatz nor his associates —including men like Hirszenberg, Lilien, Pann and Krestin— seemed to have been affected by the revolution that had been accomplished in Paris by Impressionists and Post-Impressionists; if any "influence" managed to penetrate Bezalel, it was that of Munich's formalistic *Jugendstil,* as represented by Lilien.

Though old Bezalel's teachers were unwilling, or unable, to infuse modern ideas into their pupils, the influence of the school as a whole was a salutary one. It would be unfair to think of Bezalel solely as a factory for cheap souvenirs produced for tourists. Bezalel aroused enthusiasm for art in thousands who had never before had contact with art; it made the community "art-conscious," albeit on a relatively low level. A large percentage of the "veterans" among Israel's painters and sculptors—we mention here Zeev Ben-Zvi, Nahum Guttman, Aharon Halevy, Munia Lender, Batia Lishansky, Israel Paldi, Rubin, Menahem Schmitt, Avigdor Stematzky, A. M. Sternschuss, Sionah Tagger and Jacques Zucker—availed themselves, usually for a short time, of the opportunities Bezalel offered. In addition to instruction, it provided needy students with food, lodging and even pocket money. It is significant, however, that there are few traces of Bezalel training and of Schatz's worried conservatism left in these men and women, many of whom went to Paris for their final studies. Bezalel thrived before the First World War, was completely disorganized during 1914–18, and while it again functioned during the twenties it never regained its former importance.

The New Bezalel, organized after the death of Schatz in 1932, has little in common with the old one. Its first director, Joseph Budko, was a pupil of the modern German schools, as was its present head, Mordecai Ardon-Bronstein, whose recent exhibition in New York was warmly praised by the critics.

When Schatz arrived in Palestine a much younger artist, Amedeo Modigliani, was moving from his native Leghorn to Paris. And the *Drang nach Westen* of such youngsters as Chagall, Pascin and Soutine—who formed the nucleus of what came to be known as the *Ecole Juive* of Paris—coincided with the trek to Palestine of men like Rubin, Aharon Halevy, Jacques Zucker, and other idealistic young men from the East European ghetto in the years immediately preceding World War I. Eventually, around 1925, there existed two clearly distinguishable groups of Jewish artists in the world.

The men in France were, unmistakably, the greater artists. They were by no means a homogenous group. Some of them produced what might be called ghetto art without the ghetto—a sudden, sometimes neurotic, bursting-forth of energy long suppressed under the rigidity of the iconoclastic Mosaic tradition. The artistic vocabularly of men like Chagall, Mané-Katz and Ryback was "Yiddish-French" in its expression, Yiddish-Russian in its subject matter. Others, like Modigliani, Pascin and Soutine, never indulged in nostalgic ghetto reminiscences, the first two because they had never lived in the ghetto, Soutine because he had run away from it in disgust and horror. Yet to a non-Jewish observer they all belonged to the same school. The eminent critic, Charles Terrasse, referring to this loosely knit batch of foreign-born artists, insists that "there is a form of genius which is unmistakably Jewish." He goes on to say:

"The fundamental characteristics of this genius are an indefinable sadness and remoteness, a special and exceedingly sensitive vagueness. There is an emotional nostalgia, the sound as it were of a faint chanting which seems like an echo from times now far distant. The whole school of painting which represents it has this echo of vague sadness. Neither in subject matter nor in color, nor even in suggestion, does one find in this school any note of positive joyfulness or gaiety, and in its place there is a melancholy in which the play of intellect takes an abstract form, and becomes a mental activity from which the creative eye of the painter, the eye which creates a harmony of tones by unexplained means, is absent." (*French Painting in the XXth Century*.)

To gain a fuller understanding of the *Ecole Juive*, it should be observed that its common denominator was the tendency to reveal subjective feeling rather than to portray objective truth. It is no coincidence that some of the best artistic talent among modern Jews has found its outlet in Expressionism—that movement which, to use Alfred H. Barr's definition, "rejects the imitation of the outer world of reality for the expression of an inner world of feeling and imagination."

Different conditions, however, are bound to create varied approaches to life and art, and it is no accident that quite a few Palestinian artists of the early twenties showed a greater affinity for the happily naïve "Primitive" style than for Chagallian nostalgia or Pascin's sophistication. Some of these Palestinian pioneers had a great deal in common with the early painters of North America, though they had no knowledge of the charming, if crude, work of Captain Thomas Smith, John Smibert, Gustavus Hesselius, and others who crossed the Atlantic long before the birth of the United States. It was natural that the art of America around 1700 and of Palestine around 1920 should both have been "provincial" and "colonial," with great stress on surface realism. Yet while in Colonial America portraits and conversation pieces dominated, the Palestinians, who had come from drab Russian towns, joyfully discovered the exotic countryside.

A few of those pioneers left Palestine after some years for the United States and England. Most of them never were in a position to visit other countries, and worked on in relative isolation, with all the drawbacks of an undeveloped land and far from the artistic

advantages of Europe. Rubin, who first arrived in Palestine in
1912, has traveled abroad frequently, but has always come back.

Here we might list, as one would on a sort of honor roll, the
names of the pioneer painters and their years of arrival in Palestine
—in a period roughly corresponding with the second and the third
Aliya:

Arieh Allweil (1920), Aharon Avni (1925), Arieh El-Hanani
(1922), Leon Fein (1926), Isaac Frenkel (1919), Chaim Gliksberg
(1924), Nahum Guttman(brought to Palestine as a child in 1903),
Aharon Halevy (1906), David Hendler (1924), Shimshon Holz-
mann (1922), Joseph Kossonogi (1925), Leopold Krakauer (1925),
Munia Lender (1922), Mordecai Levanon (1921), Leo Lubin
(1914), E. Luftglass (1926), Moshe Mokadi (1920), Arie Navon
(1920), S. Obadowski (1924), Israel Paldi (brought to Palestine as a
boy in 1907), Abel Pann (1920), Rubin (1912), Menahem Schmitt
(1931), Zvi Schorr (1921), Eliahu Sigard (1923), Avigdor Stematzky (1924), Hermann Struck (1922), Anna Ticho (1914), and
Joseph Zaritsky (1924).

The most successful of these pioneers was Rubin who, in 1923,
with a few colleagues arranged to hold the Holy Land's first art
exhibition in Jerusalem's historic Tower of David. Rubin has been
one of the few Israel painters who, by bringing his work to the
United States and other countries, has been able to make a living
through his art alone. Most of the others have spent years at physical labor, devoting only their spare hours to their calling. Avni
worked in the building industry in Tel Aviv, El-Hanani and Fein,
Levanon and Kossonogi toiled on the land, Halevy was a fisherman
and a gardener, Hendler worked in the quarries, Paldi was a watch-
man, Schorr a bookbinder; Nahum Guttman and Lubin spent
years with the Jewish Legion and the British Expeditionary Force
in Palestine, respectively.

There is nothing astonishing, however, in the fact that artists
everywhere find it hard to make ends meet (a sad commentary upon our society).

A few, like Moshe Mokadi (who later became Israel's first Director of Art), gained distinction as stage designers.

In addition to the problem of making a living, the pioneer artists
were facing the problems of climate and topography in Palestine.
Years before their arrival, young Martin Buber had predicted their

dilemma. From books alone he already knew about the anti-chromatic effects which an almost tropical sun can produce, particularly with the reflections from sand and stone. He feared that in Palestine everything would appear colorless:

". . . The few colors appear in glaring, abrupt isolation. All this is under the power of a sun that makes things seem remote, devours roundness, and permits no harmonious modulation of color. Thus sun gives vision, but no sight." (*Juedische Kuenstler*, 1903.)

To the layman, the problems caused by the artist's transfer from a temperate climate where the sunshine is mild, and where there are countless transitions between light and dark, to the Middle East may seem trifling. However, for the artist in Israel, with its cloudless skies and clear atmosphere, all soft colors are "swallowed up" by the ravenous sunshine. Arriving in the new land, artists have felt as the French painter, Eugene Fromentin, felt a hundred years ago when he traveled to the Orient: "No painter has yet succeeded in conquering the main handicap, which is the sun," he complained. "Yet it should be our first task to make our poor means express the abundance of light which blinds us, confuses us, which drives us mad."

The artist-pioneers grappled with the problem of the blinding light that seemed to turn everything white. They accustomed themselves to the sharp contrasts, and some eventually made excellent use of them; these replaced soft tints and hues with strong brilliant colors—colors that young Buber never dreamed of: the aquamarine of the Mediterranean, the red of the hibiscus flower, the purple of the narrow lanes in Jerusalem and Safed.

Travelers in Israel have often noted that the clearness of the atmosphere seems to abolish distance. Under these conditions, the rigid perspective of the West was an inadequate tool. Hence, some painters went back to the Far Eastern and Persian tradition of flat modeling, of two-dimensionality; this is one source of the frequently noted affinity to "Byzantine" iconography.

The men and women of the second and the third Aliya paved the way for the German-trained Central European artists who were to flee to Palestine after Hitler's rise to power. By 1933 the Bezalel School and Museum had been reorganized and modernized, and plans had been made for the establishment of the Tel Aviv Museum. Those who came during the thirties—among them M.

Ardon-Bronstein, Joseph Budko, Paul Konrad Hoenich, Ludwig Jonas, Hermann A. Kahn, Issai Kulviansky, S. Sebba, and Jacob Steinhardt—did not have to work in the fields or on the roads, but found a rapidly growing community willing to encourage them. At the same time, even during this period, there were *kibbutz* artists—like Yohanan Simon—who chose the life of the *halutz*, with its hardships and spiritual rewards.

At the beginning of the Second World War, a few artists managed to make last-minute escapes from Europe to Palestine. Among these was Marcel Janco, who had won a considerable international reputation both as a painter and an architect. He had been one of the pioneers of the modern art revolution, in 1915 at Zurich, as one of the youthful founders of Dadaism, and later in Bucharest, as the leader of the artistic *avant-garde* there. The arrival of modernists like Janco revealed new possibilities of form and composition to the country's artists, especially the younger ones.

Thus, each stream of immigration had brought talent, while the *sabra* artists who had been students in the twenties—e.g., Moshe Castel, Cille Neiman and Sionah Tagger—had grown to full maturity and were gaining proper recognition.

When, at the 1939–40 New York World's Fair, Jewish Palestine was represented by Steinhardt in an international art show at the Business Systems and Insurance Building, the catalogue had this to say:

"Palestine, old and mysterious, cannot be hurried, and generations must pass before she will have refashioned all these offerings from her children into one art which bears her likeness alone."

Nobody would have suspected then that, less than a decade later, an independent Jewish State would have come into being. But cultural developments cannot be accelerated; and it seems certain that the men and women of today will not create in Israel "one art which bears her likeness alone," nor is there any valid reason for expecting them to do so. Nevertheless, many are concerning themselves with this question. There is planning, discussion and dissension. During my inquiry into the matter, I turned to the work and utterances of three of the most noted Israel painters: a leader of the pioneer group of 1923, a mature *sabra*, and one who arrived on the scene a little more than a decade ago.

According to the first of these, Rubin, whatever a Jewish artist puts on canvas, whether it be a still life, a landscape, a portrait or a nude, is intrinsically Jewish because the artist's approach, his emotions, are Jewish:

"Just as one recognizes a Hebrew script as different from, say, Latin script, the public will eventually recognize the 'handwriting,' the craftsmanship of an Israel artist, reared in his homeland and linked with his people's past and future, as Hebrew art. But there is still a long, wearisome road before us, ere we achieve what many of us regard as a goal worth striving for: Israel art, as characteristically 'Israeli' as French art is French."

Here we again encounter the question: "But how 'French' is contemporary French art?" And how "Israeli" can Israel art be in an age in which the trend—within the democracies, at any rate—is toward greater cultural interchange? However, Rubin is clearly thinking in terms of a far-off future, of an original art to be evolved as a natural and unhastened product of increasingly "truer" Israelis.

A "national art"—with the stress on *national*—is vehemently espoused by the *sabra* Castel, who told me emphatically:

"True Israel art may be restored only upon a basis where our ancient past in this part of the world is utilized as a main factor. We have to link our creative talents directly with the artistic chain extending from Jewish antiquity."

Castel, seeking his roots in the Middle East, advises his colleagues to study the ancient art there: the frescoes of Dura Europos, the mosaics of the Beth Alpha synagogue, the Farhi Hagadah, and also Egyptian art, Arab folk painting on glass and Persian miniatures. But notwithstanding the credo which Castel has advanced with regard to the Eastern sources that ought to mold Israel art, his early training in Paris over the period of a decade has clearly been a decisive influence on his style. The fact that some of his own work seems to contradict Castel's "ideology" strengthens our belief that "national art" cannot be created synthetically.

Marcel Janco, on the other hand, has not been inclined to superimpose non-artistic ideologies upon his painting. With him, art is created by the interaction between the country—its forms and colors, its people's comedy and tragedy— and the *individual artist,* applying the craftsmanship and knowledge he has accumulated. Equipped with an original style which he evolved as one of the early abstractionists in Europe, Janco paints Israel in his own terms. While he had already been moving away from "pure" non-objectivism prior to his departure from Rumania, this trend was accelerated in Palestine. Thus, he has given highly personalized, semi-abstract expression to the scenes and the events he has witnessed, producing landscapes, but also refugees arriving in the country, Arabs in their cafés, soldiers battling amid the ruins of war. It has been instructive to observe the *effects of* the land and the people, as well as the *transformation of* the land and the people in his paintings.

All three of these Israel painters have their followers, as do other artists. But no single Israel "art concept" seems to be emerging. Nor will there be one, as long as the country is free of totalitarian direction, of *Gleichschaltung* of the left or the right.

A few marked features of style, and subject matter are, however, noticeable. The artists are preponderantly regional. They are busy with the peculiar and unique sights which the country has to offer: the austere beauty of Jerusalem; the winding, narrow streets of Old Safed; the brown-skinned Bedouins, black tents and listless camels around Beersheba; the Arab cafés where idle old men in dirty garments eternally smoke their water pipes; the fascinating immigrants from Yemen and Bokhara; the Mosque and the Citadel of Acre; and the Arab villages, with their little blue or pink dice-shaped houses. Other painters are enthusiastic about the sun-tanned faces of *sabra* girls, the husky pioneers, the world of chicken coops, cow sheds and vegetable gardens, the tractors and silos of the settlements, and the rapidly expanding factories, workshops and harbors.

The majority of Israel artists still seem to be Impressionists, Post-Impressionists or Fauvists. What Charles Terrasse said about the Parisian *Ecole Juive* and its general mood is hardly true of the large number of Israelis who indulge in strong joyous colors and have been chiefly concerned with the contemplation of the cheerful things in life.

There has been relatively little experimentation with new trends. Whereas in Europe and America Jews have been prominent in the *avant-garde* movements (Gabo and Pevsner in Constructivism, Lipchitz in Abstract Art, Blume and Chagall in Surrealism, etc.), Israel is, generally speaking, forty or fifty years "behind" the times. *Ofakim Hadashim* (New Horizons), a vanguard group formed chiefly by Janco and his followers, for a time broke away from the Association of Painters and Sculptors and served to introduce some new ideas into the art scene. For the most part, however, the Israelis do not seem especially concerned with the *dernier cri* of the Left Bank; they are not trying to be the "first" to arrive at a goal. In the large 1951 volume, *Painting and Sculpture in Israel,* edited by Haim Gamzu, one finds that only two out of sixty-three artists included—the sculptor Moshe Sternschuss and the painter Jean David—are represented by work of a modern "harshness" which may be baffling to untrained onlookers. In the earlier volumes on Palestinian art by Elias Newman (1939) and Karl Schwarz (1941), the absence of abstract and surrealist art was equally conspicuous. Yet anyone who has seen exhibitions at the Tel Aviv Museum, at the Artists' House in Jerusalem, or elsewhere in Israel would conclude that these critics have simply mirrored the facts as they are. Another critic, Miriam Tal, in an article which appeared in the *Zionist Newsletter,* reports that "attempts have been made to discourage local experiments in Cubism and Surrealism . . . on the grounds that this kind of painting, being founded on values other than the peculiar character of this country and its people, is 'foreign' in a disparaging sense." "Attempts to discourage" any form of artistic expression usually reflect provincial narrow-mindedness. We believe, however, that in Israel such an attitude represents only a small segment of the artistic population.

One characteristic has remained constant in the art of Israel throughout the years: a predilection for landscape, for the *Gruene Felder* that were more or less unknown, or, at least, inaccessible to the artists' fathers and grandfathers. Before the Emancipation, the ghetto Jew who had artistic inclinations could commune with nature only metaphysically but not through actual experience. As for the "post-Emancipation" artist—for example, Max Liebermann—who was so fond of "his" country's panorama, he often saw his landscapes disdained by chauvinists as "foreign" products. In Israel the artist, by painting the land itself, underscores, so to speak, his legal and moral right to it. In addition to this sense of rightful possession, he simply enjoys painting *his* landscape. People, when and if they are included in the canvases, are usually placed amid houses and trees, in fields and gardens, humble and almost inconspicuous in the surroundings they serve rather than dominate.

The *deracinés,* Modigliani and Pascin, painted and drew hundreds of voluptuous nudes. But in Israel—where tradition and ancient religious taboos did not permit anything resembling a Latin Quarter with its models and prostitutes—female nudes are rarely seen at exhibitions. On the other hand, such *galut* memories as Chagall, Ryback, or Mané-Katz have indulged in are also rare. The *shul,* filled with men in white prayer shawls communing with the Lord; the merrymakers of the Purim festivals turning somersaults and showing tricks in the *Judengasse;* the religious dances of the Hasidim—these themes are rare even among the older artists, and almost unknown to the younger generation. The three foremost graphic artists, Hermann Struck, Joseph Budko, and Jacob Steinhardt, continued to sketch a "ghetto" even after their own removal to Palestine, but they substituted the types and alleys of Jerusalem's Mea Shearim for those of Europe. On the whole, the old world holds no fascination for Israelis. For large numbers of them, history begins with the foundation of their state in 1948, and historical illustrations are usually confined to the recent Israel-Arab war.

While there is something refreshing about this refusal to be subdued and coerced by history, there is also the danger of provincialism, conceit, and unwillingness to learn from the great masters of the Western world as well as from the Jewish past. On the positive side, however, a new note was introduced into Israel art by soldiers of the War of Independence—in the "murals" of mess halls and barracks, and in illustrations for army magazines. New blood has also been supplied by artist-farmers in *kibbutzim,* whose schedules are adjusted so that they may take courses given by traveling art teachers. Finally, the children, whether native-born or recently brought to Israel are a source of great hope. In Ben Shemen I saw an exhibition of work by children who had come from Displaced Persons camps in Europe. I was informed by the supervisors that many of these children had experienced incredible hardships in Nazi-occupied countries; yet, judging by their artistic productions, it appeared that the gay, carefree life in this model children's settlement had enabled most of them to overcome the traumatic shock of an earlier stage. Children are "regional artists" *par excellence,* and these young people who had been in Israel for only a short time had assimilated themselves into their new surroundings with amazing speed. Nightmares of the recent past were drowned out by pictures of shepherds and watchmen, Purim carnivals, domestic animals, and activities in a *kibbutz*. While some of the graduates of academies in Warsaw, Paris, Dresden and Vienna still struggle with the colors of Israel, these children instinctively use the "right" colors to give their works a feeling of the country's light and warmth—yellow, orange, terra cotta and crimson.

From children like these will come some of tomorrow's artists. They will go to art schools modeled after those of Europe and the United States, and some will continue their education abroad (already a few Israelis are studying at New York's Art Students League). They will also, we hope, be able to view at home good works of art created by other peoples in other times—if the current efforts to collect first-class art for Israel prove to be successful. While in the past few Christian artists of note have sought inspiration in Israel (Oskar Kokoschka was among them), there should be many who will go there in the future to paint and to exhibit.

The face of the country will change. New cities, as well as beautiful forests, will arise out of what were once swamps and deserts. The human material will be different, too. The sentimentalists and romanticists from old Europe will be gone, though it is to be hoped that their qualities will not be extinct in the *sabras* of the future.

When Bialik foresaw the renaissance of Jewish art in a Jewish land, his statements did not, of course, refer to one branch of the arts alone. But what he said can be applied to tomorrow's painters and sculptors, too. While defining the artists' rights and duties, he insisted that he did not think of imposing extra-artistic burdens on them, that he wanted them "with all they have sinned and with all they have made good, with their errors and sins." A foe of narrowness, he knew, as a poet, that art cannot develop in fetters, that the artists, like the scholars, must remain free in order to be creative men:

"They should dwell with us, that is enough. Man himself, as a vessel containing the sum of life, is the most precious property of the nation. Each of them shall pour the vessel of his life into the stream of the nation and augment its power. . . ."

ZION IN CONTEMPORARY FICTION

By HAROLD U. RIBALOW

THE ZIONIST MOVEMENT, a romantic but persistent dream which culminated—as few dreams do—in fulfillment, with the establishment of the State of Israel, has inspired many and varied events and personalities. Curiously enough, however, the Jewish yearning for Zion; the existence of a galaxy of implausible personalities like Theodor Herzl, Max Nordau, Chaim Weizmann and countless others; the machinations of individuals and nations; the cloak-and-dagger tales inherent in a Middle East situation fraught with international complications—these and many more such exciting realities have elicited an astoundingly meager number of creative literary works. The novelist and the short-story writer, who, frequently with litmus-paper sensitivity, reflect and project the ideas and events of an age, fell down badly in regard to Zionism in literature. Today, some fifty years after Herzl's political vision of Jewish statehood, and nearly five years after the establishment of Israel, fiction concerning Zionism, the "Palestine problem," and Israel and the Middle East is most noticeable through its comparative absence.

Israel exists; the Jewish writer, in 1952, knows it. But, in retrospect, what has he contributed to the understanding of Zionism in his role as creative writer? The answer is: a handful of short stories; a smaller number of novels of Jewish life, which touch, ever so lightly, on Zionism; and, most recently, some four works of fiction which deal seriously with Israel, plus a group of novels written in the 1930's and 1940's which, after a fashion, suggested that at least a few Jewish writers were not entirely insensitive to the theme which, in other spheres, had proved so overwhelming, so poetic and so astonishingly successful.

To the student of American-Jewish literature it is obvious that Zionist aspirations were treated slightly, if at all, because Zionism, as such, did not exist, so far as the majority of America's Jews were concerned, until the Hitler era and, for many, not until the exciting political and military events which led to the establishment of the State of Israel. Only a devoted, small core of Jews—which, in time, grew to include some of the leading Jews of our day—were "Zionists." Strange though it may sound today, the Zionists were a minority group in American-Jewish life. And to the American-Jewish writers of the 1930's, under the influence of the anti-nationalist, proletarian mood; to the writers of the early forties, many of whom were seduced by the image of Marx and Russia; to the writers of the earlier period, the Scott Fitzgerald age, Zionism, if they heard the word, meant nothing but a crazy Jewish dream. To the Jewish writer in America, rooted in life in this country, seeking to understand and explain the wars and the depressions and the "jazz age" and the New Deal and the rise of socialism, Zionism did not matter. That writers of the caliber of Ludwig Lewisohn and Meyer Levin devoted themselves to Jewish themes in general and Zionist matters in particular meant only, to the general American reader and also to the American literary critic, that the Lewisohns and the Levins and the Maurice Samuels (few enough, alas, in numbers), were cutting themselves away from the mainstream of American writing. Thus, in the literary histories, in the critical journals, in the volumes of criticism, these Jewish writers are eliminated, as though they never existed, as though they never wrote a single worthwhile word. They were "Jewish writers," not, in consequence, "American writers." That James T. Farrell could devote himself to the Irish, William Saroyan to the Armenians, John Fante to the Italians and remain American writers was within the tradition. But that the handful of Jewish writers who concerned themselves almost exclusively with Jewish themes were American writers as well seemed contradictory to the literary brahmins. How much more true was this of the Jewish writers who limited themselves even more severely by writing about Zionism?

Nevertheless, a cursory study of the early novels and short stories of the "exclusively Jewish writers" is rewarding not only because of their themes, but also because their tales were no worse, and in some instances, far better, than stories by more widely recognized writers who described the lives of other minority groups in the United States.

Meyer Levin, who in his most recent volume, his autobiography entitled *In Search* (Horizon Press, 1950), offers a searing portrait of the Jewish writer who seeks to understand himself both as a writer and as Jew, is a perfect illustration of the Jewish novelist who steadily saw the Jewish people whole, and thereby included Zionist themes with persistence throughout his work.

In the late 1920's Levin wrote a short story called "Maurie Finds His Medium," which was published in the *Menorah Journal* (and reprinted in a collection of Jewish short stories, *This Land, These People,* which this writer edited). An unusual tale, it is significant in that Levin recognized even so long ago that the American Jew who would initially be attracted to Palestine would be the artist, the neurotic, maladjusted Jew. His hero, Maurie, goes to Palestine when he cannot succeed in America. In a curious twist, Levin shows that even in Palestine Maurie has no talent. He paints, but paints badly. He is second-rate, but in his attempt, in Palestine, he finds a happiness that eluded him in all his past life. In his most celebrated novel, *The Old Bunch* (Viking, 1937), Levin wrote a panoramic narrative of a large group of Chicago Jews. Here, too, one of the major characters looks for faith and Judaism in Palestine. Hadassah, the Women's Zionist organization, is here for the first time included as a potent factor in Jewish social life. In *Yehuda* (Cape and Smith, 1931), Levin, for the first time in the English language, presented a novel about *kibbutz* life. The only other novel on the same subject to appear in English was David Maletz's *Young Hearts* (Shocken, 1950). Levin, an American who actually lived in Palestine in a *kibbutz,* immediately caught the importance of the tragic contradictions of life in a communal settlement and projected them when he offered as his hero a violinist who has to choose between his art and his people. Even in 1931, it was possible to discover fictional themes on Jewish and Zionist issues. While the Albert Halpers and the other "proletarian" novelists who made an impact during that period were writing about American labor, Meyer Levin was discovering Jewish labor, not in the United States, but in Palestine. Curiously, Levin found less fault with *kibbutz* life than did Maletz years later, but perhaps by this time the glamour of communal life had begun to wear thin even to native Palestinians.

Levin is capable of seeing many angles of Israeli life, which is not unusual, for besides his gifts as a creative writer he has had the advantage of studying the scene more intensively than any other English-speaking Jewish novelist. In *My Father's House* (Viking, 1947), he wrote poetically about the search for security of a young boy who had no security. Levin's Daavid, in traversing the land, sees Palestine for what it is: a home as well as a refuge. And with a sure sense for the terrain of Palestine, Levin projects his own deep feeling for the soil. That Michael Blankfort more recently, in *The Juggler* (Little, Brown, 1952), often emulated Levin's story line of *My Father's House* reveals, among other things, the grasp Levin has of his techniques as well as his material.

If anyone thinks, however, that Levin is—as many Zionist writers are—an unthinking propagandist, incapable of subtlety, he should read "After All I Did for Israel," a short story published in the summer of 1951 in *Commentary*. Here Levin pulls out all stops as he writes a sardonic story of Jews who belong to various Zionist organizations, who "sacrifice" their time and their energy for Zionist causes but who are bewildered and upset when their own children indicate that they would, perhaps, like to try living in Israel. The delicious humor—which here is quite deadly—cannot be brought off in a capsule comment in a single paragraph. It must be read, if the thrust is to be felt.

This short story, incidentally, is the only "unromantic" tale in a rather meager but interesting list of stories about Zionism or Israel. In most of those that have been published, both in the "small" magazines and in the slicks," the theme has been: should an American Jew fight in the Jewish-Arab war? And in line with the pattern of fiction in these magazines, the Jew who chooses to fight is a hero. Incidentally, while the "slick," mass-circulation magazines almost always permit only Protestant Anglo-Saxon Americans to be the heroes of their stories, the establishment of Israel hurdled the wall of taboos in a few isolated cases. Thus the *Saturday Evening Post* published a story on Israel by Norman Katkov, one of its regular contributors.

In "Star in the Window" (*Saturday Evening Post*, July 23, 1949), by Norman Katkov, the conflict revolves around two brothers, one of whom wants to volunteer for the fighting and other who says that the fight is not theirs. They had fought in the American Army, of course. One brother believes that is enough; the other thinks that, as a Jew, his fight remains unfinished. The mother, an understanding woman, who had already lost one son in Iwo Jima, does not attempt to sway her Jewishly conscious son one way or the other and allows him to resolve the conflict in his own mind. The boy finally leaves for the war and the reader is given to understand that he has done the right thing. While the dialogue is forced and strained and the plot structure obvious, the writer manages to project emotion and some passion into his tale. But the most remarkable think about the story is its appearance in America's great middle-class magazine, the *Saturday Evening Post*.

A somewhat similar story, but far more subtle, is Abraham Rothberg's "Not with Our Fathers," which originally appeared in *The University of Kansas City Review* (Winter, 1949) and was reprinted by Martha Foley in her annual *The Best American Short Stories*. Here, too, a young American decides to join the Jews in Palestine in their fight for independence. Again, as in Levin's story and in Katkov's story, he finds himself opposed by his family and friends. More important, the girl he loves tries to convince him that the war is not his. Like Katkov's hero, he insists that it is. But Rothberg, not writing for a "slick" magazine, uses more explosive weapons than Katkov. His hero's girl seduces him, thus using her most effective and final weapon, against this insistent call which drives the man to Palestine. She surrenders her body and while the man takes it, he refuses to let go his dream. The story ends with the girl's gesture defeated. The man leaves.

The story ends here, but its conclusion may well be found in Deborah B. Karp's "Carmi," which appeared in a literary magazine called *Furioso* (Summer, 1950). Carmi is an American who died in the fighting. Written more as a keening memoir than a short story, "Carmi" is a fine bit of writing, representative of the output of a sensitive young American girl who saw in the sacrifice of an American-Jewish boy the poetry of Zionism in American-Jewish life.

There have been other fine short stories with Zionist themes, not all of them by Jewish writers. Both James Maxwell and Irwin

Shaw, who have written many stories for *The New Yorker* magazine, served with the American Army in the Middle East, and spent time in Palestine. Shaw—and this is not always obvious to students of his work—had been interested in Jewish themes from the very outset of his successful literary career, and some of his finest short stories about Jews were written on the basis of his Middle East experience. This is not surprising, for Shaw has always been aware of what is timely. In devoting his talents to Jewish refugees in Tel Aviv, to British soldiers in Palestine scarcely aware of the currents which led to violence and, in at least one Shaw story, to the death of an Englishman totally oblivious of the fact that he is a villain to the Jews, Shaw is, as usual, penetrating. What is more surprising is the fact that Maxwell, in his volume, *I Never Saw an Arab Like Him* (Houghton, Mifflin, 1948), has portrayed a number of situations typical of Arab-Jewish relations with more sensitivity than any other writer.

In "Arab Editor," Maxwell dissects the fanatical Pan-Arabic type, the kind that says, "We can never compromise on Zionism." Maxwell's hero, listening to this diatribe, declares that he sounds like a "corner demagogue." But one understands this Arab and regrets only that his hatred is misdirected, that he is fighting the wrong enemy. In "Strictly from the Mississippi," Maxwell tells the tale of a Jewish officer named Dave Goldstein, who is indifferent to his Jewish heritage and to Zionism as well. Asked whether he is a Zionist, Dave Goldstein says— and here speaks a representative of a number of American Jews: "Damned if I know what I am on that score. Back in St. Louis before the war I was just a guy pulling down seven or eight thousand first-year commissions selling insurance. And renewals piling up every day. My wife and kid and I lived in a pretty fair part of town and played bridge and golf with the people I did business with. Some Jews but mostly goys. Maybe once or twice a year we'd go to the temple, the way some Catholics go to midnight Mass on Christmas. Hell, with that kind of a life what do I know about Zionism?"

Later, in a discussion with another Jew, Goldstein says: "Why the hell can't European Jews go back to Europe and start over. . . . Why should you have to buck, on one hand, a gang of Arabs who hate everybody and everything that threatens their camel-dung economy and, on the other, the British who will grind out any group that gets in the way of the Empire?"

While many of the lines here already sound badly dated, the opinions aired in these sentences crop up again and again in different disguise. That Goldstein begins to change his mind when an Italian spits *"Ebreo"* at him is melodramatic, and when Goldstein slams his fist against the Italian's jaw and feels good about it, one feels that Maxwell has taken the easy way out and has not answered the questions he has raised. But this, after all, is a work of fiction, not a tract, and what remains in the mind is the portrait of an American Jew who, one is certain, relished the turn of historic events and at this time no longer questions the reasons for Zionism. One may even believe that Goldstein is the kind of American Jew who may have volunteered to fight in Palestine, much like the American Jew from New York in Zelda Popkin's novel on Israel, *Quiet Street*, who came for reasons all mixed up in his mind, but there he was, fighting in Israel.

In "Village Incident," Maxwell writes of a Jewish refugee living in Africa and of his wife and daughter. It is a touching vignette, in which the pathetic situation of this family comes through. At the end, the Arabs kill them and the narrator feels badly over their death. It is a good story, but what we remember is the remark made by the Jew in response to the question, "Do you want to live in Palestine?" His answer is important because his own indecisiveness is reflected in a number of novels concerned with Jewish displaced persons, some of whom, at the moment of decision, refuse to live in Palestine. Here, the Jew replies: "No, I do not. But I want to see the Zionist movement succeed, because I want two things very badly—a passport and the protection of a national state."

Irwin Shaw's collected stories appeared in *Mixed Company* (Random House, 1950) and while this volume omits many of Shaw's most perceptive Jewish tales, it does contain a number of his stories about Palestine and the Middle East. In "Medal from Jerusalem" Shaw captures the hopelessness of Jewish refugees caught in the toils of political maneuvering among Jews, Arabs and Americans. While his heroine here is not the idealistic Palestinian, she does portray the amoral, "survive-at-all-costs" type which was developed as a result of Hitlerism. In "The Passion of Lance Corporal Hawkins," Shaw offers a poignant account of a British

Tommy in Palestine, who saw what happened to the Jews in Belsen, yet finds himself standing guard over Jewish D.P.'s from Europe, whose ship, already in a Palestinian harbor, is supposed to go to Cyprus. The British soldier does not want to harm the Jews, but finds that he cannot help himself. He is eventually blown up on a land mine—and in this ironical conclusion one senses the horror of the British situation in Palestine. Somehow, that the Yishuv created a state out of the entire situation is not surprising, for out of such complexities and such tragedy something enormous had to grow.

But the theme of Zion occurs and recurs not only in isolated short stories; it appears, too, in novels dealing with American-Jewish life, even though it touches the fringes, and not the core, of most of these novels. In *Roots in the Sky* (Macmillan, 1937), by Sidney Meller, we find that the *shaliah* makes an appearance. The narrative is concerned with a rabbi on the West Coast and his large family. Much of the novel is stirring, although the book is one of the lamentably forgotten novels of Jewish life in this country. That Messianic Zionism is introduced seems natural and that it plays a minor role is equally natural, for these immigrant Jews were struggling to adjust themselves to the realities of American life and gave little thought to a homeland in Palestine. In Norman Katkov's bitter novel of intermarriage, *Eagle at My Eyes* (Doubleday, 1948), the Zionist organization, Junior Hadassah, comes in for cruel and unworthy remarks. The hero, a newspaperman in love with Mary, a Christian girl, is supposed to cover a tri-state Hadassah convention. The novelist says: "There wasn't an unmarried Jewish girl from twenty-one to forty-one in Minnesota and the two Dakotas who didn't make the convention her own scalping grounds." When Mary asks the Jewish newspaperman what a "Hadassah dance" is, the Jew replies: "A Hadassah dance is one thousand unmarried dogs down from the sticks trying to find a man in three days." But the streak of self-hate as a Jew is so clearly drawn throughout this novel that the cruel remarks about Hadassah are typical and register weakly. It is recorded here only to indicate that now and again a national Zionist organization makes a large enough impact on American-Jewish life to be reflected in the contemporary novel.

That Zionist personalities have come to the attention of the slick novelists is proved by the inclusion of Theodor Herzl and other Zionist leaders in such a novel as *The Pedlocks* (Simon and Schuster, 1951), by Stephen Longstreet. It is a long, melodramatic novel, escapist literature but with a streak of coarseness throughout. In the past it would have been inconceivable to have imagined that Theodor Herzl could have been included in a novel of this type.

Two other novels of Jewish interest have included material relating to Zionism in recent years. They are Charles Angoff's *Journey to the Dawn* (Beechhurst, 1951), and Laura Z. Hobson's *Gentlemen's Agreement* (Simon and Schuster, 1947). Angoff's story, the first novel of a tetralogy is concerned with the Americanization of Jewish immigrants from Europe. It is a tenderly written and conceived book, with many sharp insights into the attractions America held for the Jews who swarmed to these shores early in the century. Among the wonders of America, to these people, was the political freedom here. That the Jews actually could vote for a President was a marvel they never understood but one they deeply appreciated. For the Jews in Europe were conscious of politics, even when they had no vote or voice in the direction of the nations among whom they lived. When Moshe, one of the major characters in the book, talks with his relative Mottel, who meets him upon his arrival in America, Mottel says: "America is a good country, but people are too much Christianized." And Moshe replies sadly: "I suppose Jews really never will be able to be Jews until God gives them Palestine back." Mottel's answer, the usual answer of the Jew at the time, was: "That is true. And it will happen. Not in our time. But it will happen. Great leaders in Israel will arrive, and somehow they will get Palestine for us. Of that I am sure. I wish I were so sure of other things."

"It will happen, it will happen," Moshe joins in. And one senses that in their hope, in the hope of all the immigrants of all times, there developed the great events of the past few years.

Journey to the Dawn, because it deals with real Jews, Jews who did not attempt to deny or reject their Judaism, contains many Zionists and much talk of Zionism in its pages. Because some of these people were workers and Socialists—and Jews—it was natural for them to be Poalei Zionists, as Angoff makes clear. On the other hand, Ezra, one of the memorable characters in the novel, delivers a speech about Zionism which has nothing to do with social-ism. "I am a Zionist," he says, "but I am one more for emotional reasons than for political reasons." And here are his reasons: "I only mean that it would be thrilling, even more than thrilling, to be a Jew when Palestine is ours again, because it would then mean that Jews really are a chosen people. It would then be the first time in history that a nation in exile for almost two thousand years had been re-created. I don't mean to be chauvinistic. I only mean to say how I feel. All those centuries of prayer and suffering would then not be in vain. All the years of waiting would then mean something. All the Jews who were killed in pogroms would be avenged."

This sums it up pretty well, but Laura Z. Hobson, in her na-tional best-seller, *Gentleman's Agreement,* when she does deal with Zionism, does so negatively and sourly. A Professor Lieberman, a physicist, is introduced as the all-wise scholarly, philosophical Jew who, on the surface, at least, is unbothered by anti-Semitism. The hero of the novel is a non-Jew who, in working on a series of arti-cles on social anti-Semitism, tells everyone he is a Jew in order to record their reactions to Jews. The reader's sympathy lies with Phil Green, the hero who undertakes to become a Jew for a few weeks so that he may unmask the anti-Semites. Among the Jews he meets, Professor Lieberman is drawn as one of the wisest. When Green wants to talk with Lieberman about Zionism and Palestine, the professor retorts: "Which? Palestine as refuge or Zionism as a movement for a Jewish state?" Green answers: "The confusion be-tween the two, more than anything." Then the wise professor says happily: "Good. If we agree there's confusion, we can talk. I can't really talk to a positive Zionist any more than to a confirmed Com-munist—there is no language."

Green is impressed with Lieberman, as one feels Mrs. Hobson is impressed with him. Lieberman, by his own admission, "has no re-ligion, so I am not Jewish by religion," yet he lectures on Judaism to Green. "The man could discuss nuclear physics, attack Zionism, comment on anything, and make it rational, unexpected, amus-ing," according to Green (and the novelist). On the "Palestine solution" (and how old and jaded the phrase is today!) Lieberman remarks sharply: "Don't let them pull the crisis over your eyes. You say you oppose all nationalism—then how can you fall for a *re-*

ligious nationalism? A rejoining of church and state after all these centuries? A kind of voluntary segregation? Always for the other fellow, of course, not for the signers of the full-page ads in the *Times* and *Tribune!*"

One cannot help thinking that Professor Lieberman is the fictional counterpart of Professor Morris R. Cohen, and one cannot blame Mrs. Hobson for introducing into her problem novel the problem Jew—the one who is not Jewish by religion, who knows there is no Jewish race, who feels no connection with other Jews, but somehow cannot escape the "stigma" of being Jewish and who squirms and twists away from anything which connects and unifies Jews the world over. The Professor Liebermans are in a dilemma in a 1947 novel. We wonder where they stand today?

These, however, are the novels in which Zionism is a side act, not a major factor. There have been a small number—but an eloquent group—of books about Jews and the yearning for Zion prior to the establishment of the state which warrant analysis, for they project all the factors involving the pros and cons of Zionism. The earliest of these novels is Ludwig Lewisohn's *Breathe Upon These* (Bobbs-Merrill, 1944). While Lewisohn has written an enormous amount of words about Zionism and in some of his fiction (notably *The Island Within*) has emphasized that Jewish salvation lies in Jewish idéntification, Lewisohn has written surprisingly little fiction about Palestine and Zionism. Perhaps it is his feeling that he is most effective on Zionism in his general writings rather than in his creative writings.

In *Breathe Upon These,* Lewisohn, as he has done many times, tells a story within a story. A Christian family, feeling that something is going wrong with their own family relationship, is visited by a famous Jewish refugee and his wife and hear from their lips the terrible events experienced by themselves and other Jews. Then they are told the story of the *Struma,* which looked like "an old broken toy boat that an ill-tempered child had thrown away." The *Struma* carried 769 souls and because the British would not allow the Jews to enter Palestine, and because the ship was forced to leave a Turkish port and struck a mine and went down instantly, all the Jews aboard the ship, with one exception, died a horrible and unnecessary death. Lewisohn utilizes this terrible story within the general framework of the novel to point a moral and preach a sermon. Palestine, as the eventual home of all refugee Jews, is the heart of the story—that and the inhumanity of the British. The Jewish Agency, the members of the Yishuv, the Zionists of the world all play a role in this story, and as the *Struma* tragedy is recounted by the Jewish refugee before the "average American family," trapped in its own inadequacy, the family somehow feels more tightly knit as a family, but the British, and the dead Jews, and the sunken *Struma* stay with us.

Arthur Koestler's *Thieves in the Night* was perhaps the most widely read novel on Palestine and Zionism during the past few decades. It is now a celebrated work not only because it propounded the view of the Zionist terrorists of the Stern group, but because, of all the writers who have devoted themselves to the Zionist theme, Koestler is at the present time the best-known. He is a major writer of political novels and *Thieves in the Night,* now a dated book, rated more comment than most books on Palestine or Israel.

The major protagonist in Koestler's novel is a half-Jew named Joseph who has decided to become a full Jew by living in and identifying himself with Palestine. But actually the hero of *Thieves in the Night* is the complex Jewish people. The novel tells how a group of Jews establish a new commune in Arab territory; how they live; what kind of Jews they are; how they think politically; how they manage socially. It relates in fascinating detail much about the psychology of commune life itself. Koestler says that "the commune is a great, dense, tight-woven partnership of memories," but now and again some of his protagonists rebel against it. This revelation, harshly criticized by many Zionist writers when the novel was first published, was more or less substantiated by Maletz in *Young Hearts* and, more conclusively, by the revolution in commune life in Israel during the past few years when the settlements faced crisis after crisis as many old-time and newer settlers refused to remain in the communes and began an exodus toward the cities.

Through the characters Koestler presents the varying viewpoints on Palestine, although because of events of the past four years, the book is in many important respects dated. The terrorist viewpoint is propounded by Koestler in this book with brilliance and eloquence and is perhaps the best explanation for the emergence of the Herut Party and the success, at the time, of Menachem Beigin.

Joseph, the hero of the book, declares that he is tired of being "reasonable." "I was," he says, "the reasonable fly running in zigzags over the window-pane because there was light on the other side and I had my legs torn out and my wings burnt off with matches. I am through with your reasonableness."

There is a passage in the book which beautifully expresses the mood in which the entire volume was written: "One can reach a point of humiliation when violence is the only outlet. If I can't bite, my wrath will bite into my own bowels. That's why our whole race is ulcerated in the bloodiest literal sense. Fifteen hundred years of impotent anger has gnawed our intestines, sharpened our features and twisted down the corners of our lips."

But Koestler, like his protagonist Joseph, is less persuasive than he might otherwise be, for he dislikes the Jews about whom he writes. He was one of the first writers to attempt to differentiate between "the Jews" and "the Hebrews," and in doing so he often writes bitterly of "the Jews." "I hated," he writes, "their acid analytical faculty, their inability to relax. I hated their lack of form and ceremony and breeding, their shortcuts from courtesy to familiarity, their mixture of arrogance and cringing. *They were the slum race of the world; their slums were the ghettos, whether the walls were made of stone or prejudice.*" (Italics mine.) Again, Koestler "describes" the Jews as "the flat-footed, shifty-eyed eternal tramp." Elsewhere, Koestler writes of Joseph: "It was no good denying to himself that he disliked them, and that he hated even more the streak of the over-ripe race in himself."

Thus, in his hate, Koestler advocates terrorism and because of his hate, his message is blunted. This book is important not only because it deals with Palestine, but because it is, in a sense, the self-portrait of a brilliant man who is a Jew and whose faith is shaky within himself. Koestler represents the sort of Jew who is an artist, who is intelligent, who is sensitive; but his Judaism has been thrust upon him; he never wanted it and, having it, does not quite know what to do with it. He has no education in the fundamentals of Judaism (a matter which is proved even more easily by reading *Promise and Fulfillment*, a more recent book on Palestine by Koestler), but he does have the awareness that he cannot escape being a Jew and, therefore, he must cope with the reality. His entire Judaism, then, penetrates him with the blunt edge of negativity; it is blunt, but it goes through his heart. He is, in his confusion and despair, the spokesman for a segment of a generation. "Jewry," he says at one point, "is a sick race; its disease is homelessness and can only be cured by abolishing its homelessness." To him the logical conclusion to this statement is: "I became a Socialist because I hated the poor; and I became a Hebrew because I hated the Yid." The sickness of Jewry without a homeland may have validity; eliminate the self-hate and add the concept of Koestler's that "our nationalism is homesickness for normality" and you can find some answer to the reason why Zionism lies in the heart of all Jews. But the self-hate, which is common to men like Koestler, can vanish among Jews who know that there exists a Jewish State. The probing scalpel of Koestler has produced a disturbing, provocative and at times a true book. But the poisonous pus must first be removed if the surgery is to save the patient.

That the poison is by no means absent in later works on Palestine is proved by the novels of Alex Comfort and Ernst Pawel. Comfort in *On This Side Nothing* (Viking, 1949), and Pawel in *The Island in Time* (Doubleday, 1951), both deal with Jewish refugees who survive Hitlerian Europe, have a chance to go to Palestine, but refuse to do so. That both novels are well-written, by men who apparently have given sober thought to the problem of a new nationalism does not obviate the disturbing fact that both reject Zionism and its connotation of statehood for the Jewish people. *On This Side Nothing* is the story of Shmul Weinstock and, as the publisher notes, "of his relationship to a family he does not love, a people who do not hold him, a city that does not harbor him, a war in which he feels no stake." Shmul is a stranger on earth, who believes one place is as good—or as bad—as any other on earth. The story takes place in a North African city, from the closing of the ghetto by the German occupiers to the early days of the liberation by the British.

Shmul Weinstock, in answer to the question, "Why don't you go to Palestine," says: "At first the reason was that I didn't know enough about it. My family had come to thrive on the exile, however much they talked about Zion: also I'd not met any of the people who do the work, who farm or build houses, only the wide boys who talk politics, and also I was scared of my own people. That kind of freedom, living in a house you have built, surrounded by waste land you have reclaimed, and protected by your own courage if anyone attacks you, has come to be an achievement, not the usual way of living—Palestine Jews do it well because Jews generally do enjoy living and have had enough kicks to be free of any wish to punish themselves. I could have gone and didn't. Partly because of what I have said and partly because I had to stay and see what happened. One of them from Palestine, a brown-skinned chap with indecently big muscles, who did not look like a blood brother of mine, told me that the friends in his Youth Circle had read a book of poems I published once, but it smelt of the exile, so they burned it in the yard. I was nearly as mad at that as I was when the girl on the park bench called me a Yid and moved away. Now I know more, I see he thought that my poems threatened the freedom he had helped to make. After a while, too, as he would have said, you get used to playing up to the role which the Gentiles cast you for—somebody who is there on sufferance, clever but rather servile. They treat Jews like artists—sensitive, useless, unreliable people whom you pretend to respect because it isn't sporting to despise them. The Palestinian looked more like a Jew from further back, when Jews were rowdy, intransigent, and as militaristic as the Cossacks, and used to terrorize the Middle East. I would never be like that if I lived to be a thousand. If my kind of Jew is a Gentile fabrication, poisoned by the Exile, I can't help it." And this spokesman for Comfort adds:

"There is another reason. If I went, I would be backing the notion that freedom is something national. Some of us must go, but some genuine Jews must stay. To make a few of everyone who is being swindled. I decided to stay."

Later, when Shmul makes his decision not to go to Palestine (he ends up going to America), he rationalizes: "There are two kinds of revolutionary: the research worker, who builds up a model of living for us to see, and the other, who points to it and says, 'look.' I could not leave Exile, because, as the Zionists who didn't understand me had kept saying, I belonged there. I was the second kind."

Ernst Pawel's spokesman René, an intellectual caught with a group of Jewish refugees in a D.P. camp in Italy who await the call to go to Palestine, also refuses to go to Palestine for much the same reasons. In love with Miriam, a girl who chooses to go to

Palestine, René, knowing he will lose her by making the decision he makes, nevertheless finds himself incapable of joining the others. René thinks: "Freedom to you is law and order. . . . To you freedom is the state. You want to belong. Above all else you want to belong. The Jewish State—dream of your life. Citizens at last. Soldiers, bureaucrats, jailors. I don't blame you. But as for me, I don't want to belong. I want to be a Jew. An outcast. There is no room in Palestine for Jews." He is called "a fool, a goddamn crazy fool." And the weakness of this novel is that the author does not convince the reader that René has made the wise or the only decision.

In a discussion with Miriam, René amplifies. Palestine, he says, is for "the new kind of Jew. I'm the old kind. I'm nothing. I'm sick of national liberation, national home, national this, and national that." She asks him if he is ashamed of being a Jew. "No," he replies, "and not proud of it either." And he adds: "Streamers, pictures, slogans, uniforms, new saints, new Fuehrers. I want no part of it. The whole gang up there on the hill would have given anything to be good National Socialists, good Poles, good Hunkies, good whatever the hell happened to be around. They tried hard enough, Lord knows, but no one wanted them and so now they've turned good Jews with a vengeance. If we can't crash their party, by God, we're going to have one of our own that's just as big and brassy."

The crux of their difference lies in the next exchange. "The rest of us," Miriam states, "want to live once more—just be alive and have a place where we belong and a little peace and something to look forward to. To us these things still matter—and where can we ever hope to find them?"

"Nowhere," René says.

"Nowhere but in Palestine," the girl says.

But to the novelist, René has the final word.

The fact that history, in the few short years between the writing of this novel and its appearance, turned against the Renés and the Shmul Weinstocks is evidence that, in spite of the reservation held in the minds of thoughtful novelists, the tread of time has passed them by, and their arguments, eloquently written, become nothing more than academic hair-splittings. The freedom which Comfort and Pawel thought would be lost, has not been lost. The Jew can live in Israel as a Jew, and needn't traverse the world as an outcast, the symbol of the forever wandering Jew. The stories these men have written were drawn from harsh life. Their conclusions, however, were drawn from air, and have as little substance.

That this is so, is evidenced in other novels, in Murray Gitlin's *The Embarkation* (Crown, 1950), and in David Maletz's *Young Hearts* (Schocken, 1950). While these stories are quite different in every respect they emphasize that Palestine—which soon thereafter became Israel—represented the best hope in the world for the refugees streaming into the land and that the land itself, developed by the pioneers in the *kibbutzim,* offers enough freedom of action and thought to reject the preachments of the Comforts and the Pawels. *The Embarkation* is the tale of an American GI who deserts in Italy, is tracked down by a British agent whose job it is to keep D.P. Jews from leaving Italy for Palestine and who gives up a chance for freedom rather than betray the Jews seeking to escape Europe for Palestine. The Jews in this book *know* that Palestine is their only haven and represents their only chance for normal life again. A native-born Palestinian in the novel delivers himself of a speech which is the direct antithesis of the speeches delivered by the Hamlet-like characters in the Comfort and Pawel novels. "Be a Jew!" he declares. "I've heard that before, especially from the Americans. Be a Jew! Put on phylacteries, go to the synagogue and be a Jew or belong to a Jewish organization or give money to a Jewish cause, and be a Jew! That's being nothing, chaver. That's just being a man with a bad conscience or one of those half and half things of whom you have plenty in your country. To be a Jew means to fight for a Jewish nation—and the man who belongs to that nation is your Jew."

This proud attitude is represented in a more subtle manner in Maletz's *Young Hearts.* This novel was written before the establishment of Israel and, when it first appeared in Hebrew, it was the center of great controversy among Hebrew-reading Jews because it delineated communal settlement life as difficult, harsh, in many respects negative and without the usual sympathy the *kibbutz* and *kvutzah* life generally received in the Zionist press and propaganda. The pioneers continually ask themselves whether they are leading a "Jewish life" and they realize that their lack of religiosity makes much of their work spiritually sterile. The lack of privacy takes its toll of many settlers and the story plot—which describes the life of a young couple in a settlement—reveals that there is little to recommend life in the *kibbutz*. But it reveals something more: that the scoffers and doubters are wrong when they think that Israel must of necessity become a "police state," one in which the individual Jew must lose his freedom and one in which nationalism must rob the Jew of his "international" quality which seems so much of a treasure to some novelists. The picture of Palestinian life as drawn by Maletz is disturbing, even if it delineated life of a decade ago: commune life has faced even more serious crises since then and is in the throes of one now. But the book shows, as all honest works of fiction must, that there is nothing to fear in the very fact of Jewish statehood. The driven, the bewildered, the confused and the intellectual Jews of the world who, given the choice, decide to live in Israel need not regret it. The faults they find in Israel may well be the faults they carry within themselves.

Of quite a different nature are the four novels which have been published in English since the advent of the state. Two were written by Americans, one by a Canadian Jew and the fourth by an internationally famous literary man who used to write in German in Europe, who still writes in German in Israel, but whose latest novel is a genuinely "continental" narrative about the war between the Arabs and the Jews. The first of these novels is Zelda Popkin's *Quiet Street* (Lippincott, 1951), which was distinguished not only as being the initial American novel on Israel but also by its deep feeling for the miracle of Israel. In her novel, Mrs. Popkin chose to present a contemporary over-all view of the establishment of Israel, bringing into her story actual events that occurred in the Jewish-Arab fight, and people representing all sides in the bitter struggle in Israel. The book deals with life in the Holy Land from the period in which the United Nations debated the future of Palestine to the time that the people of Israel wrested out of the land a state of their own. It is, in part, a "journalistic" book, for so much of it comes from the headlines of recent years. While it lacks the qualities which make first-rate imaginative fiction, the author admires her people and writes an impassioned description of the fight for the creation of a Jewish State. The raw material which

Mrs. Popkin has borrowed is good material and her book is a proud book.

The second novel written by an American, *The Juggler* (Little, Brown, 1952), by Michael Blankfort, differs from Mrs. Popkin's effort, first in that it is primarily a story conceived by the novelist and not by history. Any moral that is read into it is projected from the story itself and not from headline events. *The Juggler* concerns a man who comes to Israel as a D.P., poisoned in spirit, as Comfort's and Pawel's D.P.'s are. He is unable to adjust to the new land, to the very concept that murderers are not seeking him out to kill him. It is a measure of Blankfort's ingenuity as a story-teller that his hero is a juggler. He explains the symbolism this way: "Of all things a juggler! What brought a man to become a juggler, an artist in the meaningless skill of suspension and balance? . . . Wasn't every Jew in exile more or less an artist of living in suspension and balance, never knowing when he shall fall, held up only by forces and tensions, even whims, beyond his control? . . . Jew in exile, never knowing when the hand of man that threw him high would let him fall to be broken."

Hans Muller, the juggler, sees the world as a jungle. His wife and child have been killed by the Nazis; he is homeless, for "home is a place you lose." In Israel—which contains "the endless variety of Jews," many of whom have "Nazi pneumonia, which is a sickness like typhus. . . . It attacks the will to live"—it is difficult to adjust one's self. Hans beats up a cop who, he believes, is chasing him, thinks he kills him, flees into the land, meets a young orphan, finds his way to a *kibbutz* and there he discovers a woman who believes in him, and there he finds faith in humankind again. The plot is melodramatic, but Blankfort, writing shrewdly, sparingly, re-creates the neurotic Jew and, while his conclusion is too slick, he manages to draw a world in which we can believe, an Israel we can trust.

There is in this novel an unusual character, an Orthodox Jew named Schmuel ben Yehuda, the detective who is placed on Han's trail after Hans beat another cop. Ben Yehuda, in trailing Hans, asks himself whether he has the moral right to hunt down a fellow Jew, even though that Jew had committed a crime. Ben Yehuda's comments, which may well present the views of Michael Blankfort, have been overlooked in the casual newspaper reviews of *The Juggler* and warrant emphasis here:

"What does it mean to the Jews to have their homeland back again? It means that for the first time in their lives they can be like other humans. What does it mean for a Jew to be like other human beings? It means that he can be himself—that he can consider his fellow Jews not merely as Jews but as human beings." And the monologue continues: "Is it different among Jews living in other countries, in exile? Yes, it is different. . . . Go to a Jew in exile, let's say a Jew living in New York, when a Chicago gangster is Jewish, he is not just a criminal, he is a Jewish criminal, a disgrace and a threat to other American Jews. . . . Or take Einstein. Do American Jews praise Einstein as a fellow human being who has achieved great scientific wisdom? No; they add also that his triumphs are good for the Jews. . . . Why is this? Because Jews in exile can't be themselves a hundred per cent, they are easily bruised, easily flattered, easily worried, easily made to feel inscure. And how is this different in Israel? It means that we are at last, thank God, like other people. . . . And how is this all connected up with Hans Muller. . . .? Muller is a human being who committed a crime. I am now free to say so and to think so. I can have compassion for him, as one man to another. All that I am as a Jew, if I am a good Jew, will make me have deeper compassion. In Israel, I'm free to be a complete human being because I don't have to be self-conscious of being a Jew."

In this passage one can see that in a novel, even a cops-and-robbers novel, if it deals with Israel and with the Jews, truths are perceived, and passed along.

As for the two final novels on life in Israel, both are complicated to read, for both were conceived as symbolic works of art. Max Brod in *Unambo* (Farrar, Straus and Young; Jewish Publication Society, 1952) offers the story of an Israeli film director who makes a pact with the Devil which permits him to live two lives simultaneously. Thus the director, Paul Helfin, leads one life among a group of black marketeers, immoral men and women who are making a mockery of the high ideals for which Israel was created. In his other life, he fights with the *sabras* against the enemy in the Negev. The quality of Israel life—the white and the black—both come through, although the Unambo machine—a science-fiction device which is awkwardly handled here—distracts the reader's attention from the raw material which is so well worth contemplating. Too many of the chapters include long speeches of expository prose which are in reality factual narratives of real events superimposed upon the fictional framework. The philosophical asides and the beautiful translation from the German by Ludwig Lewisohn make *Unambo* an interesting failure. Fictionally the novel fails to excite, but as a morality play it is provocative.

For that matter A. M. Klein's *The Second Scroll* (Knopf, 1951), which has been acclaimed by critics like Maurice Samuel as one of the few genuine Jewish fictional masterpieces of our time, is, in a sense, a morality play, too. It is the story of a young poet who attempts to seek out his Uncle Melech, a symbolic character who, in his own search for fulfillment, wanders over the face of the earth, becomes a great Hebrew scholar, a Communist, a near-Catholic and finally a saintly Jew who finds death in Safed, a city in Israel which has holy connotations. The poet, trying to catch up with his Uncle Melech (Klein is a Joyce scholar and may be emulating Joyce here for the search for the father-image is the key to Joyce's *Ulysses*), visits Jewish D.P. camps, Italy, the ghetto in Casablanca and, of course, Israel. The entire work—which includes two long poems, a verse play, a detailed description of the Sistine Chapel and a group of prayers—is ambitious and poetic. Israel, in this book, is not an isolated thing: it is part of the tradition of the Jewish people. Let Klein, with his sure touch for words, phrase it for us: "My sojourn in Israel was a continual going to and fro, an unremitting excitement. I wanted to take in the whole country, all at once. If a plane had been available I should have loved to have risen in it so that I might look at Dan and Beersheba simultaneously. If I could only stretch out my arms and make them the land's frontiers! For there wasn't a place, disguised though it might be under a latter-day name, that didn't speak to me out of my personal past."

It is because of his own sure knowledge of the Jewish past, of the Hebrew language, that Klein—more than anyone else who has written on Israel—understands the richness of the land as a symbol of the Jewish people. The search for Uncle Melech becomes the search of all aware Jews for their beginnings and their fulfillment. That A. M. Klein's major protagonist finds that fulfillment in this richly poetic novel may be symptomatic of our time and of the future literature on Israel.

Thus far, fiction on Israel has reflected the attitude of creative Jews toward Israel and its role in Jewish life. When Zionism attracted comparatively few Jews, the literature lagged; when the yearning for Zion was intensified, stories and novels increased in numbers and in quality. This survey emphasizes works written in English and while translations from other languages into English scarcely indicate that masterpieces exist in those other languages, there is little doubt that the literature on Zionism in, for example, Hebrew, is much greater in volume than that in English. But the American Jew today represents the largest Jewish community in the world: his reaction to Israel, creatively as well as philanthropically, may well measure the intimacy between the Israeli and the American Jew, as well as the chasm between them. The establishment of Israel already has led to a handful of novels on Israel and, inferentially, on the relationship between the Israeli and the Diaspora Jew. The wealth of the future literature on Israel, its depth, its sensitivity and its authenticity, is bound to be a true gauge of the impact of Zion reborn on a Jewish people which has survived to enjoy the miracle of Israel.

BIOGRAPHICAL NOTES

JACOB B. AGUS, rabbi of Beth El Congregation, Baltimore, Maryland, was educated at the Rabbi Isaac Elchanan Theological Seminary and Harvard University. He is the author of *Modern Philosophies of Judaism, Banner of Jerusalem,* a life of Rabbi Kuk, and *Guideposts in Modern Judaism.*

CHARLES ANGOFF, formerly managing editor of *The American Mercury* in the days of H. L. Mencken, is a prolific critic, poet, short-story writer, and novelist, whose *When I Was a Boy in Boston,* a volume of short stories, and *Journey to the Dawn, In the Morning Light,* and *The Sun at Noon* have placed him in the forefront of writers of American-Jewish fiction.

HANNAH ARENDT is the author of the monumental study *The Origins of Totalitarianism,* which includes a great deal of material on Jews and anti-Semitism, as well as her classic analysis of the concentration camps.

DANIEL BELL, an editor at *Fortune* magazine, is a sociologist and economist whose thoughtful essays have appeared in general and Jewish magazines.

NAOMI BEN-ASHER, education director of Hadassah, the Women's Zionist Organization of America, has contributed articles to many English-Jewish periodicals and has produced some excellent material for her organization.

MICHAEL BLANKFORT, a Hollywood script-writer and novelist, is the author of *The Juggler,* a story about Israel which was later made into a popular motion-picture film. During a trip to Israel, he wrote some fine articles of his impressions of the new nation for American-Jewish periodicals.

MENAHEM BORAISHA, who died in 1949, was an outstanding Yiddish poet and journalist and editorial writer for *Congress Weekly.* His narrative poem *Der Gayer* is ranked as one of the finest poems in modern Yiddish literature.

MIRIAM BRUCE has written *Linden Road,* a novel on the theme of Jewish self-hate, which was warmly received by both the critics and the public.

DAVID L. COHN is a prolific and provocative writer who was born in Mississippi and studied at the University of Virginia and at Yale. He has written many books, including *God Shakes Creation, The Good Old Days,* and *Love in America.* He has also written about Palestine and Dr. Chaim Weizmann, Israel's first president.

LESLIE A. FIEDLER has taught at the University of Montana and has written incisive literary criticism, poems, and short stories for scores of literary, scholarly, and political journals throughout the world.

ROBERT H. GLAUBER, formerly an editor with Alfred A. Knopf and with the Decker Press, is now an editor of the *Beloit Poetry Journal.*

NATHAN GLAZER is an editor with Doubleday and was formerly on the staff of *Commentary.* He co-authored *The Lonely Crowd* and *Faces in the Crowd* and has contributed articles and reviews to many magazines.

CHARLES I. GLICKSBERG, associate professor of English at Brooklyn College and a member of the faculty of The New School, is the author of *Walt Whitman and the Civil War,* editor of *American Literary Criticism, 1900–1950* and various collections of short stories. He is a versatile contributor to scholarly, literary, and English-language Jewish magazines.

HARRY L. GOLDEN has written widely on Jews of the South. He is editor of *The Carolina Israelite* and co-author of *Jews in American History.* He has written more than fifty pamphlets on American-Jewish history.

HAYIM GREENBERG, one of the most influential Zionists and brilliant Jews of recent times, was an editor, journalist, philosopher, and Zionist theoretician. At the time of his death in 1953 he headed the Culture and Education Department of the World Zionist Organization and was editor of *The Jewish Frontier.* Posthumously, his essays were collected under the title of *The Inner Eye.*

EDITH HANDLEMAN, when she wrote the essay published in this book, was a senior at Syracuse University, majoring in journalism and English and was on the editorial staff of the University's literary magazine, *Tabard.*

WILL HERBERG, who has been research director of a large A.F.L. union, has become an outstanding expounder of modern Jewish theology, both in his book *Judaism and Modern Man* and in various essays in leading American periodicals. He is a popular lecturer at academic institutions and his writings have been called, by Reinhold Niebuhr, "a milestone in American religious thought."

ABRAHAM JOSHUA HESCHEL is a professor at the Jewish Theological Seminary of America and an important theologian. His major works are *The Earth Is the Lord's, Man Is Not Alone,* and *The Sabbath.* Dr. Heschel teaches Jewish ethics and mysticism at the Seminary.

MILTON HINDUS is the author of *The Crippled Giant,* a study of the anti-Semitism of the French novelist Louis Ferdinand Céline, and *The Proustian Vision,* an analysis of the writings of Marcel Proust. Mr. Hindus is a professor at Brandeis University.

SIDNEY HOOK, author of *The Hero in History* and other significant works, is chairman of the Graduate Department of Philosophy at New York University. A prominent political thinker, he contributes to mass as well as specialized magazines and wields great influence in educational and intellectual circles in America.

IRVING HOWE, who teaches at Brandeis University, is a prominent literary critic and the author of studies on Sherwood Anderson and William Faulkner. He is a frequent contributor to quality magazines, including *Commentary* and *Partisan Review.*

HORACE M. KALLEN is one of the most distinguished Jewish philosophers and educators in the United States and the author of more than twenty books. Educated at Harvard, Princeton, and Oxford, Dr. Kallen now teaches at The New School. His books include *Judaism at Bay, Zionism and World Politics,* and *Culture and Democracy in the United States.* When he was sixty-five years old, his work was discussed by various scholars in *Freedom and Experience: Essays Presented to Horace M. Kallen.* Dr. Kallen's pungent and penetrating essays on Jewish themes have been collected in book form under the title of *Of Them Which Say They Are Jews.*

MORDECAI M. KAPLAN, the founder of Reconstructionism, has been one of the outstanding and most influential Jewish religious leaders in the United States. His books have been used as textbooks and his ideas and concepts as Judaism as a civilization have been accepted by hundreds of rabbis throughout America. His works include *Judaism as a Civilization* and *The Future of the American Jew.*

SHLOMO KATZ, managing editor of *The Jewish Frontier,* is a veteran journalist whose work has appeared in many magazines and anthologies. Born in Russia, he was brought up in St. Paul and attended the University of Minnesota. He lived in a *kibbutz* in Palestine and served in the U. S. Army in Alaska.

IRVING KRISTOL, a former *Commentary* editor, is now editor, with Stephen Spender, of the international magazine *Encounter*. He was born in New York City in 1920 and served in Europe with the U.S. Army during the last war.

MEYER LEVIN is one of the best-known Jewish writers in America. His novel *The Old Bunch* has been called by many critics the first novel on Jewish life in America and his autobiography, *In Search,* is a fascinating account of a Jewish writer's aims and struggles. He has been a war correspondent, a painter, a playwright, and a newspaper columnist, as well as a novelist and short-story writer.

LUDWIG LEWISOHN, author of *The Island Within* and more than a score of other celebrated Jewish works, is the most eloquent exponent of Judaism in American literature. As an avowed Zionist, he also has been noted for explaining Zionism to American Jews. After a lifetime of writing, lecturing, and teaching, he is now a professor at Brandeis University.

STEPHEN LONGSTREET, a Hollywood script-writer and a prominent novelist, wrote *The Pedlocks,* a novel about a Jewish family, which was a best-seller and was reprinted in a paper-back edition.

MARVIN LOWENTHAL, ex-editor of *The American Zionist,* has written such important books as *The Jews of Germany* and *A World Passed By*. He also translated *The Memoirs of Glueckel of Hameln* and has edited a book of Henrietta Szold's letters. Mr. Lowenthal has contributed thoughtful essays to *The Menorah Journal* and many other magazines, both in United States and abroad.

DAVID MILLER, a graduate of the University of Chicago, is the author of the highly praised novel of Jewish life in the Napleonic era, *The Chain and the Link,* which has been compared with the works of Thomas Wolfe.

JACOB S. MINKIN left the active pulpit for a writing career and, as a result, has written important books, including *The Romance of Hassidism, Herod: A Biography,* and *Abarbanel and the Expulsion of the Jews,* besides articles on religious, historical, philosophical, and literary subjects for learned and popular magazines. He has also contributed to the *Encyclopedia Americana* and the *Universal Jewish Encyclopedia*.

ASHLEY MONTAGU is chairman of the Department of Anthropology at Rutgers University and a popular writer on anthropological and sociological subjects. He is the author of *The Natural Superiority of Women* and *Man's Most Dangerous Myth: The Fallacy of Race*.

ZELDA POPKIN, author of *Quiet Street,* a novel about Israel's war for independence, has written detective stories and has been an editor with *Coronet.* She has also worked for the Canadian Hadassah.

HAROLD U. RIBALOW is the author or editor of eight books, including *This Land These People, These Your Children, The Great Jewish Books,* and *The Jew in American Sports.* He was also managing editor of *Congress Weekly* and *The American Zionist.*

MENACHEM RIBALOW, perhaps the most prominent Hebrew writer in the United States, was for more than thirty years and until his death in 1953 editor of *Hadoar,* the only Hebrew weekly in the world outside of Israel. He was not only the head of the Hebrew movement in America, but an outstanding literary critic of Hebrew literature, author of many books and articles, and editor of a number of anthologies of Hebrew writing.

ETHEL ROSENBERG has written two books of Jewish humor, *Go Fight City Hall* and *Uncle Julius and the Angel with Heartburn,* which became national best-sellers and earned for Mrs. Rosenberg a reputation as one of the most delightful humorists of recent times.

ABRAHAM ROTHBERG has won a wide reputation for his short stories, which have appeared in the leading literary magazines in the United States and in a number of important anthologies. He was born in New York in 1922 and was educated at Brooklyn College, the University of Iowa, and Columbia University. Much of his work is Jewish in content and he has written a book for children on the patriarch Abraham.

MAURICE SAMUEL is one of the most eloquent writers and lecturers on the American-Jewish scene and the author of many books on Zionism and Israel as well as studies on Sholom Aleichem and J. L. Peretz. He is also a noted translator and novelist. Some of his best-known titles are *Harvest in the Desert, The Gentleman and the Jew, Prince of the Ghetto, The World of Sholom Aleichem,* and *Level Sunlight.*

JOHAN J. SMERTENKO, who teaches at Columbia University, was vice-president of the American League for Free Palestine from 1945 to 1947. He has been a writer on history, with emphasis on Jewish history, and was an editor as well as a journalist.

LEON STEIN is a professor of music at De Paul University and the author of studies on various aspect of Jewish music.

MILTON STEINBERG, who was rabbi of New York's Park Avenue Synagogue when he died at the age of forty-seven in 1950, was one of the best known and most eloquent Jewish spiritual leaders of the last twenty years. His sermons, articles, and books made him one of the influential Jews of his time and his early death was a great loss to the American-Jewish community. His books include *A Partisan Guide to the Jewish Problem, Basic Judaism,* and *A Believing Jew.* He also wrote a novel on Jewish faith and apostasy, *As a Driven Leaf.*

YURI SUHL is a Yiddish poet and English-language novelist. His *One Foot in America* and *Cowboy on a Wooden Horse* are among the good Jewish novels of the past decade.

J. L. TELLER is public relations director for the Jewish Agency for Palestine and an authority on Middle East affairs. He has contributed to *Commentary, The New Republic, Commonweal* and other magazines, and is the author of *Scapegoat of Revolution.*

BENNO WEISER, a lifelong Zionist, works for the Jewish Agency for Palestine in New York. He was born in Vienna and completed his medical studies there before 1938. Since that time he has been a journalist and has worked for the Zionist cause in South America as well as in Europe.

TRUDE WEISS-ROSMARIN is editor of *The Jewish Spectator* and author of *Jewish Survival, Jerusalem,* and other volumes. She is a leading exponent of Orthodox Judaism in the United States and lectures widely on Jewish religion and literature.

ALFRED WERNER is a free-lance writer who specializes in art. He is the author of many brochures and pamphlets on this subject and books on Utrillo and Dufy. He has written for dozens of American magazines and periodicals abroad.

ELIEZER WHARTMAN is an American who fought in Israel's war for freedom, married a *sabra* girl and became a writer while serving in the Haganah. He returned to America and worked for the Israel Consulate and for various Zionist organizations. His work has appeared in *The American Zionist* and *The Reconstructionist,* as well as general magazines and newspapers. He plans to return to Israel and become a permanent resident of the Jewish State.

HERMAN WOUK, best known for his phenomenal best-seller *The Caine Mutiny,* is also a teacher at Yeshiva University and is active in Orthodox Jewish circles. He has been a radio gag-writer, Hollywood script-writer, and playwright as well as a novelist.

JAMES YAFFE, who was born in 1927, already has to his credit a fine book of Jewish stories, *Poor Cousin Evelyn,* and two Jewish novels, *The Good-for-Nothing* and *What's the Big Hurry?* He also writes detective stories with a Jewish woman as a central character. Educated at Yale, Yaffe served in the U.S. Navy.